PLYMOUTH COLONY

PLYMOUTH COLONY ITS HISTORY & PEOPLE 1620-1691

Eugene Aubrey Stratton, FASG
Former Historian General of the General Society
of Mayflower Descendants

P.O. Box 476
Salt Lake City, UT 84110

Library of Congress Catalog Card Number 86-72003
ISBN Number 0-916489-13-2   (Hardbound)
ISBN Number 0-916489-18-3   (Paperback)

First Printing 1986
10 9 8 7 6 5 4

Printed in the United States of America

Contents

List of Illustrations

Foreword

Genealogy and history interact in many ways, and early in this century J. Horace Round addressed this question in a lecture entitled "Historical Genealogy" [in *Family Origins* (reprint Baltimore 1970) pp. 1-12]. He defined three connections between the two disciplines as follows: "Genealogy as a branch of historical study, Genealogy based on the same principles as those of historical research, Genealogy in its own historical development."

"Genealogy as a branch of historical study" encompasses those instances in which the results of genealogical investigation support or enhance the work of the historian. Round describes the ways in which genealogy assists in the investigation of Domesday Book. In the United States, and in more recent years, one could point to the exploitation of genealogical literature by the social demographers.

"Genealogy based on the same principles as those of historical research" is nothing more than the pursuit of genealogy itself by modern, critical methodology, as opposed to the older, more romantic and intuitive approach so consistently excoriated by Round. In this country we would obviously point to the work of Jacobus and his colleagues and followers for the practice of this approach to genealogical research.

"Genealogy in its own historical development" comprises the history of genealogy itself—the growth and development of genealogical societies; biographies of individual genealogists; historiographical studies of certain genres of genealogical writing; and so on. Both here and in Great Britain this aspect of the interactions between genealogy and history is virtually untouched.

There exists, I would contend, yet a fourth point of contact between these two disciplines, in which the history of a given time and place is written from a genealogical perspective. The author of such a work would look at a small slice of society and tell us how the structure of that society, its customs, its religious beliefs, its economic activities, and all its other facets impinge upon the genealogical networks generated in that society. Why do first marriages take place at a certain age? What distance is a person likely to travel in his lifetime, and how does this affect the choice of marriage partner? The number of questions of this sort is endless, and all are of importance to the genealogist.

A second aspect of writing history from a genealogical perspective would be the exposition of the categories and forms of records generated by a given society, and how these might help the genealogist. In the field of religion, how did the beliefs of the Baptists, the Congregationalists, and the Quakers influence the information included in their denominational records, and how easy or difficult, therefore, will it be for the genealogist to study a family from one or another of these church groups?

This field of history written from a genealogical perspective has been explored even less than the other three areas of common interest between genealogy and history. In the present work, then, Eugene A. Stratton has undertaken a pioneering work in attempting to present Plymouth Colony history from a genealogical viewpoint.

Stratton first covers the seven decades of the existence of the colony in the usual chronological presentation, but with emphasis on the arrival of settlers, both from Holland and England, and also on the movement of those settlers once they had arrived in New England. In the second part of the volume the author then covers the same ground, but this time in topical fashion, showing us how the courts worked, how land was apportioned, how master and servant interacted, and in general explicating the operations of this small society in a way designed to assist the genealogist in his labors.

The third part of the book, while more straightforwardly genealogical, has some special surprises. This section, of biographical sketches of hundreds of the earliest settlers, draws largely on material in print, both primary and secondary, and as such serves principally as a guide to the literature. But salted throughout the pages of this section are some interesting new discoveries, and some even more interesting new suggestions for solutions to some of the most important outstanding genealogical problems of Plymouth Colony.

As noted above, *Plymouth Colony* is a pioneering work, being one of the first attempts to combine history and genealogy in this particular way. As such, it immediately becomes a standard against which future compositions of a similar nature must be judged.

Robert Charles Anderson, F.A.S.G.

Acknowledgement

T his is to acknowledge, with deep gratitude, the contribution to this book made by Mr. Robert S. Wakefield, F.A.S.G., who worked as coauthor on Part One and furnished significant material to support many of the biographical sketches in Part Three. Mr. Wakefield is one of the foremost Plymouth Colony scholars in the country, and this book could not have been written within given time constraints without his active participation. His most valued help is highly appreciated.

Introduction

S amuel Eliot Morison once observed that many historians are content to write in detail about the adventures of the *Mayflower* passengers in getting here and then leave them sitting high and dry on Plymouth Rock. He wrote: "Historians seem to lose interest in the Pilgrims as soon as they were able to have three square meals daily, and own a cow."

That rather sad situation has been corrected somewhat in recent decades. John Demos, in *A Little Commonwealth – Family Life in Plymouth Colony*, has given us an excellent specialized study of some aspects of family life in Plymouth, and in it he also comments that "There was, for example, no full-length history of Plymouth Colony, conforming to accepted criteria of professional research, until very recently. It is almost as if the aura of legend surrounding the Pilgrim settlers makes them difficult to recover as live human beings." Notice Mr. Demos's qualification "conforming to accepted criteria of professional research." He undoubtedly had in mind George E. Willison's 1945 popular book *Saints and Strangers*, which was written by a Rhodes scholar who could and did do a considerable amount of good research to write his book, and then vitiated it by throwing it together in an undocumented hodgepodge of fact and fiction so intermixed that it would be difficult for even a trained scholar to extricate the one from the other.

The recent exception noted by Mr. Demos was George D. Langdon's *Pilgrim Colony: A History of New Plymouth, 1620-1691*, about which Demos says, "This careful, admirably sound and sensible study should remain 'definitive' for a long time to come. I have myself leaned heavily upon it at several points." In the present text, too, I must acknowledge a debt to this fine book, which, at times, I also have leaned heavily upon. But that of course gives rise to the question, if definitive, then why the need for another book covering the same time and place? The answer in part is hinted at by Sumner Chilton Powell in his Pulitzer Prize-winning *Puritan Village – The Formation of a New England Town*, in which he observes "Any

1

young historian would do well to appreciate the precision and careful handling of documents, which are the *sine qua non* of any professional genealogist."

Mr. Demos in his book relies considerably, too, on the techniques of the genealogist, even though genealogy is not held in high regard in academic circles. Elizabeth Shown Mills, a superb genealogist, illustrates this point by writing in an article, "A young Southern historian began his teaching career on the university level and simultaneously showed an interest in family history. Superiors promptly cautioned him not to get involved in genealogy or his career would be ruined." (However, that young Southern historian continued his interest in genealogy, and now is highly respected by both professional genealogists and academic historians.) Genealogy has deserved its ill fame for a number of reasons, but mostly for the barbarities committed by well-intentioned, but untrained practitioners. Anyone interested in learning a bit about just how bad genealogy can be may read my article on the subject, "The Validity of Genealogical Evidence" in the December 1984 issue of the *National Genealogical Society Quarterly*.

All this obscures the fact that genealogy has been coming of age. It took some time. The late G. Andrews Moriarty and Donald Lines Jacobus have not received the attention and appreciation they deserved other than in genealogical circles. The work of some of the senior genealogists in the field today—for example, John Coddington and Milton Rubincam—is certainly on an academic level. Some of the best genealogical writers of today, Neil D. Thompson, Elizabeth Shown Mills, Robert Charles Anderson, Henry B. Hoff, and David L. Greene, just to name a few (and I feel guilty leaving out a good number of others), fully conform "to accepted criteria of professional research."

The paradox is that both historians and genealogists have plied their respective trades in that well-visited market of Plymouth Colony for years and in great, if not always comprehensive, detail. But they have plied their trades separately. There never has been a history of Plymouth Colony written from the genealogical point of view. History is made by individuals living their lives amidst other individuals. Without the trees there can be no forest. The human history of Plymouth Colony is so rich, so interesting, so pertinent to an understanding of the development of our nation, that it is a shame it has been subordinated to fairy tales such as "Speak for yourself, John Alden." There is a need for something new on the subject.

This book is intended to give a well-rounded comprehensive overview of the life of Plymouth Colony by stressing the interaction of people with history. It is not complete, in that greater detail can be found for this or that aspect in some other sources, but many of such sources are named in this book in case the reader should want to plunge deeper. A three-dimensional approach is used to tell the story. The horizontal is a chronological history, divided in chapters according to successive time periods (which has the advantage of ensuring that there will be coverage of those many years of the existence of Plymouth Colony that are usually ignored). The vertical approach slices through time to give the reader considerable detail on a given topic, such as politics, law, morality, and others. A third part adds depth by giving short sketches of several hundred colony residents between 1620 and 1691, mostly heads of families, with a short biographical sketch to show each person's contribution to the colony's history or genealogy, together with a considerable number of bibliographic references to where more information may be found in published sources, including the most recent journal articles.

Additionally, this work is intended to serve as a reference book for Plymouth Colony scholars and fans of all types. To further this goal, a general bibliography has been included, together with various appendices containing original source material of interest to historian and genealogist alike. Some such material consists of Plymouth Colony documents selected because they show who was where at different points in time. These documents are of course available individually in other publications, but they have not previously been obtainable within the covers of a single book. Further, one of the annoying facts in the lives of history scholars is that the literature of the field abounds with conclusions so repeated from book to book that they are just taken for granted as absolute fact—and in many cases they are fact—but the original source of the information remains obscure. For example, many people seriously interested in the history of Plymouth Colony have heard that Capt. Myles Standish never joined the Plymouth Church, and that William Bradford's wife committed suicide, but what are the original sources, and how reliable are they? This book attempts to go back to the original source for many of these time-hallowed traditions (the source for the statement on Standish seems quite reliable, but that for Bradford's wife is indisputably false).

A reading of all three parts of the text should give one a thorough understanding of what happened in Plymouth in colony years and who made it happen. The reader will find a greatly diversified assembly of residents. They will range from the aristocratic Edward Winslow to the theocratic William Bradford; from the introspective Roger Williams to the activist reformer William Vassall; and from the moderationist James Cudworth to the man who understood and liked the Indians so much that he could and did outfight them to the death, Benjamin Church. Others appearing are the town ne'er-do-well Webb Adey; the town drunk Thomas Lucas; the dignified widow Elizabeth Warren, who was honored by being made a "Purchaser" in the right of her late husband; those who were whipped and fined for fornication and adultery; those who were whipped and fined for being Quakers; the excommunicated popular leader John Cooke; the wards of Governor Bradford who rose to be leaders themselves; and many others. These were very human human beings.

This book will answer the question: What ever happened to those people who came over on the *Mayflower?* They will not be left high and dry on Plymouth Rock. We will follow them after they get three square meals daily and a cow, and then we will follow the ones who arrived after them, and we will follow their children, and sometimes their children's children. To do this, the book relies mainly on contemporary records, the records left by the people themselves. Two references will predominate because they cover so much material, and because there is nothing else on their scale. The first of these is the history of Plymouth written by Gov. William Bradford, which goes into considerable depth to show the origins and the early years of the colony, and then gets sparser after some twenty years or so in Plymouth. The second reference consists of the court records of Plymouth Colony, starting sparsely in the 1620s and getting more detailed with time for the duration of the colony period. These two sources give tremendous detail and insight on the life of the colony, and they are the flesh and blood of any history ever written or to be written about Plymouth Colony. There are other documents of the times such as letters, diaries, narratives, church records, wills, deeds, and a surprising number of others. All of these add to the two main sources, fill them out, and sometimes help keep them in proper perspective.

This book, then, is written to let the people of the times speak for themselves. To help this appear as authentic as possible—to give the reader a real feel for the ambience of the times—words, spellings, and punctuation are often given as found in the records themselves. This could make reading some of the quotations a bit of effort, but the effort gives such rewards that it is far superior, for the purposes of this work, to any other method. The best way to tackle the quotations is to pronounce words phonetically. You will be surprised at how similar the language of the 1600s is to today's language—e.g., "Yea, he screwed up his poor old father-in-law's account," though this will appear in the book as "Yea, he scrued up his poore old father in laws accounte." It helps, too, to keep in mind that there were no dictionaries, as we know them, in those days, and no formal rules for spelling. There was no "correct" way, but if the spelling allowed the reader of the times to understand the message, it served its purpose. For the most part their spelling is helpful, in the sense of letting us understand better how they talked. When they wrote "graunted" for "granted," it indicates that they spoke with a very broad "a," and when we see "goverment" instead of "government," it indicates to us that they dropped the "n" in their speech as well as their writing. It brings us a little closer to these people, which is one of the main purposes of the book.

They are not so far away from us. Millions of Americans have Plymouth Colony ancestry, usually being separated from these people by only some ten to fifteen generations. Technology changes tremendously, at least in modern times, in but a single generation, but human nature does not. A grandfather living today could have known his grandfather, and talked to him often. That grandfather could have talked often to his own grandfather. That grandfather could have known and engaged in conversations with Thomas Faunce, who was born in Plymouth Colony in 1647, knew personally many of the surviving *Mayflower* passengers, and died in 1746. Such a short span separates us from the people of Plymouth of the 1600s. They were much poorer than we are in material things, but they were modern people, much closer to us in mind than to those who lived before them in medieval or ancient times.

There are also millions of other Americans who are not descendants of the Plymouth colonists, though because of marriage between descendants and nondescendants, their children or grandchildren could be. But all people in this country today are the spiritual heirs of those who brought democracy to our shores centuries before it became established in the mother country. William Bradford wrote with foresight when he put down the words: "As one small candle may light a thousand, so the light here kindled hath shone to many, yea in some sorte to our whole nation."

It is easy to see far when one stands on the shoulders of giants. This book owes a great debt to the many Plymouth Colony scholars who have written earlier, for one always builds on antecedents. The greatest genealogical scholar of Plymouth Colony was George Ernest Bowman, and he must be especially acknowledged. He left a living legacy in the *Mayflower Descendant*, a timeless and unsurpassed collection of original records of the people of colonial Plymouth. Moreover, he left a methodology for precision in acquiring data that has been all too little appreciated in the past, but has been gaining recognition with time.

As shown in the acknowledgment page, some parts of this book were written in collaboration with my esteemed colleague, Robert S. Wakefield, F.A.S.G. I will only add here that I have learned much from this respected colonial Plymouth scholar in the realm of documentation. His constant reminder of the need to pin-point sources—Where did that come from? What specifically does this source say? How reliable is that reference? Are the sources in agreement?—has undoubtedly improved the accuracy of this book.

First among others who have been of great help to get this book out is Robert Charles Anderson, F.A.S.G., who saw drafts during various stages and offered much helpful advice. His extensive familiarity with the primary and secondary literature of New England history in all of its many facets has helped considerably to put the Plymouth Colony story in its broader New England context.

Many thanks are also due to Roger D. Joslyn, F.A.S.G., who saw a semi-final draft and gave it a thorough editing from the genealogical point of view, and to Linda Cunningham, who edited the book from the more conventional viewpoint. Among those most helpful in aiding me on specific aspects of the book were Ruth Wilder Sherman, F.A.S.G., editor of *The American Genealogist;* Barbara Lambert Merrick, Historian General of the General Society of Mayflower Descendants; Jane F. Fiske, F.A.S.G.; and Alicia C. Williams, editor of the *Mayflower Descendant.* I owe my wife, Ginger K. W. Stratton, a tremendous debt of gratitude not only for her patience with me while sequestering myself from my family, but also for

6   *Plymouth Colony*

her time and dedication in helping me with research and proofreading. I am also grateful to David Case, Richard L. Ehrlich, Carolyn Freeman Travers, and others of the staff of Plimoth Plantation for their helpful cooperation. Notwithstanding the help of others, though, I must of course take full responsibility for the final product.

Last, but not least, I want to thank John Sittner, publisher, Robert J. Welsh, managing editor, and the staff of Ancestry, Inc., for making it possible to satisfy my long-held dream of making this book a reality.

Eugene Aubrey Stratton

Figure 1–*Mayflower II* in full sail

Figure 2–Aerial View of Plimoth Plantation

Figure 3–Jabez Howland House in Winter

Figure 4–Interior View of Jabez Howland House

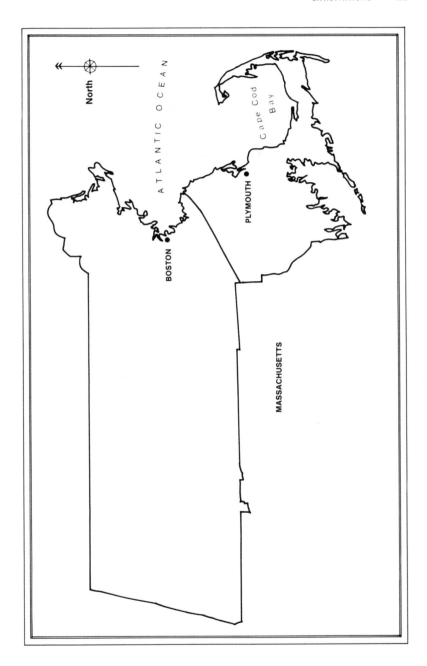

Map 1–Map of Massachusetts showing Plymouth

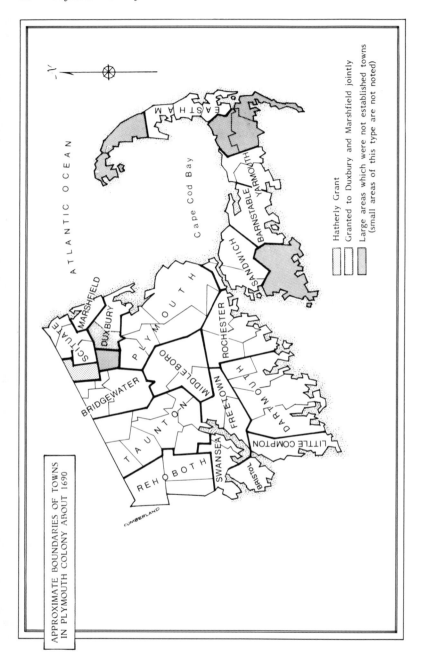

Map 2–Map of the Townships of Plymouth Colony

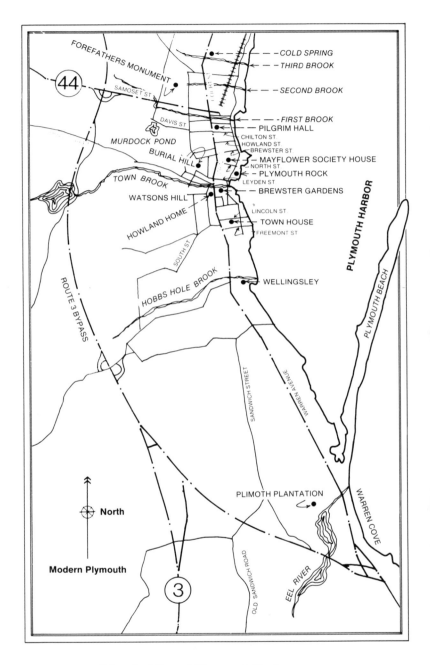

Map 3–Map of Plymouth Today

PART ONE
Chronological Histories

The Old Comers (1620-1627)

"A TIME TO PLANT"

The story of Plymouth Colony starts back in England in the early years of the seventeenth century. King Henry VIII had made the break from the Pope in the previous century, and both in England and on the continent religious reformers were asking questions and pronouncing new dogmas. Martin Luther in Germany, John Calvin in Switzerland, and John Knox in Scotland had made people more conscious of the nature of religion than ever before with the prime question: What form should organized religion take? King Henry chose a compromise answer—keeping the Catholic form, but substituting himself, instead of the Pope, as head of the Church of England. Henry was succeeded by a young sickly son, Edward VI, who died in 1553. Edward's half-sister, Mary, by some called Bloody Mary, assumed the crown and restored Roman Catholicism as the official religion. She died in 1558 and was succeeded by her half-sister, Elizabeth, who restored her father's compromise, and, as sovereign, became the head of the official Anglican Church.

When King James I succeeded Elizabeth in 1602/03, [1] England was divided between old-time Catholics, conforming Anglicans, and a great variety of Protestants. There were Puritans, who constituted a movement within the Church of England (but were not a distinct sect or denomination), and Separatists, who had gone beyond Puritan thinking and wanted to be completely separate from the official church. Perry Miller and Thomas Johnson point out that "No government in Europe at that epoch would have tolerated the existence of such a [Separatist] society, outside and independent of the established institution, and it is no wonder that the bishops and the sheriffs of England got after this congregation with vehemence." [2] Thus the Separatists, who were of several unrelated groups, came under heavy persecution from the English government. Some groups of Separatists were in England's northern counties, such as Lincolnshire, Lancashire, Yorkshire, and Nottinghamshire, where they "gathered" their own individual churches under the control of the congregation, instead of some remote bishop.

Richard Clyfton became the pastor of one such group in Scrooby, Nottinghamshire, with John Robinson as his assistant minister. William Brewster, who was master of the post station at Scrooby Manor, joined this church, later becoming its Ruling Elder. William Bradford, too, from nearby Austerfield, Yorkshire, joined the separatist religion and became a life-long follower and friend to Elder Brewster. In Bradford's own words, church members "were hunted and persecuted on every side, so as their former afflictions were as flea-bitings in comparison with these that now came upon them. For some were taken and clapt up in prison, others had their houses besett and watcht night and day, and hardly escaped their hands; and the most were faine to flie and leave their howses and habitations, and the means of their livelihood." The congregation thus decided in 1607 to move to Holland, which allowed considerable freedom to religious dissenters, and where other English religious refugees had already fled. Because of difficulty with the English government in leaving England, including imprisonment for some, such as William Brewster, they did not complete their move to Holland until 1608. [3]

At first the Clyfton-Robinson congregation lived in Amsterdam; but after about one year they decided to move to Leiden because of much quarreling between the several English churches in Amsterdam. Mr. Clyfton continued as a member of the church when it was in Leiden, but "being setled at Amsterdam and thus aged hee was loth to Remove any more," and so he remained in Amsterdam until he died in 1616. Some of the dates of events and elections in this church remain obscure, and John Robinson possibly became pastor in Amsterdam; it is certain that he held the position as soon as they moved to Leiden, and, not long after, William Brewster was known to be Ruling Elder and John Carver was a deacon. [4]

It must have been interesting to have been an Englishman living in Leiden at this time. William Brewster became a publisher of books, with Thomas Brewer as his partner, and young Edward Winslow became associated with them. John Robinson both studied and taught at Leiden's famed university. Many of their congregation worked in some fashion in the clothing trade to support themselves—Isaac Allerton as a tailor, William Bradford and William Pontus as fustian makers, Cuthbert Cuthbertson as a hat maker, Richard Masterson as a wool carder, and others in the weaving, dying, and sewing trades. A good amount of research was done earlier this century on who of the English were in Leiden, what they did, their relationship with the Dutch community, and related questions. Though the studies of Dexter and of Plooij would seem to have exhausted the subject, in recent years newer students have been combing Leiden records again. Indeed, more is being and still remains to be discovered, including new identifications of the Separatists' English origins and discoveries of colonists who had not previously been known to have lived in Leiden. [5]

Leiden was not, however, a paradise for the English. Bradford mentioned that no others would join them from England, for they would not

have been able to "endure that great labor and hard fare. . . . Some preferred, and chose the prisons in England, rather than this libertie in Holland, with these afflictions." In this he refers to economic conditions, for
most of the English were not citizens of Leiden and did not enjoy the
privileges of citizenship. Their employment possibilities were limited, and
they had to work hard just to keep up a low standard of living. Further,
"that which was more lamentable. . .was that many of their children, by
these occasions, and by the great licentiousnes of youth in that countrie,
and the manifold temptations of the place, were drawne away by evill
examples into extravagante and dangerous courses." And thus for both
economic reasons and for the welfare of their children—not for
religious freedom, which they already enjoyed in Holland—"after they had
lived in this citie about some 11 or 12 years," they decided to look for a
new place. [6]

England had known of the North American coast for years. Bartholomew Gosnold had visited Cape Cod in 1602. Martin Pring was the
first European to visit the site of Plymouth, spending six weeks exploring
the bay of Massachusetts in 1603. Jamestown, Virginia, was founded in
1607, the first permanent English settlement in the New World. Captain
John Smith was at Jamestown, but he also explored further north and made
a detailed map of the New England coast in 1616. It was probably due to
Smith's writings that the Leiden Separatists knew of the area, and most
likely when they sailed on the *Mayflower* in 1620 they had Captain Smith's
maps with them. Smith had offered his services to the people from Leiden,
but instead they chose for their captain an English soldier living in Holland named Myles Standish. Perhaps the English Separatists were cautious of Smith's reputation as a swashbuckling bragadoccio, or perhaps
they declined his offer for some other reason, but Smith himself wrote that
they turned him down to save money, "saying my books and maps were
much better cheape to teach them, than myselfe." [7]

Those who left were not known as Pilgrims at the time. The word was
first applied to them by Bradford writing his history many years later. "So
they lefte that goodly and pleasante citie which had been ther resting place
near 12 years; but they knew they were pilgrimes, and looked not much
on those things, but lift up their eyes to the heavens, their dearest cuntrie, and quieted their spirits." [8] Not all Separatists left Leiden in 1620.
Some followed later, and some stayed forever in Holland where most likely
their descendants live today. The majority of the congregation, in fact,
remained in Leiden in 1620, and that is why Pastor John Robinson, who
decided to stay with the majority, did not leave; though he planned to go
later, he died on 1 March 1624/25.

Nor was it only Separatists from Holland who crossed the ocean in
that 1620 voyage, for they were joined in England by other Separatists and
by people Bradford called "Strangers," who were not of their faith, but with
whom they had to travel in order to get support for their venture. Support came from a group of businessmen called "Adventurers," who

ventured capital into this particular New World settlement in the hope of great profits. The settlers got one share in the company for each man and woman above the age of sixteen. The Adventurers, some of whom were undoubtedly of Separatist or at least Puritan persuasion themselves, were nonetheless hard-nosed entrepreneurs, and they obtained one share in the company for each £10 they invested to transport and provision the settlers. Captain John Smith identified the Adventurers as about seventy gentlemen, merchants, and craftsmen, venturing widely varying sums of money, some great and some small. [9]

The Adventurers had obtained a patent in the name of one of their members, John Peirce, to colonize in the northern part of the Virginia territory. Though the settlers continued from England in two ships, the *Speedwell* had to return to England due to dangerous leaking, and the *Mayflower* continued alone. According to Capt. John Smith, writing in 1622, "They left the coast of England the 23 of August, with about 120 persons, but the next day the lesser ship sprung a leake, that forced their return to Plimmoth, where discharging her and 20 passengers, with the great ship and a hundred persons besides sailers, they set saile againe the Sixt of September." Among the twenty who stayed behind were Robert Cushman, one of the Separatist leaders, and William Ring, of the Leiden congregation. Cushman wrote of the short but frightful voyage aboard the *Speedwell*, "Poore William Ring and my selfe doe strive who shall be meate first for the fishes." The *Mayflower*, too, had its mishaps at sea, with a main beam splitting during a storm; a young servant, William Butten, dying; and John Howland falling overboard, but being rescued. [10]

Their destination in the northern Virginia territory was to have been roughly where Manhattan is today, but they sailed further north, outside the Virginia limits. Why they did this is not known for certain. Several theories have been advanced, including one that they deliberately avoided Virginia lands so as to be outside the jurisdiction of the Anglican Church, which was the established church in Virginia. However, Bradford and Winslow went to their graves maintaining that they arrived at New England either by accident or by the treachery of Capt. Christopher Jones. On 9 November 1620 "We espied land which we deemed to be Cape Cod, and so afterward it proved." They continued to travel around the Cape, but the winds forced them to turn back. "We put round againe for the Bay of Cape Cod: and upon the 11 of November, we came to an anchor in the Bay." They decided to look further, and on 11 December 1620 they started exploration of Plymouth Harbor. Within a few days they made the decision to settle at Plymouth, anchoring at a short distance from land, the harbor being quite shallow, and they used the shallop to go ashore. Plymouth, which had some years earlier been given its name by Capt. John Smith and had it confirmed by Prince (later King) Charles, was at that time a Wampanoag Indian village, deserted because of a disease which had killed many of the natives of southeastern New England. [11]

In 1621 a second patent, also in John Pierce's name, had to be obtained, since the colonists had settled outside the limits of their first patent. (More details on both patents are given in chapter 8.)

One hundred and two passengers sailed from England on the *Mayflower*. One died at sea (William Butten), four died at Provincetown Harbor (Dorothy Bradford, James Chilton, Jasper More, and Edward Thompson), one was born at sea (Oceanus Hopkins), and one was born at Provincetown Harbor (Peregrine White), and thus there arrived at Plymouth ninety-nine of those we say "stayed." These included John Alden, a cooper who signed on the *Mayflower* at Southampton, and who accepted an offer to stay as part of the company, and four seamen. Two of the seamen (William Trevor and _____ Ely) were hired to stay for one year, and two others (John Allerton and Thomas English) were hired to be part of the company, but the latter two died before the *Mayflower* sailed again. The entire crew stayed throughout the severe winter of 1620/21, and about half died. The surviving crew members returned to England when the *Mayflower* set sail on 5 April 1621. Of the settlers, only fifty-two, including Trevor and Ely, were still alive when the *Fortune*, the next ship, arrived in November 1621. [12]

Most of the deaths occurred during the first few months of 1621, and only six more, including Gov. John Carver and his wife, died between the sailing of the *Mayflower* and the arrival of the *Fortune*. Thereafter the condition of the settlers improved, for in 1623 Governor Bradford told a visitor from Virginia that "for the space of one whole year of the two wherein they had been there, died not one man, woman or child." Capt. John Smith wrote that the plantation in 1624 was so healthful that "in these last three yeeres, notwithstanding their great want of most necessaries, there hath not one died of the first planters." Trevor and Ely probably returned on the *Fortune* in December 1621, for Robert Cushman wrote in March or April 1623 that "William Trevore hath lavishly tould but what he knew or imagined" about the surrounding area to some of the Adventurers. [13]

While still in Provincetown Harbor, some of the group asserted that they had the right, since they had not gone as planned to Virginia territory, to live as they wished and take orders from no one. Bradford wrote of the Mayflower Compact that it was "occasioned partly by the discontented and mutinous speeches that some of the strangers amongst them had let fall from them in the ship." Winslow confirms that "some [were] not well affected to unitie and concord, but gave some appearances of faction [and thus] it was thought good. . .that we should combine together in one body, and to submit to such government and governours, as we should by common consent agree to make and choose." Thus all free adult males signed the Mayflower Compact, which stated essentially that the individual would subject himself to majority rule. After the signing, John Carver was chosen, "or rather confirmed," their governor for that year, but he died in the spring of 1621. William Bradford was chosen to succeed him, governing first with one Assistant, Isaac Allerton, and later with as many as seven, who acted as magistrates and collectively were the Council, that is, the executive and judicial body. From the beginning, all important positions were elective, and even Capt. Myles Standish, who led not a regular army, but a citizens' militia, had to be chosen for his position. [14]

The food supply in the early years was almost always critically low. Thanks to the Wampanoags, the settlers learned how to plant Indian crops, which ultimately helped them avoid starvation. Winslow described the process: "We set the last spring [1621] some twentie Acres of Indian Corne, and sowed some six Acres of Barly and Pease, and according to the manner of the Indians, we manured our ground with Herings or rather Shadds." But the first crops were not sufficient. The next ship, the *Fortune*, arrived at Cape Cod 9 November 1621 (though it took several more weeks to find Plymouth), with thirty-five new colonists led by Mr. Robert Cushman. Cushman returned on the *Fortune* when it left for England on 13 December 1621, after having given a layman's sermon on 9 December. The new colonists were ill provisioned, and Bradford wrote, "So they were all landed, but ther was not so much as bisket-cake or any other victialls for them," and "They were presently put to half alowance, one as well as an other, which begane to be hard, but they bore it patiently under hope of supply." Winslow, in May 1622, referred to the same: "Our store of victuals was wholly spent, having lived long before with a bare and short allowance: The reason was, that supply of men before mentioned, which came so unprovided, not landing so much as a barrell of bread or meal for their whole company, but contrariwise received from us for their ships store homeward." Another ship, the *Paragon*, with sixty-seven passengers sent out "by private mens purses" in October 1622, had to return to England two weeks later, damaged by a storm and leaking. The *Paragon* made at least one other unsuccessful attempt in February 1622/23, but again was driven back, and never reached New Plymouth. By 1623 Bradford was writing about their lack of food, "Yet they bore these wants with great patience and allacritie of spirite, and that for so long a time as for the most parte of 2 years." Even when new ships arrived in 1623, Bradford described how the new settlers found the old. "They were in a very low condition. . . . But for food they were all alike, save some that had got a few pease of the ship that was last hear. The best dish they could present their friends with was a lobster, or a peece of fish without bread or anything els but a cupp of fair spring water," and he added, "God fedd them out of the sea for the most parte." [15]

Relations with the Indians, at least the nearby Wampanoags under the supreme chief, Massasoit, were good. Samoset, who was not a Wampanoag, but came from Maine, had learned some English from fishing ships, and he walked in on the settlers shortly after their arrival at Plymouth and offered to help them. Through Samoset, they learned also of Squanto, who was "a native of this place," but who had been taken by a ship to England. Samoset stayed his first night at Stephen Hopkins's house, ¬robably because Hopkins had had familiarity with Indians when he was in Virginia years earlier. Through Samoset, the colonists made initial contact with Massasoit and shortly after signed a peace treaty with him, which continued until after Massasoit's death in 1662. One of Massasoit's men, Hobbamock, came to live with the settlers in Plymouth, and, along with Samoset and Squanto, became of great assistance to them. The Narragansetts, who lived to the west of the Wampanoags and were their enemies, were more numerous and powerful. During the summer of 1621 Bradford and his men kept hearing rumors from friendly Indians of an impending Narragansett attack, and following the arrival of the *Fortune,* the Narragansetts sent the Plymouth settlers a warning in the form of a bundle of arrows wrapped up in the skin of a rattlesnake. After consultation with his advisers, Bradford answered the challenge by returning the skin to the Narragansetts full of powder and shot. Under Captain Standish, Plymouth took due military precautions, including dividing the men into four companies and assigning them defensive positions, and there was no attack. [16]

Though no new ships with settlers arrived until July 1623, Plymouth was not completely isolated. English fishing ships as well as ships engaged in other colonizing ventures called on the colony from time to time. Winslow wrote, for example, that "In the end of June, or beginning of July [1622], came into our harbour two ships of Master Westons aforesaid, the one called the *Charitie,* the other the *Swan,* having in them some fifty or sixty men sent over at his owne charge to plant for him." (Bradford said sixty men.) Mr. Thomas Weston had been one of the leaders of the London Adventurers, but had quarreled with the company, sold out his interests, and begun his own enterprises. He also sent out the *Sparrow,* and a shallop from this ship brought seven passengers to Plymouth who were destined for Weston's planned colony. The settlers on the *Charity* and the *Swan* were rather rough and unruly men, and they stayed at Plymouth during the summer of 1622 until they left in September to colonize an area somewhat north of Plymouth called Wessagusset (present day Weymouth). [17]

Weston's settlers did not fare well at Weymouth and blundered considerably in their relations with nearby Indians. On one occasion they were forced to hang one of their own men to pacify the Indians from whom the man had been stealing. Finally relations got so bad that Weston's men feared for their lives. Captain Standish and some men were dispatched from Plymouth to rescue them, the Plymouth group killing several Indians in the process. Shortly afterwards Weston's group abandoned the settlement and in turn was succeeded there by newer settlers who arrived on the *Katherine,* a ship sent out by Sir Ferdinando Gorges, which arrived at Plymouth in September 1623. This ship, too, first stayed a while at Plymouth, where its passengers became one more burden to the struggling colony. Bradford wrote that Gorges's group arrived "with sundrie pasengers and families. . .and pitched upon the place Mr. Weston's group had forsaken." One of Weston's settlers at Weymouth who had arrived on the *Sparrow,* Phineas Pratt, on the breakup of the Weston settlement, moved to Plymouth. He later married Mary Priest, a daughter of the then deceased *Mayflower* passenger, Degory Priest, and a niece of Plymouth Colony Assistant, Isaac Allerton. [18]

Other ships also called on Plymouth. One visiting ship, *Discovery,* sailing from Virginia to England in 1622, carried as a passenger John Pory, an official from Jamestown, Virginia, who later wrote letters in praise of the northern colony. The next ships with passengers intended for Plymouth were the *Anne,* which arrived in July 1623, and the *Little James,* which arrived a week or so later. With the arrival of the *Anne,* Bradford observed that the Adventurers were sending over some men "on their Particular," meaning they would not have to work as the rest for the communal profit of the company. Bradford wrote that the two ships "brought about 60 persons for the generall, some of them being very usefull persons, and became good members to the body; and some were the wives and children of shuch as were hear allready. And some were so bad, as they were faine to be at charge to send them home againe the next year. Also, besides these ther came a company that did not belong to the general body, but came [on] their perticuler and were to have lands assigned them and be for them selves, yet to be subject to the generall goverment; which caused some diferance and disturbance amongst them, as will after apeare." The *Little James,* which had been built by the Adventurers to stay in New England, could have been a great boon to the colonists, but it was plagued with bad fortune, a mutinous crew, a shipwreck, seizure by creditors in England (after it was salvaged), and finally capture by Barbary pirates. [19]

Since some sixty people were said to have arrived on the two ships for the General Body, and we can calculate from the number of acres allotted in the 1623 Division of Land that about ninety people must have arrived in all, it follows that some thirty of the newcomers must have been "Particulars," who did not have to work or share with the others. In April 1624 the *Charity* arrived again with some passengers and goods, this time sent out by James Sherley, another of the Adventurers, and under the command of William Peirce, an Adventurer and frequent visitor to New England. Though a few more settlers arrived in various ships calling at Plymouth over the next few years, their numbers were limited by lack of support from the Merchant Adventurers. [20]

All was not without cheer though. In the fall of 1621, prior to the arrival of the *Fortune,* the small group of survivors celebrated what has come to be known as the first Thanksgiving. This event was described by Edward Winslow:

> Our harvest being gotten in, our Governour sent foure men on fowling, that so we might after a more speciall manner rejoyce together, after we had gathered the fruit of our labours; they foure in one day killed as much fowle, as with a little helpe beside, served the Company almost a weeke, at which time amongst other Recreations, we

exercised our Armes, many of the Indians coming amongst us, and amongst the rest their greatest King Massasoyt, with some nintie men, whom for three dayes we entertained and feasted, and they went out and killed five Deere, which they brought to the Plantation and bestowed on our Governour, and upon the Captaine, and others. And although it be not alwayes so plentifull, as it was at this time with us, yet by the goodnesse of God, we are so farre from want, that we often wish you partakers of our plentie. [21]

Winslow was writing to attract new settlers, and he might have overstated the settlers' being in general "so farre from want." This is all we have from contemporary records about the first "Thanksgiving," which was really more of a harvest festival. The word "thanksgiving," which was not used in Winslow's description, more commonly meant a day of fast and prayer.

Another early celebration was noted in a September 1623 letter from Emmanuel Altham, captain of the *Little James*, on the occasion of Governor William Bradford's marriage to Alice (Carpenter) Southworth: "And now to say somewhat of the great cheer we had at the Governor's marriage. We had about twelve pasty venison, besides others, pieces of roasted venison and other such good cheer in such quantity that I could wish you some of our share. For here we have the best grapes that ever you [saw] — and the biggest, and divers sorts of plums and nuts which our business will not suffer us to look for." Bradford, whose first wife drowned in 1620 when the *Mayflower* anchored at Provincetown Harbor, took Alice Southworth for his second wife on 14 August 1623. She was the widow of Edward Southworth, a highly respected member of the Leiden group. Alice Southworth had just arrived in Plymouth on the *Anne*, and this was the fourth marriage in Plymouth, the first having been widower Edward Winslow's on 12 May 1621 to Susanna, a *Mayflower* passenger recently widowed from William White. Bradford described how the colonists broke from the English tradition of marriage by clergy and adopted the "laudable custome of the Low-cuntries, in which they had lived, [which] was thought most requisite to be performed by the magistrate, as being a civill thing, upon which many questions about inheritances doe depende." [22]

In accordance with their agreement with the Adventurers, the settlers were to live virtually a socialistic life, sharing everything in common, for the first seven years. Then the profits of the company were to be totaled and divided according to the number of outstanding shares. But by 1623 many were complaining that the industrious ones were working to support the lazy ones. It was decided to give every man, woman, and child the use of one acre of land to be cultivated as they wished for their own crops, although they would still cultivate the greater common lands for the company. This is known as the "Division of Land," and the records of it name all the heads of household who arrived on the *Mayflower, Fortune, Anne,* and *Little James* who were still living in Plymouth, plus the names of some of the wives who arrived on the *Anne,* and of others such as Phineas Pratt, together with the number of acres each received for self and dependents. [23]

In 1624 two of the newer settlers, the Reverend John Lyford, who favored the Church of England and was an opportunist, and John Oldham, an adventurer in the modern sense of the word, brought to a head a number of complaints against the colony's government. Lyford sent letters with passing ships to various people in England in an attempt to alienate influential supporters from the colony's leaders. Bradford got word of this, and, going aboard one of the ships, he seized some letters and copied them, letting the originals go. Bradford then had a confrontation with Lyford and Oldham with the entire colony present. At first Lyford denied the accusations. When Bradford produced copies of his letters, Lyford excused himself by saying that he had merely been repeating what others were complaining about, mentioning John Billington, a rather undisciplined "stranger" who had come on the *Mayflower,* and some others whom Bradford did not identify. Billington and the others denied Lyford's accusations, saying that they might sometimes have gone to Lyford's meetings, but would not have consented to his proposals. Most likely Billington and the other dissidents had gone much further in supporting Lyford than they would admit, and many of the others are assumed to be among those who departed the colony in the next year or so. Bradford wrote to Robert Cushman on 9 June 1625, "We have rid ourselves of the company of those, who have been so troublesome unto us." Oldham and Lyford were expelled from Plymouth; Oldham left immediately, but Lyford was allowed to stay for six months. Both later were involved in other adventures in New England. Billington remained at Plymouth, though, as will be told, he eventually came to a tragic end. Bradford's decisive action undoubtedly strengthened the Separatist government for some time, but newer settlers were arriving at various times, and the population of Plymouth was becoming more diversified. [24]

Captain John Smith wrote an excellent description of Plymouth in 1624:

At New Plimouth there is about 180 persons, some cattell and goats, but many swine and poultry, 32 dwelling houses, wherof 7 were burnt the last winter, and the value of five hundred pounds in other goods; the Towne is impailed about halfe a mile compasse. In the towne upon a high Mount they have a Fort well built with wood, lome, and stone, where is planted their Ordnance: Also a faire Watch-tower, partly framed for the Sentinell, the place it seemes is healthfull. . . . The most of them live together as one family or houshold, yet every man followeth his trade and profession both by sea and land, and all for a generall stocke, out of which they have all their maintenance, untill there be a divident betwixt the Planters and the Adventurers. Those Planters are not servants to the Adventurers here, but have only councells of directions from them. . . .and all the master of families are partners in land or whatsoever, setting their labours against the stocke. . . . . They have young men and boies for their Apprentises and servants, and some of them speciall families, as Ship-carpenters, Salt-makers, Fish-masters, yet as servants upon great wages. . . . There hath been a fishing this yeere upon the Coast about 50 English ships: and by Cape Anne, there is a Plantation a beginning by Dorchester men, which they hold of those of New-Plimouth, who also by them have set up a fishing worke. [25]

The colonists' relations with the Adventurers soon became considerably strained. Because of high interest rates, poor accounting, and perhaps some self-serving by Isaac Allerton and some of the Adventurers, the colony's indebtedness to the Adventurers seemed to grow rather than decrease, in spite of some sizeable shipments of furs from Plymouth to England. For their part, many of the Adventurers were discouraged over lack of profits, and some sold out their interests to others at a loss. Since 1624 the Adventurers had been reluctant to finance more colonists, resulting in a slowing down of new immigrants, and also tending to strand those Separatists still in Leiden who wished to join their coreligionists or family. On one of his many trips to England, Isaac Allerton negotiated a new arrangement, and in late 1626 he obtained an agreement whereby the Adventurers sold for £1,800 all their interests in the colony to Allerton and the other "Planters" at Plymouth. These "Old Planters," or "Old Purchasers," were the heads of families of those then resident in Plymouth. They were later given privileges which allowed them advantageous grants of free land. The expression "Old Comers" was also used at this time, seemingly as a way of referring to those who had arrived prior to any given point in time; however, eventually this term came to encompass all who were resident in Plymouth by 1627. [26]

In 1627 eight of Plymouth's leading men, joined by four of the Adventurers in England who still wished to be associated with them, undertook the responsibility for payment of the entire debt to the Adventurers, in return for certain monopolies granted to them by their fellow colonists, such as the fur trade and other considerations. These men—called the Undertakers—were partly motivated by the knowledge that the debt rested mainly on their own credit and reputation anyway, and partly by a desire to bring more of their friends over from Holland. As Bradford wrote, "Another reason which moved us to take this heavy burthen upon our shoulders was, our great desire to transport as many of our brethren of Leyden over on to us, as we could, but without this course we could never have done it, all here being (for peace and unity's sake) made joint purchasers with us, and everyone thereby had as much interest as ourselves; and many were very opposite here against us in respect of the great charge." Bradford, Standish, and Allerton were apparently the initial Undertakers; being joined later by Winslow, Brewster, Howland, Alden, and Thomas Prence from Plymouth, and by James Sherley, John Beauchamp, Richard Andrews, and Timothy Hatherly from London. The agreement was signed on behalf of the Purchasers by twenty-seven men, Bradford noting that "some would not subscribe, and some were from home."[27]

In noting that "many were very opposite," Bradford of course meant that many of the non-Separatists were opposed to having to pay for the transportation of the Separatists' friends from Leiden. The balance between Separatist and non-Separatist was a delicate one. Though the Separatists and their supporters were in the majority and in control of the government, Bradford knew that he had to compromise at times to keep the colony together and to avoid a revolt. Bradford noted that "they had some untowarde persons mixed amongst them from the first," and even though a number of them had left for Virginia and other places, "yet diverse were still mingled amongst them," about whom Bradford and his council had serious discussions. In order to preserve "peace and union," the government decided "to take in all amongst them, that were either heads of families or single yonge men, that were of ability, and free [not servants], (and able to governe them selves with meete descretion, and their affairs, so as to be helpfull in the comone-welth,) into this partnership or purchass" that Allerton had arranged with the Adventurers. "As for servants, they had none, but what either their maisters should give them out of theirs, or their deservings should obtaine from the company afterwards."[28] Thus the Purchasers, Separatist and non-Separatist alike, became the favored ones for future Plymouth Colony land grants, but the formation of the Undertakers gave Bradford and his supporters the ability to bring over their friends without charging the costs to the entire colony. It is interesting to note that, although Myles Standish was not one of the Separatists, he played a prominent part as an Undertaker in realizing Separatist goals.

The demand for more privately-owned land was becoming quite pronounced by 1627, and probably as a by-product of the agreement between the Purchasers and the Undertakers, Bradford and the colony government agreed to give new land grants for private use to most of the settlers, excluding servants and perhaps some few not considered worthy. Each eligible single man received twenty acres, while heads of families received twenty acres per family member. Such an arrangement completely changed the original conditions of settlement.

The governor and four or five "of the spetiall men amongst them" were given the houses in which they lived, and the other houses were retained by their occupants on the basis of a valuation whereby those who had the better ones paid money for the benefit of those with the lesser ones. Now there was no longer any need to own the livestock in common, and Bradford wrote that after the agreement with the Undertakers was signed, "we made division of the cattle and other things." For the purpose of this division, settlers were placed in twelve groups of thirteen people each, with each group receiving an equal portion of the livestock as its share (a share generally included one cow and two goats). Most Plymouth Colony scholars believe that the contemporary record of this "Division of the Cattle" contains the name of every resident of the colony at the time, including even a recently born baby. Thus we have a highly significant record of most Plymouth Colony residents as of 1627. However, not every person then living in Plymouth shared in the division. It is known that there were transients in Plymouth at the time, specifically passengers from the shipwrecked *Sparrowhawk,* bound for Virginia, who were allowed to stay temporarily with the settlers and even plant crops. Two important members of this group were Mr. Fells and Mr. Sibsey, who had many servants with them. [29]

Thus, by 1627 the concept for colonizing Plymouth Colony had changed considerably. Although the settlement of the colony had no royal charter to support it, but initially only a patent to reside in the Virginia territory, Plymouth remained outside the jurisdiction of Virginia and assumed self government. With the Mayflower Compact, the colonists agreed to a form of democracy that would not be practiced in their homeland for several centuries. Though Bradford and his supporters had envisioned something close to a church-state, the large non-Separatist population prevented the full implementation of this idea as it was subsequently practiced in the adjoining Massachusetts Bay Colony. As a result, Plymouth obtained a reputation for having a less rigid and more moderate government, though it never practiced the toleration soon to come to Rhode Island. Its land policy of making grants to the many prevented it from becoming a manorial or proprietary colony, such as Virginia or other English colonies would later become. It became something unique. Unfortunately, at least for those who measure progress in terms of large-scale industrial and commercial expansion, the original choice of settlement on the shores of shallow Plymouth Harbor prevented the colony from ever achieving the size, prominence, wealth, or importance of Massachusetts Bay Colony or New York. [30] The future of Plymouth was virtually prescribed by 1627. It would be what it would be.

NOTES

1. The Old Style calendar was in use at the time of this history, and dates will be given in this fashion. The year began on 25 March and ended on 24 March of the succeeding year. March was the first month, December was the tenth month, February was the twelfth month, and so on. Because some parts of Europe, not England, had adopted the Gregorian calendar, still in use today, the New England colonists increasingly used a double year dating system between 1 January and 24 March. Though this practice adequately defines the year, it does not take into consideration the fact that the Julian calendar (Old Style) was ten days behind the Gregorian calendar during the the 1600s (until 1 March 1699/1700 Old Syle (O.S.), when it became necessary to add eleven days). Thus, to translate

Plymouth Colony dates to the new calendar, it is necessary to add ten days. For example, the Mayflower Compact was signed on 11 November 1620 O.S., which is 21 November 1620 New Style, and *Mayflower* passenger John Howland died on 23 February 1672, which could also be recorded as 23 February 1672/73, and in New Style becomes 4 March 1673. For additional details, see George Ernest Bowman, "Old Style and New Style Dating," *Mayflower Descendant* (hereafter *MD*) 1 (1899):17-23.

  2. Miller, Perry, and Thomas H. Johnson, *The Puritans*, rev. ed., 2 vols. (New York, 1963), 1:5-6, 88. The distinction between Puritan and Separatist is treated in depth by Perry Miller in *Orthodoxy in Massachusetts 1630-1650* (1933; reprint, New York, 1970).

  3. William Bradford, *History of Plymouth Plantation 1620-1647*, ed. by Worthington C. Ford, 2 vols. (Boston, 1912), 1:24-34. There are many transcriptions of Bradford's history, but the two most useful are the one edited by Ford in 1912 and William Bradford, *Of Plymouth Plantation 1620-1647*, ed. by Samuel Eliot Morison (New York, 1952). Ford keeps the original language, and Morison keeps to the spirit of the original while giving a modern version of Bradford's language. Both give excellent footnotes, Ford in considerably more detail, and Morison with the benefit of new historical interpretations. Bradford's history must of necessity be the mainstay for any modern history of early Plymouth Colony, and the present book will make considerable use of Ford's edition and some use of Morison's. References hereafter, then, will be to either *Bradford (Ford)* or *Bradford (Morison)*.

  4. *Bradford (Ford)* 1:36-42; William Bradford, "A Dialogue or the sume of a Conference between som younge men borne in New England and sundery Ancient men that came out of holland and old England Anno dom 1648," (hereafter Bradford, *Dialogue*), printed in *Plymouth Church Records 1620-1859* (hereafter *Ply. Ch. Recs.*), 2 vols. (1920-23; reprint, Baltimore, 1975), 1:139.

  5. The leading works on English Separatists in Leiden in the early seventeenth century have been Henry Martyn Dexter and Morton Dexter, *The England and Holland of the Pilgrims* (London, 1906; reprint Baltimore, 1978), and D. Plooij, *The Pilgrim Fathers from a Dutch Point of View* (New York, 1932). Recent discoveries have been made by Jeremy D. Bangs, who was Curator of the Leiden Pilgrim Documents Center in Leiden, and who became Chief Curator of Plimoth Plantation in 1986. Dr. Bangs edited *The Pilgrims in the Netherlands—Recent Research* (hereafter *Bangs's Pilgrims*) (Leiden, 1984), in which he mentions some of these discoveries and also names other new scholars in the field. Some of this information will be included in the biographical sketches in Part Three of this book (see, for example, Jonathan Brewster).

  6. *Bradford (Ford)* 1:52-55. Some of the Separatists had become citizens of Leiden, as is shown by Dexter, 648-49, and these included Bradford, Allerton, and Jonathan Brewster. Bradford and Winslow both wrote to deny charges of some of their critics that they left Holland because of a split in their own Leiden congregation or because of difficulties in getting

along with their Dutch neighbors (see, for example, footnotes in *Bradford [Ford]* 1:44, 52). On the other hand, Jan van Dorsten, "Why the Pilgrims Left Leiden," in *Bangs's Pilgrims*, 34, gives two examples of problems confronting the English in Leiden: (1) On 15 July 1619 the Dutch government published an edict prohibiting separatist religious gatherings, which was not aimed at the English Separatists, but could conceivably affect them in the future; and (2) on 28 April 1619 sixty-three year old James Chilton, later a *Mayflower* passenger, and his daughter were stoned by a group of about twenty Dutch boys, and he was hit on the head and knocked to the ground (again, this incident was apparently a result of strong reaction against Dutch non-conformists, but in this case carried over against others).

7. Samuel Eliot Morison, *Builders of the Bay Colony* (hereafter *Morison, Builders*) (Boston, 1958), 6-13. The quotation of Capt. John Smith is from his book, *The True Travels, Adventures, and Observations of Captaine Smith . . .*, as given in *The Complete Works of Captain John Smith (1580-1631)* in 3 vols., ed. by Philip L. Barbour (Chapel Hill, 1986) (hereafter *Barbour Edition*), 3:221.

8. The word "Pilgrim" is imprecise when applied to the Plymouth colonists, for, other than Bradford's reference to those people leaving Leiden with him in 1620, there is no authoritative definition of the word. Should it embrace all the *Mayflower* passengers, including the "Strangers" from England? Should it exclude the 1620 *Mayflower* Strangers, but include the Leiden people who sailed to Plymouth in the *Lyon* in 1630? Does it mean any Plymouth colonist up to a certain date, and what would be the cut-off date? Strictly speaking, it should refer only to those who accompanied Bradford in 1620 from Leiden, and thus William Ring, who had to return to Leiden when the *Speedwell* abandoned the trans-Atlantic voyage, and who never saw the New World, would be a Pilgrim; while John Alden, who sailed on the 1620 *Mayflower*, but was not from Leiden, would not be a Pilgrim. Many people quarrel with this strict definition, but are unable to agree on a replacement for it.

9. *Bradford (Ford)* 1:124, 104-06, 442-43. Robert S. Wakefield, "The Search for Descendants of Moses Fletcher," *New England Historical and Genealogical Register* (hereafter *NEHGR*) 128:161, presents evidence that Fletcher, who died in Plymouth shortly after arrival, left many descendants in Leiden. Dr. Jeremy D. Bangs believes that there is evidence of descent from Fletcher to people living in Holland today. The General Society of Mayflower Descendants has been studying the available evidence prior to making a decision on whether or not they will accept applicants on the basis of this documentation. Regarding the financial backing to establish the colony, much of Bradford's history is concerned with dealings and relations between the settlers and the Adventurers, but he presents his information piecemeal, with gaps and some confusion. A good secondary source which tries to put together the economic origins of the colony is Ruth A. McIntyre, *Debts Hopeful and Desperate* (Plimoth Plantation, 1963).

Smith's comment is from his *The Generall Historie of Virginia, New-England, and the Summer Isles. . . . (Barbour's Edition,* 2:473).

William Bradford, *Governor William Bradford's Letter Book* (Boston, 1906) (hereafter *Bradford's Letter Book*), 26, gives the agreement arranged by Allerton, dated 15 November 1626, signed by forty-two Adventurers (these names can also be found in *Bradford [Ford]* 2:6 fn):

John White	Samuel Sharp	Thomas Hudson
John Pocock	Robert Holland	Thomas Andrews
Robert Kean	James Shirley	Thomas Ward
Edward Bass	Thomas Mott	Fria. Newbald
William Hobson	Thomas Fletcher	Thomas Heath
William Penington	Timothy Hatherly	Joseph Tilden
William Quarles	Thomas Brewer	William Penrin
Daniel Poynton	John Thorned	Eliza Knight
Richard Andrews	Myles Knowles	Thomas Coventry
Newman Rookes	William Collier	Robert Allden
Henry Browning	John Revell	Laurence Anthony
Richard Wright	Peter Gudburn	John Knight
John Ling	Emnu. Alltham	Matthew Thornhill
Thomas Goffe	John Beauchamp	Thomas Millsop

Though Captain Smith mentions that there were about seventy Adventurers, we know that some had become discouraged and sold out their interests prior to the 1626 agreement. Of course all the colonists had a share in the enterprise, but they would not be Adventurers. However, it is reasonable to think that those colonists who had additionally ventured money in the company would be considered Adventurers, and Edward Winslow, with the six shares represented by his investment of £60, probably was among the seventy mentioned by Smith (see n. 19 below). Other colonists, too, then would probably have been among the seventy, and some likely ones could be Bradford, Allerton, and Warren. McIntyre, 33, adds to the above names five others who were Adventurers at one time or another: Christopher Coulson, William Greene, John Peirce, Edward Pickering, and Thomas Weston. To her list may possibly be added Mr. Gibs (*MD* 6 [1904]:143) and Joseph Pocock, Robert Reayne (though this may be a misspelling for Robert Kean), and William Thomas (*MD* 5 [1903]:10). *Bradford (Ford)* 2:82-83 shows that James Sherley, in a letter of 1629/30, mentions four men who had some intention of taking part in the venture, Mr. Fogge, Mr. Coalson, and Mr. Thomas, who "when they saw the debt and charge fell themselves off," and Mr. Collier, who "could not spare the money." *Bradford (Morison),* 390 (fn) identifies Straton and Fogge as "two of the original Adventurers who decided not to continue," but he does not give a source. These two are identified as John Stratton and Ralph Fogge by Eugene A. Stratton, "Some Stratton Notes," *NEHGR* 135:288, but though John Stratton was in some way associated with Plymouth Colony shipping matters, there is no evidence he was an Adventurer. Ralph Fogge became a resident of Plymouth, but later moved to Salem. Captain William Pierce (or Peirce) should be considered an Adventurer, too (see n. 19). The Thomas Brewer in the above list is probably the Thomas Brewer who was Brewster's partner in the printing business in Holland.

10. *Bradford (Ford)* 1:100-03; John Smith, *New Englands Trialls* (*Barbour Edition*, 4:129); *Bradford (Ford)* 1:145-46, 150-51. Bradford does not name the *Mayflower*, and we first hear of it in *The Records of the Colony of New England* (hereafter *PCR*), Nathaniel B. Shurtleff and David Pulsifer, eds., 12 vols. (Boston 1855-61; reprint 12 vols. in 6, New York, 1968), 12:4.

11. G. Mourt, *A Relation or Journall of the Beginning and Proceedings of the English Plantation Setled at Plimoth in New England, by certaine English Adventurers both Merchants and others* (hereafter *Mourt's Relation*) (London, 1622; reprint Readex Microprint, 1966), 1-2, 21; *Bradford (Ford)* 1:176-77. The largest and most informative parts of *Mourt's Relation* were written by Winslow. An illustration of John Smith's map of New England showing "Plimouth," drawn about 1617, but probably based on an earlier sketch, can be found in the *Barbour Edition* of his works, 1:319-21, together with his list of names for other New England locations. *Mourt's Relation,* 33, has the Indian Samoset telling the settlers in 1621 that the Indian name for Plymouth was Patuxet and that "about foure yeares agoe, all the Inhabitants dyed of an extraordinary plague, and there is neither man, woman, nor childe remaining. . .so as there is none to hinder possession, or to lay claim unto it." At least one Indian, however, did not die in the plague — Squanto, as told in *Mourt's Relation,* 35.

12. *Bradford (Ford)* 2:399-412; *MD* 30:1-5. The Bradford reference is his list of "decreasings and increasing," which George Ernest Bowman in "The Date of Governor Bradford's Passenger List," *MD* 1:161 calculates to have been compiled between 6 March and 3 April 1651. Bradford also kept a "register" which was more contemporary to the events which shows some of the early deaths. Though the register is no longer extant, some of the information from it can be seen in Bowman's "Mayflower Births Marriages and Deaths in Thomas Prince's 'Chronological History of New-England'," *MD* 30 (1932):1.

13. Letter of John Pory dated 13 January 1622/23, as given in *Three Visitors to Early Plymouth* (hereafter *Three Visitors*), ed. by Sidney V. James (Plimoth Plantation, 1963), 7; John Smith, *The General Historie of Virginia, New-England, and the Summer Isles . . . .* (*Barbour Edition*, 2:472); letter to Governor Bradford, as given in *Bradford (Ford)* 1:270.

14. *Bradford (Ford)* 1:189-92; *Mourt's Relation*, 2-3. The Compact is given as appendix D. References to elections are scattered throughout Bradford's history, such as *Bradford (Ford)* 1:350, "The time of new election of ther officers for this year [1624] being come. . . ." It has been questioned whether Standish was an elected or appointed military commander. It would appear that he was initially selected by the Separatist leaders for that position, probably while he was in Holland, but that he, too, had to undergo some form of confirmation by the rank and file. This is shown

by *Mourt's Relation*, 31: "Saturday the 17 day [of February 1621] in the morning we called a meeting for the establishing of military Orders amongst our selves, and we chose Miles Standish our Capitaine, and gave him authoritie of command in affayres." Also, *Bradford (Ford)* 1:392-94, gives Bradford's summary of points from Lyford's letters, which indicate that Lyford wanted to stop immigration of more Separatists from Leiden, give the vote to those on their "particular" as men likely to follow him, outvote Bradford's followers, and, choose a new captain in place of Standish. The Dutch visitor Isaac de Rasieres in *Three Visitors*, 77, also notes that "The Governor had his Council, which is chosen every year by the entire community, by election or prolongation of term."

15. *Mourt's Relation*, 60, 62; *Bradford (Ford)* 1:232, 239; Edward Winslow, "Good Newes from New England," (hereafter *Winslow's Good News*), as reprinted in *PN&Q* 4:66; Robert S. Wakefield, "The Paragon," *MQ* 43:109; *Bradford (Ford)* 1:303, 322-23. The date of the return of the *Fortune* is given by John Smith in *General Historie (Barbour Edition*, 2:450). Peter Wilson Coldham, *English Adventurers and Emigrants 1609-1660* (Baltimore, 1984), 15, contains Admiralty Court records on the *Paragon*, showing testimony by Thomas Hewes, the *Paragon's* master, that it was struck by a great storm on 8 February 1622/23 near the Western Isles on a voyage from London to New England. The ship's boat was lost, much damage was suffered, and much of the cargo was washed overboard.

16. *Bradford (Ford)* 1:198-202, 225; *Mourt's Relation*, 33-37; *Winslow's Good News*, 44-46.

17. *Winslow's Good News*, 68; *Bradford (Ford)* 1:271. Some interesting background on Weston is given in Peter Wilson Coldham, "Thomas Weston, Ironmonger of London and America, 1609-1647," *National Genealogical Society Quarterly* (hereafter *NGSQ*), 62:163.

18. *Bradford (Ford)* 1:288-94, 327. *MD* 4 (1902):87-98, gives an interesting and enlightening account of what is known of Phineas Pratt, including details of his part in alerting Plymouth Colony to the plight of the Weston colony. Much of this account comes from Pratt's own "Declaration," a petition he made to the Bay Colony Court in 1668, which is printed in *Massachusetts Historical Collections* (hereafter *Mass. Hist. Col.*), Series IV, 4:487. It is from the settlement of the *Katherine's* passengers in the fall of 1623 that Weymouth dates its distinction as the second oldest continuously-settled English habitation in New England.

19. *PN&Q* 5:38; *Bradford (Ford)* 1:314-17, 341, 350, 403, 434-35. Letters from Pory and Altham are in *Three Visitors*. Altham was one of the Adventurers who sailed in charge of the *Little James*. Both sets of letters provide a helpful supplement to our main contemporary sources on Plymouth Colony. Coldham, *English Adventurers*, 16-17, contains an interesting summary of testimony about the voyage of the *Little James*. Edward Winslow, age thirty, testified to the Admiralty Court in November 1624: "on behalf of the Treasurer and Society of Plymouth Merchants in which he has adventured £60. When the *Little James* arrived in New England, her

Captain, Emanuel Altham, and her Master, John Bridges, complained to Governor William Bradford that William Stevens and Thomas Fell behaved badly on the voyage and sought the Governor's authority for their discharge. The ship sank at Pemaguid in New England for want of a good mooring and her provisions and powder were spoiled. She was righted and repaired by her company and the people of Plymouth. The deponent has been a member of the Plymouth Company since its foundation during which time William Bradford and Isaac Allerton have been Governors." William Peirce of Ratcliffe, Middlesex, sailor, age thirty-three, testified that he had adventured £20 in the Plymouth Company, and he believed that the *Little James* sank because of disorderly conduct by Stevens and Fell. Bennet Morgan of Plymouth, New England, age twenty-seven, testified that when the *Little James* arrived in New England, her crew refused to go on a fishing voyage unless they received their wages first. Robert Cushman, yeoman, age forty-five, testified that James Sherley persuaded Stevens and Fell to go to Plymouth as colonists for shares instead of wages. James Sherley, age thirty-three, Treasurer of the Plymouth Company, testified that Stevens and Fell were to serve the Plymouth Company for five years and receive passage to Plymouth plus food, drink, and clothing.

    20. Letter from Altham to James Sherley in *Three Visitors*, 42. *Bradford (Ford)* 1:419 shows Bradford noting that in 1625 "The Company of Adventurers broak in peeces here upon [the Lyford affair], and the greatest parte wholly deserted the colony in regarde of any further supply, or care of their subsistence."

    21. *Mourt's Relation*, 61. *PCR* 11:18 gives a 1636 law which allowed the Governor and Assistants "to command solemn days of humiliation by fasting, etc., and also for thanksgiving as occasion shall be offered." Additional general information is available in W. De. D. Love, *Fast and Thanksgiving Days in New England* (1895).

    22. *Three Visitors*, 29-30; *MD* 30:4; *Bradford (Ford)* 1:218. Having his own second marriage performed by a magistrate, Bradford seems desirous of wanting to justify the custom, and he goes on to explain that "This practiss hath continued amongst, not only [the Plymouth church], but hath been followed by all the [Congregational] churches of Christ in these parts to this time, Anno: 1646."

    23. McIntyre, 17; *PCR* 12:3-6 (also in *MD* 1:227-30); *Bradford (Ford)* 1:372. The land assignments were originally considered temporary, but in 1627 when new assignments were made, the 1623 grants were confirmed as permanent. An analysis of the 1623 division can be found in Robert S. Wakefield, "The 1623 Plymouth Land Division," *MQ* 40:7, 55. The names of those sharing in the Division of Land" are given in appendix E.

    24. *Bradford (Ford)* 1:380-403; *MD* 5 (1903):77; *Bradford's Letter Book*, 12.

    25. "Smith's General History," *PN&Q* 3 (1915):124-25.

    26. *Bradford (Ford)* 2:3-6. In *Bradford (Ford)* 1:323, Bradford uses "Old Planters" to distinguish those who came before the 1623 ships: "The Old Planters were affraid that their corne, when it was ripe, should be imparted

to the new-commers, whose provisions which they brought with them they feared would fall short." In a footnote in *Bradford (Morison)*, 178, Morison writes that Bradford usually called the *Mayflower* passengers "Old Comers." In *Bradford (Ford)* 2:4, the 1626 agreement between the London Adventurers and Allerton called him agent for the "rest of the Planters there"; however, these planters, the heads of each family then resident in Plymouth, were thereafter more usually called the "Purchasers." In *Bradford (Ford)* 2:283, the March 1641 surrender of the Bradford Patent to the colony freemen referred to them as the "Purchasers" or "Old Comers." Though there might have been some looseness in the terms "Old Comers" or "Old Planters" in the beginning, ultimately they came to refer to those resident in Plymouth by the 1627 Division of the Cattle, and the terms are virtually synonymous with the "Purchasers," though Old Comers/Planters might encompass all members of the families, and Purchaser only the head. A list of the fifty-eight Purchasers is given in *PCR* 2:177, and in appendix F of this book.

27. *Bradford's Letter Book*, 38-40. Inclusion of the London men who were creditors, not debtors, would indicate that there was an awareness of profit possibilities, too. All the Plymouth Undertakers were *Mayflower* passengers except Prence, who arrived on the *Fortune* in 1621. The twenty-seven men who signed the agreement to allow privileges to the eight Undertakers in return for their assumption of the debt were:

William Brewster	Cuthbert Cuthbertson	William Palmer
Stephen Hopkins	John Adams	Experience Mitchell
Francis Eaton	Phineas Pratt	Edward Bangs
Jonathan Brewster	Stephen Tracy	Samuel Fuller
Manasseh Kempton	Edward Doty	Robert Hicks
Thomas Prence	Joshua Pratt	John Howland
Anthony Annable	Stephen Deane	John Billington
John Shaw	William Wright	Peter Brown
William Bassett	Francis Cooke	John Faunce

28. *Bradford (Ford)* 2:8.

29. *Bradford (Ford)* 2:8-17; *PCR* 12:9-13 (also in *MD* 1:148); *Bradford's Letter Book*, 39. The names of those sharing in the Division of the Cattle are given in appendix G.

30. *Bradford (Ford)* 1:229-30, said on the return of ten colonists and Squanto from an expedition to explore Massachusetts Bay that "They returned in saftie, and brought home a good quanty of beaver, and made reporte of the place, wishing they had been ther seated; (but it seems the Lord, who assignes to all men the bounds of their habitations, had apoynted it for an other use)."

Parts of Chapter 1 appeared in Stratton and Wakefield, "A Historical Background for Early Plymouth Colony Genealogical Research," *Genealogical Journal* 13 (1984-85): 135-99.

CHAPTER 2

Bringing Over Their Friends (1627-1633)

"A TIME TO EMBRACE"

I n October 1627 the Secretary of the Dutch colony recently established at New Amsterdam, Isaac de Rasieres, visited Plymouth to discuss trade. A year or two later he wrote a letter to a Dutch merchant in which he described Plymouth Colony, which he said during his visit had contained about fifty families. Plymouth was on the slope of a hill, with a wooden fortress supporting cannon on top. The lower room of the fortress was used as a church. The principal street (Leyden Street today) led down the hill to the sea, and houses along the sides were constructed of clapboards. A cross street (today Main Street) formed four corners, on one of which was the governor's house. A small stockade with four guns was placed where the streets crossed, and thus controlled the streets in all directions.

Rasieres also gave the now classic description of the colonists marching in good order to church, being called by drumbeat to assemble at the captain's door with firearms, and then marching three abreast led by a sergeant without drumbeat. Behind the sergeant came the governor in a long robe, with the preacher on his right, and, on his left, the captain with sidearms and holding a small cane. The colonists were especially strict in matters of sexual morality and enforced their morals on the Indians that lived with them. Rasieres noted that the Indians at Plymouth "are better conducted than ours, because the English give them the examples of better ordinances and a better life." [1]

By the beginning of 1628, Governor Bradford could look back and reflect that his brave band had done quite well. Their continued existence as a colony looked secure, relations with the Indians were friendly and peaceful, and they were thinking about expanding relations by setting up trading posts elsewhere. They had survived the threats of sickness, famine, and rebellion, and more recently had worked out a satisfactory solution to pay off their debts. The Undertakers would pay £1,800 to their creditors in England at the rate of £200 per year. Above this, the eight Undertakers in Plymouth owed what Bradford calculated to be not more than £400 pounds to Messrs. Sherley, Beauchamp, and Andrews. "To this pass the Lord had brought things for them," Bradford wrote. Allerton, on returning from England, "brought them further notice that their [associates in England], and some others that would joyne with them in the trade and purchass, did intend for to send over to Leiden for a competente number of them, to be hear the next year without fayle, if the Lord pleased to blesse their journey." Bradford meant that at long last they would have the opportunity of bringing over more of their friends and relatives from Leiden, Holland. Even on the other side of the Atlantic, Master John White, the Dorchester, Dorset, promoter of New England colonization, was writing in 1630, "Having passed over most of the greatest difficulties that usually encounter new planters, they [the Plymouth colonists] began to subsist at length in a reasonably comfortable manner." [2]

One of the dearest wishes of the Plymouth Separatists who had come from Leiden was to arrange for the transportation to Plymouth of their friends and relatives who had remained there. Some thirty-five of them, going via England, arrived in Plymouth in August 1629 aboard the *Mayflower* (not the original, but another ship with the same name). They had sailed with Isaac Allerton in the ships bringing new settlers to join Gov. John Endicott and the small Puritan settlements at Salem and Charlestown, the vanguard of the huge Puritan migration coming to the Massachusetts Bay Colony. A second company of people from Leiden took the *Lyon* in March 1630 and arrived, again via Salem, in Plymouth in May 1630. The "charge" for transporting the first group was over £500, which included clothing for them to the extent of 125 yards of kersey, 127 ellons of linen cloth, and sixty-six pairs of shoes, plus other items. The second group was seemingly better off financially, for the various families paid their own expenses. In addition, Bradford estimated that it cost the Colony another £500 or so to maintain these new people for up to eighteen months until they could plant and harvest their own crops. Even though the expenses for the Leiden people were to be paid by the Undertakers, Bradford noted that the "generalitie seeing and hearing how great the charge was like to be. . .began to murmur and repine." In the arrangement with the Undertakers, the Purchasers had agreed to pay three bushels of corn yearly for six years, but because of this murmuring, the Undertakers agreed not to demand payment, and it was never paid. Besides the two Leiden groups, Sherley explained in a letter of 25 May 1629, "We have allso sent some servants in the ship called the *Talbut* that went hence lately." [3]

There was a thorn in their side in the person of "Mine Host of Merrymount," Thomas Morton, who had rallied a scallywag group of servants who faced being sold to Virginians, and formed an Indian trading post a little north of Plymouth at Mount Wollaston. Morton not only sold guns and ammunition to the Indians (which was strictly against English policy), but he also set up a Maypole and with his men engaged in scandalous drinking, dancing, and "frisking togither" with Indian women. Morton ignored warnings about his behavior from Plymouth Colony.

Consequently, in 1628, the colony canvassed the other New England set-tlements in order to obtain money for the charge of sending Morton to England. When sufficient money was obtained, Captain Standish led a unit of eight soldiers to capture Morton and bring him to Plymouth to await a ship. (Bradford and his associates were shocked the following year when their own Assistant, Isaac Allerton, returned from a business trip in England with Morton as his guest; but Plymouth was soon able to "pack him away" to the newly settled Bay Colony.) We get a good idea of Plymouth's neighbor settlements in 1628 from Bradford's listing of those persons and places which helped Plymouth with Morton's ship expenses: Naumkeag (Salem), Piscatacua, Wessagusset (the future Weymouth), Thompson's Island, Shawmut (Boston), Cocheco (Dover, N.H.), and Natascot (Hull). Another settlement, Winnisimmet (Chelsea) gave noth-ing. These were all tiny settlements, mostly just a few people here and there, the largest being Naumkeag, where a year later Higginson found "about half a score houses, and a fair house newly built for the Governor," and as Bradford said, Plymouth was "of more strength than them all." [4]

But not for long though. With the Higginson Fleet to Salem in 1629, and the even larger Winthrop Fleet to Boston Harbor in 1630, the Puritan Massachusetts Bay Colony quickly outgrew the Separatist Plymouth Colony. It was impossible for the Plymouth colonists to keep this good thing — the freedom to practice religion as they wanted and the availabil-ity of extensive free or cheap land — to themselves. It was inevitable that others would invite themselves to share New England with them. The Puri-tans, under Gov. John Winthrop, though, had an advantage over Plymouth in that first, they had a charter, and second, they hit upon an idea of genius in bringing that charter to the New World with them rather than keep it with a corporation in England. In effect, they brought with them the legal right to govern themselves, while the Plymouth settlers had a more shadowy claim through their patent to a delegated right of self government. The *Mayflower* passengers originally sailed under a patent to settle in the northern part of the Virginia Company grant, but this, of course, was meaningless when they settled instead in New England. In 1621 John Pierce, the Adventurer in England who had obtained the 1620 patent, obtained a new patent in his name, which he assigned to the colonists. This patent was the justification for the colony's existence until 1629/30. The Massachusetts Bay Colony had obtained a patent in the begin-ning, too, in 1628; but they were fortunate enough to obtain a charter from the king in 1629, and in 1630 they transferred both the charter and the cor-poration possessing it to New England soil. As a practical matter — at least in these early decades — the difference did not amount to much, for England was beginning to become preoccupied with the struggle between Parliamentarians and King, between non-conformists and established relig-ion, between Roundheads and Cavaliers. As a practical matter, Plymouth could assume as much self-government as Massachusetts, for the King was getting increasingly involved in domestic matters. [5]

As the *Mayflower* people found out earlier, so the Puritans also learned that crossing the ocean was not a pleasure cruise, and establishing a new colony in the wilderness was not a painless matter. Bay Colony Deputy Gov. Thomas Dudley wrote to his erstwhile patroness, the Countess of Lincoln, on 28 March 1631, "The next year, 1629, we sent divers ships over, with about three hundred people. . . . Our four ships which set out in April [1630] arrived here in June and July, where we found the Colony in a sad and unexpected condition, above eighty of them being dead the winter before; and many of those alive weak and sick. . . the remainder of a hundred and eighty servants we had the two years before sent over coming to us for victuals to sustain them, we found ourselves wholly unable to feed them. . .many died weekly, yea, almost daily. . .not much less than a hundred, (some think many more) partly out of dislike of our government,. . .returned back again [to England]. . . . Others also, afterwards hearing of men of their own disposition, which were planted at Pascataway, went from us to them. . . . And of the people who came over with us, from the time of their setting sail from England in April, 1630, until December following, there died by estimation about two hundred at the least. . . . I should also have remembered, how the half of our cows and almost all our mares and goats, sent us out of England, died at sea in their passage hither. . . . It may be said of us almost as of the Egyptians, that there is not a house where there is not one dead, and in some houses many." [6]

Plymouth's third patent was granted to William Bradford and his associates on 13 January 1629/30 by the Council for New England (which had also granted the second Peirce Patent of 1621), and which itself existed by virtue of a royal charter. Thus, the Council for New England was delegating some of its powers to others. The new patent specifically gave Bradford the right to make laws for the colony, provided such laws did not conflict with the laws of England. Variously called the Bradford Charter, or the Warwick Charter (it was signed by the Earl of Warwick), it also gives us a good idea of the size of Plymouth Colony around the time of its signing: "William Bradford and his associatts have for these nine yeares lived in New Englande aforesaid and have there inhabited and planted a towne called by the name of New Plimouth att their own proper costs and charges: And now seeinge that by the speciall providence of god, and their extraordinary care and industry they have increased their plantacon to neere three hundred people. . . ." The almost three hundred people undoubtedly included those who had arrived on the second *Mayflower*, plus the servants on the *Talbot*, but would not have included those still to come on the *Lyon* and the *Handmaid*. [7]

Relations with the more powerful Puritan neighbor to the north were of great importance, for the Bay expanded much faster than the Old Colony. But in spite of initial religious differences, relations were good from the beginning, and became better. In 1629 some of the settlers at Salem became ill, and the Salem leader, John Endicott, requested Governor

Bradford to send the Plymouth surgeon and physician, Samuel Fuller, to help them. Subsequently Endicott wrote to Bradford, "I acknowledge my selfe much bound to you for your kind love and care in sending Mr. Fuller among us," and he added, most significantly, "I am by him satisfied touching your judgments of the outward forme of God's worshipe. . . . Being farr from the commone reporte that hath been spread of you touching that perticuler." Fuller had shown the Salem Puritans that the Plymouth Separatists were not such radicals as they had thought. From Charlestown in 1630, Fuller wrote to Bradford that he understood the Reverend John Cotton had advised the Puritans before they left England that they "should take advise of them at Plimoth, and should doe nothing to offend them. Here are diverce honest Christians that are desirous to see us, some out of love which they bear to us, and the good perswasion they have of us; others to see whether we be so ill as they have heard of us." [8]

There can be no question but that Samuel Fuller was instrumental in changing for the better the Puritans' preconceived notions of the Separatists. The two churches gradually began to resemble one another. Whether or not the Puritan church took on its congregational character as a direct result of the influence of the Plymouth Church is a matter of some controversy, but there are highly respected historians who believe this might have been the case. George Langdon agrees with Perry Miller that Massachusetts Puritans, even before they left England, had agreed on two essential elements of the Separatists' belief: the autonomy of each individual congregation, and restriction of membership (not attendance) to those predestined to be God's elect. [9] It is not necessarily true, as sometimes stated, that the Plymouth Church was more tolerant than the Puritan churches; the greater tolerance, as will be seen regarding the franchise and the treatment of Quakers, was more on the part of Plymouth Colony as a whole, not its church, which often saw eye to eye with the Massachusetts Bay Puritans.

One very practical difference between the two churches was that the Puritan churches at least had ministers from the beginning. The Plymouth Church did not get its first minister until 1629. Inasmuch as their Leiden minister, Mr. John Robinson, died before he could come to Plymouth, the Plymouth Church functioned many years under the direction of its Ruling Elder, William Brewster, who could not administer sacraments. The leadership and congregation were cautious about taking on just anyone for a minister, and did not gratify the desire of the Reverend Mr. John Lyford to head their church. In 1628 Isaac Allerton, on one of his returns from England, brought back with him uninvited a Rev. Mr. Rogers, otherwise unidentified, except by Bradford's noting that he was "crased in his braine; so that they were faine to be at further charge to send him back againe the nexte year," without having been installed as minister. In 1629 Mr. Ralph Smith came to Plymouth from Salem, and was invited to become the first Plymouth minister. Though a Separatist in thought, he showed himself too weak to be much of an asset, and in 1636 Mr. Smith "layde downe his place of ministrie, partly by his owne willingnes as thinking it too heavie a burthen, and partly at the desire, and by the perswasion, of others." The Reverend Mr. John Reyner, a happier choice, succeeded Smith as minister in 1636. [10]

Another clergyman came from Salem to reside in Plymouth in 1632, Roger Williams, who would later found Rhode Island. He did not stay long, but left in 1633 after some disagreements with the Plymouth leaders. His stay can best be described in Bradford's words: "Mr. Roger Williams (a man godly and zealous, having many precious parts, but very unsettled in judgmente) came over first to the Massachusets, but upon some discontente left that place, and came hither, (wher he was friendly entertained). . . . He this year [1633] begane to fall into some strang opinions, and from opinion to practise, which caused some controversie betweene the church and him, and in the end some discontente on his parte, by occasion wherof he left them some thing abruptly." [11]

From the beginning there was good communication and a strong spirit of cooperation between Plymouth and the Bay Colony, and Gov. John Winthrop had just barely arrived in 1630 when Plymouth consulted him on a matter of crime. One of the *Mayflower* passengers, John Billington, was found guilty of wilful murder of a recent settler, appropriately named John Newcomen, and Bradford's government was not sure what the penalty should be. They consulted Governor Winthrop and other Bay Colony leaders. Perhaps Bradford was just being cautious, for fear of possibly looking too revengeful, since Billington, by his rebellious behavior over the years, had long made himself obnoxious to them, and thus they asked for concurrence of their new neighbor for the death penalty. The Bay Colony advised that Billington ought to die and the land be purged of blood, and Billington was hanged in September 1630. In 1631 the Plymouth Colony, with help from friendly Indians, apprehended a Sir Christopher Gardiner, and sent him to the Bay Colony, where he was wanted for some small offenses, and Governor Winthrop wrote "with the true affection of a frind" thanking Bradford and "all my worthy friends with you." [12]

On 25 October 1632 Governor Winthrop and various others from Boston sailed on the *Lyon* to Wessagusset (Weymouth), where they stayed overnight. The next day they walked to Plymouth, where Bradford, Brewster, and others met them outside town and took them to Bradford's house. On Sunday, Winthrop and the Bay group attended services with the Plymouth people, took sacrament with them, and, on invitation, participated in discussing religious questions propounded by Roger Williams, who was then in the colony. Such questions and discussions were a regular feature of the Plymouth worship. During their visit the Boston men were feasted every day at various houses, and they considered themselves "kindly entertained." They remained in Plymouth until 31 October, when they left in the early morning, Bradford and others escorting them for about a half mile. [13] Such personal contact undoubtedly did much to smooth relations.

However, Plymouth Colony was never unaware that their nearby growing neighbor to the north held the power, and there was frequently a touch of arrogance on the part of the Bay Colony toward its smaller sister colony. A 1634 incident on the Kennebec River demonstrated the Bay Colony's assumption of power. The Bradford Patent gave Plymouth the right to settle or trade on the Kennebec River and to seize all persons, ships, and goods that might attempt to trade with the Indians on the Kennebec. Plymouth set up a trading post there under John Howland. A trading ship from the Piscataqua settlement under John Hocking ignored repeated warnings from Howland's group that it had no right to be there. Howland ordered one of his men to cut the moorings of Hocking's ship so it would drift down the river. Hocking shot and killed the man, Moses Talbot, and one of Talbot's companions in turn shot and killed Hocking. Since the Piscataqua settlement had lately come under the control of a powerful group in England, there was much ado about the incident. John Alden, who was at Kennebec at the time of the shooting to bring the trading post supplies, and who was not a party to the shooting, was nevertheless imprisoned when he arrived at the Bay Colony. Captain Myles Standish was sent with letters to the Bay officials acquainting them with the facts, and Alden was released, but the affair was not over, and the Bay ordered Standish to appear further at their Court. Winthrop's deputy, Thomas Dudley, tried to heal differences, and sent letters to the Plymouth leaders informing them of events. In a reply to a letter from Thomas Prence, the new Plymouth Governor for 1634, Dudley wrote that he had not wanted to show the letter to his associates, but rather wanted "to have reconciled differences in the best season and manner I could; but Captain Standish requiring an answer therof publickly in the courte, I was forced to produce it, and that made the breach soe wide as he can tell you." We can well imagine the tone of Prence's letter, since the Bay Colony had no jurisdiction over Plymouth, Piscataqua, or the Kennebec River, and their assuming a right to put themselves in the role of judge was sheer arrogance on their part. Bradford later commented, "And that their neigbours (having no jurisdiction over them) did more then was mete, thus to imprison one of theirs, and bind them to their courte. But yet being assured of their Christian love, and perswaded what was done was out of godly zeale, that religion might not suffer, nor sinne any way covered or borne with, espetially the guilte of blood. . .they did indeavore to appease and satisfye them the best they could." And thus the Plymouth attitude brought "things to a good and comfortable issue in the end." [14]

In fairness, though, it should be mentioned that the Bay Colony did not feel their action was so arbitrary. In his Journal, Winthrop in effect pleaded necessity because his people felt that it would be dangerous to let others think that Englishmen in the New World were going around killing each other for beaver. They also "feared that this type of incident would give occasion to the king to send a general governor over," which was the last thing that either the Bay Colony or Plymouth wanted. Such a dreadful possibility was not unthought of, for the Dutch Secretary Isaac de Rasieres noted after his 1627 visit to Plymouth that although "they have their freedom without rendering an account to anyone. . .if the King should choose to send a governor-general, they would be obliged to acknowledge him as a sovereign overlord." Bay Deputy Governor Dudley was not always so sympathetic to Plymouth Colony, for in 1632 he was finding fault with Winthrop for, among other matters, lending twenty-eight pounds of gun powder to Plymouth. [15]

A different kind of threat to the well-being of the Colony occurred in the person of Mr. Isaac Allerton, the first elected Assistant to Governor Bradford, and second only to Bradford in rank and authority. A Leiden Separatist, Allerton was an entrepreneur, whose negotiating ability was a needed asset to the colony, and he was used many times as a sort of "Minister of Foreign Affairs and Trade." He was instrumental in achieving the agreement whereby the Adventurers sold all their interest in the colony to the colonists (that is, the fifty-eight Purchasers) for £1,800. He became one of the eight Plymouth Undertakers assuming responsibility for the £1,800. He was of considerable assistance, being in England at the time, in arranging the passage of the 1629 and 1630 Leiden groups to Plymouth. Allerton also had a part in obtaining the Bradford Patent, together with its authority to trade on the Kennebec River. He made many trips to England to negotiate with the London partners and to arrange to bring back to Plymouth supplies necessary for the colonists (shoes, stockings, powder, shot, agricultural implements, knives, scissors, pitch, tar, ropes, nails, pots, drugs, etc.) and goods to "truck" with the Indians.

Writing about 1628, Bradford noted, "Hithertoo Mr. Allerton did them good and faithfull service, and well had it been if he had so continued." It has also been noted above that he gratuitously brought over a minister who was "crased in his braine," and he brought back the notorious Thomas Morton, which Bradford called a "great ofense" and said it was for Allerton's own "base gaine." Bradford felt Allerton could have obtained the Bradford Patent sooner, but delayed so that he could be sent to England again "for other regards." Bradford had not been pleased that in previous years Allerton had brought with him from England various goods to sell to the colonists for his own profit, "which was more than any man had yet hithertoo attempted." Because of his good services, Allerton had been excused for this; but in 1628 he brought over even more goods for personal profit, and he had them so intermixed with goods brought over for the account of the colony that they could be properly separated only on his word. Bradford observed that any casualty befalling the goods could have allowed Allerton to claim that the total loss should fall to the colony, and none to him personally. Accordingly, Allerton was instructed prior to his next trip to England, to bring over only £50 worth of shoes, stockings, and linen for the colonists, as well as a like value of trading goods. Further, supplies and goods for the colony were to be separately packed and marked. [16]

Allerton did not follow instructions, and in 1629 he brought over many kinds of goods to sell for his own profit. He failed to bring much in trading goods, saying that his expenses in England had been great, especially in arranging for the passage of the Leiden people and for his efforts to obtain a patent. Bradford suspected that Allerton was in some kind of "concurrance" with some of the English partners, but he seemed to stand so high in the partners' regard, and he also had the prestige of being married to the daughter of the much beloved Elder Brewster, that Bradford and the other leaders continued to assign him missions of importance. Bradford also suspected that Allerton was instrumental in the London partners sponsoring a competing trading post on the Penobscot River under Edward Ashley, and it did not help matters that Ashley was soon getting more supplies sent to him by the London men than Plymouth was receiving. Indeed, Plymouth was expected to help keep him supplied, too. Though Ashley was soon sent back a prisoner to England for selling powder and shot to the Indians, and Plymouth Colony obtained the Penobscot post for its own, the colonists gave no thanks to Allerton for it. [17]

What brought matters to a head was the affair of the two ships, the *Friendship* and the *White Angel*. Governor Bradford's account is garbled and difficult to understand, so we may never know the full story. But enough emerges to show that Allerton was to hire a ship to bring trading goods to Plymouth, and then to engage in fishing for profit. Allerton and some of the London partners actually arranged for two ships, without the knowledge or consent of the Plymouth leaders. One, the *Friendship*, was delayed by bad weather and was not able to engage in fishing; nor apparently did it bring many supplies, and because of the delay, its provisions were spoiled. Then the colonists learned that Allerton was sailing on another ship, the *White Angel*, to Maine. Mr. Timothy Hatherly, one of the London partners, sailed on the *Friendship*, and on arrival he let them know that although the *White Angel* carried many goods, these were mainly for Bay Colony settlers, with little for Plymouth, and further that the profit was mainly for a small group consisting of Allerton and some of the London men. Hatherly also brought a letter to the Plymouth leaders from James Sherley explaining that the London men had spent much money in the enterprise of the two ships, and the colonists would be held responsible for their share. The letter also gave them to understand that the London men had sent Hatherly over to inspect the Plymouth accounts, and "we should take it very unkindly that we should intreat him to take shuch a journey, and that, when it pleaseth God he returns, he could not give us contente and satisfaction in this perticuler, through any defaulte of any of you. But we hope you will order bussines, as neither he nor we shall have cause to complaine." Aside from the arrogance displayed by the letter, it seemed to Bradford that the colonists were expected to pay for a large share of the expenses for enterprises to which they had not agreed, and were being left out of the profits. [18]

Allerton's accounts were so "large and intrecate [that the colonists] could not well understand them." The colonists gradually learned that they had been charged exorbitant interest rates, charged for some "obscure" things, and even charged double amounts for some purchases. Bradford wrote that Allerton had even fooled his wife's father, the beloved Elder Brewster, "Yea, he scrued up his poore old father in laws accounte to above [£]200." In all, the colony, which in 1627 had owed the London men £2,200 pounds, by 1631 owed about £6,000, notwithstanding the fact that they had paid some £800 of their debt, had sent much beaver to England, and had supplied Ashley at the behest of London. Allerton was no longer trusted by either the colony or the London men, and in 1633 Mr. Sherley, whose part in some of these dealings was not so honorable either, wrote to Bradford, "Oh, the greefe and trouble that man, Mr. Allerton, hath brought upon you and us!" In spite of the shadow thus cast over him, Allerton was still an important man in Plymouth, and on 1 January 1633/34 he was elected again one of the Assistants to the governor. Perhaps realizing the cloud he was under, Allerton took some measures to restore himself in the eyes of the colonists as a whole; for example, on 24 December 1633, when the valuation of the estate of the deceased Cuthbert Cuthbertson showed that he owed more in debts than he had in assets, and the greatest part of this was owed to Allerton (Cuthbert's widow, Sarah, was Allerton's sister), Allerton stated that all other creditors should be paid first before he received anything, "desiring rather to lose all rather than other men should lose any." Eventually, after some more misadventures elsewhere in New England and after returning to Plymouth and promising "better walking," Allerton left the colony for good. [19]

Samuel Fuller, who had been so helpful to the Bay Colony in easing illness, succumbed himself to disease in 1633. Bradford wrote, "It pleased the Lord to visite them this year with an infectious fevoure, of which many fell very sicke, and upward of 20 persons dyed, men and women, besides children, and sundry of them of their anciente friends which had lived in Holand; as Thomas Blossome, Richard Masterson, with sundry others, and in the end (after he had much helped others) Samuell Fuller, who was their surgeon and phisition, and had been a great help and comforte unto them." Governor Winthrop also wrote on 24 July 1633 that there had been much sickness at Plymouth, and more than twenty of the colonists had died of pestilent fevers. The Indians, too, were attacked by the fever, and many of them died. [20]

For the most part, those of their Leiden associates who would come to Plymouth had already done so. After the 1629 and 1630 contingents, there would be no more sizeable groups making the journey together. Certainly a few individuals from Leiden made the trip one or a few at a time. An original record of the accounts of the Plymouth Company in 1628 (that is, the Undertakers) showed that they paid £3/11/4 each to bring "Mr. Rogers" (the crazed minister) and Constant Southworth to Plymouth at £1 each for their passage and four shillings, eight pence each per week for their food for eleven weeks. Once the Bay Colony began being settled, there are numerous records showing the arrival of ships from England with new colonists, such as the 1632 arrival at Boston of the *William and Francis* with about sixty passengers, including the returning Edward Winslow, and the *Charles* with about twenty passengers, including Mr. Timothy Hatherly; obviously Winslow and Hatherly were en route to Plymouth, but whether they brought with them any new settlers, either from Leiden or elsewhere, is not known. Not long before 29 October 1630, the *Handmaid* arrived at Plymouth with about sixty passengers, including two Eddy brothers from Boxted, Sussex, whose father had been vicar at Cranbrook, Kent. They continued to the Bay Colony to settle, but were rejected there for "having no testimonies." They returned to Plymouth, where John Eddy stayed about one year and then removed to Watertown, where he became a leading citizen, while Samuel Eddy remained in Plymouth. There is reason to believe that at least some, perhaps most, of the other passengers came to settle at Plymouth, for Winthrop's writings make it appear that the *Handmaid* was destined for Plymouth and did not even dock at a Bay Colony port, though whether any of these passengers were of the Leiden group cannot be said. [21]

There were undoubtedly some people who originally came to settle in the Bay Colony, but who left because they found the Puritan discipline too rigorous. Richard Silvester, for instance, who arrived about 1630, left within a few years for Weymouth, and still later, because of his "liberal" religious sentiments, found it better to live in Marshfield. There were others who came to live in Plymouth, but subsequently decided to move to the Bay. Governor Bradford wrote to Governor Winthrop on 6 February 1631/32, "Now there are diverce goone from hence, to dwell and inhabite with you, as Clement Brigges, John Hill, John Eedy, daniell ray, etc. the which if either you, or they desire their dimissions [from the church showing they had departed in good standing]: we shall be redy to give them: hopeing you will doe the like: in like cases, though we have heard something otherwise." Colony records of the next several years, such as tax lists, show many names not on the 1627 Division of the Cattle List, and some of these people are known to have been in Leiden, but for the most part, it is difficult to say which ship they came on or when. Nathaniel Morton wrote years later about some other groups arriving at Plymouth around this time which were also welcome, consisting of "severall Godly prsons; some whereof had bin of mr Laythrops Church in England and others alsoe Came to us out of England; soe that wee becaime through the Goodnes of God pretty Numerous and were in the best estate Respecting the Church that wee had as yett bine in New England." [22]

It must have seemed to Governor Bradford that no sooner did they resolve one problem than another cropped up. The settlement of the Bay Colony brought increased prosperity to Plymouth, for many of the new Bay settlers were prosperous men with more money than goods, and they soon created a profitable market for the Old Colony, especially in livestock and grain. Bradford wrote concerning 1632, "corne and catle rose to a great prise, by which many were much inriched, and commodities grue plentiful." But this kind of prosperity had its disadvantage. The nearby lands, which they had agreed in 1627 would be used by all, no longer could fulfill their needs, and they would have to start using the faraway lands which had been granted at the time, but not used. "And no man now thought he could live, except he had catle and a great deale of ground to keep them." Accordingly, the settlers "were scatered all over [Plymouth] bay, quickly, and the towne in which they lived compactly till now was left very thine, and in a short time allmost desolate." [23]

Already John Alden, Jonathan Brewster, Thomas Prence, and Miles Standish had moved across the bay to what would be called Duxbury. Aside from Bradford's disliking the dispersal for general reasons, there was also the important fact that living across the bay effectively kept the settlers there from attending church on Sunday. Among the early records of Plymouth Colony, we find under date of 2 April 1632, "The names of those which promise to remove their families to live in the towne [Plymouth] in the winter time that they the better repair to the worship of God: John Alden, Captain Standish, Jonathan Brewster, and Thomas Prence." But it was a losing battle. On 28 October 1633 it was enacted by the General Court (the whole company of freemen) with only two negative votes or abstentions, that whereas formerly each had an acre of land allotted in the town of Plymouth, but that now "the said acres lie void, the ancient inhabitants for the most part removed from thence," and whereas the absentee ownership of these vacant acres was hindering other people from settling in Plymouth, "by which means the said town is likely to be dispeopled," the owners of the vacant lots would have to surrender them, and the governor and council would make them available to other people. By 1 January 1633/34 the General Court had chosen Christopher Wadsworth and Anthony Annable as constables respectively for what they very pointedly called the "wards," not towns, of Duxbury and Scituate. A church (which Nathaniel Morton described as the "first church that sprange out of the bowells of the Church of Plymouth") was established at Duxbury sometime between December 1634 and March 1636. On 7 June 1637 the General Court passed an act that Duxbury become a township and have the privileges of a town, with the bounds to be set by the next court. [24] Other new towns would not be far behind.

We know that there were taxes, also called rates, in Plymouth Colony as early as 1623, for one of the matters agreed when newcomers arrived that year was that every male over sixteen years of age would pay a bushel of Indian wheat, or the equivalent, toward the maintenance of government and public officers. We do not hear much more about taxes until colony records show that on 2 January 1632/33 Governor Bradford, Captain Standish, John Alden, John Howland, John Doane, Stephen Hopkins, William Gilson, Samuel Fuller, Sr., John Jenny, Cuthbert Cuthbertson, and Jonathan Brewster were ordered by the court to assess taxes on the colonists, payable in grain or the equivalent. The amount of the taxes to be paid ranged from nine shillings to £3/11, and, unlike the 1623 tax which seemed limited to males over sixteen, several widows were included. Not all residents or even all landowners (e.g., Henry Sampson, Richard More) were rated, so that it is difficult to determine what the criteria were to include a given individual as a taxpayer. Perhaps, just perhaps, it was based on the value of one's crop yield plus net increase in livestock. Eighty-eight residents were rated, as follows: [25]

> 9 shillings—44 individuals
> 12 shillings—6 individuals
> 15 shillings—1 individual
> 18 shillings—22 individuals
> £1/4 shillings—2 individuals
> £1/7 shillings—8 individuals
> £1/16 shillings—3 individuals (William Bradford, Richard Church, & John Jenny)
> £2/5 shillings—1 individual (Edward Winslow)
> £3/11 shillings—1 individual (Isaac Allerton)

           ____

TOTAL   88 taxpayers

On 2 January 1633/34 rates were again assessed by the new governor, Thomas Prence, and William Bradford, Captain Standish, John Howland, Stephen Hopkins, John Doane, William Gilson, William Collier, John Jenny, Robert Hicks, Jonathan Brewster, Kenelm Winslow, and Stephen Deane. Only eighty individuals were rated this time, and we can note that some of the names on the 1632/33 list, but missing from the 1633/34 list, were among those who had died in the epidemic, though in a few cases their widows took their places. The ratings consisted of: [26]

> £0/9 shillings—45 individuals
> £0/12 shillings—7 individuals
> £0/18 shillings—13 individuals
> £1/4 shillings—3 individuals
> £1/7 shillings—8 individuals
> £1/10 shillings—1 individual (Stephen Hopkins)
> £1/16 shillings—1 individual (Isaac Allerton)
> £2/5 shillings—2 individuals (William Collier & Edward Winslow)

           ____

TOTAL   80 taxpayers

The 1632/33 and 1633/34 tax lists are interestingly quite similar, the majority of names on one being on the other. They indeed hint at little immigration after 1630, otherwise we would expect an increasing number of taxpayers each year. In fact, the number of taxpayers is less in 1633/34 than in 1632/33 because of the 1633 epidemic. We know that aside from wives and children of the rate payers, other residents of Plymouth Colony (now including Duxbury and Scituate) were various servants whose indenture agreements are found in court records. There were undoubtedly, too, various nonservant nontaxpayers; but it is doubtful that the entire population of Plymouth Colony had grown much in the early years after 1630, when the population was about 300 people plus arrivals on the *Lyon* and the *Handmaid*, perhaps 350 to 400 people in all. The next several years, though, would see a considerable increase in population.

NOTES

1. *Three Visitors*, 76-78. On p. 63, the editor points out that Rasieres took with him large quantities of wampum (also called wampumpeag, peag, or sewan), which were strings of clamshells used by the Indians for trade, hoping to spread the use of this kind of money. That the Plymouth colonists were already acquainted with wampum is shown by *Bradford (Ford)*, 2:30, in which he gives the agreement of July 1627 between the colony and the Undertakers, whereby the whole of various company stocks were given to the Undertakers, including all the wumpumpeag which was then in the store or due on account. Apparently, though, it was the large quantity brought by Rasieres which, as Bradford writes, 2:42-43, became of most profit to the colonists, Rasieres telling them how much it was desired by the Indians, for it was made only by certain tribes, but valued by all. Rasieres had earlier, in March 1627, sent a letter to Bradford (which *Bradford (Ford)* gives in 2:20, with photocopy on p. 24) stating that he would like to make a visit.

Today the town as described by Rasieres can be seen full scale, even perched on a similar slope, about three miles south of Plymouth in the 1627 replica maintained by Plimoth Plantation, Inc. A reenactment of the "Pilgrims' Progress" described by Rasieres takes place in Plymouth each Thanksgiving Day and also at scheduled times during the summer.

2. *Bradford (Ford)* 2:40; John White, "Brief Relation of the Occasion of Planting of This Colony," an excerpt from White's *The Planters Plea*, published in *Chronicles of the First Planters of the Colony of Massachusetts Bay, from 1623 to 1636* (hereafter Young, *Chronicles*) (Boston, 1846; reprint Baltimore, 1975).

3. *Bradford (Ford)* 2:64-69; *Bradford's Letter Book*, 45. The *Talbot* and the 1629 *Mayflower* were two of the five ships of the Higginson Fleet, the other three being the *Lyon's Whelp*, the *Four Sisters*, and the *George* (see Young, *Chronicles*, 215-16). There was later a sixth ship, the *Pilgrim*.

4. *Bradford (Ford)* 2:46-58, 73-74; *Bradford's Letter Book*, 41-45. The quotation from Higginson is found in Young, *Chronicles*, 258-59.

5. *Bradford (Ford)* 1:234(fn), 1:246-51. The latter reference gives the full text and a photocopy of the second Peirce Patent. The first patent, giving permission to settle in Virginia territory, (both document and text) is lost.

6. Young, *Chronicles*, 310-25. Dudley's mention of men leaving the Puritan colony for Piscataqua refers to the New Hampshire colony which was outside the jurisdiction of either Plymouth or Massachusetts. It became a haven for men who did not want to live in a structured society, and it was to Piscataqua that at least one of those sympathizing with Lyford and Oldham in 1624 subsequently went. It also became the refuge in 1638 for Daniel Cross, the only one of the four Plymouth men who killed an Indian to escape hanging. John Winthrop, *The History of New England from 1630 to 1649* (hereafter *Winthrop's History*), ed. by James Savage, 2 vols. (Boston, 1853) 1:269, mentions "The governor [Bradford] sent after him [Cross], but those of Pascataquack conveyed him away and openly withstood his apprehension. It was their usual manner (some of them) to countenance, etc. all such lewd persons as fled from us."

7. William Brigham, *The Compact with the Charter and Laws of the Colony of New Plymouth* (Boston, 1836), 21-26. Morison points out in a footnote on p. 213 of his edition of Bradford that five or six ships brought about 350 settlers to Salem in 1629, and within a year Massachusetts Bay had five times the population of Plymouth Colony. However, Winthrop in a letter to his wife mentioned about 700 passengers in his ships plus about 140 in the *Mary and John* and eighty in the *Lyon*, for a total of 920 new settlers in 1630. The Higginson Fleet had brought over about 300 settlers in 1629, and it has been estimated that there were already some fifty or sixty people in Salem at the time (Higginson mentioned finding about eleven houses there). Higginson also wrote that in 1629 "there are in all of us, both old and new planters, about three hundred, whereof two hundred of them are settled at Nehum-kek, now called Salem, and the rest have planted themselves at Masathulets Bay, beginning to build a town there, which we do call Cherton or Charles Town." Deputy Governor Dudley estimated that some eighty people died the winter of 1629/30, and about 200 people from the Winthrop Fleet died in 1630, while not less than 100 returned to England, and some left for Piscataqua. There were also a few thinly populated outposts, such as William Blaxton at Shawmut, and the people at Weymouth. Thus at the end of 1630 there would have been some 1,300 minus 400, for a net of about 900 people in the Bay Colony, while Plymouth had about 300 plus those arriving on the *Lyon* and the *Handmaid* (for these various figures, see Young, *Chronicles*, 239-59, 310-25, and note 21 below). Massachusetts must have outnumbered Plymouth in 1630 (and the next few years when not many new settlers arrived at either colony) by a ratio of less than three to one, though within a decade the ratio would grow considerably.

8. *Bradford (Ford)* 2:90, 116-17.

9. George D. Langdon, Jr., *Pilgrim Colony—A History of New Plymouth 1620-1691* (New Haven, 1966), 108.

10. *Ply. Ch. Recs.* 1:36, 52; *Bradford (Ford)* 2:58, 87-88, 236-37. Robert Cushman's letter in appendix five of *Bradford (Morison)*, 373-74, clearly shows that their associates in England entertained the possibility of Lyford being accepted as the colony's minister, but the colonists made no attempt to so engage him. The Separatists had but two sacraments, baptism and administering the Lord's Last Supper. Their spiritual mentor in Holland, John Robinson, specifically replied in a letter to Brewster dated 20 December 1623, "Now, touching the question propounded by you, I judg it not lawfull for you. . .to administer them [sacraments], nor convenient [that is, proper] if it were lawfull," and one of Lyford's complaints in 1624 was the lack of sacraments in Plymouth (*Bradford [Ford]* 1:371, 363).

11. *Bradford (Ford)* 2:161-62. Plymouth had surprising difficulty in acquiring an appropriate minister; in 1634 Winslow obtained a Mr. Glover in England to join them, but Mr. Glover died before making the trip, and a Mr. Norton, who accompanied Winslow back to Plymouth, considered the prospect of being their pastor, but after staying the winter in Plymouth he decided to go elsewhere and became minister at Ipswich (*Ply. Ch. Recs.* 1:73).

12. *Bradford (Ford)*, 2:110-12, 136-40. There are but few details available on the Billington case, but we learn a bit more from William Hubbard, *A General History of New England from the Discovery to MDCLXXX* (Cambridge, 1815, 101, "About September, 1630, was one Billington executed at Plymouth for murther. . . . [Billington] maliciously slew his neighbour in the field, as he accidentally met him, as himself was going to shoot deer. The poor fellow, perceiving the intent of this Billington, his mortal enemy, sheltered himself behind trees as well as he could for a while; but the other not being so ill a marksman as to miss his aim, made a shot at him, and struck him on the shoulder, with which he died soon after. The murtherer expected that either for want of power to execute for capital offenses, or for want of people to increase the plantation, he should have his life spared; but justice otherwise determined." Though Hubbard's book was not published until 1815, he wrote it in the second half of the seventeenth century, and thus was contemporary with some people who would have remembered the Billington affair first hand. On the other hand, Thomas Morton, no friend to the Plymouth leaders, asserted in his whimsically written satire, *New English Canaan* (1637), 216, that "Auld Woodman," that is, Billington, "was choaked at Plimmoth after hee had played the unhappy Markes Man when hee was pursued by a carelesse fellow that was new come [a punning reference to John Newcomen] into the land," and he referred to Billington as "beloved of Many."

13. John Winthrop, *Winthrop's Journal 1630-1649* (hereafter *Winthrop's Journal*), ed. by James K. Hosmer, 2 vols. (New York, 1908; reprint 1959), 1:92-94.

14. *Bradford (Ford)* 2:175-83, 186-87.

15. *Winthrop's Journal*, 1:86, 124; *Three Visitors*, 77.

16. *Bradford (Ford)* 2:40, 72-73, 59-60.

17. Ibid., 2:77-83, 107-08.

18. Ibid., 2:97-107, 109-10, 127-31.

19. Ibid., 2:129-36, 160; *PCR* 1:20-21.

20. *Bradford (Ford)* 2:171-72; *Winthrop's Journal,* 1:103. Some of the colonists who died at this time were John Adams, Peter Browne, Francis Eaton, Cuthbert and Sarah Cuthbertson, Martha Harding, Richard Lackford, John Thorp, and William Wright (for references, see Biographic Sketches).

21. *Collections of the Massachusetts Historical Society* (hereafter *MHS Collections*) 3rd Series (Boston, 1825), 1:199; Charles Henry Pope, *The Pioneers of Massachusetts* (Boston, 1900; reprint, Baltimore, 1986), 151. John Winthrop, *Winthrop Papers 1623-1630,* Vol. 2 (1931, reissued New York, 1968), 269, wrote on 29 October 1630 that the *Handmaid* arrived at Plymouth, having been twelve weeks at sea, with about sixty passengers, the ship's master having come to Boston with Captain Standish "and 2 gent passingers, who came to plant here, but havinge no testimonies we would not receive them." It has been presumed that these were the Eddy brothers. That the Eddy brothers did arrive on the *Handmaid* can be seen from the same source, 319, where in a letter to his wife on 29 November 1630 Winthrop writes, "Edy of Boxted, who came in her [the *Handmaid*] tould me a fortnight that he had many lettres in the shippe for me, but I heer not yet of them: which makes me now (havinge opportunity to send to Plimmouth) to write these few lines to thee, least the shippe should be gone before I have received my lettres." The wording of these two passages makes it appear that the ship's master, along with Standish and the two gentleman passengers, arrived at Boston via some other, perhaps smaller, vessel, and the *Handmaid* stayed at Plymouth. This would make it seem that some at least, perhaps most, of the about sixty passengers on the *Handmaid* must have been destined for Plymouth.

22. Albert Henry Silvester, "Richard Silvester of Weymouth, Mass., and Some of His Descendants," *NEHGR* 85:247-49; *MD* 9:1-3; *Ply. Ch. Recs.* 1:64. The terms "liberal" and "conservative," of course, are relative to given times and places; in this book they will be used as meaning respectively desiring to change or maintain the status quo.

23. *Bradford (Ford)* 2:151-52.

24. *PCR* 12:6; *Ply. Ch. Recs.,* 1:xxiv, liv; *PCR* 1:17, 21, 62. The *Ply. Ch. Recs.* references have a church established at Duxbury and also at Green's Harbor (Marshfield) in 1632, but this would seem erroneous—these statements are found in the Introduction, which, of course, is not a contemporary document. Certainly there was a church at Duxbury no later than 21 March 1636, when the General Court referred a matter to the two churches of Plymouth and Duxbury (*PCR* 1:41). But James Cudworth, writing from Scituate (not far from Duxbury) very specifically stated "Now these Plantations that are not yet settled [meaning that a church had not yet been organized], and are newly begun, are three: Ducks burey, where Mr. Colyer dwelles. No Pastor nor Teacher. Oures, Cittewate, to whome

the Lord has bine verey gracious, & his p'vidence has bine Admorablely sene oure beyenge to bringe us oure Pastor whome wee so longe expected—Mr. Lathrope, who the Lord has brought to us in safety, whome wee find to bee a holy Reverat & hevenly minded man. And the other is Beare Cove [Hingham], wheare is no Pastor nor Teacher." This letter was written in December 1634 and would seem to show conclusively that no church had yet been established at Duxbury. Cudworth mentioned ten established churches in Massachusetts and Plymouth Colonies, but he did not mention Marshfield at all, and the only church in Plymouth Colony was the one at Plymouth town itself. Cudworth would seem to be up to date in his information, for he mentioned that the Pastor at Salem (which was much further away from Cudworth than Duxbury), old Mr. Skelton, was dead (he died in August 1634) and Roger Williams "theare. . .dos exersies his giftes, but is in no office" (after Williams left Plymouth "something abruptly," he went to Salem, and at Skelton's death the Salem Church asked him to become its minister, but Bay authorities were opposed to him, and in 1635 exiled him from Massachusetts Bay Colony).

    25. *Bradford (Ford)* 1:327; *PCR* 1:9-11. If the same formula to determine taxability was used in 1633 as was applied in 1645, we can get a rather rough idea of it from an awkwardly worded Court record of 3 March 1645/46: "Concerneing the difference about Mr Starrs rate at Marshfeild, the Court doth not see but that it is right and equall that Mr Starr should be rated at Marshfeild pportionable to his lands improoved and stock there, and shall now pay his rate there untill that Duxborrow can make it appeare that it was understood that he should not be rated there untill hee came totally wth his famyly to dwell there, and that Marshfeild condiscended thereunto" (*PCR* 2:95). However, it should be noted that this was following the Narragansett military mission, which involved extraordinary expenses to the colony and individual towns, so that there was need for higher taxes, but whether the formula changed cannot be said.

    26. *PCR* 1:26-29.

CHAPTER 3

The Founding of Towns (1633-1643)

"A TIME TO BUILD UP"

T he next several years were a growth period, and the colony was full of growing pains. Both the Dutch from New Amsterdam and the French from Canada were encroaching on Plymouth's trading posts. A few years earlier Plymouth leaders had recommended to their Dutch friends at New Amsterdam (many Plymouth colonists had spent years in Holland and knew the language and customs well) that they begin to settle and trade with the Indians on the Connecticut River, but the Dutch declined. Then some of the leading men of Plymouth went to the Bay Colony and tried to get the Puritans to conduct trading operations jointly with them on the Connecticut River. At first the Bay refused for lack of sufficient trading goods. The Plymouth people offered to share their goods, but again the Bay refused, and it became apparent from their arguments that they were concerned about the probability of financial losses and danger from the Indians. Thus Plymouth decided to set up its own trading post on the Connecticut River near Windsor. [1]

Before they could do so, the Dutch, in a reversal of policy, opened a small trading post near the future Hartford, and when Plymouth men tried to pass them on their way to their own site, the Dutch challenged them. The Plymouth group said they would continue, even if shot at, and the Dutch held off, but later sent reinforcements in strength from Manhattan to intimidate the Plymouth outpost. Again, though outnumbered, the Plymouth men let the Dutch know they would not abandon their post, and after talks between the two groups, the Dutch left. As always, Plymouth people were careful to buy the land they required from the Indians. In 1634 Plymouth sent a bark to trade with the Dutch at Manhattan, and there they met an Englishman, Capt. John Stone, who through trickery seized their ship and set sail. Stone apparently had obtained approval for his action from the Dutch governor when the governor was drunk, but some of the Dutchmen, nonetheless, sailed after Stone and recovered both ship and goods for the rightful owners. [2]

The Plymouth colonists had also continued Ashley's trading post at Penobscot in Maine under the leadership of Thomas Willet, a capable young man of the Leiden group. This post was seized by a French group, and Willet and his men were sent away in their shallop. A detachment of men under Myles Standish was sent on a hired ship to recover the post, but the ship's captain was so blundering that the expedition was a dismal failure, and they returned to Plymouth with nothing but excuses. Plymouth then tried to get the Bay people to join them in repulsing the French, but the Bay had nothing but lip service to give them, and, worse, allowed some of their merchants to trade with the French who had seized the post, even supplying them with powder and shot. Plymouth never regained its post at Penobscot. [3]

It was the Massachusetts Bay people who terminated the expansion of the Plymouth trading post on the Connecticut. The Bay had been uninterested earlier in the area of the Connecticut River, knowing that the Indians there could pose a strong threat. After they learned that many of the Indians had been annihilated by disease, some of the Bay people, particularly from Dorchester, became interested in settling on the Connecticut, and the Plymouth people found them arriving in large numbers. Jonathan Brewster, the elder's son, wrote an alarming letter on 6 July 1635 from Matianuck (Windsor): "The Masschuset men are coming almost dayly, some by water and some by land. . . . Some have a great mind to the place we are upon." Brewster's group treated the newcomers with great care, including supplying them with the food they lacked, and he concluded his letter to Plymouth with more a hope than a conviction: "All which trouble and charge we under goe for their occasion, may give us just cause (in the judgmente of all wise and understanding men) to hold and keep that [which] we are setled upon." The Plymouth outpost was vastly outnumbered by the invading Massachusetts men, and though Bradford writes that forcible resistance was far from the thoughts of the outpost—"they had enough of that about Kenebeck"—resistance was realistically out of the question anyway because of the sheer numbers of the newcomers. The men of Plymouth finally concluded a lopsided arrangement with the Bay people which left Plymouth with the house it had built for trading and a small fraction of the land (one-sixteenth) it had originally bought from the Indians, and the Bay settlers took over all other land. [4]

By 1637 the Bay settlers in Connecticut were appealing to both Boston and Plymouth for help against Indian assaults. The Pequot Indians had first fought against the neighboring Narragansetts, and also had made occasional attacks against the English. In separate raids Indians killed two old (but not fondly remembered) acquaintances of Plymouth, Captain Stone and John Oldham, and the Bay Colony, feeling the killers should be punished, made some clumsy attempts at retribution. This in turn incited the Pequots to engage in raids against the English farmers on the Connecticut River, slaying men and women as they worked in the field. [5]

On 7 June 1637 the General Court passed an act that Plymouth would "send ayd to assist them of Massachusetts Bay and Conectacutt in their warrs against the Pequin Indians, in reveng of the innocent blood of the English wch the Pequins have barbarously shed." Lieutenant William

Holmes was to lead a force of thirty soldiers and Thomas Prence was elected by lot to be his councillor. Some forty-four men volunteered for service. As it turned out, the Connecticut and Massachusetts contingents had already vanquished the Pequots, setting their fort on fire, and killing about 400 of them with sword or fire, completely eliminating the Pequots as any menace for the future. The Plymouth men, no longer needed, stayed at home. There were other things to do at Plymouth: the same court that provided for soldiers to help the Connecticut settlers, among other actions, also fined Edward Foster and James Cole for selling less than legal measures of alcoholic spirits; gave notice to the towns of Scituate and Duxbury that they had but a limited time to set up their stocks for criminal punishments and pounds for keeping stray animals; warned those who had not yet recorded their cattle brands that they would be fined; and ordered that there would be a guard of twelve musketeers to accompany the governor on Sundays and special occasions. [6]

A more direct dispute with the Bay occurred when the towns of Scituate in Plymouth Colony and Hingham in the Bay Colony vied with each other for some marsh lands which lay between them. Sixty acres of the lands had been granted to Mr. Hatherly and his three London partners. The Hingham authorities likewise granted lots in the disputed area to its people, who staked them out, while the Scituate people pulled up the stakes. Thus the affair had to be settled by Massachusetts and Plymouth, each appointing two commissioners—John Endicott and Israel Stoughton for Massachusetts Bay, and William Bradford and Edward Winslow for Plymouth. A river south of Hingham located conveniently between the two towns was selected by the commissioners in an agreement of 9 June 1640 as the boundary, except that Massachusetts also got the sixty acres on the Scituate side at the mouth of the river (Mr. Hatherly's erstwhile sixty acres). Interestingly, we see the closeness of relationships of the people of the two colonies when we realize that one of the Massachusetts commissioners, Israel Stoughton, was the brother of the stepfather of one of Scituate's leading citizens, Mr. James Cudworth. [7]

In the meantime, a new colony had been founded. When the Reverend Roger Williams left Plymouth Colony "abruptly," he went to Salem. Though the church there invited him to become pastor, the Bay authorities thought him too radical (or perhaps too dangerous), and in 1635 he was banished from Massachusetts. Williams believed that complete separation of New England churches from the Church of England was necessary, that magistrates could have no authority over the church, and only the Indians, not the English crown, could give land rights to the settlers. He went to Rhode Island, founded the town of Providence, and showed that his town was willing to accept settlers regardless of religious belief, even Anabaptists (whom he joined briefly) and Quakers (whose doctrines he opposed even as he admitted their presence). In 1643 Williams went to England, returning in 1644 with a charter from Parliament for his colony. As dissidents from other colonies continually increased the population of

Rhode Island, so the mistrust of the other colonies grew; however, Williams was trusted by the Indians, and was able to play the part of a peacemaker between the Narragansetts and the English colonies. Though Rhode Island was not permitted to participate in the organization of the United Colonies of New England in 1643, it later joined the other colonies to fight in King Philip's War. [8]

This was the period of the great migration from England, thousands of people for religious and economic reasons coming to settle in the New World during the decade of the 1630s. But most of the new colonists were going elsewhere, and by 1640 both the Bay Colony and Barbados were much larger than Plymouth. Plymouth was growing, but growing modestly. The leaders must have known that without people in sufficient numbers to settle the land, they would not be able to hold it for long. Perhaps this was part of the reason why they decided to admit outsiders to create new towns within the colony bounds. We do not know when many towns started. In some cases but a single person or family might have moved beyond the bounds of Plymouth to become the nucleus around which others later settled. The Plymouth leaders tried to maintain tight control on the land, and there is at least one case on record where they ordered a man to return to a town from an unsettled area, threatening to demolish his habitation if he did not comply. Their policy seemed to be a mixed one of permitting a gradual movement of people from Plymouth town to new places while at the same time allowing controlled groups of outsiders "of good note," or "fit for church society," to settle other areas to the north, to the west, and on Cape Cod. There was also a policy of giving land to servants at the expiration of their indentures, and this frequently resulted in the growth of the new towns. For example, on 2 January 1633/34 the General Court ruled "that whereas by indenture many are bound to give their servnts land at the xpiracon of their terme, it is ordered that they have it at Scituate, or some other convenient place, where it may be usefull." [9]

Duxbury was the first of the new towns necessitated by the internal and external demands for land. Once the dam had been breached, it was impossible to stem the flood. In the case of some towns, such as Duxbury and Marshfield, the records give specific dates for their official recognition as towns, although it is obvious that they had been functioning more or less as towns for some time previous. Other new towns just seemed to ooze from small settlement to officially recognized township without any date of change being recorded. By 1643 Plymouth, still the largest town with 147 men age sixteen to sixty on its list of those able to bear arms, had seen seven other settlements sufficiently grow to be called towns: [10]

DUXBURY

Much has already been said in the previous chapter on the settlement of Duxbury, whose leading citizens were John Alden, Jonathan Brewster, Thomas Prence, and Miles Standish. Eventually, Elder William Brewster moved to Duxbury, too. As noted earlier, the first Duxbury Church was formed sometime between December 1634 and March 1636. Ralph Partridge became the first minister in 1636, and William Leveridge, also an ordained clergyman, stayed in Duxbury for a while, but by 5 June 1638 had removed to Sandwich. The 1643 list of men able to bear arms shows that in that year there were seventy-six men between the ages of sixteen and sixty living in Duxbury. [11]

MARSHFIELD

First called Green's Harbor, then Rexham, this settlement finally became known as Marshfield. In writing of the year 1632, Bradford noted that some lands were granted at Green's Harbor to some special men who were expected to let their servants farm there but live at Plymouth themselves. Of course, within a few years Marshfield was a town, and Edward Winslow was one of its leading residents. On 1 July 1633 the General Court ordered that Mr. Gilson, John Shaw, and the others who undertook to enlarge the passage between Green's Harbor and the sea, finish it by 1 October, or be fined £10. Whether this was done and later had to be redone, or was not done at all, is not known, but on 3 January 1636/37 the court ordered again that the passage be enlarged, and the governor, the Assistants, and John Winslow, Jonathan Brewster, John Barnes, and Christopher Wadsworth were to apportion the costs equally to "every man" and to supervise the work there, with ten men working at a time. It does not seem that "every man" would refer to the entire colony, but more likely meant every man then living at Marshfield (and possibly some living at Scituate who would have also benefitted from this access to the sea). On 5 March 1638/39, Mr. Nathaniel Thomas was appointed to exercise men at arms for Marshfield. On 2 March 1640/41 the General Court ruled that Green's Harbor would be a township and be "called by the name of Rexham, but now Marshfield." [12]

Nathaniel Morton, who was contemporary to the events, wrote that the church at Marshfield was the second to issue from the Plymouth Church, and that with the help of Edward Winslow, Marshfield procured several Welsh gentlemen of good note to settle there, with Mr. Richard Blinman as minister. However, "some desentions fell amongst them which Caused a prteing." Those who had settled Marshfield from Plymouth "with that Godly Gentleman mr Willam Thomas" continued to act as a church until Mr. Edward Bulkeley was chosen minister. Blinman had come from Chepstow, Monmouthshire, on the Welsh marches. He arrived at Marshfield sometime after 19 January 1635/36, when he received his degree at Oxford, but certainly before 10 October 1640 (probably closer to the latter date, for he first served as minister in his home parish of Chepstow), with a group known as "the Welsh party." There were disputes between the Blinman group and the settlers from Plymouth who had preceded him there, and Blinman and his followers moved to Cape Ann. "Mr. Edward Buckley" is on the Marshfield list of August 1643 of men able to bear arms, and thus he arrived there prior to this date. The total number of names from Marshfield on this list was fifty-one, giving us a good idea of the number of able-bodied males between ages sixteen and sixty living in Marshfield at this time. [13]

SCITUATE

When Mr. John Lothrop, a minister coming from England with a large group of settlers, arrived at Scituate on 27 September 1634, he noted in his records that there were nine small houses with palisaded fences already there. The owner of one house was the London Adventurer Mr. Timothy Hatherly, who had come over to settle. Another, Anthony Annable, had been in Plymouth Colony for over ten years, arriving on the *Anne* in 1623, but certainly he had not been in Scituate that long. Several had been freemen in the colony prior to 1 January 1632/33: Hatherly, Annable, Henry Cobb, William Gilson, and Humphrey Turner. The others had probably been in the colony for a while, but it is doubtful that they had been at Scituate very long. Annable had been chosen by the court to be constable of the "ward" of Scituate on 1 January 1633/34. James Cudworth, in a letter dated December 1634 to his stepfather Dr. John Stoughton in England, described Scituate as one of the "plantations that are not yet settled [that is, no church yet], & are newly begun." He mentioned the arrival of Mr. Lothrop, "a holy, Reverat & hevenly minded man," and he entreated his stepfather that "if yow doe know eny of youre frendes & acquaintances that come over hether, that youw would derect them to oure Plantation." Apparently they were eager for new settlers, though Cudworth went on to caution that they should be "such as yow judge to be fite to bee Received into Church fellowshipe." Cudworth said his house, being the largest, was the meeting house, "but wee are but few, as yet, in number – not passing 60 persons." By the time of the 1643 list of men able to bear arms, the number of men age sixteen to sixty at Scituate totaled 100, making Scituate the largest town after Plymouth. [14]

Mr. Lothrop's records show that the Scituate Church was actually organized on 8 January 1634/35, as thirteen initial members joined in covenant together, and it was apparently at that time that Lothrop was ordained their minister. Nathaniel Morton commented that, "I Can not say that the maine prte of this [Scituate] Church Came out of the Church of Plym: tho a Considerable prte of them did." Over the next three years forty-six more people became members, the great majority of them new to the colony. Since the new ones became members over rather evenly spaced intervals, it suggests a steady influx into Scituate of new families. Although we know of other families there at the same time who were not church members, including some names of nonchurch members whose marriages or deaths were recorded by Lothrop, it is difficult to estimate the number of inhabitants, or have a reliable idea of the size of the town, until the August 1643 arms list. [15]

In addition to Hatherly; Lothrop; Cudworth, who would become one of the colony's leading military figures, as well as a controversial liberal; Humphrey Turner; and William Gilson, who was an Assistant in 1633, some of the other leading men in Scituate in the early years were Nathaniel Tilden; Edward Foster, who married Hatherly's niece; William Vassall, who had earlier been an Assistant in the Bay Colony, and who would also become quite controversial; Thomas Besbeech; and Samuel Hinckley, whose son was to become a governor of the colony. Many of the newcomers were from county Kent in England (with a fair number from the town of Tenterden), and they became known as the "men of Kent" or "Kentish men." [16] Thus, unlike some of the other new towns of the 1630s which were settled almost entirely by non-Plymouth people, Scituate was settled by some who had previously lived in Plymouth town, and some who had not.

Apparently internal stress came early to the Scituate settlers. One Plymouth Colony scholar suggests that there were problems in the Scituate Church as early as 1637, and he notes Lothrop's records show that between 8 January 1634/35 and 25 February 1637/38, fifty-nine persons were admitted to church membership, but between March 1638 and October 1639, only three additional members were admitted. This suggests that membership was virtually closed for a good part of two years. Lothrop records Days of Humiliation observed by the Scituate church, including one of 7 April 1636 "in respect of present outward Scarcity & in respect of helpes in ministery, as also for the prevention of Enemies." Another Day of Humiliation occurred on 11 November 1636 "ffor a blessing uppon their consultation aboute the Lawes for Settling the State of this Patten. Some differences arising aboute some particulars in judgement, wee were by the mercye of God reconciled joyntly." On 22 January 1637/38, a Day of Humiliation took place "especially for our removeall, as alsoe the removeall of these Spreading opinions in the churches at ye Bey, as also for the preventing of any intended evil against the churches here." Scituate was the closest Plymouth town to the Bay Colony, and it is apparent that there was some rather vocal opposition in the Massachusetts churches to Mr. Lothrop's conduct of his religious duties. [17]

By 29 November 1638, Lothrop's congregation was observing a Day of Humiliation "as alsoe for our further Successe in our Removeall." On 3 January 1636/37 Mr. Timothy Hatherly had petitioned the Court "in the behalf of the Church of Scituate. . . That the place [Scituate] is too streate for them to reside comfortably upon and that the lands adjacent are very Stony and not convenient to plant upon," and he requested permission for the "said Inhabitants of Scituate" to search for lands to settle elsewhere unless other lands could be given them which would allow more comfortable subsistence at Scituate. The court approved this request on 12 January 1638/39 with a grant of land at a place called Sippican (today Rochester) to Mr. Thomas Besbeech, James Cudworth, William Gilson, Anthony Annable, Henry Rowley, Edward Foster, Henry Cobb, and Robert Linnell as a committee for the seating of a township and congregation. However, no town was founded there at this time, and apparently the grant was revoked by the court, or rejected by the grantees. Probably the court preferred to save the Sippican area for the future expansion of Plymouth town, for on 5 June 1651 the court ordered "For the continuall support of the townshipe of Plymouth, for the place and seat of government, to prevent the despersing of the inhabitants therof, it is ordered, that Sepecan bee granted to the towne of Plymouth, to bee a generall healp to the inhabitants therof, for the keeping of theire cattell, and to remayne for the common use and good of the said township, and never to bee aleanated by the townshipe from the same to any other use." The change of grant occured between 23 January 1638/39, when another Humiliation Day was observed, "Wee that were for Sippican devided into 3 companies in this service for preventing of exceptions. Wherein wee petitioned for Direction in Electing of Committyes for the Setting downe of our towne, for good order in beginning and proceeding, for more Spiritual helpe for us, as alsoe for our Brethren here," and 26 June 1639, when the Day of Humilation was for a new destination, "ffor the presence of God in mercy to goe with us to Mattakeese." Mattacheese at this time was the area on Cape Cod that became better known as Barnstable (not to be confused with Mattacheeset, which became Yarmouth). As late as 13 June 1639, Lothrop was still noting "great dissentions in general." [18]

Dissensions continued at Scituate even after the departure of the Lothrop group. In 1641 the Reverend Charles Chauncey came to Scituate from Plymouth to start a new church. He had arrived at Plymouth in 1638 and had become associated with the Reverend John Reyner in the Plymouth Church. Chauncey, acknowledged to be a great scholar, was one of the best educated men in New England, but he had a flaw. He was a believer in baptism by total immersion, which the Plymouth people were willing to allow (though with reservations about the cold climate) if Chauncey would not object to Reyner doing baptisms his way, by sprinkling. But Chauncey was adamantly for his way only, and Plymouth, after consulting with the Reverend Mr. Ralph Partridge of Duxbury and other ministers in the Bay, Connecticut, and New Haven, encouraged Mr. Chauncey to move on, so that in 1641 he accepted the invitation of people at Scituate to become the minister there. His views on baptism attracted much criticism from Bay churches, and, though he seemed to have the support of the most important Scituate citizen, Mr. Timothy Hatherly, he also had quarrels with Mr. William Vassall and others in subsequent years, which again seriously divided the Scituate Church. [19]

BARNSTABLE

We will probably never know the full reason for the Lothrop group leaving Scituate and establishing the new town of Barnstable. There seems to be more than one reason—a need for more and better land, internal dissensions, and attacks by some Bay churches. Some have advanced arguments that there was a schism between the old Plymouth colonists and the newcomer Kentish group, the former leaving with Lothrop, and the latter staying at Scituate. But Lothrop himself was a newcomer, and Hatherly, who stayed behind, was certainly one of the old Plymouth group. Most of the church members, not all, accompanied Lothrop to Barnstable, and among them were early Plymouth residents Anthony Annable, Henry Cobb, the younger Samuel Fuller (who had married Lothrop's daughter Jane), Isaac Robinson, and Henry Rowley. Another view is that Lothrop was a liberal minister, and it was a dispute between liberals and conservatives—yet William Vassall, a pronounced liberal, stayed behind. It has generally been accepted that James Cudworth, who would later show himself to be quite liberal, accompanied the Lothrop group to Barnstable, and certainly he is found there on 4 January 1641/42 as "Mr. James Cudworth of Barnestable." However, on 2 June 1640, nine months after the departure of the Lothrop group for Barnstable, Cudworth was still recorded as "Mr Cudworth, of Scittuate," who was presented by the grand jury for selling wine contrary to orders." It is interesting to note that the witness against him was Mr. Hatherly. There must have been some ill feeling between Cudworth and Hatherly, and in his 1634 letter to his stepfather, Cudworth noted that he had planted corn, "contrary to Mr. Hatherlyes mind, which I know not how I should adune." On 3 March 1639/40, Hatherly successfully sued Cudworth for a £12 debt. Sometime in 1640 or 1641, Cudworth must have decided to join the settlers at Barnstable, and he had several children born there; however, by 8 June 1649, perhaps as early as 1643 or 1644, he was back at Scituate, where he remained. [20]

Although Mattacheese was another name for Barnstable, both names are mentioned in court records of the same period. The first mention of Barnstable was in a list of 5 March 1638/39 giving names of those allowed to exercise men in arms, which for Barnstable was Mr. Thomas Dimmock. Thus there was some kind of Plymouth Colony settlement there perhaps one or more years before the Lothrop group arrived. Perhaps Barnstable was used to distinguish the settlement, while Mattacheese might have been the larger area. On 6 May 1639 the court ordered "that if Mr Callecutt do come in his owne person to inhabite at Mattacheese before the General Court in June next ensuing, that then the graunt shall remayne firme unto them; but if hee fayle to come wthin the tyme prefixed, that then their graunt be made voyde, and the lands be otherwise disposed of." Mr. Callecutt was probably Richard Collicott, a sergeant from Dorchester in the Pequot War, and he probably represented a group of potential settlers from Dorchester. At a Court meeting of 3 March 1644/45, it was ordered that since Mr. Richard Collicott had not come in person to dwell at Barnstable, the grant was void, and any land there assigned to Collicott should be taken by the Barnstable constable for the colony's use; Captain Standish, as treasurer, "shall sell and ymprove the moneys gotten or comeing of them to the colonies use." [21]

By October 1639 the settlement at Barnstable was undoubtedly considerably enlarged with the arrival of the Lothrop group. It is quite possible that the leaders at Plymouth decided to change the grant to Lothrop's people from Sippican to Barnstable not only to reserve Sippican for the expansion of Plymouth town, but also to preempt settlement in Barnstable so that "unworthy settlers," of the type they feared, would not be able to acquire lands there by default. By 1643 there were sixty names on the list of men at Barnstable between the ages of sixteen and sixty able to bear arms.

SANDWICH

On 3 April 1637 the court gave permission to ten men from Saugus, in the Bay Colony; viz., Edmond Freeman, Henry Feake, Thomas Dexter, Edward Dillingham, William Wood, John Carman, Richard Chadwell, William Almy, Thomas Tupper, and George Knott, to search out sufficient lands to settle sixty families on the conditions given them by Governor Bradford and Mr. Winslow. These families settled at Sandwich, at the beginning of Cape Cod, though apparently another, probably smaller, group already had homes there. Mr. John Vincent, a Plymouth Colony resident before the grant to the Saugus group, was appointed constable for Sandwich on 6 March 1637/38. The non-Saugus group had a minister, Mr. William Leveridge, and he and others of this group must have wondered about their own status now that so many newcomers had arrived. They sent a number of questions to the Plymouth Court, the answers to which were recorded on 5 June 1638. The court emphasized that the grants to the Saugus group were conditional; that those grantees who remained at Saugus would not have absentee land ownership at Sandwich; that they might substitute others for those of Saugus who would not be coming to settle, but it was understood from the question that these would be of the church at Saugus or neighbors of good report; that there was to be just one township, not two; and in case the Saugus men abused their privileges by monopolizing the best lands, justice would be determined by the magistrates. [22]

The inhabitants of Sandwich were presented by the grand jury to the court for such common offenses as failing to keep their hogs ringed or being defective in arms. Perhaps more than other towns, however, Sandwich appeared to be a problem for colony leaders. As early as 1 April 1639, as mentioned above, the General Court noted its great concern that Yarmouth might admit unworthy persons "Whereof the Court hath lamentable experience," and it is probable that this lamentable experience referred to Sandwich. By 3 September 1639, the General Court was sufficently concerned to rule that "Whereas, by complaint, it is very pbable that divers of the committees [what would now be called commissioners] of Sandwich have not faythfully discharged that trust reposed in them, by receiveing into the said towne divers psons unfitt for church societie, wch should have been their cheife care in the first place, and have disposed the greatest pt of the lands there already, and to very few that are in church societie or fitt for the same, so that wthout speedy remedy our cheifest end wilbe utterly frustrate, – these are to require such of the committees as are herein faulty to appeare at the next Court of Assistants, to answere the complaint, and in the meane tyme not to dispose of any more lands there, wthout further order from the Court, nor make sale nor convey any of their lands they have assumed to themselves to any pson." [23]

On 3 October 1639 Thomas Prence and Myles Standish, who were then Assistants, were delegated to hear and resolve disputes at Sandwich. Some such disputes were of an ordinary nature, but Prence and Standish particularly noted that the local Sandwich authorities, "the committees," had been negligent in admitting inhabitants "that are not fitt for church societie, & for preventing of evell for ensuinge tyme, it is ordered, that none hereafter shalbe admitted into the town, or have lands assigned them by the committees, wthout the consent & approbacon of Mr Leverich & the church first had & obtayned. And likewise such of the now inhabits as are disposed to sell their estats and depart the towne, they shall not sell their labours to any pson except he be genally approoved of by the whole towne." Further, they ordered that the town should choose one of the Assistants to join the committees and advise them on needful occasions, the first such Assistant to be Mr. Prence, which in effect meant that Prence was to be their monitor. [24]

On 5 March 1638/39, the court had ordered that meadow lands at Sandwich be divided "by equal porcions, according to eich mans estate," and that some of the townsmen join the commissioners in making the division. This would seem simple enough, but apparently there was sufficient dissension at Sandwich to make it quite a task, and finally Assistants Thomas Prence and John Alden had to go and settle the disputes which arose. It was decided that Prence and five commissioners, Edmond Freeman, Henry Feake, Edward Dillinghame, Richard Chadwell, and John Carman, would make the division, after considering "the quallyty & condicon of every pson." The results were the assignment of meadow land in amounts varying from one to forty-two acres (Mr. Edmond Freeman obtaining the largest number) to some fifty-nine people, including several conditional grants to people who had not yet settled at Sandwich. The list of recipients not only gives us a good idea of who was at Sandwich at the time, but also provides a rather loose guide as to the "quallyty and condicon of every pson." The total number of men at Sandwich able to bear arms in 1643 was sixty-eight. [25]

YARMOUTH

On 7 January 1638/39, the Court of Assistants granted lands at "Mattacheeset, now called Yarmouth" to Mr. Anthony Thatcher, Mr. Thomas Howes, Mr. John Crow, and John Coite "to be enquired of." Coite might have been the man of that name of Marblehead, but apparently he did not move to Plymouth Colony. Thatcher, Howes, and Crow were proposed as freemen of Yarmouth, along with Mr. Marmaduke Mathews, Philip Tabor, William Palmer, Samuel Rider, William Lumpkin, and Thomas Hatch. It was also specifically noted that "Old Worden (dead)," Burnell, Wright, and Wat Deville were "Psons there excepted against," probably meaning they were not eligible to be given freemen status, and showing that some form of settlement had already been in existence. In fact, on 4 September 1638 the General Court ordered the inhabitants of Sandwich and "Mattacheese or Yarmouth" to build a bridge over the Eel River (which was just a bit south of Plymouth town, and had to be crossed for travel between Plymouth and the Cape). On 5 March 1638/39 William Palmer was authorized by the General Court to be the one at Yarmouth who would exercise inhabitants in arms, and William Chase was elected constable there. It is apparent that earlier the Plymouth Court had granted land at Yarmouth to others also, for on 1 April 1639 it noted that lands at Mattacheese (another confusion of the names, for it should have been Mattacheeset) were granted to persons who should have inhabited there long ago, but did not, and the grantees "are not likely to come to inhabite there in their owne persons, and lest such as are there should receive in unto them unworthy persons, whereof the Court hath lamentable experience . . ., the Court doth order that onely such of them wch at present are there shall remayne & make use of some lands for their present necessity, but shall not divide any portions of lands there either to themselves or any others." [26]

Also on 5 March 1638/39, the General Court ordered that Mr. Nicholas Simpkins, William Palmer, Philip Tabor, and Josiah Barnes of Yarmouth be added to Thatcher, Howes, and Crow as commissioners. They were to make a division of planting lands "to eich man according to his estate and quallitie." Joshua Pratt of Plymouth and John Vincent were also appointed to determine if lands occupied by Andrew Hallett were prejudicial to the other settlers, in which case some rearrangement would be made. On 3 September 1639 the court decided that Mr. Andrew Hallett could have his great 200-acre lot. Otherwise, though, the court prohibited anyone in Yarmouth from purchasing two or more house lots and putting up a single house on them. On 7 October 1639 the General Court ordered the town of Yarmouth to build a pair of stocks and a pound, and the constable was authorized to confiscate goods from anyone who refused to pay an assessment for the costs of these, as well as for the travel of Yarmouth commissioners to attend the court at Plymouth. Probably reacting from the experience at Sandwich, on 3 March 1639/40 the General Court ordered that Yarmouth could accept no more inhabitants unless "they bring certificate from the places whence they come, under sufficient mens hands of the sd places, of their religious and honest carriage, wch certyficate shall first be allowed by the govnr and assistants before such psons be admitted there." At the same time, complaints against Yarmouth commissioners Thatcher, Crow, and Howes for unfair division of lands were rejected, the court approving of their work. By 1643 Yarmouth had forty-nine names on the list of men able to bear arms. [27]

TAUNTON

Taunton was originally called Cohanett, and again by the time we first see mention of the town in contemporary records, it already has some settlers. A marginal note in contemporary *Plymouth Colony Records* states that "Taunton began here to be added to this booke. June 5th 1638." A list of Plymouth Colony freemen of 7 March 1636/37 contains seven names of men identified as being of Cohannett: Mr. William Poole, Mr. John Gilbert, Sr., Mr. Henry Andrews, John Strong, John Deane, Walter Deane, and Edward Case. However, other records show that these seven were first made freemen on 4 December 1638, so that the names were additions to the 1636/37 list. Thus we know there were seven freemen at Taunton in December 1638, probably with families and servants, and there most likely would have been others there who were neither freemen nor servants. A shipping list shows that Elizabeth Poole (William's sister) left Weymouth, Dorset, on 22 April 1637 on the *Speedwell*, traveling with two friends, fourteen servants, goods valued at £100, and twenty tons of salt for fishing provision. Walter Deane and six servants sailed to New England on the same ship at the same time. Another ship, the *Prosperous*, left Dartmouth, Devonshire, on 27 April 1637, carrying bullocks and heifers for various planters in New England, including William and Elizabeth Poole. William Poole had probably preceded his sister across the Atlantic. On 5 March 1638/39, Captain Poole was authorized to exercise the men at Cohanett in arms. [28]

The General Court, noting on 3 March 1639/40 that the inhabitants of Taunton had complained of a need for meadow land, agreed that without such additional land they could not survive. Accordingly, the court granted them new lands between Taunton and Assonett, providing that the ministers and people "now there which are fitt. . .continue in a church estate there the space of seaven yeares." The court further ordered that Mr. William Hooke, Mr. Nicholas Street, and Mrs. Poole have competent meadows and uplands laid out for them by Captain Standish and others appointed for this purpose. Hooke and Street were ministers, and it would appear that in Taunton, at least, the Plymouth leaders had obtained new settlers who were strong in the church. On 1 June 1641 the General Court ordered that the first seven freemen of Taunton, who had suffered great personal expense in traveling to attend the courts and in laying out lands to the town's inhabitants, should have some additional lands assigned them, provided the additions not exceed forty acres apiece. On 6 June 1643 Taunton asked the court for additional land and timber rights. The timber could not be granted without detriment to "another plantation intended below that," but otherwise the request was granted, provided that "leave can be obtained from Ussamequin [Massasoit], and all payments to be made by themselves." In 1643 Taunton had fifty-four men on the list of those able to bear arms. [29]

The settling of new towns brought new problems to the colony. Some problems arose because of the deportment of new residents, but some were created by mere distance alone. Deputies had existed as a political institution in Massachusetts since 1634, when the towns, led by Watertown, protested taxes being determined by the Bay Colony Assistants alone. The residents of the towns thereupon elected deputies to represent them at court, becoming in fact a second legislative chamber. Plymouth did not have deputies until 1638, and even then the need for them had more to do with distances than an enraged populace. On 5 March 1638/39 the General Court observed that many freemen considered it a costly inconvenience to have to attend the General Court, and it enacted a law providing that each town elect annually two deputies, with Plymouth electing four, to represent the freemen of the towns at the courts. While in the Bay the institution of deputies resulted from a kind of revolution by the townspeople demanding more representation, in Plymouth, which had a much higher percentage of its total citizenry as freemen, it seemed more to be a desire on the part of the leaders to get more effective representation, for too many freemen were not coming to court meetings because of the expense. By voting for deputies who would represent their collective views, the townspeople were assured of a voice at the courts. It was true that only a freeman could serve as a deputy, but the court specifically allowed non-freemen town residents to vote for the deputies, not so much in recognition of the nonfreemen's right to have political representation, but rather out of a concept of economic fairness, since the non-freemen would have to help bear the expenses of the deputies' travel three times yearly to Plymouth. Such was the solution to one of the difficulties created by expansion. [30]

While the leaders of Plymouth had to ponder over problems involving the pattern of settlement of the colony, other matters also occupied their attention. Plymouth Colony's external debt—owed by the eight Undertakers (though Allerton was no longer in the colony) to their four London partners (though Hatherly was now residing in Scituate)—continued to be a curse. It seemed that no matter how much beaver and other skins the Undertakers sent to England, the debt constantly increased. Though Hatherly had told Plymouth colonists that the English partners would not hold them responsible for a share of the debts of the *Friendship,* the other three men in London continued to press them for payments of expenses resulting from both the *Friendship* and the *White Angel.* Winslow, on a trip to England, told the Londoners that this part of the debt was rejected. On his return to Plymouth in 1635, Winslow persuaded his colleagues to send another 1,150 pounds of beaver plus other skins to England, even though the Londoners had still sent them no accounting, and Bradford writes somewhat peevishly, "Though [we] thought his [Edward Winslow's] grounds but weake. . .yet by his importunitie [we] yeelded, and sent the same." In 1636 Bradford calculated that Plymouth had sent more than 12,000 pounds of beaver and over 1,000 pounds of otter skins over a six year period to England, so that they should have been credited with more than £10,000. All their previous debts, even including the expenses of the *Friendship* and *White Angel*, would come to no more than £4,770, and they might owe up to another £2,000 for supplies sent from England, so there should be some difference owing them. But, London claimed they still owed money. This might have been due in part to some lowering in the price of beaver, and certainly the extremely high interest rates of the times for risky overseas ventures contributed to their indebtedness; but the colonists' failure to keep accurate accounts, and some shoddy practices by both Allerton and Sherley, such as double and even triple charging for supplies, made the debt much worse than would otherwise be. At the behest of the Londoners, Edward Winslow's brother, Josias Winslow, came to Plymouth to serve as the Undertakers' accountant, but, in Bradford's words, "did wholy faile them, and could never give them any accounte." [31]

One study points out that Governor Bradford's account has to be our main guide, but unfortunately in writing about this particular topic, Bradford "is repetitious, sometimes confusing, and yet omits certain business details." To make matters more confused, the three partners in England now quarreled among themselves. Beauchamp and Andrews accused Sherley of receiving some £12,000 worth of furs from Plymouth, but refusing to give them an accounting of the proceeds. They went to court and Sherley won. Andrews turned over his part of the debt to have it paid in kind to the Bay Colony for the support of poor ministers and other godly men. The others still pressed for settlement of the debt. Businessmen already in the colony, John Atwood, William Collier, and Beauchamp's brother-in-law Edmond Freeman, were used as arbiters, and on 15 October 1641 terms satisfactory to most were reached, with the Plymouth men promising to pay another £1,400 to the English partners in full payment of all debts. The final end to the debt did not come about until 1645, when Beauchamp, the last of the London men to hold out, settled his claim for £291 worth of lands in Plymouth, Rehoboth, and Marshfield. [32] It is to their credit that in spite of all difficulties, including questionable practices on the part of their creditors, the Plymouth colonists did not repudiate their indebtedness for their original passage across the Atlantic and some subsequent sustenance, but, after repaying a considerable amount in valuable skins, negotiated a final settlement to which all concerned could agree.

There were other problems. Economically, the escalation of prices brought on in the 1630s by continual arrivals of large contingents of new settlers to the Bay Colony began to reverse as the Puritan Revolution in England slowed immigration to but a comparative trickle. Bradford noted for 1638 that cattle were selling for £20 to 28 each, but by 1641 he writes that "catle and other things begane greatly to fall from their former rates and persons begane to fall into more straits." In 1642 Bradford observes that wickedness was breaking forth in the land, and he gives a number of examples (which will be discussed in subsequent chapters). Though the

Pequot problem was over, another threat of an Indian War, this time with the powerful Narragansetts, brought about a confederation agreed to on 29 August 1643 by the colonies of Massachusetts Bay, Connecticut, New Haven, and Plymouth, calling themselves the United Colonies of New England. Their avowed purpose was for "preserving and propagating the truth [and liberties] of the Gospell and for their owne mutuall saftie and wellfare." Various articles provided for two commissioners from each colony to make decisions under the treaty, including making war if all eight, or at least six, of the commissioners were agreed. One article provided that all servants or criminals fleeing from one colony, who were caught in another, would be returned to the original colony. Another article provided that each colony would, from time to time, "bring a true account and number of all the males in every [settlement]. . .of what qualitie or condition soever they be, from 16 years old to 60, being inhabitants ther." The resulting list compiled by Plymouth is another of those important original documents which have fortunately been preserved, for virtually all adult males age sixty or under are on the list—ministers, government officials, freemen, other free residents, and servants. We know of one case where George Pidcock of Duxbury was specifically excused by the Court of Assistants on 2 January 1643/44 because he, "by reason of a cold palsy that his body is subject unto, is unable to beare armes to exercise wth a peece [that is, a musket]." The very fact that this exemption appears in court records by itself is a good indication of the thoroughness of the list. Consequently we have a good idea of the total male population between sixteen and sixty in Plymouth Colony in 1643—about 600 (after eliminating some duplicates). We have their names, we know the towns they lived in, and we have a basis for an educated guess as to the total population, including women, children, and men over sixty: probably around 2,000 people. [33]

NOTES

1. *Bradford (Ford)* 2:164-67.

2. Ibid., 2:167-71, 190-91.

3. Ibid., 2:206-24.

4. Ibid., 2:216-24. When Bradford comments that they of the New-Towne group "delt more fairly" with Plymouth Colony, he is referring to the settlers moving to Connecticut under the Reverend Thomas Hooker.

5. Ibid., 2:191-92, 232-36, 242-43.

6. *PCR* 1:60-62; *Bradford (Ford)* 2:247-53.

7. *Bradford (Ford)* 2:274-82; *NEHGR* 14:101.

8. *Encyclopaedia Britannica*, 1971 edition (hereafter *Encyc. Brit.*), 23:541-42.

9. On 16 September 1643 the United Colonies voted that the quota for soldiers from the different colonies be based on their population, and since Massachusetts was to contribute 150 soldiers to Plymouth's thirty

(and New Haven's twenty-five), it would seem that Massachusetts was then roughly five times larger than Plymouth. *PCR* 3:102 records that "Wheras Joseph Ramsdan hath lived long in the woods, in an uncivil way, in the woods, with his wife alone, wherby great inconveniencies have followed, the Court have ordered, that hee repaier downe to sum naighborhood betwixt this and October next, or that then his house bee pulled down." *PCR* 1:23 gives the order that servants would be granted land.

10. *PCR* 8:187-89.

11. *Ply. Ch. Recs.* 1:69-70; *PCR* 1:41, 8:189-90.

12. *Bradford (Ford)* 2:152-53, *PCR* 1:13-14, 11:25, 31, 37. Could the "but now Marshfield" have been added later in the same hand and ink? Plymouth records contain many later additions, which are known because either the handwriting or the ink changes, but where they do not change, it is virtually impossible to tell what additional word or phrase might be tacked on.

13. *Ply. Ch. Recs.* 1:71; David L. Greene, FASG, "Mary, Wife of the Rev. Richard Blinman of Marshfield, Gloucester, and New London: An Unsolved Problem," *The Genealogist* (hereafter *TG*) 4:173; *PCR* 8:196.

14. *NEHGR* 9:279, 10:42, 14:101-04; *PCR* 1:21, 8:190-92.

15. Amos Otis, "Scituate and Barnstable Church Records," *NEHGR* 9:279-87; these are the records of Rev. John Lothrop, the original of which is no longer extant, which were taken by Otis from a copy of the original made by Ezra Stiles in 1769. *Ply. Ch. Recs.* 1:71; *PCR* 8:190-92.

16. Samuel Deane, *History of Scituate, Massachusetts, From Its First Settlement to 1831* (Boston, 1831), 8. See also Eben Putnam, *Two Early Lists 1635-1637* (Baltimore, 1964), which documents many early settlers from Kent.

17. Robert Charles Anderson, FASG, "Notes of Early Scituate Church History" (not yet published); Otis, *NEHGR* 10:37.

18. *PCR* 11:25, 1:108, 2:170. Otis, *NEHGR* 10:37. *PCR* 1:121 gives a Court order "to set forth the bounds betwixt Mattacheese and Mattacheeset."

19. *Bradford (Ford)* 2:300-07. Chauncey remained minister at Scituate until 1654, when he changed his views on baptism and was elected president of Harvard College.

20. *PCR* 2:30, 1:156; *NEHGR* 14:103; *PCR* 1:156; *NEHGR* 9:282, 285; *PCR* 2:144. Possibly Cudworth returned to Scituate in 1643, for his name was canceled from the 1643 list of men from Barnstable able to bear arms (see appendix J) and added to the Scituate list.

21. *PCR* 11:31, *PCR* 1:121; Pope, 111; *PCR* 2:81. *PCR* 1:93, 95, show Stephen Hopkins, Gregory Armstrong, and Gabriel Wheildon were granted land at "Mattacheese," but this is a confusion in the records with the name "Mattacheeset." *PCR* 1:107 gives a record referring to Mr. John Crow, Mr. Thomas Howes, Mr. Anthony Thatcher, and Mr. Marmaduke Mathews at "Mattacheese, als Yarmouth," while *PCR* 1:108 has another record giving the names of those granted lands at "Mattacheeset, now

called Yarmouth," and included the four men mentioned on the previous page. Yet see n. 18 above where a contemporary Court order clearly distinguished between the two names. See appendix J for the list of men able to bear arms, keeping in mind that some names might have been added after 1643.

22. *PCR* 1:57, 80, 88-89.

23. Ibid., 1:97-98, 120, 131.

24. Ibid., 1:133-34, 147.

25. Ibid., 1:147-50 gives the fifty-nine names of those receiving grants, and *PCR* 8:192-93 (shown in appendix J) gives the Sandwich men able to bear arms.

26. *PCR* 1:108-09; Pope, 108; *PCR* 11:28, 30-31, 1:116, 120. That Coit might have been the one of Marblehead is strengthened by the fact that Thacher was of Marblehead, too. Winthrop, *History*, 1:260, under date of 30 March 1638, shows the Reverend Stephen Bachelor had also been at Yarmouth: "Another plantation was now in hand at Mattakeese ['Now Yarmouth' is written in the margin], six miles beyond Sandwich. The undertaker of this was one Mr. Batchellor, late pastor at Sagus, (since called Lynn,) being about seventy-six years of age; yet he walked thither on foot in a very hard season. He and his company, being all poor men, finding the difficulty, gave it over, and others undertook it."

27. *PCR* 1:117, 130-31, 135, 142, 8:1.

28. *PCR* 11:27, 1:53; *NGSQ* 71:177; *PCR* 11:31.

29. *PCR* 1:142-43; Pope, 239, 439; *PCR* 2:18-19, 58, 8:195.

30. Morison, *Builders*, 87-89, 93; *PCR* 11:31.

31. *Bradford (Ford)*, 2:226-32. It would seem a remarkable coincidence that the London partners might press Edward Winslow's brother upon the Undertakers as their accountant unless we consider that Allerton might not have been the only Plymouth representative to use his visits to London to obtain personal advantages. It would seem likely that Edward Winslow found a way to bring his brother over at the expense of the Undertakers.

32. McIntyre, 57-65; *Bradford (Ford)* 2:259-60, 268-71, 294-300; *PCR* 12:127-30.

33. *Bradford (Ford)* 2:269, 307, 354-62; *PCR* 2:67. Many calculations of total population in 1643 are possible, depending on the assumptions one makes. A very rough estimation of some 2,000 people would seem plausible, based on reasoning too complicated to be given here.

CHAPTER 4

A Loss of Leaders (1643-1657)

"A TIME TO MOURN"

Plymouth was founded mainly by young people. After the death of Governor Carver in 1621, all the other leaders were in their twenties and thirties, except Elder William Brewster, who was fifty-three on arrival at Plymouth. Now time was catching up with them. Bradford, who became governor at age thirty-one, was now in his fifties. Brewster died in April 1644, and his loss was deeply felt by his companions. Bradford, who had been Brewster's protege and friend in England, Holland, and Plymouth, wrote about him:

> He was wise and discreete and well spoken, having a grave and deliberate utterance, of a very cherfull spirite, very sociable and pleasante amongst his freinds, of an humble and modest mind, of a peaceable disposition, under valleving himself and his owne abilities, and some time over valewing others; inoffencive and innocente in his life and conversation, which gained him the love of those without, as well as those within; yet he would tell them plainely of thier faults and evills, both publickly and privatly, but in shuch a maner as usually was well taken from him. . . . For the govermente of the church, (which was most proper to his office,) he was carfull to preserve good order in the same, and to preserve purities, both in the doctrine and comunion of the same; and to supress any errour or contention that might begine to rise up amongst them; and accordingly God gave good success to his indeavors herein all his days, and he saw the fruite of his labours in that behalfe. [1]

Many writers have commented on the difficulty Plymouth had in getting and keeping good ministers. And yet with a man such as William Brewster as ruling elder of the church, there was not as much need for ministers as some other settlements might have. Indeed, it is apparent from Bradford's History and from other contemporary records that Brewster was the guiding light behind the Plymouth Church. It is fair, then, to raise the question: Could their difficulty with ministers have been in good part because they had such a strong, respected, and dedicated ruling elder? Unlike Brewster, the ministers coming to Plymouth had a university

73

degree, and, being ordained, they could administer the sacraments. But they could not have had the intimate relationship with people and institutions that Brewster had. Did it fall to Brewster to "preserve puritie both in the doctrine and comunion" and "supress any errour or contention that might begine to rise up amongst them" because the various ministers coming to Plymouth were weak, or were they weak because the real authority in the church was Brewster? Would Brewster tell these ministers "plainely of their faults and evills, both publickly and privatly"? This is not to detract from the many great qualities and services of the elder, but he would indeed have had to possess the forebearance of a St. Francis not to have kept a heavy guiding hand on the church he had brought to these shores.

Of the adult male *Mayflower* pasengers who had survived that first year at Plymouth, Gilbert Winslow returned to England after a few years and died there; Richard Warren died in 1628; John Billington was hanged in 1630; Peter Brown, Francis Eaton, and Samuel Fuller succumbed to an infectious disease in 1633; William Latham and Edward Leister separately left Plymouth after a number of years and died in Bermuda and Virginia respectively; and William Brewster and Stephen Hopkins died in 1644. Writing about 1644 Bradford deplored both the deaths and the dismissal of members to other settlements. "And thus was this poore church left, like an anciente mother, growne olde, and forsaken of her children, (though not in their affections,) yett in regarde of their bodily presence and personall helpfullnes. Her anciente members being most of them worne away by death, and these of later time being like children translated into other families and she like a widow left only to trust in God. Thus, she that had made many rich became her selfe poore." [2]

Within a few years, another Plymouth stalwart was lost to the colony forever, not by death, but by compliance with duty. Edward Winslow was twenty-five years old when he arrived at Plymouth in 1620, and he was thirty-seven when he became governor some twelve years later. One of only two men to alternate as governor with Bradford (the other being Thomas Prence) during the 1630s and 1640s, he was probably the most aristocratic of the *Mayflower* passengers in upbringing, and certainly in outlook (his correspondence with Bay Governor Winthrop shows a thorough underlying belief that some by birth were intended to govern). Following the disabling mistrust engendered by Allerton's questionable dealings, Winslow became the colony's main emissary to England, and he engaged in numerous diplomatic and trade negotiations with the other New England colonies. In 1646 he was chosen by Governor Winthrop and the Bay Colony magistrates to go to England as their representative to defend the Bay General Court from the charges being made to Parliament by William Vassall and Robert Child (detailed later in this chapter). In this he was successful, but his presence in England coincided with the height of the Puritan Revolution in England, and people of his experience and competence were needed. After performing various tasks for the Parliamentarians, Winslow was assigned a joint command of the 1655 English expedition which won Jamaica from the Spanish, his fellow commanders being Robert Venables and Sir William Pen (father of the Quaker founder of Pennsylvania). Winslow died during the expedition. At the time Bradford ended his History, Edward Winslow was still alive in England, and the last words of the History are "So as he [Winslow] hath now bene absente this 4 years, which hath been much to the weakning of this govermente, without whose consente he tooke these imployments [that is, Parliamentarian service] upon him," a double lament. [3]

These were fast moving times in England, as the Puritans there took more and more control. Bradford wrote, "Full little did I thinke, that the downfall of the Bishops, with their courts, cannons and ceremonies, etc. had been so neare, when I first begane these scribled writings (which was aboute the year 1630, and so peeced up at times of leasure afterward)." It was a dual struggle; on the one hand the Divine Rights of Kings versus a demand for popular representation through Parliament, and on the other hand a battle for religious domination between the King's church with bishops and an uneasy coalition of "non-conforming" Puritans, Presbyterians, Levellers, and Anabaptists, among others. Civil war broke out in 1642, and at first the King and Cavaliers held their own. But in July 1644 the Royalists lost to the Roundheads at the Battle of Marston Moor. Oliver Cromwell, in command of the Parliamentarian New Model Army, most decisively defeated the Royalist army at Naseby in June 1645, and finally captured the Royalist headquarters at Oxford in June 1646. King Charles I was captured, attempted an escape, and finally was beheaded on 30 January 1648/49. [4]

The New England colonies were, of course, pro-Parliament, but not to the extent that they wanted a victorious Parliament to send governors general over to rule them. It was during the Puritan control of England that Roger Williams was able to get his charter for Rhode Island. But most colonists were affected in a more indirect way, such as getting less money for crops and livestock as immigration trickled to insignificance. Some settlers had gone back to England to fight for the Puritans there, but not a substantial number from Plymouth Colony. In spite of Governor Bradford's joy in seeing the downfall of the bishops, when it came to active measures, Plymouth seemed content to revise the beginning of the oaths of its officials, "You shall sweare to be truly loyall to our Soveraigne Lord King Charles," by crossing out the reference to the King and replacing it with "to the state and Govrment of England as it now stands"; and later, after the restoration of Charles II in 1660, by striking over "the present state and Govrment of England," and substituting "our Sovr Lord King Charles. [5]

A major change in land policy had taken place in 1639 and 1640. The Bradford Patent gave all rights in Plymouth Colony to William Bradford and his associates. His associates were not defined, but Bradford governed the colony mainly with a small group, among them his fellow Undertakers, who were agreed on the proper relationship of church, state, and citizen. In a broader sense, his associates could be considered to be all the

Purchasers, or Old Comers. The narrow group predominated in the Court of Assistants, and, among other things, controlled the distribution of land. In 1639 their right to grant land was challenged, and a compromise worked out whereby Bradford agreed to turn over the Patent to the Court of Freemen, and the court agreed to reserve three large tracts of land for the Purchasers. By the early 1640s, it was the court which decided who would receive grants to unreserved land in the colony, and the court listened to petitions from resident and outsider alike. [6]

We have already seen much of the rush from Plymouth to new lands in the colony. The land at Plymouth was not the best, being sandy and rocky, much like Cape Cod, of which Plymouth is geologically a part. There were at least two attempts to move the town itself. The first may have been for religious reasons. At a General Court meeting of 21 March 1636/37 there was consideration of moving Plymouth a little northward, and Duxbury a little southwesterly, to join in a new town at the Jones River. Captain Standish, Manasseh Kempton, George Kenrick, John Jenney, and Edward Bangs for Plymouth, and William Collier, Stephen Tracy, John Howland, Edmond Chandler, and Joshua Pratt for Duxbury, had been appointed to report on a fit place for the move. Seven of these believed "Jones River to be the fittest place for the uniting of both pts into a neerer society, & there to build a meeting howse and town." However, the matter was referred to the churches concerned, and apparently that was the end of it. [7]

THE FOUNDING OF EASTHAM

Perhaps a more serious attempt to move Plymouth came about in 1644, when because of the "straightnes and barrennes of [Plymouth] and their finding of better accomodations elsewhere, more suitable to their ends and minds; and sundrie others still upon every occasion desiring their dismissions, the church begane seriously to thinke whether it were not better joyntly to remove to some other place." After many meetings, the Plymouth people gave their attention to moving to Nauset on Cape Cod, one of the three areas reserved to the Purchasers, who were in agreement for the move. There then occurred a change of heart, for "now they begane to see their errour, that they had given away already the best and most commodious places to others, and now wanted them selves." Nauset was too small and too remote, so Plymouth remained as it was. Still, this was the occasion for the establishment of yet another new town, and an undated list probably made in the 1640s shows that the freemen there were Thomas Prence, John Doane, Edward Bangs, Nicholas Snow, John Jenkins, Josiah Cooke, Samuel Hicks, John Smalley, Joseph Rogers, and Richard Higginson. On 3 March 1644/45 the General Court granted to the Plymouth Church "or those that goe to dwell at Nosett," all the land between sea and sea "from the Purchasors bounds at Naumskeckett to the Hering Brooke at Billingsgate." The court on 2 June 1646 ordered that "Nawsett" be made a township, and Samuel Hicks was appointed as constable. On 7 June 1651 the court ordered the name of the town of Nauset to be changed to Eastham. [8]

REHOBOTH

Another town that began settlement around the same time, perhaps a bit earlier, was Rehoboth, originally called Seekonk, in the southwest corner of the colony, touching the Massachusetts and Rhode Island borders. This was part of one of three large areas of land reserved by the General Court for the Purchasers in 1639. When it first began to be settled is unknown, but at least one person was living at Seekonk as early as 2 August 1642, when the Court of Assistants issued a warrant for John Hazell "that lives at Sickuncke" to answer a charge of contempt. He seemed to be a squatter from elsewhere (possibly being the John Hassell who was earlier living at Ipswich), and on 1 November 1642 the Court of Assistants ordered him either to take the Oath of Fidelity or to remove his dwelling. On the same date, Hazell testified to the Assistants that Massasoit chose ten fathoms of beads "at Mr. Williams, and put them in a basket, and affirmed that he was fully satisfyed therewth for his lands at Seacunck, but he stood upon it that he would have a coat more, & left the beads wth Mr. Williams, & willed him to keepe them untill Mr. Hubberd came up." From Rehoboth town records it can be seen that Edward Winslow and John Brown bought the entire Rehoboth area, eight miles square, from Osamequin (Massasoit) in 1641. [9]

At the 2 August 1642 Assistants' meeting, some men from Hingham — John Porter, Thomas Loring, Stephen Payne, and the Rev. Nicholas Baker — requested permission to settle at Seekonk. Though the records do not show how the request was answered, Payne, at least, was later living there, being chosen by the General Court on 4 June 1645 as constable. On 6 July 1641 the General Court had noted that the Bay Colony "would have Sicquncke from us." The Bay disputed Plymouth's right to Rehoboth, and the issue was referred to the Commissioners of the United Colonies to decide. At a meeting at Hartford on 5 September 1644, the commissioners decided in favor of Plymouth, unless Massachusetts could produce better evidence to support its claim. Richard Wright, a supporter of Governor Winthrop, was elected the first deputy from Rehoboth to the Plymouth Court, but refused to serve. One of the Plymouth Assistants, Mr. John Brown, played a leading role in Rehoboth's affairs, and some of the Massachusetts men left the town. On 28 October 1645, the General Court noted that the "townes" of Taunton and Rehoboth had been excused from sending men to fight against the Narragansetts "in regard they are frontire townes, and billited the souldiers during the tyme they were forth," and Rehoboth was not assessed with the other towns for the expenses of the campaign. At the same court meeting, Walter Palmer of Rehoboth was admitted a freeman and chosen a commissioner to represent Rehoboth at court meetings. Other early residents at Rehoboth included Richard Bowen and Robert Martin. At the 2 June 1646 court meeting, Peter Hunt was chosen constable for Rehoboth, and Thomas Cooper was made a highway surveyor. There is no record of when Rehoboth was made a town, but the General Court's decision of 4 June 1645 "That Seacunck be called Rehoboth" has been taken as the official date. [10]

Leonard Bliss, Jr. in *The History of Rehoboth. . .,* shows that although the Plymouth Court first granted lands at Rehoboth to some colonists from Hingham for the settlement of a town, they were soon joined by Mr. Samuel Newman "and the majority of his church at Weymouth," and that the town was given the name Rehoboth, "a roomy place," by Mr. Newman. Bliss gives a list of fifty-eight names from the Proprietors' Records as the landowners at Rehoboth in the year 1643. In addition to Newman's, another name on the list is that of Obadiah Holmes, who had earlier been excommunicated at Salem for Baptist activity. On 29 October 1649, Holmes complained to the General Court at Plymouth that Mr. Newman had slandered him by saying that he had taken a false oath. Mr. Newman claimed that he had just repeated what he heard from others, namely from Thomas Cooper, Stephen Paine, Robert Sharp, Jonathan Bliss, Thomas Wilmoth, and William Sabin, but now he knew the charge was not true, and he acknowledged he had done Holmes wrong and promised to pay costs. The court advised Newman to give the facts at some meeting in his town so as to clear the record for Holmes. Holmes was later arrested and severely whipped in Lynn for attending a Baptist meeting, and he subsequently moved to Newport, Rhode Island, where he became a Baptist minister. [11]

DARTMOUTH

Another of the three large tracts reserved to the Purchasers was southwest of Plymouth on Monument (now Buzzard[s]) Bay. Like so many other places, its earliest settlement went unrecorded, but on 5 October 1652 Dartmouth appeared on a list of rates charged to "the severall Townes within this Jurisdiction for the Officers Wages." On 7 March 1652/53 a list was made of the original proprietors of Dartmouth lands, which were divided in thirty-four shares. Almost everyone on the list was one of the Old Comers. However, as Langdon points out, by 1694 only five of the fifty-six men then owning land shares had a surname identical to one of the original proprietors. Thus it would appear that many of the original proprietors had sold their interests to others. Apparently Dartmouth did not officially become a town until 8 June 1664, when the General Court ordered that the tract of land commonly called Acushena, Ponagansett, and Coaksett be made a township, and that it be called Dartmouth. Somewhat before this time, perhaps in 1661, the court advised that such places as Saconeesett (which was also part of the Dartmouth area) and Acushenett should apply themselves in some effective way "to procure a godly man for the dispensing of Gods word amongst them. To induce those already settled there to attract new settlers to join them so that the tax base for the support of a minister would be broadened, the court ruled that the inhabitants would be taxed proportionately even for the uninhabited lands. In June 1670 Dartmouth still had no acceptable minister, and the court ruled that the town would have to pay £15 yearly for the support of a minister and meeting house. [12]

BRIDGEWATER

The settlement of Bridgewater was unique in that the area was specifically given to the town of Duxbury for its expansion. In October 1645 the General Court granted to the inhabitants of Duxbury "a competent pporcion of lands about Saughtuckquett, towards the west, for a plantacon for them, and to have it foure miles every way from the place where they shall sett up their center, (pvided it entrench not upon Winnetuckquett, formly graunted to Plymouth,) and have nominated Captaine Miles Standish, Mr John Alden, Georg Soul, Constant Southworth, Joseph Rogers, and Willm Brett to be feoffees in trust for the equall devideing and laying forth of the said lands to their inhabitants." These lands soon became known as Duxbury New Plantation, and on 3 June 1656 the court ordered that "henceforth Duxburrow New Plantation bee allowed to bee a townshipe of yt selfe, destinct from Duxburrow, and to bee called by the name of Bridgwater, prvided that all publicke rates bee borne by them with Duxburrow upon equall proportions." On 3 July 1656 the court ordered Bridgewater to pay one-third of the combined taxes with Duxbury for public expenses, from which we might assume that it already had roughly half the population of its mother town. By 1 June 1658 Bridgewater was asking the court for more land, and the court agreed "to consider of the resonablenes of theire desire in reference to the accomodateing of some usefull men that may be usefull in church and comonwealth." [13]

In discussing an event which occurred before his arrival at Scituate, the Reverend Mr. Charles Chauncey wrote that following John Lothrop's departure, "there was a day of humiliation kept at Mr. Hatherly's house, by the rest of the brethren that purposed to stay at Scituate, and as some of them do constantly affirm they entered into Covenant with god and Christ and with one another, to walke together in the whole revealed will of God and Christ." One writer understands this to mean that they formed a new church as distinguished from continuing on with a fragment of the previous church. Chauncey arrived at Scituate in 1641, and almost from his arrival there was dissension with some of the members of the old church who stayed behind. William Vassall wrote on 2 February 1642/43, that when some of the members "called Mr Chauncy to be their Pastor, . . .William Vassall, Thomas King, John Twisden, Thomas Lapham, Suza King, Judith White [daughter of William Vassall and wife of Resolved White], and Anna Stockbridge refused to do so," and they therefore entered a new covenant together "as a Church of Christ." The Vassall group called their church the "Second Church" of Scituate, though there are some who believe it was more a "Third Church," the first being the one that had moved to Barnstable, and the second being Chauncey's. [14]

Chauncey, strongly supported by Timothy Hatherly and his followers, refused to acknowledge Vassall's church, and both sides appealed to church leaders in other towns. The Vassall church obtained the willingness of Rev. William Witherell, then pastor of the Duxbury Church, to come to Scituate as their pastor. He was ordained on 2 September 1645, in spite of objections of some other churches and of the refusal of the Duxbury Church to dismiss him. John Cooke had been sent by the Plymouth Church to try to dissuade them, and Josias Winslow, the future governor, was sent for the same purpose by the Marshfield Church. Winslow might have been an unwilling messenger, for Deane asserts that shortly after this, Winslow began attending Witherell's church, even though he lived ten miles away, and brought his children to be baptized by Witherell. Chauncey remained at Scituate in control of his church until 1654, when he became discouraged and was on the verge of returning to England. At that point in time, he was invited to become President of Harvard College, on condition that he abandon, publicly at least, his views on baptism by total immersion. He accepted the Harvard invitation, interestingly replacing its first president, Henry Dunster, who had been invited to leave for having embraced Baptist ideas on baptism. Dunster then settled in Scituate. [15]

William Vassall is especially known for his support, perhaps even leadership, of the remonstrance of 1646, in which Robert Child and others petitioned the Bay Colony General Court for greater suffrage, more liberal policies on church membership, and closer adherence to the laws of England. It was to answer such charges as these, plus the still pending charges of Samuel Gorton, that Edward Winslow went to London on behalf of Winthrop and Bay Colony leaders in 1646. This type of internal dissension had begun earlier with Samuel Gorton, who had arrived in Boston in 1637, but who went to Plymouth almost immediately. As early as 5 November 1638, Gorton was in trouble with the Court of Assistants (with Edward Doty putting up £40 as a surety for him), and on 4 December 1638 he was fined £20 and ordered to depart the colony within a fortnight for "misdemeanrs in the open Court towards the elders, the Bench, & stirring up the people to mutynie in the face of the Court." He then moved to Portsmouth, Rhode Island, where he began gathering a few other discontents around him, and again got in trouble with local magistrates. Moving to Providence, he tested Roger Williams's generous nature with his extreme theological views and open contempt for authority. Ultimately, he stirred up the Narragansetts against the Bay Colony, was seized by Colony authorities, brought to Boston for trial, and just narrowly missed being put to death. Going to England, Gorton pleaded his case before the Commission for Foreign Plantations with some success, but did not return to New England. Such agitation in England was dreaded by both the Bay and Plymouth, for it was treading on sleeping dogs, in this case a Parliament that had not been making use of its ultimate power over the colonies. [16]

William Vassall, one of the original Bay Colony Assistants in 1630, returned to England, but later came back to New England, this time residing at Scituate in Plymouth Colony. His brother in England was a member of the Commission for Foreign Plantations. Without question Vassall was aware of the way Gorton was twisting the Bay Colony tail and of the inherent weakness in the governments of the New England colonies, which ruled as if they were de facto independent countries. Though Vassall is known for behind-the-scenes involvement in the famous 1646 Bay Colony remonstrance, he was earlier the chief participant in a related incident which occurred in Plymouth Colony in 1645, an incident completely unknown in official records, but which was fortunately recorded in a letter Edward Winslow sent to Massachusetts Gov. John Winthrop. In 1645 Vassall initiated a petition to the Plymouth General Court asking for full religious toleration for all well-behaving men. The division in court on this petition interestingly gives us an indication of the liberal-conservative split that existed there. Many of the town deputies, plus Assistants John Browne, Edmond Freeman, Timothy Hatherly, and Myles Standish, were in favor of the Vassall petition. Governor Bradford and Assistants William Collier, Thomas Prence, and Edward Winslow were the opposition. It could have passed, but for arbitrary action by Bradford, which gave the conservative side time to maneuver effectively against it. Winslow happily commented in his letter to Winthrop on its defeat, "You would have admired to have seen how sweet this carrion relished to the palate of most of the deputies." [17]

In 1646 Robert Child, Samuel Maverick, and some others in Massachusetts sent a remonstrance and petition to the Bay Colony Court asking for religious freedom and wider suffrage. It was not well received. Shortly after, one of the signers sailed to England in the *Supply* with a petition to Parliament asking that the Presbyterian Church be allowed in Massachusetts and that the laws of England be established in the Bay under a governor general. The Reverend John Cotton, Sr., preached a sermon just before the ship sailed in which he called the petition a Jonah and advised that the passage would be extremely rough and the passengers should toss the petition in the sea. The passage did get rough, and some of the passengers did toss what they thought was the petition into the sea, though actually a copy was saved. When the ship reached England, Robert Child's brother, John Child, wrote a pamphlet entitled "New Englands Jonas Cast Up at London," in which he repeated many of the petitioners' grievances, and denied that a miracle had happened to quiet the sea after the so-called "Jonas" had been thrown overboard. It was in part to answer this attack that the Massachusetts Bay Colony authorities engaged Edward Winslow to go to England for what would be his last trip. [18]

Winslow responded to "New Englands Jonas" in a pamphlet of his own which he called "New Englands Salamander," in which he identified William Vassall as both the "salamander" and the real author of "New Englands Jonas." Winslow's pamphlet and his personal influence as agent for Massachusetts were quite successful, and the petitioners' attacks came to nothing. "New Englands Salamander" itself was a brilliant political document, and in it Winslow shed new light on both Massachusetts and Plymouth. In answering Vassall's charge that Winslow was a "Principall opposer of the lawes of England in New England," Winslow stated that "our Salamander having labored two years together to draw me to his party, and finding hee could no way prevaile, he then casts off all his pretended love." Winslow pointed out that the laws of England were respected in New England to the extent that they were compatible with the changed conditions there, and they were certainly in force as much or more than was the case in other New World colonies, such as Virginia and Barbadoes. "But I have been so farre from sleighting the law of England as I have brought my owne booke of the statutes of England into our court, that so when wee have wanted a law or ordinance, wee might see what the statutes provided in that kind, and found a great willingnesse in our generall court to take all helpe and benefit thereby." To answer the charge that "there are many that are not free amongst us," he replied that it was their own fault if they would not ask to be made freemen, and he suggested that they wanted to shirk the responsibilities of freemen. For the petitioners' main charge that "wee have not penall lawes exactly set downe in all cases," he confessed that neither could they find any commonwealth under heaven where there were not some things reserved to the discretion of judges, and "in case any misdemeaner befall where no penaltie is set down, it is by solemn order left to the discretion of the bench, who next to the word of God take the law of England for their [precedent]." Still, though the defense was brilliant, it did not alter the fact that, as Morison wrote, "the period 1647-70 was the most intolerant in the history of Massachusetts." And for the most part in Plymouth Colony as well. [19]

Territorial expansion continued. Douglas Edward Leach points out that the Indians did not understand land ownership in the same terms as the English. "To the Indians, the mere signing of a paper did not transfer exclusive rights to a piece of uncultivated land." Land was something to roam in, hunt in, fish in, build a temporary home in. Land "belonged" to the one making use of it. Leach writes, "Basic to the whole problem of interracial friction, of course, was the fact that the English were gaining control over more and more land which had formerly belonged to the various tribes, thereby pushing the Indians into an ever-decreasing extent of territory." The leaders at Plymouth were scrupulous about paying the Indians for all the land they obtained from them. The law was clear on this: "It hath been the constant custome from our first beginning That no pson or psons have or ever did purchase Rent or hire any lands herbage wood or tymber of the Natives but by the Majestrates consent." The concept was often reinforced that land could not be taken, but had to be bought from the Indians, and then only with the consent of the Assistants, whose purpose was to avoid the "dangerous consequence" of stealing land from the Indians, or obtaining it by fraud. But did the Indians really understand the real reason for which they were getting paid? In some cases, an Indian tribe would be on better terms with the white men than with a neighboring tribe on the other side of them. Frequently the colonists bought large tracts of land from them, and then left the land unused for many years before dividing it into individual lots. Since the Indians could still make use of this land, they must have thought the white men rather foolish at times. But then the settlers came to take over exclusive rights to the land, and the Indian sellers, perhaps a bit astonished now, had to retreat to a constantly diminishing piece of territory. [20]

The Bay Colony was on the north, and the ocean was on the east, so Plymouth's expansion had to be to the south, much of it occupied by the Wampanoags under Massasoit, and to the west, occupied by the Narragansetts. The United Colonies of New England had been formed for the mutual security of the signatories against any Indian menace in general, and against the Narragansett danger in particular. In 1644 trouble started in Connecticut. A runaway English servant was murdered by Indians, and in a separate case an Englishwoman named Phelps was assaulted by an Indian and left for dead. The white settlers reacted, and the Indians in general became hostile. The commissioners of the United Colonies advised that war should not be hastened, but neither should the settlers bear such "insolencies" too long. Bradford tells us that these early troubles ended when the murderers were delivered to justice. Now a new threat arrived. The Mohegans and their chief, Uncas, living on the other side of the Narrangansetts, had been friendly to the English. The Mohegans had captured and executed the Narragansett chief, Miantonomo. In spring 1644 the Narragansetts attacked and killed many of the Mohegans, who appealed to the English for help. The United Colonies called both parties together and examined the complaints of the Narragansetts against the Mohegans, that the Mohegans had killed Miantonomo after accepting a ransom for him. The commissioners then made a decision, declaring that they had not found any proof of a ransom; that if the Narragansetts could prove their charge, they would get Uncas to make satisfaction; but if the Narragansetts continued attacks against Uncas, the United Colonies would have to assist him. The Narragansetts agreed they would commit no hostile act against Uncas or his tribe, at least until spring planting, following which they would give the English thirty days warning of their intentions. [21]

In 1645 the Narragansetts, contrary to their promise, again attacked the Mohegans. Again the United Colonies commissioners insisted on both sides coming to them, but the Narragansetts refused. Roger Williams sent a letter telling the commissioners that war would soon engulf the entire country, but that the Narragansetts had made a treaty of neutrality with the Rhode Island colonists. The commissioners decided that, in spite of such a dreadful possibility, they were clearly bound to aid Uncas, and not just defensively, but offensively as well. Three hundred men would be raised, of which Plymouth would be expected to contribute forty. The Narragansetts informed the commissioners that there could be no peace without their having Uncas's head, and further that if the United Colonies persisted, the Narragansetts would procure as allies the Mohawks, who lived still further west on the other side of the Mohegans. The commissioners asked Plymouth to send their forty men at once to Seekonk, which Plymouth did, their contingent being under the command of Captain Standish. At this point the Massachusetts General Court balked, asking if the massing of soldiers was legal without their specific vote. The court was finally convinced with the argument that they had already agreed that the commissioners could "determine" all affairs of war, and this implied sufficient authority for their actions. Now once again united and in full position for making war, the colonies offered the Narragansetts one more opportunity to treat for peace. As it turned out, the chiefs of the Narragansetts agreed to go to Boston, where they concluded a treaty accepting all of the colonies' terms, including payment of wampum, cessation of hostilities with the Mohegans, turning over hostages to the colonies, and agreeing to deliver any Indian who had murdered an Englishman to the colonies. Once again a major Indian war was averted, at least for the time being. [22]

A new generation was rising, and some members remained in Plymouth, while others dispersed to far corners. John Cooke, who came over on the *Mayflower* as a boy with his father, Francis Cooke, was now a deputy representing Plymouth and a deacon in the Plymouth Church. In 1645 he had been sent with a message telling William Vassall not to continue with his Second Scituate Church, but Cooke himself would later be excommunicated from the Plymouth Church. Jonathan Brewster, the Elder's son who had arrived on the *Fortune* in 1621, had been in charge of the trading post in Connecticut in 1635. He must have liked Connecticut, for he returned in the late 1640s, establishing himself at New London, where he set up his own private trading post (for which he was censured) and became a close friend of Governor Winthrop's son, John Winthrop, Jr. Richard More, arriving at Plymouth as a boy of about six, married in 1636, sold land at Duxbury in 1637, and two months later was admitted as an inhabitant at Salem. He worked as a seaman and ultimately became a sea captain. Nathaniel Morton, who sailed to Plymouth with his parents on the *Anne* in 1623, was raised, after the death of his father, by Governor Bradford, and around 1647 became Clerk for the General Court. Edward Winslow's younger brother, John Winslow, came to Plymouth on the *Fortune*, married *Mayflower* passenger Mary Chilton, and moved to Boston in the 1650s, where he became a prosperous businessman and shipowner. Edward Doty, arriving on the *Mayflower* as a servant to Stephen Hopkins, became a prosperous land owner and employer of servants himself, but also displayed a temper and argumentative nature which frequently brought him into the court as both complainant and defendant. Thomas Cushman, a boy of about twelve years when he arrived on the *Fortune*, married a daughter of Isaac Allerton and, in 1649, replaced the late Elder William Brewster as Ruling Elder of the Plymouth Church.

Following the death of his father Cushman, like Nathaniel Morton, was raised by Governor Bradford. In fact, Bradford raised a fair number of future Plymouth leaders, for the Southworth brothers, Constant and Thomas, were his stepsons, Constant later becoming a military leader and Assistant. Josias Winslow, son of Gov. Edward Winslow, was already an Assistant by 1657, and Thomas Hinckley, son of Samuel, became an Assistant in 1658; both would later become governors.

Governor Bradford himself laid down his duties and died on 9 May 1657, making a nuncupative will the same day. Of all those who came to Plymouth shores in 1620, he was foremost. He was Plymouth. A learned man, though without much formal training, he was the archetypal American puritan, educating himself so as better to understand the ways of his deity, teaching himself Latin and Hebrew so as better to read the Bible and religious commentaries. Like Governor Winthrop, his counterpart in the Bay Colony, Bradford had a vision of a city on a hill, and he must have suffered disappointment time and again as he discovered anew that not all his companions shared his vision. We know this because he tells us so in his History, in words of simple eloquence. He was theocrat more than democrat, but it was through him that Plymouth survived. George Langdon summed up his handling of his trust:

> He believed in the vigorous exercise of leadership and, in consultation with the men whom he trusted, he made the decisions at Plymouth. But Bradford also did not forget that, in the absence of police power, he needed the confidence of the men who settled the plantation. Had he forgotten this, Plymouth could well have destroyed itself, and the landing of the Pilgrim Fathers have been only one more in a series of dreary failures to establish settlement in America.

There were still others alive from that 1620 voyage—indeed, the last would not die for almost half a century yet—but with Bradford's death, it would now be a different Plymouth. [23]

NOTES

1. *Bradford (Ford)* 2:348-51.
2. Ibid., 2:369.
3. Ibid., 2:394; Morison, *Builders*, 259, 299. It was at this time that Winslow wrote *New Englands Salamander* as an argument against the claims of the radicals. Morison writes, "As a result of Winslow's efforts the Lords Commissioners for Plantations gave Massachusetts Bay a clean bill of health." Winslow also obtained from the 1649 Rump Parliament a charter for The Society for the Promotion and Propagating the Gospel of Jesus Christ in New England to raise funds in England to be used especially for bringing the gospel to the Indians, with the Commissioners of the United Colonies of New England to disburse the funds. See also Robert Emmet

Wall, Jr., *Massachusetts Bay: The Crucial Decade, 1640-1650* (New Haven, 1972), for more on the three New England rebels—Samuel Gorton, William Vassall, and Robert Child.

4. *Bradford (Ford)* 1:14; *Encyc. Brit.*, 8:502-03.

5. *PCR* 11:10, 83; Morison, *Builders*, 248-49, states that "New England, very wisely, determined to keep out of it [the English Civil War], although their sympathies were with the Roundheads. A considerable number of Massachusetts men, like Saltonstall, Leverett, Hugh Peter, and Nathaniel Ward, went back to England to take part in the struggle, but the colony remained officially neutral." Morison gives an example of authorities in Boston forcing a Parliamentarian-armed ship to respect its neutrality, and he comments that the Roundheads "were divided into two religious camps, both of which were obnoxious to the New Englanders," the Presbyterians, and the Independents. Though the latter had something in common with Congregationalism, they were also radically different in that they were for religious toleration, necessarily so because they were composed of many differing sects.

6. *Bradford (Ford)* 2:282-83; *PCR* 2:4-5, 10-11.

7. *PCR* 1:41.

8. *Bradford (Ford)* 2:367-68; *PCR* 8:177, 2:81, 102, 11:59.

9. *PCR* 2:49-50, 83; Loenard Bliss, Jr., *The History of Rehoboth, Bristol Co., Massachusetts. . .* (Boston, 1836), 22.

10. *PCR* 2:43, 83, 23, 9:38; Bowen, 1:27-28; *PCR* 2:91-92, 89, 94, 12:177, 2:102, 11:46.

11. Bliss, 24-31; *PCR* 2:150-51; John Adams Vinton, *The Giles Memorial* (Boston, 1864), 181.

12. *PCR* 3:19; *MD* 4:185-88; Langdon, 47; *PCR* 4:65, 11:141, 227.

13. *PCR* 2:88, 3:101, 143. It is interesting to note the court's emphasis on some "usefull" men who can be "usefull" in church and commonwealth. This is similar to the phraseology of Mr. Leveridge's question to the court in 1638 about new settlers coming to Sandwich: "Whether the undertakers have a full guift of the lands at Sandwiche, or whether a condiconall graunt onely, for the setling of such a convenient number there that may be usefull for the common wealth, & cheifly fitt for church fellowship."

14. Samuel Deane, *History of Scituate, Massachusetts* (Boston, 1831; reprint, Scituate, 1899), 63, 60-61; *Bradford (Ford)* 2:306; Anderson, "Notes of Early Scituate Church History." We are indebted to Mr. Anderson for allowing us to see his paper suggesting that Chauncey's church in Scituate was not a continuation of the Lothrop church.

15. Deane, 66-83; Morison, *Builders*, 215-16.

16. Wall, 121-56; *PCR* 1:100, 105-06.

17. *Winthrop Papers*, 5:55-56. In his *History of New England*, 260-62, Winthrop calls Vassall "a busy and factious spirit, and always opposite to the civil governments of this country and the way of our churches." He describes Vassall's several petitions to the Bay Colony and Plymouth courts, and to Parliament, as asking that "the distinctions which were

maintained here, both in civil and church estate, might be taken away, and that we might be wholly governed by the laws of England." Vassall, as a resident of Plymouth, did not sign the Bay remonstrance of 1646, but neither Winthrop nor anyone else had any doubts that he was behind it.

18. Morison, *Builders*, 250-59.

19. Edward Winslow, "New Englands Salamander, Discovered By An Irreligious And Scornful Pamphlet, Called New-Englands Jonas Cast Up At London, etc. Owned by Major John Childe, But Not Probably To Be Written By Him," in *Collections of the Massachusetts Historical Society*, Third Series, vol. 2 (Cambridge, 1830), 110-45; Morison, *Builders*, 260.

20. Douglas Edward Leach, *Flintlock and Tomahawk—New England in King Philip's War* (1958; republished paperback, New York, 1966), 16, 14; *PCR* 11:41.

21. *Bradford (Ford)* 2:370-75.

22. Ibid., 2:376-88.

23. *Bradford (Morison)*, xv (rear of book); Langdon, 25.

CHAPTER 5

Quaker Ranters, Baptist Schismatics, and Indians with Tongues Running Out (1657-1675)

"A TIME TO GATHER STONES TOGETHER"

P rior to the mid-1650s, trouble with "radical" Protestant religious groups had been mainly with Anabaptists and with those liberal thinkers of the colonies who advocated more religious toleration. At a mild extreme of toleration was William Vassall of Scituate, who wanted to admit nonchurch members to the sacraments, but still insisted that they show some sign of being God's elect. At the other end was Roger Williams of Rhode Island, who wanted tolerance for all to practice their religion as they saw fit. Now a new sect came to embroil the colonists' emotions as nothing before. Quakerism represented "the extreme left wing of the Puritan movement." The essential belief of the Quakers was a need for unmediated living in accordance with Christ's teachings. The Separatists said, "No bishops!" The Quakers said, "No ministers, and no magistrates, either!" And no oaths, and no fighting, though they were willing to resist passively, expound their doctrine publicly, and die for it if need be. Some sixty Quaker missionaries arrived in the New World from England between 1655 and 1662. They were not welcomed. [1]

The general feeling of historians is that since laws in Plymouth affecting personal liberty became more severe when the leadership passed from Bradford to Prence, Prence was more totalitarian than Bradford. But the death of Bradford coincided almost precisely with the onslaught of the greatest threat ever posed to the qualified homogeneity which the leaders of Plymouth and most other New England colonies were pledged to maintain. Whether Bradford could have confronted this threat with greater tact and less reverberation must be conjectural, but it is likely that he, too, would have been driven to uphold new, more drastic laws. A letter from the governor and magistrates of Massachusetts dated 1656 to the commissioners of the United Colonies (Bradford and Prence were commissioners this year) complained that "our Naighbours collonie of Plymouth our beloved brothers" seemed to be "wanting" in "Incurragement to the Minnesters of the Gosspell soe as many pious Minnesters of the Gospel have (how Justly wee know not) deserted their stations," and they desired that some action be taken to prevent a "flood of Error and principles of anarchy." Further, the Bay authorities expressed their horror at the arrival of persons "professing themselves Quakers fitt instruments to propagate the kingdome of Sathan," and they wished to see more laws to prevent "the coming in amongst us from foraigne places such Notorious heretiques as quaker Ranters etc." [2]

In looking first at the way in which Plymouth reacted to the Quaker assault, we can learn much about the attitudes and behaviors of both the leaders and the people of the times. In good measure, the Quakers were to Plymouth what the Separatists had been to England, only now the roles were reversed.

Perhaps the first mention of Quaker activity in Plymouth Colony records occurred on 3 February 1656/57, when two separate complaints were made at the Court of Assistants against people at Sandwich. Jane, the wife of William Launder, and Sarah, the daughter of Richard Kirby, were summoned to appear at Court for "disturbance by them made in the publicke worship of God on the Lords day att Sandwidge, by opposing and abusing the speaker amongst them." Both were sentenced to be be whipped, but Jane Launder had her sentence suspended and was given a warning to offend no more. Nicholas Upshall, Richard Kirby, the wife of John Newland, and William Allen were accused of frequently meeting "at the house of William Allen, att Sandwich, on the Lords day, and att other times, att which meetings they used to invey against the minnesters and majestrates, to the dishonor of God and contempt of govment." Upshall was in the especially disadvantageous position of having been licensed by the court to stay at Sandwich only until the extreme of winter was over. Now he was ordered to leave the colony by 1 March, and Tristram Hull, who had aided him in coming to Plymouth, was ordered to see that he left. The others were subsequently fined at various times for Quaker activity. [3]

Though undoubtedly there were existing laws to cover such a situation, the officials were often ones to put a fine point on it, and so we are not surprised to see in the law books some specific anti-Quaker enactments of 3 June 1657. All men in the colony who had not taken the Oath of Fidelity who were free to do so (that is, not servants, etc.) were required to take the oath, leave the colony, or pay a fine of £5. Of course, Quakers— their religion not allowing them to "swear"—could not take the oath. Further, anyone who "shall bring in any quaker rantor or other Notoriouse heritiques either by land or water into any pte of this Govrment shall forthwith upon order from any one Majestrate returne them to the place from whence they came," or pay twenty shillings for each week that they stayed after having received a warning. New laws of 1657 and 1658 readdressed the situation concerning those "commonly called Quakers whose doctrine and practises manifestly tends to the Subversion of the fundamentals of Christian Religious Church order and the Civell peace of this Govrment as appeers by the Testimonies given in sundry depositions and otherwise." Those giving hospitality to a Quaker would be fined £5 or whipped, unless they could show they did not know the person was a Quaker. Any person suspecting that someone was a Quaker, but not reporting it, would be subject to disciplinary action. The General Court further provided that "Noe Quaker Rantor or any other such corupt pson shalbee admited to bee a freeman of this Corporation." The court then ordered that any Quaker or "manifest Incurragers of them," or anyone speaking contemptuously of the court or the colony's laws, or anyone judged by the court as "grosly scandalouse as lyers drunkards Swearers etc. shall lose theire freedome of this Corporation." Further, Quakers or manifest encouragers of same would not be allowed to vote in local town elections either. [4]

For all the laws and horrified words against Quakers, Plymouth Colony was more tolerant of them than Massachusetts, where four Quakers were hanged between 1659 and 1661. But in spite of the savageness of words against the Quakers by magistrates and ministers even in the Bay Colony, the desire was more to get rid of their presence than to kill them. The trouble was that after being exiled they kept coming back, knowing full well that they faced death. So it was at Plymouth, though Plymouth never executed a Quaker. But any punishment short of death seemed ineffective. On 3 June 1658 two Quakers, Humphrey Norton and John Rouse, were presented to the General Court, presided over by Gov. Thomas Prence. Norton and Rouse at times acted as if Prence were on trial. "Thow lyest," exclaimed Norton; "Thomas, thow art a mallicious man." What could be done with a man who would tell the governor, "Thy clamorouse toungue I regard noe more then the dust under my feet; and thou art like a scoulding woman; and thow pratest and deridest mee."? Norton and Rouse were sentenced to be whipped, but afterward refused to pay the under-marshal the customary fee required of those whipped, and they were sentenced to jail, where after a week they "made composition in som way with the said marshall, and soe went away." On 2 February 1657/58 John Copeland and William Braind, Quakers, were charged with verbally abusing men, John Alden and Thomas Southworth being specifically mentioned, and they were ordered to leave the colony within forty-eight hours; but by 8 February they were back in Plymouth, and accordingly were publicly whipped. [5]

Not all Plymouth officials, though, joined together in the persecution of Quakers. On 2 March 1657/58, the General Court noted a petition from "sundry prsons of the towne of Scituate" complaining against Capt. James Cudworth, head of the Scituate military company, for entertaining Quakers in his home. Cudworth was relieved of his command, and Lt. James Torrey and Ens. John Williams were ordered to act in his place. Cudworth was not an ordinary resident. In 1656 and 1657 he had been an Assistant, and had probably been present at the court which sentenced Upshall, Kirby, Allen, and Goodwife Newland. He had also served in 1657 as one of Plymouth's two commissioners at the United Colonies, the other commissioner being Thomas Prence, who now presided over the court which tried him. After losing his military position in 1657/58, Cudworth was again elected a deputy to represent Scituate, but the Court refused to allow him and a man from Sandwich to serve. In 1660 Cudworth was accused of abetting and encouraging Quakers, especially in two letters, one of which he sent to England. Colonial governments were always aghast at the thought of any influential person on this side of the ocean sending a letter of complaint to friends or authorities in England for fear of stirring up the English government. In his long letter to England of December 1658, James Cudworth expressed his indignation and many grievances:

> He that will not Whip and Lash, Persecute and Punish Men that Differ in Matters of Religion, must not sit on the Bench nor sustain any Office in the Common-wealth. Last Election, Mr. Hatherly, and my Self, left off the Bench, and my Self Discharged of my Captainship because I had Entertained Some of the Quakers at my House (thereby that I might be the better acquainted with their Principles). . . . But the Quakers and my self cannot close in divers Things; and so I signified to the Court, I was no Quaker . . . . But withal, I told them, That as I was no Quaker, so I would be no Persecutor.

He went on to say that

> In the Massachusets (namely, Boston-Colony) after they have Whipp'd them, and Cut their Ears, they have now, at last, gone the furthest step they can, They Banish them upon pain of Death. We expect that we must do the like; we must Dance after their Pipe: Now Plimouth-Saddle is on the Bay-Horse.

In a closing remark, he echoed what some Quakers had said about John Alden, from whom they had apparently expected more sympathy than they received, "Mr. Alden hath deceived the Expectations of many, and indeed lost the affections of such, as I judge were his Cordial Christian Friends; who is very active in such Ways, as I pray God may not be charged him, to be Oppressions of a High Nature." [6]

On 6 June 1660 Cudworth and Isaac Robinson, son of the beloved Pastor Robinson of Leyden, were disenfranchised, though both were later restored to freeman status. Robinson had also got into trouble because of a letter, in this case one that he had sent to Governor Prence asking for a more temperate policy toward Quakers. Even Ens. John Williams, one of the officers ordered to replace Cudworth in the Scituate military company, was fined forty shillings for entertaining a foreign Quaker and permitting a Quaker meeting in his house, though the Court did not take away his office because of his excuse that he had been hoping to reform some of the Quakers. Cudworth was the man the colonists of Plymouth would make their commander-in-chief some fifteen years later in King Philip's War. [7]

The number of people charged and fined for Quaker activity, or for refusing to take the Oath of Fidelity, which in most cases at this time amounted to the same thing, multiplied without cease. Though Sandwich seemed to be the home of the greatest number, converts were made in all towns. Repressive measures did not stop them, but seemed to aid their growth. On 2 October 1660, twenty-four people were fined ten shillings each for being at Quaker meetings, and these included John Soule of Duxbury, Rodulphus Elmes of Scituate, and John and Deborah Smith and Lydia Hickes of Plymouth. On 1 June 1658 the General Court appointed a special marshal for Sandwich, George Barlow, with jurisdiction also at Barnstable and Yarmouth, to assist the county marshal, meaning to see that the laws against Quakers were kept. On 2 October 1660 the court further spelled out Barlow's responsibilities and expanded his jurisdiction, ordering that "marshal Gorge Barlow shall have libertie to apprehend any forraigne Quaker or Quakers in any pte of this Jurisdiction and to be procecuted according to order provided in that case." Barlow carried out his functions apparently with relish, and a number of claims were made against him, such as on 13 June 1660 when Thomas Clarke "affeirmed in open Court, that Gorg Barlow is such an one that hee is a shame and reproach to all his masters; and that hee, the said Barlow, stands convicted and recorded of a lye att Newberry." A number of men were fined for refusing to assist Barlow in the execution of his office, including Sandwich's eminent citizen, Mr. Edmond Freeman, who was fined ten shillings on 6 October 1659. [8]

Yet the court was far from devoid of fairness. On 13 June 1660, the occasion when Thomas Clarke spoke out against Barlow, Barlow and Obadiah Eddy had accused John Newland, whom we have already seen as a Quaker, of saying that he was as holy and perfect as God was holy and perfect. The record shows that "The Court, being unsatisfied in some respects about the testimonies, have, for the psent, freed the said Newland," with a caution that he would have to answer if more satisfying testimony came in. In a case of 5 March 1660/61, Barlow himself was fined twenty shillings for cruelty to Benjamin Allen, making him sit in the stocks at Sandwich for most of the night without cause, and "for other wronges done by him unto the said Allin." Allen was a Quaker, but nonetheless in this case the court protected him, and, further, turned over the twenty-shilling fine to him. At the same time, Barlow was ordered to return to Ralph Allen a shirt and other clothing he had taken from him. Still more retribution came to Barlow on 4 March 1661/62 when the court severely reproved him and his wife for their "ungodly liveing in contension one with the other." In May 1665 Barlow was accused of "attempting the chastity of Abigaill, the wife of Jonathan Pratt, by aluring words and actes of force," and on 6 March 1665/66 he was fined ten shillings for being drunk the second time. [9]

Thomas Prence, that "Terrour to evill doers," was not known for his compassion towards Quakers. And few families were more identified with the Quakers than those of Arthur and Henry Howland, the two brothers of *Mayflower* passenger and erstwhile Assistant, John Howland. As early as 22 December 1657, Mr. William Collier and Capt. Josias Winslow, having knowledge of a Quaker meeting to take place at Arthur Howland's house in Marshfield, sent Constable John Phillips of Marshfield to interrupt the meeting and arrest a Quaker leader, Robert Huchin. As Phillips testified, he could not apprehend Huchin, being hindered by Howland, who told Phillips "hee would have either a sword or a gun in the belly of him." Seventeen-year-old Samuel Hunt testified that Zoeth Howland, son of Henry, had told him he would not go to a church meeting with him "to hear lyes, and that the devill could teach as good a sermon as the minnisters." Henry Howland himself was disenfranchised, along with William Newland, on 6 October 1659 for being an abettor and entertainer of Quakers. [10] Governor Prence would not have relished being related to this conglomeration of radicals.

On 5 March 1666/67, the General Court, presided over by Gov. Thomas Prence, fined Arthur Howland, Jr. £5 for "inveigling of Mistris Elizabeth Prence and makeing motion of marriage to her, and procecuting the same contrary to her parrents likeing, and without theire consent, and directly contrary to theire mind and will." He was also ordered to find sureties for his future good behavior, and "in speciall that hee desist from the use of any meanes to obtaine or retaine her affections as aforsaid." On 2 July 1667 Arthur Howland, Jr. "did sollemly and seriously engage before this Court, that he will wholly desist and never apply himself for the future, as formerly he hath done, to Mistris Elizabeth Prence in reference unto marriage." In spite of his pledge not to speak of marriage to Elizabeth Prence again, on 9 December 1667 Arthur Howland, Jr. married Elizabeth Prence, and thus the governor acquired Quaker in-laws. Many of the other Howlands continued their Quaker ways in the new town of Dartmouth, but Arthur Howland, Jr. remained in Marshfield, and on 5 June 1671 he was made a constable of Marshfield, where presumably his duties could have included seeing that Quakers fully complied with the law. [11]

However, by this time an accommodation had been reached, and the Quakers were no longer so menacing, nor so menaced. Even in 1659, Humphrey Norton had told in England a powerful story of suffering and wrongs. Following the restoration of Charles II, the English government indicated a desire for leniency toward Quakers, ordering the New England colonies to send them back to England for trial. One writer describes such a situation:

> Christopher Holder and his companions, John Copeland and John Rous, were now in England, visible 'witnesses,' with their cropped ears, of the way the bearers of the gospel of inward Light were treated in the Puritan Colony. . . . When the news of William Leddra's execution reached the Friends in England, Edward Burrough sought an interview in person with the king. He said to the king, 'There is a vein of innocent blood opened in thy dominions which will run over all, if it is not stopped.' To which the king at once replied, 'but I will stop that vein. . . . Call the secretary and I will do it presently.' Burroughs

at once named Samuel Shattuck, the Salem Quaker who had been banished from the colony on pain of death and the king appointed him as royal messenger. [12]

On 2 October 1660 the General Court ordered that fines would no longer be levied on those not coming to the colony's church meetings. This was of course of benefit to Quakers, as well as other non-Congregational church-goers. However, on 4 June 1661 the court ordered that all qualified men refusing to take the Oath of Fidelity would be fined £5. On the same date, it enacted laws that any "Quakers or other such like Vagabonds" coming into any colony town would be whipped by a marshall or constable, and there would be a penalty of forty shillings or a whipping for those allowing Quaker meetings in their houses, or speaking at such meetings. Significantly, the law also specified "and incase any Constable of this Jurisdiction shalbee unwilling or cannot procure any to Inflict the punishment aforsaid that then they shall bringe such psons to Plymouth to the under Marshall and hee shall enflict it," thus recognizing that Quaker persecution was not so popular among colony rank and file. Probably not long after, though, these laws, though not formally repealed, were just crossed out, as if they had not existed. After 1661 the records show but few monetary or bodily punishments of Quakers. On 2 October 1660 Henry Howland was fined £4 for entertaining Quaker meetings in his house twice, but on 7 May 1661 the court merely noted that at Sandwich several people had entertained foreign (probably English) Quakers, William Allen entertaining Christopher Holder, William Newland entertaining one foreign Quaker, and Peter Gaunt entertaining two foreign Quakers. [13]

Along with the Quaker problem emerged another serious challenge to maintaining the colony properly as its leaders desired. Most towns now had churches and ministers, but ministers had families with mouths to feed and bodies to clothe. While it might be assumed that church members in good standing paid their tithing, not all others would be so inclined. On 5 June 1655 several inhabitants of Rehoboth petitioned the General Court to assist them to raise maintenance money for the ministry, as done in other colonies. The court observed that those inhabitants not signing the petition seemed to be the ones not subscribing any significant sums for this purpose. Some dispute then took place over enforceable ways to compel inhabitants to pay a given sum each year. Finally, for Rehoboth, Mr. John Browne, one of the magistrates, suggested that those not signing the petition be asked to contribute, but if any would not contribute, Browne would undertake to pay their rates himself for the next seven years. This resolved Rehoboth's problem, and for the other towns the court ordered "Whereas there hath been many Complaints of want of due maintenance of the minnesters as some have reported; It is therefore Enacted That noe Pastor Teacher of any Congregation shall remove before his Complaint hath been Tendered to the Majestrates and they have heard both sides; That upon such Complaints if there appeers to bee a reall defect in the hearers of the minnesters soe complaining; the Majestrates shall use all gentle meanes to [persuade] them to doe their duty heerin; But if any of them shall not heerby bee reclaimed but shall [persist] through plaine Obstinacye against an Ordinance of God that then It shalbee in the power of the Majestrate to use such other meanes as may put them upon their duty." [14]

The Commissioners of the United Colonies in their reply of September 1656 to the letter of the Bay authorities complaining that Plymouth had been found "wanting" in its responsibilites to keep ministers, noted that "an able Orthodox minnestrey is. . . necessary for the sperituall good of [Christ's] people and to bee duely sought after in every societie or Township." They agreed further that "a competent Mayntenance proportionable to the abillitie of the place and necessitie of the minnester is a Debt of justice and not Charitie. . . . The reference or relation of a Minnester being to the whole Societie Joyntly whether in church order or not; his expectation of Mayntanance and the Debt of Justice is from the whole Societie Joyntly." [15] Given the basic premises of the founding of those colonies which were members of the United Colonies (Rhode Island, of course, would be an exception), it is difficult to see how the authorities could have viewed their situation in any other way.

By 3 June 1657 the General Court was determined to take more specific action. It noted that in several townships there was a lack of a ministry to the great prejudice of the souls of many. The very granting of the right to form townships was conditioned upon maintaining the "Publicke worshipe and service of God," and therefore the court judged that both the church and the town were "mutually Ingaged to Support the same." In each town having a minister "approved by this Govrment," four men would be chosen to make "an equall and just proportion upon the estates of the Inhabitants according to theire abilities to make up such a Convenient [that is, fitting] maintainance for his Comfortable attendance on his worke as shall be agreed upon by the Church," and if the town did not appoint the four men, or the four men did not do their duty, then the magistrates would apportion this tax. The towns were given an out if they should be able to find any other way to maintain their ministers. One such other way was later suggested, not ordered, by the court concerning the windfall that towns received when whales were beached on their shores, not an infrequent occurrence: "They Judge it would bee very comendable and benificiall to the townes where Gods Providence shall cast any whales if they should agree to sett appart some pte of every such fish or oyle for the Incurragement of an able Godly minnester amongst them." [16]

Various other laws were passed in an attempt to find a working solution to raise money for the maintenance of ministers. One such law provided that anyone not paying his rates could be fined double the amount. Another provided that ministers would no longer have to collect the rates themselves, for that might prejudice people against them and their work, but rather two townsmen would be appointed to collect the rates for them. A law of June 1670 attempted to plug up an obvious loophole, for the rates applied only to towns having a minister, and there had been no discomfit to any town without a minister. The court observed that there was "great reason to feare" that some towns might not desire to engage a minister for "worldly & covetuous principles," and therefore towns without ministers would henceforth be rated a yearly sum by the court to provide a fund for the building of future church meeting houses or for the encouragement "of a minnester to labour amongst them." At the same time this law was passed, the town of Dartmouth was specifically and conspicuously rated £15 for this purpose. [17]

These laws for the maintenance of ministers were not popular among nonchurch members. On 2 October 1658 Lt. Matthew Fuller, son of *Mayflower* passenger Edward Fuller, was fined fifty shillings for speaking reproachfully to the court and saying the law about maintenance of ministers "was a wicked and divillish law, and that the divell satt att the sterne when it was enacted." On 31 October 1666 a complaint was made to the court that although the town of Scituate had agreed about a rate for the maintenance of their ministers, Walter Briggs, late constable of Scituate, had failed to bring in the money. Accordingly, the court fined Briggs £5 and ordered him either to collect the money or pay it all himself. On 2 July 1667 Nicholas Nickerson was brought before the court for speaking against the minister of the Yarmouth Church, Mr. Thomas Thornton. Nickerson said Thornton had declared that if a man did not have money to pay towards the minister's maintenance, he must borrow it of his neighbor. At the court hearing, Nickerson acknowledged that he had done Thornton wrong and promised to repeat his apology publicly, and the court released him in view of his promising reformation. On 29 October 1669 Arthur Howland, Philip Leonard, William Norcutt, and William Hincksman were charged with not paying their rates for the ministry, and all were ordered to pay their portions except Howland, who was excused because of his age and low condition. On 1 March 1669/70 Nathaniel FitzRandolph was fined forty-two shillings for not paying his rates of twenty-one shillings for the ministry at Barnstable. On 7 June 1670 Capt. Nathaniel Thomas of Marshfield was charged with not paying his ministry rates of £1/7/9, and he was ordered to pay double, £2/15/6. [18]

As mentioned above, in June 1670 Dartmouth was conspicuously mentioned in connection with the law that towns without ministers would have to start paying for future maintenance, and was rated at £15. Dartmouth had paid nothing by 1 July 1672, when the court noted it had neglected to do so under the excuse that those appointed to collect it refused, and the order to pay £15 was repeated. Dartmouth was a special case. Sometime after its founding it effectively became, no doubt in good part due to its location, the "Rhode Island" of Plymouth Colony, the place where religious dissenters could go without much disturbance from colony officials. James Cudworth had written that "almost the whole Town of Sandwich is adhering" to the Quakers, but by the 1670s there were a number of Quakers in Dartmouth, too, coming from Scituate, Duxbury,

Plymouth town, and other places. Many of the families associated with Plymouth in its earliest days removed to this newly opened area, including the adjoining Saconnet, later to be called Little Compton, where land was granted on 4 June 1661 to some of the former servants who had been promised land by their contracts. There were Howlands, from the families of Arthur and Henry, the brothers of John; several third-generation Aldens; some Soules; some Samsons; a Cuthbertson, now shortened to Cutbert; the Jenney family; Palmers; Delanos; and others. Of course, not all these were necessarily religious dissenters, but it is a fact that Baptist and Quaker meetings were active in Dartmouth and Little Compton, but no Congregational Church was established in either during the lifetime of Plymouth Colony. As of 29 May 1670 Dartmouth had only seven freemen residents: John Cooke, John Russell, James Shaw, Arthur Hathaway, William Spooner, Samuel Hicks, and William Palmer. [19]

One of the leading men at Dartmouth was John Cooke, who had a varied career in Plymouth Colony. In his life, which was virtually coextensive with the life of the colony, can be seen much of Plymouth's history. He came over on the *Mayflower* in 1620 with his father, Francis Cooke, and he died 23 November 1695, perhaps the last male survivor of the first Plymouth colonists. He was old enough to be made a freeman on 1 January 1633/34 and he was on the 1632/33, but not the 1633/34, tax list, being called John Cooke, Jr. to distinguish him from John Cooke, Sr., who must have been older, but no relationship is known. On 28 March 1634/35 he married Sarah Warren, daughter of *Mayflower* passenger Richard Warren. Since both the Cooke and Warren families were fairly large, he was allied with a good number of Plymouth families, though he must have had ability of his own to be singled out for leadership. Nathaniel Morton wrote that Cooke, Mr. John Doane, and Mr. William Paddy were deacons under the Reverend John Reyner, and John Dunham became a deacon later. Reyner became minister in 1636, and John Doane was a deacon at least as early as 2 January 1633/34, when he resigned his office as Assistant because of his deaconship. Thus John Cooke must have been a relatively young man when he became a deacon. On 16 May 1639 the townsmen of Plymouth elected four "comittes" to be added to the governor and council to make laws: John Doane, Manasseh Kempton, John Dunham, and John Cooke, Jr. [20]

Though we know nothing of their earlier relations, Nathaniel Morton, when he wrote the records of the Plymouth Church, did not like John Cooke, Jr. Morton wrote that long after the election of Thomas Cushman as Ruling Elder of the Plymouth Church (he was elected in 1649), "troubles Came on apace Not to mension againe the troubles which were occasioned by some of the Church at Barnstable which was blowne up by John Cooke and others." A few pages further on, Morton added:

By Reason or occation of the before mensioned devision and decention of the Church of Barnstable one of the Church of Plymouth whoe was formerly a deacon therof; fell into the error of Anabaptistry and falling in with some of those that Carried on that Scismaticall devison; att length was Called in question by the Church; and Continewing in his obstanacie and sequestration from the Church Comunion att times of sollemne worshipp was alsoe Cast out of the Church and soe Remaineth untill this day. This John Cooke although a Shallow man became a Cause of trouble and decension in our Church and Gave Just occation of theire Casting of him out. [21]

Morton, who wrote his church history in the early 1680s, was not fussy about chronology, and so we must use other means to approximate the time of Cooke's excommunication. On 14 April 1645 John Cooke signed a letter to William Vassall on behalf of the Plymouth Church concerning the ordination of Mr. William Witherell as pastor of Scituate's Second Church, which stated "The Church of Plymouth is of the same mind together with the Elders which sent unto you, hoping in charity that you will desist upon it, from your present and intended proceeding; but in case you should go on notwithstanding the advice given, the Church of Plymouth shall question communion with you." In a deed of 21 March 1647 Mr. William Paddy, James Hurst, and John Cooke, "deacons of the church of Christ at plimouth," sold a house and land to Nathaniel Morton, and so Cooke was still in good standing with the church at that date. For most, if not all, of the years between 1641 and 1656, John Cooke was an elected deputy from Plymouth to the General Court. The freemen and nonfreemen voters did not always elect as deputies the men most acceptable to Plymouth state and church leaders; but when they made particularly objectionable choices, as for example on one occasion James Cudworth, the court could refuse to allow them to take their positions. It would certainly seem that an excommunicated deacon, at least in the 1650s, would have been objectionable to the Plymouth leaders. On the other hand, James Cudworth, in his famous letter to England of 1658 which brought him prosecution in Plymouth, wrote that "Brother Cook told me, one of the Brethren at Barnstable certified him, That he was in the Weaver's House, when cruel Barloe [Sandwich marshal] came to demand the sum." Brother Cook must be John Cooke, and he therefore most likely defected from the Plymouth establishment sometime between 1656 and 1658. [22]

On 8 June 1664 the General Court granted fifteen acres of land near Dartmouth to John Cooke, and on 3 October 1665 the treasurer (at the time Constant Southworth), Nathaniel Warren, and John Cooke were appointed to treat with the late Massasoit's son, Philip, for the purchase of land for the colony. In 1666 John Cooke became a deputy to represent Dartmouth at the General Court, and in 1667 he was appointed to solemnize marriages at Dartmouth and act as a pretrial magistrate. He had disputes with some of the inhabitants of Dartmouth, which like the towns in Rhode

Island must have been quite heterogeneous. These disputes involved land that he had purchased on behalf of himself and some others, and on 1 July 1672 the court ordered that he could keep possession of Ram Island, and the town would also pay him £11 for money he had paid out in its behalf, plus £3 for damages. He in turn would deliver up deeds to the town for other lands. These disputes did not seem to affect his popularity with the inhabitants of Dartmouth, for they were still electing him deputy in 1673 and subsequent years. In spite of his excommunication, Cooke seemed to be respected by the General Court in Plymouth and did not suffer the persecutions that were the lot of others. Perhaps his background as a *Mayflower* passenger had something to do with it. Still, he was not immune to the law, as can be seen from the ten shillings he was fined on 29 October 1670 for unnecessary traveling on the Sabbath. In the 1680s Cooke went to Boston on at least two occasions to speak by invitation at the Baptist Church there. In 1684 he and his associates formed a Baptist Church in Dartmouth, with Cooke as its preacher, which position he kept until his death eleven years later. [23]

THE FOUNDING OF SWANSEA

By this time the towns of Plymouth Colony were fairly well established. On 5 March 1667/68, the court approved that the township granted to Capt. Thomas Willett and his neighbors at Wannamoisett be called Swansea. The town leaders were Captain Willett, Mr. Stephen Paine, Sr., Mr. James Browne, John Allen, and John Butterworth. The first minister was Mr. John Myles. Willett quickly made three proposals to the Plymouth Court concerning Swansea: (1) that no "erroneous" person be allowed in the town as either inhabitant or transient, (2) that no man of evil or contentious behavior be admitted, and (3) that no one be admitted who was likely to become dependent on the town for support. The newly gathered church expanded on his proposals, stressing that they were meant to keep out people advocating damnable heresies or beliefs contrary to those necessary for salvation, but not to preclude anyone just for holding opinions different from others in disputable matters. [24]

Captain Willett and the Swansea Church found themselves in agreement, and on 22 February 1669/70 all the inhabitants of Swansea signed the agreement. It looked like any other orthodox establishment of town and Congregational Church, but it was not, for Mr. Myles's church was Baptist. Myles, a university-educated Baptist who had served in Cromwell's church and aided the Protectorate, had come to Rehoboth around 1665. He took a liberal view toward those churches which practiced infant baptism (opposition to which was the main difference distinguishing the Baptists from the Congregationalists), making it possible for Congregationalists to participate in his services. On the death of Mr. Samuel Newman at Rehoboth in 1663, the Reverend Zachariah Symes took his place, and occasionally Myles preached in the place of Symes. He also preached to his own meeting of Baptists, and on 2 July 1667 the Plymouth Court fined

Mr. Myles and Mr. Brown £5 pounds each "for their breach of order in setting up of a publicke meeting without the knowlidge and approbation of the Court." Mr. James Browne was the son of the late liberal Plymouth Colony Assistant John Browne. The court went on to observe that the continuance of Myles and Brown at Rehoboth was prejudicial to town and church; however, if they would remove their meeting to some other place where there was no church, and would "give us any reasonable satisfaction respecting their principles, wee know not but they may be pmitted by this govment soe to doe." Hence their founding of nearby Swansea with Thomas Willett. Recently discovered Swansea Church records mention the name of Thomas Willett several times, but do not necessarily show that he was a member, and he probably attended the Swansea Baptist Church without joining. The nine freemen residents in Swansea as of 29 May 1670 were Thomas Willett, James Browne, John Allen, Nicholas Tanner, Nathaniel Peck, Hugh Cole, Zachariah Eddy, Samuel Luther, and John Myles, Jr. [25]

MIDDLEBOROUGH

In 1633 the court had enacted a law that the children born at Plymouth, "& next to them such as are heer brought up under their parents and are come to age of discretion" would be granted land before any subsequent newcomers. This promise was kept on 4 June 1661 when the court authorized the "first born children" to purchase two large tracts of land, one next to the Massachusetts bounds, and the other between Namassakett and Bridgewater. On 3 June 1662 the court approved a list of "first born children" to share in the lands to be purchased. Actually, one tract of land at Namassakett had already been purchased from Indians on behalf of the colony by Capt. Thomas Southworth on 7 March 1661, and this became known as the Twenty-Six Men's Purchase. Another acquisition, called the Pachade Purchase, of 9 July 1662 by Maj. Josias Winslow on behalf of himself and others seems to be the specific tracts referred to on 4 June 1661. However, many names of the first proprietors of both purchases are the same. These and subsequent purchases in the Namassakett area gradually began to be inhabited, and on 1 June 1663 the court ordered that those settlers at Namassakett would be considered as belonging to the town of Plymouth. On 1 June 1669 the court granted township status to Namassakett and changed its name to Middleborough, its bounds being set between Plymouth, Taunton, and Bridgewater, and touching unincorporated land on the south. Middleborough had only six freeman residents as of 29 May 1670: John Morton, Henry Wood, Jonathan Dunham, Francis Coombe, William Nelson, and Samuel Eaton. [26]

As the settlers pressed further into new lands, relations with the Indians worsened. Between 1652 and 1660 Indians at Rehoboth complained often about the white man's livestock destroying their corn. At Sandwich, Indians complained in 1657 about some of the settlers allowing their horses to eat much of their corn, and though the court ordered the town to make restitution, it again showed the Indians that they were dependent on the Englishman's justice. Massasoit died in 1660 and was succeeded by his son Wamsutta, who showed some signs of wanting to continue the friendly relations enjoyed by his father. He continued to appeal to the Plymouth Court in disputes with the Narragansetts, and at one point asked the court to give him and his brother English names (the court bestowed the name Alexander Pokanokett on him, and gave his brother the name Philip). But the new Alexander also showed an independent streak. On 4 March 1661/62 Capt. Thomas Willett was directed by the court to speak to Wamsutta about turning land over to others instead of selling it to the colony, as had been the custom. In 1662, in response to a demand by the Plymouth government, Wamsutta went to see the Plymouth leaders to answer charges about rumors of an Indian uprising, which he denied. Unfortunately, while away from home he came down with a fever from which he later died. His younger brother Metacomet, called Philip by the English, now became the chief of the Wampanoags. [27]

Within a short time of the elevation of Philip, rumors began to circulate of an impending Indian rising. To answer these suspicions Philip was summoned to Plymouth, and on 6 August 1662 he attended a meeting of the Court of Assistants, where he professed his earnest desire to continue the friendship that had theretofore existed between the Wampanoags and Plymouth Colony. He promised allegiance to the king of England, and he agreed not to make war nor dispose of lands without the agreement of the Plymouth government. But the rumors continued, and in 1667 the court was informed by an Indian that Philip planned to act in concert with the French against the English. Major Josias Winslow and Capt. Thomas Southworth ordered Philip again to appear at Plymouth. A delegation consisting of Major Winslow, Captain Southworth, Treasurer Southworth, and others had gone to Philip earlier and charged him with declaring himself, in spite of his alliance with Plymouth, willing and ready to join the French or the Dutch against the English. The accuser was one of Philip's own Indians, who repeated the accusation to his face, but Philip stiffly denied it and said that Indian was in the pay of Ninigret, the Narragansett chief. On 4 June 1667 Philip appeared before the court at Plymouth and repeated his denial and made a counter accusation that it was all a plot by Ninigret, his professed enemy. Philip produced testimony in his behalf, including a letter from Mr. Roger Williams asserting that the Indian who accused Philip was a very vile fellow. The court, on consideration of all the evidence, was "not willing to desert [Philip] and lett him sincke, though there was great probabillitie that his tongue had bine runing out." [28]

In the meantime Plymouth prepared for war. On 2 April 1667 the Council of War assembled at Plymouth, consisting of Governor Prence, Mr. John Alden, Maj. Josias Winslow, Capt. Thomas Southworth, Capt. William Bradford (son of the late governor), Mr. Thomas Hinckley, Mr. Anthony Thacher, Mr. Constant Southworth, and Mr. Nathaniel Bacon. It was decided that every commissioned officer of the military companies should have a formal commission delivered to him, and the draft of commissions to captains, lieutenants, and ensigns was prepared. Towns were ordered to maintain a military watch during any possibility of danger. The alarm would be given by firing three muskets. Arms and ammunition were to be checked to see that they were in a state of readiness. Plans to evacuate women and children were to be made. Orders of war were prepared for the horse and foot soldiers. It was specifically stated that the Dutch and French were to be looked upon as the common enemy, but there could be little doubt that the preparations also had the Indians in mind. On 7 July 1671 Capt. Matthew Fuller, Lt. Ephraim Morton, Ens. Mark Eames, Cornet Robert Stetson, Secretary Nathaniel Morton, Mr. James Walker, Mr. Thomas Huckens, Mr. Isaac Chittenden, and Mr. Josias Winslow (the uncle of Maj. Josias Winslow) were added to the Council of War. Incongruously, on 2 March 1668/69, the General Court, in discussing means of raising more revenue, had considered allowing monopolies in each town to trade powder, shot, and guns with the Indians. However, no further mention of such trade is found in the records. [29]

Efforts were made to engage the most trusty of the Indian tribes as their allies, and to disarm, if at all possible, other tribes. There was fear that Philip and his Wampanoags would join with the Narragansetts. Philip was ordered to surrender his arms, and on 23 August 1671 it was decided to summon Philip to appear to explain why he had not done so. Mr. James Walker was sent to him with a letter of summons, and Mr. Roger Williams and Mr. James Browne were requested to accompany him. Instead of appearing, Philip went to the Bay Colony to complain against the treatment accorded him by Plymouth, and the Bay officials offered to mediate between the two sides, noting, however, that they did not feel as strongly as Plymouth that Philip owed Plymouth allegiance. The United Colony commissioners for Massachusetts and Connecticut, and some others, came to Plymouth, along with Philip, on 13 September 1671, and Plymouth officials presented their case that Philip had broken his agreement with them. Specific charges were that Philip had not surrendered his arms as he had promised, that he had refused to come to the Plymouth Court for discussions, that he had harbored some Indians who were enemies to Plymouth, that he had misrepresented his case to the Massachusetts authorities, and that he had shown much insolence to Plymouth emissaries, especially Mr. James Browne. The officials from Massachusetts and Connecticut agreed that Philip had wronged Plymouth and had lied to the Massachusetts authorities. The meeting ended with Philip again promising that he and his people would acknowledge themselves to be subjects of the King of England, that he would pay £100 damages to Plymouth, that he would send the Plymouth governor five wolf's heads yearly, that he would come freely to Plymouth to settle any future differences, that he would not make war with anyone without the approval of Plymouth, and that he would not dispose of lands without such approval. [30]

Plymouth records as kept by Secretary Nathaniel Morton show two consecutive items of interest:

> The 23th of February, 1672[/73], Mr John Howland, Senir, of the towne of Plymouth, deceased. Hee was a godly man and an ancient professor in the wayes of Christ; hee lived untill hee attained above eighty yeares in the world. Hee was one of the first comers into this land, and proved a usefull instrument of good in his place, & was the last man that was left of those that came over in the shipp called the May Flower, that lived in Plymouth; hee was with honor intered att the towne of Plymouth on the 25 of February, 1672.
>
> Thomas Prence, Esquire, Govr of the jurisdiction of New Plymouth, died the 29th of March 1673, and was interred the 8th of Aprill following. After hee had served God in the office of Govr sixteen years, or neare therunto, hee finished his course in the 73 yeare of his life. Hee was a worthy gentleman, very pious, and very able for his office, and faithful in the discharge therof, studious of peace, a welwiller to all that feared God, and a terrour to the wicked. His death was much lamented, and his body honorably buryed att Plymouth the day and yeare above mensioned. [31]

John Howland had been part of Plymouth above fifty years. Though there were still a few *Mayflower* passengers surviving outside Plymouth, virtually all the old guard were gone now. Governor Prence, too, having arrived in 1621 on the *Fortune,* had spent more than fifty years intertwining his life with that of the colony. Though reputed to be a strict man, a severe man, he must have been in some way representative of at least the freemen of the colony, for after the death of Bradford they continually reelected him governor until the day he died.

NOTES

1. *Encyc. Brit.,* 9:938; see also Arthur J. Worrall, *Quakers in the Colonial Northeast* (Hanover, N.H., 1980).

2. *PCR* 10:155-56.

3. Ibid., 3:111-12, 130, 200.

4. Ibid., 11:68, 100-01.

5. *Encyc. Brit.,* 9:938; *PCR* 3:139-40.

6. *PCR* 3:130, 115, 162; George Bishop, *New England Judged by the Spirit of the Lord* (London, 1703), 168-76.

7. *PCR* 3:183, 189, 185, 5:175.

8. Ibid., 3:200, 140-41, 11:130, 3:190, 173.

9. Ibid., 3:206, 190, 4:10, 88, 117.

10. *Ply. Ch. Recs.* 1:147 (the words are Nathaniel Morton's); *PCR* 3:125, 176.

11. *PCR* 4:140, 158-59; Robert M. Sherman and Ruth Wilder Sherman, *Vital Records of Marshfield, Massachusetts to the Year 1850* (Warwick, R.I.,

1978), 10; *PCR* 5:28. His marriage to Elizabeth Prence did not afford an end to the troubles of Arthur Howland, Jr., though he might have been given some measure of protection while Governor Prence lived, and he might have "walked better" during his father-in-law's lifetime, too. On 6, 4th mo., 1684, Arthur and Elizabeth Howland joined in a letter, he writing from Plymouth jail, which they entitled "The Sufferings of Arthur Howland." He told how around the beginning of 1679, because of some scruples of his conscience, he refused to partake sacrament with the Marshfield Church. After trying to get him to change his mind, church officials excommunicated him, and ordered all church members not to eat or drink with him, nor be on any familiar terms with him. They then tried to turn his wife against him, and she told them she could not partake with them in such an un-Christian act without sinning against her conscience. Later the constable came to their house to collect their rate for the maintenance of Samuel Arnold as minister, and when Howland would not pay it, he was taken to prison (Joseph C. Hagar, *Marshfield — The Autobiography of a Pilgrim Town* [Marshfield, 1940], 39-41, contains a photocopy of the original letter).

12. Langdon, 20, citing *Cal. State Papers, Col. Ser., 1661-1668,* #168; Rufus M. Jones, *The Quakers in the American Colonies* (New York, 1966), 90-94.

13. *PCR* 11:129-30, 3:201, 213.

14. Ibid., 3:81, 11:64.

15. Ibid., 10:156-57.

16. Ibid., 11:67, 135, 207-08.

17. Ibid., 11:224, 226-27.

18. Ibid., 3:150, 4:135-36, 158, 5:28, 31, 38.

19. Ibid., 5:59,98; Bishop, *New England Judged,* 171. *PCR* 3:216; Langdon, *Pilgrim Colony,* 120; *PCR* 5:279.

20. Dartmouth VR 3:25; *PCR* 1:21; *MD* 13:83; *Ply. Ch. Recs.* 1:73; *PCR* 1:23, 121. Peregrine White survived John Cooke, dying on 20 July 1704 (*MF* 1:102), but he was born on the *Mayflower* after it reached Cape Cod. The last surviving female passenger was Mary (Allerton) Cushman, who died 28 November 1699, and thus was really the last *Mayflower* survivor.

21. *Ply. Ch. Recs.* 1:76, 92.

22. Deane, *Scituate,* 82; *PCR* 12:153, 2:31, 57, 63, 68, 72, 94, 123, 3:23, 31, 44, 49, 63, 79, 99. *Ply. Ch. Recs.* 1:lii, footnote 1, mentions that "Mr. John Cotton gave the names of the deacons down to 1760 [*sic*]. In a copy of [Cotton's] account owned by Mr. Lord, in the margin of 4 is written, in the hand of Mr. Cotton, 'Mr. James Hirst.' There was a James Hirst (or Hurst) at Plymouth in the early days, but his name apparently does not occur in church records, and the authority for Mr. Cotton's statement is unknown." The 1647 deed should leave no doubt that James Hurst was a deacon. John Cooke seems to have played a Saul/Paul role as a prosecutor joining the prosecuted. In a footnote to *Bradford (Ford)* 2:394, Ford

transcribes a letter from Samuel Gorton to Nathaniel Morton in which he mentions a dispute he had with the Reverend Ralph Smith, from whom Gorton was renting quarters. Smith wanted to evict him, though Gorton claimed he had a four-year lease, and they put the matter to arbitration. Cooke, "an eminent member of your Church," was one of the arbiters to whom Gorton had delivered his papers (presumably the lease), and who told him that the governor had commanded the papers out of their hands, so that they, the arbiters, could do nothing for him. Cudworth's comment is found in Bishop, 173.

23. *PCR* 4:67, 109, 122, 153, 163, 5:97-98, 114, 144, 165, 256, 51; William G. McLaughlin, *New England Dissent 1630-1833, the Baptists and the Separation of Church and State*, 2 vols. (Cambridge, 1971), 1:166-67.

24. *PCR* 4:175; Otis Olney Wright, *History of Swansea, Massachusetts* (Swansea, 1917), 47-48.

25. McLaughlin, *New England Dissent*, 1:128-34; *PCR* 4:162; Robert C. Anderson, "Swansea, Massachusetts, Baptist Church Records," *NEHGR* 139:21-49; *PCR* 5:279.

26. *PCR* 11:16, 3:215-16, 4:20; Thomas Weston, *History of the Town of Middleboro, Massachusetts* (Boston & New York, 1906), 584-86, 594-96; *PCR* 4:41, 5:19-20, 279.

27. *PCR* 3:21, 106, 119, 192, 132, 192, 4:8; Leach, *Flintlock*, 23-24.

28. *PCR* 4:25-26, 151, 164-66.

29. Ibid., 4:142-47, 5:73. Just six years after considering monopolies to sell weapons and ammunition to the Indians, the Council of War voted on 1 June 1675: "Forasmuch as by frequent and sad experience it is found, that selling, etc, of armes and amunition to the Indians is very [pernicious] and destructive to the English, it is therfore ordered, decreed, and enacted by the councell of warr for this jurisdiction, that whosoever shalbe found to sell, barter, or give, directly or indirectly, any gun or guns, or amunition of any kind, to any Indian or Indians, and the same legally proved against them, every such pson or psons shalbe put to death" *PCR* 5:173).

30. Ibid., 5:70-72, 74, 76-79.

31. Ibid., 8:34.

CHAPTER 6

King Philip's War (1675-1676)

"A TIME TO HATE"

T he point has been well made by a number of historians that the English settlers at Plymouth were honorable in their treatment of the Indians. Their policies were not arbitrary, and in general they treated the Indians with respect and fairness. They did not steal their lands, but scrupulously paid for them, and they had a well-enforced policy of having the colony government supervise all land transactions with the Indians. There was a mutual benefit in Plymouth's treaty with their immediate neighbors, the Wampanoags, in that the settlers were known as allies of the Wampanoags, and quite possibly saved them from being annihilated by their enemies the more powerful Narragansetts. Then why was it that the Wampanoags, after more than fifty years of peaceful coexistence, rose up against the colonists? Because the two groups were on an inevitable collision path. The English grew in number and had to spread out, the land stayed constant, and the Wampanoags were hemmed in on all sides. Their plight was shared by their neighbors, too, for the Narragansetts were squeezed between the colonies of Massachusetts, Connecticut, and Rhode Island, and, not far away, was the Connecticut River, on the other side of which lived their fierce enemies, the Mohawks. The Nipmucks in central Massachusetts were also being pushed further toward the Connecticut River by the ever-expanding towns of Massachusetts Bay Colony. [1]

Exclusion of the Indians from the lands they had sold was not the only complaint the Indians had against the English, but it was the prime one. Certainly the colonists thought of the Indians differently from their own kind. We see this especially in the case of Sam, an Indian sentenced to be whipped for raping a white woman. The court observed, "Hee deserved death, yett considering hee was but an Indian, and therfore in an incapasity to know the horiblenes of the wickednes of this abominable act . . ."; which was admitting that the law, though striving for fairness in general, had a somewhat different policy for whites and Indians, although in this case it worked to the advantage of the Indian. The races were kept separate, and though there might have been a stray marriage between a white backwoodsman and an Indian woman, there is virtually nothing in the records to show so. This is very much in contrast to the conquest of Latin America by the Spaniards, where mixed marriages were somewhat common, usually on a class basis with rank seeking rank—the historian of the Incas, Garcilaso de la Vega, was the product of the marriage of a Spanish noble-man with an Inca princess. And even in Virginia, John Rolfe had married Pocahontas. [2]

Colonists were forbidden to trade alcohol and munitions with the Indians and the records are full of penalties for those who disobeyed. The reasoning behind the alcohol prohibition was explained in a 1654 court order, "Wheras there hath been great abuse by trading wine and other strong liquors with the Indians, wherby they drinke themselves drunke, and in theire drunkenes comitt horred wickednes, as murthering theire nearest relations, etc., as by sadd and woefull experience is made mani-fest, it is therfore ordered, that noe pson or psons whatsoever, from this time, trade any strong liquors, directly or indirectly, to the Indians." On 2 October 1658 Lydia, the wife of Henry Taylor, was fined five shillings for selling strong water to an Indian; on 5 March 1660/61, James Cole and Gyles Rickard, ordinary keepers, were each fined ten shillings for selling wine or strong liquors to Indians; on 3 March 1662/63 Ephraim Doane, Thomas Ridman, John Knowles, and John Wilson were each fined twenty-five shillings for trading liquors with the Indians; on 2 July 1667 Samuel Fuller, Jr. was fined twenty shillings for selling liquor to the Indians; and there were many other such cases. [3]

The policy of not trading munitions with the Indians varied consider-ably, and apparently there were many exceptions depending on the period and the type of occasion. On 2 March 1651/52, Nicholas Hyde was fined £25, a severe penalty, for selling a gun to an Indian; however, he was also ordered to satisfy Chief Massasoit about a gun "hee had of him," which probably meant that he had also sold a gun to Massasoit, who was not com-pletely satisfied with the transaction, though the wording could also mean that Hyde had obtained a gun from Massasoit. In either case there is the implication that it was all right for Massasoit to possess a gun. On 9 June 1653 the grand jury presented Mr. William Leveridge of Sandwich for "changing" a gun with an Indian. On 3 June 1652 Joseph Harding of Eastham was presented for "carrying an Indians gun unto the smith to bee mended, in his unkels name," and John Bryant of Taunton was presented for "exchanging of a muskett for a fowling piece with the Indians." How-ever, on 4 October 1655, when Teague Jones accused an Indian of having stolen a gun from him, the court could not find that the gun belonged to Jones, and ordered the constable to return it to the Indian, while on 3 June 1668 Peter Pitts of Taunton was ordered to return a gun he had detained from an Indian. And on 1 October 1661 the court, noting an increase in the harm done to cattle by wolves, ordered the towns to pay to an Indian bringing in a wolf's head one-half pound of powder and two pounds of shot or lead, in addition to the customary coat awarded for evidence of killing a wolf. [4]

The court endeavored to apply justice to everyone, and it demonstrated this determination dramatically to the Indians in 1638 when four white men robbed and murdered an Indian on the highway. Arthur Peach, Thomas Jackson, Richard Stinnings, and Daniel Crosse were indicted, and, though Crosse managed to escape custody, the other three were hanged. On 6 March 1654/55 the court sentenced John Woodcock of Rehoboth to sit in the stocks and to pay a forty shilling fine for going into an Indian's house and taking away some goods plus the Indian's child as satisfaction for a debt the Indian owed him. Adonijah Morris, who also seized some goods from the same Indian for a debt, was likewise fined forty shillings. On 5 October 1663 three Indians came to court to answer a complaint against them by Ephraim Doane, but when Doane did not appear to prosecute, the court awarded the Indians five shillings each for their trouble. On 1 March 1669/70 Thomas Matthews was fined three shillings four pence for beating up an Indian named Ned, and he was further ordered to pay fourteen shillings to Ned toward his cost of having to travel to court. The Plymouth Court also took it upon itself to act as judge and jury over cases of Indians injuring other Indians within the court's jurisdiction, and on 27 October 1674 it tried an Indian named Matthias, alias Achawehett, for the murder of an Indian named Joseph, alias Chachapanucke. The jury found Matthias guilty of manslaughter "by chance medley," and accordingly the court cleared him of willful murder and released him. [5]

It might have been this impartial striving for justice that brought about the opening volley of King Philip's War. On 1 June 1675 a trio of Indians — Tobias, his son Wampapaquan, and Mattashanamo — were tried for having on 29 January 1674/75 "wilfully and of sett purpose, and of mallice fore thought, and by force and armes, murder[ed] John Sassamon, an other Indian, by laying violent hands on him and striking him, or twisting his necke, untill hee was dead; and to hide and conceale this theire said murder, att the time and place aforesaid, did cast his dead body through a hole of the iyce into the said pond." This was a particularly sensitive case, for Sassamon was a Christianized, educated Indian who had once served as Philip's secretary. He later left Philip, became a teacher to friendly Indians near Middleborough, and, shortly before his death, warned the Plymouth government of a Wampanoag conspiracy to wage a general war. One of his murderers, Tobias, was a counselor to Philip. Accordingly, the Plymouth authorities were very circumspect, and they added six of the "most indifferentest, gravest, and sage Indians" to the usual jury, and all six of these concurred with the verdict, which was that the three accused Indians were guilty of murder. The court sentenced the three to be hanged, and Tobias and Mattashanamo were executed on 8 June 1675. Wampapaquan was reprived briefly for some unspecified consideration, but within a month was shot to death. Right after the hangings, Plymouth authorities began hearing reports of pronounced Indian unrest. [6]

Following the death of Governor Prence in 1673, Josias Winslow, son of *Mayflower* passenger Edward Winslow, became the new Plymouth governor. He had been born in the colony around 1628, and he grew up in that second generation which was assuming leadership more and more. He had been an Assistant from 1657 to 1673, became governor in 1673, and in 1675, at the start of King Philip's War, he governed with the aid of Assistants John Alden, now a senior statesman; William Bradford, born in the colony, a son of the late governor; Thomas Hinckley, who had arrived in the colony with his parents as a young boy and was rapidly rising in importance; John Freeman, who had also arrived as a young boy, the son of the late Assistant Mr. Edmond Freeman, and the husband of Mercy Prence, daughter of Governor Prence and granddaughter of Elder Brewster; Constant Southworth, Bradford's stepson who had served in a number of important positions; James Browne, son of the late Mr. John Browne, who had been one of the more liberal Assistants; and James Cudworth, another liberal leader who had once failed to get reelected as an Assistant because of his tolerant views toward Quakers, and had even been disenfranchised for a number of years. Josias Winslow was also the major of the colony's militia, and he had been commander-in-chief of a military expedition ordered in 1671 to convince the Indian tribes under the squaw sachem Awashuncks and others at Saconnet to surrender their arms and continue peaceful relations. 7

The war that began following the execution of two of the murderers of Sassamon was initially Plymouth's war. Josias Winslow and Thomas Hinckley, as commissioners to the United Colonies (now consisting of three colonies, Massachusetts, Plymouth, and Connecticut, the former colony of New Haven having merged with Connecticut), prepared a brief narrative of the early events of that war. Plymouth had been aware of reports that Philip was arming his people and attracting outside warriors to his camp, but the authorities thought he was acting bellicose out of fear that the Plymouth Court might bring him to trial "with the other Murderers" of Sassamon. The feeling was that when the court adjourned without calling him, Philip would stop being apprehensive and "the cloud might blow over." Plymouth's "innosensy" was disturbed when Lt. John Browne of Swansea reported that Philip and his men were still in arms, that many strange Indians from various places had joined him, that they had sent their wives to be under the protection of the Narragansetts, and that they were often alarming the settlers around Swansea with the noise of guns and drums. One of the squaw sachems in Rhode Island, Weetamo, had told Benjamin Church that Philip intended a war against the English, and some of her people would help him. Mr. James Browne visited Philip twice on 14 and 15 June, to persuade him to be peaceful, and brought from the Plymouth Council an "amicable frindly letter to Phillip therin shewing our dislike of his practices," and advising him to dismiss the outside Indians and command his own people to fall quietly to their business. But, Browne could obtain no answer from him. On 17 June Mr. Paine of Rehoboth and several other Englishmen went unarmed to Mount Hope, the peninsula south of Swansea, which was Philip's home, and Philip's men threatened them by pointing their guns at them. On 18 and 19 June the Indians looted the house of Job Winslow, and on 20 June burned and looted other houses south of Swansea. Plymouth troops marched to relieve Swansea, but on 23 June a dozen more houses were set afire. On 24 June Thomas Layton was slain by Indians at Fall River, and on 25 June a number of people at Swansea were slain. A force dispatched from Massachusetts joined the Plymouth troops, but were not able to punish the Indians. Winslow and Hinckley concluded their report by noting that "wee had deserved better" of the Indians. [8]

It actually appears that the first man killed in the war was an Indian. John Easton, deputy governor of Rhode Island, wrote a narrative in which he described events in the Swansea area of 23 June 1675. The Indians were looting various deserted houses when two white men, an old man and a boy, appeared on the scene. Seeing three Indians run out of a house, the old man told the boy to shoot, which he did. One Indian was hit, but got away. Later some Indians came to the garrison and asked why they shot the Indian, letting them know that he had died. The boy said it was no matter. Some of the others tried to let the Indians know that they did not feel so callous about the death, but the Indians went away in haste. Easton wrote that the next day, 24 June, Indians returned and killed the boy who had shot the Indian, his father, and five other white men. A contemporary letter from an unidentified Boston merchant to a friend in London reported something similar, saying that a man at Swansea, his wife, and his son of about twenty were shot by Indians. The wife was defiled by the Indians, who also "skinned her head, as also the son." Richard LeBaron Bowen, in his history of Rehoboth, noted that records showed only one father and son killed, William and John Salisbury, on 24 June. Thus, Bowen concluded that John Salisbury started the war, prompted by his father, whom Bowen called "a third rank inhabitant of Swansea." However, as is shown by her appearance in later records, Mrs. Salisbury did not die in this fight, which brings into question whether Bowen's supposition was correct. Benjamin Church later recalled that on a march of 30 June past the burned houses south of Swansea, the English troops witnessed this gruesome sight: "And soon after, eight more at Mattapoiset, upon whose bodies they [the Indians] exercised more than brutish barbarities, beheading, dismembering, and mangling them and exposing them in the most inhuman manner, which gashed and ghostly objects struck a damp on all beholders. . . . They marched until they came to the narrow of the neck, at a place called Keekkamuit, where they took down the heads of eight Englishmen that were killed at the head of Metapoiset Neck and set upon poles, after the barbarous manner of the savages." Vital records sent to Plymouth by Nicholas Tanner, Swansea Town Clerk, showed that nine males were buried at Swansea on 24 [*sic*] June: Gershom Cobb, Joseph Lewis, John Salsbury, John Jones, John Fall, Nehemiah Allen, Robert Jones, William Lohun, and William Salsbury (a tenth, William Hamon, was killed later, and buried on 29 June). [9]

Massachusetts had been quick to respond to Plymouth's appeal for help. While sending troops, the Bay Colony also sent emissaries to try to reconcile Plymouth and Philip, but the discovery of the mutilated bodies of the first colonists killed in the war convinced Massachusetts that mediation could not be successful. Plymouth particularly wanted the Bay to try to persuade the Narragansetts and the Nipmucks to keep neutral. It had hoped to keep the war confined to Philip's home area of Mount Hope, and Capt. James Cudworth, with about one hundred Plymouth men and two hundred Massachusetts men, was given the assignment. But Philip crossed the water separating Mount Hope from Saconnet on the mainland, and the war could no longer be contained. Within a short period of time, Philip and his men destroyed the town of Dartmouth. Middleborough had to be evacuated. Philip and his warriors escaped the nets spread out against them and fled to the Nipmucks in central Massachusetts. Now war spread to endanger Massachusetts towns on two sides, both the ring of towns west of Boston and those settlements on both sides of the Connecticut River. Using a hit and run tactic, the Indians could quickly fall on a town and either destroy it, or loot and burn the outlying houses and steal the livestock while the townspeople defended themselves from a few garrison houses. Massachusetts forces undertook a preventative offensive to keep the Narragansetts from joining Philip, but succeeded mainly in arousing these powerful tribes against all the English, except for one group called the Niantics led by Philip's traditional enemy, Ninigret. Another of Philip's traditional enemies, the Mohegans, joined the English, and in the west the Mohawks maintained a deep-seated hostility that sometimes led to excursions against the tribes allied with Philip. But, a wide expanse of territory in Rhode Island, Connecticut, and Massachusetts was subject to frequent and ferocious Indian raids. [10]

Plymouth reacted strongly. On 4 August 1675 the Council of War deliberated over the fate of some 112 Indians, men, women, and children, who had fallen into custody. They concluded that "whereas, upon examination, it is found that severall of them have bin actors in the late rising and warr of the Indians against us, and the rest complyers with them therin, which they have done contrary to the engagement and covenant made and plighted with this colonie, which they have pfidiously broken, as appeereth further alsoe in that they did not discover that pnisious plott which Phillip, with others, completed against us, which has caused the destruction of severall of us, by losse of lives and estates, and still held in danger therby," most of the Indians would be sold as slaves, while because of special considerations a few would be otherwise disposed of. On 2 September 1675 the Council of War ordered that fifty-seven Indians who had come in to surrender be sold into perpetual servitude. On 6 December 1675 the council decided that great damage could potentially occur from the Indians south of Plymouth, and these were ordered to come no closer to Plymouth than Sandwich, under penalty of death or imprisonment. Throughout the colonies, all Indians, even the friendly Praying Indians, were looked upon with suspicion and hatred by many, while a few white men risked their careers, if not their lives, in pleading for moderation. [11]

Plymouth's governor, Maj. Josias Winslow, was made commander-in-chief of the United Colonies forces, and he planned a campaign to inflict a serious blow against the Indians. James Cudworth, now promoted to major, took Winslow's place as commander of all Plymouth forces; Cudworth was much older now than when he had put in his plea for toleration for the Quakers, and so far in this war he had accomplished very little. On 6 December 1675 the Council of War directed the commissioned officers of Plymouth Colony to rendezvous their men at Plymouth on 7 December, proceed to Taunton on the eighth, Rehoboth on the ninth, and Providence on the tenth. All men were to be able and fit and provided with clothing for the season, knapsacks, and ammunition. The order ended tersely, "Fayle not." [12] Winslow won a considerable victory on 19 December at the Great Swamp Fight, killing many Narragansetts in a palisaded Indian village in Rhode Island and separating the survivors from their food supplies. But Winslow's losses were heavy, too, and he could not sustain the momentum.

Plymouth's troops in general were not well provisioned, nor were they trained for the type of guerrilla warfare they encountered with the Indians. Over the years each town had had its military company with captain, lieutenant, and sergeant, and the men were regularly drilled in the best manner prescribed by European training methods to prepare men for fighting on the plains of Europe. The Indians were not acquainted with such techniques, but fought as they always had by falling suddenly on one of an opponent's weak areas, doing as much damage as possible, and then running for the woods and dispersing. The raids came closer: Scituate, on the sea between Boston and Plymouth was attacked, and on 12 March 1676 a group of Indians even raided the garrison house of William Clark on the Eel River only three miles south of Plymouth. On 7 July 1676, after a squaw had given information against two Indians, Woodcocke and Quanapawhan, they were tried for the "bloody murder" of Mrs. Clarke, and they in turn accused a third one, John Nun, who owned also that he was of the group that had murdered Jacob Mitchell and his wife and John Pope. The three Indians were found guilty and immediately executed. The court tried to make it clear that in looking with favor on Indians coming in to surrender, they would make a distinction between those who had killed colonists in the field in a soldier-like way, and those who had committed murders such as in the Clarke raid. A fourth Indian, Keeweenam, was implicated by the others. According to their story, he had scouted out the Clarke house and instigated the murder by telling Tatoson, the leader of the group, that the Clarke house was but poorly defended. Keeweenam was found guilty, and his sentence, that his head should be severed from his body, was immediately executed. [13]

The first part of the war definitely went to the Indians, whose victories terrorized the English settlers throughout southern New England. Further, food was in short supply, and famine threatened. Even in the summer and fall of 1675, the men recruited to fight could ill be spared from the harvests, and when spring 1676 arrived, the colonies, reeling under devastating Indian raids, found themselves often forced to choose between sending men to fight or keeping men to sow. Military contingents were raised by the assignment of quotas from the United Colonies to the individual colonies, with quotas being further broken down within the colony and assigned to the towns. In the early part of the war, for example, 1,000 men were to be raised, with 527 assigned to Massachusetts, 315 to Connecticut, and 158 to Plymouth. Some quotas assigned by Plymouth to the towns were as follows (Indian raids had made it impossible for colonists to live safely in Dartmouth, Swansea, and Middleborough which were by now deserted, and some of their men were undoubtedly recruited from towns to which they had fled): [14]

	4 October 1675	30 December 1675	29 March 1676
Plymouth	15	11	30
Duxbury	8	6	16
Scituate	23	17	50
Sandwich	16	11	28
Taunton	20	13	30
Yarmouth	15	10	26
Barnstable	16	13	30
Marshfield	13	10	26
Rehoboth	15	15	30
Eastham	8	9	18
Bridgewater	8	7	16
TOTAL	157	122	300

While volunteers were preferred, when not enough were available others were impressed. This was not an arbitrary pressing, though, no clubbing indiscriminately at anyone coming down the street. It worked more like a draft board system, with each town being assigned certain men to determine who would be pressed into service. On 6 December 1675, for example, the Plymouth Council of War appointed Maj. James Cudworth, Cornet Robert Stetson, and Isaac Chittenden as press masters to obtain enough able and fit men at Scituate for an expedition against the Indians. On 30 December 1675 the council further ordered that any person being pressed into the colony's service who neglected or refused to go forth on such service would be fined £10, and in case he did not have enough money or goods available to raise such an amount, he would be committed to prison not to exceed six months. If a man tried to evade service by going to another town, the constable of the latter town would be required to turn him over to the constable of the first town. A number of men were fined on 10 March 1675/76 for various military related offenses, including some who had been pressed, but refused to serve. The largest amount that these men were fined, however, was £8, and many fines were less. Interestingly, the constables of Bridgewater were fined £2 for not pressing John Willis and another £2 for illegally pressing Samuel Lathrop, a man unfit for service. The constables of Taunton were also fined £4 for pressing Joseph Deane, who was unfit for service. [15]

The defeat that probably affected Plymouth more disastrously than any other military action of the war occurred on 26 March 1676 on the Pawtucket River. A Plymouth Colony company under the command of Capt. Michael Pierce set out from Rehoboth to fall upon a group of Indians who were reported nearby. With about sixty-five Englishmen and some Indians, Pierce suddenly found himself facing perhaps one thousand Narragansett warriors, and though the colonists fought bravely, the situation was hopeless. Only a few of the Plymouth troops and their Indian allies escaped with their lives, the town of Scituate alone counting at least fifteen dead. The Reverend Noah Newman, who had taken the place of his father, Samuel Newman, in Rehoboth's church, wrote a letter the day after the battle in which he noted the names of those killed. For Plymouth Colony, this must have been the low point of the war, and the loss of morale can be seen in a record of the Council of War of 11 April 1676. The Council met to proceed with preparations for the expedition for which Plymouth had a quota of 300 out of 1,000 men total. "But many of the souldiers that were pressed came not to goe forth, especially Scituate and Sandwich proved very deficient, which caused a frustration of the whole designe, soe as they did not agree to goe forward in any thinge for publicke good, either for the healp and defence of Rehoboth, then in straites, or otherwise for our offence of our enimie or defence from them." [16]

The lowest point had been reached and the colonists' fortunes began to climb. In addition, the Indians were not as well supplied with men, material, or food. The Englishmen, after their initial defeats, were beginning to learn how to fight Indian style, thus nullifying in good part the Indians' major advantage. Since they were never unified, the various tribes never really subordinated their individual interests to a total war effort. As the war progressed, many of the friendly Indians were of great help, and the colonies were fortunate that they had overcome their fear mixed with prejudice and begun relying more on their Indian auxiliaries. Friendly Indians made up substantial parts of the colony's forces, and their ability and numbers were a definite contributing factor to the final victory. Rhode Island was no longer threatened by the war, and after an initial raid by Indians on Providence, the colony, which was not a member of the United Colonies, played a lesser part in the war. Connecticut was rapidly gaining control of its territory. Bay Colony troops increasingly restored order in the arena of central Massachusetts. Philip and his allies began losing more men in their encounters with colonial troops, something they could ill afford to do, and the troops also had good fortune in finding large Indian food caches, thus depriving the enemy of what was becoming its greatest need. Too, more and more of the Indians were coming over to the colonists, sometimes even turning around and fighting their former allies. Philip and his immediate followers were finding themselves increasingly alone.

The hero of the war for Plymouth was Capt. Benjamin Church, son of Richard Church and his wife, Elizabeth, the daughter of *Mayflower* passenger Richard Warren. Church had early distinguished himself in fighting at Swansea, at the Pease Field near Saconnet, in the Great Swamp Fight, and in guerrilla-type operations throughout Plymouth Colony. Church understood the Indians, had been on quite friendly terms with them before the war, and during the war was able to make good use of them, sometimes being able to get them to change sides almost instantly. His son wrote:

> When he [Church] took any number of prisoners, he would pick out some that he took a fancy to, and would tell them, he took a particular fancy to them and had chose them for himself to make soldiers of; and if any would behave themselves well, he would do well by them and they should be his men and not sold out of the country. If he perceived they looked surly, and his Indian soldiers called them 'treacherous dogs,' as some of them would sometimes do, all the notice he would take of it would only be to clap them on the back and tell them, 'come, come, you look wild and surly, and mutter, but that signifies nothing. These, my best soldiers, were a little while ago as wild and surly as you are now. By the time you have been but one day along with me, you'll love me too, and be as brisk as any of them.' And it proved so. For there was none of them but, after they had been a little while with him, and seen his behavior, and how cheerful and successful his men were, would be as ready to pilot him to any place where the Indians dwelt or haunted (though their own fathers or nearest relations should be among them), or to fight for him, as any of his own men. [17]

Church persuaded Queen Awashuncks and her Saconnet tribe to surrender and sent them to Plymouth. On 1 August 1676 Church just narrowly missed capturing Philip on the Taunton River, but had to be satisfied with the capture of his wife and son. After a quick return to Plymouth, Church was out in the field again, determined to capture the Indian who had given his name to the war. The war had completed a full circle, and Philip, now destitute and with but a few tired, hungry men, had come back to where it all started, his one-time home at Mount Hope. Church was across the water at Aquidneck Island when a deserter from Philip's camp told him where the Wampanoag chief was hiding. Profiting from past mistakes of colonial troops, before leading a charge on Philip's camp, Church posted pairs of men in a circle surrounding the camp. When his main force charged, Church knew Philip would have nowhere to flee except into ambush. A waiting pair of men, a white and an Indian, saw someone run-ning toward them. The white man aimed his gun first, but his gun misfired. The Indian shot and stopped the runner dead. It was Philip. A victorious Church ordered Philip's head severed and his body cut into quarters. [18]

On 28 June 1676 the Saconnet Indians led by Awashuncks, who had been persuaded by Church to surrender, appeared before the Council of War with Awashuncks's son, Peter, as spokesman. They appealed for peace and for their lands at Saconnet. The following dialogue took place: [19]

Council: What reason have you to expect that youer request heerin should be graunted, since you have broken youer engagements with us by joyning with the Sachem Philip att Mount Hope and other Indians, our professed enimies, and have bin copartenors with them in all assaults and enterprisses against us, in which said hostile attemptes many of ours have lost their lives, habitations, and estates? And you must not thinke that wee can passe over matters of such a high nature soe shighly. We are not willing to vallue the blood of our English friends att soe low a rate. You are never able to make satisfaction for the wronge, nor make good the damage you have don us by youer pfiduous dealings in this respect. Youer way had bine, when you saw the said Philip and other our enimies to rise up in rebellion against us, to have declined them and repaired to the English, and place youer selves under our protection.

Peter: [We had] not bin active in fighting with the English, but fledd away for feare.

Council: Why did you feare the English?

Peter: When the English army went out, wee were afraid, and desired to go over to Rhode Iland; but the younge men there kept such a strict watch that wee could not get over in safety. Then wee were forced to hyde ourselves in swampes; and the English army came and burnt our houses; and wee understanding that the Narragansetts were friends to the English, wee went to them.

Council: Did the Indians burne the English houses before the army came?

Peter: Yee, they burned theire forsaken houses.

Council: Did the English doe you any wrong att any time, or speak high or threating words to you that scared you? Speake freely, with-out feare.

Peter: The English never did us any hurt or wronge to this day; if they had, wee would speake of it.

The Saconnets again desired the government to allow them to live within colony limits, promising to be subject to the English, and they asked for terms. The council answered that they had found the Saconnets so perfidious, they would have to have some good security to guarantee their fidelity. Chowohumma, alias David, another of the tribe, offered to do anything they could to fight Plymouth's enemy, and further to capture Succanowassucke, the first of the Saconnets to stir up the others. The council gave them terms to place themselves at the disposal of the colonial army, to surrender any arms not needed for this purpose, to leave Peter as a hostage, and to turn over such of their comrades who had engaged in raids to murder any English or destroy their property. The council in turn promised them a temporary abode where they could be in safety until the war ended, followed by a more permanent place to reside within the colony. [20]

Shortly after the death of Philip, the war ended with Church's capture of Annawon, the most important of Philip's surviving lieutenants. Now came the time to settle affairs, to reward the good and punish the evil. On 22 July 1676 the Council of War ordered that it would be legal for magistrates to dispose of the children of those Indians who had surrendered by assigning them as servants to colonists until the children reached the age of twenty-four or twenty-five (to protect the children, the magistrates later ordered that their masters give them written indentures setting out the terms of their servitude). On the same day it was ruled that volunteer soldiers who had brought in captured Indians could keep half of them to sell as slaves. It was also ruled that no Indian male captive above the age of fourteen could be allowed to remain within colony limits, and thus the slaves would have to be sold outside Plymouth; in fact, probably most were sold to the West Indies. There were not many executions, though Annawon was sentenced to death. On 6 March 1676/77 three Indians, Timothy Jacked, Nassamaquat, and Pompacanshe were charged with murdering John Knowles, John Tisdale, Sr., and Samuel Atkins. While the jury had strong suspicions that the first two were guilty, the evidence against them was not sufficient, and there was no evidence against Pompacanshe. However, the penalty turned out to be the same: Timothy Jacked and Nassamaquat were sentenced to be sent out of the country, and Pompacanshe, as a prisoner taken in war, was also to go. On 13 July 1677 Popanooie was found to be guilty of great cruelty and outrage toward the Dartmouth settlers, and particularly in participating in the murder of several of the children of Thomas Pope, late of Dartmouth, and others. His wife and children being found partners with him in the rebellion, the whole family was sentenced to perpetual servitude and were sent out of the colony. Possibly the acrimonies of the war still remained on 12 November 1678 when three Sandwich Indians were convicted of stealing £25 from Zachariah Allin's house and, having lost the money, they were sentenced to be sold as "lawfull slaves for tearme of theire naturall life." [21]

On the other hand, Mamanuett, an Indian sachem at Saconnet, was able to convince the General Court that he and some fifteen of his men had been faithful to the English during the rebellion, having been in service for the colonials, and the court granted that they could return to repossess their lands. It was perhaps a fitting aftermath of the war that in

March 1678/79 the commissioners of the United Colonies ordered a sister of John Sassamon, the Indian murdered by Philip's men, to be freed from being a servant to Joseph Burge, who was to receive £10 for his loss. Captain Benjamin Church was able to ameliorate the plight of about five or six Indians when, at his initiative, the court overruled their being sold as lifetime slaves and permitted them to reside in Plymouth. [22]

The colony's soldiers were rewarded with land, as had been promised by the court. On 10 March 1675/76 the court observed that soldiers sent out on the first expedition had been promised money or land, and, there being no money, certain tracts of land valued at £1,000 would be given them. On 21 July 1676 a list of names of twelve men from Scituate was approved by the Council of War to receive lands ranging in value from £2/1 for William Hatch to £10 for Lt. Isaac Buck. Captain Roger Goulding of Rhode Island, who had proved to be a constant and real friend in the late war, on 1 November 1676 was awarded 100 acres of land, and on the same day David Lake and Thomas Lake, who had been very useful and of much service to the colony, were given 100 acres, with David, who "hath bine most healpfull," getting sixty, and Thomas the rest. Captain Benjamin Church was commissioned as a magistrate. In the race among the colonies to take over Indian lands, Plymouth won the Mount Hope peninsula, which became known as Bristol, and Captain Church became the new town's deputy. In 1682 the court was still giving out awards, such as £4/4 to Capt. John Williams for his services in the late war, and Mr. William Clarke, who lost his wife and child at Eel River, was given the contract to supply food and lodging for the magistrates at £40 yearly. [23]

The cost of the war to the colony was incalculable. Losses of houses and other property, plus crops, have never been reckoned, but just the increase in colony taxes alone will illustrate the magnitude of the financial cost: [24]

	1665	1676	1677
Plymouth	£13/17/06	£351/03/09	£19/00/00
Duxbury	12/12/06	164/19/00	11/06/06
Scituate	22/13/09	586/07/04	30/10/00
Sandwich	12/12/06	327/15/06	22/16/00
Taunton	12/12/06	327/15/06	16/00/00
Yarmouth	10/15/03	266/01/00	18/10/00
Barnstable	3/14/00	351/03/09	24/05/00
Marshfield	2/17/04	266/01/00	18/10/00
Rehoboth	18/18/09	485/05/04	12/00/00
Eastham	10/02/06	236/05/00	15/18/00
Dartmouth	7/10/00		

Sowams/ Swansea	6/00/00	165/00/00	05/00/00
Bridgewater			10/00/00
TOTAL	£134/06/07	3,692/16/02	£203/15/06

It is of interest to note that "divers Christians in Ireland" raised £124/10 for the relief of those in Plymouth Colony who had been impoverished and distressed as a result of the war. [25]

It has been estimated that the colony lost upwards of one hundred lives (including a few women and children), but, again, total figures have never been obtained, and this does not include men from other colonies. One list of documented Plymouth Colony casualties shows some ninety people dead, and it does not claim to be complete. [26] Additionally, there were probably some who survived the war, but died later of wounds received during it. The Indian deaths for all areas have never been calculated with any precision, and it would be next to impossible, even if such figures were available, to sort out deaths of Plymouth Colony Indians. Certainly Indians died during the war by the hundreds, if not more. The sad fact is that this was not a war that could have been avoided—it had to happen.

NOTES

1. Leach, *Flintlock,* 14, as noted earlier, believes the basic problem was that English control of more and more land was pushing the Indians into less and less space. Langdon, 157, points out that there was no reason to question Gov. Josias Winslow's sincerity in saying that Plymouth had dealt fairly with the Wampanoags on land transactions, but "What Winslow never understood was that protection of the Indian in a particular sale was not the crucial issue; rather it was the proximity of settlement."

2. *PCR* 6:98; *Encyc. Brit.* 22:932, 18:85.

3. *PCR* 3:60, 150, 207, 4:32, 162.

4. Ibid., 3:4, 36, 10, 90-91, 4:183, 6.

5. *Bradford (Ford)* 2:263; *PCR* 1:96-97, 3:74, 4:46, 5:31, 156.

6. *PCR* 5:167-68; Leach, *Flintlock,* 30-33. Since Philip began his armed attacks just a matter of days after the execution of two of Sassamon's murderers, it is quite possible that the court planned not to execute Wampapaquan initially, but then felt forced to have him shot to death because of outraged public opinion following Philip's raids.

7. *PCR* 5:163, 73-75.

8. Ibid., 10:362-64.

9. Richard LeBaron Bowen, *Early Rehoboth, Documented Historical Studies of Families and Events in the Plymouth Colony Township,* vol. 3 (Rehoboth, 1948), 10-11, which also gives verbatim extracts from the John Easton and the Boston merchant letters; Suffolk Co., Mass. PR 5:270; *PCR* 8:61. The quotations from Benjamin Church are from *Diary of King Philip's*

War 1675-76, with an introduction by Alan and Mary Simpson (hereafter Church) (Chester, Conn., 1975), 75-76, 79. This is a modern edition of Benjamin Church's version of the war by his son, Thomas Church, *Entertaining Passages Relating to Philip's War Which Began in the Month of June 1675,. . .etc.* Because Church was not reticent about crediting his own exploits, some writers have been a bit cautious in accepting the details of his personal actions; however, there is no question of his successes. On 30 June 1675 Church was serving in a Plymouth group headed by James Cudworth. The Swansea town clerk might have confused day of burial with day of death, for it would seem that the bodies Church saw on 30 June were of the men said to have been buried on 24 June.

10. The summary of the war presented here is mainly based on Leach, *Flintlock,* and on Langdon, 164-87, and these two sources will not be referenced further except for special purposes.

11. *PCR* 5:173-74, 183. Among leading men in Massachusetts who pleaded for better treatment of the Indians were Maj. Daniel Gookin, Capt. Daniel Henchman, Rev. John Eliot "the apostle to the Indians," and Thomas Danforth. Gookin and Danforth even had their lives threatened in an anonymous letter circulated in Boston (Leach, *Flintlock,* 147-51).

12. *PCR* 5:175, 183.

13. Ibid., 5:204-06.

14. Ibid., 5:176, 185, 193.

15. Ibid., 5:183, 185, 190.

16. *PCR* 5:189-90, 193. Robert S. Wakefield, "Plymouth Colony's Casualties in King Philip's War," *TAG* 60:236-42, collates material from different sources to show as many as possible of Plymouth's total casualties.

17. Church, 139.

18. It has been said that the white man of the pair that stopped Philip was Caleb Cooke, a grandson of *Mayflower* passenger Francis Cooke. However, this is apparently based more on family tradition than contemporary record. In the 1975 edition of Church's memoirs, this is given as a footnote by the Simpsons on p. 211: "Probably Caleb Cook, grandson of Mayflower Francis Cook. According to family tradition, he traded his gun for the Indian's gun that shot Philip. From his descendants in Kingston, Mass., the lock made its way to the Massachusetts Historical Society and the barrel to the Pilgrim Society in Plymouth." The claim is also found in Bradford Kingman, *Epitaphs from Burial Hill — Plymouth, Massachusetts* (Brookline, 1892; reprint, Baltimore 1977), 11, which shows from the epitaph on his tombstone that he died on 5 February 1721/22. Kingman, in a footnote, states, "Caleb Cook, son of Jacob and Damaris (Hopkins) Cook, born March 29, 1651, and resided at Rocky Nook, Kingston. . . . He was a soldier under the lead of Col. Benjamin Church, and while closely pressing the Indians, Cook, and an Indian named Alderman, of the Seaconet tribe were placed on duty to watch Philip, lest he should get out of a swamp, where he had hidden, and if possible to kill Philip. He soon had a chance, and fired at him, but his gun missed. He then bid Alderman to

fire, and he soon became their victim, having been shot through the heart. Mr. Cook exchanged guns with the Indian, and the gun which did the fatal work has been kept in the Cook family until quite recently. The old flint lock was taken off and presented to the Massachusetts Historical Society. Part of the gun is in the Cabinet of Curiosities in Pilgrim Hall, Plymouth."

19. *PCR* 5:201-03.
20. Ibid., 5:203.
21. Ibid., 5:207, 223, 210, 224, 244, 270.
22. Ibid., 5:224-25, 10:366, 11:242.
23. Ibid., 5:224-25, 191, 206, 214-15, 234, 6:77, 85, 106, 128, 5:7, 93.
24. Ibid., 4:118, 5:207, 243.
25. Ibid., 5:222.
26. Wakefield, *TAG* 60:236-42.

CHAPTER 7

The End of a Colony (1676-1691)

"A TIME TO PLUCK UP THAT
WHICH IS PLANTED"

T he events following a war are often more cataclysmic than the war
itself. Change is in the air, new questions are being asked, traditions
may be discarded, and new demands must be faced. For Plymouth
Colony, some of the new demands came from England, which had under-
gone many changes since its own war between King and Parliament. Oliver
Cromwell died in 1658. His successor as Lord Protector, his son Richard,
was ineffective in the role. Great masses of people chafed under puritani-
cal rule, and even leaders of the Protectorate yearned for a restoration of
the monarchy. Charles II was invited to return from exile, and the Restoration period began in 1660. The second Charles was an easy going man
who reigned in an uneasy partnership with Parliament until he died in
1685. He was succeeded by his brother, James II, who was determined at
a minimum to achieve coexistence between Catholic and Protestant in
England. However, his rash pro-Catholic policies and attempts to revital-
ize the concept of the Divine Right of Kings soon brought him exile at the
instigation of his daughter and her Dutch husband, Prince William of
Orange, who in 1689 began a joint reign as William and Mary. [1] The fall-
out from these events naturally affected Plymouth.

Plymouth did not act with the speed or enthusiasm of Rhode Island,
which was motivated by self-interest, in recognizing the Restoration, but
neither did it delay as much as Massachusetts, which virtually looked upon
itself as a free state and had to be threatened by the English Privy Council. In April 1664 England sent out four commissioners to visit Massachusetts, Connecticut, Plymouth, and Rhode Island. The commissioners
were received in Massachusetts with barely hidden distaste, but Plymouth
succeeded in making a good impression on them, the court ordering on
8 June 1664 that whether "they shall either arive in this harbour or come
by land, that some psons be deputed to bee in a reddines to accomodate
them in a civill manor behoofull to theire condition; and for that end that
the Treasurer bee provided with nessesaries for theire intertaiment," and
if needed a tax would be levied to defray the costs. The commissioners were
Col. Richard Nichols, Sir Robert Carr, George Cartwright, Esq., and
Samuel Maverick, Esq. Maverick was well known in both Plymouth and

Boston as a former Bay resident who had removed to New York some time after signing the Childs/Vassall Remonstrance in 1646. In August 1664 an English expedition captured New Amsterdam from the Dutch and renamed it New York. Even though Plymouth's Thomas Willett became the first mayor of New York (returning to Plymouth Colony after a few years), the fact that New York was now a proprietary colony ruled by a governor appointed in England made it more a threat to New England's freedom than it had been under the Dutch. [2] The third governor of New York, Edmond Andros, would see that threat come true.

In spite of Massachusetts's lukewarm attitude following the visit of the commissioners, the royal charter of Massachusetts was confirmed by King Charles II. Connecticut and Rhode Island, both having charters granted by the Commonwealth, were uneasy enough about it so that shortly after the Restoration they sent their governors, John Winthrop, Jr. and Roger Williams, in person to seek royal charters from Charles, and they succeeded in getting them. Plymouth, with its rather weak rights vested solely in the Bradford Patent, was strangely dilatory and did not request a royal charter at this propitious moment. Had they been more lively in seeking their charter, they probably would have obtained it at this time. Instead, on the arrival of the four commissioners, the Plymouth Court voted that an address should be made to His Majesty for a further confirmation of the patent. The commissioners suggested in 1665 that Plymouth might be given more secure rights in return for allowing the King to appoint a governor from a list of three men nominated by the colony, a proposal Plymouth could not accept. [3]

Following King Philip's War, there was criticism in England that Plymouth had unreasonably provoked Philip into starting the uprising. In 1677 Gov. Josias Winslow wrote to King Charles to answer these charges, also putting forth Plymouth's claim to the Mount Hope lands as being included in the Bradford charter. Winslow also sent King Philip's crown as a present to Charles, but unfortunately he entrusted it to the care of his brother-in-law, Waldegrave Pelham, who failed to put either the present or the letter in the hands of the King. Court records show that "Letters were received from his matie, our dread sov[ereign], which were publickly read, wherby it appeered that his matie had not received a pticular accoumpt of the transacting of matters relateing to our late warr with the Indians, which befell our collonie by reason of the miscarryage of our letters directed to his matie in anno 1677." The court therefore "saw cause to speed away another addresse to his matie, therin to psent him with a true intelligence of matters, and to remove the misinterpretation of our intensions and proceedings." The English government sent Edward Randolph on several visits to the New England colonies, and, though Randolph did not report favorably to England on Massachusetts, he acquired good impressions of Plymouth. In fact, Randolph told his superiors that Winslow believed New England could not be safe for the King until it was under a royal governor general, a change Winslow felt Plymouth would support. In this Winslow seems to have had the same kind of feeling as his father, one of abhorring the general long-range trend of government control slipping more and more out of the hands of conservative elements. This was not a feeling to make public, though, and Josias Winslow later had to repudiate Randolph's report when word of it became known. [4]

On 7 July 1680 Plymouth admitted Randolph as a freeman of the colony. Randolph supported Plymouth in its general desire to get a charter, continuing his support after the death of Governor Winslow on 23 December 1680. Winslow was succeeded as governor by Thomas Hinckley. In the meantime, Plymouth had engaged William Blathwayt, a high ranking official in England, to pursue its interests. Blathwayt wrote favorably to Hinckley about the patent, noting, however, that the Massachusetts charter would be revised so as to provide for a greater dependence on the King, and the revised charter would be the model for Plymouth:

> In acknowledgement of so great favors, such provisions may be inserted as are necessary for the maintenance of his majesty's authority, which, as I am confident, you will most readily embrace, with the continuance of that loyalty his majesty has already commended in you. So will you thereby obtain a pre-eminence before others, whose behavior has been less dutiful.

Edward Randolph wrote to Hinckley from Boston on 29 May 1683:

> By the enclosed papers, you will see what transactions have been in England, and how far his majesty is resolved to deal with this Colony [Massachusetts]. It therefore stands you in hand to be very careful to improve the present opportunity; for, be confident, what regulation is made here will pass through all New England. I was no way wanting with Mr. Blathwayt in your behalf. He is very full of great business, and cannot but with great difficulty be spoken with.

Randolph went on to say that he had "verbal instructions for a petition to his majesty from your government, and how you must make your further applications for a settlement of your Colony." And he warned, "If you neglect this present opportunity, you may be concluded without any hopes of a revocation." As a postscript he noted, "This letter contains only the hints of such things as you [and] I must discourse." Apparently an original copy of the Bradford Patent could not be found in England, and even a copy sent over by Josias Winslow had been "mislaid, or quite lost" (bureaucracy changes but little over the centuries), and Randolph had to ask Hinckley to send still another copy to him. [5]

Even at this date, Plymouth's treatment of Quakers was damaging the colony's reputation in England, and in a letter to William Blathwayt of 22 November 1683 Hinckley tried to assure him that "since we had any hints of his majesty's indulgence toward them," Plymouth had not been extracting severe penalties, "only, of late, some few of them have had a small fine executed on them for their perverse, disorderly carriage" of marrying themselves in their own meetings and refusing to be married by magistrates. Randolph, in writing to Hinckley on 24 November 1683 to rebuke the colony, was very blunt:

> I am not a little concerned to find that not only the complaint that the Quakers in your Colony are whipped and fined for not marrying according to your law, but that you have countenanced the late arbitrary, and till now unheard-of, proceedings against Mr. Saffin, by imprisoning him. . .and [I] assure you nothing could so much impede the getting-out your patent as this. For how will the Lords of his Majesty's Council argue, that if you who have no grant of power to govern (all you can pretend to by your grant from the Earl of Warwick is only the soil in your Colony, and no color for government): so that you have very much exposed yourself.

There it was—the Bradford Patent stripped down to naked reality. The Plymouth colonists had the right to occupy land, but no right to govern themselves. Meanwhile Massachusetts refused to compromise with the crown on revising its charter. Randolph, as crown representative in Boston, continued to send adverse reports to England regarding the independent attitude maintained by the Bay Colony. Finally, in October 1684, Massachusetts's charter was judged by an English court to be forfeit. There the matter rested for a while. [6]

In 1685 Plymouth Colony began an innovation in its form of government, dividing the colony into three counties, Plymouth, Barnstable, and Bristol, each named after its county seat. Government administration had grown considerably since the days when Governor Bradford had Isaac Allerton as his only Assistant. In 1685 the administrative officers for the colony as a whole consisted of one governor, one deputy governor, six Assistants, twenty-eight deputies from seventeen towns (most towns had two), twenty-three constables from seventeen towns, twenty-seven grand jury members from eighteen jurisdictions (the eighteenth being Manamoit, later called Chatham), thirty-eight highway surveyors in seventeen towns, fifty-seven selectmen in seventeen towns, six associate magistrates, three each for Plymouth County and Bristol County (Barnstable County is not shown to have any at this time), six additional members of the Council of War, two from each county, and three majors, one for the military forces of each county. In addition there were such appointed positions as the secretary for the General Court, a marshal and deputy marshal, and several lesser offices. The treasurer was usually one of the Assistants. The venerable John Alden was still one of the Assistants in 1685, the last of the *Mayflower* passengers to occupy this position, and he was elected again in 1686, but Judge Sewall noted in his diary for 1687 "Monday, Sept. 12. Mr. John Alden, the ancient Magistrate of Plymouth, died." [7]

THE FOUNDING OF BRISTOL

On 1 June 1680 a letter from King James was read at General Court, "wherin was expressed his maties favorable aspect on this collonie, with his settlement of Mount Hope theron." This was a victory for Plymouth, whose claim for the former home area of King Philip was contested by Massachusetts. On 28 September 1680 the governor, deputy governor, and treasurer were appointed a committee to arrange the sale of these new lands, and the court also voted to distribute £300 from the proceeds of the sale to the several towns according to their proportional share of 1680 taxes. The purchasers of Mount Hope were four merchants, Capt. John Walley, Mr. Nathaniel Byfield and Mr. Nathaniel Oliver, of Boston, and Mr. Stephen Burton, formerly of Boston. At their request, the court ordered on 28 October 1681 that they and those whom they have admitted or would admit to the lands would be a town and enjoy all the liberties and powers of a town, and that town would be called Bristol. Early Bristol County land records show the subdivision of this rather large area by the four purchasers to various buyers, and the entire transaction thus became unique in the development of Plymouth County, the closest similar transaction being Mr. Hatherly's subdivision of his large tract at Scituate. [8]

LITTLE COMPTON

Though transferred in the next century to Rhode Island, Little Compton originally was settled as a Plymouth Colony town from the lands formerly called Saconett. Benjamin Church recalled how Capt. John Almy of Rhode Island in 1674, "with great importunity," invited him to ride with him and view the area, trying to persuade him that the land was rich and the situation pleasant. Subsequently Church made a purchase and built a farm there. With great industry Church settled in and by the next spring he was hoping his success would attract other men to become his neighbors. Then, "Behold! The rumor of a war between the English and the natives gave check to his projects." Mr. Constant Southworth of Duxbury sold land at Saconett on 29 April 1675 to a large group of men, including Benjamin Church. The town would have been well settled had it not been for the war, and when the war was over many of the original proprietors had changed their minds. On 6 June 1682 it was formally established as a town. [9]

FREETOWN

A court order of July 1683 provided that the inhabitants of the freemen's land at Fall River would be a township and have a constable and grandjurymen. It would be called Freetown, and John Bayley was its first deputy, William Makepeace its first constable, and Mr. Thomas Terrey its first lieutenant. Richard LeBaron Bowen wrote that in 1660 "the twenty-six ancient freemen who had purchased the tract of land, later known as the township of Freetown, divided it into twenty-six lots, and for the next twenty-three years the propriety was generally known as 'ye ffreemen's land at Taunton River. . . .' Apparently none of the twenty-six original proprietors became actual settlers of this freemen's land. About half the lots came into possession of sons, some of whom settled. About a quarter of the lots were purchased by Rhode Island men, mainly from Portsmouth. These twenty-six divisions were long narrow strips. . .200 rods (3,300 ft.) wide and four miles long." [10]

ROCHESTER

The area called Sippican was originally granted to some inhabitants of Scituate for their expansion. However, their grant was later changed to Barnstable, and the General Court ordered that Sippican be reserved for grazing lands for the residents of Plymouth, and it was "never to bee aleanated" for any other use. Never is a long time, and over the years some of those using the land for grazing must have in effect taken up residence there, for on 4 June 1686, "upon the request of the inhabitants of Scippican, alias Rochester, to become a township and have the priviledges of a town, the Court granted theire desires." [11]

It is possible to get an idea of population figures around this time by looking at estimates calculated for Plymouth County towns for 1690, as follow: Plymouth 775, Scituate 865, Bridgewater 440, Duxbury 410, Marshfield 400, and Middleborough 165, for a total of 3,055. During the last half of the colony period, as can be seen from various quotas for men and taxes, Scituate—the main point of contact with the Bay Colony—was always the wealthiest and most populous of the towns. In 1690 the General Court recorded the value of rateable property of the various towns and settlements, as a basis for determining taxes, with this result (given in £s):

Plymouth County		Barnstable County		Bristol County	
Plymouth	2260	Barnstable	3000	Bristol	1049
Scituate	4360	Yarmouth	2777	Taunton	2689
Marshfield	1804	Sandwich	2500	Rehoboth	2117
Duxbury	1500	Eastham	2506	Dartmouth	2200
Bridgewater	1430	Rochester	367	Swansea	1500
Middleborough	582	Manamoy	505	Little Compton	2000
		Succonessett	405	Freetown	349

Since these values were based on a given formula, some idea of the wealth of colony towns can be obtained from the prices of the following, which were used in the formula:

Ox	£2/10	2-year-old colt	1/00
Cow	1/10	1-year-old colt	/10
3-year-old steer or heifer	1/10	1 year or older swine	/06
2-year-old " " "	1/00	1 year or older sheep	/05
1-year-old " " "	/15	1 acre of land in tillage	/05
Horse or mare	2/00	1 acre meadow or pasture	/05

Ships and trading goods were valued at not more than half price, and thus the rated value for livestock and land might have been only half the true value. [12]

There had grown up a system of town, or select, courts whereby a town's selectmen could hear and decide minor civil cases. When such a suit involved residents of two towns, the matter could be tried in either town, as initiated by the plaintiff. A new codification of laws of 1685 provided for intermediate courts between the select courts and the Court of Assistants. These were county courts, coming into existence in 1686, one called the Court of Common Pleas, to hear all cases involving common law where the amount was more than a specified minimum, and the other called the Court of General Sessions, which handled most criminal matters and many county administrative matters. At least three magistrates or assistant magistrates had to be present for a county court to function. Although normally this type of court would not hear divorce suits or criminal cases where the penalty could be death, mutilation, or banishment, in one case the court at Bristol condemned John Delaforest to death for murdering a fellow Frenchman. Delaforest escaped, was recaptured and returned to Plymouth from Boston, and the Court of Assistants, acting as a court of final appeal (there was no jury, for the jury trial had taken place at Bristol), ordered the chief marshal to hang him the next day, 31 July 1690, which was done. A county court could hear appeals from the select courts, and its own verdicts could be appealed to the Court of Assistants. With three layers of courts, the system of justice grew more complex, and we see the effect of this in such matters as the suit of John Doty versus John Bradford, both of Plymouth, which was brought to the Court of Assistants in 1686, but the action was barred "because it ought first to have been tryed at a County Court." On 1 June 1684 the General Court also ordered that the governor with three or four Assistants "and such other substantiall psons as the Govr for the time being shall commissionate under the seal of the collonie, shall have full power to acte as a Court of Admiralty." [13]

Charles II died on 6 February 1684/85. It took some time for news to get to Plymouth, and it was not until 24 April 1685 that the court noted that "James the Second, Kinge of England, Scotland, & Ireland, etc, was proclaimed at Plimouth according to the form required by his majesties most honorable privy councell." The signs were ominous, and the court noted parenthetically in an order of 2 June 1685 regarding payments to a war veteran for life "(if there be a continuation of this goverment)." In 1686 Joseph Dudley was appointed by the King as president of a provisional government in Massachusetts pending a more complete reorganization. Later in the year Sir Edmond Andros, a former governor of New York described in the *Encyclopaedia Britannica* as "one of the ablest English colonial governors in 17th-century America," but better known in the colonies as "the usurper Andros," became royal governor of the Dominion of New England, which would include Massachusetts, Maine, Plymouth, Connecticut, Rhode Island, and New Hampshire, and whose jurisdiction two years later would extend to New York and New Jersey. Edward Randolph became secretary of the new government, and he proposed that Thomas Hinckley, John Walley, William Bradford, Barnabas Lothrop, and

Nathaniel Clark be the Plymouth representatives to the governor's council. Though the Andros government brought a certain degree of efficiency to New England as a whole, the imposition of taxes without representation and the introduction of quitrents, whereby new landholders had to pay an annual rent to the crown for their lands, were obnoxious to a people accustomed to many years of self-rule. The Andros government also encouraged old landholders to apply for confirmation of their grants with provision for them to pay quitrent, too. Further, Andros required that all estates valued at more than £50 be probated at Boston, not only a hardship for people then, but the reason why even now some Plymouth Colony wills and administrations of the period can only be found in Boston. Ultimately, the Plymouth councillors refused to attend council meetings anymore, except for Nathaniel Clark, a former secretary to the Plymouth Court, who used his influence with the council to get Clark's Island in Plymouth Bay granted to him. [14]

When word reached New England that King James II had been overthrown in England, a minor revolution took place in Boston. William Bradford and Nathaniel Thomas wrote on 20 April 1689 to Thomas Hinckley:

> We just now received the printed paper (herewith sent your honor), together with the certain advice (of those who were then present at Boston and in action), that on Thursday last Sir Edmund Andros was seized, and Randolph, Palmer, West, Graham, and divers others of that party. The country coming in that morning—six companies of colors over Charles Ferry, and four over Boston Neck,—the whole town of Boston rise in arms, and this declaration read in the Townhouse gallery. The Governor was sent to, to surrender; who at first denied, but, for fear of storm, after some treaty came out of his fort, with those who were with him, and surrendered themselves; and afterwards the Fort and Castle were surrendered without bloodshed. 'Tis said the Governor is kept prisoner in the Fort, in irons. The rest are in the common jail.

A former Massachusetts deputy governor wrote to Hinckley on the same day that Andros and "West, Graham, Randolph, Sherlock, Palmer, and about fifty more persons obnoxious to the people for joining with them in their violent and arbitary practices are secured, some in the Fort, some in the Castle, and the rest in the common jail. . . . How far these motions may have influence on yourselves, you will best judge. I yet fear what the consequences thereof may be. I heartily pray that no more bitter fruits may spring forth from this root. . . . It will be wisdom to hasten our address to those that are now supreme in England for pardon of so great an irruption, and for a favorable settlement under the sanction of royal authority." [15]

The moment was well chosen. The new king, William III, did not care for rebellion (except his own) any more than any other sovereign would, but it was not his nose which had been rubbed in the dirt, and in fact the colonists claimed they were merely rising against a usurper forced on them by the discredited James. In New York, Jacob Leisler, who had seized the colony in the name of William and Mary, was not so fortunate; making himself governor, Leisler was later defiant to the governor appointed from England, Col. Henry Sloughter, and though he finally surrendered the fort, he was tried for treason and hanged (John Walley wrote Hinckley from Bristol in 1691 that "Leisler, and seven more condemned and sentenced, were executed, or like to be speedily"). Massachusetts shipped Andros to England for trial for his "usurpation," but after being duly tried, Andros was immediately released. A few years later he was sent out again, this time by William III, as governor of Virginia, where he promoted the establishment of William and Mary College. [16]

On 4 June 1689 the General Court proclaimed, "Whereas, through the great changes divine Providence hath ordered out, both in England and in this countrey, we, the loyall subjects of the crown of England, are left in an unseted estate, destitute of goverment, and exposed to the ill consequents thereof; and having heretofore enjoyed a quiet settlement of goverment in this their maties colony of New Plimouth for more than three-score and six years without any interruption; having also been by the late Kings of England from time to time, by their royall letters, graciously owned and acknowledged therein, whereby notwithstanding our late unjust interruption and suspention therefrom by the illeagall arbitrary power of Sr Edmond Andros, now ceased, the Generall Court held here in the name of their present maties, William and Mary, King and Queen of England, etc., together with the encouragement given by their said maties gracious declarations, and in humble confidence of their sd maties good liking, doe, therefore, hereby resume and declare their reassuming of their said former way of goverment, according to such wholsome constitutions, rules, and orders as were here in force in June, 1686, ..." The court also directed the honorable Gov. Thomas Hinckley, Esq., to make address to the King and Queen "for the reestablishment of their former enjoyed liberties and priviledges, both sacred and civil," and also to attempt to recover the colony's seal, which had been taken away. [17]

From the time Andros took over until the court meeting of June 1689, there had been no Plymouth Colony government, and between 15 October 1686 and 4 June 1689 there are no colony court records. Still, life had to continue, and we see this in other records involving those by now second and third generation descendants of the early settlers. In the combined Plymouth County Court of General Sessions and Common Pleas of June 1688 before Judge Nathaniel Thomas and Justices of the Peace Peregrine White, John Cushing, and Ephraim Morton, Joseph Rogers of Duxbury was fined £5 for refusing to be a constable. In Duxbury on 14 May 1688 Samuel Seabury, Edward Southworth, Samuel West, Jonathan Alden, John Soule, and Josiah Howland met to renew the bounds on some land they had acquired by sale or inheritance. In Marshfield, John Besbey and Joanna Brookes were married on 13 September 1687. The heirs of the estate of John

Alden, Esq., lately deceased, were among the earliest to be recorded, on 13 June 1688, in the probate records maintained by the new Plymouth County Court. On 26 December 1686 Thomas Faunce (a man who was born early enough, 1647, to know personally many of the *Mayflower* passengers, and who lived long enough, to 1746, that he could have known George Washington) was ordained a deacon of the Plymouth Church: "The Pastor prayed, & then gave the charge, & then the Elder prayed, and all [t]his was done, whilst the hands of the Eldership were upon him." Judge Sewall noted in his dairy for 13 April 1688 that Elder (John) Chipman visited him and told him that the Indian meeting house at Sandwich had been raised. [18] The people of Plymouth Colony kept busy, even though technically, there was no Plymouth Colony, only three counties that had control over themselves but for small matters, while the important decisions were being made at Boston.

After the fall of Andros, the colony slowly started to put itself together. There was some doubt even as to whether there existed any legality for the General Court to meet. Hinckley assumed he was governor again, and called the court meeting for 4 June, but Barnabas Lothrop refused to accept office, at least in June, though he took his place by October. The "unsetled estate" noted by the court was reflected in the court having to order some towns to elect new selectmen to replace those who "are not accepted," and substantial signs of unrest continued for the remaining life of the colony. [19] King Philip's War had taken its toll, not just in lives and money, but in spirit as well. If such dreadful things could happen, what might occur next? The Andros government occurred next, and showed the colonists, among other things, that old forms of government did not necessarily have to endure. Once Andros was gone, a new specter presented itself: uncertainty.

A new matter was coming to occupy the attention of the court and the people. On 25 December 1689 the court noted:

> Wheras, by our many provocations, we, by the just hand of Him who is the wise Disposer of all things, are fallen into perrillous times by reason of the depredations of the French on this countrey, together with the rebellious insurrections and cruel massacres the barbarous heathen, abetted alsoe by the French, whereby great mischiefe hath already ensued, and much more may be justly feared and expected, — it doth, therefore, much concern us to take some most speedy and effectuall course to defend outselves by putting the millicia into good order, and making such other provision needfull in such imergentcies.

Relations between British New England, New York, and the French in Canada had been deteriorating, and hostilies broke out in 1688. Most of the fighting and the Indian raids took place in the northern border areas, but King Philip's War had shown Plymouth how quickly such danger could spread. When Massachusetts offered Benjamin Church command of a company of Indians, he became the first from Plymouth to assist the Bay State in its new troubles. [20]

By 20 May 1690 the Plymouth Court was ordering that sixty-two men be raised under the command of Maj. John Walley, one of the Assistants, to join with the forces of New York, Massachusetts, and Connecticut to go to Albany or wherever needed against the common enemy. Each of twenty towns or settlements was given a quota to furnish one to six men for this purpose. Further attacks by the enemy resulted in another appeal by Bay Gov. Simon Bradstreet, and Canada became the soldiers' destination. The Plymouth Court decided to raise fifty Indians and 153 English soldiers, which included the earlier quota. The town quotas now ranged from two to sixteen Englishmen. Joseph Silvester and John Gorham were chosen as captains under Major Walley, and Jabez Snow and Samuel Gallop were the lieutenants, with Samuel Lucas and either Preserved Abel or John Butterworth as ensigns. The Plymouth troops participated in the expedition to Quebec in the fall of 1690, under the command of Sir William Phips, but the army could not take Quebec, and the campaign was a disaster, resulting in great financial losses for both Massachusetts and Plymouth. [21]

There were human losses, too. As a pure statistic, twenty-two Plymouth men killed in that war does not seem a large number. But when we associate the number with names and feelings, recognizing so many Plymouth families, we can perhaps understand a little better what this statistic meant to so many people. The following are only those war deaths that can be identified by Plymouth County probate records: Benjamin Wood, also called Atwood, of Middleborough, "being prest upon their maties service. . .if it should so please God that he should not Return againe. . . ."; Moses Simons of Scituate "being bound out a soldier to Canada. . .in case he does not return. . . ."; Samuel Bryant of Scituate; Samuel Dwelly of Scituate; Thomas Hiland, Jr. of Scituate, whose estate included "his wages Due to him on the Canada Expedition"; Arthur Loe of Marshfield; Matthew Stetson "deceased in the Expedition to Canada"; Nathaniel Parker of Scituate, "Prest to go out a Souldier in the Expedition to Canada and Dyed while he was out in said Expedition"; Lazarus Turner of Scituate; Capt. Joseph Silvester was heard to say "that he was going out to warr And had not made any Settlement of my Estate but he said that it is my will that my Son Joseph shall have [certain land] and all the Rest of my Estate I leave and Give to my welbeloved Wife Mary Silvester to be at her Disposing to bring up my Little Children. . ."; John Stetson, whose inventory was presented by Abigail Stetson, "Relict Widdow of Ensign John Stetson late of Scituate"; Robert Finney of Plymouth, "bound for Canada to ffight against the ffrench and not knowing what may Happen to me in the voyage. . ."; William Eaton, "being Cald forth to go against the ffrench I give 1 Cow and Calf to my father and mother"; Joseph Knapp of Plymouth; Zachariah Soule of Duxbury; Mark Lothrop, "being Designed into the Warrs against the ffrench enemy and knowing my life and Breath to be in the hands of God. . ."; Benjamin Washburn, "having some Days since listed himself in order to Goe against the ffrench Enemy and considering the difficulty of the voyage that therein it might please God to take him away either by the sword or other ways. . ."; James Haward of Bridgewater; John Witherell of Scituate, "Being now bound forth to the service of the wars for God and my Countrey leaves to his children. . ."; James Glass, "Being Going into ye warr [declared] that if he the said Glass Did never Return againe home. . ."; and James Snow of Bridgewater, "who dyed in ye Expedition to Canada." [22]

A few months before the abortive expedition, rumors had circulated in Plymouth that the English government was planning to have Plymouth Colony become a part of New York. On 24 June 1690 the General Court noted it had had information that Plymouth had already been joined to New York, but the Reverend Mr. Increase Mather, who was in England as an emissary from Massachusetts, had prevented this undesirable event. "We are also informed that after that we were like to be annexed to Boston, but the same hindered by Mr Wiswall for the present; being also informed there is a possibility that we may obtain a charter for our selves if we speedily address to their maties imploy a suitable person to manage & rayse sufficient moneys to cary the same an end." The Reverend Mr. Ichabod Wiswall of Duxbury was Plymouth's own agent in England, and he was quite determined to preserve Plymouth's independence. But this would have been a task of great magnitude. Even in the wording of the court record of 24 June 1690, there can be seen the pessimism prevalent in the colony: "This Court thinking it their duty to informe the several inhabitants in the severall towns in this colony thereof, that they may not hereafter say they had no notice," gave warning to the towns that they must decide whether "we should sit still & fall into the hands of those that can catch us," but they warned that to do otherwise would require raising at least £700. [23]

The war against the French and Indians was not popular, and as early as 25 December 1689 the court noted that the towns of Bristol, Dartmouth, Swansea, and Eastham "refused or neglected" to pay their taxes for the costs of the war. The towns of Bristol County were especially obstreperous. One of the first orders of the reconvened court in June 1689 was to recommission the officers who had commanded the county regiments and town military companies in 1686, before Andros took power. In the very beginning Marshfield and Swansea objected to their captains, and before long, especially in Bristol County, there was considerable dissension over who would officer the troops. In Taunton feeling was so high that the court on 1 April 1690, "for composing the uncomfortable differences that have been and yet continue there, — in respect to their chief officers," ordered the formation of two companies, each officered by one of the two opposing sides. This was not a satisfactory solution, as was noted by Walter Deane and some of the other leading men at Taunton in a letter to Hinckley of 7 April 1690, in which they stated "that the liberty granted to all to list under whom they pleased, it will make such a division in the town as portends nothing but confusion and ruin"; and, they also noted that "the contempt of authority by one party seems to be too little discountenanced." Major Walley was also unhappy about the Taunton matter, and he wrote to Hinckley that a great many people ere long would be "ready to oppose all that doth not please them . . . . You have given such a precedent as never was in N[ew] E[ngland], and other towns are a-pleadin for the benefit of it; and we shall want, not only two, but ten captains in a town." He commented also on difficulties with military companies in Swansea, Little Compton, Rehoboth, and Dartmouth, noting that in the last town, "by one neglect or other, all orders and warrants come to nothing." [24]

It was not just the military companies. Even the weather seemed to have gone against the colony. On 19 April 1690 Governor Hinckley wrote to Governor Bradstreet, "Our crops generally failing by the sore drought this last year hath reduced us to great straits," and they just narrowly missed having famine conditions. Hinckley wrote to Increase Mather in 1691 that many, "especially in the county of Bristol. . .deny us to have any authority," and he stated it was "feared there would be blood shed, if endeavors should be used to subject them to their duty." In writing to Ichabod Wiswall, Hinckley wrote that Governor Sloughter of New York had written to Joseph Church, an associate magistrate for Bristol County, concerning complaints Sloughter had received from some inhabitants of Dartmouth and Little Compton about having taxes levied on them "without authority." Church relayed Sloughter's words, "if he hears of any more complaints of that nature. . .he will take such methods to ease the subject as 'will otherwise affect you than you are aware of.' " [25] Coming from the man who earlier in the year had hanged Jacob Leisler, this seemed something more than just an idle threat.

Fear of being absorbed by New York became an obsession with many Plymouth men. Increase Mather's son, Cotton Mather, wrote to Hinckley on 26 April 1690, "Governor [Sloughter] of New York had Plymouth put into his commission; but, purely through my father's industry and discretion, he procured the dropping of it." But the threat of New York continually cropped up. It seemed to Hinckley that the possibilities came down to three: absorption by New York, absorption by Massachusetts, or self government under a royal charter. But self government in turn might lead to continuation of the colony's internal unrest, perhaps even anarchy, and that in turn could lead to reconsideration by England, this time with but two choices, absorption by either New York or Massachusetts. Certainly, given but two choices, Hinckley would have preferred being taken over by Massachusetts than New York. He wrote to Increase Mather in 1691 thanking him for his services "in keeping us from New York," and he said, "though it would have been well pleasing to myself and to sundry others of the most thinking men, which are also desirous to support the ministry, and schools of learning, to have been annexed to Boston, yet the greatest part of the people and of our deputies are most desirous to obtain a charter for themselves, if possible to be procured." [26]

Hinckley's reluctance to give strong leadership to the quest for a charter became obvious to others. John Cotton, Plymouth's minister and a nephew of Increase Mather, wrote to Hinckley on 6 February 1690/91 that he hoped he would "stand forth, and play the man." Cotton further said that some men of "wisdom, prudence, and piety. . .with great unanimity" wished Hinckley would think favorably "of taking a voyage to Old England." A personal appearance in England by a determined governor might have obtained the charter. Cotton noted that "a prudent messenger might (if there himself, with such friends as I believe he would there find) suggest such arguments as would either obtain a distinct charter, or, at least, such privileges and immunities in our affixing us to Boston as would render our condition very comfortable." And he concluded by sighing, "Never did poor Plymouth. . .need more help from heaven and earth than at this day." [27]

Plymouth's own agent in London, Rev. Ichabod Wiswall, was also continually trying to prod Hinckley to action. "When some consider the spirit which animated the first planters to venture their all," he wrote to Governor Hinckley on 6 July 1691, "that Plymouth, under its present circumstances, should sit silent so long, (may I not say, sleep secure?) is a great riddle." He continued, "If you desire to return to the late experience of the miseries of an arbitrary commissioned government, a little longer neglect of your opportunity may hasten it." Reference to the silence from Plymouth occurred often in Wiswall's letters. Earlier, on 17 October 1690, he had written Hinckley, "Considering how often your Court hath advised concerning a patent from England, I wonder now that there is so much silence, and want of further motion in that affair." [28]

On 3 March 1690/91 the court ordered Governor Hinckley to express the colony's hearty thanks to the Honorable Sir Henry Ashurst of England and to the Reverend Mr. Increase Mather and Mr. Ichabod Wiswall for their services for the good of the colony. The court gave £25 each to Mather and Wiswall, and fifty guineas (£52/10) to Ashurst, along with a request to the latter to use his influence to procure them a charter from the king, for which purpose they voted another £100. But it was too late. A new charter was already being prepared for Massachusetts, and Wiswall believed that Mather was using his influence to get Plymouth included as part of the Bay Colony. Indeed, Savage credited Mather with being the one who worked on Hinckley to frighten him with the prospect of being joined to New York, convincing Hinckley that Plymouth would be better under Massachusetts. There seemed to be no spirit of unity to hold Plymouth together as a colony, and it can be argued that the inhabitants of such places as far apart as Scituate and Taunton both had more in common interest with Boston than with Plymouth. Wiswall continued writing in vain to seek more action, but the annexation could not be stopped. The new Massachusetts charter, incorporating the three counties formerly making up Plymouth

Colony, was approved in England on 7 October 1691, and in early 1692 the Massachusetts court ordered the Bay Colony's towns, including those of Bristol, Barnstable, and Plymouth Counties, to send representatives to the Massachusetts Assembly. Sir William Phips, a native New Englander, became the new royal governor. [29]

On 4 November 1691, after the fact had been accomplished, Wiswall wrote again from London to Hinckley that Massachusetts, Plymouth, Maine, and some other areas were now "clapped up into one Province, under such restrictions as I believe will not be very acceptable to those inhabitants who must lose their ancient names." Again he reflected on the lack of assertive action from Plymouth: "There is a time to speak, and a time to keep silence. We might have been happy, or, at least not so miserable, had some been able or willing to be taught their proper seasons." [30] But for Plymouth it was over now. Now was the season for silence.

NOTES

1. *Encyc. Brit.* 8:504-07.

2. David Ogg, *England in the Reign of Charles II*, 2nd ed., (Oxford 1956, reprint, 1967), 168, 680-81, 676-77; *PCR* 4:62; *Hubbard*, 665; *Bradford (Ford)* 2:84(fn).

3. Langdon, 190-91; *PCR* 4:62. Langdon, chapter 14, goes into much more detail on Plymouth's attempts to improve its legal status.

4. Langdon, 188, 192-94; *PCR* 6:20. Edward Winslow, in his letters to Massachusetts Gov. John Winthrop, often expressed his feelings against democratic tendencies in both colonies. In 1645, following the abortive Vassall attempt to obtain more civil and religious freedom, Winslow wrote Winthrop, "I utterly abhorred it," and he added that if such a change came about, he would move from Plymouth to Massachusetts, "I trust that we shall finde (I speake for many of us that groane under these things) a resting place amongst you for the soules of our Feet" (*Winthrop Papers*, 56).

5. *PCR* 6:46; *NEHGR* 8:228; *PCR* 6: 55, 58; *Mass. Hist. Col.*, 4th Series, vol. 5 (Boston, 1861), *The Hinckley Papers. . .*, 1676-1699 (hereafter Hinckley), 91-94. Although relations between the colony governments and Quakers had improved over the years, the Quakers still maintained their proselytizing ardor, and Judge Sewall notes at Boston in 1676, "Quaker marcht through the town, crying, 'Repent, etc.,' " (*Sewall's Diary*, 15). What could Randolph be referring to when he writes that his letter only contains hints of things they must discuss? The two most likely things would be payment of money or their desires for features in the charter which they might not want to become public knowledge.

6. Hinckley, 95-97; Ogg, 682-83. John Saffin, the son-in-law of the late Capt. Thomas Willett, and a resident of Boston who owned some land in Bristol, was imprisoned by Plymouth Colony for refusing to pay a tax in Bristol (*PCR* 6:116-17).

7. *PCR* 6:164-69, 185; *Sewall's Diary*, 190.

8. *PCR* 6:36, 50, 77.

9. Church, 67-69; *Bristol Co. LR* 3:455-57; *PCR* 6:88. For a list of settlers of Little Compton, see Robert S. Wakefield, "Little Compton RI Marriages: An Analysis," *TAG* 61:133-40.

10. *PCR* 6:113, 165, 189; Bowen, 83-84.

11. *PCR* 6:189.

12. Evarts B. Greene and Virginia D. Harrington, *American Population Before the Federal Census of 1790* (New York, 1932), xxiii, 21; *PCR* 6:251-52, 221. In the year 1690, because of costs for the campaign against the French and Indians, taxes were high, being 3.75 percent of the rated value (*PCR* 6:254-55).

13. *PCR* 6:92, 115, 193-94; *The Book of the General Law of the Inhabitants of the Jurisdiction of New Plimouth* (Cambridge, 1672); Langdon, 206; *PCR* 6:202, 139, 7:305-07; David Thomas Konig, editor, *Plymouth Court Records 1686-1859* (Wilmington, Del., 1978) (hereafter Konig), 1:3.

14. *PCR* 6:160, 169; *Encyc. Brit.* 14:1029, 1:912-13; Langdon, 213-18.

15. Hinckley, 190-92.

16. *Encyc. Brit.* 13:926-27, 1:913; Hinckley, 285.

17. *PCR* 6:208-09. The "threescore and six years" in the court's proclamation could make it appear that the proclamation had initially been written in the last previous year of the court's meeting, 1686.

18. Konig 1:196; *Copy of the Old Records—Town of Duxbury, Mass.* (Plymouth, 1893), 61-62; *PCR* 8:89; *Ply. Co. PR* 1:16; *Ply. Ch. Recs.* 1:259; Sewall, 210. The identification of what is considered today to be "Plymouth Rock" relies on the accuracy of a story verbally brought down to us concerning Elder Thomas Faunce. When Faunce was ninety-five, he told a group of people he had been present when Mary Chilton came to Plymouth and visited the Rock before she died. She set foot on it and laughed, and said she was the first woman of the *Mayflower* to step upon that rock, and now, at seventy-five, she was stepping on it for the last time.

19. *PCR* 6:204-05, 217, 209.

20. *PCR* 6:223; Langdon, 226-27.

21. *PCR* 6:231-32, 248-51; Langdon, 231-32.

22. The names and extracts from the probate records of Plymouth County were published in the *Genealogical Advertiser*, ed. by Lucy Hall Greenlaw (reprint, Baltimore, 1974), 1:116-20, 2:26, 60-62.

23. *PCR* 6:259.

24. *PCR* 6:226, 210, 237; Hinckley, 235-36, 240-41.

25. Hinckley, 246, 291, 296.

26. Ibid., 248, 287-88.

27. Ibid., 279-80.

28. Ibid., 285, 276.

29. *PCR* 6:260; Savage 4:615-16; Langdon, 240-43. Savage, 3:419-23, collates a good bit of information from various sources on Phips.

30. Hinckley, 299.

PART TWO
Topical Narratives

CHAPTER 8

Political Structure and Government

T he legal basis for Plymouth Colony was a series of patents: the patent of 2 February 1619/20 issued by the Virginia Company to John Peirce, who was acting on behalf of the Adventurers; the patent of 1 June 1621 issued by the Council for New England to John Peirce and his associates; and the patent of 13 January 1629/30 issued by the Council for New England to William Bradford and "his heirs, associates, and assigns," sometimes referred to as the Bradford Patent, or the Warwick Patent, after the Earl of Warwick, one of the grantors. Bradford wrote that John Peirce, "by reason of acquaintance and some aliance with some of their freinds," took out the first patent in his name, "but his name was only used in trust." The 1620 Peirce Patent was lost, so its provisions are not known. It would no longer have had validity anyway after the colonists settled outside the Virginia territory. However, when Peirce saw them successfully settled, he went to the Council of New England and obtained a second patent, "but he meant to keep it to him selfe and alow them what he pleases, to hold of him as tenants, and sue to his courts as cheefe Lord." This very real threat fortunately for the Plymouth colonists did not come about. Peirce was the principal financial backer of the *Paragon,* whose voyages to bring new settlers to New England were aborted at least twice in 1622 and 1623 by tempestuous storms, and Peirce suffered great losses as a result. This appears to be the reason why, as one of the Adventurers wrote to Bradford on 9 April 1623, that at great cost "we have got Mr. John Peirce to assigne over the grand patente to the companie," he charging them £500 for what had cost him £50. [1]

The second Peirce Patent noted that "John Peirce and his associates intend and have undertaken to build Churches, Schooles, Hospitalls Towne howses, and such like workes of Charytie." Upon request to the council (and apparently such request was never made), the patentees would be granted liberty "to make orders Lawes Ordynaunces, and Constitucons" to govern the colony. "And in the meane tyme untill such graunt made, Yt shalbe lawfull for the said John Peirce his Associates Undertakers and Planters their heires and assignes by consent of the greater part of them to establish such Lawes and ordynaunces as are for their better goverment,

and the same by such Officer or Officers as they shall by most voyces elect."
Somewhat retroactively, this wording gave authority to the Mayflower
Compact signed by all males, except the very youngest, which provided
for the colonists to "combine" themselves into a civil political body and to
make laws for the "general good" of the colony. [2]

If the compact was the colonists' guide, it was not very specific. It has
been understood to mean that they intended to set up a democratic form
of government, but even that is not spelled out. It is important to keep in
mind that for the first seven years they were at least in theory under the
control of the Adventurers in England. As a practical matter, though, that
control was most effective in prescribing initial constraints on the colonists.
They could not own land or personal property for seven years. The one
acre of land allotted to each colonist in 1623 was held in trust for the company, and not until 1627 was it confirmed that the possessors could do completely as they pleased with it. [3] There was no need for deeds until 1627.
It is surprising how much of laws in general pertain to regulating the
orderly possession and transfer of land and other property. We do not in
truth know a lot about how the colonists were governed in the early years,
but lack of concern for property probably tended to simplify government.

On first setting out in the two ships, *Mayflower* and *Speedwell*, they
"chose a Gov[ernou]r and 2 or 3 assistants for each shipe, to order the people by the way, and see to the disposing of there provissions, and shuch
like affairs. All which was not only with the liking of the maisters of the
ships, but according to their desires." A footnote by Bradford stated that
Christopher Martin "was governour in the biger ship, and Mr. Cushman
assistante." Bradford described Martin as one of the "Strangers" sent by
the Adventurers, and the Holland group thought it fitting to have the
Strangers appoint someone to work with John Carver and Robert Cushman in receiving money and buying provisions in England, "not so much
for any great need of their help, as to avoyd all susspition, or jelosie of any
partiallities." Bradford does not note who was governor when the
Mayflower continued alone, but the fact that after the compact was signed
he writes "they chose, or rather confirmed, Mr. John Carver. . .their
Governour for that year" might indicate that Carver had replaced Martin
as governor on the *Mayflower*. Of course, we do not know, and it could
be that governor of a ship and governor of the colony were two entirely
different matters. Certainly Bradford's wording makes it appear that Carver
was appointed or confirmed governor before Martin died on 8 January
1620/21. [4]

Shortly after Governor Carver died (not long after 5 April 1621),
William Bradford was "chosen" governor, and, since he had not yet recovered of an illness, Isaac Allerton was chosen to be an Assistant to him.
Edward Winslow, in tesifying in England in 1624 regarding the *Little James*,
said he was a member of the Plymouth Company since its foundation, during which William Bradford and Isaac Allerton had been governors. Carver
is conspicuously missing here, and Allerton appears only this one time on

record as governor; it is possible that, since Bradford was ailing, Allerton had served on occasion as acting governor. Bradford said that he and Allerton continued as governor and Assistant "sundry years togeather, which I hear note once for all." Apparently the governor and the Assistant were all the formal offices needed until 1624, but it is obvious that there was earlier some kind of informal council, for Edward Winslow wrote that in 1622, when there were reports of possible trouble with the Indians, "The Governour, together with his Assistant and Captaine Standish, called together such as were thought most meet for advice in so weightie a business." Bradford wrote for 1624 that "The time of new elections of ther officers for this year being come, and the number of their people increased, and their troubles and occasions therwith, the Govr desired them. . .also to adde more Assistans to the Govr for help and counsell. . . . They now chose 5 [Assistants] giving the Govr a duble voyce." [5]

It is apparent from these records that they had annual elections, and that the governor, having a double vote, would most likely not have had a veto power. Isaac de Rasieres noted that in 1627 "Their government is after the English form. The Governor has his Council, which is chosen every year by the entire community, by election or prolongation of term." But it was not the entire community, for Bradford wrote on 8 September 1623 to the Adventurers, where apparently some criticism had been made, "You are mistaken if you think we admite weoman and children to have to doe in [our governemente], for they are excluded, as both reason and nature teacheth they should be; neither doe we admite any but such as are above the age of 21 years, and they also but only in some weighty maters, when we thinke good; yet we well like of your course, and advice propounded unto us, and will as soon as we can with convenience bring it into practice, though it should be well it were so ordered in our patent." [6] In the ensuing years, the franchise even for adult males became more restricted.

Sometime during the early years the colony's highest governing body began to be called the "court," a term used in corporations at the time to describe the totality of stockholders. Gradually there came to be two courts, the General Court (also called Court of the Freemen after the word "freeman" was in use), and the Court of Assistants, or council, or bench, consisting of the governor and the Assistants. The latter acted as the executive and judicial authority between meetings of the former. The governor and Assistants had the authority to call the General Court at any time, and a special meeting could also be called at the request of a given number of the rank and file court members. Regular meetings of the General Court were originally scheduled quarterly, but in subsequent years a pattern emerged of having three sessions annually, with at first the March session being known as the Election Court, and this later being changed to the June session. [7]

In 1633 the number of Assistants was increased to seven, and this number was never exceeded to the end of the colony, though at times one or more Assistant positions might be vacant. On 5 June 1651 the General Court voted that "Liberty is allowed unto the Gover to make choise of and to depute any one of the Assistants whom hee shall think meet to bee in his rome, when hee is ocasioned to bee absent, as deputie Gover." A law of 1679 made it necessary for a deputy governor to be given an oath as such, and therefore to be chosen separately from the other Assistants, and thus the Assistants became six in number. We do not know the nominating procedure for governor and assistants, but at least for the latter there could be more candidates than positions. In 1638 when Timothy Hatherly was reelected as an Assistant, but refused to serve, "Mr. John Browne, being the next in the number of votes, was by the genall consent elected to the office of an Assistant in his stead" (Mr. Hatherly was liable to a fine for refusing to serve). In 1646 Edward Winslow wrote to Governor Winthrop in the Bay Colony, "Our election is over. Mr. Bradford Governor; the Assistants the same, save only Mr. Thomas insteed of Mr. Freeman, whom I suppose the country left out in regard of his professed Anabaptistry & Separacon from the Churches." Winslow implies that these were unmanipulated elections, which they may well have been; however, it should be noted that in 1645/46 Freeman had just concluded acting as agent for his brother-in-law in England, John Beauchamp, the last of the Adventurers to whom the Undertakers owed money, and whose demands for disputed amounts were most irritating to Bradford, Winslow, and the others of the Undertaker group. [8]

The governor and the Assistants were the colony's magistrates as well. One of the earliest laws on record is of 17 December 1623, which provided that "all Criminall facts, and also all of trespasses and debts betweene man and man" (that is, civil cases) should be decided by "the verdict of twelve Honest men to be Impanelled by Authority in forme of a Jury upon their oaths." A law passed in 1636, but which may have been first enacted earlier, provided that the governor and two Assistants at the least would determine trivial cases of a civil nature between individuals where the amount involved was under forty shillings, "as also in offences of small nature," which probably meant minor criminal cases. Quite possibly the "small nature" did not have to be spelled out, for cases falling within this category could have been well known by custom. Another law passed or reiterated at this time provided that transfers of houses and land had to be acknowledged before the governor or any one of the Assistants and committed to public record. The magistrates also performed marriages, for the Separatists believed marriage was not a sacrament, but a civil function. While Winslow was on a trip to London, the Archbishop of Canterbury, on charges made by Thomas Morton, attacked him on several matters, including the fact that he had performed marriages, and Winslow was committed to prison for about four months. [9]

A 1636 codification of laws provided, in addition to a governor and seven Assistants, for the annual election of a clerk of the court (also at times called the secretary), a coroner, and a constable. One of the Assistants or some other "sufficient" person was chosen as treasurer. The messenger of the court was apparently an appointed position for someone to act as warrant server, jailer, executioner, and custodian of standard weights and measures; in June 1645 the title of this position was changed to marshal. Other appointed positions were grand jurors, trial jurors, highway surveyors, and military officers (though in earlier years we know that Standish was "chosen" by the settlers as captain). A law of 1636, repassed in 1658, provided that the governor could appoint nonfreeman landowners, as well as freemen (who did not have to own land) to juries. These positions were initially for the colony as a whole, but as more towns were formed, the highway surveyors were selected by the towns, and military officers were proposed by the towns and confirmed by the court. The court could also appoint special commissions for various tasks, such as in October 1636 when the General Court appointed William Brewster, Ralph Smith, John Doane, John Jenney, Jonathan Brewster, Christopher Wadsworth, James Cudworth, and Anthony Annable as a special committee to join with the governor and Assistants in reviewing all laws to make recommendations for changes at the next court meeting. [10]

As is apparent from the above events, the political structure of Plymouth Colony was not planned; it just evolved. The main features seem to have been a gradual changing to keep up with the increasing population, and a groping for balance to continue a peaceful coexistence between members and nonmembers of the Plymouth Church. This can especially be seen in Bradford's words of 1627, that "diverse were still mingled amongst them," but to preserve "union and peace," the Separatist-controlled government would "take in all amongst them," that were of ability, not servants, and able to act with discretion. However, within a few years after 1627, there would be some changes, and in subsequent decades the laws governing the franchise and freedom in general became more strict. The laws of 1636 were a restructuring to keep some old laws found to be worthy, to reject other old laws, and to enact new laws considered necessary. One of these laws, probably a reiteration of an old one, provided that "the lawes & ordnances of the Colony & for the Governmt of the same be made only by the ffremen of the Corporacion & no other." It was also provided that "at the day & time appointed a Govr & seaven Assistants be chosen to rule & governe the said plantacons wthin the said limits for one whole yeare & no more. And this eleccon to be made onely by the freemen according to the former custome." There is a change here from the Mayflower Compact, which was signed by all free adult males, as well as others, and all free adult males in Plymouth in 1636 were not freemen. [11]

The concept of freeman went back centuries in England to describe one who was not a serf, but who enjoyed the freedom of a town. The term later became expanded and was applied to a shareholder in a corporation. Morison points out that the charter of the Massachusetts Bay Corporation called for a governor, deputy governor, and eighteen Assistants to be elected annually, "and the freemen, in General Court, had the supreme legislative power." Though this could sound quite democratic, Morison also points out that of the hundreds of people who crossed the Atlantic in the Winthrop Fleet, the only ones who were freemen were the governor, deputy governor, and some of the eighteen Assistants. In October 1630 more than one hundred of the Massachusetts colonists demanded the right to vote, and in May 1631 they and a few others were made freemen, but it was also ruled that henceforth only church members could be freemen, which restricted the future proportion of freeman to nonfreeman considerably. Thus, in view of the large number of colonists coming to the Bay, the institution of the freeman concept was a restriction of the vote. [12]

Bradford in his History does not give us any idea as to when the institution of freemen occurred in Plymouth. The word is not mentioned in the few early records we have. The earliest list of freemen is one of 1633, and there are sixty-eight names on that list, with others added apparently afterwards in the order they were admitted. Four of the sixty-eight men are shown in another record to have been admitted as freemen 1 January 1632/33, thus implying that the others were admitted earlier. There are missing from the list such names as Thomas Blossom and Richard Masterson, who indeed could have been expected to be admitted as freeman, except that they died before October 1633. On the other hand, the list has names of others, such as John Adams, Peter Browne, Francis Eaton, Samuel Fuller, Godbert Godbertson, and William Wright, who died in an epidemic in October, possibly some in November, 1633. Thus this list was made between 1 January 1632/33 and October 1633, and the institution of freemen in Plymouth most likely began in 1632. [13]

We might have expected to see as freemen all the surviving adult male *Mayflower* passengers as well as those adult males from the 1627 Division of the Cattle list, and for the most part we do. There are a few exceptions, though. Some of the children on the earlier two lists were likely over twenty-one years of age by 1633, but the minimum age might have been older than that. Henry Sampson seems to fit into this category, for he was admitted as a freeman not long after. Francis Billington, son of John Billington who was hanged for murder, is not on the list; he never became a freeman. *Mayflower* passenger William Latham is not on the list, and he never became a freeman (he had not been one of the Purchasers either, though probably he was still a servant in 1626). Among Purchasers who were in the 1627 division, we find Edward Bumpas, Edward Holman, Moses Simonson, and Francis Sprague. Sprague and Simonson were freemen by 1637, but the absence of Edward Bumpas and Edward Holman is a bit surprising. Holman, the records show, was a ne'er do well, but, still, he had been a Purchaser. There were, then, restrictions on who could be a freeman in 1632/33. [14]

In fact, the freeman concept appears to have been adopted only after the Plymouth leaders had seen how it could be used restrictively in the Bay Colony. Was it then a device adopted from the Bay to limit the franchise? This is a legitimate question, for it appears that all free adult males had a voice in the government in the beginning years, but that by 1632 the franchise had become limited to freemen. Though there was no church membership requirement to be a freeman, as in the Bay Colony, nor any early property qualification, not everyone coming into Plymouth could expect to become a freeman, for one had to be elected to this privilege by the General Court. By the early 1630s, there were free (nonservant) adult male residents in Plymouth Colony who did not have the right to vote (for example, Webb Adey, Francis Billington; and Edward Holman), yet we see no records anywhere to show them losing the vote. It was just that they were not freemen and from 1632 onward only freemen could vote. The trend seemed to be in the early years toward a small reduction in the number of people enjoying the franchise, probably eliminating only the most obvious rebels or ne'er-do-wells as voters. But apparently with hindsight, the colony leaders realized that the reduction had not gone as far as they really wanted, and they wished they could have been more restrictive. In 1646, writing to Bay Governor Winthrop, Edward Winslow seemed to deplore the fact that important Plymouth Colony decisions could be made only after much deliberation by a large number of people, "We are so many (since we followed your example in one particular, which we too late repent,) to consult, as tis very hard for any to say what will be done tho' he should know what is most wholsome for us." Though nowhere is the particular Bay Colony "example" specified, from the context it most likely was the institution of the freeman concept. Unlike the Bay, Plymouth was constrained both by the fact that church and nonchurch residents were somewhat equal in numbers and by the precedents set in the past, giving the franchise to a much higher percentage of its people. These differences undoubtedly influenced Plymouth's character. [15]

Thus, the general policy of admission to freeman rank, at least in the beginning, was on the whole quite liberal, and most of the male Old Comers achieved freeman status. The Leiden group and the non-Leiden group seemed roughly evenly matched. Bradford dominated the government, but under him the majority of the leadership seemed to consist of non-Leiden men, as can be seen in 1633 (the first year for which we have records showing all seven Assistants), when Edward Winslow was governor, and the Assistants were William Bradford, Myles Standish, John Howland, John Alden, John Doane, Stephen Hopkins, and William Gilson. Of these, only Winslow and Bradford had definitely been of the Leiden group (Standish had spent time in Leiden, but he never became a member of the Separatist Church). John Doane, who became a deacon in the Plymouth Church, was probably a Separatist, for church membership and Separationism went hand in hand. Many of the non-Leiden group (Alden and Howland for instance) very early became pillars of the Plymouth community. Hopkins, frequently an Assistant, was known to be independent minded and would not have been considered a Separationist. We see a balance here, and our view of this balance is strengthened by our knowledge that Standish voted against Bradford, Prince, and

Winslow in the 1645 Vassall dispute, and also by later Quaker charges that Alden had betrayed his past moderate reputation. Too, the inclusion of such people as James Cudworth, Timothy Hatherly, John Browne, and Edmond Freeman in the government at various times shows why Plymouth Colony had more moderate policies than the Bay. These policies never reached the live-and-let-live policies of Rhode Island, and, as stated before, the Plymouth Church was probably as conservative as the Bay churches, but there existed a balance of political power from the very early years in Plymouth that determined its course of forced moderation.

The fact that the great majority of heads of families enjoyed the franchise made the institution of deputies in Plymouth different from the system of deputies in Massachusetts. The government of the Bay Colony had deputies forced on it as the towns demanded more representation. Morison shows that at the first meeting of the Massachusetts General Court, "consisting of exactly six Assistants besides the two chief magistrates, it was decided that the Governor and Deputy-Governor be elected out of the Assistants, by the Assistants. In other words, the first Board of Assistants, not one half of the legal number, arrogated to themselves complete legislative, executive, and judicial power. And for the first four years of the settlement they exercised it." Many of the Bay settlers demanded the franchise, and more than one hundred were made freemen in 1630, but after that the franchise became restricted to members of the church. Even then, initially, the only function of the freemen was to vote in the annual elections for the Assistants, and, in 1632, for the governor and deputy governor also. By 1634 the freemen in the towns were demanding more representation, and they chose deputies for this purpose. The deputies examined the charter and found that the General Court, consisting of all the freemen, had the supreme power. Thereafter the deputies, sitting as representives of the whole body of freemen, joined with the Assistants to make laws, admit new freemen, raise money and taxes, and dispose of land. [16]

There was no need for this type of thing in Plymouth, where the General Court already consisted of all the freemen and already decided the important matters. On 5 March 1638/39 the General Court ruled:

> Whereas complaint was made that the ffreemen were put to many inconveniencies and great expenses by their continuall attendance at the Courts It is there fore enacted by the Court for the ease of the sevall [settlements] and Townes within the Govment That every Towne shall make choyce of two of their ffreemen and the Towne of Plymouth of foure to be Committees or Deputies to joyne wth the Bench to enact and make all such lawes and ordinances as shalbe judged to be good and wholesome for the whole Provided that the lawes they doe enact shall be propounded one Court to be considered upon untill the next Court, and then to be confirmed.

The inconvenience having been transferred from all the freemen to just the deputies, by 20 October 1646 the court ruled that all the freemen would be required to attend the annual June Election Court, following which only the deputies need stay for the remaining sessions of that court, and that the other two annual courts would be only for judicial matters, with only the magistrates needing to attend. The court also ruled that any township not electing deputies would be fined forty shillings, and any elected deputy not appearing at court on the required days would be fined twenty shillings. The court made it quite clear that the deputies of the towns "must arise out of their freemen," although it allowed all adult male residents, who were not servants or otherwise disqualified, to vote in the election of the deputies. [17]

Though there was considerable democracy in Plymouth, the governor and the Assistants had substantial authority and influence, and they apparently could delay matters from coming to a vote, stalling for time to persuade more of the deputies to agree with them. But legally the freemen had the power, and if enough of them wanted to exercise it they could frustrate the designs of the governor and Assistants. Bradford seems to have used his ultimate power of persuasion when right after his virtually routine reelection as governor in June 1655, he presented the court with a list of "particulares" showing why he would not accept the position for the full year, "unlesse som speedy course bee taken for the redresse of the same." Much of his complaint had to do with the deputies not giving satisfaction in such matters as mandatory maintenance of ministers and "suppression of error" (error meaning heretical ideas). His threat of leaving the government seemed to have had some effect, and Bradford continued as governor for the full year. [18]

Of course, this example is extreme in that it was meant to stir the deputies to a positive course of action. Bradford and the Assistants did not have the power, especially in matters concerned with raising money, to override the lethargy of the deputies. But in matters where he and the Assistants could take the initiative, and where it would require a positive act by the deputies to defeat the government, the governor and Assistants obviously had substantial power. However, in Plymouth there was a strong counterbalance to arbitrary government in that institution known as the Grand Inquest or Grand Jury. It first appears in Plymouth records in 1636 when a law provided that a "great Quest" be appointed by the governor and Assistants for "enquiring into the abuses & breaches of such wholsome lawes & ordnances as tend to the preservacon of the peace & the good of the subject." That responsibility was further defined to have the "grand Enquest" inquire into all wrong actions of any person or persons tending to hurt "society Civility peace & neighborhoods," and to present such disturbers to the court for punishment. Though there probably was some forewarning of so drastic an action, Bradford and the Assistants must have been somewhat astonished when on 5 March 1638/39 the Grand Inquest delivered to the court the following radical inquiries:

1. Wee desire to be informed by what vertue and power the Govr and Assistants doe give and dispose of lands either to pticuler psons or towneshipps and plantacons.

2. Wee further desire to be informed what lands are to be had, or is reserved for the purchasers as hath beene form[er]ly agreed in Court too.

3. Wee further desire to be informed of the undertakers of the trade what wilbe allowed to the colony for the use of the said trade during the years past.

4. Wee further desire to be informed why there is not a Treasurer chosen for this yeare, as other officers, seing by an order in Court there should be yearely one chosen, to take up the fynes and moneys wthin the whole colony. [19]

The names of the Grand Inquest members are given from time to time, and it would appear that there was considerable change in the composition of the membership. The twenty-two members for the year in which the above contretemps occurred included Jonathan Brewster, son of the elder; Kenelm Winslow, Edward's brother; William Paddy, who had been treasurer (and perhaps was responsible for the fourth inquiry); Henry Howland, whose brother John was an Assistant; Thomas Cushman, who would succeed Brewster as ruling elder of the church; and several others who were Old Comers. It did not appear to be a group made up of rebels, but most likely they were asking questions that a good majority of the freemen wanted to have asked, but perhaps feared to ask as individuals. In this sense, the Grand Inquest, or Jury, added considerably to the cause of moderation at Plymouth. In another sense, though, it also contributed to orthodoxy, for over the years the Grand Jury presented numerous people to the court to be tried not only for criminal offenses, but also for deviations from the standards of the community, such as going out to sea on a Sunday, for smoking tobacco contrary to order, for living alone disorderly, for not grinding corn well enough, or for swearing. In good part also, the Grand Jury functioned as the community gadfly, taking towns to task for not mending roads or maintaining an animal pound, prodding the government to provide just and equal weights and measures, or asking to know by what power the court prohibited inhabitants from seining for bass at Cape Cod. [20]

The growth of towns made another innovation necessary by 1665. Towns were ordered to chose three to five selectmen from the freemen, their choices to be approved by the General Court, and these selectmen would hear small legal disputes between individuals, where the amounts involved did not exceed forty shillings; settle small disputes between the colonists and Indians, such as disputes about livestock damaging Indian crops; issue summons and give oaths; see that newcomers to a town properly applied to the court for permission to live there; require everyone to attend church meeting; and see that all single people lived with some well-governed family. Where the parties to a civil suit tried by the selectmen lived in different towns, the complainant could pick which town's selectmen would hear the case. Appeals could be made from a select court to the General Court, or, after their formation, to county courts. [21]

At no time could the government be separated from the personalities of the governors. Certainly in the beginning, and possibly in the end, the same political structure under a different governor could have led to a different history of the colony. Governor William Bradford dominated the government of Plymouth Colony from the beginning until his death in 1657. He was chosen governor every election between 1621 and 1657 except 1633, 1634, 1636, 1638, and 1644, and when he was not governor, he was an elected Assistant. Edward Winslow was elected governor in 1633, 1636, and 1644, and Thomas Prence was elected in 1634 and 1638. There is no hint in the records of any effective political opposition to Bradford in 1633 and 1634, nor any hint of rivalry between Bradford and Winslow or Prence. Nor is there any reason to believe that Bradford wanted to get away from public affairs. From his own writings it can be clearly seen that he was in the beginning obsessed with setting up an idealized church-state at Plymouth, and when it became necessary to compromise with that objective, he still continued his deep commitment to keeping the colony, as it had evolved, a viable state. In other words, at no time was Bradford anything other than totally and deeply concerned with Plymouth affairs. Consequently, we must assume empirically that the elections of Winslow in 1633 and Prence in 1634 were events that Bradford desired, and probably even orchestrated. In his early forties, Bradford still had many useful years left, but he must also have realized, as happens to many leaders, that he could not go on forever, and he must have given some consideration to a successor. Winslow and Prence were his proteges, and Prence eventually won the successorship, while Winslow returned to England and a different life in the service of the Puritan Commonwealth there. From the time of his election as governor in 1633 until his death in 1673, Prence was continuously either governor or an Assistant, with an unprecedented streak of sixteen years as governor from 1657 to 1673.

Thomas Prence, a young man of about twenty-one when he arrived at Plymouth in 1621, must have had some excellent qualifications for his advancement. He obviously had some form of good education, and he had to be a man worthy of respect. His first wife, Patience, was a daughter of Elder Brewster, and in 1627, while not yet thirty, he became one of the eight Plymouth members of the inner group called the Undertakers. No successor is ever a precise copy of his predecessor, and although Prence was completely orthodox in the Bradford sense, he did not share Bradford's views on the necessity of living in the town of Plymouth, being one of the first of those who moved to Duxbury. After Prence was elected governor for 1638, he refused to move back to Plymouth from Duxbury, even though there was a law requiring the government to be in Plymouth and the governor to reside there. However, he indicated willingness "(at the request of the Court) to condiscend thereunto," provided that Bradford would continue as governor until Prence could find a fit place, and that in case he could not find a place without detriment to himself, the court would waive the requirement and let him continue to reside at Duxbury. He was known for his strictness, and his attitude against the Quakers was particularly stringent. Nathaniel Morton referred to him as a "terror to evil-doers." Prence governed with a strong hand and in his years as governor starting in 1657 he presided over the court while it tightened considerably the requirements for becoming a freeman. But the fact that he was elected governor continuously after the death of Bradford shows that he had very real political support in the colony, and that he was taking the colony where it wanted to go.

Josiah Winslow, the fifth governor, and Thomas Hinckley, the sixth and last governor, seemed to be not as strong as their predecessors. It was as if the colony – and its leaders – were growing tired with the increasing years. Both Winslow and Hinckley were born and raised in the colony, and perhaps were more conditioned to follow the mood of the colony than to innovate. Winslow was a military man, and his time in office, 1673 to 1680, was when a military man was most needed. Both Winslow and Hinckley seemed to acquiesce to the circumstances which were leading Plymouth to its destiny. Plymouth probably could not have maintained its separate identity. Its division into counties some years before it was absorbed into the Bay shows that its parts were already disparate. Plymouth town was not even the largest town in the colony, and there was nothing in the colony to act as the magnet that Boston was in keeping the parts of the Bay Colony together. If Plymouth was fated to become a part of the Bay, Hinckley seemed almost providentially the man for the job.

NOTES

1. *Bradford (Ford)* 1:305-08. On 20 April 1622 John Peirce obtained still another patent from the council from New England, but on complaint by the Adventurers, the council reconfirmed the second patent (of 1 June 1621) "as if the [new one] had never bin." For additional information on the *Paragon*, see Robert S. Wakefield, "The Paragon," *MQ* 43:109.

2. *Bradford (Ford)* 1:246-51 gives the verbatim second patent, together with a photocopy of it. It is given in this book as appendix A, and the Mayflower Compact is given as appendix D. The second Peirce Patent, dated 1 June 1621, is phrased to meet the new circumstances of the pioneering group; that is, it was granted for a settlement in New England, and the Mayflower Compact seems to be precisely justified by the appropriate wording. The *Mayflower* departed Plymouth on 5 April 1621, and, according to Capt. John Smith (*Bradford [Ford]* 1:214[fn]) arrived in England on 6 May, and thus there was opportunity for the Adventurers to gather and digest the news and to prepare for a new patent.

3. *PCR* 12:13: "That the first devision of the Acers should stand, and continue firme, according to the former devision made unto the possessers ther of, & to their heirs for ever."

4. *Bradford (Ford)* 1:135-36, 142 and fn, 192 and fn. Martin was responsible for spending all or most of £700 in Southampton, but "saith he neither can nor will give any accounte of it, and if he be called upon for accounts he crieth out of unthankfullnes for his paines and care, that we are susspitious of him, and flings away, and will end nothing." Martin's early death probably saved the Separatists much squabbling and difficulty.

5. *Bradford (Ford)* 1:216; Coldham, *English Adventurers*, 16; *Bradford (Ford)* 2:350; Winslow, *MD* 25:161.

6. *Three Visitors*, 73; *Bradford (Ford)* 1:350(fn).

7. *PCR* 11:39, 79. *PCR* 11:39 shows that the General Court sessions started at 9:00 in the morning and ended at 4:00 in the afternoon. The Court of Assistants met on the first Tuesday of each month except when there was a General Court session (*PCR* 11:37), and this was later changed to the first Tuesday of August, December, February, and May (*PCR* 11:79).

8. Hubbard, 91; *PCR* 2:169, 11:249; 1:86; *MHS Collections*, 4th Series, 6 (1863):178. In 1665 a proposition was referred to the towns for consideration that there be but five magistrates (Assistants) chosen annually, but this failed to become law, and seven Assistants continued to be chosen (*PCR* 4:102).

9. *PCR* 11:4, 12; *Bradford (Ford)* 2:202-03.

10. *PCR* 11:6-12.

11. *Bradford (Ford)* 2:8; *PCR* 11:7, 11.

12. Morison, *Builders*, 84.

13. *PCR* 1:3-5; *Bradford (Ford)* 2:171; *MD* 1:24-28, 79, 154, 157, 197-98, 200.

14. *PCR* 1:3-4, 2:177.

15. *MHS Collections*, 4th Ser., 6 (1863):182-83.

16. Morison, *Builders*, 84-86, 89.

17. *PCR* 11:31, 54.

18. Ibid., 3:80.

19. Ibid., 11:11, 18, 1:119.

20. Ibid., 1:87, 3:47, 1:118, 3:96, 82, 10.

21. Ibid., 11:143, 217-18, 223, 6:92, 115.

CHAPTER 9

Law and Order

Plymouth Colony was a land of law, though not necessarily of lawyers. Perhaps it was just an extension of the Englishman's respect for and faith in the law that we see in New Plymouth, but even detractors of the colony must admit that the colonists' concern for the law was not just lip service. We do not see here the law applied hypocritically according to rank. We do not see here the coups and unpunished rebellions that existed in other colonial lands – the murder of Viceroy Francisco Pizarro in Lima, Peru, is a case in point. Nor do we see here the presumption of Roman law that the authorities would not charge individuals with crimes if they were not probably guilty in the first place, for there was an abundance of acquittals in the Plymouth Court.

No one was above the law. That does not mean that we see Governors Bradford and Winslow, or Elder Brewster being punished, but we would not expect to, for they set themselves as examples And, though the laws represented more of a compromise than they would have liked, they were not going to ride roughshod over them. If there is need for an exception to test the rule, it was in 1645 when Bradford defeated the Vassall proposal even though most of the deputies were for it. Winslow described it to Winthrop: "but our Governour and divers of us having expressed the sad consequences would follow, especially my selfe and mr. Prence, yet notwithstanding it was required according to order to be voted: But the Governour would not suffer it to come to vote as being that indeed would eate out the power of Godlines etc." But had enough of the freemen been unswervingly in favor of the religous freedom proposal, they could have passed it at the next election (that is, full) Court. Even in reporting the incident to Winthrop, Winslow did not know but what the proposal would eventually pass, and it was on this occasion that he hoped, if the proposal did pass, "we shall finde. . .a resting place amongst you for the soules of our Feet." [1]

Certainly Bradford and his lieutenants were going to use all the persuasion they could exert to get their way, and they would thrust their views forward with the utmost vigor. But Bradford knew that "though they had some untowarde persons mixed amongst them from the first," they would give them fair participation in the colony's government and economy, for "they saw not how peace could be preserved without so doing, but danger and great disturbance might grow to their great hurte and prejudice other wise." Winslow answered Vassall's subsequent criticism of the colony:

> As for our trialls between man and man, hee knowed wee goe by jury there [in Plymouth] as well as here [in England]: And in criminalls and capitalls wee goe by grand jury and petty jury. And where the death of any is suddaine, violent, or uncertaine, the crowner sits upon it by a quest, and returneth a verdict, etc. and all according to the commendable custome of England, whom wee desire to follow. But their maine objection is, that wee have not penall lawes exactly set downe in all cases? 'Tis true I confesse, neither can they finde any Commonwealth under heaven, or ever was, but some things were reserved to the discretion of judges, and so it is with us and no otherwise, our Generall Courts meeting together twice a yeere at least hitherto for that very end, and so continuing so long as their occasions and the season will permit: and in case any misdemeaner befall where no penaltie is set down, it is by solemne order left to the discretion of the bench, who next to the word of God take the law of England for their president before all other whatsoever. . . . And yet I dare affirme that Virginia, Barbadoes, Christophers, Nevis, and Antiego have not all of them so many lawes as New-England, nor so many expresse penalties annexed. [2]

That no one was above the law can be seen in the 1636 conviction of Stephen Hopkins, who was at the time an Assistant and magistrate himself, but still was fined £5 for battery against John Tisdale, the court observing that Hopkins should have especially been one to observe the king's peace. On 7 March 1636/37 the court awarded Francis Cooke, a *Mayflower* passenger who was never high in government position, £3 damages in a civil case against Mr. John Browne, who had just been an Assistant and magistrate the previous year, and would be so again. When Browne did not pay fast enough, on 7 June 1637 the court reaffirmed its verdict and ordered him to pay. On 2 October 1637 William Gilson, who had been an Assistant and magistrate in 1633, was fined twenty shillings for not appearing to serve on the grand jury (the fine was later remitted). On 3 June 1640 Mr. James Cudworth was presented by the grand jury for selling wine contrary to order. On 1 March 1641/42 Mr. Edmond Freeman, leading resident of Sandwich, was presented by the grand jury for lending a gun to an Indian. On 1 December 1640 Kenelm Winslow, brother to Edward Winslow who had already been governor twice, was fined ten shillings for neglecting his position as surveyor of the highways. In 1645, the year after his brother had served his third term as governor, Kenelm Winslow complained to the court that he could not get justice in his suit against John Maynard, and a committee appointed by the court, consisting of Myles

Standish, William Paddy, Edmond Eddenden, Edward Case, Anthony Annable, Anthony Thacher, and Thomas Tupper, determined that "the sayde charge of injustice is altogether untrue." On 3 March 1645/46, Roger Chandler successfully sued Kenelm Winslow in court, and Winslow was ordered to return to Chandler's daughter (who apparently had been his maid) her clothes which he had retained. On the same day Winslow was committed to prison for uttering opprobrious words against the church at Marshfield, saying they were all liars. [3]

It has already been related how the grand jury in 1638/39 dared to ask by what authority the governor and Assistants held the power to dispose of lands. In most countries of this time such effrontery could have led to serious punishment, but in Plymouth it led to the surrender by the governor and Assistants of their power to make land grants. In some cases in Plymouth it can be deduced that Bradford and other high officials were not above the law by what did not happen rather than what did. In October 1636 Bradford went to court to charge four men with trespass; that he won his case is not so important as the fact that he had to go to the court in the first place, for he was not powerful enough on his own to get his way. In 1647 Thomas Prence won a case of trespass against Edward Holman and Nicholas Hodges, and in 1650 Prence won a case of slander with the defendant, Strong Furnill, making a public apology, but Prence was obviously not powerful enough by himself to get such an apology—he had to rely on the law to do it. [4]

Winslow once stated, "I have been so farre from sleighting the law of England as I have brought my owne booke of the statutes of England into our court, that so when wee have wanted a law or ordinance wee might see what the statutes provided in that kind, and found a great willingness in our generall court to take all helpe and benefit thereby. And never did I otherwise oppose the law of England: nor ever stand against the liberties of the subject, but am ready to sacrifice my life for the same." One scholar has suggested that the Plymouth settlers used the *Eirenarcha: or of the Office of the Justices of the Peace,* by Elizabethan jurist William Lambarde, and a copy of that book was apparently handed down for some time by justices of the peace in later Plymouth County. The provenance of the book is such (it once belonged to William Cecil) that D. C. Parnes feels it must have been given by Cecil to Brewster. However, Winslow's statement that he brought his "owne book of the statutes of England" could give support to the *Eirenarcha* theory, but not to its introduction in Plymouth by Brewster. [5] In any event, there are more than sufficient differences between the *Eirenarcha* and the record of dispositions of cases in the Plymouth Court to show that it would have served as no more than a guide at best, just as Winslow's words suggest that his book served as no more than background information.

There were certainly major differences between English law and Plymouth law, not the least of which was that justice in Plymouth was not dependent on finding an appropriate ready-made writ, though some of the more common classifications of crimes and torts established in England by writs appear in court records, such as trespass and trespass on the case. The evidence seems to indicate that the colony leaders were determined from the beginning to use that part of English law which was convenient to them, and change English legal concepts when they were inconvenient; hence, the abolition of primogeniture, the recording of deeds, and the adoption of the Dutch custom of civil marriage. As can be seen in the Granger bestiality case (discussed in chapter 12), the court could refer to ministers for an interpretation of the Bible on how to prosecute a given crime. It was the Granger case which specifically "occasioned these questions" which were answered by ministers John Reyner, Ralph Partridge, and Charles Chauncey. The questions were:

1. What sodomitical acts are to be punished with death, and what very fact (ipso facto) is worthy of death; or, if the fact itself be not capital, what circumstances concurring may make it capital?

2. How far a magistrate may extract a confession from a delinquent to accuse himself of a capital crime, seeing [that "no man is required to incriminate himself"]?

3. In what cases of capital crimes one witness with other circumstances shall be sufficient to convince? Or is there no conviction without two witness? [6]

The Granger case bothered them, as well it might, for it is an undeniable blot on Plymouth's reputation for living according to laws. The Plymouth magistrates were well aware that one year earlier, in 1641, in the Bay Colony, two daughters of John Humfry, an Assistant who had gone to England, were raped by a former servant and a hired hand, and both men were punished with no more than a fine and a whipping since it was not a capital offense under Massachusetts law. Not only would Granger's crime seem to be a lesser offense, but his conviction would seem to be highly irregular under Plymouth's own laws. He was convicted on testimony "by one that accidentally saw his lewd practices towards the mare. . . ." plus "his free confession. . .though at first he strived to deny it." It was well understood, though it did not become a part of Plymouth's written law until later, that no one should be condemned "without a second witness or concurring circumstances." Nor could one be required to indict himself. Two of the questioned ministers, Reyner and Partridge, agreed that a magistrate was obliged, when he knew of a crime and had reason to believe he knew who the criminal was, not to "neglect diligent inquisition" or "by force of argument to draw [the suspect] to an acknowledgment of the truth," but he could not extract a confession by any violent means. However, Mr. Chauncey conceived "that in matters of highest consequence, such as do concern the safety or ruin of states or countries, magistrates may proceed so far to bodily torments, as racks, hot irons, etc. to extract a confession, especially where presumptions are strong." We do not know whether torture was used on Granger, but the fact that Bradford said he denied the offense at first, but then confessed, plus the very need to question ministers on the legality of torture, show that it might have been considered. Given the confession, whether freely made or not, Granger's life depended on the answer to the third question, the need for a second witness. Reyner believed that a man who made an "unforced confession" would be his own second necessary witness. Partridge's answer seems to disagree, for he felt that conviction on the testimony of one witness was not "safe," and he seemed to imply that he could not accept a man's confession as adequate substitute for the second witness. Chauncey gave a strong argument that a man could not be convicted on the strength of only one witness, but he fully accepted that "if a man witness against himself, his own testimony is sufficient." [7]

Unlike the Bay Colony, Plymouth had a written law defining rape as a capital crime, as were also treason or rebellion; wilful murder; "solemn Compaction or conversing with the devil by way of witchcraft"; wilful burning of ships or houses; sodomy, rapes, or buggery; and, at first, but later changed, adultery. [8] It is to Plymouth's credit that it never executed or otherwise punished any person for witchcraft, unlike the Bay Colony and Connecticut. In fact, when in 1661 Dinah Silvester accused the wife of William Holmes of being a witch, it was the accuser who was sentenced by the court to be whipped, be fined, or make a public apology. On 6 March 1676/77 it was charged that Mary Ingham, wife of Thomas of Scituate, "by the healp of the divill, in a way of witchcraft or sorcery, malliciously procured much hurt, mischeiffe, and paine unto the body of Mehittable Woodworth, the daughter of Walter Woodworth, of Scituate aforsaid, and some others, and particularly causing her, the said Mehittable, to fall into violent fitts, and causing great paine into severall partes of her body att severall times, soe as shee, the said Mehittable Woodworth hath bin almost bereaved of her sences, and hath greatly languished, to her much suffering thereby, and the procuring of great greiffe, sorrow, and charge to her parents." Mary asked, as was her right, for trial by jury, and the jury found her not guilty, "and soe the said prisoner was cleared as abovesaid." [9] Capital punishment was never used in Plymouth Colony for arson or, after the death of Granger, for sex crimes. No Englishman was ever executed in Plymouth Colony for treason or rebellion, and, until King Philip's War, the same was true of Indians. Willful murder was the charge responsible for all executions other than those of Granger and cases related to the war.

John Billington was hanged for the murder of John Newcomen in 1630. Arthur Peach, Thomas Jackson, and Richard Stinnings were hanged for the murder of an Indian in 1638, and Daniel Cross would have been had he not escaped. The execution of three Indians in 1675 for the murder of another Indian was the *casus belli* of the King Philip tragedy. In 1690 a Frenchman, Deleforest, was hanged for murdering a fellow Frenchman. The details of these cases are given in Part I. Otherwise there was but one execution in the colony. In July 1648 a coroner's jury reported that "coming into the house of the said Richard Bishope, wee saw at the foot of a ladder which leadeth into an upper chamber, much blood; and going up all of us into the chamber, wee found a woman child, of about foure yeares of age, lying in her shifte uppon her left cheeke, with her throat cut with divers gashes crose wayes, the wind pipe cut and stuke into the throat downward, and a bloody knife lying by the side of the child, with which knife all of us judge, and the said Allis hath confessed to five of us att one time, that shee murdered the child with the said knife." Rachel Ramsden testified that when she went to Richard Bishop's house on an errand, "the wife of the said Richard Bishope requested her to goe fetch her some butter-milke at Goodwife Winslows, and gave her a ketle for that purpose, and shee went and did it; and before shee went, shee saw the child lyinge abed asleepe. . ., but when shee came shee found [Alice Bishop] sad and dump-ish; shee asked her what blood was that shee saw at the ladders foot; shee pointed unto the chamber, and bid her looke, but shee perseived shee had killed her child, and being afraid, shee refused, and ran and tould her father and mother. Moreover, shee saith the reason that moved her to thinke shee had killed her child was that when shee saw the blood shee looked on the bedd, and the child was not there." The child was Alice (Martin) (Clarke) Bishop's daughter, Martha Clarke, by Alice's first hus-band, George Clarke. On 1 August 1648 Alice Bishop confessed she had murdered her daughter and said she was sorry for it. And on 4 October 1648 she was sentenced to be hanged, "which accordingly was executed." [10]

Though not a written law, there was apparently an underlying con-cept that cruelty of a grown child against a parent could be a capital crime, too. Although only one case is in the records to support specifically this assumption, the principle is stated unequivocally. On 4 July 1679 Edward Bumpas was charged with striking and abusing his parents, and he was sentenced to be whipped at the post, the court noting that it had been leni-ent, "in regard hee was crasey brained, otherwise hee had bine put to death or otherwise sharply punished." [11]

Though Plymouth was not a land of university-trained lawyers—the only university graduates during the early decades were ministers—Plymouth law allowed for a party at law to be represented in court by someone else, presumably someone more knowledgeable and/or more articulate. As an example, on 7 November 1643 when John Hearker sued Josias Checkett for a house and land in Scituate, Jonathan Brewster acted as attorney for Hearker and Samuel Fuller acted as attorney for Checkett. On 7 June 1670 John Williams appeared at court in behalf of Nathaniel Man of Scituate to enter an appeal from the court of the Selectmen of Scituate. On 27 October 1674 the court observed that at the last court "John Barker, attorney to Samuell Hieland, as attorney to the said Hiland, by processe of law obtained a verdict and judgment of fourteen pounds of Israell Hubert." The court also encouraged arbitration by disinterested parties, sometimes named by the individuals concerned, and sometimes by the court. That such arbitration was not, however, mandatory is seen in a court record of 6 February 1665/66, when Mrs. Rachel Davenport "with her arbetrator refuseth to refer the controversy now depending betwixt Thomas Little and her unto an arbetration, but rather refers the case to the determination of the Court." The case concerned rents due her from Thomas Little for land previously owned by William Holmes, and the court on 1 May 1666 made a compromise judgment whereby Little was to pay her £15, considerably less than she was demanding. [12]

The focus of Plymouth law seemed to be deterrence, not vengeance. This is shown by the number of killings in which the jury found "misadventure," and the defendant was freed. The object was also to right the wrong, to make one who had lost something whole again. Though the law made a distinction between crimes against the state, called "criminal facts," and trespasses and debts "between man and man," the distinction was not always apparent, for when the individual was injured, so was the state. However, sometimes in criminal matters it seemed to be the individual who did the prosecuting, and both types of cases were determined by the verdict of a twelve-men jury. A case in point was when, following the conviction of Robert Latham for cruelty leading to his servant boy's death, his wife Susanna Latham, on 8 June 1655, was presented by the grand jury for complicity in the crime with her husband; five years later the Court observed that she would be tried on this charge "if any will come in. . .to procequte against her," and she was released when none appeared. [13]

What may appear to be cruelty in punishments was actually the application of the requirements of justice to economic feasibility. In the early years there is seen the punishment of tieing one's neck and heels together, though later whipping or sitting in the stocks were more common forms of physical punishment. This was more expediency than thirst for cruelty. A community living just above the subsistence level did not have surplus wealth to invest in penitentiaries for long-term prison sentences. Monetary fines were a frequent punishment, too, but there was a limit as to how much money could be extracted from the more habitual offenders, such as Webb Adey or Thomas Lucas. As a case in point, Thomas Lucas was fined ten shillings on 2 October 1658 for being drunk the second time. On 6 October 1659 he was fined ten shillings again for being drunk. On 2 October 1660 Lucas was fined ten shillings for being drunk twice. On 5 March 1660/61 Thomas Lucas was found guilty of being drunk a third time, but this time he was sentenced to find sureties for his good behavior. John Wood and George Bonham each put up £10 to assure his appearance at the next court, but on the same day Lucas presented himself at court distempered with drink, and for his unseeming behavior both in words and gestures he was committed to prison and fined forty shillings. Though no duration of imprisonment was given, it can be understood to be short term, and probably was only a day or so. He broke his bonds for good behavior when on 7 May 1661 he was found with Ann Savory, wife of Thomas, at the time of public worship on the Lord's day drunk and under the hedge in an uncivil and beastly manner, and he was to appear at the next court.

On 10 June 1661 his sureties lost some of their money when the court called his bond of £20 forfeit, but on further consideration remitted £10 of the same. [14]

On 3 March 1662/63 Thomas Lucas, "it being the third time he hath ben convicted and sentanced in the Court for being drunk," was sentenced to be publicly whipped; demonstrating rather clearly its concern for deterrence, not vengeance, the court ordered that the sentence be stayed "untill hee shalbee taken drunke the next time, and then hee is to bee forthwith taken and whipt, without further presenting to the Court." Though the court seemed to have difficulty in keeping count, it apparently was referring to the higher seriousness of being found drunk three *or more* times. On 1 March 1663/64 Thomas Lucas was publicly whipped for being drunk a third time: "Hee was sentanced formerly for being drunke the third time; nevertheles the execution therof was [respited] untill hee should bee found drunke againe, which accordingly was witnessed against him, and soe the said punishment was inflicted on him as aforsaid." On 30 March 1664 he was charged with abusing his wife, and Stephen Bryant and George Bonham each put up £5 for his appearance at court. On 8 June 1664 Lucas was sentenced to sit in the stocks for swearing. On 9 June 1665 he was sentenced to be imprisoned for twenty-four hours for swearing by the wounds of God. On 3 October 1665 Thomas Lucas was fined ten shillings for being drunk. On 2 March 1668/69 he appeared in court to answer the charge of abusing his wife and children. He promised reformation, and, his wife testifying that since his presentment he had not abused them as aforesaid, the court cleared him with an admonition. On 7 June 1670 Lucas was fined three shillings, four pence for striking Samuel Jenney. Again it can be seen that the court was not seeking vengeance, but in the case of Thomas Lucas it finally appeared to abandon its efforts toward deterrence, for on 3 June 1673 Lucas was found guilty of being drunk again, but the court released him with a warning. On 1 June 1675 the court tried a new tactic, and when Lucas was charged for being distempered with drink, the court noted, "it being soe oftens, and that hee hath borne severall particular punishments gradually, and can not be reclaimed, it was ordered concerning him, that all that sell drinke be stricktly ordered and prohibited to lett him have none." But on 30 October 1675 Lucas, for reviling some deceased magistrates and for being drunk, was sentenced to be whipped at the post, which was accordingly done. He died as he lived, and on 6 January 1678/79 a coroner's jury reported that Thomas Lucas, "being very ancient & decrepid in his limbes, and it being very cold, and haveing drunk some drinke, gott a violent fall into a ditch, in a very dangerous place, could not recover himselfe, but bruised his body, and lying all night in the cold, soe hee came by his end." When he died, some of the the color must have gone out of Plymouth. [15]

The range of legal matters considered by both the Court of Assistants, which usually tried lesser cases only, and the General Court, which tried all manner of cases, was considerable. Slander, illegal dealings with

Indians, violation of liquor laws, engaging in prohibited activities on Sunday (especially during meeting time), stealing, refusing to serve in a public office, murder, lying, drunkenness, vagrancy, making false accusations, assault and battery, lascivious carriages toward another – these were some of the charges which could bring one to face the court. In 1639/40 James Till of Scituate confessed that he had purloined corn and a shirt from William Parker when he was a servant to him, and purloined corn from John Emerson and others when he was a servant to them, for which he was sentenced to be whipped and be burned on the shoulder. In 1649 Mr. Samuel Newman, teacher of the church of Rehoboth, was presented for saying things in his preaching that tended to defame the colony's magistrates. In 1651 George Russell of Scituate was found guilty of beating Katherine Winters and required to pay twenty shillings to the constables for her benefit. In 1653 Lieutenant White was fined fifteen shillings for neglecting to give speedy notice of danger and for not speedily delivering a letter sent by the commissioners. In 1654/55 Lt. Samuel Rider was reduced to the rank of a common soldier for resisting and making threatening speeches to a constable (though within the year this sentence was reversed and he was restored to his position as a lieutenant of the Yarmouth military company). In 1651 the grand jury presented Jonathan Coventry of Marshfield for making a motion of marriage to Katherine Bradbury, a servant to Mr. Bourne, without her master's consent. In 1654/55 Joan, the wife of Obadiah Miller of Taunton, was presented for "beating and reviling her husband, and egging her children to healp her, biding them knock him in the head, and wishing his victials might choake him." [16]

In 1656 Michael Turner was fined twenty shillings for refusing to serve on the grand jury. In 1658 an Indian named Repent was found guilty of speaking words which intimated that he would have shot the governor, and he was sentenced to be whipped. In 1659 Thomas Ewer, for tumultuous and seditious speeches in court, was sentenced to be tied by his neck and heels, but when the court learned that he was infirm and had a rupture, it suspended the sentence with a warning for him to carry himself better. In 1659 Richard Beere of Marshfield, for being a grossly scandalous and debauched person, and having been formerly convicted of filthy, obscene practices, was disenfranchised. In 1660 Caleb Lambert was sentenced to sit in the stocks for abominable cursing and swearing. In 1662 the wife of George Crisp was presented for lying, but the court found that although she spoke a falsehood, it did not "come under the notion of a pernisious lye," but was only unadvised, and thus she was not fined. In 1667/68 Joseph Turner was sentenced to be publicly whipped or pay a £5 fine for publishing lascivious and filthy verses. [17]

Of course at certain periods the court's activities reflected important concerns of the community, such as the Quaker invasion around 1660 and the growing threat of an Indian uprising in the early 1670s. It was always concerned with matters of citizenship and with maintaining peace and decorum in the community. The court was very family oriented, and it felt that single people were less apt to cause disturbances if they lived with families. On 9 June 1653, for example, the court ordered Teag Jones and Richard Berry (or Beere, the same who is shown above as being disenfranchised in 1659), and others with them, to part their uncivil living together. People without means were not wanted in the colony, and typically such a person would be treated as was Robert Pinion, who in 1667 was taken up as a vagrant, publicly whipped, and ordered to depart the colony forthwith. The court also continued century-long practices in England of regulating weights, measures, prices, and interest rates. In 1654/55 Thomas Clarke of Plymouth was presented for requiring £6 interest on a loan of £20 for one year, which the grand jury considered "great extortion, contrary to the law of God and man"; however, the record is annotated "Cleared by traverse," which meant that Clarke exercised his right to ask for a jury trial and was found not guilty. In 1653 the court took notice of complaints that some of the coopers were selling bad casks which had caused great damage to various buyers, and it ordered that henceforth any cooper making a faulty cask would be required to pay anyone for any damages that resulted. In 1671 the court ordered that no rum could be sold in the colony for more than five shillings a gallon, or if retailed no more than two pence a gill. [18] John Barnes and Stephen Hopkins were sometimes punished for charging more than a fair price.

Plymouth was not an especially litigious community for its times, and so John Williams, Jr. was not a small exception, but an exception on a grand scale. Through his legal adventures can be seen some of the various uses and abuses of the law available in Plymouth, and no one in the colony ever engaged in such activities to an extent even remotely approaching that of Williams. He was the son of John Williams, Sr., who was in Scituate as early as 1637, became a freeman in 1637, and was a deputy in 1640. John, Jr. was proposed as a freeman in 1651 and became one in 1653. In 1653 he joined his sister, Anna Barker, in posting security for her to administer the estate of her late husband, John Barker. Williams became an ensign of the Scituate military company in 1655. In 1657/58, when the court dismissed James Cudworth as captain of the Scituate company, Lt. James Torrey and Ens. John Williams were ordered to command the company in Cudworth's place. In 1658 Williams became one of the advisers to the Council of War. [19]

Thus far the career of John Williams is similar to that of a number of other relatively wealthy second-generation Plymouth men. The first notice of any difference was when he appeared at court in 1659 to answer the charge of Robert Barker and Deborah Barker, brother and daughter respectively to the late John Barker, that he had misused Deborah, who was his niece and had been put out to him. He produced considerable evidence in his behalf, and the court found him not guilty, but ordered that Deborah Barker need not return to live with him and she could pick her own guardian; she chose Thomas Bird of Scituate. In 1660 he was summoned to court to answer charges of entertaining a foreign (that is, from outside the colony)

Quaker and permitting a Quaker meeting in his house. He refused to answer the accusation, saying that he had further evidence to clear himself, and he refused to acknowledge the legality of proceedings against him. A month later he was fined forty shillings, but the court did not take away his military rank because of his excuse that he had been hoping to reform some of the Quakers. In 1662/63 at Mr. Hatherly's request, the court appointed a jury to divide the lands which John Williams, Sr. and John Williams, Jr. had owned in partnership—a rather unusual occurrence, for ordinarily a father and son would have been able to effect such a division among themselves. In 1663/64 Williams and John Bayley were fined three shillings, four pence each for striking each other. In 1664 Edward Jenkins complained against Williams, who had erected a fence prejudicial to Jenkins's land and the common highway. [20]

By this time Williams had married an Elizabeth, who might have been an unrecorded daughter of Rev. John Lothrop. On 7 June 1665 the court noted that there had been various complaints about Williams's disorderly living with his wife, his abusive and harsh carriages toward her by both words and actions, his keeping himself away from the marriage bed, his accusing his wife of being a whore, and his denial that the daughter born to his wife was his. Williams was not able to prove his charges against his wife, and the court admonished both of them to try to recover peace and love between them. He appeared in court again on 3 October 1665 to answer the charge of Mr. Barnabas Lothrop, in behalf of his sister, who was Williams' wife, that Williams had been unkind, churlish, and of unworthy behavior toward his wife. The court noted that Williams had not made the reformation expected of him, and though at first he seemed willing to let the matter be decided by a jury, he later refused. The court "being earnestly desirous of a renewed closure of his hart and affections to his wife, and that his future conversation with her might bee better than his former," decided to be lenient with him, with exhortations to mend his ways. His wife Elizabeth asked that her name be cleared of the accusations made against her in court by her husband, and the court ruled that it could find no cause of blame in her, and that she had behaved herself faithfully in the bond of wedlock and had been much wronged. [21]

On 6 March 1665/66 Williams was discharged from his rank as ensign. On 1 May 1666 Williams appeared at court again to answer the charges of his continuing to abuse his wife by his accusations and actions. Williams agreed to a jury trial and promised to supply his wife with money and necessities and to allow her to remain with friends until the trial. On 5 June 1666 a jury found Elizabeth Williams's complaint against her husband to be true. The court observed that it too was satisfied by the evidence, Williams also "declaring his insufficiency for converse with woemen," and the court, deciding that it was not safe for her to live with her husband, gave her the right to depart from him until he behaved better toward her. Williams was ordered to keep her in clothing and bedding and pay her £10 a year to maintain herself, and the court required him to put up one-third of their estate as security for her livelihood and comfort. On 5 June 1667 Capt. James Cudworth and Mr. Joseph Tilden were appointed by the court to demand Elizabeth Williams's allowance from her husband. On 30 October 1667 the court ordered Williams to renew his bond for the assurance that he would pay his wife the yearly allowance. She was apparently living at his house in Scituate, and he elsewhere, for in 1668 John Williams engaged to pay towards his wife's maintenance a barrel of beef, a barrel of pork, a good cow not over eight years old, and as much corn to make up the total value £10, and these were to be delivered to her at his house in Scituate. [22]

In 1670 John Williams appeared at court as the attorney for Nathaniel Man. On 29 October 1670 the court ruled that Rowland Wills who had been brought into Scituate by John Williams, and who had lived apart from his wife for years, could stay in Scituate until the next harvest, Wills having agreed to send for his wife in the interim. Provided she came, and provided that the town of Scituate approved, Wills could then stay, but otherwise would have to depart. John Williams engaged to spare the town of Scituate any expenses that might accrue to them as a result of Wills living on Williams's farm. In 1671 Ens. John Williams was granted the administration of the estate of the deceased Edward Williams, which indicates his rank was reinstated. On 1 July 1672 John Williams of Scituate was in court to answer charges of doing servile work on the Sabbath, and he read a petition to the court which was considered. The court noted that he had excepted against one particular in the charges in that the place where he was supposed to have committed the offense was not given, and the court offered him a trial by jury, but he declined. The court sentenced him to a forty shilling fine. On 29 October 1672 John Williams and William Rogers agreed to settle a dispute between them concerning accounts and other matters by arbitration. On 1 March 1674/75, John Cowin of Scituate was released on bond on charges of assaulting and abusively wounding Ens. John Williams. In 1676 John Williams, now a captain, was in court as a deputy. [23]

On 4 July 1679 the court, after considering the petition of Elizabeth Williams that she was stricken in years and so often confused by what the court ordered for her maintenance, which had proved short of comfortable support, ordered Williams to pay the full sum of £10 to her every year in money, and if Williams did not pay it, the constable was to levy £15 against his estate. In 1681 Capt. John Williams was a selectman for Scituate, and a deputy. The court ordered in 1681/82 that two Indians who had stolen property from John Williams were to be his servants for four months each and then depart from Scituate. On 7 July 1682 the court awarded £4/4 to Capt. John Williams to express gratification for his services in the late war. In 1682/83 the court found an Indian, George Partridge, guilty of stealing and running away from Williams, and of threatening to kill him. In 1685 Capt. John Williams of Scituate obtained a judgment of £16/7 against Thomas Waid and Timothy White, and the constable was ordered, if they did not pay, to levy a distress on their estates. The constable asked Williams to select an appraiser, but Williams "utterly refused" and urged the constable to arrest White, assuring him that the court order was sufficient. The position of constable was always a difficult one, and Williams made it no easier. Explained the constable, "And I, being ignorant of the law, seized the body of the said White," and took him to the jail keeper, who refused to accept him. Then the constable again told Williams he would assure him of full execution of the court order if Williams would choose an appraiser, but Williams again utterly refused. [24]

In 1686 Thomas Waid and Timothy White sued Capt. John Williams, and the jury found it could go either way, depending on a point of law. The court, however, resolved the matter in favor of Williams. In the same year Williams sued Capt. John Briggs and Nathaniel Tilden, and the action was nonsuited, with Williams being ordered to pay the defendants forty-two shillings. At the same time he sued Samuel Holbrooke, who was the unfortunate constable in the Waid and White case, with the jury finding in Holbrooke's favor. Then he sued John Holbrooke and was awarded £11. Later in 1686 Williams appealed the most recent Waid verdict, and won, and he obtained a review in the Samuel Holbrooke case, and lost. In 1691 Barnabas Lothrop, Esq., in behalf of his sister Elizabeth Williams, went to the General Court in connection with his sister's maintenance allowance to be paid by her husband Capt. John Williams, but the court determined that the case more properly belonged to the County Court. [25]

This completes a brief summary of the cases in which Williams appeared in Court Orders. In addition, in the volume of Judicial Acts, that is, civil cases, John Williams was a plaintiff or defendant in almost one hundred pages, including actions against Gowin White, John Bayley, John Sutton, Thomas Summers, Constant Southworth, James Cudworth, Nathaniel Turner, Ann Bird, Peter Worthylake, Joseph Turner, William Rogers, James Doughtey, Michael Peirse, Robert Standford, John Barker, Samuel Hiland, Edward Jenkins, John Barker, John Buck, Samuel Nash, Israel Hobart, Thomas Wade, Gershom Ewell, Thomas Man, William James, Edward Wanton, Timothy White, Henry Josselyn, John Briggs, Samuel Holbrooke, John Holbrooke, John Cushen, Thomas Turner, William Randall, Nathaniel Turner, Daniel Hicke, John Silvester, Ralph Chapman, John Hoare, and Joseph Tilden. That the court tolerated so many suits by one man indeed shows that Plymouth was governed by law, not individuals.

NOTES

1. *Winthrop Papers* 5:56.
2. *Bradford (Ford)*, 2:7-8; Winslow, *New Englands Salamander*, 139-40.
3. *PCR* 1:42, 156, 2:36, 4, 85, 98.
4. Ibid., 1:44, 2:117, 152.
5. Winslow, *New Englands Salamander*, 138; D. C. Parnes, *Plymouth and the Common Law (1620-1775)* (Pilgrim Society, 1971), 22-33.

6. *Bradford (Morison)*, 320, 404-13.

7. *Bradford (Morison)*, 320 and fn; *PCR* 11:93; *Bradford (Morison)*, 404-13.

8. *PCR* 11:12, 95.

9. Ibid., 5:223-24.

10. Ibid., 2:132-34, 7:5, 1:108, 2:79.

11. Ibid., 6:20.

12. Ibid., 2:66, 5:38, 153, 4:113, 119.

13. Ibid., 3:82, 143.

14. Ibid., 3:150, 173, 200, 206-07, 212, 220.

15. *PCR* 4:33, 51, 55, 66, 101, 106, 5:16, 39, 118, 169, 182, 6:5, 7. For information on the family of Thomas Lucas, see Mrs. Barclay, "Mary [2] Lucas, Probable Wife of Nathaniel [2] Atwood," *TAG* 41:200.

16. *PCR* 1:143, 2:140, 172, 3:37, 74, 5, 75.

17. Ibid., 3:101, 138, 175, 176-77, 199, 4:29, 177.

18. Ibid., 3:37, 4:154, 3:75, 38, 5:60.

19. Ibid., 3:37, 80, 130, 153.

20. Ibid., 3:171-72, 185, 189, 4:27, 30, 50, 75.

21. Ibid., 4:93, 106-08.

22. Ibid., 4:117, 121, 125-26, 153, 167, 191.

23. Ibid., 5:38, 50, 81, 87, 89, 99, 107, 163, 214.

24. Ibid., 6:18, 59, 61, 81, 93, 104, 174.

25. Ibid., 6:198-99, 202, 267.

CHAPTER 10

Land and Inheritance

Though Separatist and Puritan alike had powerful religious motivation to persuade them to immigrate to New England, anyone who underestimates the importance of land as a like enticement fails to comprehend the value system of these seventeenth-century Englishmen. Sumner Chilton Powell in his Pulitizer-Prize-winning study of the men who settled Sudbury in the Bay Colony gives detailed attention to their English homes, noting that in one such home, Berkhamsted, Hertfordshire, in a twenty-five year period over one thousand acres of land were traded in countless transactions. "If the men of Berkhamsted were doing nothing else, they were trading land," Powell observes, and he shows that use of such Berkhamsted records "is excellent documentation for the general study of the land hunger of New England's first settlers." [1]

Bradford, to whom Plymouth was a Zion, deplored the trend of his friends, colleagues, and fellow settlers to desert Plymouth in favor of greater acres elsewhere. He wrote that in 1623 "they began to think how they might raise as much corn as they could," and "after much debate of things, the Governor (with the advice of the chiefest among them) gave way" and "assigned to every family a parcel of land." By 1627 the pressure for land was becoming so great that Bradford and his advisers had to give twenty additional acres to every person (excluding servants, and perhaps some others). "But yet seeking to keep the people together as much as might be," Bradford wrote, they agreed that the owners of the near acres would share their land with the owners of the far acres, and thus Plymouth could be kept as a compact community. We can calculate that if about 156 people obtained twenty acres of land, plus previously granted one-acre lots, then, aside from public and common areas, Plymouth now would have included more than 3,120 acres, or more than five square miles. Bradford wrote that the lots were to be five acres in breadth by the waterside and four acres in length, and, though apparently there were to be more than one lot going back from the coast, overall the lots must have rather hugged the coastline. Some land must have been skipped over as not so suitable, and so the total acreage extended northward to the future Duxbury and southward toward Manomet. [2]

In his account of the year 1632, Bradford laments that "there was no longer holding them together, and they must of necessity go to their great lots. . . . First, those that lived on their lots on the other side of the Bay, called Duxbury, they could not long bring their wives to the public worship and church meetings here, but. . .they sued to be dismissed and become a body of themselves." And he writes ruefully, "And so they were dismissed about this time, though very unwillingly." These people, of course, were led by some of Bradford's closest friends – Alden, Jonathan Brewster, Prence, and Standish. Still trying to keep Plymouth together as much as possible, Bradford records that "to prevent any further scattering from this place and weakening of the same, it was thought best to give out some good farms to special persons that would promise to live at Plymouth." The scheme here was to give out land on the other side of Duxbury, the area which later became Marshfield, where no allotments had been made, to people such as Edward Winslow. These favored people would keep their cattle and farms there, maintained by servants, but would themselves continue living in Plymouth. "But, alas," cried Bradford, with the benefit of hindsight, "this remedy proved worse than the disease," for in a few years the Marshfield settlers began a nagging to "rent themselves away," and the choice was either to allow them, or to suffer "continual opposition and contention." And still others "broke away," and Bradford concluded, "This I fear will be the ruin of New England, at least of the churches of God there." In a footnote, Morison comments that "Bradford's efforts to stop what would now be called 'progress' are amusing and pathetic." [3]

Among the laws reconfirmed in 1636 was one which read, "That Inheritance do descend according to the comendable custome of Engl. & hold of Est Greenwch." Unfortunately the wording here has led to some confusion, for it seems to refer to two separate ideas, the way land was to be inherited, and the way it was to be held. The "comendable custome of England" is particularly obscure, because from the earliest time land in Plymouth was not inherited by the custom of England, which was in most cases by primogeniture, all to the oldest son. We know this because Dutch visitor De Rasieres in 1627 wrote about Plymouth that "In inheritances they place all the children in one degree, only the oldest son has an acknowledgment for his seniority of birth." Since subsequent records show the oldest son getting a double portion of the inheritance, De Rasieres's observation undoubtedly means that this "acknowledgment" was in effect in 1627, as soon as the colonists had private ownership. Though much of the law in Plymouth and the Bay Colony was a continuation of English law, from the very beginning the new colonists in both places seized the opportunity of changing that part of English law which did not please them – one such part being the practice of primogeniture. [4]

The second separate idea in the wording of the Plymouth law was of tenure. The Massachusetts Bay Company 1629 charter provided that Bay land would be held of the King, as of the manor of East Greenwich in county Kent, in free and common socage, and not in Capite or by Knights Service. This reserved to the King one-fifth of any gold or silver which might be found there. To put it in simpler words, this meant essentially that the land would be held in fee simple, not subject to any rents, services, fines for livery, wardships, or other annual and occasional obligations, and was as close to outright ownership as could be conceived under English law. The manor of East Greenwich, then, referred to how the land would be held, and not to inheritance. [5] We can only guess that though the Plymouth law did not mean exactly what it said, the framers must have understood it to mean what they subsequently practiced: land would be held in fee simple, and inheritance would be equally shared by all the children, except that the oldest son would get a double portion.

A Plymouth law of 28 October 1633 required wills and testaments to be proved before the Governor's Council within one month of a testator's decease. Also within one month a full inventory of property had to be valued and presented, in cases of one dying either testate or intestate. The 1636 codification of laws provided that a deceased man's wife would have a third part of his land during her lifetime. This law at first also gave her a third of his personal property if he died intestate, but permitted a man leaving a will to dispose of his personal property as he wished. However, this was later changed in such a way as to imply that the wife had to get one-third of both real and personal property, regardless of a man's will. The implication further was that she could dispose of the personal property as she wished, whereas her right to one-third of the land was for her lifetime use, and on her death the land would then go to her husband's heirs, who would not necessarily be her own heirs (for example, where he might have had children by an earlier wife). The same code required that all sales or other transfers of land must be acknowledged before the governor or one of the Assistants, and must be publicly recorded, for which a fee was charged. [6]

In Plymouth the law did not have to be hard and unyielding, for having no royal governor, and being composed of all the freemen, the Plymouth General Court was as free as conceivable in making, changing, interpreting, and ignoring the law. In many cases, it is obvious that the court was guided primarily by a concept of fairness, and this is certainly true in the inheritance case of Naomi Silvester, widow of Richard. On 5 October 1663 the court recorded a memorandum that it would consider the condition of Naomi Silvester, widow, "her deceased husband having by his last will and testament left, in an absolute way, but a smale, inconsiderable parte of his estate unto her." By the testimony of neighbors it appeared that she was a frugal and industrious woman who helped build up her husband's estate, and the court felt that some prudent (though unspecified) measure should be taken to give her a more appropriate part of the estate. [7]

An undated law provided that sales of houses and lands must be acknowledged before an Assistant and recorded with all convenient speed.

"And that the wyfe hereafter come in and consent & acknowledg the sale also; but that all bargaines and sales of houses and lands made before this day to remayne firm to the buyer notwithstanding the wife did not acknowledg the same." In point of fact, most land sales were recorded, though not always speedily; however, some were not recorded, and every now and then either an original deed appears transferring land ownership which was never officially recorded, or reference is found in an official deed to some earlier deed no longer extant. The requirement that the wife sign a deed would have been a boon to genealogists, but unfortunately this was one law more honored in the breach, for it was relatively infrequent that the wife did sign. Often when she did, it was for a land transaction where she had some title other than as a wife, such as when she had inherited the land from her parents, and even in these cases the wife did not always sign with her husband. [8]

There were several grants of large tracts of land to proprietors who had been instrumental in developing the colony. The four Adventurers who had joined in 1627 with the eight Plymouth men to form the Undertakers—Richard Andrews, John Beauchamp, James Sherley, and Timothy Hatherly—had been promised land in the area of Scituate. On 1 July 1633 the General Court ordered that the whole tract of land between Scituate and Conihasset be left undisposed of until these four men presented their wishes. On 3 October 1637 the General Court gave further definition to their grant, provided that it did not prejudice the town of Scituate. Mr. Hatherly, one of the few Adventurers to settle in Plymouth Colony, was already a resident of Scituate, and was one of the Assistants. In a deed of 1 December 1646, Timothy Hatherly noted that he had acquired the shares of Andrews and Beauchamp, while Sherley's part of the tract had been divided into thirty equal shares. Hatherly divided his three quarters of the tract into thirty parts, retaining three himself, and selling for £108 the other twenty-seven parts to Charles Chauncy, Thomas Chambers, John Williams, James Cudworth, Joseph Tilden, Henry Merritt, Thomas Rawlins, Thomas Tarte, John Hoar, Richard Sillis, Thomas Ensign, Thomas Chittenden, John Stockbridge, John Allin, Thomas Hiland, John Whitcomb, John Woodfield, Edward Jenkins, John Hollet, Ann Vinall, William Holmes, John Weston, Gowen White, John Daman, Rodolphus Elmes, and Richard Mann; Joseph Tilden received two shares, and the rest one share each. [9]

The aftermath of the 1638 grand jury inquiry as to what power allowed the governor and Assistants to grant lands to any given person or town was the surrender of the Bradford Patent to the corporation; that is, to the colony in the persons of the freemen. Bradford describes this as "Whereas the Patent was taken in the names of William Bradford (as in trust). . .and now the number of freemen being much increased, and divers townships established and settled. . .it was by the Court desired that William Bradford should make a surrender of the same into their hands. The which he willingly did." First there was a cessation of any further land grants. Then at a General Court of 3 March 1639/40, in order to put a stop to all controversies and differences about the Patent between Purchasers, freemen, or others, it was decided that Bradford and "those that held the trade" (that is, the Undertakers), would be paid up to £300 for their expenses in acquiring the Patent. Further, the Purchasers or Old Comers "shall make choyce of two or three places [that is, large areas of land] for themselves & their heires," and following their selection, all the residue of land not previously granted to individuals or towns "shalbe assigned & surrendred into the hands of the whole Body of the freemen to be disposed of either by the whole Body" or by their delegates. It was also provided that the governor and Assistants continue to grant land to residents in Plymouth and Duxbury until the following December. [10]

On 1 December 1640 the Purchasers informed the General Court that for their "two or three places," they would choose (1) an area on Cape Cod three miles long and from sea to sea between present-day Yarmouth and Eastham, (2) the area which was later Dartmouth and Little Compton, and (3) the area which later was Rehoboth and Swansea. The Bradford Patent was surrendered to the freemen on 2 March 1640/41, when Bradford and his fellow Purchasers gave all their rights in the Patent to "the whole Court, consistinge of the freemen of this corporacon of New Plymouth." Bradford formally handed over the document to Nathaniel Sowther, who acted on behalf of the whole court, and the court then ordered the document handed back to Bradford for its safekeeping. [11] These large proprietary tracts, as with Hatherly's tract in Scituate, could have allowed the owners to develop in New England the types of manorial plantations characteristic of Virginia, and, later, other colonies; however, though some fairly large estates were retained by their various owners, most of the tracts were subdivided for sale to other colonists, and Plymouth remained essentially a small farmer colony.

There was overwhelming sentiment, at least among the freemen, that the early residents of Plymouth should be given preferential treatment in the granting of land. Not only were the Old Comers provided for, but there was concern, too, that their children should receive some special treatment. This is shown in a law of 1633 which stated "that such children as are heer borne & next unto them such as are heer brought up under their parents and are come to age of discretion allowed, and want lands for their accomodacon be provided for in place convenient before any that either come from England or elsewhere. then to seeke as they are." There must have been some foot-dragging on carrying out this law, for it was not until 3 June 1662 that the General Court approved a list of thirty-three names "as being the first borne children of this govment," to receive two tracts recently purchased by the colony from the Indians. The list was broader than just the "first born," for it included several of the original settlers, such as John Howland, John Alden, and Francis Cooke, presumably on behalf of their children. Some of the names on the list are husbands of the daughters of some of the early colonists. At least one name, William Pontus, appears to be there only because he was of the Leiden group, though he did not arrive in Plymouth until after 1627. The two tracts purchased were in the area later called Middleborough and were known as the Twenty-six Men's Purchase and the Purchade Purchase. [12]

All such purchases had to be made from the Indians, who were deemed the rightful owners, although they had no concept of private property such as the English had. A law of 6 June 1643 provided that "Whereas it is holden very unlawfull and of dangerous consequence and it hath beene the constant custome from our first begining That no pson or psons have or ever did purchase Rent or hire any lands herbage wood or tymber of the Natives but by the Majestrates consent. It is therefore enacted by the Court that if any pson or psons do hereafter purchase rent or hyre any lands herbage wood or tymber of any of the Natives in any place wthin this Govment wthout the consent & assent of the Court Every such pson or psons shall forfeit five pounds for every acree Wch shalbe so purchased hyred rented and taken And for wood & tymber to pay five tymes the value thereof to be levyed for the Colonies use." On 2 October 1660 this prohibition was expanded, "In reference unto the law prohibiting buying or hiering land of the Indians directly or Indirectly bearing date 1643 the Court Interpretts those words alsoe to comprehend under the same penalty; a prohibition of any mans receiveing any lands under pretence of any gift from the Indians without the approbation of the Court." [13] In many cases, especially in dealing with large tracts such as for the "first born children," the court appointed several men to bargain with the Indians for the sale of the land.

Sometimes land was granted to the towns, which in turn would parcel out various lots. In January 1638/39 the General Court granted to Thomas Besbech, James Cudworth, William Gilson, Anthony Annable, Henry Rowley, Edward Foster, Henry Cobb, and Robert Linnell a tract of land at a place called Sippican "for the seating of a township for a congregation there," and they were to act as a committee to dispose of lands lying there. The location of Sippican was later changed, but the procedure of the court making the overall grant ("committees," usually consisting of some of the leading men who expected to live in the area, subdivided the grant) is noted in other towns as well. In Sandwich in 1638/39 the court granted additional meadow lands to the residents, letting certain residents decide who would get what; however, because of widespread dissension, it became necessary to have Assistants Thomas Prence and John Alden go to Sandwich to supervise. Though in general the towns could make additional grants of land within town boundaries, the colony was in a continual, though uneven, state of expansion, and the General Court was almost constantly awarding new grants to individuals and groups. It seemed that any resident could petition the court for land, and was reasonably assured of getting it if he was "ancient freeman" or servant, or to show a "want"; that is, need, for land. [14]

One of the most interesting court orders regarding land was made on 3 September 1639. The court noted that "many do want [i.e., lack or need] lands which were heare when the division of lands and goods were made about twelve yeares since," and it ruled that they "shall have liberty to go & seeke out a convenient place, or two, or three, for their accomodacon, that, upon report thereof unto the Court, the said lands may be confirmed unto them." The court was obviously referring to the 1627 division of live- stock and the simultaneous granting of twenty acres to most of the then residents of Plymouth. Bradford wrote that at that time servants were not to share in the land division, and he hinted that even nonservants who were not "able to governe them selves with meete discretion" would be passed over in the awarding of twenty shares per person. It appears from Bradford's words that only the fifty-eight Purchasers shared in this land award, a single man getting one twenty-acre lot, and a head of family get- ting as many twenty-acre lots as he had family members. The records include a list of the Purchasers, and it would appear that anyone who was not on this list (or not a member of the family of someone on the list) did not get land, and these were probably the "many" who in 1639 had been in Plymouth twelve years earlier, but were not awarded land then. It is known, for example, that William Latham, Richard More, and Robert Bart- lett were in Plymouth at the time, but were not Purchasers. Unfortunately no list can be compiled of "many" similar people. Although the wording is uncertain, it appears an unknown number of people who shared in the 1627 livestock division might not have shared in the 1627 land division. [15]

Examples of the land transactions of just a few individuals might illus- trate that Powell's observation was as true in Plymouth as in England that "if they were doing nothing else, they were trading land." *Mayflower* pas- senger Edward Doty's transactions are probably typical of those who were moderately concerned with land ownership. He had been a servant, became a freeman, did not serve in high office, was more than ordinarily aggressive in his dealings with others, and he left many children to pro- vide for. He was an unmarried Purchaser in 1627, and so would have been granted twenty acres in addition to his one acre from 1623. In 1637 he and his father-in-law Tristram Clarke were to receive parcels of land at Mount's Hill. Also in 1637 Doty sold to Richard Derby for £150 all his houses and tenements at High Cliff, plus four lots of land and three other acres he had purchased of Joshua Pratt, Phineas Pratt, and John Shaw. In 1637/38 he was granted sixty acres plus a garden place at Derby's Pond. In 1638 he relinquished his right to the sixty acres and received in turn six acres of meadow plus "all that parcel of upland" before the meadow. In 1639 he sold twenty acres at High Cliff to Richard Derby for £22. In 1640 he received six more acres, plus upland, from the court. The court allowed Doty in 1641 to increase his upland at High Cliff to forty acres. He paid Joshua Pratt in 1642 forty shillings for one acre of upland at High Cliff. In 1643 Doty sold forty acres of upland at High Cliff to Stephen Bryant and John Shaw, Jr. for £16. These are the transactions that appear in the records, but it is doubtful that they are all that he had. It is known that he owned land in central Plymouth where the Mayflower Society House now stands. [16]

John Barnes, an early Plymouth resident who arrived no later than 1633, was not a Purchaser, but he became a freeman by 1636/37. He was a general merchant engaged in many commercial activities, and like Doty he was also engaged in frequent legal disputes. He was disenfranchised for drunkenness in 1659. His land transactions, rather numerous even for Plymouth, will be treated only briefly. In 1633/34 he sold Richard Higgins a house and twenty acres of land in Plymouth for £10 plus twenty acres of land in Scituate. In 1637 he was granted seven acres of land in Plymouth. In June 1639 Barnes bought four acres of land from John Winslow for £8, and in July 1639 he sold the same land to Robert Hicks for £9/15. In November 1639 he bought two acres of meadow from Edward Holman for forty shillings. The court in June 1640 granted Barnes 100 acres of upland and ten acres of meadow. In August 1640 he bought from John Combes and Phineas Pratt two acres of upland for £3. In October 1640 he bought a house, garden, upland, and two acres of marsh meadow from Josias Winslow for £52. One month later, in November 1640, Barnes bought a house and land at Eel River from Mark Mendlove for £12. In January 1640/41 Barnes paid £20 to Thomas Hill for a house, garden, and land at Wellingsley. In February 1640/41 he sold a house and lands he had bought from Mark Mendlove to William Baker for £18 — seemingly a large profit for three months, though he let Baker pay the money over a four-year period. In December 1642 Barnes sold Edward Edwards the properties he had purchased both from Thomas Hill and from Combes and Pratt for £16. Whether he took a loss on this transaction is hard to say, for the earlier Hill transaction involved a number of fruit trees which Barnes could have sold separately. Barnes was a shrewd merchant, and surely the idea occurred to him that he could have sold off property attached to real estate, such as fences, timber, or household goods in his other businesses. In the Edwards transaction, the deed provided that Edwards was to pay Barnes money, stockings, shoes, or other merchantable commodities. In October 1644 Edwards sold the same lands to Thomas Whitney for £9/2/6, which Whitney was to pay to Barnes. In 1649 Barnes sold some land at Eel River formerly belonging to Mark Mendlove to George Bonham for £3, and it is possible that when he sold Mendlove's house to Baker, he might not have included all the land. [17]

Barnes was not the biggest real estate dealer in Plymouth, and his holdings were probably not very significant compared to some of the large possessions of Timothy Hatherly or John Browne. William Bradford, Edmond Freeman, Robert Hicks, Thomas Prence, Joseph Tilden, and Edward Winslow, among many others, had a considerable number of land transactions. In chapter 11 it is shown that the promise of land grants was an important inducement in attracting servants to Plymouth Colony, and some of these servants eventually acquired considerable land holdings. In the beginning a servant coming out of servitude would be given an individual lot in some place assigned by the court, but in 1661 the court provided for a collective purchase of lands at Saconett for former servants. [18] In general, the earlier one arrived at Plymouth, the easier it was to get free land grants. Most of the Purchasers did quite well, but even people arriving in the 1630s were sometimes included under the heading "ancient freemen" to whom numerous land grants were made. In fact, a perusal of court records shows the court handing out grants as if land were one of the world's cheaper commodities, a procedure which could not continue indefinitely. Though towns still had some undivided holdings from earlier grants by the court, the division of lands at Mount Hope after King Philip's War marked a realistic end to large scale distributions. The abandonment of primogeniture from the beginning guaranteed that holdings would on the average get smaller as a number of sons inherited from a father. By the end of the colony period, free grants become fewer and fewer, but sales of land from one individual to another continued to be a marked feature of the colony, so that land transactions in Plymouth resembled those in the places from which the immigrants came, and if nothing else, they were still trading land.

NOTES

1. Sumner Chilton Powell, *Puritan Village — The Formation of a New England Town* (Middletown, Conn., 1963), 22.

2. *Bradford (Morison)*, 120, 187-88. The example in the text of 156 people times twenty acres obviously is based on 156 people sharing in the division of the livestock, but it is just an example, a very rough approximation, for it is by no means certain that every person receiving livestock in the division also received twenty acres of land.

3. Ibid., 253-54.

4. PCR 11:12; *Three Visitors*, 77.

5. George L. Haskins, "Gavelkind and the Charter of Massachusetts Bay," *Publications of the Colonial Society of Massachusetts, Transactions 1937-1942*, Vol. 34 (Boston, 1943), 483-98 has an excellent discussion of land tenure and inheritance in the Bay Colony, with observations also on Plymouth Colony.

6. PCR 1:17, 11:12-13.

7. Ibid., 4:46.

8. PCR 11:52. See also Eugene A. Stratton, "A Note on Terminology: Spinster: An Indication of Legal Status," *TAG* 61:167-70.

9. PCR 1:13, 68, 12:158-60.

10. *Bradford (Morison)*, 308; PCR 11:34-35. In a footnote on p. 429, Morison states that the General Court voted on 5 March 1639/40 to pay the fifty-eight Purchasers or Old Comers £300 for the surrender of the Patent, but PCR 11:34-35 clearly shows that it was on 3 March 1639/40, and that the £300 were to be "payd to those that held the trade viz: Mr Bradford

Mr Prence Capt Standish and the rest of the ptners," the "partners" being an alternate way of referring to the Undertakers.

11. *PCR* 2:4-5, 10-11.

12. *PCR* 11:16, 4:18-19, 3:215-16; Thomas Weston, *History of the Town of Middleboro, Massachusetts* (Cambridge, 1906), 584-600.

13. *PCR* 11:41, 129.

14. Ibid., 1:108, 147.

15. *PCR* 1:131; *Bradford (Ford)* 2:8; *PCR* 2:177 (see also appendix F for a list of the Purchasers).

16. *PCR* 1:69, 12:20, 1:76, 99, 12:46, 1:166, 12:81, 2:26, 12:91.

17. Ibid., 1:24, 71, 12:45, 49, 1:154, 12:61, 63, 64, 68, 69, 87, 88, 166.

18. Ibid., 3:216.

CHAPTER 11

Man and Master

One of the least known aspects of Plymouth Colony is the distinction made between classes. There were "freemen" and there were "free men" who were not "freemen," but the most pronounced difference was between free men and "unfree men;" that is, servants, apprentices, and slaves. Slavery was not introduced until the later period, but servants and apprentices were present from the beginning. Apparently there was little difference between a servant and an apprentice, and at times the records seem to treat them interchangeably, and yet at other times there was a distinction. It might not be inaccurate to say that all apprentices were servants, but not all servants were apprentices. The distinction seemed to be that apprentices tended to be young and were expected to be taught a trade or given some form of education.

Of the 104 people called 1620 *Mayflower* passengers, at least twenty were servants or wards: William Button, Robert Carter, "Carver's maidservant," Edward Doty, William Holbeck, John Hooke, John Howland, John Langmore, William Latham, Edward Lester, Desire Minter, the four More children, Solomon Prower, George Soule, Elias Story, Edward Thompson, and Roger Wilder. Of these, twelve died during the first year, and thus there is no way of knowing what they might have become. Servants were employed by both Separatist and non-Separatist alike. Carver's maidservant married and died within a few years. Edward Doty became a freeman and quite prosperous, as did John Howland, who also rose to some distinction as a leader and Assistant. William Latham and Edward Lester left Plymouth and apparently were not too successful elsewhere. Desire Minter returned to England and died there. Of the four More children, only Richard More survived the first year, and he eventually moved to Salem, where he became a prosperous merchant and sea captain. George Soule became a freeman and prosperous. Thus from the beginning there was upward mobility, at least for some.

Whether servants came over on the next few ships is difficult to say, for our knowledge of the next passengers comes from lists of people in the 1623 land division and the 1627 livestock division. According to Bradford, servants were not to share in the land grants of 1627, [1] and we can see, for example, that Richard More, probably still a servant or ward at age thirteen, and William Latham, probably still a servant at age eighteen, were not on the list of Purchasers. However, they were on the list of those participating in the 1627 division of livestock, and that list was apparently a complete list of all residents (not transients) in Plymouth in 1627, including servants. The difficulty is that we do not really know which people were still in a servant status that year. Several people in the livestock division, but not on the Purchaser list, may be accounted for by assuming they were included in a related family; besides More and Latham, though, only Robert Bartlett was neither a Purchaser nor had any known family connection in 1627, and thus Bartlett, who arrived in 1623 on the *Anne* before the land division, conceivably may have been a servant in 1627. Certainly more servants arrived on the *Talbot* in 1629. [2] It was shown in chapter 3 that in 1637 Elizabeth Poole sailed to Plymouth with no less than fourteen servants, and even people not considered particularly rich, such as Gyles Rickard, often brought over two or three servants.

In the England of this time servants were very common in all but the poorest of families. Conditions of living were such that the supply of laborers exceeded the demand, and so with even a modest income one could always hire someone a little further down the economic ladder to do the menial work in return for food, lodging, some simple clothes, and perhaps a very little money. There was thus in England a "servant class" that could be characterized generally as poor, uneducated, and often not overly concerned with moral scruples. This class would have been an important source of supply of workers for Plymouth Colony. Another source of servants, both in England and in Plymouth, came from both apprentices, who were often of more prosperous families, and from poorer members of once successful families that had been visited by distress. However, Plymouth could offer something that England could not, the possibility of acquiring free land. This opportunity undoubtedly also attracted some servants from England who perhaps had been craftsmen or otherwise free there. Thus there were servants of different types and backgrounds in Plymouth.

How were servants recruited? Again there is so much we do not know. We know that some servants in effect recruited themselves by coming from the Bay Colony and offering their services, but many came directly from England. Frequently their passages were paid by the person in Plymouth for whom they would be working. In at least one case, we see the process both before and after recruitment. On 12 July 1637 Edward Doty sold some land to Richard Derby, and, using the deed as a general contract, they agreed between them "that the said Richard Derby shall procure one able man servant to be brought over to serve the said Edward Doty for the terme of five six or seaven yeares for whose passage the said Edward Dotey shall pay five pounds to the said Richard Derby & performe such other covenants to the said servant as the said Edward shall agree upon with twelve bushells of Indian graine at thend of his terme." On 31 August 1638 the court recorded a memorandum:

> that whereas William Snow was lately brought over out of Old England by Mr. Richard Derby, and is his covenant servant for five yeares, as appeares by his indenture, beareing date the xxth of Februar., 1637 [i.e., 1637/38], –now the said Richard Derby hath assigned over the said William Snow unto Edward Dotey, to serve him the residue of the said terme of five yeares, and two yeares longer, that is to say, for the terme of seven yeares from the xxth day of October next ensuing unto the end of the terme of seaven yeares thence next ensuinge, the said Edward performing such condicons as on his part are to be performed, and shall, in the end of the said terme, pay the said William Snow one lievely cow calf of two months old, and eight bushells of Indian corne, and a sow pigg of 2 or 3 months old, with two suits of apparell, and find him meate, drink, & apparell during his terme. [3]

Snow married Rebecca Browne, daughter of *Mayflower* passenger Peter Browne, and though he never became a freeman, he did own land and he certainly improved his status. Not long after Mr. Derby's transaction of 31 August 1638, on 24 October 1638 he turned over his servant Richard Clark to Mr. Atwood. [4]

William Spooner of Colchester, co. Essex, by contract of 27 March 1637, apprenticed himself to John Holmes, gentleman, of Plymouth for six years, and later in 1637 Holmes, with the consent and liking of Spooner, assigned Spooner's contract to John Coombs of Plymouth. At the end of the term Coombs was to give Spooner "one comely suit of apparell for holy dayes and one suite for workinge dayes and twelve bushells of Indian Wheate, and a good serviceable muskett, bandiliers and sword fitt for service." There are hints that Holmes might have been from Colchester, too, and might have recruited Spooner as a servant for Coombs. Could Holmes have known, perhaps through a letter from home, that Spooner was desirous of finding employment in Plymouth? [5] So, too, Edmond Weston in 1636 had his contract to serve John Winslow turned over to Nathaniel Thomas, on behalf of the latter's father Mr. William Thomas, with Thomas paying Winslow £10, and promising to give Weston at the end of two years £6 and fourteen bushels of corn, plus whatever else Weston would be due by virtue of his covenant with Winslow. [6] We know that even a prosperous man might arrange to have a relative work as a servant, for on 13 February 1639/40 Henry Cogan transferred the five-year contract of his servant James Glass (who was also his nephew) to Manasseh Kempton. [7]

It would be unwise to read too much into scant records. There are more specific cases where the transfer of a servant from one person to another was not by earlier arrangement. Twyford West, who had been under a six-year contract to serve Edward Winslow, was transferred by Winslow to Nicholas Snow, but then deciding that he disliked working for Snow, asked Winslow to take him back. West was even willing to have one year added to his term of service if Winslow would do so; hence on 12 February 1635/36 Winslow recorded an agreement whereby he compounded with Snow and agreed to take West back into his service. [8] Transfers from one master to another were common; for example, on 10 January 1638/39 Thomas Bordman turned over the remaining term of William Barden's seven-year covenant to John Barker, bricklayer, and one of the terms was that Barker was to teach Barden the trade of a bricklayer. [9] On the other hand, Kenelm Winslow's servant, John Gardiner, by the agreement of all concerned, was turned over on 22 February 1635/36 to George Kendrick, and Kendrick was to assume Winslow's obligations to Gardiner, except that Gardiner, in return for an extra six bushels of corn at the end of his term, was willing to free Kendrick of being obligated to teach him the trade of joinery. [10] On 26 August 1634, by agreement between Gov. Thomas Prence and John Barnes, Prence's servant John Rouse, "having a desire to forsake the service of his master," and Barnes's servant Richard Willis, "having inclination to dwell with the sayd Thomas Prince," changed places. [11]

One important source of servants was the practice of some families of "putting out" one or more children. Samuel Eddy, for example, although the son of an English minister and university graduate, did not seem to prosper in Plymouth, and he and his wife, "by reason of many wants lying on them," were forced to put out several children as servants. So, too, Samuel Eaton and Benjamin Eaton, after the death of their father, *Mayflower* passenger Francis Eaton, were placed out by their stepmother and were apprenticed respectively to Widow Bridget Fuller and John Cooke, Jr. On 13 August 1636 Mary Moorecock, by her own voluntary will, and with the consent of her stepfather, was apprenticed to Richard Sparrow for nine years. Six-year-old Elizabeth Billington, with consent of parents, on 18 April 1642 was apprenticed for fourteen years to John and Mary Barnes. Sarah Hoskins was apprenticed on 18 January 1643/44 with the consent of her father, to Thomas and Winifred Whitney until she became twenty years old. Thomas and Anne Savory put their five-year-old son Thomas Jr. out on 2 August 1653 as an apprentice with Thomas Lettice, carpenter, until he reached twenty-one. Young Thomas was to receive meat, drink, apparel, washing, lodging, and all other necessities, and was to be taught the trade of a house carpenter, and be taught to read the English langauge. In turn he was to give his master faithful and respectful service, not absent himself by day or night without license, not marry or contract marriage during his term, not embezzle, purloin, or steal any of his master's goods, nor give away any of his secrets, and to be obedient. On completing his term, he would be given two suits of clothes and various specified carpenter's tools. The same Thomas and Anne Savory in November 1653 put out their nine-year-old son Benjamin to John and Alice Shaw until he reached twenty-one, and the father was to receive thirty shillings. Benjamin was to be taught to read and write, and at the end of his term he would get £5 or a cow. [12]

The attraction of future land grants occurs frequently in servant contracts. Such grants were provided for by law, and apparently a colonist could commit the government to honor his covenant to give a servant so much land at the end of his term, though not necessarily in a timely way. John Irish's contract of 20 April 1629 with Mr. Timothy Hatherly called for Irish to receive twenty-five acres of land at the end of five years. On 4 March 1643/44 the court ordered that John Irish should receive his twenty-five acres from the town of Duxbury, for it had been agreed that servants promised land by covenant would receive the land from the towns where they lived. He still did not get the land at that time, and on 29 September 1658 the court authorized him to seek out land elsewhere, noting that "the like is graunted by the Court to any other in like condition that are able to claime the like libertie by the like right as the said Irish hath done." He later obtained land at Saconett. [13]

A court record of 2 January 1633/34 shows that "whereas by indenture many are bound to give their servants land at the xpiracon of their terme, it is ordered, that they have it at Scituate, or some other convenient place, where it may be usefull." By October 1636 the court decided to put a restriction on the amount of land that could be so covenanted, and it ordered "that such servants as come out of their time, & are by their covenants to have lands, have onely five acres apeece, if fownd fit to occupie it for themselves, in some convenient place." [14] On 22 August 1636 Peter Talbot, having land due him because of his service as a former servant to Edward Doty, assigned his right to the land to James Skiffe for six bushels of corn, and on 31 August 1636 William Phips, the late servant to the Undertakers, sold his land due him for his service to Josiah Winslow for fifty shillings. [15]

The contract or covenant was an almost inviolate part of servitude, and was to be strictly observed by both parties. Though this was not always honored by one or the other party, whenever any breaches came to the attention of the court, it almost invariably decided in favor of strict compliance. Even a relatively short-term period of service could be by covenant, such as when Richard Bishop hired himself to Love Brewster for the term of one whole year from 25 November 1638 and was to have for his service £3 in money and twenty bushels of Indian corn. [16] A classic case of compliance involved *Mayflower* passenger Stephen Hopkins, whose unmarried servant Dorothy Temple, on showing signs of pregnancy, named the father as the recently executed Arthur Peach (who was therefore not available to marry her). The court ordered on 4 February 1638/39 "in regard by her covenant of indenture shee hath yet above two yeares to serve him, that the said Mr. Hopkins shall keepe her and her child, or provide shee may be kept with food and rayment during the said terme; and if he refuse so to doe, that then the collony provide for her, & Mr. Hopkins to pay it." On the same day the court ordered "Mr. Steephen Hopkins is committed to ward for his contempt to the Court, and shall so remayne comitted until hee shall either receive his servant Dorothy

Temple, or els provide for her elsewhere at his owne charge during the term shee hath yet to serve him." On 8 February 1638/39 the court noted that Hopkins had concluded an agreement with Mr. John Holmes for £3 and other considerations to discharge Hopkins and the colony of responsibility for the support of Dorothy Temple and her child, and the said Dorothy was to serve the remainder of her time with Holmes. [17] Hopkins had been an Assistant as recently as 1636.

On 4 May 1658 Robert Sprout complained to the court that his former master, Walter Briggs, was keeping the document of his indenture from him to avoid complying with his obligations, and the court ordered Briggs to give Sprout the indenture. A different type of case was recorded on 5 June 1667 when Benjamin Bartlett complained to the court that his servant John Cooper refused to serve him because the indenture agreement could not be produced, and Bartlett thought that it had been stolen. In this case the court understood by other sufficient evidence that Cooper was to serve his master for three more years, and it ordered Cooper to agree on conditions of his continued service with Bartlett or be publicly whipped and then returned to his master—"after this they renewed the conditions, and soe the mater for present is ended." One instance where the court did agree to change the terms of an indenture was on 10 June 1661 when William Hiferney, an Irishman and servant to John Hollett of Duxbury, complained that he had been stolen from his own country, and he engaged himself to Hollett for twelve years because he was unacquainted with the English language; the court "perswaded" Hollett to agree, if Hiferney would perform faithful service, to remit two years of the contract time. In another case, Jonathan Briggs complained that his master, William Hailstone of Taunton, did not perform his covenants to him, in that he did not teach him the trade of a tailor, and on 6 June 1654 the court ordered Hailstone to pay his servant £15 in lieu of the training. [18]

There were frequent complaints of master against servant, servant against master, and government against servant. After more than twenty years in Plymouth, Bradford asked, "How came it to pass that so many wicked persons and profane people should so quickly come over into this land?" and one of the chief reasons in his answer was "Men being to come over into a wilderness, in which much labor and service was to be done about building and planting, etc., such as wanted help in that respect, when they could not have such as they would, were glad to take such as they could; and so, many untoward servants, sundry of them proved, that were thus brought over, both men and womenkind who, when their times were expired, became families of themselves, which gave increase thereunto." [19] The records show continued concern over the distinction between "desireable" servants and "undesirable" servants, such as the 1636 law "That no servant comeing out of England or elswhere and is to serve a master for some tyme be admitted his freedome or to be for himself untill he have served forth his tyme either with his master or some other although hee shall buy out his tyme, except he have beene a house keeper or master of a famyly or meete & fitt to bee so." [20] The "meete & fitt to bee so" implied a subjective morality judgment.

Servants could be rude to their masters, as in the case of Thomas Williams, who served Widow Warren. On 5 July 1635 Williams was accused of speaking profane and blasphemous speeches. There being some dissension between him and Mrs. Warren, she exhorted him to fear God and do his duty, to which he answered that he feared neither God nor the devil. On humble acknowledgment of his offense he was released with a warning, even though the governor was in favor of corporal punishment "as ye case seemed to require." More often, though, masters could be mean, and even cruel, to servants. On 3 March 1639/40 John Crocker of Scituate was "proved to have corrected his servant boy, Roger Glass, in a most extreame and barbarous manner," and the court took Glass from Crocker and placed him with John Whetcomb to serve out his six years (Whetcomb happened to be his uncle by marriage – see under James Glass in Part III). On 1 August 1654 Robert Ransom complained that he was badly used and unreasonably dealt with by his master, Thomas Dexter, Jr., and though the court considered the charge unproved, it allowed Thomas Clarke of Plymouth to buy out Ransom's remaining time. On 8 June 1655 John Hall of Yarmouth complained that Francis Baker was abusing Samuel Hall, servant of Baker and son of John Hall, by kicking him and unreasonably striking him. The court took Samuel away from Baker, putting him in the custody of his father, and the father was to pay Baker £8 for Samuel's remaining term. When a servant of Mr. Thomas Gilbert, Jr. complained that he was ill used by his master and in want of proper clothing, the court ordered the town of Taunton to take notice of the boy's condition and use its best prudence to see that the boy was competently provided for and especially that he be provided with shoes and stockings in the winter, "and wee likewise desire you seriously to remember that some speedy course may bee taken for the curing of the boyes foot, being in danger of perishing." [21] The problem of males in a household taking advantage of female servants is discussed in chapter 12.

By far the most extreme case on record of a master mistreating a servant involved Robert Latham, whose wife Susanna was the daughter of John Winslow and his wife, *Mayflower* passenger Mary Chilton. On 31 January 1654/55 a coroner's jury was called to view the body of Latham's servant boy, John Walker. The jury found:

> that the body of John Walker was blackish and blew, and the skine broken in divers places from the middle to the haire of his head, viz, all his backe with stripes given him by his master, Robert Latham, as Robert himselfe did testify; and also wee found a bruise of his left arme, and one of his left hipp, and one great bruise of his brest; and there was the knuckles of one hand and one of his fingers frozen, and alsoe both his heeles frozen, and one of the heeles the flesh was much

broken, and alsoe one of his little toes frozen and very much perished, and one of his great toes frozen, and alsoe the side of his foot frozen; and alsoe, upon the reviewing the body, wee found three gaules like holes in the hames, which wee formerly, the body being frozen, thought they had been holes; and alsoe wee find that the said John was forced to carry a logg which was beyond his strength, which hee indeavoring to doe, the logg fell upon him, and hee, being downe, had a stripe or two, as Joseph Beedle doth testify; and wee find that it was some few daies before his death; and wee find, by the testimony of John Howland and John Adams, that heard Robert Latham say that hee gave John Walker som stripes that morning before his death; and alsoe wee find the flesh much broken of the knees of John Walker, and that he did want sufficient food and clothing and lodging, and that the said John did constantly wett his bedd and his cloathes, lying in them, and so suffered by it, his clothes being frozen about him; and that the said John was put forth in the extremity of cold, though thuse unabled by lamenes and sorenes to performe what was required; and therefore in respect of crewelty and hard usage he died.

This of course is not a typical case, and must be weighed against the probable hundreds of unrecorded cases where relations between master and servant were mutually pleasant and beneficial. In the Latham-Walker case, the community view can can be seen in the aftermath, when on 4 March 1654/55 Latham was indicted for felonious cruelty to his servant John Walker, age about fourteen, by unreasonable correction, by withholding necessary food and clothing, and by exposing Walker to extremities of the seasons, whereby he died. The trial jury found him guilty of "manslaughter by chaunce medley," and he was sentenced to be burned in the hand and, having no lands, to have all his personal property confiscated. Latham's wife, Susanna, as noted in chapter 9, was presented by the grand jury for being in great measure guilty with her husband in exercising extreme cruelty toward their late servant John Walker. In her case, however, the presentment continued without trial for three years, until the court on 1 June 1658 ordered that she would be held for trial if anyone wished to prosecute her for the offense, but no one came forth, and the court ordered the presentment erased from the records. [22]

In view of the varying conditions under which servants worked, it is not surprising that runaway servants were a frequent problem, such as the case of Thomas Byrd, a servant to Mr. James Cudworth, who on 4 January 1641/42 was sentenced to be whipped once at Barnstable and once at Plymouth for running away from his master and breaking into a house and stealing clothes. According to Bradford, three of the four men who murdered an Indian in 1638 were servants who ran away at night from their masters, "and could not be heard of, for they went not the ordinarie way, but shaped shuch a course as they thought to avoyd the pursute of any." Runaway servants became such a problem in all colonies that one of the articles of the United Colonies provided "if any servante rune away from his maister into an other of these confederated jurisdictions, that in shuch case, upon the certificate on one magistrate in the jurisdiction out of which the said servante fledd, or upon other due proofe, the said servante shall be delivered, either to his maister, or any other that pursues and brings such certificate of proofe."[23]

Involuntary servitude was more associated with nonwhites, but an Englishman, too, could find himself in this situation. Webb Adey could only be described as a ne'er-do-well (see Part III). On 2 October 1637 he and several others were presented for disorderly living and were ordered to give an account of how they lived. On 5 June 1638 he was presented again for working on two Sundays and for disorderly living in idleness and nastiness, and he was sentenced to sit in the stocks. Further, he was ordered to find himself a master, and if he could not, the court of Assistants would find a master for him. In order to have fitting clothes and be ready for service, he was ordered to raise some money by selling or leasing his house. On 2 July 1638 Adey was ordered to become a servant to Gov. Thomas Prence on trial, and if Prence then did not want him, the court would find him another master. His house and lands would be sold to anyone offering the most for them, and his personal property was to be inventoried by the constable and sold to pay his debts. On 9 June 1653 the court noted that Thomas Brayman and his wife because of his "distracted condition" were out of any employment that might conduce to their maintenance and subsistence, and it therefore ordered that the town of Taunton should take care of him in such way as they thought fit for one in his condition, and his wife be put to service, being young and fit for same, and having no other way that was so likely to procure her maintenance.[24]

The first record we have of a black in Plymouth records is the list of 1643 of those men between sixteen and sixty able to bear arms. The list is quite thorough, ranging from the governor and ministers to servants (for example, Benjamin Eaton is on the list, and he was placed out as a servant for fourteen years in 1635; Webb Adey is on the list; Thomas Williams is on the list; and William Snow is on the list). Also on the list is "the blackamore," and though attempts have been made to identify him with Abraham Pierce, who arrived at Plymouth in 1623, the evidence against the identification is substantial. We still do not know who "the blackamore" was, what his status in Plymouth was, or how long he had been or remained in Plymouth. In the first three printings of this book, a "highly speculative" case was made to indicate that possibly the 1643 blackamore' had been a Hercules Hill or Hills. There was such a person first mentioned in the records on 5 March 1643/4 when the court "upon hearing of the differrence betwixt William Hatch, of Scituate, & his servant Hercules, for the terme he should serve him, whether six or seaven yeares . . . having heard the evedences on both sides, do order that the said Hercules is to serve the said William six yeares, which wilbe untill the third day of July next & then to be free from him."

Hercules Hill was one of eight men from Scituate who went forth on 23 August 1645 on the Narragansett campaign. Thus he was in Plymouth Colony both before and after the 1643 list, but he was not named by name on that list, though he was able to bear arms. Further, the use by the court of his first name only, and the fact that William Hatch came over the records with a last name, and non-whites sometimes had classical names bestowed on them by their masters. However, this argument cannot be very convincing in light of a transcribed parish record of Boughton-under-Blean, Kent, showing a Hercules Hills, son of Hercules Hill, was baptized there on 27 April 1595. There is no evidence that Hercules Hill of co. Kent was identical with Hercules Hill of Scituate, but certainly the name was not impossible for a white man.

There is good evidence that there was a black as a transient in Plymouth Colony as early as 1622. Hoten shows that among the inhabitants of early Elizabeth City, Virginia, was a servant called "John Pedro a Neger and aged 30 in the *Swan* 1623." We have Bradford's words to show that the *Swan* arrived in Plymouth in early summer 1622, or he was taken aboard after the ship left for Virginia, the former is much the more likely."

It is not possible to tell how many blacks might have been in Plymouth Colony, for they would usually appear in records only when involved in some kind of legal situation. But gradually it can be seen that the black population was growing. On 3 May 1653 "A neager maide servant of John Barnes, att this Court accused John Smith, Senior, of Plymouth, for receiving tobacco and other things of her which were her masters, att sundry times, in a purloineing way"; later both were cleared for lack of sufficient evidence and admonished. On 1 November 1676 "A negro named Jethro" who had been captured by the Indians and then retaken by the colonists, was ordered to remain a servant to the successors of his deceased master, Captain Willett, for two years, and then to be freed and set at liberty. During this term he was to receive meat, drink, and apparel "fitting for one in his degree and calling," following which service he was to be provided for competently with apparel. On 1 July 1684 Robert Trayes of Scituate, described as a "negro," was indicted for firing a gun at the door of Richard Standlake, thereby wounding and shattering the leg of Daniel Standlake, which occasioned his death. The jury found the death of Daniel Standlake by "misadventure," and the defendant, now called "negro, John Trayes," was cleared with admonition and fine of £5. On 27 October 1685 Nimrod, a Negro, was found guilty of fornication with Hannah Bonney, and sentenced to be severely whipped and to pay eighteen pence weekly to Hannah for the maintenance of her child for one year, and "if he, or his master in his behalfe, neglect to pay the same, the said negro to be putt out to service by the Deputy Governor."[26]

Most, if not all, of the above cases could be indentured servitude rather than lifetime slavery, and the black servant, like the white, at the end of the term of service could expect to be freed. However, in 1691 a Negro named John was found guilty of burglary and sentenced to stand on the gallows an hour and have his hand burned with the letter "B," and he was described as a slave belonging to Capt. John Williams. John Demos shows that there were other black servants in Plymouth Colony who probably were slaves, judging from the fact that they were passed in wills to heirs in an absolute sense, whereas indentured servants had their remaining term of servitude mentioned. But in general we do not see many black slaves in the colony period, and it is obvious that some blacks, after serving out an indenture, became free. Though outside the colony period by a few years, a document entered in the probate record book on 15 November 1694 is of interest: "I John Saffin of Bristol 'Out of meer love to & for the Incoragment of my Negro man Adam to goe on Chearfully in his Busines and Imployment by me Now put into the Costadie Service and Command of Thomas Sheapard my tennat on Bound feild farme in Bristoll Aforesaid for and Dureing the term of Seaven years from the Twenty fifth Day of march last past 1694.' At the close of that time I do 'Enfranchise, Clear and mak free my said Negro man Named Adam to be fully at his own Dispose and Liberty as other freemen are or ought to be.'" By the 1691 will of Thomas King of Scituate, King set his Negro servant Roben free and gave him £5 and his bed.[27]

Indians, at least in the aftermath of King Philip's War, did not fare well. The bitterness and hatred engendered by the war overflowed into the wholesale perpetual enslavement of Indians, who were frequently sold outside the colony to owners in the West Indies, where they usually died after a short while. Such treatment was not just meted out to those who directly or indirectly might be called war prisoners, but also to any Indian unfortunate enough to be involved in a crime. An example was noted in chapter 6 of how three Indians in 1678 were accused of stealing £25 from Zachariah Allin of Sandwich, and Allin was authorized to sell them into perpetual slavery. But gradually the wounds of war healed, and we see in 1679 the brothers of an Indian woman whom Jonathan Hatch had bought of Captain Church were to pay Hatch £3 and buy freedom for her and her husband; a third Indian purchased by Hatch was to remain with him until he reached twenty-four years of age. Though Indians could still be put into servitude for crimes or for debt, perpetual slavery became rarer. For the most part, in the context of the times, Plymouth Colony's reputation for moderation applied as well to the treatment of servants.[28]

NOTES

1. *Bradford (Ford)* 2:8.

2. Sherley's letter of 25 May 1629, as given in *Bradford's Letter Book*, 45.

3. *PCR* 12:21, 1:94.

4. Ibid., 1:100.

5. Ibid., 12:19; see also Eugene A. Stratton, "The Descendants of Mr. John Holmes, Messenger of the Plymouth Court," *NGSQ* (June and September, 1986).

6. *PCR* 1:45.

7. Ibid., 1:139.

8. Ibid., 1:37.

9. Ibid., 1:110.

10. Ibid., 1:37.

11. Ibid., 1:30.

12. See under Samuel Eddy in Part III; *PCR* 1:36, 43, 128, 2:38, 67; *MD* 3:139, 5:90.

13. See under John Irish in Part III.

14. *PCR* 1:23, 44.

15. Ibid., 1:43.

16. Ibid., 1:103.

17. Ibid., 1:111-13.

18. Ibid., 3:133, 4:154, 3:220, 51.

19. *Bradford (Morison)* 321.

20. *PCR* 11:33.

21. Ibid., 1:35, 141, 3:63, 83, 88, 119. In the case of the Gilbert servant, apparently Gilbert left the colony right after the court's order, and the aftermath is given in chapter 13.

22. *MD* 2:148; *PCR* 3:71-73, 82, 143.

23. *PCR* 2:30, *Bradford (Ford)* 2:264, 359.

24. *PCR* 1:68, 87, 91, 3:37-38.

25. Ibid., 2:69, 90, 8:182 (the indexer erroneously assumed that this is a list of freemen, but the list itself very clearly shows it is those who had taken the Oath of Fidelity). Pope is the source for Hatch arriving on the *Hercules. NEHGR* 66 (1912):87 transcribes the parish register (the IGI shows Hills's baptism in the same parish on 12 April 1589). The John Pedro reference is from John Camden Hotten *The Original List of Persons of Quality, etc.* (London, 1874), p. 258.

26. *PCR* 3:27, 39, 5:216, 6:141, 177.

27. Konig 1:189; Demos, 110-11; *Bristol Co. PR* 1:230; Pope, 271.

28. *PCR* 5:270, 6:14.

CHAPTER 12

Morality and Sex

We are always trying to make puritans of the Puritans and the Plymouth colonists, and then we call them hypocrites if we find they did not always act in the manner we have chosen for them. The people of Plymouth Colony were very human, and they had very human appetites. In some cases they do not resemble the twentieth-century human because of a difference in prevailing knowledge and philosophies, but in others they differed only because of environmental constraints. In matters of sexuality, the Plymouth colonists were subject to all the desires of the flesh inherent in all human beings, but in matters of morality they placed inhibitions on their desires, using the Bible as the justification for the greatest restraints. They emphasized the avoidance of temptation through Bible study, sermons, laws, and, when necessary, after the fact, punishments. They were well aware of how powerful the sex drive could be, and they tried to tame it, for they knew that they could not suppress it. [1]

An example of the conflicting views in the mind of one person can be seen in Rev. John Cotton, the son of the distinguished Rev. John Cotton who has been called "the patriarch of New England," and the uncle of the also justly famed Rev. Cotton Mather. The younger John Cotton graduated from Harvard in 1657, and in 1666 he was invited to become minister of the Plymouth Church, a position he held from 1669 to 1697. For his ordination "Elder Thomas Cushman gave the charge, and the aged Mr. John Howland was appointed by the church to join in imposition of hands." Cotton himself writes that when he arrived at Plymouth in 1667, there were forty-seven church members in full communion (not to be confused with the greater number of attendees) and that during the next thirty years 178 new members were admitted to the church. He was a highly respected minister, known for his sermons, and described by Nathaniel Morton as "a man of strong prtes and Good Abillities to preach the word of God. . .from whom wee have Received many very proffitable truthes." Yet it must have been known by the Plymouth fathers that in 1664 Cotton had been excommunicated from the Boston Church for "immoral conduct," being restored a month later after making penitential acknowledgment. As his son later wrote in a praiseful biography, "And yet what man is there without his failings?" After twenty-eight years of service in Plymouth, Cotton resigned his ministry in 1697, ostensibly over a difference within the church about Isaac Cushman preaching in the area later called Plympton before being designated a ruling elder. However, Judge Sewall in his *Diary* gives as one of the reasons for Cotton's resignation "his notorious Breaches of the Seventh Comandmt." *Thou shalt not commit adultery!* Sewall also played a role in the resolution of the matter, for when he came to Plymouth on 10 March 1697/98, he had a long discourse with Cotton, and told him "a free confession was the best way." After tarrying more than a year at Plymouth, Cotton became minister at Charleston, South Carolina, where he died in 1699 of yellow fever. [2]

There was probably some hypocrisy in the handling of this affair, in that the Reverend Mr. Cotton was not tried by the court for his notorious breaches, but such hypocrisy would have been necessary, for it would not do to expose publicly the inconsistencies of the teacher of morals. Lesser people under suspicion, from the beginning of the colony to the end, faced a trial, and if found guilty, a financial penalty or physical punishment, or both. One of the earliest records we have of punishment involving a sexual offense was from a court of 1 April 1633 when John Hewes and his wife Joan were sentenced to sit in the stocks because Joan conceived a child by him before they were married. At the same court John Thorp and his wife Alice were sentenced to sit in the stocks and fined forty shillings because Alice conceived a child before marriage; however, because of their poverty, they were given twelve months to pay the fine. On 23 July 1633 the governor and council sentenced William Mendlove, the servant of William Palmer, to be whipped for "attempting uncleanes wth the maid servt of the said Palmer, & for running away from his master." A similar case was tried by the Court of Assistants on 21 August 1637, when John Bundy, an apprentice bound to William Brewster, was found guilty of "lude behavior & uncivill carriage" towards Elizabeth Haybell, in the house of her master, Mr. Brewster, and was sentenced to be severely whipped. [3]

It would appear that in Plymouth, as in England, female servants were objects of male lust. On 29 March 1655 John Peck of Rehoboth was presented, and later fined fifty shillings, for "attempting the chastitie of his fathers mayde to satisfy his fleshly, beastly lust, and that many times for some yeares space, without any intent to marry her, but was alwaies resisted by the mayde, as hee confesseth." In the case of a maid who did give in to the importunities of a male servant, Jane Powell, servant to William Swift of Sandwich, confessed to a charge of fornication with David Ogillior, an Irishman, servant to Edward Sturgis, saying she was lured into it "by him goeing for water one evening, hopeing to have married him, beeing shee was in a sadd and miserable condition by hard service." [4]

By far the easiest way to come under suspicion in Plymouth Colony was for a woman without a husband to show signs of pregnancy. The Court of Assistants on 7 August 1638 sentenced Thomas Bordman to be severely whipped for begetting Luce with child before they married, and

Luce, now his wife, was to be sentenced as the court might see fit after delivery. Dorothy Temple, a servant to Stephen Hopkins, was sentenced on 4 June 1639 to be whipped twice for "uncleaness and bringing forth a male bastard," but she fainted after the first whipping, and so the second one was canceled. She was not of course whipped until she had been delivered of the baby and recovered. She named the baby's father as Arthur Peach, who shortly before had been hanged for murdering an Indian. One wonders also what happened in a case like this, where it was impossible for the child's father to marry her. In Dorothy Temple's case, her master, Stephen Hopkins, was ordered to keep her and her child for the duration of her indenture—about two years. However, Hopkins refused to do so, and the Assistants, of whom he himself had been one just a few years earlier, committed him to house arrest until he would either take her back or otherwise provide for her. Mr. John Holmes, the Messenger of the Court, for £3 and other consideration, agreed to take her and her son into his house according to her indenture, and discharge both Hopkins and the colony of any further obligation for their support. It can be assumed that when her indenture was finished, she and her child, if he survived, went elsewhere. [5]

On 1 September 1640 Thomas Pinson and his wife Joan were convicted of incontinency before marriage, he to be whipped and she to sit in the stocks. On 2 November 1640 Francis West and Margery his wife were found guilty of incontinency with one another before marriage, and both were sentenced to sit in the stocks; interestingly, Francis was also sentenced to build a pair of stocks in Duxbury within two months. On 1 March 1641/42 John Caseley and his wife Alice of Barnstable were sentenced for fornication before their marriage, he to be whipped, she to sit in the stocks. On 4 June 1645 John Ellis of Sandwich was sentenced to be whipped at the public post for uncleaness with his wife before marriage, and his wife Elizabeth was sentenced to stand and watch his punishment. On 6 March 1648/49 Peregrine White, born on the *Mayflower*, and his wife Sarah, both of Marshfield, were fined for fornication before marriage. [6]

For church members, sexual offenses could lead not only to physical or financial punishment by the law, but also to excommunication, which was not a light matter, for, aside from religious considerations, it could mean isolation from relatives, friends, and neighbors. In Mr. Lothrop's Barnstable Church, David Linnell and Hannah Shelley confessed to the truth of their "publique ffame touching carnall & uncleane carriages betwixt them," and on 30 May 1652 they were "pronounced to bee cutt off from that relation wch thye hadd formerlye to the church"; they were also on 8 June 1652 punished with scourges for the same offense by the sentence of the magistrates. Again, at Lothrop's church, William Carsley (or Kersley) was "excommunicated & cast out of the church att Bernestable for carnall carriages" on 5 September 1641. Nine lines of the original record are missing, but from the court record given later in this chapter it is clear that his offense was homosexuality." [7]

Judging from the records, two things seem apparent: (1) sexual relations between a single man and single woman were quite common in Plymouth, and (2) in the majority of such known cases, discovery of pregnancy was followed by marriage, though it cannot be said in general whether the intent of marriage existed before the pregnancy. These two conclusions were true in the early days of the colony, and the number of such cases increased as the population of the colony increased. On 30 October 1667 Thomas Delano was fined for "haveing carnall coppulation" with his wife before marriage, his wife being Rebecca, the daughter of *Mayflower* passenger John Alden.The *Delano Genealogy* has the child of that relationship born on the same day his father was being sentenced (official records show that this son died on 5 April 1738 in his seventy-first year, and so would have been born circa 1667). The parents obviously felt the shame of their situation, for they named him Benoni, a Hebrew name meaning "child of sorrow," more commonly used by New England colonists for a son whose mother died at his birth. In June 1688 Nathaniel Parker and Lois Rogers were found guilty of fornication, "but being married together at this Court, were sentenced to pay a fine of five pounds." [8]

On 17 January 1671 Mary Churchill confessed that she was gotten with with child by Thomas Doty, son of *Mayflower* passenger Edward, with whom she had "carnall coppulation" three times. The first occasion was about 15 July last, the second was on 8 August last, and the third was about a "senight" after. Sergeant Ephraim Tinkham testified that around the stated second time, he had gone to Joseph Churchill's house to speak to him, but no one answered his knock. He went in and after he heard some noise from another room, Mary Churchill came forth. He apparently had reason to suspect that Thomas Doty was there, for he asked Mary if Thomas was in the house, and after some pause she said he was. Tinkham and Doty went away together, Tinkham warning him to take heed lest evil come of such carriages. Mary Churchill later was fined £6. At the time of her court hearing, Thomas had fled the colony, but records show that they later married sometime after their first child was born. [9]

Toward the end of the colony period such cases were appearing with regularity in the courts. In the 26 October 1686 Court of General Sessions and Common Pleas, Mary Sutton of Scituate confessed fornication with Joseph Booth, and was sentenced to a £5 fine or be whipped; John Dwelly and his wife of Scituate were ordered to pay £5 each or be whipped for fornication before marriage; Isaac Samson and Lydia Standish confessed committing carnal copulation with each other before marriage and were ordered to pay a £5 fine. At the March 1687/88 session, Jeremiah Hatch of Scituate was bound over for his wife's having a child at nine and twenty weeks after marriage, but he was charged only prosecution and court fees, "he making it appear a possibilyty that the said child might be born before the time of Nature, And that it dyed in some short time after its birth." At the same session John Merritt and his wife Elizabeth of Scituate were fined fifty shillings and costs for premarital fornication, their child "being born twelve weeks too soon, That is to say, at twenty-seven weeks after marriage or thereabouts." At the June 1688 session, John Cole and wife Susanna of Plymouth were found guilty of pre-marital fornication and fined £5. In December 1688 John Rickard and his wife Grace were fined £5 for premarital fornication. In March 1688/89 James Newell "negro" and his wife Mary were fined £5 for fornication. In the County Court of March 1689/90, Susanna Clark of Plymouth was fined fifty shillings for fornication; in September 1690 Sarah Sutton of Scituate was presented for fornication, but left the area, and Martha Doty of Plymouth, daughter of the Thomas Doty and Mary Churchill above, confessed to having committed fornication and was ordered to pay a £5 fine or be publicly whipped. In the March 1690/91 County Court John Kingman, Jr. and his wife were fined £5 for fornication, but on his petition pleading great weakness and also his losses occasioned by his military service in Canada, the court remitted half the fine. Elizabeth Thomas, daughter of John Thomas of Marshfield, too, had half of a £5 fine remitted for "weakness both of body and minde." [10]

In the case of Mary Sutton, above, she made oath that Joseph Booth was the father of her child, and she charged him with having "Divers times bodily and Carnall Knowledge of her within the months of April and May in 1686." The court ordered Booth to pay maintenance for the child. Mary would keep her child until it reached eight years of age, and Booth would pay to the selectmen of Scituate eighteen pence a week for the first year, and twelve pence a week for the next seven years. [11] Presumably the maintenance was based on eight years, because at the age of eight the child would be old enough to be put to work and be able to earn its own living.

As can be seen from the above, the penalties were decreasing as the number of cases increased. And in fact, when there was a previous contract of marriage between the accused couple, the penalty was often less. When the father was unknown, it was customary for midwives at the time of childbirth to get the mother in her weakness to disclose the name of the father. Efforts were made to get the father to marry the mother, and this was not just a matter of morals, but also of economics, so as to prevent the mother and child from becoming public charges. Such a marriage did not always take place, though, as when Elizabeth Warren, a granddaughter of *Mayflower* passenger Richard Warren, accused Joseph Doty, a son of *Mayflower* passenger Edward Doty, of fathering her child. Doty put up a bond of £80 on 27 October 1674 to ensure his answering the charges, but no more appears about it in the records; however, Doty was apparently married at the time, and Elizabeth Warren later married William Green. Doty married Deborah Ellis, whose parents, Lt. John Ellis and Elizabeth Freeman, daughter of Sandwich's leading citizen, Edmond Freeman, are mentioned above as being fined themselves for fornication before marriage. In a similar case, Elizabeth Soule, daughter of *Mayflower* passenger George Soule, and Nathaniel Church, grandson of *Mayflower* passenger Richard Warren, were fined on 3 March 1662/63 £5 for fornication, and on 5 October 1663 Elizabeth Soule sued Nathaniel Church for £200 for failing to marry her, with the court awarding her £10. On 2 July 1667 Elizabeth was in court again "for comitting fornication the second time," and this time she was sentenced to suffer corporal punishment by being whipped at the post. [12]

In some of the records showing how sexual offenses were punished, we see hints of double standards revealing underlying attitudes of colonists, not only toward Indians, but also toward women. On 3 September 1639 Mary, the wife of Robert Mendlove of Duxbury, was charged "with dallyance divers tymes wth Tinsin, an Indian, and after committing the act of uncleanesse wth him as by his owne confession by sevall interpters is made apparent, the Bench doth censure the said Mary to be whipt at a carts tayle through the townes streets, and to weare a badge upon her left sleeve during her aboad wthin this govnt; and if shee shalbe found wthout it abroad, then to be burned in the face wth a hott iron; and the said Tinsin, the Indian, to be well whipt wth a halter about his neck at the post, because it arose through the allurement & inticement of the said Mary, that hee was drawne thereunto." On 26 October 1686 Ruth Everett of Scituate was convicted "of having a bastard child Born of her Body which by the complexion appears to have been begotten by an Indian and she will not confess who the father of it is," and thus she was sentenced "to be whipt 30 stripes: 15 now at Plimouth and 15 at Sittuate. . .unless she in the meantime confess who the father of her child is." Hannah Tubbs, wife of William Tubbs, Jr. of Duxbury, was sentenced in 1687 to a £5 fine or thirty stripes for agreeing with James Brown, an Indian, to commit adultery with him. Yet in June 1688, when Thomas Wild of Marshfield was charged with getting Hannah, the Indian servant of Joseph Waterman, with child, he was ordered only to pay Waterman twenty shillings "toward the charge occasioned thereby," and nothing more appears in the records about the case. [13]

Whipping at a cart's tail while the cart was drawn through town was considered a more severe punishment than whipping at the post, and was used for aggravated offenses. On 3 October 1665 Sarah Ensign was convicted of committing "whoredom" aggravated with diverse circumstances, and sentenced to be whipped at a cart's tail, with the number of stripes not to exceed twenty to be determined by whichever magistrate would oversee the punishment. In Scituate on 3 September 1639 Christopher Winter was sentenced to be whipped at the post at the governor's discretion for committing uncleaness with Jane Cooper, whom he later married. For her part, Jane was sentenced to be whipped at a cart's tail, but Jane was apparently a woman with a past. In 1638 Winter had been fined ten shillings for engaging to marry Jane Cooper "contrary to order & custome of this govment." He was also excommunicated from Mr. Lothrop's church "for marrying of one Mrs Cooper a woman of scandalous carriage, beeing vaine, light, proud, much given to scoffing." He had been warned not to marry her and part of his crime was to have broken his promise that he would not do so. Interestingly, William Vassall and Timothy Hatherly, known for their liberal sentiments, and "Goodman Raylings" (probably Thomas Rawlings, but possibly Henry Rowley), disagreed with the decision to excommunicate. [14]

Very strangely, on 4 October 1648 Christopher Winter "and his wife haveing been presented, the 8th of June, 1648, for haveing knowlidg each of other before publicke mariage," paid a fine to the treasurer, Captain Standish, and were cleared. To be punished again ten years later for the same offence for which he had previously paid the penalty by being whipped, seems highly unusual. Could Jane have died, and Christopher have married another wife after having previous sexual relations with her, or could this be his nephew Christopher following in his uncle's footsteps? Unfortunately, not much is known about this Winter family. It would be easy to think of Catherine Winter of Scituate, who was presented for fornication with her "father-in-law" James Turner (actually her stepfather) on 2 March 1651/52 as Christopher's daughter; but she was in fact the daughter of John Winter of Scituate, thought by some to have been the brother of Christopher. [15] Christopher Winter will appear again.Though in some cases it appears that the records confuse the meanings of fornication and adultery, most of the time the courts made a careful distinction between the terms. For sheer numbers, cases of fornication far exceeded cases of adultery, but it is clear that adultery was quite visibly present in the colony. On 7 December 1641 Thomas Bray of Yarmouth, a single person, and Anne, the wife of Francis Linceford, were charged with having "comitted the act of adultery and uncleanesse, and have divers tymes layne in one bed together in the absence of her husband, wch has beene confessed by both pties." Being found guilty, they were sentenced to be severely whipped immediately at the public post and again at Yarmouth, where the offense was committed, and they were to wear as long as they were in the colony the two letters "AD" for "Adulterers" on a conspicuous part of their upper garments, and if they were found anywhere in the colony without the letters, they would be whipped on each such occasion. On 5 March 1656/57 William Paule, a Scotsman, was sentenced to be whipped and to pay the costs of his imprisonment and punishment for his "unclean and filthy behaviour with the wife of Alexander Aines." Katherine Aines was sentenced to be whipped at both Plymouth and Taunton and to wear a red letter "B" on her upper garment. Alexander Aines, for leaving his family and exposing his wife to such temptations, was sentenced to sit in the stocks while his wife and Paule were being whipped, and also to pay the costs of his wife's imprisonment and punishment. [16]

On 10 June 1662 Thomas Bird was sentenced to be whipped twice for making several adulterous attempts on Hannah Bumpas, and she was sentenced to be publicly whipped for yielding to him and not making such resistance as she should. Bird was also to pay £10 to her as part satisfaction for the wrong he had done her. Jane Halloway, wife of Samuel, of Taunton, was sentenced on 1 March 1669/70 to be publicly whipped following her recovery from delivery of the baby she was then carrying. She had accused Jonathan Briggs of committing adultery with her, and her husband later sued for divorce because of her "audacious asserting and affeirming that shee had comitted adultery." On 29 October 1671 a jury found John Buck and Mary Atkinson guilty of adultery, but the court changed the charge to fornication, since it was not known if her husband was alive at the time the act was committed; they were sentenced to be publicly whipped at the post or to pay a fine of £10 each. They chose the latter. On 4 March 1673/74 the court noted that Nathaniel Soule was to be summoned to its next meeting to answer the charge of committing adultery with an Indian woman. [17]

Of course, barring confession or a couple being caught *in flagrante delicto*, it would have been harder to prove adultery than fornication resulting in pregnancy. The Plymouth courts were probably as fair as any courts of the time could be, and the Plymouth magistrates found themselves at times in a very delicate balance between their desire to punish morality crimes and their sense of not wanting to injure the innocent. Sometimes they found a compromise. On 2 March 1651/52 the Court of Assistants ordered Edward Holman, who had been observed to frequent the house of Thomas Shrive "at unseasonable times of the night, and at other times, which is feared to bee of ill consequence," to keep away from Shrive's house, and ordered Shrive's wife not to frequent the house of Holman, and to avoid his company. In another case, on 1 June 1663 the court went one step further, ordering Joseph Rogers to remove his dwelling from Namassakeesett, because he had been keeping company with Mercy, the wife of William Tubbs "after such manor as hath given cause att least to suspect that there hath bine laciviouse acts comitted by them." William Tubbs was ordered not to allow Rogers to come to his house, and Rogers was told that if he should be found at Tubb's house or in the company of his wife, he would be severely whipped. On 6 March 1665/66 the court required a bond of £20 from John Robinson, plus £10 each from two sureties, for his future good behavior, he having been convicted of some lascivious speeches and actions toward Frances, the wife of Thomas Crippin. Crippin was also accused of being a "pandor of his wife in lightnes and laciviousenes," and he, not being able to find sureties, was required to bind over to the court £40 in livestock and other property. Jonathan Hatch was convicted of unnecessarily frequenting the house of Thomas Crippin, giving rise to "suspision of dishonest behavior" towards Crippin's wife, and he was warned to keep away from her or "hee will answare it att his peril." [18]

We find very few cases of clearly identified rape. Certainly some of the cases where a man is accused of "attempting the chastity of" someone might have been attempted or actual rape, but the wording frequently leaves room for doubt. One clear cut case was tried on 30 October 1677, when Ambrose Fish was accused that he did "by force carnally know and ravish Lydia Fish, the daughter of Mr. Nathaniel Fish, of Sandwich aforsaid, and against her will." Rape was a capital offense and the "verdict of the jury of life and death" was that "if one evidence with concurring cercomstances be good in law, wee find him guilty. But if one evidence, with concurring cercomstances, be not good in law, wee find him not guilty." This apparently meant that Lydia Fish herself was the only witness of the act. The court hedged, sentencing him to be publicly whipped. Lydia was a granddaughter of the Reverend John Miller, and Ambrose Fish was possibly her brother. Another case (mentioned in chapter 6) involved an Indian named Sam, who on 31 October 1682 was found guilty by his own confession and by the jury of raping an English girl, "wickedly abusing the body of Sarah Freeman by laying her downe upon her backe, and entering her body with his. Hee was centanced by the Court to be severly whipt att the post and sent out of the country [colony]." What appears to be attempted rape was described in a presentment of 5 March 1655/56, when Richard Turtall was accused of lascivious carriage toward Ann Hudson, the wife of John Hudson, "taking hold of her coate and inticing her by words, as alsoe by taking out his instrument of nature that hee might prevaile to lye with her in her owne house." [19]

Though fair-minded in determining guilt, the Plymouth leaders themselves acknowledged that their punishments were severe. Bradford wrote concerning the year 1642 that it was surprising to see how wickedness was growing in the colony, "wher the same was so much witnesed against, and so narrowly looked unto, and severly punished." He admitted that they had been censured even by moderate and good men "for their severities in punishments." And he noted, "Yet all this could not suppress the breaking out of sundrie notorious sins. . .espetially drunkennes and unclainnes; not only incontinencie betweene persons unmaried, for which many both men and women have been punished sharply enough, but some maried persons allso. But that which is worse, even sodomie and bugerie, (things fearfull to name,) have broak forth in this land, oftener then once." [20]

The event which apparently provoked these observations from the governor was mentioned very briefly in court records of 7 September 1642: "Thomas Graunger, late servant to Love Brewster of Duxborrow, was this Court indicted for buggery wth a mare, a cowe, two goats, divers sheepe, two calves, and a turkey, and was found guilty, and received sentence of death by hanging untill he was dead." The executioner was Mr. John Holmes, the Messenger of the court, and in his account he claimed as due him £1 for ten weeks boarding of Granger, and £2/10 for executing Granger and eight beasts. Bradford described Granger as about sixteen or seventeen years of age. Someone saw him in the act with the mare, and he was examined and confessed. The animals were individually killed before his face, according to Leviticus 20:15, and were buried in a pit, no use being made of them. Bradford relates that on examination of both Granger and someone else who had made a sodomitical attempt on another, they were asked where they learned such practices, and one confessed he "had long used it in England," while Granger said he had been taught it by another, and had heard of such things when he was in England. [21]

The Granger case, as discussed in chapter 9, was severe, and there may have been revulsion against it, for it is a fact that never again in Plymouth Colony was anyone executed for a sex crime, regardless of its nature. When on 6 March 1665/66 William Honeywell was tried on suspicion of "buggery with a beast," he "stiffly" denied it, and "wheras noe sufficient evidence appeered to convict him of the said fact, hee was sett att liberties." On 28 October 1681 the court found Thomas Saddeler of Portsmouth, Rhode Island, guilty of the same crime, noting "a certaine mare of a blackish couller then and there being in an obscure and woodey place, on Mount Hope aforsaid, neare the ferrey, then and there thou didst tye her head unto a bush, and then and there, wickedly and most abominably, against thy humaine nature, with the same mare then and there being felloniously and carnally didest attempt, the detestable sin of buggery then and there felloniously thou didst comitt and doe," and he was sentenced to be severely whipped, to sit on the gallows with a rope around his neck, to be branded on the forehead with a Roman "P" to signify his abominable pollution, and to be exiled from the colony. [22]

There were a few specific homosexual cases at Plymouth, and some suspicions of a few others. We should be careful not to read too much into the records, which could be quite specific when the facts were available to justify fine details, but could be rather vague when the facts themselves seemed flimsy. On 6 March 1648/49 the wife of Hugh Norman and Mary Hammon of Yarmouth were presented by the Grand Jury for "leude behavior with each other upon a bed." Mary Hammon was later cleared with an admonition. On 2 October 1650 (apparently the delay was at her own request "by reason of som hinderances"), Hugh Norman's wife was tried for lewd behavior with Mary Hammon on a bed "with divers lasivious speeches by her allso spoken," and she was ordered to make a public acknowledgment of her "unchast behavior" and to take heed "lest her former cariage come in remembrance against her to make her punishment the greater" in any future offense. There had been earlier charges made by Richard Berry, who accused Teague Jones of committing sodomy and other unclean practices with Sarah, the wife of Hugh Norman; however, on 6 March 1649/50 Richard Berry acknowleged before the General Court that he had given false witness under oath, and he was sentenced to be whipped at the post. [23]

Somewhat more specific, though a bit confusing also, is the case of Lydia Hatch, Jonathan Hatch, Edward Mitchell, Edward Preston, and John Keene. On 1 March 1641/42 Lydia Hatch was sentenced to be whipped for "suffering Edward Mitchell to attempt to abuse her body by uncleanesse," and for not reporting it, and also for lying in the same bed with her brother Jonathan. Edward Mitchell was sentenced to be whipped at both Plymouth and Barnstable for "his lude and sodomiticall practices tending to sodomye wth Edward Preston, and other lude carryages wth Lydia Hatch." Edward Preston was sentenced to be whipped at Plymouth and Barnstable at the same time as Mitchell for his lewd practices tending to sodomy with

Edward Mitchell, and for "pressing John Keene thereunto (if he would have yeilded)." John Keene "because he resisted the temptacon, & used meanes to discover it, is appoynted to stand by whilst Mitchell and Preston are whipt, though in some thing he was faulty." Jonathan Hatch "was taken as a vagrant, & for his misdemeanors was censured to be whipt, & sent from constable to constable to Leiftennant Davenport at Salem." A few days later it was determined that Jonathan Hatch would dwell with Mr. Stephen Hopkins, with Hopkins to have a special care of him. [24]

Considerably more specific was the charge against John Alexander and Thomas Roberts, who were found guilty on 6 August 1637 "of lude behavior and uncleane carriage one wth another, by often spendinge their seede one upon another, wch was proved both by witnesse & by their owne confession; the said Alexander found to have beene formly notoriously guilty that way, and seeking to allure others thereunto." Alexander was sentenced to be severely whipped and burned on the shoulder with a hot iron, to be perpetually banished from the colony, and to be whipped again anytime he might be found in the colony. Thomas Roberts was sentenced to be severely whipped and to return to his master, Mr. Atwood, to serve out his time with him, but he would forfeit any possibility of being granted lands in Plymouth (a later annotation stated "except hee manefest better desert"). In another case, mentioned above in connection with his excommunication from the Barnstable Church, William Kersley (or Carsley) on 7 December 1641 was required to post a £20 bond, with Henry Rowley and Anthony Annable as sureties for an additional £10 each, to ensure his appearance to answer charges for "uncleane carriages towards men that he hath lyen wthall." However, nothing more is heard about this case, and he later married "Mrs. Matthew's syster of Yarmouth." [25]

We see the surety system at work in the case of George Wright, a planter of Rehoboth, who, having been presented by the grand jury for "attempting the chastity of diverse women by lacivious words & carriages," was found guilty, and was required to put up a bond of £40, with Richard Church and Samuel Nash as sureties for an additional £20 each, to ensure his appearance at the October 1647 court. When he did not appear in October, Richard Church and Samuel Nash were given license to bring in George Wright to the court which would be held the following March. On 7 March 1647/48 Lieutenant Nash and Sergeant Church were respited (from losing the money they posted) until the next court, at which time they were to require Capt. George Wright to appear "for whose personall apeerance and good behavior they stand bound." Presumably all they could recover of their £20 each was £5/8, which was a debt owing George Wright by John Dogged of Rehoboth. On 7 June 1648 the court ordered Dogged to provide that much money for the use of Nash and Church "in consideration of the damage befaling them by the abovesaid Gorg Wright, the breaking of his bands for the good behavior." Nothing more appears in court records on Wright, who apparently absconded. He is probably the same Capt.

George Wright mentioned by Roger Williams in a letter to John Winthrop, Jr. as having stabbed Walter Lettice at Newport in January 1649. [26]

In view of all the above, the question will naturally arise about whether there were cases of record of incest in Plymouth Colony. One such case was not strictly speaking in the colony, for Thomas Atkins, the accused, lived on the Kennebec River, an area not in, but under the control of Plymouth. His daughter Mary accused him of having incestuous relations with her many times, which he denied. On 2 October 1660 the trial jury brought in a verdict that he was not guilty "of the said fact," but the court sentenced him to whipping because in his examination he confessed that while drunk he "offered some unclean, insestious attempts to his owne daughter." [27]

Another such case the court viewed with considerable suspicion, but was reluctant to determine conclusively. Christopher Winter, whose marriage to Jane Cooper was so opposed by church and state, was brought to court on 2 March 1668/69 with his daughter Martha Hewitt, the wife of John Hewitt, and charged with incest. The court noted that "it can not be att present proved by full and cleare testimony," but the circumstances were quite suspect. Winter had rejected the suit of two men for his daughter's hand, but shortly after she conceived a child, he invited either one of them to marry Martha. Martha would not divulge the identity of the child's father. When Winter learned that his daughter was with child, he did not seem much upset about it, and did not "reprove or beare witnes against her wickednes, as would have become a father that was innosent." Though formerly very strict with his children, he became indulgent to her "since this wickednes." He talked about going to England about the time her pregnancy became noticed. He told Hewitt that his daughter was frightened of him and one time fell into a swoon because of fright. Hewitt's father testified he went to talk to Winter within one week's time "as I was informed of her being laid," but Winter refused to answer who the father was. The husband testified that once Winter asked him what kind of constitution he had, and John Hewitt replied that he was subject to be angry as well as other men, but did not usually express it in raging terms. Winter also told Hewitt during Martha's delivery that she had a hard time, and "hee feared the midwife should charge it upon her now to tell whose the child was; and I, the said Hewitt, replyed, shee would make her tell if shee could. Hee said, if hee had spoke to her, shee would not, nor durst not, for shee should tell in time convenient." The grand jury decided not to hold Winter for trial, and he was released. On 5 June 1669 John Hewitt tried to divorce his wife, "shee haveing bine detected of whordom; but notwithstanding what evidence was produced by them att this court, the case appeered very diffucult in reference to some pticulars." [28] Perhaps the court felt there was a possibility that Hewitt himself could have been the father, and it was afraid to act either way for fear of making a mistake. Again, it is prudent not to read more into these cases than appears in the records, for it is obvious in many of them that there was more information available to the court at the time than is recorded.

For miscellaneous cases the records show such matters as James Till on 3 September 1639 being sentenced to be whipped for lying and alluring John Bryan to drinking, and for "slandering his dame Emson [his employer, Mrs. Emerson], saying he would go whome & lye wth her." On 8 June 1651 John Bumpus was sentenced to be whipped for "idle and lacivius behavior." On 7 October 1651 Goodwife Ramsden was cleared with an admonition of the charge of "lacivius goeing in the companie of young men," and on the same date Samuel Eaton and Goodwife Halle were presented for "mixed daunsing." In a reversal of the usual sex complaint, John Williams, Jr., who from other records appears to have been a stubborn man, was admonished in 1665 for "sequestration of himselfe from the marriage bed." [29]

Bigamy, too, was found in Plymouth Colony. Nicholas Wade of Scituate in 1680 complained his daughter Elizabeth had married Thomas Stevens not knowing of his earlier marriages. It appeared that at the time Stevens married her, he already had a wife at Boston, a wife and children in England, and another wife in Barbadoes. The court agreed that this was sufficient reason to dismiss Elizabeth from the aforesaid marriage bond, and it dissolved the covenant of marriage between them. Elizabeth was granted the liberty of marrying again, while Stevens was sentenced to be severely whipped at the post. [30]

Governor Bradford wondered "how came it to pass that so many wicked persons and profane people should so quickly come over into this land?" Part of his answer was directed at the servant class, but he could not blame it all on servants. Thomas Cushman, son of the ruling elder who had succeeded Brewster, was ordered in 1664 to pay £5 for "carnall coppulation" with his later wife, Ruth Howland, the daughter of *Mayflower* passengers John and Elizabeth (Tilley) Howland, though the court observed in this case the sin had occurred "before marriage but after contract." It would seem an unusually long contract, for, the child being born on 4 October 1664, the sin would have occurred in January 1663/64, but the marriage did not take place until 17 November 1664. On 3 October 1665 James Cudworth, Jr., son of one of the colony's distinguished leaders, was fined £5 for copulation with his wife before marriage. In 1671/72 Samuel Arnold, Jr., the son of Marshfield's minister, was fined £10 for fornication with his wife before marriage. [31]

In the above records appear the names of Edward Winslow's stepson Peregrine White; the children of magistrates such as John Alden, Edmond Freeman, and John Howland; and grandchildren of highly respected *Mayflower* passengers such as Richard Warren and Myles Standish. Many of these cases were, as was the case of Rev. John Cotton, after Bradford's time, and perhaps they were symptomatic of a second or third generation behaving laxly in the comforts created for them by the hardships of the first generation. Regardless of the reason, though, the records clearly show that Plymouth Colony was in practice no less human than other places at both the same and at other times.

NOTES

1. Edmund S. Morgan, *The Puritan Family* (New York, 1944, 1966), 62-64, points out that the Puritans "have gained from their modern descendants a reputation for asceticism that is not easily dispelled. . . . As a matter of fact the Puritans were a much earthier lot than their modern critics have imagined. . . . In short, the Puritans were neither prudes not ascetics. They knew how to laugh, and they knew how to love." He also points out with examples that a genuine and touching love existed between many married Puritan couples, and there is no reason to believe that the Plymouth settlers were any different.

2. *Encyc. Brit.* 6:612; John Langdon Sibley, *Biographical Sketches of Graduates of Harvard University* (Cambridge, 1873), 1:496-508; *Ply. Church Recs.* 1:111, xxxi-xxxii, 143, 180; *Diary of Samuel Sewall,* vol. 1, 1674-1700, *Mass. Hist. Col.,* 5th Series (Boston, 1878), 5:460, 473. Sibley states that during Cotton's first year in the ministry at Plymouth the number of members increased from twenty-seven to seventy-four, which would seem to differ from some of Cotton's figures.

3. *PCR* 1:12, 15, 65. Concerning the lack of court charges against Mr. Cotton, Judge Sewall, 461, noted that one minister had told others "that they had dealt too favourably with Mr. Cotton." Concerning the charges brought against couples having children born less than nine months after marriage, many apologists for the colonists say that the Plymouth authorities had no concept of premature birth, but the records clearly show that people in the colony well knew the difference between a nine-month baby and a seven-month one, or a six-month one, or a five-month one, etc. Such apologists would prefer to think of their ancestors as stupid rather than immoral.

4. *PCR* 3:75, 91.

5. Ibid., 1:93, 111-13, 127.

6. Ibid., 1:162, 164, 2:37, 85, 138.

7. *NEHGR* 10:40-41.

8. *PCR* 4:168; Joel Andrew Delano, *The Genealogy, History and Alliances of the American House of Delano 1621 to 1899* (New York, 1899), 154; *MD* 9:160; David Thomas Konig, ed., *Plymouth Court Records 1686-1859* (Wilmington, Del., 1978), 1:196.

9. *PCR* 5:83-84, 94; Mrs. John E. Barclay, "Notes on the Dotey and Churchill Families," *TAG* 36 (1960):1-4, gives much more detail about this entire matter, including mention of records showing that Thomas Doty apparently had planned marriage with someone else, for he had contracted to have a house built for him just before he fled, and Mary sued him for support before their marriage.

10. Konig 1:189-90, 194, 196, 199-200, 205, 207.

11. Ibid., 1:190.

12. *PCR* 5:156; Barclay, *TAG* 36:9-10; Robert C. Anderson, "Elizabeth Soule, Wife of Francis Walker and Their Posterity," *MQ* 50:31. Concerning the distinction between fornication before a marriage contract and after a contract but before marriage, *PCR* 11:95 gives a 1645 law that provides that anyone who "shall comitt Carnall copulation before or without lawfull contract shalbee punished by whiping or els pay ten pounds fine a peece and bee Imprisoned during the pleasure of the Court soe it bee not above three daies but if they bee or wilbee married the one to the other then but ten pounds both and Imprisoned as aforsaid; and by a lawfull Contract the Court understands the mutuall concent of parents or guardians if there bee any to bee had and a sollemne promise of marriage in due time to each other before two competent witnesses." As can be seen from the varying sentences, this type of law was probably used more as a guideline than an invariable rule, for the same law continued to contradict what it had just said by stating, "And if any pson or psons shall comitt Carnall Copulation after contract and before marriage they shall pay each fifty shillings and bee both Imprisoned during the pleasure of the Court soe it bee not above three daies; or els in case they cannot or will not pay the fine then to suffer corporall punishment by whiping."

13. *PCR* 1:132; Konig 1:190, 192, 196.

14. *PCR* 4:106, 1:132, 97; *NEHGR* 10 (1856):40-41.

15. Ibid., 2:135, 3:5.

16. Ibid., 2:28, 3:111-12. We do not know what the "B" stood for. A possible clue is in *PCR* 2:57, recording that on 6 June 1643 John Walker, stepson of Arthur Howland, Sr., was bound over to answer charges of "lying with a bitch."

17. Ibid., 4:22, 5:31, 41, 81-82, 140.

18. Ibid., 3:6, 4:42, 116-17.

19. Ibid., 5:245-46, 6:98, 3:97.

20. *Bradford (Ford)* 2:308-9.

21. *PCR* 2:44, 51; *Bradford (Ford)* 2:328-29. In a footnote, Ford states that Granger left a wife and children, and Shurtleff in the index to *PCR*, vol. 2, also assumes that the young Granger was married and a father. However, this seems unlikely for a boy of sixteen or seventeen, and it is probable that the Thomas Granger of Scituate whose administration was granted on 3 January 1642/43, and who was survived by a wife and children, was the executed boy's father.

22. *Bradford (Ford)* 2:315-28; *PCR* 4:116, 6:74-75.

23. *PCR* 2:137, 163, 148. As an example of the type of case where it could be possible to read too much into it, *PCR* 2:170 shows that on 8 June 1651 the grand jury presented John Shaw, James Shaw, Samuel Cuthbert, Benjamin Eaton, Goodwife Gannett, Martha Haward, and William Snow for "vaine, light, and lacivius carriage at an unseasonable time of the night." This was probably something considerably short of a sexual orgy. It is doubtful, too, that sexual misconduct was involved when Ann, the wife

of Thomas Savory, was presented on 7 May 1661 for being found during the time of a church meeting drunk with Thomas Lucas "under an hedge in uncivell and beastly manner" (*PCR* 3:212). Lucas was notorious as a town drunk, and from the general tenor of the records, it can be seen that had there been any sexual connotation, the wording would have been different.

24. Ibid., 2:35-36, 38.

25. Ibid., 1:64, 2:28; Pope, 89.

26. *PCR* 2:112-13, 121, 127; Savage 4:658.

27. *PCR* 3:197-200.

28. Ibid., 5:13-14, 21, 23.

29. Ibid., 1:132, 2:170, 174, 4:93.

30. Ibid., 6:44-45.

31. *Bradford (Ford)* 2:329-30; *PCR* 4:83; Joseph Augustine Cushman, *The First Seven Generations of the Cushman Family in New England* (1964), 13; *PCR* 4:106, 5:86.

CHAPTER 13

Everyday Life and Manners

O ne of the most important facts to keep in mind about Plymouth is that it was a poor colony. In terms of twentieth- century life, so was the seventeenth-century Bay Colony, but Plymouth was even poorer. So much in everyday life was geared to hard economical reality. Welfare and charity were high virtues, but where were they to come from? An interesting illustration may be seen in a court record of 2 March 1657/58:

> Concerning Josepth Gray, servant to Mistress Gilbert, of Taunton, whoe was somtimes since frozen on his feet, and still is lame therof. These are from the Court to the towne of Taunton, to request them, that wheras there is hopes that this spring hee may bee cured, if endeavors be used for that end, that they would please to take some course, either into the Bay or elswhere, for his cure; and what expence they shalbee att about the same, in regard that his said mistress is not in a capacitie to defray the charge, incase hur husband doe come againe into the countrey, and bee found able, hee shall satisfy the said charge; if not, the Court hopes it will not bee unrewarded of God.

The town of Taunton could ill afford the expense the General Court was asking it to incur, and the court pointed to the possibility that Taunton might be reimbursed by a return of Mr. Gilbert, but if not, the court was saying, Taunton must not look to the General Court for any money. Perhaps God would help. Actually, in the case of Joseph Gray, the court decided two months later that the town of Taunton should levy a tax on its residents to pay the costs of his cure. [1]

Whenever anything untoward occurred, the first question was "Who will bear the charge?" There were a number of clearly understood levels of responsibility. First, the person responsible for the expense was responsible for its payment. Next, the family was responsible for its members. Finally the community, usually the town, under some circumstances could be responsible. Numerous records show the concern of the court that a resident bringing a nonresident into the colony must be bound legally to pay any expenses relating to the nonresident. The community had but scant funds to do it. But if a responsible individual could not be found, or if the responsible individual was incapable of bearing the expense, then the community would have to do it. In one case, town residents of Yarmouth complained in 1661 that Richard Childs had erected a cottage within town limits contrary to an order of the court; however, Childs "put in cecuritie to save harmless the towne of Yarmouth from all charge that may arise by the children hee now hath," and the court let him stay and keep his cottage. [2] There is an implication here that the town, once Childs was allowed to become a resident, would accept the financial responsibility, if it ever came down to that, for any new children that Childs might have as a resident.

When in 1654 Robert Titus sold his house and land at Rehoboth and planned to move out of the colony, he found that Mr. Browne, the magistrate there, attached part of his estate to the extent of £50. The court observed that it appeared Titus had, contrary to the mind of the town, received into his house Abner Ordway and a woman, persons of evil fame, with children. The court therefore ordered that when Titus and his family left town, they were to take these people with them, or else put up such security as necessary "for the saveing the inhabitants of the towne harmles from any determent that may befall them by Abner Ordway, or any such as belong unto him." Though there may seem a harshness about such policies, they actually reflect a certain amount of understood charity. The community could not stand by and see an individual or family without food, shelter, or clothing, and if no one else paid the costs, the community would. There was a limit as to how much cost the community could bear, and therefore the policy was to keep the possibility of such events occurring as low as possible. The arguments were to determine who was responsible, but the fact that there would be responsibility was understood. Sometimes the solution to the problem of responsibility seems unfair, such as when a pregnant unmarried girl accused a man of being the father, but the matter could not be proved. Elizabeth Doxey, a servant to the recently deceased Joseph Tilden in Scituate, in 1670 accused Nathaniel Tilden of fathering her child; he denied it, and he could not be found guilty, but the court required him to post security for the child's support "untill another father appeereth." [3]

If a family became destitute, usually because of the inability of the head of the family, through illness or misfortune, to earn the family's subsistence, the town took charge. The Braymans of Taunton are a case in point. They apparently had no children, and Thomas Brayman, "by reason of a distracted condicon in which hee is," could not support himself. The court therefore ordered that the town of Taunton find a place for his wife, who was young, in another home as a servant, and "to dispose of Brayman as they shall thinke meet for one in such condition." The records do not reveal what might have been "meet" under these circumstances, but it is likely that the town was required to support Brayman, perhaps, as was common in eighteenth-century Plymouth, by paying some other family to provide him with food and shelter. A court order of 6 June 1683 (and these orders often repeated what had long been understood to be law or custom) specified in order "that the poor may be provided for as nessesity requireth, this Court ordereth that the celect men in each towne shall take care and see that the poor in theire respective townes be provided for, and are heerby impowered to releive and provide for them, according as nessesitie in theire discretion doth require, and the towne shall defray the charge therof."[4]

Sometimes it was difficult to determine just which town had the responsibility for a given individual or family. In 1680 the court discussed the case of John Harmon, "a decriped man," about whom there had been debate by Taunton and Plymouth as to "which place of the two hee should belonge" and as a temporary measure split the costs evenly between both towns. Harmon came to the court's attention in 1682 as one "whoe hath bin for severall yeers wandering from one towne to another, and not fixed to any place. . .where in justice he ought to be fixed." This was not then a case of a poor man wandering into Plymouth Colony from some other colony, for clearly he was recognized as a colony resident. The court noted that immediately before King Philip's War Harmon had lived in Dartmouth, "wherby hee seemed as probably to belong to that towne as to any other," and Dartmouth was ordered to provide for him at least until the next court session. Beyond the town, it was the colony itself that bore responsibility, as was shown in 1680 when the court handled the case of "a poor orphan, named Sarah Nesfeild. . .whose father was slaine by the Indians." The court allowed Tristram and Anne Hedges of Manamoit (Chatham) £5 for the care of the six-year-old Sarah, and ordered that "of right it belonges to each towne in this govment to releive theire owne poor, yett forasmuch as the village of Mannamoiett is in its infancye, and therfore not soe able to doe as others," Manamoit would pay £3 and the colony treasurer would pay the difference. Some six months later, though, the court ordered Manamoit to remove Sarah from the Hedges and find a fit place for her, and it freed the town from having to pay the £3.[5]

When possible, the court endeavored to prevent a person from becoming a public charge. One example of this can be seen in an order of 1682 to the Duxbury selectmen that they "take some course with Henery Clarke and Thurston Clarke, whoe are like to be in great want, that what stocke they have may be improved for theire benifitt and comfort, soe as not to be a burthen to themselves or theire naighbours." As a preventative measure, towns used a "warning out" process to prevent a person from becoming a public charge. A new person coming into town would invariably come to the attention of the selectmen. It can be inferred from the records that when such a person was wealthy enough (such as if the person bought a farm), or was well known and respected, or if some other resident offered to become financially responsible, there would be no problem. But if a person seemed to have no visible long-term means of support, the selectmen would order the constable to give that person a "warning" to depart from the town within so many days. The warning served two purposes, for it both told the person to leave, and, if the person stayed anyway, it had a legal effect of relieving the town from any financial responsibility. On 28 October 1684, for example, Lieutenant Morton and Joseph Warren, selectmen of the town of Plymouth, informed the court that they had given warning to John Hoskins to depart the town, he being likely to become a public charge. On the same day the selectmen of Scituate complained to the court that toward the end of July, when William Parslow had been in town not above six weeks, they had warned him out of town, yet he remained there. [6]

Since the colonists enjoyed few, if any, luxuries, the conduct of their daily lives exposed them to many hazards. People had to go from one place to another, but travel by foot—by far the most common and necessary means of transportation—was dangerous. A coroner's jury in 1653 found that Thomas Bradley died while walking to Rhode Island by the extremity of heat. Henry Drayton in 1654/55 died while hunting "through the violence of the season." Richard Mann coming from his own house to the farms by walking over a frozen pond in winter fell through the ice and died. Falling through the ice was a frequent cause of accidental deaths, and it occurred because people chanced thin ice in preference to the long way around. Nathaniel West in 1658/59 was on his way to Rhode Island and the coroner's jury reported that "goeing upon the iyce, it brake, and hee fell in and was drowned." In 1662 Thurston Clarke, Sr. died while walking home from Plymouth to Duxbury by getting lost in the snow. Mary Totman, wife of Thomas, died in 1666 by eating a root she thought was good food, but was really poisonous. Many children drowned by falling into brooks, ponds, or rivers. People lived in the open air much more than today and were more subject to accidents caused by nature. Seamen, especially by the nature of their work, lived dangerous lives. [7]

A large percentage of even the most common articles had to be imported, if not from England, then from the Bay Colony, increasing prices considerably. All the books in the various inventories had to be transported from elsewhere, mostly from England. It is not strange then that little is seen of published works by Plymouth authors. Winslow had his works printed in England. Bradford's history remained in manuscript form. When Mr. Charles Chauncey published his *Retractation* in 1641, while he was living in Plymouth Colony, it had to be done in London. Eventually Cambridge acquired a printing press, and when Nathaniel Morton wrote his *Memoriall,* he had it published there. It is evident that Morton could not afford to publish the book himself, and the General Court ordered that money obtained from the ransom of an Indian prisoner be used to defray the cost of printing. Later the court approved the amount of £25 for this purpose, and it is interesting to see that there were cost overruns even in those days, for on 5 July 1669 the court ordered the treasurer "to make good a barrel of marchantable beefe to Mr. Green, the printer att Cambridge, which is. . .more then is due by bargaine, but the Court is willing to allow it on consideration of his complaint of a hard bargaine about the printing of the booke aforsaid." There is no record of any printing press in Plymouth during the colony period. [8]

The inventories left by the colonists give a reasonable approximation of their wealth, though they must be used cautiously, for frequently real estate was not included in inventories, and sometimes testators gave much of their property to their heirs during their lifetimes. Though such inventories illustrate considerably the general poverty of the colony, compared to other places or other times, they also reveal a surprising difference in possessions between the richest and poorest residents. Webb Adey, for example, left a small house and garden valued at £1/10, a twelve-acre lot of land, a small birding gun, a small cracked iron pot, a stock lock, and other small items valued at two shillings. His total estate was valued at £3/7, and he had £4/0/10 due him in debts, while he owed £2/6, including funeral expenses. The 1661 inventory of Thomas Hatch of Barnstable was valued at £14/18. On the other hand, Thomas Lucas, who appears numerous times in court records as the Plymouth town drunk, left a more middling estate of £141/10, of which £39 consisted of real estate, and £30/10/9 consisted of the shovels, hoes, pothangers, etc., in his blacksmith shop. Christopher Winter, who from his frequent problems with church and state might have seemed to have been poor, left a respectable estate of over £237, exclusive of housing and land. At the upper end of the economic ladder, John Browne, Sr. of Rehoboth had an inventory of £655/1/2, and in addition bequeathed well over 2,700 acres of land to his heirs. [9]

The inventories reveal much of everyday life in the colony. Feather beds were a prized possession, passed down from one generation to another. John Browne, Sr. had a bed in the parlor which must have been a featherbed, for it was valued at £24/10, more than some people might pay for a house, and was described as having red curtains and valence with a red worsted rug and coverlid and blanket with pillows. He had three other featherbeds, not so expensive, but one valued at £13 had a bolster with four down pillows, a red stag rug, an old coverlid and blanket, with curtains and valence with a flockbed under it. He left two suits valued at £10 and £9, both with cloak and trooper's coat, and one had a waistcoat and the other a hat. He left other clothes, considerable household equipment, including much pewterware, some weapons, tools, farm equipment, and much livestock, as well as some expensive horses, one mare alone being valued at £17. There is no carriage or indication of any horse-drawn conveyance, but there are a side saddle and a hackney saddle. Valued at £1/4 were three East India tablecloths. Browne also had a looking glass, six red leather chairs plus other chairs, and a case of liquors. Surprisingly, he does not seem to have left any books.

Captain Myles Standish, though not often thought of as an intellectual, was probably as well read as any person in Plymouth Colony. He left an inventory of £358/7, including a house and land valued at £140. His books included a *History of the World* and a *Turkish History*, a *Chronicle of England* and *The Country Farmer*, a *History of Queen Elizabeth*, *The State of Europe*,

Eusebius Dodine's *Herbal*, Dr. Hall's *Works*, Calvin's *Institutions*, Wilcox's *Works*, "Mayors," Rogers's *Seven Treatises*, the *French Academy*, three old Bibles, Caesar's *Commentaries*, Bariffe's *Artillery*, Preston's *Sermons*, Burrough's *Christian Cententment, Gospel Conversation, Passions of the Mind, The Physician's Practice, Earthly Mindedness* and *Discovery*, Ball *On Faith*, Brinsley's *Watch*, Dodd *On the Lord's Supper*, Sparke's *Against Heresy*, Davenport's *Apology*, *A Reply to Dr. Cotton on Baptism*, *The German History*, *The Swedish Intelligencer*, *Reasons Discussed*, a *Testament*, a *Psalmbook*, *Nature and Grace in Conflict*, a law book, *The Mean in Mourning*, *Allegation Against B.P. of Durham*, Johnson, *Against Hearing*, a parcel of old books on diverse subjects in quarto, another parcel in octavo, Wilson's *Dictionary*, Homer's *Iliad*, a *Commentary on James*, and catechisms. [10] Elder Brewster left more books, but they did not show half the breadth of interest or intellectual curiosity as those of Standish.

George Barlow, the cruel special marshal at Sandwich, left a house valued at £2, three swine, two mares, four cows, plow irons, tooles valued at six shillings, two chains, three kettles, two sickles, a ring and double hooks, a staple and hook, a door hinge, four pails and trays, rings and wedges for scythes, one barrel, one saddle, one gun, one bed valued at two shillings and ten pence, two pitchforks, one pair of pothooks and hangers, two oxen, eight acres of upland, three calves, one bed and bolster, pillow and sheets with blankets, two pewter dishes, one coat and waistcoat and britches, two glass bottles, three trays, a staple and ring, one hoe, one frying pan, one bedstead with cord and matts, two hats, two axes, two bags, two old chairs and one new chair, and a pair of spectacles, books, and a brush grouped together at six shillings. [11]

The inventory of Gov. Josias Winslow was not itemized in great detail, but grouped like items together. His purse, rings, apparel, and watch were valued at £54/1, and his personal arms and horse equipment at £18. His silver plate had a value of £45, and he left books valued at £31/7. By his will of 1691, Tooto, a Negro man, left his house and land to John Baxter, and all his movables and riding horse to Temperance Baxter. He left his young horse to Mr. Thacher and his mare, colt, and an iron kettle to Lydia Taylor, two cows to Mercy Denison, one cow to James Gorham, and the increase of his cattle and his oxen to Mr. Baxter to pay for his burial at the burying place "neer his mistres feet as may Conveniantly be." Mr. William Sergeant left a house and land at Barnstable valued at £50 and a house and land at Malden valued at £176. It is known that Mr. William Vassall had a surveying instrument, and the inventory of his neighbor in Scituate, James Cudworth, shows that Cudworth had a pocket compass. [12] The inventory of merchant John Barnes could be expected to be both interesting and unusual, and is given as appendix K. Virtually all inventories showed farming equipment, for even when a colonist worked in town, he would usually also engage to some extent in farming.

Plymouth was mainly a group of farm communities. Fishing was an important industry, and an iron works was developed in Taunton, but the real business of the colony was agriculture. The towns had a small collection of stores and shops, but they existed mainly to serve the surrounding farms. There were blacksmiths and rope makers, coopers and wheelwrights, barbers and bricklayers, carpenters and butchers, tanners and nailers, and there were tailors, too. They served each other and their fellow townsmen, but all were supported in one way or another by agriculture. The various trades can be seen from the legal documents of the times: wills, deeds, court records, and others, where frequently the individual had to be identified or defined. A prosperous farmer tending land that he owned was a yeoman, the backbone of the community, the social level just below the gentry. Above the yeomen were the gentry, the gentlemen, who were addressed as "Mr.," and were identified in the records with the abbreviation "gent." after their names. The minister, the higher officials, the richest farmers, if not gentlemen by birth, in the tradition of English social mobility would become gentleman by accomplishment and position. [13]

Next below the yeoman was the husbandman, the one who cultivated the soil for himself, though frequently on leased land. Often the sons of a yeoman cultivating land borrowed from their father would describe themselves as husbandmen. The distinction does not seem like much today, but it had meaning then; the husbandman might aspire to be a yeoman, but the reverse would not be true.

Merchant was an occupation that might mean anything involving the buying and selling of a variety of products. An occupation of considerable importance was that of innkeeper, for the state recognized the need to provide comfortable lodging, food, and drink for visitors. James Cole became Plymouth's best known innkeeper with his establishment on Cole's Hill on the north side of Leyden Street. His worth to the community was shown in 1659 when the court awarded him £10 to repair his house "soe as it may bee fitted as an ordinary for the entertainment of strangers." Further down the social ladder were laborers, free men, not servants, who hired themselves out for daily wages. [14]

From yeoman on down the social scale, a man was called "goodman," and a women "goodwife," the latter familiarly shortened at times to "goody" (and could be abbreviated as "G" in the records). Men above yeoman status were addressed as "Mr.," pronounced "Master," and their wives were addressed as "Mrs.," or "Mistress." A young girl coming from a higher class family would also be called "Mrs.," even though unmarried.

Much of the early life of Plymouth is reenacted on a daily basis about eight months out of the year at Plimoth Plantation in modern-day Plymouth, where a full-size reproduction of the village exists as it was in 1627 insofar as it can be reconstructed from the records. "Interpreters" representing people known to have lived in 1627 Plymouth speak in an old English dialect as they go about their daily business of mending sails, hoeing gardens, killing chickens, cooking codfish cakes, milking goats, and performing all the other activities of life in a small frontier agricultural village. To go beyond 1627, one has to use imagination, for with time the village grew into a town and changed. Wearing apparel for the richer residents undoubtedly became more luxurious. The small one-room houses with lofts were enlarged with lean-tos and an extra story. The better houses acquired glass windows, and there would have been more houses combined with shops. The early meetinghouse-fort was left to decay, and it is said that some of the timbers were used in the construction of Sgt. William Harlow's house, a house that still exists in today's Plymouth.

One could imagine Mr. John Browne coming to Plymouth on a handsome horse from Rehoboth, perhaps to attend a court session. He might stay at James Cole's inn in the town center, as Judge Sewall, according to his *Diary,* would later stay there. Webb Adey might be nonchalantly leaning against a building as Mr. Browne passes, and one wonders if he would tug at a forelock as a sign of respect, as was done in England. Probably not, for there was more of a leveling influence at work in the new world, though Adey might have murmured a respectful greeting, for, who knew, but what he might be the defendant in a case where Mr. Browne could be one of the judges. There would be others at the inn, so Browne would not lack for company for supper. He would probably merit a room, or at least a bed, to himself, and so he could get a good night's rest. He might have visitors in the morning, perhaps the governor would drop by to say hello and tell him about current concerns. It would be a short walk to the courthouse, and Browne would take a seat of honor. After a day of give and take at court, in the afternoon he might drop by John Barnes's general store and buy some imported fabric to bring back to his wife, and then perhaps he might sup with the minister. Leaders from other towns would want to get his attention during his stay at Plymouth, and there would be talk about the Bay Colony, the danger of Indian uprisings, the division between church members and nonmembers, or the increasing number of undesirable people coming into the towns from elsewhere. After the daily sessions at court, Browne might visit a blacksmith for his horse, see a tailor about a new cloak, buy some Spanish wine to bring home with him, or complain to another Assistant about a bridge between Plymouth and Rehoboth left unrepaired.

At court he would give an account of his activities as a magistrate at Rehoboth, and would defend the interests of his town in obtaining fairness in the levying of taxes and troops. He would ride out of town, no doubt, with more than he had come, and perhaps he would tow a smaller horse laden with goods behind him. Plymouth was not Boston, but it had more contact with Boston than Rehoboth did, and so more goods would have been available there. Browne would ride back on dusty roads, but they would be passable, for each town's highway supervisors would bear responsibility for their care. He would probably travel by way of Taunton, and, though there would at this time be more wilderness than cultivation along the way, every now and then he would pass a farm and perhaps wave to a goodman in the fields, or he might even stop and have a mug of cider at the house of someone he knew well. He would not be alone on the road, for there would have been occasional horsemen and an abundance of people walking from one town or farm to another town or farm, most of them colony residents, including some Indians. There would be a number of strangers, too, wondering who he was, for his horse and his dress would have told them he was somebody of importance. Everywhere he went there might be a feeling of bustle and busyness, for this was a growing colony, and for many there would have been a feeling of enterprise in the air.

It is a subject of much debate as to just how much New England resembled old England in its manners, customs, economy, and everyday life. Certainly there was no complete break with the past. This could be seen in the wages of a laborer, which were regulated in Plymouth as in England, as were the prices charged by the merchant, or the beer sold by the innkeeper. Though inflation was known in the colony, especially in those years of the mass migrations to the Bay Colony when Plymouth exports were in great demand, there was more usually a stability of prices, so that a given object could be said to have a customary, or fair, price. These prices were enforced by the court, and sometimes set by committees appointed by the court. As early as 5 January 1635/36, John Doane, John Winslow, Manasseh Kempton, Kenelm Winslow, John Jenney, John Browne, and John Barnes were chosen to assist the governor and council to set rates on goods to be sold and wages to be paid laborers. The court not only regulated prices, but sometimes quality. In 1665 the court required the clerk of the Taunton iron works to inform the owners that there was complaint of bad iron being produced there, and ordered him that henceforth the iron must be "good and marchantable" so that the colony would no more be injured. *Mayflower* passenger Stephen Hopkins was presented by the grand jury on 5 June 1638 for selling beer for two pence a quart that was not worth a penny a quart. Much of what was done in Plymouth Colony, as elsewhere at the time, was not done on the basis of scientifically objective testing, but rather by experience, or "common fame," which was a well understood expression to indicate collective experience—the grand jurors knew the quality of beer when they tasted it, just as they did not need breath analyzers to tell if Thomas Lucas was drunk again. In 1640 John Barnes was presented for buying rye at four shillings per bushel and selling it for five shillings "without adventure or long forbearance"; or, in other words, a twenty-five percent profit was justified only when the merchant was taking a sizeable risk, or was deferring recovery of his investment for a long period of time. [15]

Though there was respect for the law in Plymouth Colony, it did not necessarily carry over to the law enforcers. A law of 20 October 1646 ordered that "any person [casting] contempt & reproch on the Marshall or any of his by reason off and concerning his office shalbe fined for every such default to the Goverments use [ten shillings]." The marshal, of course, was a colony office, and it is clear that he might not have always enjoyed respect. Each town had one or more constables, and it is obvious that this could be an onerous position. In 1652 George Russell was fined £3 for abusing the constable of Scituate in the execution of his office. In 1654/55 William and Elizabeth Randall were presented for abusing the constable of Scituate, Walter Hatch, who, "when he strained for the majestrates table, [the] wife tore the destresse out of his hand, and hurt his hand soe as blood was sheed." When the constable chosen at Sandwich in 1655 refused to come to Plymouth to be sworn in, the court threatened him with a fine. In 1658 the court awarded William Bassett, the Constable of Sandwich, £5 "in regard of the much trouble" he had had, and the "great losse that hee hath lately sustained." In 1659 Thomas Butler was fined fifty shillings for refusing to serve as constable. In 1669 Robert Parker was chosen as constable by the town of Barnstable, but refused to serve. In 1674 William Hatch and Jeremiah Hatch were fined for refusing to serve as constables. In 1675 Robert Crossman, Sr. of Taunton was fined forty shillings for abusing the constable, throwing a stick at him, and drawing a knife and threatening to stab him. In 1680/81 Nathaniel Southworth and Joseph Warren, Jr. were fined ten shillings each for refusing to aid the constable of Plymouth in the execution of his office. The constable was probably the most common interface between the law and the individual, and resentment against some types of laws, such as paying tax for the magistrates' meals or the ministers' maintenance, or the harsh treatment given to Quakers, made this a most undesirable position. [16]

As time went on, Plymouth Colony resolved some old problems and acquired new ones. The court could not satisfy all complaints. Though people were frequently punished for slander, in 1677 when Captain Goulding, David Lake, and Thomas Lake complained that they were meeting with opposition and threatening speeches from neighbors to disturb them in their peaceful enjoyment of lands granted them by the court, the court said it would maintain their title to the lands, "but as for words, they must beare with them when they meet with them." In 1670 the court ordered that profits from fishing with nets at Cape Cod would go to provide a free school for the training of youth in literature for the good and benefit of posterity, and in 1678 it gave £5 from fishing profits to the schoolmaster at Rehoboth, and it expressed an intention to have a grammar school in each town of the colony. People complained of high taxes, and some towns were using tax methods that the court found odd. In 1668, at the complaint of Mr. Nicholas Byram that Bridgewater was overtaxing people with dormant lands and undertaxing those who used the town's common lands, the court told the town to find some more equitable way. In 1670 the court, in answer to the complaint of land owners at Rehoboth, ordered the town not to tax them more than thirty shillings for a £40 rating. [17]

These court records have left to posterity so much about the everyday life of Plymouth that, in part, it makes a reconstruction of that life relatively easy. But at the same time they also leave a very incomplete picture. They give us almost nothing of the humor of life that must have been there. We see married couples fighting, but we do not see them enjoying each other's company. It is a pity there was no Judge Sewall in Plymouth, or no Samuel Pepys, both contemporaries to the colony, to record the pleasures that people might get from eating together, singing together, or playing together. Other than a very infrequent reference to merriment, such as Emanuel Altham's comment on Governor Bradfords' wedding, the contemporary records about Plymouth Colony might lead us to suppose that no one in the colony ever laughed. But we know otherwise, for the records show a very human people, and all our experience tells us that very human people do laugh and have fun. We must supply from our imagination much that is missing from the records, but we are fortunate to have as much as we do.

NOTES

1. *PCR* 3:132, 134.
2. Ibid., 3:220.
3. Ibid., 3:52, 5:43.
4. Ibid., 3:37-38, 6:109-10.
5. Ibid., 6:54, 94, 54, 56.
6. Ibid., 6:99, 147, 145.
7. Ibid., 3:39, 70, 93, 158, 4:12, 130, 5:101, 122-23, 3:16, 195-96.
8. *Bradford (Ford)* 2:301; PCR 4:173, 186, 189, 5:25.
9. *MD* 11:8; *MSR*, 529; *Ply. Colony PR* 4:1:14, 4:2:61; *MD* 18:18.
10. *MD* 3:153.
11. *Ply. Colony PR* 4:2:82.
12. *MD* 5:82, 12:188; *Ply. Colony PR* 4:2:20, 4:2:10.
13. For an excellent study on agriculture in Plymouth Colony, see Darrett B. Rutman, *Husbandmen of Plymouth — Farms and Villages in the Old Colony 1620-1692* (Boston, 1967).
14. *PCR* 3:166.
15. Ibid., 1:36, 4:98, 1:87, 2:5.
16. Ibid., 11:53, 3:10, 75, 84, 137, 174, 5:20, 225, 169, 6:56.
17. Ibid., 5:242, 107-08, 259-60, 4, 48. More details on everyday life and manners can be found in Demos's *Little Commonwealth*.

CHAPTER 14

Writers and Records

W e are fortunate that the people of Plymouth believed in keeping records, though we could wish that they had kept more, especially during the early years. There are two general types of written sources for contemporary information on Plymouth Colony. The first consists of narratives written by people who either were there or were in contact with people there. The second consists of official records or statistics kept by institutions, such as courts, towns, and churches.

The earliest extant narrative record is known as *Mourt's Relation* (see Bibliography), although its proper title is *A Relation or Journall of the beginning and proceedings of the English Plantation setled at Plimoth in New England, by certaine English Adventurers both Merchants and other. With their difficult passage, their safe arivall, their joyfull building of, and comfortable planting themselves in the now well defended Towne of New Plimoth.* It is difficult to know where the title ends and description of the contents begins, for there is more on the title page, including "With an answer to all such objections as are any way made against the lawfulnesse of English plantations in those parts."

Published in England in 1622, and containing various letters and narratives, including a letter from Edward Winslow dated 11 December 1621, *Mourt's Relation* was obviously sent via the *Fortune* on its return voyage from Plymouth. A preface "To the Reader" is signed "G. Mourt," which is almost certainly George Morton. The curtailing of the last syllable frequently occurs at this time, such as "Coop" for "Cooper," and Richard More's wife was frequently called Christian Hunt, for it is that way in the records, though Mrs. Barclay has shown that it was really Hunter. Morton could not have written such firsthand narratives of early life at Plymouth, for he did not arrive there himself until 1623, but this is consistent with his introduction, in which he states that shortly he hopes to effect a visit to Plymouth, "these relations comming to my hand from my both known and faithful friends." Edward Winslow appears to be the author of most of the material, though William Bradford probably wrote some. The whole was intended, at least in part, to attract new settlers, and thus emphasizes the peaceful relations with the Indians, the availability of food, and the pleasant living conditions, though it also relates enough of the new colonists' sufferings and hardships to indicate that it is an honest history.

A word would be in order here on the language of contemporary writers. They used an English akin to that used by Shakespeare and the writers of the King James version of the Bible, though not so literary. Thus Plymouth writings can appear a bit more modern to us than these other works, and this can be misleading. It is tempting to give familiar words their modern-day meaning, though in some cases they meant something else to the people using them. In the full title of *Mourt's Relation*, for example, "Adventurers" meant people who were putting themselves or their capital at risk, hoping for a gain—it did not mean thrill seekers. When Bradford called John Howland a "lusty" man, he meant lively or happy, without sexual connotation (see *Bradford [Morison]*, 59 fn). When Pastor Robinson wrote to Brewster that it was not "convenient" for him to give the sacraments, he did not mean that Brewster had more important things to do, but that it was not fitting or proper. If the meaning of a word, either familiar or unfamiliar, is important, it is helpful to look it up in the *Oxford English Dictionary*, where examples of its use in the sixteenth and seventeenth centuries are often found. For instance, a number of times Plymouth documents refer to someone's "meerstead," where the connotation is vaguely that of a land holding, but what type of land holding? The *Oxford English Dictionary* shows that the word "mere" was sometimes spelled "meer" and it referred to staking out boundaries, as was written in 1598 "Wee. . .have sett downe certain stakes wch meyre out ye saide landes," and in 1621 "This purchase will. . .meare and bounde his owne [property]." Thus a meerstead was a plot of land which had been staked out as belonging to someone. It is especially helpful in reading about land grants to know that "want" could mean "lack," and "all those who want land," means "all those who lack land." [1]

In 1624 Edward Winslow published his *Good Newes from New England: Or a true Relation of things very remarkable at the Plantation of Plimoth in New England* (London, 1624), in which he continues the narrative begun in *Mourt's Relation* up to September 1623, when Winslow sailed on the *Anne* for England. Inasmuch as Winslow wrote in some detail about relations with the Indians, how war with the Narragansetts was averted, the arrival of new ships, and Weston's colony at Wessagusset, he fills in many of the gaps in Bradford's writings. In 1662 Phineas Pratt submitted a paper to the Massachusetts General Court called "A Declaration of the Afaires of the Einglish People [that first] Inhabited New Eingland," in which he gives considerably more details on the sad plight of the Weston settlement and of the rescue of the settlers by Captain Standish.

Winslow felt compelled to write justifications, and he continued with *Hypocrisie Unmasked* (London, 1646), which was reissued in 1649 as *The Danger of Tolerating Levellers*. The main object of the book can be seen from a subtitle of the *Levellers* edition: "An Historical Narration of the dangerous

pernicious practices and opinions, wherewith Samuel Gorton and Level-
ling Accomplices so much disturbed and molested the severall Plantations
in New-England." The year 1646 was of course the year that Winslow sailed
to England to represent the Massachusetts Bay Colony against charges
made by Gorton. Winslow also includes in his book, however, "The
Ground or Cause of our first planting in New-England," and some pages
on the churches in Leiden and New England. It was during the same
period that Winslow wrote his *New-Englands Salamander, Discovered by an
Irreligious and Scornfull Pamphlet, called New-Englands Jonas Owned by Major
John Childe, But Not Probable to be Written by Him*, which gives a scathing
answer to William Vassall's *New-Englands Jonas*. Vassall himself was the
salamander, whom Winslow bitterly mocks in such passages as "For our
Salamander having labored two years together to draw me to his party,
and finding hee could no way prevaile, he then casts off all his pretended
love." We also find here helpful information on the conduct of the Court
of Assistants in Plymouth, which "next to the word of God take the law
of England for their [precedent] before all other whatsoever."

The most important single document for the events that led up to the
colonization of New Plymouth, together with a narrative of the colony's
history to 1646, is Bradford's history, which he penned mainly between
1630 and 1646. Bradford's manuscript, rediscovered in the middle of the
nineteenth century, included many letters from others and some official
documents of various types, plus his annotated list of *Mayflower* passengers. The story of how the manuscript was lost and then many years
later found is worth repeating. It apparently passed from Governor Bradford to his son Maj. William Bradford, thence to the latter's son Maj. John
Bradford, and thence to his son Samuel Bradford. Increase Mather had
once borrowed the book, his son Cotton Mather made some use of it, and
we know Rev. William Hubbard copied from it. Later Judge Samuel Sewall
borrowed it. In 1728 Rev. Thomas Prince noted on a blank page that he
learned of the book from Maj. John Bradford, who told him it was in
Sewall's hands and suggested that he get it from Sewall to use in the
Chronicles Prince was writing. It stayed with Prince until the Revolution,
and he kept it in his library in Boston's Old South Church. It then disappeared, but knowing that the British occupied the Old South Church, since
it was later found in the Bishop of London's palace, it would seem that
someone on the British side took it to England with him. Bishop Samuel
Wilberforce had access to it in writing a book, and this and other published
clues allowed two men in Boston to recognize that the Bradford manuscript
was in England. After some negotiation it was returned to Massachusetts
in 1897.

The Bradford title of the manuscript is *Of Plimoth Plantation*, and there
are a number of different editions of varying quality. The best two are used
in the present text and are called, after their editors, *Bradford (Ford)* and
Bradford (Morison). Bradford probably wrote his history from a combination
of memory and writings he had at hand. We know he kept miscellaneous

records in a "register" of births, deaths, and marriages of the earliest times in Plymouth, which has long been lost, but which was at least partially transcribed by Rev. Thomas Prince in his 1736 *Chronological History of New England in the Form of Annals.* Prince listed his sources, describing some material from Bradford as "A Register of Gov. Bradford's, in his own Hand, recording some of the first Deaths, Marriages and Punishments at Plymouth: with Three other Miscelaneous volumes of his," all unfortunately lost. [2] We also have some letters to and from Bradford which are not included in his history (see *Bradford Letter Book* in the Bibliography). *Bradford (Ford)* 2:420-21 shows the location of other extant short writings of William Bradford.

Sydney V. James, Jr. put together in *Three Visitors to Early Plymouth* (Plimoth Plantation, 1963) seven letters of early outside visitors: John Pory, an official of Jamestown, Virginia; Emanuel Altham, one of the Merchant Adventurers who was also captain of the *Little James;* and Isaac de Rasieres, an official of Dutch New Amsterdam. These letters, all from the 1620s, give firsthand impressions of curious and articulate men of experience, and are generally favorable to the fledgling colony. They are especially important for the aura of authenticity they give to the fuller writings of Bradford and Winslow; that is, they give a picture that is fully consistent with that derived from the Plymouth writers.

Nathaniel Morton published his *New Englands Memoriall* in 1669, but it was taken in great part from Bradford's history, as Morton himself acknowledged. Since Bradford left off his story in 1646, and Morton continues through 1668, we might expect that we would at least have more contemporary history for the last twenty-two years, but alas the years get scantier as he writes, and the largest part of them are filled with Morton's encomiums on the deaths of prominent individuals, especially ministers. His entire account of the year 1660, for example, gives the election of the governor and Assistants, and then enlightens us with "This year James Pierce, a yong man that belonged to Boston coming on Fishing, and upon occasion putting into Plimouth Harbour, it pleased God that a storm of Thunder and Lightning arose, and by a blow thereof he was slain of a sudden, being much scorched and burnt thereby, although his Clothes were made fast and close about him: so strange was this great work to the wonderment of all that beheld it." The year 1661 was not so memorable, as far as Morton was concerned, for he left us for the year only the election of the governor and Assistants. Still, there are bits here and there that supplement our other sources. For example, under 1662 Morton mentioned King Philip briefly, commented on an earthquake, and told of the death of Mr. John Brown, who "in his younger Years travelling into the low Countries, he came acquainted with, and took good liking to the Reverend Pastor of the Church of Christ at Leyden as also to sundry of the Brethren of that Church, which ancient amity induced him (upon his coming over to New England) to seat himself in the Jurisdiction of New-Plimouth," a fact we would not have were it not for Morton.

Morton was apparently criticized for not including more information about the Plymouth Church in the *Memoriall*, and he therefore wrote *A Breife Eclesiasticall History of the Church of Christ Att Plymouth Anno Domi 1680*. As Morton himself said, referring to his *Memoriall*, "I occasionally took Notice of Gods Great and Graciouss worke in erecting so many Churches of Christ in this wildernes; But it was Judged by some that were Judicious that I was too sparing and short in that behalf; The consideration wherof put mee on thoughts of Recollecting somthing more p'ticularly Relateing to the Church of Plymouth."[3] In his church history, Morton borrowed freely from Bradford's history and incorporated another writing of Bradford's, the "Dialogue or the sume of a Conference between som younge men borne in New England and sundery Ancient men that came out of Holland and old England Anno dom 1648," in which Bradford discussed some of the antecedents of the Plymouth Church. Morton also includes letters, such as from Pastor Robinson, which add to our knowledge of the Separatist movement, and he gives some of his own views on events taking place within the church, so that, for example, it is from Morton that we learn Deacon John Cooke was excommunicated for falling into the error of Anabaptistry.

There are historical narratives by contemporary, or near contemporary, writers who lived outside Plymouth. The Reverend William Hubbard's *A General History of New England from the Discovery to MDCLXXX* (Cambridge, 1815), in spite of the publication date, was actually written in the late seventeenth century by a man who would have had the opportunity to speak directly with a good number of the participants in the making of Plymouth Colony history. Though the pages devoted to Plymouth are not many, and it is apparent that Hubbard, too, had access to Bradford's history, still he gives some details not found elsewhere, such as a description of how Billington murdered the man Hubbard called "his mortal enemy."[4] Hubbard also wrote *A Narrative of the Indian Wars in New England* (Danbury, Conn., 1803), in which he gives us a point of view more favorable to the Indian side of the conflict with the Englishmen than we find in other writings of the time. The Reverend Cotton Mather, in *Magnalia Christi Americana* (Cambridge, 1702), has occasional comments on events and persons of Plymouth Colony that are of interest.

Two early works which should be read by the serious student are William Wood, *New-Englands Prospect* (London, 1634), and Thomas Morton, *New English Canaan* (London, 1637). Wood describes geography, flora, and fauna much more than political and historical events. Morton, the master of Merrymount (see chapter 2), was no friend to the Plymouth Separatists, as he plainly showed in his allegorical and sarcastic book of verse. There is not a lot to add to our knowledge of Plymouth, but as Morison said, "We are heavily in debt to Morton for the jolliest contemporary account of early New England."[5] Morton at times gives us the opposite side of the coin when, for example, he calls Standish "Captain Shrimp," and when he tells us that John Billington, although a continuing problem to Bradford and his followers, was "much beloved by many." Whether we can believe Morton's highly subjective uncorroborated views is another matter. For the later colony years, *The Hinckley Papers,* a collection of letters from and to Gov. Thomas Hinckley, give us a wide perspective of what was happening in and around Plymouth Colony.

There were contemporary writings on the adjacent Bay Colony which contain little of direct interest to Plymouth scholars and much of background interest. Governor John Winthrop's writings are of prime importance here (see Bibliography). The Reverend Alexander Young, *Chronicles of the First Planters of the Colony of Massachusetts Bay,* from 1623 to 1636 (Boston, 1846), gives an excellent sampling of excerpts from some of the other writers, such as John White, Francis Higginson, and Thomas Dudley. Young's companion volume, *Chronicles of the Pilgrim Fathers of The Colony of Plymouth from 1602 to 1625* (Boston, 1844), is not of much interest today, for the reason that its excerpts are mainly a repeat of writings from Bradford and Winslow, where even the casual reader might be better advised to read the originals. Samuel Purchase, *Purchase His Pilgrims* (London, 1626), is another excellent, informative account of early voyages to New England. Far from least are the references to Plymouth and its New England environment to be found in the collected works of Capt. John Smith, recently put together for the first time in a three-volume set (see Bibliography). Smith's writings are most interesting for their own sake, but here and there he also adds firsthand knowledge to better our understanding of early Plymouth, as some of the references in the present text show.

Institutional records are of course drier than some of the lively narratives of Bradford, Winslow, or Thomas Morton, and they can be a danger to us because they are so often single-faceted, but read with a discriminating eye they can tremendously enrich our knowledge of people and events. *Records of the Colony of New Plymouth in New England,* edited by Nathaniel B. Shurtleff and David Pulsifer, 12 vols. (Boston, 1855-1861; reprint, New York, 1968), are indispensable for an understanding of Plymouth Colony and its people. The set is easily accessible to anyone who has a well-stocked public or university library nearby. The first six volumes are Court Orders from 1633 to 1691; volume seven, Judicial Acts, is a record of private law suits, what Plymouth laws called "man against man," from 1636 to 1692; volume eight consists of Miscellaneous Records, that is, births, marriages, deaths, treasury accounts, lists of freemen, at various times, and other lists; volumes nine and ten are the Acts of the Commissioners of the United Colonies; volume eleven consists of the Laws of Plymouth Colony from 1623 to 1682; and volume twelve is our earliest recordings of Plymouth Deeds, covering the years 1620 to 1651. The coverage in the earliest years is spotty, but most informative, giving us such valuable information as the participants in the 1623 land division and the 1627 livestock division (volume twelve). The volumes of Court Orders give us the records of the proceedings of both the General Court and the Court of Assistants. Since both courts governed so much of the everyday life of the colony, we have here far more than mere summaries of cases of the state versus individuals. It would seem as if nothing was beyond the concern of the courts — elections, weights and measures, land grants, permits for ordinaries, excuses from military service, public and private purchases and other transactions, the levying of taxes and troops, fines for absence from church meetings, the recording of apprentice and servant indentures, divorce, regulation of prices and wages, the laying out of streets, the reaction against Quakers, and of course criminal trials.

On the one hand, these *Plymouth Colony Records* are our most valuable resource in trying to reconstruct the everyday life of Plymouth Colony residents, and in trying to grasp their underlying manners and mores. It is through these records that we can attempt to make an important evaluation and answer the questions of how much were these people like us and how different were they from us. How much has human nature changed in some three to four centuries? But the same records can be dangerous in that they might lead us into oversimplifications. They are not the complete records or the sum of the lives of the individual residents. No matter how much courts regulate human activity, they still tend to emphasize the rawer side of life, the negative, the deviations. We can learn much from such records, but we should be careful that the conclusions we form from them are not too general or too all-embracing.

The most important records from the genealogist's point of view, and also of considerable value to the historian and sociologist, are the probate records and land records. Ruth Wilder Sherman and Robert S. Wakefield, *Plymouth Colony Probate Guide* (Plymouth, 1983) [6], is invaluable for learning if there are probate documents for a given individual, and where those documents may now be found. This book also contains explanatory material describing the various present repositories of colony probate records. Most of the probate records are in four Plymouth Colony volumes, and the contents of the first two and part of the third have been published in the various issues of the *Mayflower Descendant*. The remaining ones are to be published by Plimoth Plantation. The original clerk's copies are preserved in the offices of the Plymouth County Commissioners. Sherman and Wakefield mention the little-known fact that Plymouth Colony probate documents for the period 1685-91, if an estate was valued at more than £50, had to be handled at Boston, and thus are now located in Suffolk County.

The probate records of Barnstable and Bristol counties are located at the county courthouses in Barnstable and Taunton. For Barnstable, volume one and part of volume two were abstracted in the *Mayflower Descendant*, and for Bristol, some of volume one are in the *Genealogical Advertiser*, and the rest of volume one are in *NEHGR*, volumes sixty-two through sixty-four (the *NEHGR* material is also in *Mayflower Source Records*). Plymouth County probate records from 1685 to 1691 which are not in Suffolk County are at the Plymouth County Registry of Probate on North Russell Street in Plymouth. Some have been published in *PN&Q*, *Genealogical Advertiser*, and *NEHGR.* See also below on land records. Additionally, some early Plymouth Colony probate material not available elsewhere has been published, together with some other early documents, as *The Plymouth Scrap Book,* edited by Charles Henry Pope (Boston, 1918). Some other early probate material is located at Pilgrim Hall in Plymouth, and some of these documents have been published in the *Mayflower Descendant.*

Plymouth Colony land records are found in eleven original record books which have been collected in six volumes called Plymouth County Deeds, and are located in the offices of the Plymouth County Commissioners on South Russell Street in Plymouth. The first original record book, 1627-51, plus some documents of transactions involving Indian lands, were published in volume twelve of *Plymouth Colony Records.* Record book two and part of record book three were published in the *Mayflower Descendant,* and publication is continuing in the original *Mayflower Descendant.* A few probate records are also found among these land records, mainly in record book five. The land records of Plymouth, Barnstable, and Bristol counties are located respectively in the Registries of Deeds in Plymouth, Barnstable, and Taunton. Most Barnstable County land records were destroyed in an 1828 fire, though some were subsequently rerecorded.

It should especially be noted that all Plymouth Colony probate records and land records have been microfilmed by the Genealogical Library of the Church of Jesus Christ of Latter-day Saints and can be obtained at L.D.S. branch libraries throughout the country. For land records, the overall index and volume one, are found on microfilm no. 567788. Volumes two to four are on microfilm no. 567789. Volumes five and six are on microfilm no. 567790. The four volumes of Plymouth Colony probate records are found on microfilm no. 567794.

County records do not begin until 1685, and thus contribute but little to Plymouth Colony. Abstracts of county court records (no wills or deeds) called *Plymouth Court Records 1686-1859,* edited by David T. Konig (Wilmington, Del., 1978-1981) are in sixteen unindexed volumes, but only the first volume has any records of the colony period, and then very few. The originals of these are kept at Pilgrim Hall in Plymouth. The court records of Barnstable and Bristol counties have not been published, but may be found respectively at the county offices at Barnstable and Taunton. *Abstracts of Bristol County, Massachusetts, Probate Records,* volume one, 1687-1698, were published by H. L. Peter Rounds in 1984.

On 20 October 1646 it was "enacted by the Courte That there shalbe in every Towne within this goverment a Cleark or some one appointed & ordayned to keepe a register of the day & yeare of the marriage, birth, & buriall of every man woeman & child within their towneshippe & to have 3 [pence] a peece for each particular person soe registred." Parents, people getting married, and masters of the families where someone died were ordered to report the births, marriages, and deaths to the town clerk or pay a three-shilling fine. [7] Plymouth records contain some such vital statistics prior to 20 October 1646, but the law of this date made it henceforth mandatory. However, the law is not clear as to who was to pay the clerk three pence, and if it meant the person making the report, not the government, this would have been a deterrent in some cases. It is obvious from studying vital records that they are not complete, and sometimes they may be in error, such as when different dates are given for the same event in town records and church records. Ages given at death are quite likely to differ from fact by as much as several years.   While the original vital records of Plymouth Colony towns are invaluable as genealogical and historical sources, they vary somewhat in accuracy because of the human factor, both of individuals making reports and of clerks recording them. We may get some feeling of the problem from the following notation in court records: "Lett none marvell att the promiscuous and disorderly setting downe of the names of such as are or may be married, or doe or may be born, or may dye; for they are sett as they were brought to mee, as disorderly as they are sett downe. If the Courts order had bin minded respecting this matter, they had bine otherwise placed then they are." This disclaimer appears to have been written by the colony clerk. We see the town clerk's side in a submission from Taunton of 3 March 1683: "To the honored Court att Plymouth, the first Tusay in March. Heer followeth the Names of the Beirth, Marriages, & Deathes that have bin in Taunton in the Year past; all that are brought in to mee, but many doe neglect to bring them to mee to bee recorded." [8]

The earliest vital records are in volume eight of *Plymouth Colony Records,* and some additional marriages are found in volume one of the same. The vital records of many Plymouth Colony towns have been published as individual books, some exceptions being Eastham, Barnstable, Sandwich, Swansea, and Freetown, and strangely the town of Plymouth itself, though many of the exceptions, including Plymouth, have been printed in part in the *Mayflower Descendant.* Bristol and Little Compton, Rhode Island, were published in *Vital Records of Rhode Island 1636-1850* (Providence, 1891-1912), but Little Compton records were compiled with errors, some of which are corrected by Robert S. Wakefield in an article in *TAG* 61:133 (January/April 1986). The first volume of *Middleborough Vital Records,* which includes all the colony period, was published in 1986. Vital records of Plymouth, Freetown, Sandwich, and Swansea are now being transcribed, and will probably be published in a year or so. Most of the vital records are in alphabetical sequence by surname, not literal sequence as recorded, even though literal sequence can yield more to genealogists.

Some death records of the late colony period are found in *Plymouth Church Records.* Some Scituate and Barnstable records as recorded by Reverend Lothrop are in volumes nine and ten of *NEHGR.* Marshfield Church records were published in *MQ,* volume forty-six, and some Plymouth Church records were published in *MQ,* volume forty-nine. Bradford Kingman, *Epitaphs from Burial Hill, Plymouth, Massachusetts, from 1657 to 1892* (Brookline, Mass., 1892) contains some information of interest to the

genealogist as well as the historian. Other church records giving genealogical information include those of the Bristol Church published in *NEHGR*
34:132 (though the transcription was not done well), and those of the
Swansea Baptish Church published by Robert Charles Anderson in
NEHGR 139:21. Baptisms in the Second Scituate Church (which became
the First Unitarian Church of Norwell) were published in *NEHGR* 57:82,
178, 318.

Some town records are of considerable value, such as *Records of the
Town of Plymouth*, 3 vols. (Plymouth 1889-1903), but only volume one has
to do with the colony period. *Copy of the Old Records of the Town of Dux-
bury, Mass. from 1642 to 1770*, was compiled by George Etheridge
(Plymouth, 1893). Some Barnstable town records may be found in the
Library of Cape Cod History and Genealogy. Unpublished town records are
located at the town halls of Bridgewater, Marshfield, Middleborough,
Rehoboth, Dartmouth, Taunton, Little Compton, Barnstable, Eastham,
Sandwich, and Yarmouth; however, not all records survived.

Much miscellaneous material of interest can be found in volumes one
to thirty-four of the *Mayflower Descendant*, such as gravestone information
from various towns, and the current *Mayflower Descendant* continues to publish original source material. George D. Langdon, Jr.'s "Bibliographic
Essay," *Occasional Papers in Old Colony Studies* (Plimoth Plantation, July
1969), gives additional sources, and should be required reading for anyone making a serious study of Plymouth Colony. [9] Much material from
NEHGR articles having to do with Plymouth Colony has been republished
in book form in *Mayflower Source Records*. In short, original records concerning Plymouth Colony are abundant and easily accessible to the
interested researcher.

NOTES

1. As well as understanding the language, being able to read the
handwriting of original seventeenth-century records is indispensable.
Books which may be used for self study of colonial handwriting are E. Kay
Kirkham, *The Handwriting of American Records for a Period of 300 Years*,
(Logan, Ut.: Everton Publishers, 1973), and Harriet Stryker-Rodda, *Under-
standing Colonial Handwriting* (1980; reprint, Baltimore, 1986).

2. *MD* 30:1.

3. *Ply. Ch. Recs.* 1:xv-xvi.

4. Hubbard, *History*, 101.

5. Morison, *Builders*, 18.

6. Published by the Plymouth Colony Research Group, 128 Massasoit
Drive, Warwick, RI 02888.

7. *PCR* 11:52.

8. Ibid., 8:74, 83.

9. Langdon's important bibliographic essay is also found in the second edition of his *Pilgrim Colony*, but not the first.

PART THREE
Biographical Sketches

Biographical Sketches

T hese biographical sketches do not comprise a list of all residents of Plymouth during the colony period, nor do the descriptions of individuals necessarily include all available information. The sketches do give a representative idea of people in the colony as we can understand them from the records. The criteria for inclusion of a name in this section are several. Biographical sketches are included for virtually all those people who were in Plymouth Colony by the time of the 1634 tax list. Following this time, the choice is somewhat arbitrary, but preference is given to residents who made important contributions to the history of the colony, or who are known to have many descendants, especially where material has been published on the family. Those who might be typical of people arriving at different periods after 1634, or who by their recorded actions might help give an understanding to the variety of people in the colony are also included. There is no intention to slight any individual by not including him or her. Sometimes an individual on whom much information exists is treated briefly because considerable information has already been published. In this case, reference is made to the published material. Emphasis is given in all cases to providing known bibliographic details, but again such information is not intended to be exhaustive. The desire here is to present sufficient information on enough individuals to contribute to a representative understanding of Plymouth Colony from the historical viewpoint, while also giving considerable genealogical information to aid genealogists and historians in conducting future research. For the full title of frequently used books, see the Bibliography. Where some evaluation of a source is given, it is intended to help the reader know how much reliance to place in that source. Negative evaluations should remind the reader that not everything appearing in print is true.

ADAMS, JOHN – Arriving in 1621 on the *Fortune*, John Adams later married Ellen Newton, who arrived on the *Anne* in 1623. They and their first child, James Adams, received shares in the 1627 livestock division. Robert S. Wakefield, "Men of the Fortune, John Adams," *TAG* 55:212, gives additional information on the family, including children John Adams, who married (1) Jane James, and (2) Elizabeth _____; and Susan Adams, who disappears from the records. Son John Adams probably moved to Flushing, Long Island. Son James Adams married Frances Vassall, daughter of William Vassall, q.v., had issue, and was known to have had interest in Barbadoes. On 15 May 1672 Frances Adams, the wife of James Adams, and daughter to the late William Vassall, petitioned the Massachusetts Court for, and was granted, 150 acres of land, and on 7 May 1673 the court noted that a farm of 150 acres belonging to her, wife of James Adams of Concord, was returned to the court (Nathaniel B. Shurtleff, *Records of the Governor and Company of the Massachusetts Bay in New England* (1854; reprint, New York, 1968), 4:2:524). John Adams, the father, died 1633, probably in the epidemic of that year, and his widow took inventory of his property on 24 October 1633 (*MD* 1:157). He was on the 1633 tax list, and his widow, Ellen Adams, was on the 1634 tax list. Widow Ellen Adams married (2) Kenelm Winslow, q.v. Later Adams families in Plymouth are likely not of this family, but of the family of Francis Adams, who arrived in Plymouth much later (see George Adams, *Genealogy of the Adams Family of Kingston, Mass.* [Boston, 1861], for information on the Francis Adams family).

ADEY, WEBB — Arriving in Plymouth between 1627 and 1633, Webb Adey is of interest as an example of a ne'er-do-well who came to the colony. There is no record of a marriage or children. He was one of the few longtime early residents who never became a freeman. Interestingly, on 7 November 1636, eight men were granted "diverse portions" of land, seven of them getting six acres each, but Webb Adey got only three acres (*PCR* 1:46). He was one of four men charged with "disorderly liveing, & therefore to be required to give an account how they live" in 1637 (*PCR* 1:68). In 1638 he was charged several times with not observing the Sabbath, and once was sentenced to sit in the stocks, and was whipped. He was ordered to find someone to take him into service, and on 2 July 1638 the court ordered his house and goods to be sold to pay his debts, and he was to work as a servant to Mr. Thomas Prence (*PCR* 1:68, 86-87, 91-92). On 29 August 1638 he sold his house in Plymouth plus three acres of land in the new field for £17 to John Jenney (*PCR* 12:35). In 1639 Ralph Gorham was charged with beating Webb Adey (*PCR* 1:118). In 1642 Adey was sentenced to jail for licentious and disorderly living (*PCR* 2:36, 42). In 1645 he bought six acres of land from John Harmon for thirty shillings (*PCR* 12:113). He died 4 March 1651/52 (*PCR* 8:13), and in a nuncupative will of the same day he bequeathed to Mr. John Reyner, Goodman Pratt, Goodman Savory, and Goodman Shrive from debts owed him, and left his house to the poor in town (*MD* 11:8). He is also found in the records less frequently as Adey Webb.

ALDEN, JOHN — In spite of various writings attempting to identify his English origin and parentage (e.g., Harry Hollingsworth, "John Alden — Beer Brewer of Windsor?," *TAG* 53:235. Nothing is known for certain of his English background other than Bradford's words that Alden "was hired for a cooper, at South-Hampton, wher the ship victuled; and being a hopefull yong man, was much desired, but left to his owne liking to go or stay when he came here; but he stayed, and maryed here" (*Bradford [Ford]* 2:400). The Hollingsworth article also pointed out that Charles E. Banks had claimed that Alden was from Harwich, Essex, because an Alden family there was related by marriage to the master of the *Mayflower*, Christopher Jones. Alden is not a particularly common name, and researchers should keep in mind the fact that one of the Adventurers was a Robert Allden. John Alden married Priscilla Mullins, q.v.; became one of the Purchasers and the Undertakers; was for many years an Assistant; and presided as deputy governor on at least two occasions (*PCR* 4:81, 5:245). His progeny are among the most numerous of all *Mayflower* descendants. His house in Duxbury may still be visited today. There is no thorough Alden genealogy, and *Memorial of the Descendants of John Alden* by Ebenezer Alden, (Randolph, Mass., 1867) is neither very complete nor very accurate. In 1660 the General Court noted that "In regard that Mr Alden is low in his estate, and occationed to spend much time att the courts on the countreyes occations. and soe hath done this many yeares, the Court have alowed him a smale gratuity, the sume of ten pounds, to bee payed by the Treasurer" (*PCR* 3:195). He may have become more than ordinarily conservative with the years. James Cudworth wrote in 1660 that "Mr. Alden hath deceived the Expectations of many, and indeed lost the Affections of such, as I judge were his Cordial Christian Friends, [and he is] very active in such Ways. . .to be Oppressions of a High Nature," referring to the treatment of Quakers (Bishop, p. 176).

John Alden died at Duxbury 12 September 1687 and left no will, having disposed of most of his estate during his lifetime. His children were Elizabeth, John, Joseph, Rebecca, Ruth, Sarah, Jonathan, David, Mary, Priscilla, and an unnamed child which probably died young. Daughters Mary and Priscilla were unmarried as of 13 June 1688 (*MD* 3:10). That Rebecca was the daughter who married Thomas Delano has been controversial—see under Thomas Delano. The only direct proof for the existence of Rebecca Alden is *PCR* 4:7, showing that on 1 October 1661 Abraham Pierce, Jr. apologized to the court for having foolishly told Ruth Sprague and Bethiah Tubbs at Francis Sprague's house that Rebecca Alden and Hester Delano were with child and that "wee should have young troopers within three quarters of a yeare."

ALLERTON, BARTHOLOMEW—Coming to Plymouth on the 1620 *Mayflower* with his parents, Isaac and Mary Allerton, Bartholomew later returned to England where, Bradford wrote, he married, but how many children he had was unknown. Banks, *English Ancestry*, p. 29-30, mentions that "A chancery suit of 1657 in which Bartholomew Allerton was a defendant relates to property in Suffolk, the parties being residents in Norfolk. It would seem that this son became a preacher, as the will of a Bartholomew Allerton, clerk, of Bamfield (probably Bramfield), co. Suffolk, was proved in 1659. He mentions late wife Margaret, present wife Sarah and his 'children' without naming them, unfortunately (P.C.C. 92 Pell)." Banks may be right that this testator was the *Mayflower* passenger, but it is of course not yet sufficiently proven.

ALLERTON, ISAAC—Isaac Allerton was born ca. 1586, (he said he was about fifty-three years old in September 1639 [*Small Descendants* 2:756] gives a good account of his career and family). A Leiden Separatist and 1620 *Mayflower* passenger, Allerton was second in authority only to Bradford in the early years of the colony. However, Bradford felt that Allerton had abused the trust the colonists placed in him (see text), and Allerton left the colony in the 1630s for other parts. A most enterprising man, he engaged in commercial pursuits at Marblehead and in Maine and later resided at New Amsterdam. He cleared his debt to the Adventurers by a contract of 12 May 1646 in which he ratified what William Bradford, Edward Winslow, and Myles Standish, as agents for Sherley, Andrews, and Beauchamp, had done or would do about the sale of his lands, goods, and cattle "provided they do clearly acquit him from all debts and demands" (*Small Descendants* 2:783). He died at New Haven in February 1658/59, leaving little estate except debts he claimed were due him.

After the death of his first wife, Mary Norris, he married (2) Fear Brewster, and (3) widow Joanna Swinnerton. Walter S. Allerton, *A History of the Allerton Family, 1585 to 1885, and a Genealogy of the Descendants of Isaac Allerton* (revised, 1900), contains considerable errors, some of which are clarified by Newman A. Hall in "The Unproven Allerton Family Lineage," *MQ* 45:23. (See also Hall's "The Children of Isaac Allerton," *MQ* 47:14 and his "Joanna Swinnerton: The Third Wife of Isaac Allerton, Sr.," *NEHGR* 124:133. Also see James R. Case, "Isaac Allerton, The First Yankee Trader," *MQ* 48:170.) Allerton left a number of descendants in New England, and his son Isaac migrated to Virginia, where the line was carried on under the Allerton, Lee, and Travers surnames.

ALLERTON, JOHN—A seaman on the 1620 *Mayflower*, John Allerton was hired to stay, but died during the early months. No relationship to Isaac Allerton is known, but it is not precluded, given the custom of people to migrate in family groups. There was a John Allerton living in Leiden who buried a child there on 21 May 1616. He lived in the Pieterskerkhof section, as did Isaac Allerton, and the Dexters believed he was identical with the *Mayflower* seaman (Dexter, p. 601).

ALLERTON, MARY—The wife of Isaac; see under Mary Norris.

ALLERTON, MARY—A daughter of Isaac and Mary, Mary Allerton married Thomas Cushman, q.v. When she died in 1699, she was the last survivor of the *Mayflower* trans-Atlantic passengers (Peregrine White died in 1704, but he was born at Provincetown).

ALLERTON, REMEMBER—Born at Leiden ca. 1614 to Isaac and Mary, Remember Allerton accompanied them on the 1620 *Mayflower*. She married before 6 May 1635 Moses Maverick of Marblehead (*NEHGR* 96:358), and she died between 12 September 1652 and 22 October 1656. See also *MD* 5:129.

ALLERTON, SARAH—A sister of Isaac Allerton, Sarah Allerton married (1) John Vincent, (2) *Mayflower* passenger Degory Priest, and (3) Cuthbert Cuthbertson. She did not sail to Plymouth with Priest, but remained in Holland where, after hearing of the death of Priest, she married Cuthbertson, and accompanied him to Plymouth in 1623 on the *Anne*, along with her son Samuel Cuthbertson and her two daughters by Degory Priest, Mary Priest and Sarah Priest. Both she and her husband, Cuthbert Cuthbertson, died before 24 October 1633, when their inventories were taken (*MD* 1:154).

ALLERTON, SARAH—The young Sarah Allerton was previously thought to have arrived at Plymouth with her aunt, Sarah (Allerton) (Vincent) (Priest) Cuthbertson on the *Anne*. However, Newman A. Hall gives convincing reasons in *MQ* 47:17 to show that she more likely was the daughter of Isaac Allerton by his marriage to Fear Brewster, and was born in Plymouth Colony. She was not known to be married or have descendants.

ANNABLE, ANTHONY—William P. Greenlaw, *NEHGR* 65:380, shows that Anthony Annable married Jane Momford at All Saints Church, Cambridge, Cambridgeshire, 26 April 1619. He arrived at Plymouth in 1623 on the *Anne*, and, since he had four acres in the 1623 land division, his wife and two children probably came with him. On 9 June 1630 he sold a dwelling house and garden plot at Plymouth to Daniel Ray (*PCR* 12:17), and it was possibly at this time that he moved to Scituate, becoming one of the earliest settlers there. He was on the 1633 list of freemen, and on 1 January 1633/34 he was chosen constable for Scituate (*PCR* 1:21). He and his wife Jane were original members of the Reverend Lothrop's Scituate Church, and probably left Scituate with Lothrop (*NEHGR* 9:279). He was a deputy for Scituate 4 June 1639 and a deputy for Barnstable 2 June 1640 (*PCR* 1:126, 155). His wife Jane died in December 1643, and he married Ann Clarke 1 March 1645/46 (*MD* 2:212). He made his will 24 February 1672/73, with codicil dated 23 April 1674, sworn 4 June 1674, in which he named his wife Ann, son Samuel, daughter Desire, and other unnamed daughters (*MD* 25:90). Pope was wrong in calling his second wife Ann Alcocke and in giving him a third wife Hannah (or Ann) Barker. His children by Jane were Sarah and Hannah (both in the 1627 livestock division), a daughter who died young, and Deborah, and those by Ann were Samuel, Ezekiel (who probably died young), and Desire (*NEHGR* 9:281; *MD* 2:212-13). Also, the Susanna Annable who married William Hatch at Scituate 13 May 1652 is shown in the vital records as the daughter of Anthony Annable (*MD* 2:33). Anthony Anable published a recent family history, *The Anable Family in America 1623-1967* (Stamford, Conn., 1967).

ANDREWS, HENRY—One of the first settlers and freemen of Taunton, Henry Andrews was there in 1636/37 and 1638, and was elected a deputy for Taunton in 1639 (*PCR* 1:53, 105, 126). In his will dated 13 March 1652/53, proved 6 June 1653, he called himself a yeoman, and he named his daughter Mary, wife of William "Hedges" (Hodges) and their son John

Hedges; his daughters Sarah and Abigail; his son Henry; and his wife Mary (*MD* 11:152). His wife Mary Andrews dated her will 14 February 1653/54, proved 15 March 1654/55, and she stated that she was forty-three years of age. She gave real estate left by her deceased husband Mr. Henry Andrews to son Henry, to daughter Abigail, and to son-in-law William Hedge and daughter Mary Hedge (*MD* 12:246). Their daughter Mary married (1) William Hodges and (2) Peter Pitts, q.v.

ATKINSON, THOMAS—The name of Thomas Atkinson was added to the freeman list sometime after 1 January 1632/33, but no later than 7 March 1636/37 (*PCR* 1:53). On 7 November 1636 Atkinson was among those granted six acres each of land in Plymouth which was to belong to their dwelling houses and not be sold separately (*PCR* 1:46). He served on a coroner's jury 5 June 1638 (*PCR* 1:88). On 4 December 1638 he posted £40 as a surety bond that Samuel Gorton would leave Plymouth Colony within fourteen days—Gorton was fined £20 and also gave surety for another £40 after being charged with misdemeanor in open court towards the elders and the bench, and with stirring up people to mutiny (*PCR* 1:105-06). On 28 February 1639/40 William Honeywell was to be released from his indenture to Mr. Thomas Prence in return for setting, planting, and weeding Mr. Prence's crops, promising not to loiter or work for others, and Honeywell would have one-half the crop at harvest. Thomas Atkinson would provide room and board and would be paid by Prence until settlement at harvest (*PCR* 1:139-40).

A Thomas Atkins was presented along with John Wood on 1 December 1640 for delivering only five score herring per hundred when they should have delivered six score and twelve, and they were discharged after being ordered to make restitution (*PCR* 2:4-5). Since names were sometimes cut short (e.g., Cuthbertson to Cuthbert), this could be the same person, though not necessarily. After 1640 Thomas Atkinson disappears from the records, but by 20 June 1654 another Thomas Atkins appears to take the Oath of Fidelity (*PCR* 3:58). This one would probably not be the same person, for a freeman would not have to take the Oath of Fidelity, only a new resident. The one taking the oath was probably the Thomas Atkins, an inhabitant of Kennebec, who was charged with committing incest with his daughter in 1660, found not guilty, but whipped anyway (*PCR* 3:197, 199-200). The latter Atkins was married to an Elizabeth; see also Mrs. John E. Barclay, "The Ten Daughters of Thomas Atkins of Kennebec," *NEHGR* 121:241. Neither Thomas Atkinson nor Thomas Atkins was on the 1643 ATBA list, and thus it is likely that Atkinson died or left the colony between 1640 and 1643.

ATWOOD, JOHN—This is the Mr. John Atwood who was an Assistant in 1638, not the John Wood, alias Atwood, who also lived in Plymouth. He apparently had planned before 8 April 1633 to come to Plymouth, for on that date John Doane sold the indenture of Walter Harris—who had bound himself to serve Mr. Atwood of London under the command of Mr. John Doane of New Plymouth—to Henry Howland (*PCR* 1:12). On

30 December 1636 John Atwood, late of London, gentleman, bought John Doane's half interest in a house and land near Plain Dealing that they had jointly owned for £60 (*PCR* 1:47). Mr. John Atwood was made a freeman on 3 January 1636/37 (*PCR* 1:48). He served on the grand jury in 1636/37 (*PCR* 1:54). In 1637 he was on a committee to determine what to do with the beaver trade (*PCR* 1:62). On 6 August 1637 Thomas Roberts was sentenced to be severely whipped and to be returned to his master, Mr. John Atwood, for the rest of his term, and he was not to get any future land grants (but an added note provided, "except hee manefest better desert" (*PCR* 1:64). Atwood had various land grants at Plymouth (*PCR*, passim). On 24 October 1638 Mr. Atwood hired John Long as a servant (*PCR* 1:100). On 5 March 1638/39 Mr. John Atwood assigned the indenture of William Taylor, son of William Taylor of Boddington, Cornwall, England, a carpenter, to Thomas Little (*PCR* 1:119). Apparently, Atwood entered into other indenture agreements. On 16 May 1639 he agreed that since Job Cole had paid the passage of Thomas Gray and given him clothing, he would assign all of his interest in Gray's services to Cole (*PCR* 1:121). Atwood was chosen in 1641 to serve on the committee which replaced the Court of Assistants in administering land grants (*PCR* 2:25, 29). In 1641 he was chosen as a deputy for Plymouth (*PCR* 2:16), and in 1641/42 he became the colony's treasurer (*PCR* 2:34). In his will dated 20 October 1643, sworn 5 June 1644, he gave twelve pence to any of his brethren and their children who asked for it, and he named a kinsman William Crow; his brother and sister Lee and their children Ann and Mary; and his wife Anne Atwood (*MD* 5:153). His wife dated her will 27 April 1650, sworn 3 December 1654, in which she named her brother and sister now living in New Plymouth, Robert and Mary Lee, and their children, and her loving nephew William Crow (*MD* 11:200). A memorandum dated 3 March 1642/43 on a deed from Francis Billington to Mr. John Atwood was witnessed by a Harmon Atwood (*PCR* 12:95). Pope has a Herman Atwood of Sanderstead, co. Surrey, cordwainer, as a servant to brother Buttall in Boston, who became deacon of the second church, but there is nothing else in the records to indicate any possible relationship with John Atwood.

BAKER, WILLIAM – On 16 February 1632/33 Richard Church hired William Baker from the first of March to the last of September for fourteen bushels of corn and twelve shillings money. Church was also to give him one month of meals after the term, and to provide him with sufficient help to saw timber, with the sawed boards to be divided equally between Church and Baker (*PCR* 1:8). On 5 November 1638 a William Baker of Watertown, who may or may not be the same William Baker, was licensed to dwell within Plymouth Colony "provided he bring good testimony of his good conversation" (*PCR* 1:102). On 5 April 1641 John Barnes leased a house and lands to William Baker from 5 April to the last of October for fifty shillings in money or corn (*PCR* 2:13). Pope believed him to be identical with the William Baker who was admitted as an inhabitant of Boston on 28 July 1651, and who married (1) Mary, daughter of Edmund

Eddington and (2) Pilgrim, daughter of John Eddy of Watertown (brother of Samuel Eddy of Plymouth Colony).

BANGS, EDWARD—Arriving at Plymouth in 1623 on the *Anne*, Edward Bangs was probably born ca. 1591, for he said he was age eighty-six in 1677. *Dawes-Gates* (2:61-68) has a section on him and cites the evidence to show that he was probably identical with the Edward Bangs who was baptized on 28 October 1591 in Panfield, Essex, England, the son of John and Jane (Chavis) Bangs. He married (1) after 1627 Lydia Hicks, daughter of Robert and Margaret Hicks (she may have been the second wife, for *Dawes-Gates* suggests that he may have had an earlier one, and, (2) Rebecca (?Hobart). He was one of the Purchasers, and he was on the 1632/33 freeman list. He was one of those chosen to lay out the twenty-acre lots in the 1627 division, along with William Bradford, Edward Winslow, John Howland, Francis Cooke, and Joshua Pratt (*PCR* 12:14). With Myles Standish and others, Edward Bangs was chosen in 1633 to divide the meadow in the bay equally (*PCR* 1:14). He was also on committees to assess the entire colony for public costs (*PCR* 1:33, 38), and he served on various juries and other public service committees (*PCR*). He appears to be a man who was responsible and trusted. In a record where he was surety for another, he was called a yeoman (*PCR* 1:103). In 1641 he was granted eighty acres of land at Warren's Wells, and in 1642 he was allowed to exchange some of it for land closer to his house (*PCR* 2:25, 48). He moved to Nauset with the Prence group, and in 1647 he was a supervisor of the highways there (*PCR* 2:115).

In 1652 he became a deputy for Eastham (*PCR* 3:9)and in 1657 was licensed to sell wine and strong waters at Eastham "provided it bee for the refreshment of the English and not to bee sold to the Indians" (*PCR* 3:123). In a deed of 22 June 1651, he was joined as grantor by his wife Rebecca (*PCR* 12:209). He made his will on 19 Oct. 1677, calling himself aged eighty-six years, and he named his sons: Jonathan, John, Joshua; his daughter Howe, daughter Higgens, daughter Hall, daughter Merrick, and daughter Atwood; the children of his daughter Rebecca, deceased; and his son Jonathan's oldest son Edward (*Ply. Colony PR* 3:2:106). In an agreement of 6 March 1677/78, Jonathan Bangs agreed that the land bequeathed to his son Edward could be used by Jonathan's brother John until Edward came of age (PR 3:2:105). *Dawes-Gates* 2:67 gives his children from his marriage to Lydia Hicks as: John, who married Hannah Smalley, and, from his marriage to Rebecca (possibly Hobart), Rebecca, who married Jonathan Sparrow; Sarah, who married Thomas Howes, Jr.; Jonathan, who married (1) Mary Mayo, (2) Sarah _____, and (3) Ruth (Cole) Young; Lydia, who married (1) Benjamin Higgins, and (2) Nicholas Snow; Hannah, who married John [2] Doane; Joshua, who married Hannah Scudder; Bethia, who married Rev. Gershom Hall; Mercy, who married Stephen [2] Merrick; and Apphia, who married (1) John Knowles, and (2) Stephen Atwood.

There was also a John Bangs in Plymouth in the early years, who was assigned hay ground on 20 March 1636/37 (*PCR* 1:56), and thus he would seem to have been too old to have been a son of Edward Bangs, unless he was born to an earlier wife, and came over after his father. Of course, he could just as well have been a brother or no relation at all. There seems to be no other record of this John Bangs, and the name could even have been a spelling error for some other name, such as John Barnes. On 1 May 1660 George Watson asked the court on behalf of his son John Watson and his nephew John Bangs to correct a mistake in the records about a purchase of land in the Dartmouth area that should have been in the name of Mr. Robert Hicks (*PCR* 3:186); this John Bangs would have been the son of Edward, for Robert Hicks was his grandfather, and George Watson had married Hicks's daughter Phebe. This John Bangs was also mentioned as a grandson in the wills of both Robert Hicks and his wife Margaret Hicks (*MD* 8:143, 16:157). A genealogy of the family can be found in Dean Dudley, *History and Genealogy of the Bangs Family in America* (Montrose, Mass., 1896).

BARKER, ELIZABETH—Elizabeth Barker accompanied her husband Edward Winslow on the 1620 *Mayflower*, but died at Plymouth 24 March 1620/21 (*MD* 30:3). Leiden records show that Edward Winslow from London, a printer, accompanied by Jonathan Williamson (i.e., Jonathan Brewster) and Isaac Allerton, registered marriage intentions 27 April 1618 with Elizabeth Barker, single, from Chatsum, England (probably Chattisham, Suffolk), who was accompanied by Janie Hazel, her niece, and Mary Allerton (Dexter, p. 640). Dexter (p. 642) shows that there was also a Dorothy Barker (or Baker) at Leiden, with a daughter Mercy who married Samuel Buckingham.

BARKER, ROBERT—The first record of Robert Barker in Plymouth is on 20 January 1632/33 when he complained to the council that his master, John Thorpe, did not keep him in sufficient clothing. The complaint was found just, and Thorpe was ordered to provide him apparel or turn over his contract to another (*PCR* 1:7). By 15 August 1633 Thorpe had died, and his widow Alice turned over Barker's apprentice term, running until 1 April 1637 to William Palmer, a nailer, who promised to teach him his trade and give him two suits (*PCR* 1:7, 16). On 4 December 1638 Robert Barker of Jones River was fined twenty shillings for drawing blood in a fight with Henry Blague (*PCR* 1:106). He was a highway surveyor for Marshfield in 1645 (*PCR* 2:84). The Barker article, cited below, states that he, his brother John Barker, and two others in 1641 bought a ferry for £60 from Jonathan Brewster. On 28 October 1645 he sought money from the government for ferrying prisoners and passengers over the North River (*PCR* 2:89). He was one of two constables for Marshfield in 1646 (*PCR* 2:102), and in the same year he was licensed to keep an ordinary at Marshfield (*PCR* 2:105). He became a freeman 6 June 1654 (*PCR* 3:48). On 4 March 1661/62 he and his wife and son were fined £10 for exchanging a gun with an Indian, but £5 was later remitted (*PCR* 4:11, 17). On 5 June 1666 he was accused by the court of not keeping his ordinary fit for the entertaining of strangers, and he was ordered to forbear (*PCR* 4:129).

Robert's brother John Barker drowned at their ferry in 1652. On 6 October 1659 Robert Barker complained in court against Ens. John Williams for misusing Deborah Barker, daughter of John Barker (and his wife Anne, sister of John WIlliams). Williams produced sufficient evidence to be cleared by the court, but the court also ordered that Deborah would not have to return to the house of her Uncle Williams, and she chose Thomas Bird of Scituate to be her guardian instead (*PCR* 3:171-72). On 7 March 1681/82 Lt. Robert Barker (the son) was fined £2/10 on behalf of his mother, the wife of Robert Barker, for selling cider to Indians. Robert Barker, Sr. was living in Duxbury at the time he made his will, 18 February 1689/90, sworn 16 March 1691/92 (*MD* 31:102), in which he named his sons Francis and Robert; his daughters Rebecca Snow and Abigail Rogers; his grandsons Samuel Barker, Francis Barker, Robert Barker, Jabez Barker, and Isaac Barker; and his son Isaac's six daughters Rebecca, Mary, Lydia, Judith, Martha, and "the youngest of all," all under twenty-one. Torrey shows Robert Barker married to Lucy Williams. James Atkins Noyes, "Barker Pedigree," (*NEHGR* 53:426) shows that his son Isaac married Judith Prence, daughter of Thomas; son Francis married Mary Lincoln; son Robert married (1) an Alice, and (2) Hannah Wanton; daughter Rebecca married William Snow; and daughter Abigail married Joseph Rogers. Robert's wife has since been shown to have been Alice Snow, daughter of Anthony and Abigail (Warren) Snow, and granddaughter of 1620 *Mayflower* passenger Richard Warren (Lucy Williams and Hannah Wanton are doubtful).

BARNES, JOHN—On 25 March 1633 Timothy Hatherly, merchant, of London, sold a heifer to John Barnes of Plymouth (*PCR* 1:9). On 26 August 1634 Barnes and Gov. Thomas Prence exchanged servants, John Rouse going from Prence to Barnes, and Richard Willis going from Barnes to Prence (*PCR* 1:30). On 19 December 1634 the court "turned over" Simon Trat to serve John Barnes until age twenty-three (*PCR* 1:32), and on 13 August 1639 Barnes assigned Trat's indenture to Thomas Clark (*PCR* 1:129). Barnes was a member of a committee in 1635/36 to advise the governor and council on setting prices for goods and wages for laborers (*PCR* 1:36). Although he was not on the earliest freeman list, he became a freeman before 7 March 1636/37 when his name appears on another list (*PCR* 1:52). On 4 August 1638 Barnes transferred the unexpired term of his servant Thomas Shrive to Robert Bartlett (*MD* 3:108). On 4 December 1638 he was presented for inordinate drinking, but the case was dropped for insufficient evidence (*PCR* 1:107). On 25 September 1639 Mr. Henry Feake of Sandwich assigned to John Barnes the remaining term of his servant Edmond Edwards (*PCR* 1:132). He engaged in many land transactions (see chapter 10), and in 1640 he was granted a rather large amount of land, 110 acres (*PCR* 1:154). He appears very frequently in the records, and Darrett B. Rutman, *Husbandmen of Plymouth* (Boston, 1967), uses him as an example of a general merchant in early Plymouth, adding (p. 25) that he was also a brewer, baker, innkeeper, land speculator, and farmer. Gyles Rickard was his friend, neighbor, customer, and occasional drinking partner. Barnes was often involved in legal disputes (*PCR*, passim). On 6 October 1659 he was disenfranchised for frequent and abominable drunkenness (*PCR* 3:176).

Barnes married Mary Plummer on 12 September 1633 (*PCR* 1:16). Mary was probably a sister of Ann, who was married to Henry Sampson. Mary died 2 June 1651 (*PCR* 8:13), and he then married (2) Joan _____. Mrs. Joan Barnes was sentenced on 1 March 1652/53 to sit in the stocks for frequently slandering the children of Captain Willett and the daughter of George Watson (*PCR* 3:23). Barnes died prior to 30 August 1671, when his inventory was taken (appendix K). A coroner's inquest determined that while he was stroking his bull, the bull suddenly turned and gored him in the right thigh, and he died about thirty-two hours later (*PCR* 5:88). His will dated 6 March 1667/68 (appendix K) mentioned his wife Joan; son Jonathan; grandson John Marshall; deceased daughter Lydia; cousin "the wife of Henry Sampson," and kinswoman Esther Rickard (*MD* 4:98, 19:61). His daughter Mary married Robert Marshall in 1660, and son Jonathan married Elizabeth Hedge, daughter of William, 4 January 1665/66 (*PCR* 8:22, 31). He also had a son John, who died 25 December 1648 (*PCR* 8:5). On 24 August 1651 he gave livestock to his children Jonathan, Mary, Hannah, and Lydia, and in the deed he mentioned his trusty and well beloved friends Constant Southworth, Lt. Thomas Southworth, and Josiah Cooke of Eastham (*PCR* 12:214). On 5 March 1671/72 Mrs. Joan Barnes complained that she could not provide for John Marshall and Robert Marshall, the sons of Mr. Robert Marshall, who were then in her custody, and the court gave notice that Marshall should appear to provide for them, or it "will take course for the disposall of them" (*PCR* 5:85).

BARTLETT, ROBERT—Paul W. Prindle, "The Probable Ancestry of Robert Bartlett of Plymouth," *TAG* 55:164, suggests the Robert Bartlett who arrived at Plymouth on the *Anne* in 1623 was identical with the Robert Bartlett baptized at Puddletown, Dorset, England, on 27 May 1603. The fact that he was not one of the 1626 Purchasers might indicate that he arrived as a servant and was still in this status in 1626 (see text). Bartlett married Mary Warren, daughter of *Mayflower* passenger Richard Warren, ca. 1629 (Wakefield, *Plymouth Marriages*, p. 4). On 1 July 1633 he and Mrs. Elizabeth Warren were assigned mowing rights on the same land they had used the previous year, probably close to where Mrs. Warren and her other two sons-in-law lived (*PCR* 1:15). On 28 May 1635 Thomas Little, who had married Mary Warren's sister Anna, gave his brother-in-law Robert Bartlett a parcel of land beyond Eel River to build a house on (*PCR* 1:34). On 1 December 1635 Richard Stinnings (later hanged for murdering an Indian) apprenticed himself to Robert Bartlett for nine years (*PCR* 1:35). On 4 August 1638 John Barnes sold Robert Bartlett the remaining three years of Thomas Shrive's indenture (*PCR* 12:32). Though Bartlett held such positions as grandjuror and highway surveyor (*PCR*, passim), he did not serve in the higher positions of government.

On 7 October 1652 Bartlett petitioned the court because "sondry speeches have pased from som who pretend themselves to bee the sole and right heires unto the lands on which the said Robert Bartlet now liveth, at the Ellriver, in the townshipp of Plymouth, which hee, the said Robert, had bestowed on him by his mother in law, Mis Elizabeth Warren, in marriage with her daughter; by which said speeches and passages the said Robert had ben dishartened in his proceeding either in building, fencing, etc.," and the court confirmed his right to the lands (*PCR* 3:19). On 1 June 1658 the court appointed several men to settle the bounds between Bartlett's land and that of his brother-in-law Nathaniel Warren (*PCR* 3:142). On 1 May 1660 Bartlett was convicted by the Court of Assistants for speaking contemptuously about the ordinance of singing psalms, and he said he hoped it would be a warning to him, and he promised to acknowledge his fault to those he had earlier spoken to (*PCR* 3:186). On moving to Nauset in 1649, Richard Church sold his real estate at Eel River to Robert Bartlett for £25 (*PCR* 12:165). Bartlett made a nuncupative will 19 September 1676, sworn 29 October 1676, leaving his estate to his wife to dispose of to their children (*MD* 3:114-15). Their children were Benjamin, Rebecca, Mary, Sarah, Joseph, Elizabeth, Lydia, and Mercy (*MD* 3:116-17), all of whom married and had descendants. After the second generation, Bartlett descendants have sometimes "suffered grievously at the hands of various writers," as Mrs. Barclay wrote in "The Family of Samuel Bartlett of Duxbury, Mass.," *TAG* 37:141. (Also see Eugene A. Stratton, "Mary, Wife of Nathaniel Atwood," *MQ* 48:127, which corrects a widely disseminated error regarding Bartlett descendants, and Barbara Lambert Merrick, "Sarah (Brewster) Bartlett, *MQ* 51:131.)

BASSET, WILLIAM – William Basset, of the Leiden Separatists, arrived in 1621 on the *Fortune*. In Leiden records, he is shown as a master mason, from Sandwich, Kent. He was a widower of Cicely Bassett, and he was betrothed in Leiden in 1611 to Mary Butler, with William Brewster, Roger Wilson, Anna Fuller, and Rose Lisle as witnesses, but Mary died before the marriage. He was betrothed on 29 July 1611 to Margaret Oldham, with Edward Southworth, Roger Wilson, Elizabeth Neal, and Wybra Pontus as witnesses, and they married 13 August 1611. He married in Leiden a third time to Elizabeth _____ (Dexter, p. 165), and he brought her and their son William to Plymouth. Wife Elizabeth and children William and Elizabeth were in the 1627 division, but the wife died later. Basset married at Plymouth a fourth wife after 5 June 1651 Mary (Tilden) Lapham, for on that date Timothy Hatherly proved the will of Thomas Lapham, deceased. The widow Lapham, being weak, was not able to appear in court (*PCR* 2:169). Earlier, 22 June 1650, Mary Lapham, widow of Thomas Lapham of Scituate, confirmed the sale of land in Tenterden, Kent, to Thomas Hiland (*MD* 10:199; *PCR* 12:194). The will of Timothy Hatherly dated 12 December 1664 (*MD* 16:158-59), left £5 to the wife of William Basset, "my wifes Daughter," and thus Mary would have been the daughter of Nathaniel Tilden of Scituate.

On 8 November 1666 William Basset, who described himself as a black-smith of Bridgewater, sold four lots to John Sprague of Duxbury, and Basset's wife Mary gave her consent, John Sprague being her husband's son-in-law (*Ply. Colony LR* 3:66). In his will, dated 3 April 1667, sworn 5 June 1667, William Basset mentioned his unnamed wife (Mary swore to his inventory), his son Joseph, and his son William's son William (*MD* 16:162); the inventory shows an interesting collection of books. On 2 June 1669 William Basset of Sandwich, oldest son of William Basset some-time of Bridgewater, deceased, confirmed land to his youngest brother, Joseph Basset of Bridgewater (*Ply. Colony LR* 3:140). William Basset, Sr. also had a daughter Sarah, who married Peregrine White, q.v.; a daugh-ter Ruth, who married John, son of Francis Sprague, q.v. (*TAG* 41:178); and a daughter Elizabeth, who married Thomas Burgess in 1648 (*PCR* 8:6) and divorced him in 1661 after he was brought to court for an act of uncleanness with Lydia Gaunt (the first divorce in Plymouth Colony), and the Court allowed Elizabeth to keep small things "that are in William Bas-set's hands" (*PCR* 3:221). On 6 June 1683 Goodwife Sprague and her son John agreed about land which formerly belonged to John Sprague's grand-father Basset (*PCR* 6:109). Ruth (Basset) Sprague married (2) a man whose surname was Thomas (*TAG* 41:179). William, Sr. also had a son Nathaniel [2] Basset. Robert Ray King, "The Family of Nathan Basset of Chatham," *NEHGR* 125:7, has to do with Nathan [3] Basset, the son of Nathaniel [2] Basset and his wife Dorcas Joyce, daughter of John. (Note: In correspondence, Robert S. Wakefield questions whether it was the same William Basset in all four marriages, and it is a surprisingly large number of Englishmen sharing a name with someone else that was resident in Leiden.)

BEALE, WILLIAM – Arriving at Plymouth on the *Fortune* in 1621, Wil-liam Beale was paired with the young Thomas Cushman in the 1623 land division, the two of them receiving two acres. Beale was not in the 1627 cattle division. A William Beale with family is later found in Marblehead in the Bay Colony.

BEAVAN, JOHN – On 25 July 1633 John Beavan contracted to serve John Winslow for six years as an apprentice, and at the end of the term Winslow was to give him twelve bushels of Indian corn and twenty-five acres of land (*PCR* 1:15-16), but Beavan does not appear any further in Plymouth records. Beavan is obviously a Welsh name, and he may have moved out of Plymouth Colony with the Welsh party led by the Rever-end Mr. Blinman (see text).

BECKET, MARY – Arriving on the Anne in 1623, Mary Becket is said to have married *Mayflower* passenger George Soule prior to the 1627 cat-tle division (*MF-3*). Nothing is known about her origins in England, and her identification as George Soule's wife is based on her known presence in Plymouth in 1623, on Soule being unmarried that year, on her disap-pearance from the records thereafter, on Soule having a wife named Mary in the 1627 division, and on there being no other known Mary to assign as his wife.

BENNET, WILLIAM – William Bennet complained on 3 January 1632/33 that Edward Doty had cheated him by giving him bacon not worth the price they had agreed upon (*PCR* 1:7). On 1 April 1633 he accused Doty of slandering him by calling him a rogue, and the jury found in his favor, ordering Doty to give Bennet thirty shillings (*PCR* 1:12). Thereafter he disappears from Plymouth records, but Savage wrote that he was the William Bennett of Salem of 1636. An Edward Bennett was proposed as a Plymouth freeman in 1645 (*PCR* 2:84), but there is no known relationship.

BESBECH, THOMAS – Elizabeth French, "Genealogical Research in England – Besbeech," *NEHGR* 67:33, shows that Thomas Besbech was baptized at Biddenden, Kent, on 3 March 1589/90, the younger son of John and Dorothy (Foster) (Austen) Besbeech. He married Anne Baseden at Biddenden 14 January 1618/19. He was made a freeman of Plymouth Colony 2 January 1637/38 (*PCR* 1:74). The records show many variations in the spelling of his surname. He is usually shown in records with the honorific "Mr.," though in Lothrop's notes on the members of the Scituate Church he is shown as "Goodman Besbech," who joined on 30 April 1637 (*NEHGR* 9:280). He was one of the Scituate residents given a grant in 1638/39 at Sippican (*PCR* 1:108); however, on 1 March 1641/42 he was chosen a grand-juror from Duxbury (*PCR* 2:34). In 1642 he was fined five shillings for departing the court without license and was warned to serve in his grand jury position (*PCR* 2:42). A committee was directed in 1642 to set the bounds between the lands of Mr. Thomas Besbeech and John Washburn and to use Mr. William Vassall's surveying instrument for this purpose (*PCR* 2:39, 52). In 1643 he was a deputy for Duxbury (*PCR* 2:57). He was a resident of Sudbury in the Bay Colony on 2 April 1647, when he sold his house and land in Duxbury to Mr. John Reyner for £30 (*PCR* 12:141). Pope has him as a proprietor at Barnstable in 1638/39, and has him moving from Sudbury to Marshfield and then back to Sudbury, where he died 9 March 1673/74. His will dated 25 November 1672, proved 7 April 1674, names his children and grandchildren (Pope).

BIDDLE, JOSEPH – Although Joseph Biddle (also seen as Beadle) is first mentioned in the Plymouth records on 4 July 1635, when he paid £6 to Isaac Robinson for some land which Robinson had bought of Edmond Chandler (who had bought it from John Barnes) (*PCR* 1:34), there is reason to believe that Biddle was in Plymouth at least several years earlier. The inventory of his estate, dated 26 September 1672, included lands "graunted to him by the Court as hee was a servant of the first Comers into the Countrey" (*MD* 19:163). On 28 October 1636 he married widow Rachel Deane (*PCR* 1:45). Joseph Biddle of Marshfield dated his will 17 April 1671, inventory 26 September 1672, and named Mr. Samuel Arnold, the poor of the town, his recent servant Jacob Bumpas, Edward Bumpas, and John Branch, leaving the rest of his estate to his wife Rachel and her daughter Martha Deane (*MD* 19:163).

BILLINGTON, ELEANOR—The wife of John Billington, Eleanor was with him in 1620 on the *Mayflower*. Her maiden name is not known, though some have speculated that it might have been Newton, since her son Francis inherited land in Lincolnshire, England, with a co-heir named Newton. However, Billington researcher Harriett Hodge thinks that the surname could be Longland. On 1636 Eleanor was fined £5 and sentenced to sit in the stocks and be whipped for slandering John Doane (*PCR* 1:42). She was married between 28 August 1638 and 21 September 1638 to (2) Gregory Armstrong (*PCR* 12:33. 37), but there is no record of her having any children by him.

BILLINGTON, FRANCIS—The son of John and Eleanor Billington, Francis accompanied his parents on the 1620 *Mayflower*. See the three articles under his father for his probable English origin and his American descendants. When the *Mayflower* was anchored at Cape Cod, "one of Francis [*sic*, should be John] Billingtons Sonnes [presumably son Francis], who in his Fathers absence, had got Gun-powder, and had shot of a peice or two, and made scuibs, and there being a fowling peice charged in his fathers Cabbin, shot her off in the Cabbin, there being a little barrell of powder halfe full, scattered in and about the Cabbin, the fire being within foure foote of the bed betweene the Deckes, and many flints and Iron things about the Cabbin, and many people about the fire, and yet by Gods mercy no harme done" (*Mourt's Relation*, p. 15). The same source, p. 26, relates how Francis Billington climbed a tree and saw what appeared to be a great sea, but on close inspection it turned out to be a very shallow pond, which is called to this day the Billington Sea. He married Christian (Penn), the widow of Francis Eaton, in July 1634 (*PCR* 1:31).

BILLINGTON, JOHN—One of the non-Separatists on the 1620 *Mayflower*, John Billington increasingly got into trouble with the Plymouth leaders. In 1621 he was tried before the whole company for disobeying a lawful command of Capt. Myles Standish, and was sentenced to have his neck and heels tied together, but on humbling himself and craving pardon, and it being his first offence, he was forgiven (*Bradford [Ford]* 2:112 fn). In 1624 John Lyford named him as one of his supporters, but Billington denied it. In 1625 Bradford wrote to Robert Cushman, "Billington still rails against you, and threatens to arrest you, I know not wherefore; he is a knave, and so will live and die" (*Bradford, Letter Book*, p. 13). In September 1630 Billington was hanged for murdering John Newcomen. His wife was Eleanor or Ellen, and he arrived with her and their two sons, John and Francis. *NEHGR* 124:116 gives good evidence that his family probably came from around Spaulding, Lincolnshire. The most comprehensive study of his descendants is Robert S. Wakefield, "Some Descendants of Francis [2] Billington of the *Mayflower*," *TG* 3:228-48. See also Harriet W. Hodge, "Desire Billington and Her Grandfather Francis Billington's Estate," *MQ* 52:137.

BILLINGTON, JOHN—A son of John and Eleanor, John Billington sailed with them on the 1620 *Mayflower*. In 1621 he wandered off and was lost for five days before being taken by Indians to Nauset. On learning his location from Massasoit, the colonists sent ten men to rescue him, and they found him with some Indians they recognized as those who had attacked them when they first came to Cape Cod. However, the Indians returned the boy peacefully, thus averting a possible cause for war (*Bradford [Ford]* 1:222-24; *Mourt's Relation*, pp. 49-52). We know the younger John Billington died sometime between the 1627 cattle division, when he obtained a share, and September 1630, when *Bradford (Ford* 2:407) stated that he died before his father was hanged.

BLOSSOM, THOMAS – A Separatist at Leiden, Thomas Blossom gave his wife Ann a power of attorney to sell houses in Cambridge, England, which she had inherited from her mother's father (Dexter, p. 603). He joined in signing a letter of 30 November 1625 from Leiden Separatists to Bradford, and he was sole signer of a letter of 15 December 1625 to Bradford (*Bradford, Letter Book*, p. 18, 21). In the December letter he deplores the difficulty the Leiden people had in reuniting with the Separatists in Plymouth, and he states that the only way the Leiden group could join the others would be with the means coming from Plymouth. He had set out on the *Speedwell* in 1620 and had to return to Leiden; he writes that the son who was with him in the ship had since died, and he only had two children living, both born since he last saw Bradford. Blossom and his family reached Plymouth probably on the 1629 *Mayflower.* Sometime prior to August 1631 he witnessed the undated will of Mary Ring (*MD* 1:31). He died in the sickness of 1633, as *Bradford (Ford)* 2:171 noted, calling him one of "theire anciente friends which had lived in Holand." His widow, Anna, married 17 October 1633 Henry Rowley (*PCR* 1:16), and lived in Scituate. His son Thomas's marriage at Barnstable 18 June 1645 to Sarah Ewer, with Edmond Freeman performing the ceremony, was noted by Rev. John Lothrop (*NEHGR* 9:286).

BONHAM, GEORGE – On 29 August 1640 George Bonham, also spelled Bonum, and Bonam, bought a house and land from Thomas Pope (*PCR* 12:61). On 5 January 1640/41 a dispute between Bonham and George Bower was sent to arbitration, with Manasseh Kempton and James Hurst on Bonham's side, and John Winslow and William Paddy on Bower's side (*PCR* 2:6). Bonham bought a house and land at Eel River from Richard Willis, who had recently purchased it from William Dennis (*PCR* 12:69). He married on 20 December 1644 Sarah Morton (*PCR* 2:79), daughter of George and Juliana (Carpenter) Morton. In 1649 he bought additional land at Eel River from John Barnes (*PCR* 12:166). In 1658 he became a freeman and was a grandjuror (*PCR* 3:135, 137). In 1659 the court found Bonham's charges that John Smith had made opprobrious speeches against him to be frivolous, and ordered Bonham and Smith to choose some of their neighbors to hear the controversy and make an end to it (*PCR* 3:169). On 3 June 1662 he was on the list of ancient freeman and others to get land at Taunton (*PCR* 4:20), and on 7 June 1665 he was granted a thirty-acre share in land near the Nemasket River (*PCR* 4:94). He was a surety for

Thomas Lucas twice and John Dunham the younger once, and on several occasions he was chosen to act with others in determining land boundaries (*PCR,* passim).

On 8 March 1678/79 the court, in referring to the settlement of the estate of Richard Willis, mentioned land which Willis's "father in _____," had given him (*PCR* 6:4), obviously his father-in-law, for he married Patience Bonham (*PCR* 8:33). She married (2) John Holmes, son of the Messenger John Holmes (Bertha W. Clark, "John Holmes's Two Wives Patience," *TAG* 38:235). John K. Allen, *George Morton of Plymouth Colony and Some of His Descendants* (Chicago, 1908) names Bonham's children as Ruth, who married Robert Barrow; Patience; Sarah three born with this name, but two died young); and George; but this work is not adequately documented. The combination of Miss Clark's article plus the *PCR* 6:4 Willis settlement gives sufficient proof that George Bonham, Jr. was his son. There was another man of the same surname in the area, Nicholas Bonham of Barnstable, but no relationship is known.

BONNEY, THOMAS—Thomas Bonney was proposed as a freeman 5 March 1638/39 (*PCR* 1:117), but he never became one. In 1640 he was among those granted lands in Duxbury, and later in the same year he was granted thirty acres of land lying on the Namassacuset River (*PCR* 1:144, 161). He was a constable of Duxbury in 1642/43 and 1644 (*PCR* 2:53, 72). On 3 March 1645/46 Bonney was presented for uncivil carriages and lascivious actions towards women and maids, but was released; on the same day he made a public apology to John Farnyseede and his wife Elizabeth for saying that Mrs. Farnyseede tried to tempt "him into lust," and he admitted that it was his own "base heart" that made him misinterpret her actions (*PCR* 2:96-98). On 4 August 1646 Bonney complained against John Willis and John Farnyseede for damaging his garden, and he was awarded seven shillings damages (*PCR* 2:107). In 1653 he was a highway surveyor for Duxbury (*PCR* 3:32), and in 1661 he was on a coroner's jury (*PCR* 3:223). On 1 October 1661 he was charged by Christopher Wadsworth with wounding his mare (*PCR* 4:7). Thomas Bonney, shoemaker, dated his will 2 January 1688/89, sworn 1 May 1693, and he mentioned his wife Mary, son Thomas Bonney, and "my children" (*MD* 34:182). He is said to have married (1) Mary Terry and (2) Mary Hunt, but the evidence is not conclusive. Howard Dakin French, "The Family of Thomas Bonney of Duxbury," *NEHGR* 89:220, gives him eight children. His son Thomas married (1) Dorcas Sampson, daughter of 1620 *Mayflower* passenger Henry Sampson, and (2) Sarah Studley, and he had three children by his first wife, Ebenezer, Elizabeth, and Mercy, all of whom would be *Mayflower* descendants. It has been claimed that Thomas [2] had other children by Dorcas Sampson, but on analysis these have been found to be the other children of Thomas [1], and thus they were siblings to Thomas [2] and would not be *Mayflower* descendants (see French's article).

BOREMAN, THOMAS—His first mention in the records is on the 1633 tax list. On 13 March 1634/35 he contracted with the court to repair the fort for £30, work to be done by 31 May 1635. All posts were to be ten inches square and not to stand above ten feet asunder, with three rails between every post, of fit thickness, and all posts and rails to be sawn (*PCR* 1:33). He was living in Barnstable when he married Hannah Annable, but the date of marriage is variously given as 3 March 1644, 10 March 1645, and 1 March 1645 (*PCR* 2:80, *MD* 3:51, *PCR* 8:41), showing that the official records are not always necessarily correct. On 8 June 1655 he was a highway surveyor at Barnstable (*PCR* 3:79). On 4 June 1661 he was among some Barnstable men granted lands at Saconesset (*PCR* 3:216-17). The births of his children are given in *PCR* 8:41: Hannah, Thomas, Samuel, Desire, Mary, Mehitabel, and Tristram. In his will dated 9 May 1663, sworn 4 June 1663, he mentioned his wife without naming her (wife Hannah submitted the inventory), his sons Thomas, Samuel, and Tristram, and his daughters Hannah, Desire, Mary, and Mehitabel (*MD* 18:63). His son Thomas was fined £5 on 8 March 1678/79 for "being marryed in a clandestine way" (*PCR* 6:6). The name is also found as Burman, but Bordman is a different family.

    BOURNE, RICHARD—The definitive history of the family of Richard Bourne, carried out for five generations, is Lydia B. (Phinney) Brownson and Maclean W. McLean, "The Rev. Richard Bourne of Sandwich, Mass.," *NEHGR* 118:83, 197, 275, 119:26, 313, which also summarizes previous efforts to find his family in England and possible connections with other New England families named Bourne. Hotten, p. 38, shows that a Richard Borne, age twenty-four, and a Thomas Borne, age twenty-two, were on a list of people to go to St. Christophers and Barbadoes in Jan. 1634/35, but, though some writers have stated that these were Richard of Sandwich and Thomas of Marshfield, and that they were brothers, there is no adequate evidence of this, nor is there any evidence that either of these two Bournes was related to Henry Bourne of Barnstable. Richard Bourne was granted seven acres of land on 2 January 1636/37, along with Josiah Winslow, James Cole, and John Bourne on behalf of his father Mr. Thomas Bourne, and this land was to belong to their dwelling houses in Plymouth and could not be sold separately (*PCR* 1:49). This shows that Richard Bourne and John Bourne—and implies that John's father Mr. Thomas Bourne—were in Plymouth by this time, but it does not show any relationship between the Richard Bourne and the Thomas Bourne families. We again see the heads of the three Plymouth Colony Bourne families, Henry, Richard, and Mr. Thomas, together on a list of freeman dated 7 March 1636/37 (*PCR* 1:53), but again such a fact is neither direct nor indirect proof of any relationship among the three families. Richard Bourne was among those granted hay ground rights on 20 March 1636/37 (*PCR* 1:57). On 2 May 1637 he was on a jury to lay out highways (*PCR* 1:58). These facts would put into question Savage's statement that Richard Bourne was in Lynn in 1637. On 5 June 1638 he was on a Plymouth grand jury (*PCR* 1:87). On

4 September 1638 he was fined eighteen pence for keeping three pigs unringed (*PCR* 1:98). On 4 June 1639 he was a deputy for Sandwich (*PCR* 1:126).

He served in various other public ways, often being associated with Mr. Edmond Freeman (*PCR,* passim). In 1670 he was ordained the pastor of the Indian Church at Mashpee, his parish covering from Provincetown to Middleborough, where his efforts to work in a cooperative fashion were most important in motivating the Indians not to fight on King Philip's side in the war (*NEHGR* 118:86). His first wife has not been positively identified, but some writers have claimed that she was Bathsheba, daughter of Andrew Hallett, Jr. – again, the evidence is insufficient. He married (2) in 1677 Ruth (Sargent) (Winslow), daughter of Mr. William Sargent, and widow of Jonathan Winslow; she was some thirty years younger than Bourne, and after his death she married (3) John Chipman. Some interesting correspondence from Bourne to the widow Ruth Winslow before their marriage, and a letter from William Sargent to his daughter, are shown in *NEHGR* 118:87. He died intestate before 18 September 1682, and a final settlement of his estate showed that his son Job predeceased him, but left children; and Richard's sons Elisha and Shearjashub survived him. He also had a son Ezra, who was living on 9 March 1672/73 when he witnessed a deed. All children were by his first wife, and Brownson and McLean give the early descendants of all but Ezra, who apparently died without issue.

BOWMAN, JOHN – He appeared on the 1633 and 1634 tax lists, and on 2 January 1636/37 forty acres of land were granted to Edmond Chandler on the east side of Moses Simonson's land, where "Morris form[er]ly begann to cleare for Mr. Bowman" (*PCR* 1:49). Mr. Bowman may or may not have been John Bowman. Thereafter John Bowman disappears from the records, though there were later Bowmans in Plymouth.

BRADFORD, WILLIAM – William Bradford was baptized at Austerfield, County York, 19 March 1589/90, the son of William and Alice (Hanson) Bradford (William B. Browne, "Ancestry of the Bradfords of Austerfield, County York – Records Extending the Ancestral Line of Gov. William Bradford," *NEHGR* 83:439, 84:5). He became an early convert to the Separatist Church at nearby Scrooby, Nottinghamshire, and he left with the church for Holland ca. 1607. Cotton Mather relates that he was living in Holland when he became of full age and sold his lands in England (*NEHGR* 4:44). He married (1) at Leiden 10 December 1613 Dorothy May, q.v., and he listed himself in the marriage intentions as age twenty-three (*MD* 9:115-17. He married (2) at Plymouth 14 August 1623 Alice (Carpenter) Southworth, q.v. under Carpenter (*MD* 30:4). His child by his first wife was John Bradford, who married twice, but left no children. By his second wife, William had William, Mercy, and Joseph Bradford. Mercy married Benjamin Vermayes, and there is no record of any surviving children. Sons William and Joseph both left descendants, and William became a colony leader, often serving as an Assistant. Governor Bradford's nuncupative will is given in *MD* 2:228. Ruth G. Hall, *Descendants of Governor William Bradford* (1951) covers the first seven generations, but with many errors.

BREWSTER, JONATHAN – The oldest son of Elder William and Mary Brewster, Jonathan arrived at Plymouth in 1621 on the *Fortune*. The *Brewster Book*, a part of which contains family birth, marriage, and death records, was begun by Jonathan Brewster and continued by members of his family, and it is transcribed in *MD* 1:1 and continuing issues. The first family entry is "Johnnathan Brewster was borne at Scroby in Nottinghamshyre the 12th of August 1593 yeaes." He lived in Leiden with his parents, and considerable information on his life there can be found in Jeremy D. Bangs, "Jonathan Brewster in Leiden Documents," *MQ* 51:161, 52:6, 57. He was a ribbon maker and exporter in Holland, and in 1617 he formed a partnership with Thomas Brewer, who later became one of the Adventurers. In this series of articles, Dr. Bangs effectively counters the claim of the Dexters that Jonathan Brewster had a wife and child who died in Holland. In Plymouth, Jonathan engaged in various activities, acting at times as an attorney, starting a ferry service, and engaging in coastal shipping to Virginia. In 1635 he was in charge of a trading post in Connecticut on behalf of Plymouth Colony, later returning to Plymouth. In 1652 he started his own trading post in Connecticut, and was censured by the local government for doing it without permission, but was allowed to keep his post. He was a close friend of Connecticut Gov. John Winthrop, Jr. and a fellow experimenter and scientist with his own laboratory at his trading post (Morison, *Builders*, p. 283). He married Lucretia Oldham, q.v., at Plymouth 10 April 1624 and they had William, Mary, Jonathan, Ruth, Benjamin, Elizabeth, Grace, and Hannah. (See also Barbara Lambert Merrick, "Jonathan Brewster and His Family," *MQ* 52:72-83.)

BREWSTER, LOVE – A 1620 *Mayflower* passenger, he arrived with his parents William and Mary Brewster. He married Sarah Collier (*PCR* 1:30), daughter of William Collier, q.v., 15 May 1634. His children were Sarah Brewster, who married Benjamin 2 Bartlett; Nathaniel, who married, but whose wife's name is not known; William, who married Lydia Partridge, daughter of George; and Wrestling, who married a Mary, whose maiden name is not known (*NEHGR* 53:113-14, 285). He named his wife and four children in his will dated 6 October 1650, inventory 31 January 1650/51 (*MD* 2:203).

BREWSTER, MARY – The wife of Elder William Brewster, Mary arrived on the 1620 *Mayflower*. Walter Burgess, *John Robinson, the Pastor of the Pilgrims* (1920), p. 80, advanced the view that she was the daughter of Thomas Wentworth. This was supported by John G. Hunt, "New Light on the Brewsters of Scrooby and New England," *TAG* 41:1, and has been tenaciously clung to by numerous Brewster descendants, who would like to claim a Wentworth royal line. However, the evidence for such an identification is too scant to serve for a judgment, and Hunt himself abandoned the Wentworth claim when he wrote more recently in *Of Mary*

Brewster, three parts (privately published, 1984, 1985) that Elder Brewster's wife was a Mary Wyrral; but again the evidence is not adequate. A review by E. A. Stratton published in the Spring 1985 issue of the *Detroit Society for Genealogical Research Magazine* argues that the parentage of Mary Brewster is still unproven (see also Dr. Bangs in *MQ* 51:165-66, fn 1). Mary died at Plymouth 17 April 1627 (*Brewster Book*—see under Jonathan Brewster, above).

BREWSTER, WILLIAM—For all that we know about him, there is much more that we do not know; for example, we do not know the dates of his birth and death. Various accounts differ showing birthdates in 1559, 1560, 1563, 1564, or 1566-67, and death dates ca. 18 April 1643, or ca. 16 April 1644. Dexter, "The True Date of the Birth and Death of Elder Brewster," *NEHGR* 18:18, gives good reasons for believing that he was born in 1566 or 1567, and that he died in April 1644. John G. Hunt, "The Mother of Elder William Brewster of the Mayflower," *NEHGR* 124:250, makes a good case that his parents were William and Mary (Smythe) (Simkinson) Brewster of Scrooby, Nottinghamshire. He entered Peterhouse, Cambridge University, on 3 December 1580, but apparently did not graduate. He became an assistant to William Davison, one of Queen Elizabeth's Secretaries of State, and he went to Holland with Davison in 1585 on a diplomatic mission. When Davison was imprisoned by Queen Elizabeth as a scapegoat for the execution of Mary Queen of Scots, Brewster returned to Scrooby and subsequently was appointed to his father's old post there as postmaster, holding that position until 1607. He was imprisoned as the result of the betrayal of a ship's master when he was leading a group of Separatists fleeing England for Holland. On being released, he went to Holland, where he became ruling elder of the separatist church, supporting himself and his family by running a printing business (Lucy Hall Greenlaw, "Early Generations of the Brewster Family," *NEHGR* 53:109; *Bradford [Ford]* 2:342-50).

William Brewster arrived at Plymouth on the 1620 *Mayflower* accompanied by his wife Mary and their sons Love and Wrestling. He continued as ruling elder of the Plymouth Church until he died. Bradford summed up his work: "He would labour with his hands in the feilds as long as he was able; yet when the church had no other minister, he taught twise every Saboth, and both powerfully and profitably, to the great contentment of the hearers, and their comfortable edification. He did more in this behalfe in a year, then many that have their hundreds a year doe in all their lives. . . . He had a singuler good gift in prayer, both publick and private, in ripping up the hart and conscience before God, in the humble confession of sinne, and begging the mercies of God in Christ for the pardon of same" (*Bradford [Ford]* 2:348-50). His inventory (*MD* 3:15) shows a private library of hundreds of books, mostly religious, but displaying a considerable breadth of interest for a man of his times.

His children were Jonathan, Patience (who married Thomas Prence), Fear (who married Isaac Allerton), Love, Wrestling, and a child that died in Leiden. Wrestling, Patience, and Fear predeceased him, the two daughters having had children, and Wrestling dying without issue. An excellent short account of Brewster's life is given in *Dawes-Gates* 2:143-56, and, in a footnote on p. 151, documented information is included to support the good possibility that Brewster had had some interest in the Virginia settlement, and that he might have been the father of the Capt. Edward Brewster who was a resident of that settlement and who returned to England in 1618. A contemporary, Nathaniel Brewster of Brookhaven, Long Island, in spite of claims to the contrary, has been shown most likely not to have been related to Elder Brewster's family (Donald Lines Jacobus, "The Family of Rev. Nathaniel Brewster," *TAG* 12:199). The most comprehensive family history to date is Emma C. Jones, *The Brewster Genealogy*, 2 vols. (1908), which is good, but with some errors. A fully documented account of Brewster's first five generations is being prepared for the General Society of Mayflower Descendants by its Historian General, Barbara Lambert Merrick. A recent biography by Mary B. Sherwood, *Pilgrim: A Biography of William Brewster* can be obtained from the author at P.O. Box 6541, Falls Church, VA 22046.

BREWSTER, WRESTLING—A 1620 *Mayflower* passenger, he arrived with his father Elder William Brewster, q.v. *Bradford (Ford)* 2:402, wrote that Wrestling Brewster died as a young man, unmarried.

BRIAN, THOMAS—On 10 January 1632/33 Thomas Brian, a servant of Samuel Eddy, was charged before the Court of Assistants with running away from his master. Getting lost in the woods, he was returned by Indians, and for his offense was privately whipped (*PCR* 1:7). Pope states that as a servant to Mr. Allerton he was also brought before the Bay Court in 1642 (Allerton's servant was called Thomas Briant, and this may not be the same man).

BRIDGES, WILLIAM—He married John Oldham's daughter Mary Oldham and was living in the Bay Colony. Though he is not shown in early Plymouth Colony by name, he may have been represented by one of the ten shares that John Oldham received in the 1623 land division (*MQ* 40:60).

BRIGGS, CLEMENT—Arriving in the *Fortune* in 1621, Clement Briggs later moved to Dorchester, where he married (1) Joan Allen, and (2) an Elizabeth whose maiden name is unknown. He later moved to Weymouth. On 7 June 1659 Thomas Briggs, son of Clement, deceased, was granted 150 acres of land and, if available, twenty acres of meadow (*PCR* 3:164), and on 29 October 1668 Remember Briggs, Clement's son, on behalf of himself and Clement's other children, was granted twelve acres of swamp land near Bridgewater (probably in lieu of the original twenty acres) (*PCR* 5:5). Edna Anne Hannibal, *Clement Briggs of Plymouth and His Descendants 1621-1965* (1966), is a good family history, well documented with probate and land records. (See also *MD* 4:131 and Mrs. John E. Barclay, "The Briggs Families of Taunton, Mass.," *TAG* 33:76-86, which has a section subtitled "Clement Briggs Notes" on pp. 83-86.)

BRITTERIDGE, RICHARD – A 1620 *Mayflower* passenger, Richard Brit-teridge died 21 December 1620 without known descendants, the first person to die after the *Mayflower* reached Plymouth. Bradford listed him together with several others without further comment. He does not appear in Leiden records.

BROWNE, JAMES – The son of Mr. John Browne of Rehoboth, James Browne is mentioned in the series of articles on his father by French given below. He probably arrived at Plymouth with his parents in 1632, later becoming prominent among the second generation leaders of the colony. He was made a freeman on 1 June 1658 along with his brother John Browne, Jr., both being called "Mr." (*PCR* 3:136). On 10 June 1661 he was on a coroner's jury investigating the death of Robert Allen in Rehoboth (*PCR* 3:222). He became a selectman for Swansea on 7 June 1670, and on 29 October 1670 he was one of a committee appointed to dispose of lands and grant admission to new inhabitants of Swansea (*PCR* 5:35, 49). He was a selectman for Swansea on 5 June 1671 (*PCR* 5:57). On 23 August 1671 he was appointed to accompany Mr. James Walker and Mr. Roger Williams on a mission to King Philip (*PCR* 5:76). He became an Assistant for the first time on 3 June 1673 (*PCR* 5:112), a position to which he was reelected many times. He married Lydia Howland, daughter of 1620 *Mayflower* passengers John and Elizabeth (Tilley) Howland, and they had James, Jabez, Dorothy, and Joseph; Joseph probably died young, and the first three were named in the will of their grandmother, Elizabeth Howland (*MD*, 3:54), dated 17 December 1686. James Browne, Sr. died at Swansea 29 October 1710, and his will, dated 25 October 1694, proved 11 January 1710/11, named his wife Lydia and children James Browne, Jabez Browne, and Dorothy Kent (wife of Joseph Kent, Jr.) (*MD* 7:163-66).

BROWNE, JOHN – A good idea of John Browne's impressive career can be had from Robert L. French, "John Browne of Plymouth Colony, Obstructionist and Libertarian," *MQ* 49 (1983):109, 161, 50:5, 57, which contains some interesting possibilities for the origin of his family in England. He arrived at Plymouth possibly on the *Lyon* in 1632 with his wife Dorothy and their children, though Savage writes that this was a different John Browne. Nathaniel Morton in *New Englands Memoriall*, pp. 163-64, wrote that Browne in his younger years traveled in the Low Countries and made friends with the minister John Robinson and others of the Separatist church; on arriving in New England, because of his former friendships, he decided to settle in Plymouth. He was then about fifty years old and his wife forty-nine. He was on the 1633 tax list, and he became a freeman not long after (*PCR* 1:4). In 1635/36 he became an Assistant (*PCR* 1:36), a position to which he was elected many times. He could write to Governor Winthrop as "Loving Friend," and was on good terms with many of the leading men of Plymouth, Massachusetts, and Rhode Island, and also of England. He was a Commissioner of the United Colonies and was used by Plymouth in many inter-colony negotiations. In 1645 he joined Freeman, Hatherly, and Standish in their unsuccessful support of Vassall's petition (see chapter 4). In 1652 Browne sued Rev. Samuel Newman, minister of the Rehoboth Church, for defamation, and was awarded £100 plus costs which Browne later remitted. Browne was the resident of Rehoboth who in 1655 offered to make up the deficiency for seven years of residents who did not want to pay for maintenance of the church. In 1655 he left for England, staying there four years, during which he served as executor for the estate of the senior Sir Henry Vane, father of the former governor of the same name of the Bay Colony, later one of the leading men in Commonwealth England. He returned to Plymouth in 1660.

He dated his will 7 April 1662, and his inventory was taken 19 April 1662 (*MD* 18:18, gives the will and a very substantial inventory). He left his wife Dorothy, and named his son James, his daughter Mary, wife of Thomas Willett, and his grandchildren John Browne, Joseph Browne, Nathaniel, Lydia Browne, and Hannah, and also his granddaughter Martha Saffin, wife of John Saffin. To daughter Mary Willett he left but twelve pence "to bee payed att the end of every yeare During her life for a memoriall unto her; and it shalbee in full of all filiall portion which shee or any in her behalfe shall Claime," which would seem to be such a pointed slight that the court felt compelled to write on the back of the will, "Least any thinge mencioned in this will in reference to mistris Mary Willett the wife of Capt: Thomas Willett might bee by any mis Construed to the prejudice of of [*sic*] the said mistris Willett; wee thinke it meet to Declare that out of the longe experience of her Dutifull and tender respect to her said father from time to time expresed there hath never appeered to us the least ground of any such thinge to this prsent." That Browne died a rich man can be seen in the fact that to one grandson alone he left over seven hundred acres of land.

His widow Dorothy Browne dated her will 17 December 1668, sworn 29 March 1674, and she mentioned her daughter Mary Willett; Mary Willett's children; Sarah Elliott, daughter of Sarah Elliott, deceased; son James Browne; grandson John Browne; the latter's two brothers Joseph and Nathaniel; granddaughter Dorothy Browne; daughter-in-law Lydia Browne; daughter-in-law Dorothy Browne; and granddaughters Lydia Browne and Anna Browne (*MD* 18:94). John and Dorothy Browne had a son who predeceased them, John Browne, Jr., and his will was dated 31 March 1662, inventory 19 April 1662. He mentioned his father-in-law William Buckland, his wife (not named), his oldest son John Browne, and "all my Five children," with his father John Browne to be executor (*MD* 18:14). The author of the *MQ* articles above also believes that a William Browne was either the son or nephew of John Browne, Sr.

BROWN, JOHN—A weaver who lived in Duxbury, John was the brother of of the 1620 *Mayflower* passenger Peter Brown, as is shown by PCR 2:89, where Priscilla Browne, daughter of Peter Browne, deceased, having finished the term she was to dwell with William Gilson of Scituate, chose John Browne, "her unckle," to be her guardian. This was the John Brown who married Phebe Harding on 26 March 1634 (*PCR* 1:26), not the Mr. John Browne who was an Assistant, as stated by Pope. The Duxbury John Browne dated his will 15 April 1672, sworn 5 June 1684 (Ply. Colony PR 4:2:128). He left a daughter Remember, who married Josiah Wormall. Evidence to show which John Brown was the brother of Peter Brown is given in an article in the October 1986 issue of *NEHGR*.

BROWN, PETER – A 1620 *Mayflower* passenger, Peter Brown was not a Leiden Separatist, but not much else is known about his background. We read in *Mourt's Relation*, p. 27, that he and John Goodman were cutting thatch on 12 January 1620/21 about 1 1/2 miles from the Plymouth settlement and wandered away and got lost. The next day the colonists sent ten to twelve armed men to seek them, going out as far as seven or eight miles, afraid that they had been captured by Indians. Finally, after the searchers had given up, Brown and Goodman found their way back to the Colony. Brown was on the 1633 freeman list. On 1 January 1632/33 he was fined three shillings for not appearing at court, and on 2 January 1632/33 he was fined the same amount again for the same reason (*PCR* 1:5, 7). On 7 January 1632/3 a dispute between him and Samuel Fuller was referred by the court to Robert Hicks and Francis Cooke for arbitration (*PCR* 1:18). He probably died in the 1633 sickness, for his inventory was taken on 10 October 1633 (*MD* 1:79).

He married (1) Martha Ford, q.v., in 1626 and (2) Mary _____ ca. 1630 (*TAG* 42:41). He had two surviving children by each wife. He died intestate, and his widow Mary was made administratrix of his estate on 11 November 1633, at which time she was ordered by the court to pay £15 to Mr. John Doane for benefit of Peter's daughter Mary, and £15 to Mr. William Gilson for benefit of Peter's daughter Priscilla, the court having placed Mary with Doane for nine years and Priscilla with Gilson for twelve years; widow Mary was allowed the rest of the estate for her own third and for bringing up her own two children (*PCR* 1:17-19). One of Mary's children died young, and the other, Rebecca Brown, married William Snow and had issue. Of the older daughters, Mary married Ephraim Tinkham and had issue (*TAG* 42:39), and Priscilla married William Allen, but left no issue. In a deed of 27 October 1647 Ephraim Tinkham and his wife Mary sold to Henry Sampson land adjoining Sampson's land in Duxbury which was one-third of the land belonging to Peter Brown, deceased; on 8 June 1650 William Allen of Sandwich and his wife Priscilla sold to John Brown of Duxbury, weaver, land in Duxbury which was one part of three which belonged to the children of Peter Brown, brother of John Brown, q.v. (*PCR* 12:146, 186); and on 25 March 1668 William Snow of Bridgewater and his wife Rebecca sold to Ephraim Tinkham one-third of a share of land in Dartmouth which was granted to Peter Brown as a Purchaser (another deed from William Allen sold to Henry Tucker on 15 April 1668 a one-third share of land in Dartmouth which was granted to Peter Brown as a Purchaser) (*MD* 5:34-37). Claims of a son Peter were shown to be baseless by Donald Lines Jacobus, "Peter Brown of Windsor, Conn.," *TAG* 33:214, and Robert S. Wakefield, "Peter Brown of Windsor, Conn., Not a Mayflower

Descendant," *NGSQ* 67:253. Robert S. Wakefield, *Mayflower Families in Progress—Peter Brown of the Mayflower and His Descendants for Four Generations* (1986), was recently published and is available from the General Society of Mayflower Descendants.

BUCK, ISAAC—Isaac Buck was in Scituate no later than 1643. In 1650 he accused John Hewes of stealing four hoes from him (*PCR* 2:160). On 4 October 1655 the General Court noted that the members of the train band at Scituate had carried themselves unworthily "in that they voted for divers unmeet persons" to be sergeants, and demoted to a sergeant the ensign earlier assigned by the court, and therefore the court ordered them to choose fit sergeants and warned them against any such other "contempt of the govment." Isaac Buck, the clerk of the band, was charged with unworthily demeaning himself and was required to make a public announcement of the fact at the head of the company; on the same day he was fined twenty shillings for refusing to shoe horses to be used by a United Colonies commissioner from New Haven, but the following year the fine was remitted (*PCR* 3:89-90, 106). Buck was made a freeman in 1658, and in the same year he was a constable for Scituate (*PCR* 3:136-37). In 1659 the Court of Assistants noted complaints against him by Constant Southworth and Nathaniel Morton for not paying charges due for the "majestrates table" (that is, their meals), and for Morton's wages, and now he was ordered to pay these charges (*PCR* 3:161). On 1 March 1669/70 Sgt. Isaac Buck was approved by the court as the lieutenant of the Scituate military company (*PCR* 5:33). In Scituate he was often elected a deputy to the court, a selectman, and town clerk (*PCR* 4, 5, and 6, passim; *MD* 1:233, 19:62), holding the latter office until he died in 1695, when he must have been quite old.

His wife was Frances _____, who along with their son Isaac, Jr. was among the heirs in 1672 of Esther Woodfield, widow of John Woodfield (*MD* 17:156, 19:62). Isaac Buck died intestate in 1695, leaving his wife Frances and nine children: Isaac, Joseph, Jonathan, Thomas, Benjamin, James, Elizabeth Whitcomb, Ruth Garrett, and Deborah Merritt (*TAG* 24:104). The *TAG* article, by Mrs. Barclay, also shows that Allerton Cushman's wife Mary was James[2] Buck's daughter, and Abigail Buck who married Nathaniel Harlow was probably James[2] Buck's widow.

BULKELEY, EDWARD—Edward Bulkeley was baptized at Odell, Bedfordshire, 12 June 1614, the son of Rev. Peter and Jane (Allen) Bulkeley, and his father migrated to Massachusetts in 1635, becoming pastor of the church at Concord. Edward graduated from Cambridge University, England, and came to America after his father, becoming minister of the church at Marshfield no later than 1643. His wife was Lucian _____, and they had issue, with many descendants living today. He later became minister at Concord following the death of his father, and he died at Chelmsford on 2 January 1695/96. Edward Bulkeley is one of the very few early Plymouth residents with a documented and proven royal line. An excellent family history was written by Donald L. Jacobus, *The Bulkeley Genealogy* (1933).

BUMPAS, EDWARD—Edward Bumpus arrived in Plymouth as a young man in 1621 on the *Fortune*, and he shared in the 1623 land division and the 1627 cattle division. In 1629/30 he married a Hannah, whose last name is unknown. There is no record that he was ever made a freeman, and in 1656 he was described as "one of the town's poor" (Mrs. John E. Barclay, "The Bumpus Family of New England," *TAG* 43:65). He died before 5 March 1683/84, and his wife survived him. They had at least twelve children between 1631 and 1654. His early descendants are given in Mrs. Barclay's article, above. A family history compiled by Carle Franklin Bumpus, *Bompasse, Bumpas, Bump, Bumpus and Allied Families 1621-1981*, rev. (Baltimore, 1985), was reviewed in *TAG* 60:189.

BUNDY, JOHN—Born in England ca. 1617, John Bundy died in Taunton in 1681. His mother was a sister to Susanna Alley, the wife of Philip Alley of Boston (*MF* 2:12). On 6 March 1636/37 the court of Assistants noted he was bound as a servant to Griffin Mountegue (of the Bay Colony) for eight years from 14 March 1635/36, and approved, with Bundy's consent, his remaining term being transferred to William Brewster, who had made a settlement with Mountegue (*PCR* 1:51). On 21 August 1637 Bundy was found guilty of lewd and uncivil carriage towards Elizabeth Heybell, in the house of her master, William Brewster, and was sentenced to be severely whipped (PCR 1:65). On 8 January 1638/39 William Brewster assigned his interest in John Bundy's remaining five years of service to his son Jonathan Brewster (*PCR* 1:107). On 15 August 1645 John Bundy was one of the soldiers from Plymouth who went on the expedition against the Narragansetts (PCR 2:90). He married (1) Martha Chandler, daughter of Roger and Isabella (Chilton) Chandler and (2) Ruth (?Ratchell) Gurney, and he had children by both wives (*MF* 2:12). On 3 June 1662 he was granted land in Taunton with some "first-born children" and others, and on 3 October 1665 his request was granted that three daughters of Roger Chandler be given fifty acres each near Taunton (*PCR* 4:20, 110). His will dated April 1681, proved 29 October 1681, stated he was aged sixty-four or thereabout, and he mentioned his wife, "the children," son James Bundy, "my sons," and "the sons by this wife." See *TAG* 27:1, 37:212; *MF* 2:12.

BURCHER, EDWARD—Edward Burcher arrived at Plymouth in 1623 and received two shares in the 1623 land division, presumably for himself and his wife. He was not in the 1627 cattle division, and was probably not the man Pope had later living in the Bay Colony. In 1648 Samuel Fuller with the consent of his mother Bridget Fuller deeded two acres of land at Strawberry Hill in Plymouth to Lt. Matthew Fuller, the land being described as sometimes belonging to Edward Burcher.

BUTTON, WILLIAM—A young servant to Samuel Fuller, William Button died without known descendants on 6 November 1620 when the *Mayflower* was still at sea, but nearing Cape Cod.

CANNON, JOHN—John Cannon arrived at Plymouth in 1621 on the *Fortune,* and he was paired with William Tench in the 1623 land division, the two of them receiving a total of two acres. On 14 September 1638 a memorandum in the land records showed that William Tench and John Carman had bequeathed two acres of land to John Billington, deceased, and the land was now being sold by Billington's widow, Eleanor, and son, Francis (*PCR* 12:37). Neither Cannon/Carman nor Tench were in the 1627 cattle division, and their leaving land to Billington is an indication that they were of the dissident faction that left the colony in the wake of the Lyford controversy (see chapter 1) even though Billington himself did not.

CARPENTER, ALICE—Born Alice Carpenter, the daughter of Alexander Carpenter of Wrington, Somerset and Leiden, Holland, she married Edward Southworth at Leiden (*MD* 10:1). After the death of Southworth, she sailed to Plymouth on the *Anne* in 1623, and shortly after arrival married Gov. William Bradford as his second wife. She had four sisters associated with Plymouth Colony, Juliana, Priscilla, Agnes, and Mary (Mary Lovering Holman, *The Scott Genealogy* [Boston, 1919]). All the sisters eventually came to Plymouth except Agnes, who married Samuel Fuller, but died before he sailed on the 1620 *Mayflower.* Alice's two sons by her first marriage, Constant and Thomas Southworth, came to Plymouth after her. Her sister Priscilla's husband, William Wright, mentioned in his will his "brother Will Bradford," who had also been mentioned in the will of Samuel Fuller, her sister Agnes's widower, (*MD* 1:200, 24).

CARPENTER, JULIANA—A sister of Alice Carpenter, q.v., Juliana married (1) George Morton, and arrived in Plymouth in 1623 on the *Anne* with him and their children. Following Morton's death she married (2) Manasseh Kempton, but had no children by him. Ann Cooper, the daughter of Juliana's sister Priscilla, married Juliana's son Ephraim Morton. Juliana died 19 February 1664/65, age eighty-one (*PCR* 8:25).

CARPENTER, MARY—A sister of Alice Carpenter, q.v., Mary never married, but came to live in her later years at Plymouth, where she died 19/20 March 1687/88 in her ninety-first year, "a godly old maid, never married" (*Ply. Church Recs.* 1:260). Frederic Kidder, "Letter of Mary Carpenter," *NEHGR* 14:195, transcribes a letter addressed to Mary at Wrington, Somerset, from Governor Bradford in which he writes, "Sundrie of our ministers (hearing of the peace and liberty now in England and Ireland) begine to leave us and it is feared many more will follow. We do not write these things to discourage you (for we shall be glad to see you if God so dispose) but if you find not all things here according to your expectation when God shall bring you hither that you may not thinke we delt not plainly with you." A footnote in *NEHGR* 14:196 suggests that the date of the letter, 19 August 1664, in the oldest extant copy must be wrongly transcribed. Internal evidence would place it ca. 1644 or 1646.

CARPENTER, PRISCILLA—A sister of Alice Carpenter, q.v., Priscilla arrived at Plymouth sometime after the 1627 cattle division, but before 1633. She married (1) William Wright and (2) on 27 November 1634 John Cooper

(*PCR* 1:32). She died 29 December 1689 in her ninety-second year (*NEHGR* 14:378).

CARTER, ROBERT – A 1620 *Mayflower* passenger, Robert Carter was a servant to William Mullins, and he died during the first year at Plymouth without known descendants. Mullins in his will dated 21 February 1620/21, which was apparently copied 2 April 1621, mentioned "my man Robert," thus indicating that Carter was still alive then (*MD* 1:230-32). He was probably one of the six people who died between the sailing of the *Mayflower* and the arrival of the *Fortune*.

CARVER, JOHN – A Leiden Separatist and the first governor of Plymouth Colony, John Carver was one of the organizers of the voyage on the *Mayflower* which resulted in the settlement of Plymouth. *Bradford (Ford)* 1:216) wrote that in April 1621 "whilst they were bussie about their seed, their [Gov. John Carver] came out of his feild very sick, it being a hott day; he complained greatly of his head, and lay downe, and within a few howers his sences failed, so as he never spake more till he dyed, which was within a few days after. . . . He was buried in the best maner they could, with some vollies of shott by all that bore armes; and his wife, being a weak woman, dyed within 5 or 6 weeks after him." A footnote on the same page refers to a comment in Hubbard's *History*, that Carver was "a gentleman of singular piety, rare humility, and great condescendency; one also of a public spirit, as well as of a public purse, having disbursed the greatest part of that considerable estate God had given him, for the carrying on the interest of the company." His wife was Katherine, q.v. He left no surviving children, but Dexter, p. 608, states that Carver buried one child in St. Pancras 10 July 1609 and another there on 11 November 1617.

CARVER, KATHERINE – The wife of Gov. John Carver, q.v., Katherine Carver accompanied him on the 1620 *Mayflower* and died in late spring 1621. Banks, *English Ancestry*, p. 44, states that Carver married Mrs. Catherine (White) Leggatt, widow of George, and daughter of Alexander White of Sturton-le-Steeple, Nottinghamshire, but this has not been confirmed.

CARVER, ROBERT – Robert Carver has been called a brother of Gov. John Carver, but this is speculation, for there is no evidence for it. In fact, it is not known whether he was related to Governor Carver in any way. He is first shown in Plymouth records on 3 September 1638, when he was granted twenty acres of land at Greene's Harbor (*PCR* 1:94). He lived in Duxbury for a while, but moved back to Marshfield. He was a grandjuryman in 1643 (*PCR* 2:53), and he became a freeman in 1648 (*PCR* 2:122). He married Christian _____, who died in 1658, and they had but one known child, a son John who predeceased his father. Son John had married Millicent Ford, daughter of William and Ann Ford, and had ten children. Robert made an arrangement with Millicent after the death of John to live with her, and she and her children could have the improvements of his estate during his life, with half the estate going to John and Millicent's oldest son, William, during Robert's lifetime, and the other half going to William after the death of Millicent; he died in April 1680, eighty-six years old, and was buried in Marshfield (William Jones, "Robert Carver of Marshfield, Mass., and Some of His Descendants," *NEHGR* 88:215, 311, 89:34, 96:304.)

CARVER'S MAIDSERVANT—Never mentioned by name this woman is referred to twice as "a maidservant." "His [Carver's] maidservant married and died a year or two after, here in this place." It is thought that she might have been the unnamed second wife of Francis Eaton, and that they had no surviving children (*MF* 1:3).

CHANDLER, EDMOND—Edmond Chandler was probably related to Roger Chandler, for he was in Leiden during the same period, appearing in the records there in 1613, 1615, 1619, 1623, and 1626. He was a say-weaver (as was Roger), and was later listed as a draper and then a pipe-maker. He buried a child in Leiden in 1619 (Dexter, p. 609). As was Roger, Edmond was on the 1633 freeman list. He moved to Duxbury, and in 1635/36 he was one of the Duxbury members of a committee to look into possibilities of uniting Duxbury with Plymouth (*PCR* 1:41). He served on other commissions and juries, and engaged in a good number of land transactions (*PCR, passim*). On 1 January 1636/37 he became a constable for Duxbury (*PCR* 1:48). On 24 January 1638/39 John Edwards put himself as an apprentice to Edmond Chandler of Duxbury, yeoman, for five years (*PCR* 1:110). On 4 June 1639 Chandler became a deputy for Duxbury (*PCR* 1:126).

Edmond apparently had two wives, but their names are not known (Lora Altine Woodbury Underhill, *Descendants of Edward Small of New England*, 2 vols. [Boston & New York, 1934 2:1027-95]. He dated his will 3 May 1662, proved 4 June 1662, and in it he named sons Samuel, Benjamin, and Joseph; and daughters Sarah, Anna, Mary, and Ruth. The first three daughters were to get 3,500 (pounds?) of sugar belonging to him at Barbadoes (*MD* 14:68). He also had a son John, who apparently died without issue, but in his 1653 will, while at sea heading for Barbadoes, he named his father Edmond Chandler of Plymouth (Sherman and Wakefield, *Plymouth Colony Probate Guide*, p. 21). As Bowman comments, there have been many serious errors written about Chandler descendants of colonial Plymouth, some of which he sorts out in "Chandler Notes," *MD* 14:65 (also see *MD* 14:140-41). Note in particular that although Edmond [3] (Joseph [2]) Chandler married Elizabeth [3] (Jonathan [2]) Alden, they did not have any surviving children, in spite of claims to the contrary.

CHANDLER, ROGER—Roger Chandler, possibly related to Edmond Chandler, q.v., was in Leiden records as a say-weaver from Colchester, England, and he was married at Leiden on 21 July 1615 to Isabel Chilton. He and his wife and two children, Samuel and Sarah, were living at Leiden on 15 October 1622 (Dexter, p. 609), having arrived at Plymouth sometime after the 1627 cattle division. His wife was the daughter of 1620 *Mayflower* passenger James Chilton, and their descendants are given in *MF* 2, which gives references for additional information. He was on the 1633 freeman list, and he later moved to Duxbury.

CHILLINGSWORTH, THOMAS – Thomas Chillingsworth is first noted in Plymouth records on 21 March 1637/38, the date of the will of Thomas Hampton of Sandwich, who died without family, and left his estate to several people, with Thomas Chillingsworth as one of the main beneficiaries (*MD* 3:74). On 4 December 1638 he was fined for keeping a hog unringed (*PCR* 1:107). According to Savage, he had been earlier at Lynn. The Plymouth Court noted on 3 October 1639 that he had sold a lot at Sandwich to Joseph Winsor (*PCR* 1:133). On 16 April 1640 he was among the residents of Sandwich granted meadow land, receiving two and a half acres (*PCR* 1:150). He became a freeman on 5 June 1644 (*PCR* 2:71). On 4 June 1645 he was a surveyor of highways for Marshfield, and on 2 June 1646 he was a constable of Duxbury (*PCR* 2:84, 102). He served on various juries (*PCR*, passim), and on 7 June 1648 he was chosen for the first of two times as a deputy for Marshfield (*PCR* 2:123). On 4 October 1648, Thomas Chillingsworth of Marshfield, shoemaker, bought from Mr. Edmond Freeman the one-half tract of land, about three hundred acres, that Freeman owned, Freeman having previously sold the other one-half to Arthur Howland (*PCR* 12:154). Chillingsworth seemed to be associated at Lynn, Sandwich, and Marshfield with John Dingley, q.v., but, contrary to some reports, Chillingsworth's daughter Sarah was not Dingley's wife.

Chillingsworth died before 1 March 1652/53 when the court ordered Mr. Alden and Captain Standish to take portions from his estate for his children, and on the same day his wife Joan was made administratrix of his estate (*PCR* 3:21-22). On 7 March 1653/54 Joan Chillingsworth informed the court that she had arranged to have her four daughters given £10 each at the time of their marriages, and Thomas Doged (Doggett) joined her as a surety (*PCR* 3:45). She married Thomas Doged 17 August 1654 (*NEHGR* 6:347), and Doged was later involved in land disputes with Arthur Howland until they were able to agree on their boundaries (*PCR* 3:97, 102-05). Savage names Chillingsworth's daughters as Sarah, Mary, Mehitable, and Elizabeth. Mehitabel Chillingsworth married at Marshfield 20 May 1661 Justice Eames, and Elizabeth Chillingsworth, daughter of Thomas, died at Marshfield 28 September 1665 (*NEHGR* 6:347, 8:191). Savage states that Thomas's daughter Sarah Chillingsworth was the second wife of Samuel Sprague, and his daughter Mary Chillingsworth married John Foster. On 3 October 1665 Justice Eames complained against Samuel Sprague and his wife Sarah, and against John Foster, for concealing a document concerning lands sometime belonging to Thomas Chillingsworth and for withholding the lands by violence (*PCR* 7:124), which would tend to confirm Savage.

CHILTON, ISABEL – The daughter of James and Susanna Chilton, Isabel was baptized at St. Paul's Parish, Canterbury, County Kent, on 15 January 1586/87. She married at Leiden 21 July 1615 Roger Chandler, q.v., and they came to Plymouth sometime after the 1627 cattle division. *Bradford (Ford)* 2:400 recorded under James Chilton and his wife that "They had an other doughter, that was maried, came afterward." Isabel's children and their descendants are given in *MF* 2.

CHILTON, JAMES – James Chilton has been erroneously lumped together with the "Strangers" on the 1620 *Mayflower*, but he was in fact a Leiden Separatist, as is shown by Jan van Dorsten in "Why the Pilgrims Left Leiden," in Bang's *Pilgrims*, p. 34. Leiden records reveal that on 28 April 1619 the sixty-three-year-old James Chilton was returning to his house with his daughter when about twenty boys began throwing rocks at them, and James was hit on the head and knocked to the ground. He never saw Plymouth, for he died on 8 December 1620 when the *Mayflower* was still at Provincetown Harbor. His wife Susanna and daughter Mary came with him, and a daughter Isabella came later. He probably had another daughter, "Engeltgen," who married in Leiden in 1622 (see *MF* 2 which gives his first five generations in America). He was also known to have had other children in England, but no descendants from them have been traced. James Chilton was the son of Lionel Chilton, and he was a resident of Canterbury, where he worked as a tailor, and of Sandwich, Kent before going to Holland. His English background is given by John G. Hunt, "Origins of the Chiltons of the Mayflower," *TAG* 38:244.

CHILTON, MARY – A daughter of James and Susanna Chilton, Mary sailed with them on the 1620 *Mayflower*, and she has been called the first woman to step on Plymouth Rock (see Charles T. Libby, *Mary Chilton's Title to Celebrity*, [reprint. Providence, R.I., 1978]). She was baptized at St. Peter's Parish, Sandwich, Kent on 31 May 1607. She married at Plymouth Edward Winslow's brother John Winslow, q.v., and they later moved to Boston, where she died before 1 May 1679. Her family is given in *MF* 2. See also Robert M. Sherman, "The Baptism of Mary Chilton," *MQ* 43:56, and Hunt's article under her father, James Chilton.

CHILTON, SUSANNA – A 1620 *Mayflower* passenger, Susanna accompanied her husband James Chilton and daughter Mary to Plymouth. Her maiden name is not certain. Hunt thought it was Furner; see his article under James Chilton. She died shortly after arriving at Plymouth.

CHIPMAN, JOHN – A declaration by John Chipman to the Plymouth Court dated 8 February 1657/58 giving substantial background about himself is transcribed in *NEHGR* 35:127-28. In 1657 he had been out of England for twenty-one years and he supposed that he was thirty-seven years old. Thus, he was born ca. 1620, and probably arrived in New England between 12 July 1637 and 31 August 1638 (see William Snow). He was the son of Thomas Chipman of Brinspittle (also called Bryant's Puddle), Dorset, and he alleged that his father had been cheated out of some property in England by a kinsman, Christopher Derby, as was acknowledged by Christopher's son, John Derby, who came to Plymouth Colony, resided at Yarmouth, and was lately deceased. Chipman desired the court to make an inquiry in England about this matter and also to see if his sisters, Hanner and Tamson (Hannah and Thomasine), could be located.

On 2 March 1641/42 Ann Hinde, wife of William Hoskins, age about twenty-five years, made a deposition to Edward Winslow in a case between John Derby and John Chipman. Ann was living in the house of Mr. Derby's father with John Chipman at the time Chipman left for New England to serve Mr. Richard Derby, brother of John Derby. Ann left later also to serve Richard Derby, and old Mr. Derby requested her to commend him to his cousin Chipman and tell him "if hee were a good boy hee would send him over the money that was due him when hee saw good." Ann also deposed that John Derby affirmed that this money had already been paid to Chipman's mother, but Ann knew that the mother had been dead a quarter of a year before the time that old Mr. Derby sent his message to Chipman (*PCR* 4:98). It is not known if anything further became of this matter.

Chipman was strangely not on the 1643 ATBA. He was proposed as a freeman in 1649 (*PCR* 2:141), and, though there is no record of when he became a freeman, he appears on a 1658 freeman list and is recorded under Barnstable (*PCR* 8:200). He served as a grandjuryman (*PCR* 3:9); in 1663 he became a deputy (*PCR* 4:37); and in 1665 he became a selectman for Barnstable (*PCR* 4:112). He was one of two men chosen as ruling elders of the Barnstable Church on 14 April 1670. He married (1) Hope Howland, daughter of *Mayflower* passenger John Howland, by whom he had all his children, and (2) Ruth Sargent, daughter of Mr. William Sargent and widow of both Jonathan Winslow and Rev. Richard Bourne. He died 8 April 1708, age eighty-eight, and his headstone still exists in Sandwich Cemetery. His will dated 12 November 1702 named wife, children, and some grandchildren. There have been several family histories of the Chipman family, a recent one being John Hale Chipman, *A Chipman Genealogy* (Norwell, Mass., 1970), which, though not adequately documented, is generally good. See also *TAG* 61:2-6.

CHURCH, RICHARD – A family history, John A. Church, *Descendants of Richard Church of Plymouth, Mass.* (Rutland, Vt., 1913), is not sufficiently documented and contains known errors. There have been confusing accounts of Church's children, and Robert S. Wakefield, "The Children and Purported Children of Richard and Elizabeth (Warren) Church," *TAG* 60:129, analyzes the contemporary evidence to sort out the facts. Governor Bradford mentioned Church in a letter of 6 February 1631/32 to Bay Governor Winthrop, in which he stated "Richard Church came likewise as a soujournour to worke for ye present; though he is still hear residente longer than he purposed; and what he will doe, neither, we nor I thinke himselfe knowes; but if he resolve here to settle we shall require of him to procure a dismission; but he did affirme to us at ye first, that he was one of mr webbs men, and free to goe for England or whither he would, ye wch we ye rather beleved because he came to us frome wessagasscusett upon ye falling out with his parttner" (*MD* 9:1).

Documentation for the following is in the Wakefield article. Church had earlier, 19 October 1630, applied for freeman status in Massachusetts Bay Colony. On 2 January 1632/33 he was made a Plymouth freeman. He married Elizabeth Warren, daughter of *Mayflower* passenger Richard Warren, the marriage probably taking place before 14 March 1635/36. On 7 March 1636/37 widow Elizabeth Warren mentioned land she had given to her sons-in-law Richard Church, Robert Bartlett, and Thomas Little. On 7 March 1647/48 he was referred to as Sergeant Church. He moved to Nauset ca. 1649. Later he moved to Charlestown in the Bay Colony, where he was called a carpenter on 24 January 1653/54 in a deed in which he purchased half a corn mill in Hingham. He moved to Hingham and became a selectman. On 25 August 1664 he deposed that he was aged about fifty-six years. He died at Dedham 26 December 1668. The will of Richard Church, dated 25 December 1668, sworn 26 January 1668/69, named his wife Elizabeth Church and his children, unnamed except for one, Joseph. His wife Elizabeth died at Hingham 9 March 1669/70. His children were Elizabeth, Joseph, Benjamin, Nathaniel, Charles, Caleb, Abigail, Sarah, Mary, Deborah, and possibly Richard. His son Benjamin married Alice Southworth, daughter of Constant and Elizabeth (Collier) Southworth, and became the famous fighter of King Philip's War.

CHURCHILL, JOHN—John Churchill married on 18 December 1644 Hannah Pontus (*PCR* 2:79), daughter of William Pontus (*MD* 11:93). On 18 August 1645 he bought land from Richard Higgins (*PCR* 12:111). On 1 May 1649 the court allowed John Churchill to dispose of the house and land of George Clarke, deceased, for the use of Clarke's daughter, Abigail Clarke (*PCR* 2:138). On 5 June 1651 he became a freeman (*PCR* 2:167). On 3 May 1664 widow Hannah Churchill was awarded one-half of the land of her deceased father, William Pontus (*PCR* 4:58). John Churchill died 1 January 1662/63 (*PCR* 8:23). He made a nuncupative will, which was exhibited to the court on 3 March 1662/63, and Abigail Clarke, age about twenty, deposed that on 24 December 1662, her kinsman John Churchill willed that his sons Joseph and Eleazer should have all his lands except fifty acres which he would give to his son John, and some land at Punckateesett that he would give his son William. His wife would have a lifetime interest in his house and lands, and he named a Hannah (see *PCR* 8:7 for birth of his daughter Hannah on 12 November 1649). He also mentioned unnamed children, who might include, but not necessarily, some of the above (*MD* 18:40). *PCR* 8:16 also shows that he had a daughter Mary born 1 August 1654. On 25 June 1669 his widow Hannah Churchill married Gyles Rickard, Sr. (*PCR* 8:32). The descendants are quite numerous, and a family history is Gardner A. Churchill and Nathaniel W. Churchill, *Churchill Family in America* (1904), which is not well documented.

CLARKE, FAITH—The daughter of Thurston Clarke, Faith married at Plymouth (1) *Mayflower* passenger Edward Doty, q.v., and (2) John Philips, q.v. She dated her will 12 December 1675, sworn 8 June (probably 1676), and, calling herself the wife of John Philips of Marshfield, she named her daughters Mary, Elizabeth, and Desire, and her son John. On 4 November 1676 letters of administration were granted to John Rouse, Jr. of

Marshfield on behalf of himself, his wife (Elizabeth Doty), and sisters Desire Sherman and Mary Doten; see *MD* 3:90-91.

CLARKE, RICHARD — A 1620 *Mayflower* passenger, Richard Clarke died in the general sickness soon after arrival at Plymouth (*Bradford [Ford]* 2:410). No descendants are known.

CLARKE, THOMAS — Arriving in 1623 on the *Anne*, Thomas Clarke later married (1) Susanna Ring (daughter of Mary Ring, q.v.), who was the mother of all his children, and (2) Alice (Hallett) Nichols. He is believed (by John Insley Coddington, F.A.S.G., among others) to have been the Thomas Clarke who was baptized at St. Dunstan's, Stepney, Middlesex, on 8 March 1599/1600, son of John and Mary (Morton) Clarke (see Jacobus, "Thomas Clark[e] of Plymouth and Boston in the Line of Nathaniel [3] of Lyme, Connecticut," *TAG* 47:3, and Coddington, "The Clark Family of Beverly and Rochester, Mass.," *TAG* 43:19). There has been speculation that his father might have been the John Clarke who was a pilot on the 1620 *Mayflower*; however such a relationship has not been recognized by the Mayflower Society. Others believe that he was the son of the *Mayflower* pilot, but that he was born at Rotherhithe, Surrey. His children were William, Andrew, John, James, Susanna, and Nathaniel, as given by Alfred H. and Katharine W. Radasch, *The Thomas Clark Family* (1972), a partly documented family history covering the early generations. See also John G. Hunt, "Origins of Three Early Plymouth Families: Cole, Collier, and Clarke," *TAG* 42:119 and Prentiss Glaizer, "Clark-Clarke Families of Early Connecticut," *NEHGR* 128:22. The Radasch book gives a brief background for Thomas Clarke, showing that he was described variously as a carpenter, yeoman, merchant, and gentleman. He was chosen a constable, highway surveyor, and Plymouth deputy. He removed from Plymouth to Boston after 1655 and before his second marriage, and returned to Plymouth ca. 1678. He died at Plymouth in March 1697/98.

CLOUGH, RICHARD — Richard Clough was on the 1633 freeman list as Richard Cluffe. He was a tailor by occupation, and he appeared before the court several times for trespass, stealing, and calling the grand jury "rogues" (*PCR* 1:44, 91, 97, 118, 300). In 1637 he was a volunteer for the Pequot War (*PCR* 1:61). There is no record of any wife or children, and after 1640 he disappears from the records.

COBB, HENRY — Since Henry Cobb's first child was born 7 June 1632 (*PCR* 8:42), the year of his marriage (1) to Patience Hurst, daughter of James Hurst, q.v., was probably 1631, and he thus probably arrived at Plymouth between 1627 and 1631. He was on the 1633 freeman list. He moved to Scituate in its early years, having one of the nine houses already existing there when Rev. John Lothrop arrived around late September 1634 (*NEGHR* 10:42). He and his wife were among those who founded the First Scituate Church on 8 January 1634/35 *NEHGR* 9:279), he being called in the records "Goodman Cob". He was among those granted land at Sippican 22 January 1638/39 (*PCR* 1:108), and he went with Lothrop to Barnstable, where his daughter Patience was born 13 March 1641/42 (*NEHGR* 9:282). He was an elder in the Barnstable Church (shown in his will). He became a deputy for Barnstable in 1652 (*PCR* 3:9), an office he held six times until 1662 (*PCR* 4:14). On 8 June 1664 he became an excise officer for Barnstable (*PCR* 4:67).

His first wife was buried 4 May 1648, and a year and a half later he married (2) 12 December 1649 Sarah Hinckley (*PCR* 8:42), daughter of Samuel Hinckley. The births of ten of his children (not all) from both wives at Plymouth, Scituate, and Barnstable between 1632 and 1660 were recorded in *PCR* 8:42. He dated his will 4 April 1673, codicil 22 February 1678/79, proved 3 June 1679, and he named his wife Sarah; his sons John, James, Gershom, Eleazer, Samuel, Jonathan, and Henry; daughters Mary, Hannah, Patience, and Sarah, and unnamed children by his second wife, who may also be among those named (Ply. Colony PR 4:1:22). Administration was granted on the estate of his widow, Sarah Cobb, on 2 March 1679/80 (*PCR* 6:32).

COGAN, HENRY – P. W. Coldham gives a shipping list (*NGSQ* 71:176) showing Henry Cogan, his wife, seven men servants, and two maidservants sailed to New England from Weymouth, Dorset, 22 April 1637 on the Speedwell. He had on 6 July 1635 shipped a load of stockings to New England, and he may have been related to the William Cogan who sailed to New England from Dartmouth, Devon, 27 April 1637 on the Prosperous. G. E. McCracken (*NEHGR* 111:174-77) shows that Henry was baptized at Taunton, Somerset, 6 April 1607, a son of Henry and Joane (Boridge) Cogan; that he married at Bridport, Dorset, 14 March 1636/37 Abigail Bishop, daughter of Thomas and Avis (Abbott) Bishop; that they had children Abigail Cogan (married at Billerica, Mass., John French), Thomas Cogan (died young), John Cogan (baptized at Barnstable 12 February 1642/43, married Mary Long and had issue), Mary Cogan (died young), and Henry Cogan (died young); and that his wife's sister Anne Bishop also came to New England and married at Dorchester (1) John Holman and (2) Henry Butler. The article also shows that Henry Cogan may have first come to New England before 1 July 1634 and settled at Dorchester before moving to Barnstable. He may have been a sea captain. He took the Oath of Fidelity on 5 June 1644 (*PCR* 2:72), and he was on an undated list of men who had taken the Oath from Scituate (*PCR* 8:183) but was then of Barnstable (thus indicating he may have settled first at Scituate). A Thomas Cogan (Coggin) on the 1643 ATBA list for Taunton may have been a relative, though there is no evidence for it. On 2 March 1646/47 Francis Crocker petitioned the General Court to marry Mary Gaunt, a kinswoman of Mr. Cogan of Barnstable (*PCR* 2:112). On 29 October 1649 Henry Cogan's widow submitted an inventory to the Court, stating that he had died in England ca. 16 June 1649 (*MD* 9:226). She married (2) John Phinney 10 June 1650, and she died before 26 June 1654 (*PCR* 8:47). The name is also given as Coggen, Coggin. (See also James Glass.)

COLE, JAMES – James Cole was not on the 1633 freeman list, but was made a freeman by the time of the 1636 list. He first appears in Plymouth records on the 1634 tax list. During the 1637 Pequot War he was not a volunteer, but was one of three men noted as "such as will goe if they be prest" (*PCR* 1:61). In 1662 he was one of the former servants and ancient freemen granted land at Saconett Neck (*PCR* 4:18), and in deeding land at Saconett to his son Hugh of Swansea, he refers to that granted to "the old servants, whereof I am one" (Pope). Pope called him a shoemaker, innkeeper, proprietor, and town officer, and he is best known as the owner of Cole's Tavern on Cole's Hill in central Plymouth. He appears frequently in the records licensed as a retailer, fined for selling less than legal measure, presented for breach of the peace, fined for selling wine to an Indian, etc. (*PCR*, passim). Keeping a tavern was a public service, and on 7 June 1659 the court gave Cole £10 "towards the repaireing of the house hee now liveth in, soe as it may bee fitted as an ordinary for the entertainment of strangers" (*PCR* 3:166). He had a wife Mary, who was fined with him on 2 March 1668/69 for selling strong liquors to an Indian and £3 for allowing people to drink on Sunday during public worship (*PCR* 5:15). He had at least two children, Hugh and James, Jr. (Pope), both of whom must have been born before 1627, since they appeared on the 1643 ATBA.

COLE, JOB – Job Cole was in Plymouth at least as early as 14 September 1633, when Richard Langford died, and his inventory included a debt he owed to Job Cole (*MD* 1:86). He was probably the Job Cole named as a brother in the will of Zaccheus Cole on 16 November 1630, and was probably then living in St. Olave, Southwark, Surrey (see John G. Hunt, "Origin of Three Early Plymouth Families: Cole, Collier, and Clarke," *TAG* 42:119). He was clearly identical with the Job Cole named in will of his brother John Cole, q.v., and the bequests by the family-less John also to several of Mr. Collier's men shows a possibility that John, and therefore perhaps Job, too, were the ones called on the 1633 tax list "Mr. Colliers men." This possibility is increased by the fact that Job Cole mar. on 15 May 1634 Rebecca Collier (*PCR* 1:30), the daughter of William Collier She had been baptized at St. Olave, Southwark, Surrey, 10 January 1614/15 (*TAG* 49:215), the parish associated above with Job Cole. Rebecca Cole, the widow of Job Cole, died at Eastham 29 December 1698, about eighty-eight years old (*MD* 6:204).

On 16 May 1639 Mr. John Atwood agreed that since Job Cole paid the passage of Thomas Gray and gave him some clothing, Cole could have the remainder of Gray's indenture (*PCR* 1:121). Cole became a freeman 3 March 1639/40 (*PCR* 1:140). He had land in Duxbury (*PCR* 1:66, 85) and Green's Harbor (*PCR* 1:91), and he was a constable for Duxbury 2 March 1640/41 (*PCR* 2:9). He was a deputy for Yarmouth 5 June 1644 and a constable for Nauset (Eastham) 7 June 1648 (*PCR* 2:72, 124). He was a surveyor of the highways for Eastham 6 June 1654 (*PCR* 3:50). He was known to have had at least two children, the Rebecca Cole who was born at Eastham 26 August 1654 (*PCR* 8:15), and the Daniel Cole, Jr. (Job Cole's brother Daniel would have been Sr. – see John Cole, below), who was called the son of Job and was fined for cursing on 5 June 1672 (*PCR* 5:94). On 29 October 1671 the court ordered that Daniel Cole should have certain items from the estate of William Collier that were specified in a paper given to him by Collier (*PCR* 5:80).

COLE, JOHN—John Cole's undated will was proved on 7 January 1637/38, and he named his brother Job, q.v.; his brother Daniel; his sister Rebecca; Elizabeth Collier (most likely the sister of his brother's wife Rebecca); and each of Mr. Collier's men, Edward, Joseph, Arthur, Ralph, and John (*MD* 2:209).

COLLIER, WILLIAM—One of the few Adventurers to come to live in New England, he was praised by Nathaniel Morton (*New Englands Memoriall*, p. 91): "This year [1633] likewise Mr. William Collier arrived with his Family in New-England, who as he had been a good Benefactor to the Colony of New-Plimouth before he came over, having been an Adventurer unto it at its first beginning; so also he approved himself a very useful Instrument in that Jurisdiction after he arrived, being frequently Chosen, and for divers years serving God and the Country in the place of Magistracy, and lived a godly and holy life untill old Age." He was often elected an Assistant between 1634/35 and 1665, and he appeared to side with the more conservative leaders, such as in the 1645 fight with Vassall. James Cudworth wrote that "Mr. Collier last June would not sit on the Bench, if I sate there" (Bishop, p. 176). He was on the Council for War, and he served at times as a commissioner of the United Colonies. He resided in Duxbury, and in 1649/50 he deeded ten acres of land in Duxbury to "my kinsman William Clark" (*PCR* 12:182).

Collier married Jane Clark at St. Olave, Southwark, 16 May 1611, and he and his wife had four daughters with them in Plymouth Colony: Sarah, who married (1) Love Brewster and (2) Richard Parke of Cambridge; Rebecca, who married Job Cole; Mary, who married Thomas Prence; and Elizabeth, who married Constant Southworth. Robert S. Wakefield, "More on the Children of William Collier," *TAG* 49:215 and 51:58, identified eight other children in England (all of whom had died young there), and he showed that Collier had lived in St. Mary Magdalen Parish, Bermondsey, Surrey, and St. Olave Parish, Southwark. In the St. Olave register he was called a grocer. Bradford referred to a "brew-house of Mr. Colliers in London" (*Ford* 2:125). On 7 June 1653 Mrs. Jane Collier made a claim on behalf of her grandchild, the wife of Nathaniel [2] Warren (*MD* 3:141). The grandchild was Sarah (Walker) Warren, who was baptized at St. Olave, Southwark, 10 November 1622, the daughter of William Walker (*TAG* 51:92). On 2 December 1661 William Collier of Duxbury, gentleman, with the consent of Mrs. Jane Collier, sold all his house and land that he was living on in Duxbury to Benjamin Bartlett, who was not to enter into possession until the death of both William and Jane Collier. Collier died before 5 July 1671, when men were appointed to administer his estate (*PCR* 5:68). An excellent documented narrative of various aspects of his life is given in *Moore Families*, p. 196-205. (See also John Cole, above, and the Hunt article shown under Job Cole, above.)

CONANT, CHRISTOPER – Christopher Conant, a brother of Roger Conant, q.v., arrived in Plymouth in 1623, and received one share in the 1623 land division. He was not in the 1627 cattle division, and he probably left with his brother. Pope has him as a juryman in Charlestown in 1630.

CONANT, ROGER – He was baptized at East Budleigh, Devonshire, on 9 April 1592, the son of Richard and Agnes (Clarke) Conant, and he later moved to London and became a salter. There is an excellent account of Roger Conant in *Dawes-Gates*, 2:221-28. Though best known for being, in effect, the first governor of the English settlers at Salem in 1626, replaced in 1628 by Gov. John Endicott, he had arrived first at Plymouth, some say, as early as 1622. Evidence of his early arrival at Plymouth comes from Hubbard, *General History* (p. 102, 106-07), "There (Nantasket) Mr. Roger Conant, with some few others, after Mr. Lyford and Mr. Oldham were, (for some offence, real or supposed) discharged from having any thing more to do at Plymouth, found a place of retirement and reception for themselves and families, for the space of a year and some few months, till a door was opened for them at Cape Anne, a place on the other side of the Bay. . . . That were lately removed from out of New Plymouth, out of dislike of their principles of rigid separation, (of which number Mr. Roger Conant was one, a religious, sober, and prudent gentleman. . .)". Conant is not named in the 1623 land division, nor indeed in any of the Plymouth Colony documents, but he is thought by some to have been represented by three of the ten shares of land assigned to "Mr [John] Ouldam & those joyned with him". (See below for further discussion of this possible connection.) By 1623 Conant would have had a wife, Sarah (Horton) Conant, and a son, Caleb, who had been baptized at London on 27 May 1622. An earlier daughter Sarah had died young, and after the land division Conant had Lot, Roger, Sarah, Joshua, Mary, Elizabeth, and Exercise.

It seems reasonable that Conant might have been part of Oldham's group, for he was later associated with Oldham and Lyford at Nantasket and Cape Ann, and it is possible he left Plymouth as a result of the abortive Oldham-Lyford rebellion. However, Bradford's history, including letters sent to him from the London Adventurers, mentioned an unnamed salter, who would seem to have been either a master or journeyman of that craft. The evidence suggests that this salter may have arrived in the *Charity* in March 1623/24. In a letter of 24 January 1623/24, Robert Cushman wrote to Bradford, "We have now sent you, we hope, men and means, to setle these 3 things, viz., fishing, salt making, and boat making. . . . The salt-man is a skillful and industrious man, put some [helpers] to him, that may quickly apprehende the misterie of it." The same letter mentioned that the Adventurers were sending Mr. Lyford over, and that they had obtained a patent for Cape Ann (*Bradford [Ford]* 1:356-58). Bradford did not like the salter, whom he described as "an ignorante, foolish, self-willd fellow" who, after making a survey of the possibilities, assured Bradford that he could make a profitable salt works if he could have eight to ten full-time workers, which he was given, "but in the end all proved vaine." Bradford continued, "the next yere [1625] he was sente to Cap-Anne," but burned the house and spoiled the salt pans, "and this was an end of that chargeable bussines" (*Bradford [Ford]* 1:378-79). It seems unlikely that two salt masters were at Plymouth at the same time, but only one was used, and the second was not called to correct the first when he made costly mistakes. Indeed a second salter was not even mentioned by Bradford. It would seem reasonable that Bradford was describing Conant, and that therefore Conant arrived in 1624 and had not been in the 1623 land division.

CONER, WILLIAM—William Coner, or Conner, arrived at Plymouth in 1621 on the *Fortune*, and he received one share in the 1623 land division. He was not in the 1627 cattle division, and does not appear further in colony records.

CONVERSE, SARAH—Sarah Converse was mentioned in the 1633 will of Samuel Fuller as being in his charge (*MD* 1:24-29), but there is no other record of her.

COOKE, FRANCIS—A 1620 *Mayflower* passenger, Francis Cooke married Hester Mayhieu at Leiden 30 June 1603, the records there describing him as a woolcomber, unmarried, from England (*MD* 8:48). Thus he was in Holland before the arrival of the Clyfton/Robinson Separatists. He was probably born no earlier than 1583, for he must have been under sixty in 1643 when he was on the ATBA for Plymouth, and yet not much after 1583 if he married in 1603. He appears frequently in Plymouth records on grand and trial juries, as a surveyor of the highways, on various ad hoc committees, and in a number of land transactions. (See Bowman's "Francis Cooke and His Descendants," *MD* 3:95.) He came to Plymouth with son John, and Francis's wife and their daughter Jane and son Jacob arrived on the *Anne* in 1623. Two more children, Hester and Mary, were born at Plymouth. Jane married Experience Mitchell; Hester married Richard Wright; and Mary married John Thompson. Francis's son Jacob married Damaris Hopkins, daughter of Stephen. *Dawes-Gates*, 2:239-57 gives a good account of both father Francis Cooke and son Jacob Cooke. Another good account of the Francis Cooke family can be found in *Small Descendants*, 2:601. Francis died 7 April 1663 (*PCR* 8:23). Son John Cooke has a separate entry below. See also Walter J. Harrison, "New Light on Francis Cooke and His Wife Hester Mayhieu and Their Son John," *MD* 27:145. Some confusion about the marriage of Francis Cooke's son Jacob's daughter Mary Cooke, is cleared up by Stratton, "Which John Rickard Married Mary Cooke?," *MQ* 49:122.

COOKE, JOHN—He was called John Cooke, Sr. on the 1634 tax list to distinguish him from Francis Cooke's son, John Cooke, Jr., but there is no known relationship between the two families. A John Cooke was made a freeman on 1 January 1633/34 (*PCR* 1:21), but this may have been John, Jr., for it would seem that a deacon in the Plymouth Church would have also been a freeman. Both Johns appear on the 1643 ATBA, but

Savage has John, Sr. moving to Rehoboth this year and then later to Warwick, Rhode Island.

COOKE, JOHN—John Cooke was baptized at Leiden between January and March 1607/08 (*MD* 27:153) and was, thus, about thirteen years old on arrival at Plymouth with his father Francis Cooke in 1620 on the *Mayflower*. He became a deacon of the Plymouth Church in the 1630s, but he was excommunicated from the church ca. 1657. He served on juries and on various special assignments, and was a long-time Plymouth deputy (see chapter 5). Probably around the time he was excommunicated, he became a Baptist. In 1664 he was granted fifteen acres of land near Dartmouth (*PCR* 4:67), and he had other significant land dealings in the area. In 1666 he was a deputy for Dartmouth (*PCR* 4:122). He was one of the advisers for the defense of Dartmouth against the Indians (*PCR* 4:146). He became a magistrate for Dartmouth authorized to marry, to administer oaths, and to issue warrants for court trials at Plymouth (*PCR* 4:163). Though Nathaniel Morton called him "a shallow man," he appeared to be a populist-type leader who was also able to command the respect of the authorities. He married Sarah Warren, daughter of *Mayflower* passenger Richard Warren 28 March 1634 (*PCR* 1:29), and they had five children. Cooke died 23 November 1695, (*Dartmouth VR* 3:25), having lived through the entire life of Plymouth Colony. He was frequently mentioned in Plymouth records as John Cooke, Jr., which was to distinguish him from John Cooke, Sr., see above, who was apparently no relation.

COOKE, JOSIAH—Though not taxed in 1633, Josiah Cooke's name is on the 1634 tax list. On 24 March 1633/34 he and Edward Doty were fined six shillings eight pence each for breaking the peace, and since Doty drew blood from Cooke, Doty was to pay him three shillings four pence for it (*PCR* 1:26). He married widow Elizabeth Deane 16 September 1635 (*PCR* 1:35). He became a freeman on 3 January 1636/37 (*PCR* 1:48). Bowman, in *MD* 3:97 footnote, shows that he could not, as some have claimed, have been a son of 1620 *Mayflower* passenger Francis Cooke, for no court would have allowed a son to sit on the jury in a case where his father was plaintiff, nor would a court have allowed the agreement signed by Francis Cooke's children if one of them had not signed, and Josiah was alive then, but not a signer. John Insley Coddington, "The Widow Mary Ring, of Plymouth, Mass., and Her Children," *TAG* 42:193, shows that he was among those moving to Nauset (Eastham) ca. 1645. He had been a grandjuror, surveyor, and constable, and he became a deputy from Eastham starting 1647. In his will dated 22 September 1673, and proved 29 October 1673, he called himself aged about sixty-three years, and he named his wife Elizabeth, his son Josias, his sons(-in-law) Joseph Harding and William Twining, daughter Bethiah Harding, grandson Joseph Harding, grandson Amaziah Harding, granddaughter Anne Snow, grandchild Stephen Twining, (step)daughter Meriam Deane, and grandsons Josiah and Richard Cooke. William Twining had married his stepdaughter Elizabeth Deane (*MD* 15:34). His daughter Anna Cooke had married Mark Snow, son of Nicholas and

Constance² (Hopkins) Snow; his son Josiah had married Deborah Hopkins, daughter of Gyles² Hopkins; his daughter Bethia had married Joseph Harding, ward and presumed nephew of John Doane; and he may have had other children (see Coddington above, and *Dawes-Gates*, 2:503-06, which continues the line through Josiah² Cooke for two more generations).

COOMBS, JOHN—On 12 October 1630 Ralph Wallen sold his house and garden plot to Mr. John Coombe. He married ca. 1631 Sarah Priest daughter of 1620 *Mayflower* passenger Degory Priest, (*MD* 4:96, where she is called a "daughter" of Godbert Godbertson, but was in fact his daughter-in-law). On 24 January 1633/34 John Coombs, gentleman, exchanged thirty acres of land, which he possessed in the right of Sarah his wife, with Mr. Thomas Prence (*PCR* 1:25). Though he was referred to as "Mr." and "Gentleman" in various land and other transactions (*PCR*, passim), and he was on the earliest freeman list, Coombs became one of the few recorded freemen of Plymouth Colony to be disfranchised (for drunkenness in his case) on 3 September 1639 (*PCR* 1:132); however, he was readmitted as a freeman on 5 June 1644 (*PCR* 2:71). On 4 December 1638 he was among a group of nine men fined three shillings for not appearing at court, but he and Francis Sprague were not listed with the other seven who were fined again for not appearing the second time, and again for not appearing a third time (*PCR* 1:104). On 5 April 1642 Mr. John Coombs agreed he owed £3/4/6 demanded by John Gorham, and Gorham agreed that he would give Coombs four or five bushels of wheat to sow his ground with, so that Coombs could repay his debt with the proceeds of the harvest. On the same day Coombs for £14, forty shillings [*sic*], transferred the unexpired term of his servant William Launder to Mr. William Thomas (*PCR* 2:38).

He died sometime prior to 1 August 1648 when the court ordered that the one-third part of the English corn due Mrs. Coombs from William Spooner be turned over to Thomas Cushman. The court noted that Mr. John Coombs was indebted to the estate of Godbert Godbertson, which in turn owed Isaac Allerton, who had turned the debt over to his son-in-law Thomas Cushman (*PCR* 2:131-33); from a document dated 27 October 1646 by Allerton, it appeared that the debt was quite large (£100 sterling). Also on 1 August 1646 the court noted that Coombs's children were now with William Spooner, who was ordered to keep them for the present and not dispose of them without further court order (*PCR* 2:131). Coombs had taken over the indenture of William Spooner, of Colchester, County Essex, England, from John Holmes in 1637 for six years. On 6 March 1642/43 the court ordered William Spooner to pay the debt of ten shillings of his master Mr. Coombs to Mr. William Hanbury (*PCR* 2:51). (See also *TAG* 46:130.)

COOPER, ANN (or Agnes)—Ann Cooper was the wife of Edward Tilley, whom she accompanied to Plymouth on the 1620 *Mayflower*, and she died soon after arrival. She was the daughter of Edmund and Mary (Wyne) Cooper of Henlow, Bedfordshire, where she married Edward Tilley on 20 June 1614 (see *TAG* 52:206).

COOPER, HUMILITY – Bradford called Humility Cooper, a 1620 *Mayflower* passenger, a child and cousin both to Edward Tilley and his wife and to Henry Sampson. Henry Sampson's mother and Edward Tilley's wife were sisters, Martha and Agnes Cooper. See the Ward articles under John Tilley. Mr. Ward also showed in "The Baronial Ancestry of Henry Sampson, Humility Cooper, and Ann (Cooper) Tilley," *TG* 6:166, that Humility Cooper, daughter of Robert Cooper, was baptized as an adult at Holy Trinity Minorities, London, on 19 March 1638/39. The entry states she was then age nineteen, and had been born in Holland. Ward points out that this was probably the same woman, for there was a Robert Cooper in the Cooper family associated with Edward Tilley and Henry Sampson, and he married Joan Gresham and was known to have been in Holland with the Separatists. Thus Humility would have been but an infant when she arrived at Plymouth and, if she had been orphaned in Holland, it would be natural for her to be in the family of Edward and Agnes (Cooper) Tilley, for Agnes would have been her father's sister. Dr. Bangs, *MQ* 52:9, shows Robert Cooper as one of the witnesses to a 1618 agreement concerning the apprenticeship of a "Robert Hagges," a young man over twenty-one years of age, to Edward Tilley. The agreement concerned a trip Hagges had to make to England to collect an inheritance. In Ward's earlier article, *TAG* 52:206, he shows the married at Henlow, Bedfordshire, on 22 November 1615 of Robert Cooper's brother, Benjamin Cooper, to a Rose Haggis. Humility died before 1651 when Bradford wrote that she "was sent for into England and dyed ther" (*Ford*, 2:408). There is no evidence that she did or did not have children.

COOPER, JOHN – John Cooper was not on the 1633 or 1634 tax lists, but he was married at Plymouth on 27 November 1634 to Priscilla (Carpenter) Wright (*PCR* 1:32), widow of William Wright, and he became a freeman 1 January 1634/35 (*PCR* 1:32). In January 1634/35 a servant of Nicholas Snow said that he was willing to serve out the time of his indenture with John Cooper (*PCR* 1:33). Cooper later moved to Scituate, and sometime between September 1634 and 1637 "Goodman Cooper" acquired John Hewes's house in Scituate (*NEHGR* 10:42). On 1 January 1637/38 John Cooper was one of a group of men at Scituate who complained about not having enough land to subsist on, and the Court of Assistants granted them additional land between the North and South Rivers (*PCR* 1:72). He was chosen a constable of Barnstable in 1639/40 (*PCR* 1:141, 155) and became a deputy there in 1642 and 1643 (*PCR* 2:46, 57). He dated his will 28 December 1676, sworn 25 February 1683/84, and he named his loving wife Priscilla, the children of his sister Alice Bradford, and the surviving children of his sister Lydia Morton (*Ply. Colony PR* 4:2:59). Alice (Carpenter) Bradford was the sister of his wife Priscilla (Carpenter) Cooper, and Lydia Morton was the Lydia Cooper who married Nathaniel Morton, q.v., on 25 December 1635. There is no known relationship with the Cooper family of Henlow, Bedfordshire, allied with the Sampson and Tilley families (see Humility Cooper, above), but John's marriage to a member of the Leiden

Separatist Carpenter family, his being made a freeman probably shortly after arrival, and his sister's marriage to a member of the Leiden Separatist Morton family would indicate membership in the Separatist church, along with a possibility, which needs further research, that John and Lydia Cooper were connected with the Henlow Coopers. This John Cooper should not be confused with the John Cooper who was fined ten shillings on 5 July 1666 for profane and abusive carriage toward another, and who was a servant to Robert Bartlett on 4 July 1663, Bartlett complaining that Cooper refused to serve him because he had lost the indenture papers (*PCR* 4:133, 154).

CRACKSTON, JOHN—A 1620 *Mayflower* passenger, John Crackston was one of the Leiden Separatists. He died the first winter at Plymouth, leaving his son John, below, as his only known child in America. He also had a daughter Anne, who registered marriage intentions at Leiden 12 December 1618 with Thomas Smith, in the presence of her father, John Crackstone. John was described as being from Colchester, England, and Anne was accompanied by her friend Patience Brewster (see Dexter, pp. 610, 634, and Robert S. Wakefield, "Pilgrim John Crackstone—A Search for His Ancestry and Posterity," *MQ* 40:117). No descendants of her marriage have been found.

CRACKSTON, JOHN—The son of John Crackston, q.v., the younger John accompanied his father from Leiden to Plymouth on the 1620 *Mayflower*. According to *Bradford (Ford)* 2:405, the younger John died five or six years after arrival; however, it must have been somewhat later, for he was among those sharing the 1627 cattle division. He was not known to have issue.

CROSBY, THOMAS—The Cape Cod Crosbys go back to Thomas Crosby who was baptized at Holme-on-Spaulding Moor 26 February 1634/35, as shown in Eleanor D. Crosby's well-documented *Simon Crosby The Emigrant: His English Ancestry and Some of His American Descendants* (Boston, 1914). The English research for this volume was done by the highly respected Elizabeth French Bartlett. Hotten, p. 62, shows Thomas Crosby on the *Susan and Ellen* of 18 April 1635 as an eight-week-old child sailing to New England with his parents Simon and Ann (Brigham) Crosby. The family settled in Cambridge, where the father died when Thomas was a boy. Thomas graduated from Harvard College in 1653, and in 1655 he was engaged at £50 annually to preach at the Eastham church, where he continued until 1670, even though he was never ordained. On 8 March 1678/79 the residents of Manamoit (Chatham), having requested township status and indicating that they would like to procure Mr. Crosby or some other orthodox minister, were told by the court to apply the next year (*PCR* 6:4). Crosby later became a merchant at Harwich. He died while visiting Boston 13 June 1702. He married Sarah _____; she later married (2) John, son of the Reverend John and Lydia Miller. Thomas and Sarah had twelve children born at Eastham between 1663 and 1680 (*MD* 4:31). Additional information on the Crosby and related families in England can be found in Paul W. Prindle, "The Yorkshire Ancestry of the Three Crosby Sisters of Rowley, Mass.," *NEHGR* 119:243; Walter Lee Sheppard, "The Watson Ancestry of Constance (Brigham) Crosby of Holme-on-Spaulding Moor, Yorkshire, and Rowley, Mass., and Notes on the Sotheron and Millington Families," *NEHGR* 120:21; and same author, "Notes on the Yorkshire Ancestry of the Three Crosby Sisters of Rowley, Mass.," *NEHGR* 120:225; and O. Day, "Crosby Correction," *TAG* 42:209 (but see also *TAG* 43:128).

CUDWORTH, JAMES – One of the most important and interesting men in Plymouth Colony, James Cudworth served as a deputy, Assistant, commander of the colony's armed forces in King Philip's War, and deputy governor. He was the owner of one of nine houses in Scituate already existing when John Lothrop arrived there at the end of September 1634 (*NEHGR* 10:42). We are fortunate in having some of his letters which show him to be an intelligent and thoughtful man, as is demonstrated by his frequent appearance in the text. This sketch will concentrate on his family. His mother married Mr. John Stoughton, the rector of St. Mary's Church, Aldermanbury, London, whose brothers were Thomas Stoughton and Bay Colony Assistant Israel Stoughton, both of Dorchester (*NEHGR* 14:101-04). In his will dated 15 September 1681, inventory 20 June 1682, Cudworth named his sons James, Israel, and Jonathan; daughter Mary's four children Israel, Robert, James, and Mary Whetcombe; and daughter Joanna Jones. His inventory included almost £8 worth of books, unfortunately not named. His will impossibly left two-thirds of his lands to his oldest son James, and one-third each to Israel and Jonathan (*Ply. Colony PR* 4:2:8), but this would probably have been more correctly understood as two-fourths to the oldest and one-fourth each to the others. A rather elaborate narrative in *NEHGR* 64:84-87 states that James Cudworth was a brother to the famous English theologian Dr. Ralph Cudworth, whose wife was the widow of Thomas Andrews, son of Adventurer Thomas Andrews, and daughter of Matthew Craddock, first governor of the Massachusetts Bay Colony (however, see p. 72 of McIntyre for a different interpretation of the Andrews/Craddock connection; at any rate, Cudworth had interesting family connections (see also *NEHGR* 53:433 for mention of another brother in England). Pope states that he also called Rev. Zachariah Symmes of the Bay Colony his cousin.

CUSHMAN, ROBERT – One of the Leiden Separatist leaders, Robert Cushman's English origins are given by Elizabeth French, "Genealogical Research in England – Cushman," *NEHGR* 68:181. He was baptized at Rolveden, Kent, 9 February 1577/78, son of Thomas and Elinor (Hubbard) Couchman. He was an apprentice to George Masters; was excommunicated from St. Andrews Church, Canterbury, after saying that he could not be edified by going to that church; was received back in the church in 1605; and in the same year became a freeman of Canterbury, being described as a grocer. His first wife was Sara Reder, by whom he had son Thomas, q.v., and he married (2) at Leiden in 1617 Mary (Clarke) Shingleton. He and John Carver were chosen by their fellow Separatists to go to England to negotiate for a patent to go to America, and Bradford in his History has much to relate about him. In 1621 he arrived at Plymouth on the *Fortune* with son Thomas, but returned to England with the *Fortune*, leaving Thomas in the care of Governor Bradford. Cushman died in 1625 before having the chance to return to Plymouth. A good account of his family can be found in *Small Descendants*, 2:669, which mentions also that a Sarah Cushman who married William Hoskins on 6 October 1636 was thought to be the daughter of Robert Cushman (Hoskins married [2] on 21 December 1638 Ann Hynes [*PCR* 1:45, 107]).

CUSHMAN, THOMAS—The son of Robert Cushman, q.v., Thomas was baptized at Canterbury 8 February 1607/08, and he was taken by his father to Leiden shortly after. He arrived at Plymouth on the *Fortune* in 1621, and became a ward of Governor Bradford. He was a Purchaser and received a number of land grants. He was admitted a Plymouth freeman 1 January 1633/34 (*PCR* 1:21). On 1 July 1634 he successfully sued Mr. John Combes for £10 (*PCR* 1:30). He served on various juries and committees and was a highway surveyor (*PCR*, passim). On 1 December 1640 he, Nicholas Snow, and Josias Cooke were presented by the grand jury for not mending the highways, but were freed on condition that they make the repairs within a year (*PCR* 2:5). On 3 March 1645/46 Cushman made a successful motion in court that Mr. Isaac Allerton be allowed a year's time to recover his debts in the colony (*PCR* 2:95). Allerton was his father-in-law, Cushman having married Mary Allerton at an unknown date. By a letter of 27 October 1646, Allerton had assigned to his son-in-law Thomas Cushman a debt of £100 owed Allerton by Mr. John Coombes (*PCR* 2:130-33). On 1 August 1648 the Court of Assistants assigned part of some grain due the widow of John Coombes toward satisfying the debt of her late husband to Cuthbert Cuthbertson, whose estate was a debtor "of considerable sume" to Isaac Allerton.

Cushman succeeded William Brewster as Ruling Elder of the Plymouth Church on 6 April 1649, the position having been vacant since 1644 (*Ply. Ch. Recs.* 1:165). He had differences with the pastor, John Cotton, as the latter noted in church records in 1683, writing that the elders met with the pastor and decided to put their differences to some other churches for advice, and the Elder (Cushman) moved that the magistrates be invited to meet with and advise them. In succeeding months there are additional intimations of differences in which "the Elder showed discontent" (*Ply. Ch. Recs.* 1:251, 253-54). He became ill in his old age and languished for some eleven weeks before he died on 10 or 11 December 1691, another man whose life was virtually coterminal with that of Plymouth Colony (*Ply. Ch. Recs.* 1:165-66; George E. Bowman, "Elder Thomas Cushman's Will and Inventory, and the Records of His Death," *MD* 4:37). In his will dated 22 October 1690, sworn 16 March 1691/92, he named his wife Mary, sons Thomas, Isaac, Elkanah, and Eleazer; daughters Sarah Hawks and Lydia Harlow; and the three children of his daughter Mary Hutchinson. He also had a daughter Fear (*PCR* 8:15), who predeceased him without issue.

Family histories, not sufficiently documented, are Henry W. Cushman, *Historical and Biographical Genealogy of the Cushmans* (Boston, 1855), and Joseph A. Cushman, *The First Seven Generations of the Cushman Family in New England* (1964). An important article is Mrs. John E. Barclay and Anna M. Gurney, "Rebecca, Wife of Reverend Isaac Cushman" (*TAG* 26:144), which shows the error in undocumented published claims that the wife of Thomas Cushman's son Isaac was an Abigail Rickard; she was much more likely Rebecca [2] Harlow. Newman A. Hall, "Mary Cushman, Wife of Francis Hutchinson, An Isaac Allerton Line," *MQ* 52:28, convincingly clears up the question as to which Hutchinson she married, showing that it had to be Francis, not Edward. See also *TAG* 24:105 and *NEHGR* 122:48, 249, 128:193 and the account of the Cushman family given in *Small Descendants*, 2:669. From the cited sources it can be seen that Cushman's daughter Mary married Francis Hutchinson; Thomas married Ruth Howland, daughter of Mayflower passenger John Howland; Sarah married John Hawkes; Isaac probably married Rebecca Harlow; Elkanah married (1) Elizabeth Cole and (2) Martha Cooke; Fear died without issue; Eleazer married Elizabeth Combes; and Lydia married William Harlow.

CUTHBERTSON, CUTHBERT—Also called Godbert Godbertson, Cuthbert Cuthbertson was said by Edward Winslow to be a member of the Dutch Church who could speak English and who took communion with the Separatist church in Leiden (*Plooij's Dutch*, p. xxx,xlvii; Winslow, *Hypocrisie*, p. 63). In Leiden, he worked as a hatmaker. On 27 May 1617 he was betrothed to Elizabeth Kendall, and on 25 October 1621 he was betrothed to Sarah (Allerton) (Vincent) Priest, widow of *Mayflower* passenger Degory Priest (Dexter, p. 611-12). He arrived at Plymouth in 1623 on the *Anne*, along with his wife Sarah, their son Samuel, and his wife's two daughters by her second married, Mary Priest and Sarah Priest. Both Cuthbertson and his wife died in the 1633 sickness, and their inventories were taken on 24 October 1633 (*MD* 1:154).

CUTHBERTSON, SAMUEL—The son of Cuthbert and Sarah Cuthbertson, he later shortened his name to Samuel Cuthbert. He arrived on the 1623 *Anne*. Following the death of his parents, he put himself out as an apprentice on 1 April 1634 for a term of seven years to Richard Higgins of Plymouth. Richard Higgins on 31 August 1639 transferred his apprenticeship to John Smalley for Samuel to learn tailoring (*PCR* 1:129). He was granted lands at Marshfield, and later moved to Dartmouth. A deed shows him resident at Acushnet (Dartmouth) and the heir of Godber Godberson, deceased (*MD* 16:182). He had one known son, Samuel, who died at Middleborough on 17 April 1699, age forty-two (Wood, *Middleborough Deaths*, p. 52).

DAMON, JOHN—John Damon was the servant and heir in Scituate of his mother's brother, William Gilson, q.v. His descendants are numerous, and many are covered in six typescript volumes undocumented of a Damon family history, a set of which is kept at the Mayflower Society library in Plymouth, Massachusetts, with another set at the New England Historic Genealogical Society in Boston.

DAMON, HANNAH—Hannah Damon was a servant and heir in Scituate of her mother's brother, William Gilson, q.v.

DEANE, JOHN—A brother of Walter Deane, q.v., John Deane in his will dated 25 April 1660, proved 7 June 1660, called himself aged about sixty years, and he named his wife Alice; oldest son John; second son Thomas; third son Israel; youngest sons Isaac and Nathaniel; his daughter Elizabeth; and his brother Walter Deane (*MD* 17:158). He became a freeman on 4 December 1638, with the other principal men of Taunton, including his brother Walter (*PCR* 1:105). He served on many juries, as constable of Taunton, and as highway surveyor for Taunton (*PCR*, passim). He became a selectman of Taunton for the year 1657 (*PCR* 3:122). He and his brother were on a list of ancient freemen and sundry others to get land to the north of Taunton in 1662 (*PCR* 4:20; this was after his death), and in 1667 Alice Deane, widow of John Deane, was on a list (in the right of her husband) of ancient freemen to get land west of the Taunton River (*PCR* 4:160). On 3 June 1662 widow Alice Deane and Lt. James Wyatt posted a bond to hold the court harmless in the matter of their permitting a legacy of £10 to be paid by Thomas Trowbridge of New Haven to Isaac Deane, underage (*PCR* 4:16). Their son Lt. Israel Deane died between 7 August and 27 September 1677 (his will is *Ply. Colony PR* 3:2:96), and widow Alice Deane died intestate shortly after in the same year (Ply. Colony PR 3:2:97); the heirs of Alice and her son, Israel, were Isaac, John, and Thomas Deane, and Josiah and Elizabeth Edson; and Israel mentioned also his sisters-in-law Sarah and Katherine. A widow Rachel Deane married Joseph Beadle 28 October 1636 (*PCR* 1:45), but nothing has been found to connect her to any of the other Deanes living in Plymouth Colony. *TAG* 59:227 (see under Walter Deane, below) gives the marriages of the children of John and Alice Deane as follows: John Deane married Sarah Edson; Thomas Deane married Katharine Stevens; Israel Deane died unmarried; Isaac Deane married Hannah Leonard; Nathaniel Deane died without issue; and Elizabeth Deane married Josiah Edson.

DEANE, STEPHEN—Arriving on the *Fortune* in 1621, Stephen Deane became one of the Purchasers. In January or February 1632/33 the court gave him permission to build a grist mill with monopoly rights if he could handle all the colony's needs, but on condition that he charge no more than one pottle out of every bushel of ground grain (*PCR* 1:8). On 24 March 1633/34 he was one of a committee chosen to rate the colonists for taxes (*PCR* 1:26). He married Elizabeth Ring (see John Insley Coddington, "The Widow Mary Ring, of Plymouth, Mass., and Her Children," *TAG* 42:193). He died in September 1634, and on 16 September 1635 Elizabeth Deane, widow, married Josias Cooke (*PCR* 1:35). The children of Stephen and Elizabeth (Ring) Deane were Elizabeth (married William Twining and had children), Miriam (married John Wing as second wife but no issue), and Susanna (married first Joseph Rogers and second Stephen Snow, and had children by the second husband) (*TAG* 42:193). The name of Stephen Deane on a list of first born children to get land in 1662 (*PCR* 4:19) was probably his "right" to land and would have passed to his heirs.

DEANE, WALTER—Walter and John Deane, q.v., were brothers, as shown in the latter's will. They are believed to be the sons of William Deane of Southchard, Somerset, whose will dated 22 July 1634 named sons William (oldest), Thomas, John, Walter, and Isaac, and daughters Susan Deane, Eleanor Deane, Margery Strong, and Elizabeth (youngest), and grandson John Strong (one of the witnesses was William "Cogam") (*NEHGR* 51:432-34). A Walter Deane, son of William Deane of South Chard, Somerset, was baptized at Chard 13 May 1612 (*NEHGR* 80:336). Walter Deane sailed for New England on the *Speedwell* from Weymouth, Dorset, on 22 April 1637 with six servants, the same ship carrying Elizabeth Poole, Henry Cogan, and Giles Rickard (*NGSQ* 71:176). His wife was Eleanor, who joined him in a deed of 20 August 1693 (*NEHGR* 3:375). The will of William Cogan of Southchard, Somerset, dated 24 April 1654, named his daughter Eleanor Deane, wife of Walter Deane in New England; however, he named another daughter Eleanor Cogan (*NEHGR* 51:434), and this has given rise to much speculation about the identity of Walter Deane's wife. George E. McCracken, "Early Cogans English and American," *NEHGR* 110:267-68, points out that Eleanor Deane had been supposed on other grounds to have been the daughter of Richard Strong of Taunton, Somerset. Bristol County, Mass. LR 1:152, dated 26 January 1690/91 shows Walter Deane of Taunton, a tanner, sold land for his beloved brother John Strong, living in Northampton, New England.

Mary Lovering Holman, *Ancestry of Col. John H. Stevens. . .*, (Concord, N.H., 1948), pp. 348-49, gives a verbatim excerpt from the will of this William Cogan, who may have been the Cogam witness of the William Deane will, above, and identifies Eleanor, the wife of Walter Deane, as a daughter of John Strong of Chard, Somerset, and sister of the John Strong of Northampton, Massachusetts. However, Mrs. Holman also shows the younger John Strong had for his first wife Margery Deane, the sister of Walter Deane, and thus the "beloved brother" relationship between Walter Deane and John Strong may be a "brother-in-law" relationship. No Eleanor appears in the will of the older John Strong. The will of William Cogan actually left his house and land "(after the death of my daughter Eleanor Deane wife of Walter Deane in New England) unto Eleanor Cogan my daughter and to the heires male of her bodie," and for default of male issue to "Joane Cogan my daughter and to the heires males of her bodie," and for default of male issue to Joane then to "the heires male of the said Eleanor Deane of her bodie." This peculiar set of conditional inheritances suggests that Eleanor Deane had a lifetime interest in the house and lands, perhaps because she had been married earlier to William Cogan's son, but without having male issue by him. If she had also been a cousin to William Cogan's son (not a rare occurrence at the time), this could be a possible explanation as to why the sequence of inheritance would be first to her for life, then to the male issue of two daughters of William Cogan in turn, and finally, if they had no male issue, then to the male issue of Eleanor Deane. It is significant that female issue are excluded, and the facts seem to indicate that Eleanor Deane was of the Cogan male line, but was not a blood daughter of William Cogan (even though he called her "daughter." If she had been a blood daughter, then the male issue of the other Eleanor Cogan and her sister Joane Cogan, would not have been intermediate in the line of succession between the lifetime possession by Eleanor Deane and the final conditional inheritance by her own male issue with any husband). It is an interesting problem that obviously requires more research. For more information on John Strong, who had earlier been a resident and constable of Taunton, see Donald Lines Jacobus, *Descendants of Robert Waterman* (New Haven, 1939 1:640-43, and the references therein.) Not available when that book was published is the fact that John Strong sailed to New England from Dorset on 8 May 1635, with his family, aboard the *Hopewell* (*NGSQ* 71:173).

Walter Deane became a freeman of Plymouth Colony 4 December 1638 (*PCR* 1:105), and he became a deputy for Taunton on 2 June 1640 (*PCR* 1:155). He served at various times on grand juries and coroner's juries, and he was a selectman for Taunton for many years between 1666 and 1686 (*PCR*, passim). On 1 October 1661 Joan, widow of Obadiah Miller (former wife of Thomas Cogan), obtained permission to sell some land for the relief of her daughter, Bathsheba Cogan (Coggin), with Richard Williams and Walter Deane of Taunton as overseers, and the rest of the land was reserved for the use of the other children of the deceased Thomas Cogan (*PCR* 4:4-5, 10). On 30 October 1678 Mary, widow of Lieutenant Wyatt, was to have land leased out for her benefit by Mr. James Walker, William Harvey, Sr., and Walter Deane, or any two of them (*PCR* 5:272). Walter was living on 20 August 1693 when he and his wife joined together in a deed (Pope). David Kendall Martin, "First Wife of Shadrach Wilbore and Children of Walter Deane of Taunton Ma," *TAG* 59:227-30, gives Walter Deane's children as Mary Deane, who married Shadrach Wilbore; a child who died without issue; a daughter who married Bartholomew Tipping; Ezra, who married Bethiah Edson; James, who married Sarah Tisdale; Benjamin, who married Sarah Williams; and Joseph, who married a Mary.

DELANO, PHILIP—He was a member of the Separatist Church at Leiden, born of French parents, and had been in communion with the French (Walloon) church (Winslow, *Hypocrisie Unmasked*, p. 64). He arrived at Plymouth on the *Fortune* in 1621, was a Purchaser, and was on the 1633 freeman list. He made the first recorded land sale in Plymouth after the institution of private property; in 1627 he sold to Stephen Deane for £4, one acre of land (obviously his share of the 1623 land division) on the north side of town between the first and second brooks, adjoining the land of Moses Simonson on one side and Stephen Deane on the other (*PCR* 12:7). Delano deposed in 1641 that he was about thirty-six years old (*Lechford's Notebook*, p. 420). In 1637 he volunteered for the Pequot War (*PCR* 1:61).

On 2 October 1637 he was given forty acres of land in Duxbury, adjoining the lands of John Alden and Edward Bumpus (*PCR* 1:67). He served on various juries and commissions, especially grand juries (*PCR*, passim). He was on the 1662 list of first-born children to get land at Middleborough (*PCR* 4:19).

Philip Delano married (1) Hester Dewsbury on 19 December 1634 (*PCR* 1:32). He married (2) Mary (Pontus) Glass, widow of James, sometime between 3 September 1652 (death of James Glass—Pope) and 3 December 1659 (when his wife Mary joined him in a deed—*Ply. Colony LR* 2:2:41). On 3 May 1664 Hannah Churchill, widow, asked that one-half the lands granted to William Pontus be given to her; the court, with the consent of Philip Delano and his wife Mary, the other daughter of William Pontus, granted her request (*PCR* 4:58). On 5 July 1682 Philip's sons Thomas and Samuel (Samuel was called the only son of the second wife) agreed to follow what they knew to be the intent of their father, now deceased, for the distribution of his estate; his other children sharing the estate were John, Jane, Rebecca, and Philip (*MD* 11:250). Besides the six named children, he also had Jonathan, Mary, and Esther. A comprehensive family history with a large number of errors and awkward manner of presentation is Joel Andrew Delano, *The Genealogy, History, and Alliances of the American House of Delano 1621 to 1899* (New York, 1899). (See also Kerry William Bate, "Some Delano Questions," (*TAG* 52:91), and "Some Delano Answers," (*TAG* 53:172).

One of Philip's sons, Thomas Delano, married a daughter of John Alden, as is shown by signatures on Alden's estate settlement dated 13 June 1688 (*MD* 3:11), but which daughter has been controversial. Daughter Mary had been accepted, but in 1947 the Society of Mayflower Descendants decided that it had to be daughter Rebecca instead. The matter had been thoroughly aired in 1932-33 by letters from various genealogists to the *Boston Transcript* genealogy column. Daughter Mary had signed the 1688 Alden settlement as Mary Alden, with her signature immediately above Thomas Delano's. This in itself would show that in 1688 she was still an Alden, not a Delano. Thomas Delano was married before 30 October 1667 when the court fined him £10 for copulation with his unnamed wife before marriage (*PCR* 4:168). On 5 February 1929 at an auction at the American Art Galleries of New York there was sold for $800 an unrecorded deed of 2 July 1685 in which William Clarke sold land to John Thomas, Jr., and the sale was acknowledged by John Alden, Assistant. The deed was witnessed by Thomas De Lano and Rebecca De Lano (*Boston Transcript*, 30 December 1632). John Alden, q.v., had a daughter Rebecca, and there was no record of her death or marriage by that name. The evidence is indirect, but the preponderance is that Thomas Delano's wife was Rebecca.

DINGLEY, JOHN—John Dingley may have resided earlier at Lynn (*Moore Families*, p. 227), but he first appears in Plymouth records at Sandwich on 4 December 1638, when he was fined ten shillings for being defective in arms, and was also presented for keeping two hogs unringed

(*PCR* 1:107). On 16 April 1640 he was granted five and one-half acres of meadow lands allotted at Sandwich (*PCR* 1:149). On 5 June 1644 he was chosen constable of Marshfield (*PCR* 2:72). Since he was on the 1643 ATBA for both Sandwich and Marshfield, it would seem that he moved from the former to the latter about this time. He also served as grandjuror (*PCR* 2:84, 116, 3:78, 4:37, 91, 148, 5:91), and as a highway surveyor (*PCR* 2:102, 4:124), and on grand and trial juries (*PCR,* passim). He became a freeman on 5 June 1644 (*PCR* 2:71). On 22 October 1650 Richard Church sold Dingley some land in Marshfield, and Dingley was described as a smith (blacksmith) in the deed (*PCR* 12:197). On 1 November 1679 John Dingley and his fourteen-year-old servant Arthur Loe appeared in court and Arthur covenanted to live with Dingley and his wife as an apprentice and servant until he became twenty-one (*PCR* 6:25). Administration of Dingley's estate, dated 18 March 1689/90, shows that he was survived by son Jacob, and Jacob's son Joseph; Sarah, the wife of William Ford; and Hannah, the wife of Josiah Keane (*PN&Q* 5:92).

His wife has been called Sarah _____. The accounts of John Dingley's origins as the son of an armigerous family of Cropthorne, Worcestershire, with several fairly recent royal lines, as given by Edward N. Dingley, *Ancestors of Edward N. Dingley* (1954), are colorful, but unsupported by evidence and not very logical. Some of the reasons for doubting this Dingley ancestry are given by Eugene A. Stratton, "Search for the English Ancestry of John Dingley," *TAG* 56:207; however, this article gives an incorrect surname for Dingley's wife and the author fell into the mistake made by others, such as Savage and Arthur Adams, of thinking that Dingley died some thirty-one years earlier than he actually did. An updated article by Stratton, "Another Look at John Dingley of Marshfield," will appear in *TAG,* 61:234. *Moore Families,* p. 227-32, gives a well-documented narrative of Dingley's life and some of his early descendants, and shows that he also had two sons named John who died young, and a daughter Mary, who married Capt. Myles Standish's son Josiah, but died without issue.

DIXE, ANTHONY—He arrived at Plymouth in 1623 and received land in the 1623 land division, but the number of shares he received is illegible. He did not share in the 1627 cattle division and is believed to be the Anthony Dix (or Dikes) who later appeared at Salem, and whose widow, Tabitha, married Anthony Pickman (Pitman) (*MQ* 40:60; Pope).

DOANE, JOHN—John Doane was born ca. 1590 (he called himself aged about eighty-eight in his will, dated 16 May 1678, given below). He arrived at Plymouth probably between 1628 and 1632. There is no record of him being at Leiden, but he served as a deacon in the Plymouth Church. He was an Assistant in 1632/33, but he was "freed from the office" on 2 January 1633/34 so that he could devote his full time to his church functions. He still served on various government committees, including the one that revised the laws in 1636, and he later became a deputy for Plymouth. In 1636 he shared an allotment of hay ground with the widow Ellen

Billington, and this might have led to his suing her the same year for £100 for slander; she was sentenced to pay him £5 and to sit in the stocks and be whipped (*PCR* 1:40-42). He was usually given the honorific title "Mr.," and in one document he referred to himself as "Gent., Tayler" (*Dawes-Gates*, 2:305). He had business connections with Mr. John Atwood, though the exact relationship is unclear. He acted as Atwood's agent in obtaining the indenture of Walter Harris as a servant in 1633, and in 1636 Atwood bought Doane's share of a house and land at Plain Dealing which they had held in partnership (*PCR* 1:12, 47). Doane was granted a license to sell wine in 1639, and in 1640 he was presented for selling wine contrary to the court's order, though this apparently was a misunderstanding, and the charges were dropped (*PCR* 1:127, 156). He was one of the men appointed to buy land at Nauset from the Indians, and he became one of the first settlers there (*PCR* 2:144, 154, 168).

His earliest known wife was called Ann in a 1648 deed, but in a later deed (of 1659) his wife was Lydia (*Dawes-Gates* 2:304; *MD* 13:232). His inventory in 1686 was sworn to by an Abigail Doane, whom some have taken as a third wife, though *Dawes-Gates* 2:305 has good arguments to show that Abigail was more likely his daughter. Torrey suggests that wife Ann might have been a Perkins. In his will dated 18 May 1678, inventory taken 21 May 1686 and sworn to by Abigail Doane 29 May 1686, he named his "loving wife," daughter Abigail, sons John, Daniel, and Ephraim, and granddaughter Margaret Hicks, and he left the remainder of his estate to "all his sons and daughters" (*MD* 3:177). He described himself in the will as "aged eighty and eight or there about," and in the inventory he was said to have died 21 February 1685/86, "aged about a hundred years" — thus in eight years he had aged twelve years, which is a typical overstatement of age which occurred in these times as someone began approaching the century mark. His daughter Lydia married Samuel Hicks; Abigail married Samuel Lothrop (in 1690 — she was unmarried in 1686 when Doane's will was sworn to); son John married (1) Hannah Bangs and (2) Rebecca Pettee; Daniel married (1) unknown and (2) Hepsibah (Cole) Crispe; and Ephraim married (1) Mercy Knowles and (2) Mary (Smalley) Snow (*Dawes-Gates* 2:305, which carries the line of Daniel [2] Doane forward two more generations). *Dawes-Gates* 2:302 gives good reason for believing that John Doane's ward, Joseph Harding, was his nephew, and Joseph's mother, the widow Martha Harding, was Doane's sister. In addition to the account in *Dawes-Gates* 2:299-313, another good account of what is known of his life and family is given in *Moore Families*, p. 233-43.

DOTY, EDWARD — Edward Doty arrived at Plymouth on the 1620 *Mayflower* as a servant to Stephen Hopkins, but he probably completed his term of service by the 1627 cattle division, in which he shared. For which purpose he was assigned to the company not of Hopkins (as would have been expected if he were still a member of Hopkins's household) but of John Howland. He had earlier fought a duel with swords with another Hopkins servant, Edward Leister, for which both were sentenced to be tied neck to heels; Hopkins successfully pleaded to have the punishment end after one hour (this story has appeared with much embellishment from time to time, but the earliest, most authentic version seems to be from Prince, *Chronological History*). He was on the original 1633 freeman list. On 2 January 1632/33 John Washburn sued Doty for wrongfully taking a hog from him, but the court found Washburn's case to be faulty and dismissed it; on the same day Joseph Rogers complained that Doty did not comply with a contract where he owed Rogers six young pigs, and Rogers was awarded four bushels of corn; and also on the same day William Bennett complained against Doty for various injuries, and the matter was referred to the council for resolution (*PCR* 1:6-7). The last case was resolved on 1 April 1633 when a jury found Doty guilty of slandering Bennett by calling him a rogue, and Doty was fined fifty shillings, thirty to Bennett and twenty to the court (*PCR* 1:12). On 2 January 1633/34 John Smith, who had bound himself as an apprentice to Doty for ten years, complained to the Court that Doty had disbursed but little for him; the court ruled Smith should continue being bound enough time to make a total of five years, after which Doty would have to give him double apparel, and "so be free of each other" (*PCR* 1:23). On 24 March 1633/34 Doty was fined six shillings, eight pence for fighting with Josias Cooke and drawing blood, and required also to pay Cooke three shillings four pence (*PCR* 1:26). On 28 March 1634 Doty sued Francis Sprague and was awarded six shillings six pence and half a peck of malt (*PCR* 1:29).

On 6 January 1634/35 Doty married Faith Clarke (*PCR* 1:32), daughter of Thurston (or Tristram) Clarke; on 4 December 1637 Edward Doty and Tristram Clake "his father in law" were to view land for a grant to them (*PCR* 1:69). On 22 August 1636 Peter Talbot, who until recently had been Doty's servant, being due an allotment of land for his service, assigned his right to James Skiffe for six bushels of corn (*PCR* 1:43). On 5 October 1636 a dispute between Doty and Joseph Beedle was referred to arbitration (*PCR* 1:44). On 2 January 1637/38 Doty was presented for breaking the King's peace by assaulting George Clarke and was fined ten shillings. On 6 March 1637/38 he was fined another ten shillings. (The fine on 6 March may just be the order to pay for the 2 January appearance or it may be the result of a second assault on Clarke) (*PCR* 1:75, 80). On 5 November 1638 Edward Doty, yeoman, posted £40 as a surety for Samuel Gorton (*PCR* 1:100). Also on 5 November 1638 George Moore was allowed to live with Edward Doty (*PCR* 1:102). On 4 June 1639 Doty and John Coombes posted £20 each as sureties for Richard Derby, who was charged with endangering the lives of others by giving them poisoned drinks (*PCR* 1:128). On 4 January 1641/42 the court settled differences between Doty and Thurston Clarke (father-in-law or brother-in-law?) by ordering Clarke to pay corn and money to Doty (*PCR* 2:30). On 7 September 1642 Doty and Kenelm Winslow acted as sureties for £20 each for John Hasell of Seekonk (*PCR* 2:44). On 7 December 1647 Doty was ordered to pay seven shillings damages to Samuel Cuthbert and court costs for taking away some wood from Cuthbert's land

(*PCR* 2:120). On 7 May 1650 James Shaw and John Shaw, Jr. were ordered to pay court costs and thirty-five shillings damages to Doty (*PCR* 2:149). On 7 August 1650 Doty was ordered to pay a bushel of corn each to Edward Gray and Samuel Cuthbert for letting his cattle damage their corn (*PCR* 2:161).

Doty was involved in other law suits concerning private individuals, but seemed seldom to get in trouble on official matters. He also engaged in various land transactions, as shown in the text. According to known records, Doty did not serve in public positions, which was unusual for one who was a Purchaser and early freeman. Doty died 23 August 1655 (*PCR* 8:17). His will dated 20 May 1655, inventory 21 November 1655, mentioned his wife, his son Edward, and his other unnamed sons (*MD* 3:87). *Bradford (Ford)* 2:411 stated that Doty "by a second wife hath seven children, and both he and they are living." His first wife is unknown. The seven children noted by Bradford would have been Edward, John, Thomas, Samuel, Desire, Elizabeth, and Isaac. Two other children were Joseph, born 30 April 1651 (*PCR* 8:12), and Mary. Edward's son Isaac Doty moved to Oyster Bay, Long Island, and son Samuel Doty moved to Piscataway, New Jersey. Ethan A. Doty, *The Doty-Doten Family in America* (1897), is an impressively large family history, but with many known errors. It is especially wrong in having son Joseph Doty married to Elizabeth Warren, granddaughter of 1620 *Mayflower* passenger Richard Warren, though we know from *PCR* 5:156 that Joseph had fathered a child by her (see Mrs. John Barclay, "Notes on the Dotey and Churchill Families," *TAG* 36:1). Nor did Joseph [2] Doty marry a Deborah Hatch, as has often been claimed. Joseph's wife was Deborah Ellis, as was shown by Mrs. Barclay in the same article, p. 10-11; see also "Lt. John and Elizabeth (Freeman) Ellis of Sandwich, Mass.," *NEHGR* 119:161. At least one publication has the widow of Edward's son Thomas Doty, Mary (Churchill) Doty, marrying Henry Churchill, who was in fact her brother. The explanation was given by Mrs. Barclay in *TAG* 36:1 that Thomas [2] Doty married twice; both wives were named Mary, the first being Mary Churchill, and the second, of unknown surname, married (2) Henry Churchill. The early generations of Edward Doty's family need much more research. Edward's widow, Faith, married (2) John Phillips, q.v., on 14 March 1666 (*PCR* 8:31).

DUNHAM, JOHN — John Dunham was born ca. 1589 (age at death in 1668/69 was given as eighty). He was a Leiden Separatist who came to Plymouth between 1628 and 1632, probably with those who arrived from Holland in 1629 and 1630. A deacon in the Plymouth Church, he had married (1) Susanna Kenny, who died in Holland, and (2) Abigail Barlow, daughter of Thomas in Leiden on 22 October 1622. He had three children by his first wife: John, Humility, and Thomas, and eight by his second wife: Samuel, Abigail, Persis, Jonathan, Hannah, Joseph, Benajah, and Daniel. All the children are mentioned by Mrs. John E. Barclay, "Notes on the Dunham Family of Plymouth, Mass.," *TAG* 30:143, and she carries four of them forward: John, who married a Mary; Thomas, who Mrs. Barclay believed never married, in spite of what Savage and others wrote; Samuel, who married (1) Martha (Beal) Falloway and (2) the widow Sarah Watson; and Joseph, who married (1) Mercy Morton and (2) Hester Wormell. Of the other children, Abigail married Stephen Wood; Persis married (1) Benajah Pratt and (2) Jonathan Snow; Jonathan married (1) Mary Delano, and (2) Mary Cobb; Hannah married Giles [2] Rickard; Benajah married Elizabeth Tilson; and Daniel married a Hannah. Isaac Watson Dunham's *Deacon John Dunham of Plymouth, Mass., 1589-1669, and His Descendants* (1907) is a very poorly written book, confusing, difficult to use, and often erroneous.

EATON, FRANCIS—A 1620 *Mayflower* passenger, Francis Eaton arrived with his wife Sarah and son Samuel. Bradford wrote "his first wife dyed in the generall sicknes; and he maried againe, and his 2 wife dyed, and he maried the 3 and had by her 3 children. One of them is maried and hath a child; the other are living, but one of them is an ideote. He dyed about 16 years agoe. His son Samuell, who came over a sucking child, is allso maried, and hath a child" (*Bradford [Ford]* 2:400, 410). Some genealogists believe that Eaton's second wife was Carver's unnamed maid servant who "maried, and dyed a year or two after, here in this place" (*Bradford [Ford]* 2:402). Eaton's third wife was Christian Penn. The first five generations of his descendants are given in *MF* 1. He died in the 1633 epidemic. His children were Samuel, Rachel, Benjamin, and a child, called by Bradford an idiot, of whom there is no further record. The first three children had issue. Eaton's inventory called him a carpenter and itemized a number of carpenter's tools (*MD* 1:197-99). Banks, *English Ancestry*, p. 52, found a record apprenticing a John Morgan to Francis Eaton, of Bristol, England, carpenter, but this was dated after Eaton was in Plymouth. However, first names and occupations frequently recur in the same family, and Waters, *Genealogical Gleanings,* 2:1034, summarizes the will of Christopher Cary of Bristol, England, dated 30 October 1615, in which he leaves to his wife a lodge and garden in the parish of St. Philip's, "now in the occupation of Frances Eaton, house carpenter;" this fact may be useful for further research. For additional information on the family of his daughter Rachel Eaton, who married Joseph Ramsden, see Robert S. Wakefield, "The Ramsden Family of Plymouth, Mass.," *MD* 36:187.

EATON, SAMUEL—A 1620 *Mayflower* passenger, Samuel came to Plymouth with his parents, Francis and Sarah Eaton, q.v. He married (1) Elizabeth _____ and (2) Martha Billington, daughter of Francis and Christian (Penn) (Eaton) Billington (that is, the daughter of his stepmother). He worked as an apprentice to John Cooke, Jr. (*MF* 1:5, which also gives his descendants).

EATON, SARAH—The wife of Francis Eaton, q.v., she sailed with him and their son Samuel on the 1620 *Mayflower,* and she died in the illnesses of the first year. Her maiden name is not known.

EDDY, SAMUEL—The son of the Reverend William and Mary (Fosten) Eddy, Samuel was baptized at Cranbrook, Kent, 15 September 1608 (Parish Register). He and his older brother John Eddy arrived at Plymouth on the *Handmaid* in 1630, as is shown in the text. The Eddy Family Association, Inc., has published one of the better family histories, *The Eddy Family in America* (Boston, 1930, with occasional supplements), which gives the results of much research on the English antecedents of the two brothers and on their descendants in America. John Eddy moved to Watertown in the Bay Colony after a year or so in Plymouth. Samuel was a tailor by trade, having been apprenticed in England after his father's death. He bought a house at Plymouth 9 May 1631 from Experience Mitchell (*PCR* 12:18), and he was made a freeman 1 January 1632/33 (*PCR* 1:5). On 10 January 1632/33 Thomas Brian, the servant of Samuel Eddy, was brought before the council for running away from his master, and was privately whipped (*PCR* 1:7). Though Eddy was of gentry status, and though he received land grants, he did not seem to prosper in Plymouth, as can be seen from his putting his children out as servants. On 3 April 1645 Samuel Eddy put his seven-year-old son John to dwell with Francis and Katherine Goulder until John reached twenty-one (*PCR* 2:82). The court noted on 2 March 1646/47 that Samuel and Elizabeth Eddy, having many children and "by reason of many wants lying on them," were not able to bring up their children as they desired, and thus they put their seven-year-old son Zachary out with Mr. John Browne of Rehoboth to be brought up in the employment of husbandry "or any busines he shall see meete for ye good of theire child" until age twenty-one (*PCR* 2:112). On 4 March 1652 Samuel and Elizabeth Eddy for their "many wants" put out their nine-year-old son Caleb with Mr. John Browne (*MD* 2:30). Samuel also had a daughter Hannah born 23 June 1647 (*PCR* 8:4), and a son Obadiah, as given in the *Eddy Family* book, which also gives reason to wonder if he might have had a son Samuel.

The *Eddy Family* book, which is well documented in the early generations, shows that although Samuel had land rights elsewhere, he lived in Plymouth until the family moved to Swansea ca. 1680. Samuel died at Swansea 12 November 1687 in his eighty-seventh year (*Ply. Ch. Recs.* 1:262 — as often happens, his age at death could be wrong, for it would seem unlikely that his clergyman father would not have baptized him shortly after birth); and his wife Elizabeth died at Swansea 24 May 1689 at the end of her eighty-second year (*Ply. Ch. Recs.* 1:265). The maiden name of Samuel's wife Elizabeth is unknown. From *PCR* 2:82 we know that son John (the oldest known child) was born 25 December 1637, and thus it seems reasonable to suppose that Samuel and Elizabeth were married after his arrival in Plymouth. There is a mystery about Samuel Eddy appearing on a list of 3 June 1662 of "first born children" who received land purchased by Major Winslow and Captain Southworth (*PCR* 4:18-19). The list is a bit misnamed, for the original act from *PCR* 11:16 provides that "such children as are heer borne & next unto them such as are heer brought up under their parents. . .be provided for . . .before any that either come from England or elsewhere." A good reason can be found for virtually all the names on the 1662 list. The "first born" seems to be any needy child (or a parent for the child) of those who were in Plymouth by 1627. One person on the list does not fit the pattern, William Pontus, but we might suppose that he was included because he and his wife were of the Leiden Separatists and needed land. Some men are on the list because they married "first born" children, such as William Hoskins (married Sarah Cushman), William Nelson (Martha Ford), George Partridge (Sarah Tracy), and Andrew Ring (Deborah Hopkins). Edward Gray was the only person receiving a double share, and he was the husband of Mary Winslow, daughter of two Old Comers (Mary Chilton and John Winslow). But why was Samuel Eddy's name on the list?

Samuel did not qualify for inclusion by any right of his own. Therefore it is reasonable to suppose that he qualified by right of his wife, and that she must have been the daughter of some Old Comer family. Which Old Comer families had daughters named Elizabeth who can not otherwise be accounted for? Only one. *Bradford (Ford)* 2:408-09 gives Bradford's words that "Thomas Rogers dyed in the first sicknes, but his sone Joseph is still living, and is maried, and hath six children. The rest of Thomas Rogers [children] came over, and are maried, and have many children." Yet not all of Thomas Rogers's other children at Plymouth have been identified. Besides Joseph, who came over with Rogers, his son John came over ca. 1630, but that is all that is known about his children in New England. *MF* 2:153 cites Leiden records to show that Rogers also had in Holland Lysbeth (Elizabeth) and Grietgen (Margaret). It might seem reasonable then to think that Samuel Eddy's wife was Elizabeth Rogers, except for one other fact. As shown by *Plymouth Colony LR* 4:311, Samuel Eddy was a brother-in-law of Thomas Savory, q.v. All would be neat if Savory were married to a Margaret, but his wife was Anne or Annis. One could suppose that Savory married (1) a daughter of Thomas Rogers and (2) Anne, or that he married Anne, a daughter of Thomas Rogers not given in the Leiden records, but this is just speculation (a Margaret Savory was in Leiden in 1613 and 1619 [Dexter, p. 633]). Pope has Thomas Savory arriving in New England in the *Mary and John* in 1633/34. He was at Kennebec in April 1634 with John Howland (*MD* 2:11), and there is no record any earlier of him in Plymouth. Thus he would not qualify as a "first born" either. Yet on 7 June 1665 he was one of five men receiving land in the Major's Purchase, and while the other four received the land for themselves, Savory received it "for his children" (*PCR* 4:95). Though nothing in the records shows that the Major's Purchase was reserved for the children of Old Comers, the other four receiving land were William Clarke of Duxbury, a kinsman of Adventurer and Purchaser William Collier (*PCR* 12:182); Benjamin Eaton, a son of 1620 *Mayflower* passenger Francis Eaton; Jonathan Dunham, a son of Leiden Separatist Deacon John Dunham, q.v., and his wife, Abigail Barlow, who was also in Leiden; and Joseph Dunham, a brother of Jonathan. There are possibilities here, but obviously this theory needs more support before it can be considered fact.

ELLIS, JOHN—Lydia B. (Phinney) Brownson and Maclean W. McLean have complied a definitive family history, "Lt. John[1] and Elizabeth

(Freeman) Ellis of Sandwich, Mass.," *NEHGR* 119:161, 260, 120:26, 97, 187, 272, 121:37, 127, 152, 260, 122:51, 131, 196, 254, which contains much detail about John Ellis's life and resolves some problems in earlier writings. John Ellis first appears in the 1643 ATBA for Sandwich. On 20 August 1644 he was accused of fornication before marriage to his wife Elizabeth, daughter of Sandwich's leading citizen Edmond Freeman, and he was sentenced to be whipped and fined £5. In 1653 he was approved to be the lieutenant of the Sandwich military company. He engaged in various business enterprises, such as participating in a monopoly for profiting from beached whales, building a mill, and building a meeting house. In 1657/58 several men were summoned before the court to answer for a tumultuous carriage at a Quaker meeting in Sandwich, but Lieutenant Ellis and two others were "found not soe faulty as was supposed," and were admonished and cleared. He seems to have had a son, John Ellis, Jr., by an earlier wife. He died before 23 March 1677, when an inventory was taken of his estate. His wife Elizabeth exhibited his inventory and also that of John Ellis, Jr. (though she was too young to be his mother), and the authors of the Ellis article wonder if the two John Ellises could have been unrecorded casualties of King Philip's War. Elizabeth Ellis later moved to Sippican, where some of the land was part of a grant made by the court to the veterans of the war, and she probably died there, perhaps not long before 20 April 1714. Of their children, Deborah Ellis is believed, on the strength of good indirect evidence, to have married Joseph [2] Doty—see also Mrs. Barclay, "Notes on the Dotey and Churchill Families," *TAG* 36:9.

ELY, _____ – A 1620 *Mayflower* seaman, Ely contracted to stay at Plymouth for a year, which he did, and then left. He may of course have descendants, but none is known. Dr. Jeremy Bangs (*MQ* 51:59) suggests that this seaman may have been either John or Christopher Ely, or Ellis, who are documented in Leiden.

ENGLISH, THOMAS – A 1620 *Mayflower* seaman who was hired by the Pilgrims to be master of the shallop, Thomas English died before the *Mayflower* left Plymouth in April 1621, leaving no known descendants. Dexter, p. 614, stated that Thomas England, who appeared in Leiden records in 1613, was "undoubtedly the Thos. English of the *Mayflower*."

ENSIGN, THOMAS – Thomas Ensign was one of the "men of Kent" who settled at Scituate, and he first appears in the records when he bought James Cudworth's house there sometime between 1634 and 1637 (*NEHGR* 10:42). He left a son Thomas in Cranbrook, County Kent, England, who predeceased him, mentioning in his will dated 3 September 1657 his father Thomas Ensign, a brother John, and sisters Hannah and Sarah, all in New England (*NEHGR* 66:87). Thomas, Sr. married Elizabeth Wilder in Plymouth Colony 17 January 1638/39 (*PCR* 1:108), and the circumstances would indicate that Elizabeth was his second wife. (MacKenzie, *Colonial Families* 3:584-85, calls her the daughter of Thomas Wilder of Shiplake on the Thames, England, who died in England in 1634, and his wife Martha, who came as a widow to Hingham in 1638/39 with a daughter Mary, the other children having preceded her.) Ensign did not take the 1638/39 Oath of Fidelity, and he is unusual in that he was proposed for freeman five times, 5 March 1638/39, 1 December 1640, 5 June 1651, 4 May 1652, and 8 June 1655 (*PCR* 1:116, 2:3, 167, 3:7, 78), but was never made a freeman. Yet he was a grandjuror on at least three occasions, 1 March 1641/42, 7 June 1642, and 4 June 1645 (*PCR* 2:34, 41, 84). On 7 June 1653 the court ordered him to pay thirty shillings to John Hoare which he had obtained by a mistake of a trial jury (*PCR* 3:35). On 4 August 1658 John Ensign, son of Thomas, chose Capt. James Cudworth as his guardian until he reached legal age (*PCR* 3:148). On 1 March 1663/64, John Ensign was given the administration of the estate of Thomas Ensign, deceased (*PCR* 4:55). Thomas Ensign dated his will 16 July 1663, proved 9 June 1664, and he mentioned his wife Elizabeth, his son John, "my Daughter hanna my Coult that was foaled this year and my great old bible that was my fathers," his daughter Hannah's son Thomas Sheppard, "my Daughter Sarah my yeare old Coult" and £10, and his wife's sister's daughter Sarah Underwood (*MD* 16:23-24). From the will of his son John, given below, it would appear that Thomas, Sr. must have had two living daughters named Hannah, perhaps one by each wife.

Son John Ensign was killed on 26 March 1676 in King Philip's War, (Newman's Letter, *Early Rehoboth*, 3:14-15), along with Joseph Wade (see Thomas Wade, below). The will of this John Ensign was dated 5 July 1676 [*sic*], sworn 28 October 1676, and he named his mother Elizabeth Ensign; daughter Hannah Ensign; sister Hannah Sheppard's son Thomas Sheppard, Jr.; sister Hannah Wade's sons Jacob and Joseph and daughter Silence; sister Sarah Wade, to get "the ten pound legacye that my father Gave her"; and Sarah Underwood. His mother and his brother Thomas Wade were to be joint executors (*Ply. Colony PR* 3:2:16). There were obviously close family ties between the Ensigns and the Wades, and these will be discussed further under Thomas Wade. Thomas, Sr.'s daughter Sarah Ensign probably married (1) Joseph Wade and sometime after Wade was killed in King Philip's War (2) Thomas Mann (see *TAG* 61:46). One of his daughters named Hannah must have married a brother of Joseph Wade, either John or Jacob.

FAUNCE, JOHN—John Faunce arrived at Plymouth in 1623 on the *Anne*. Banks guessed that he came from Perleigh, County Essex because he could find the surname only in that area, but others have found it elsewhere. He was a Purchaser and on the 1633 freeman list. Faunce married Patience Morton, daughter of George and Juliana (Carpenter) Morton. He served on juries and obtained various land grants (*PCR*, passim). His house was located in the southern part of Plymouth near the Eel River. He died 29 November 1654 (*PCR* 8:16). His children are given in *Moore Families*, p. 244-47, and the line is further carried forward by James F. Faunce, *The Faunce Family History and Genealogy* (Akron, Ohio, 1967). One of John's sons was the famed Elder Thomas Faunce, who lived to be almost 100, dying in 1746. A well known story originated in a talk given in the nineteenth century at Plymouth's Old Colony Club that at age ninety-five Elder Faunce was driven to town in an open wagon from Eel River and taken to Plymouth Rock. He told the people gathered there how he had talked to John Howland and his wife, John Alden, Giles Hopkins, George Soule, Francis Cooke and his son John, and Mrs. Cushman, born Mary Allerton, who "died but yesterday." All of these, he said, told him that upon that rock they had stepped ashore, and John Winslow's wife, Mary (Chilton), had come there on her seventy-fifth birthday and laughed as she stepped on the rock and said she was the first woman to have stepped on it. This story, relayed to posterity verbally by one who claimed to hear it from a person who had been in Elder Faunce's audience that day, is as far back as we can go to authenticate that what we call today Plymouth Rock was in fact the first land at Plymouth touched by the *Mayflower* passengers. For other information on Faunce's descendants, see James Freer Faunce, "The Faunce Family," *NEHGR* 114:115; Rachel E. Barclay, "The Faunce Family: Addenda and Corrections," *NEHGR* 116:188; and Rachel E. Barclay,"Correction to Faunce Article," *NGSQ* 48:184.

FELL, THOMAS—Although he arrived at Plymouth in 1623 on the *Little James,* he was not named among those sharing the 1623 land division. Perhaps he was included with others who received shares without being named; however, it is quite possible that he was left out because he had been specifically hired to work for the company for a five-year period, along with William Stevens, q.v. Fell and Stevens were sent home in 1624, apparently because they had behaved badly when the *Little James* sank. For additional details see chapter 1, note 18.

FELLS, _____—Called "Mr. Fells" by Bradford (*Morrison* p. 189-92), Fells and Mr. John Sibsey were the chief among many passengers aboard the *Sparrowhawk* bound for Virginia in 1627 when it was wrecked off Cape Cod. They were all allowed to stay at the colony until they could get a ship for Virginia, and in the meantime were permitted to plant a crop for their subsistence. Most of these passengers were servants, many of whom came from Ireland. According to Bradford, Fells was accused of keeping a maidservant as a concubine, and the two of them were questioned, but nothing could be proved. Later the maidservant appeared pregnant, and Fells ran away. Apparently all this group left the colony when they were able. They would have been present during the 1627 cattle division, but did not share in it.

FLAVEL, THOMAS—Thomas Flavel arrived at Plymouth with an unnamed son in 1621 on the *Fortune,* and his wife arrived in 1623. The family received three shares in the 1623 land division, but they were not in the 1627 division.

FLETCHER, MOSES—A Leiden Separatist from Sandwich, Kent, and a 1620 *Mayflower* passenger, Moses Fletcher died shortly after arrival at Plymouth. Robert S. Wakefield, "The Search for Descendants of Moses Fletcher," *NEHGR* 128:161, gives evidence that he married (1) Mary Evans and left ten children, thirteen grandchildren, and twenty great-grandchildren in Holland and married (2) Sarah Danby. Mr. Wakefield concludes that it would be reasonable to suppose descendants of Fletcher are living today in the Netherlands or elsewhere. Dr. Jeremy D. Bangs, former curator of the Leiden Pilgrim Documents Center, believes he has evidence of such descendants living today. Though an application from a claimed descendant is pending with the Mayflower Society, the Society has not yet recognized the claim. None of Fletcher's family is known to have come to colonial New England.

FLOOD, Edmond—He arrived at Plymouth in 1623 and received one share in the 1623 land division, but he was not in the 1627 cattle division.

FOGGE, RALPH—Regarding the dealings of Allerton, Sherley wrote Bradford in 1631 that Allerton "and Straton and Fogge were above a month" trying to straighten out the accounts, and in a footnote Morison identifies Straton and Fogge as "Two of the original Adventurers who decided not to continue" (*Bradford [Morison]*, p. 390); see also "Some Stratton Notes," *NEHGR* 135:288). *Lechford's Notebook*, p. 335, has Ralph Fogge of Salem, New England, giving a deposition that he saw Mrs. Ann Stratton deliver documents to her son John Stratton at Dedham, England, ca. 1631, and Fogge deposed that he was then aged about forty years. Waters, *Genealogical Gleanings*, p. 654, shows a John Bancks, mercer of London, giving in his 1630 will "To Susan ffoge the wife of Raffe ffoge, the daughter of my sister Susan Draper [wife of Edward Draper, girdler]," mother of John Fogge, and Waters comments that this may have been the Ralph Fogge of Salem (see also Waters, p. 742 for another will mentioning Ralph Fogg). *Bradford (Ford)* 2:82-83 footnote, gives a letter in which James Sherley mentions Mr. Fogge, Mr. Collier, Mr. Coalson, and Mr. Thomas as having intended to take part in the adventure, "although they seemed earnest to be partners, yet when they saw the debt and charge fell themselves off."

Fogge was on the Plymouth 1633 freeman list and on the 1634 (but not 1633) tax list. On 1 July 1633 Mr. Fogg was given use with Mr. Weston of a watering place for mowing; on 28 October 1633 Mr. Raph Fog was granted a "misted" (that is, a staked-out lot) formerly granted to Richard Warren, deceased, but on condition that Fogge build a dwelling house within twelve months; and on 2 January 1633/34 Ralph Fogge was granted a small parcel of land on an island at Newharbour Marsh (*PCR* 1:14, 18, 24). Pope, p. 171, shows that he was made a Massachusetts freeman 3 September 1634, and that he had a wife Susanna, and children John, Elizabeth, and David; he was probably living in 1656 when a Ralph Fogg, of London, skinner, bought land and warehouses in Boston. Fogge was town clerk for Salem in 1636, and kept records for the Quarter Court at Salem (Essex Inst. Hist. Col. 2nd Ser., vol. 1, pt 1, p. 18).

FORD, MARTHA—*Mourt's Relation*, p. 63, says about the passengers of the 1621 *Fortune* "these came all in health unto us, not any being sick by the way. . .the good wife Ford was delivered of a sonne the first night shee landed, and both of them are very well." In the 1623 land division, the widow Ford had four shares. By the time of the 1627 cattle division she had married Peter Browne and along with her and her husband in the company headed by Samuel Fuller were John Ford and Martha Ford. It would appear that her first husband came with her, but died before the 1623 division, and thus John Ford would have been the child born immediately after arrival. Mrs. Barclay believed ("Goodwife Martha Ford Alias 'Widow' Ford, Her Second Husband, Peter Browne, and Her Children," *TAG* 42:35) that the newborn child was a fifth Ford, who was living in 1623, but this supposes that Martha did not obtain a share for a deceased husband, and such a supposition is open to question (see Wakefield, *MQ* 40:55). She probably died by 1630, for Browne had two children by a second wife before he died in 1633. Martha's children are given in the Barclay article. (See also Wakefield, "Men of the Fortune: Ford," *TAG* 56:32.) Her son John Ford disappears from the records after 1640/41, and her daughter Martha Ford married William Nelson. There is no evidence that the William Ford subsequently found in Marshfield was her son, and what we know of early Plymouth Colony argues against it (he would have had to have been born by 1623, but have been absent from the 1627 cattle division—very unlikely).

FORD, WILLIAM—William Ford first appears in Plymouth records on the 1643 ATBA for Duxbury. *Moore Families*, pp. 264-75, gives an account of his life and his family. In 1671 he gave his age as sixty-seven, and thus was born ca. 1604. His wife Anna, or Hannah, _____ died in 1684; Mrs. Barclay (*NEHGR* 119:23) thought Ford's wife might be Hannah Eames (Torrey suggests the daughter of Anthony Eames). Ford was a miller in Duxbury, and he later moved to Marshfield where he owned a mill in partnership with Josias Winslow, Jr. In 1652 he became a freeman, and he served in various public capacities such as highway surveyor and constable. On 3 October 1662 he was fined five shillings for allowing Samuel Howland to breach the Sabbath by carrying grist from the mill. In 1665/66 he became a selectman for Marshfield for the first of several times. His will, dated 12 September 1676, sworn 4 November 1676, mentioned his wife, sons William and Michael, daughters Margaret and Millicent, Margaret's unnamed husband, and grandsons John Ford, William Carver, and John Carver (*Ply. Colony PR* 3:2:22). Daughter Margaret is believed to have married Zachariah Soule and to have had no issue (see *MF* 3 and Torrey). Daughter Millicent married John[2] Carver, son of Robert, and their children are given by Mrs. Barclay, "The Ancestry of Experience, Wife of Cornelius[4] Washburn of Bridgewater, Mass.," *NEHGR* 119:24. Son Michael married Abigail Snow, daughter of Anthony and Abigail (Warren) Snow, and son William married Sarah Dingley, daughter of John Dingley.

FREEMAN, EDMOND—*Dawes-Gates*, p. 349-64, gives a well-documented account showing that Edmond Freeman was baptized 25 July 1596 at St. Mary's Church, Pulborough, Sussex, the son of Edmond and

Alice (Coles) Freeman, and he died 2 November 1682 at Sandwich, Plymouth Colony. He married (1) at Cowfold, Sussex, on 16 June 1617 Bennett Hodsoll, daughter of John and Faith (_____) (Bacon) Hodsoll, who died in 1630 at Pulborough and (2) Elizabeth, whose surname is not known, but who may have been the Elizabeth Raymer who married Edmond Freeman on 10 August 1632 at Shipley, Sussex (parish register). He sailed for New England with four surviving children and some other people with his surname on the *Abigail* in July 1635, and he settled first at Saugus (Lynn) in the Bay Colony. He was evidently the leader of the Saugus men who moved in 1637 to Sandwich, and it was to him that a deed was granted as agent for the others. He became an Assistant in Plymouth Colony, but was not reelected in 1646, and Edward Winslow wrote to Gov. John Winthrop in Boston that "I suppose the country left [Freeman] out in regard of his professed Anabaptistry & Separacon from the Churches" (*MHS Collections*, 4th series, 6:178). The *Dawes-Gates* account shows also that he was of an unorthodox nature for his time and place, and was later sympathetic to the Quakers. He had business interests of his own in New England, and he had a power of attorney in behalf of his brother-in-law, John Beauchamp, who had continued as one of the four London Undertakers after the other Adventurers sold out their interests.

His will dated 21 June 1682, proved 2 November 1682, named his three "sons," Edmond Freeman, John Freeman, and Edward Perry (whose wife Mary has sometimes been assumed to have been a daughter of Edmond Freeman though no evidence has been found). Also named were his daughter Elizabeth Ellis, and his grandsons Matthias Freeman and Thomas Paddy (*MD* 12:248). His son Edmond married (1) Rebecca Prence, daughter of Thomas and (2) Margaret Perry. His son John married Mercy Prence, daughter of Thomas. His daughter Elizabeth married John Ellis. His other children were Alice Freeman, who married William Paddy, and a daughter Bennett and a son Nathaniel, both of whom died young. For additional comments on the Perrys, see Lydia B. (Phinney) Brownson and Maclean McLean, "Ezra Perry of Sandwich, Mass. (c. 1625-1689)," *NEHGR* 115:86.

FULLER, _____—The wife of Edward Fuller, who accompanied him on the 1620 *Mayflower*, she has sometimes been called Ann Fuller, but there is no evidence that that was her name, nor is her maiden name known. She died during the early months at Plymouth.

FULLER, EDWARD—It has been assumed in the past that Edward Fuller, unlike his brother Samuel, was not in Leiden, but Jeremy D. Bangs in *MQ* 51:58 cites a contemporary Leiden document to show that, in fact, he was there. Edward arrived at Plymouth on the 1620 *Mayflower* with his wife (see above) and son Samuel, q.v., and both he and his wife died shortly after arrival. Another son, Matthew, came to Plymouth Colony later. Though there have been claims that Matthew was not Edward's son, there is good indirect evidence in support of the relationship—see Bruce Campbell MacGunnigle, Robert M. Sherman, and Robert S. Wakefield, "Was Matthew Fuller of Plymouth Colony a Son of Pilgrim Edward Fuller?"

TAG 61:194. Matthew became a captain and a colony leader. He married a Frances, whose surname is unknown, and they had Samuel, John, Mary, Anne, and Elizabeth, as is shown by Matthew's will (*MD* 13:7). Additional information on Edward Fuller can be found in Homer W. Brainard, "Edward Fuller and his Descendants" and Francis H. Fuller, "John Fuller of Redenhall, England, and his Descendants in New England," *NYGBR* 33:171, 211. For other published material, see Edward's brother Samuel.

FULLER, SAMUEL—It has been accepted that Samuel Fuller and his brother Edward, q.v., were the sons of Robert Fuller, a butcher of Redenhall with Harleston Parish, County Norfolk; however, current research may put this in question, and, if so, the results will appear in a forthcoming *TAG* article. Samuel married (1) Alice Glascock (2) Agnes Carpenter, q.v., and (3) Bridget Lee (*MD* 8:129). Of his children by his third wife, only son Samuel is known to have descendants, and the first five generations of the Samuel Fuller family are given in *MF* 1. The senior Samuel Fuller was among the English Separatists living in Leiden. He came to Plymouth on the 1620 *Mayflower*, his wife Bridget coming later in the 1623 *Anne*. He was the colony's physician and surgeon, and he is frequently mentioned in the text. See the articles given under his brother Edward. Herbert and Florence Fuller, *The Fuller Family in England and America*, 2nd ed. (1971), covers the families of both Samuel and Edward, but is known to have errors. Additional articles of interest on the Fuller families are Francis H. Fuller, "Early New England Fullers," and "Fullers of Redenhall, England," *NEHGR* 55:192, 410.

FULLER, SAMUEL—A son of Edward, Samuel accompanied his parents on the 1620 *Mayflower* to Plymouth. He married Jane Lothrop, daughter of rev. John Lothrop (*MD* 16:129). Though the 1627 cattle division list should have covered the senior Samuel Fuller plus two second generation Samuel Fullers, the son of the senior Samuel and the son of his brother Edward, only one second generation Samuel is actually on the list, and this most likely is Samuel, son of Edward, who was indisputably living in 1627. The evidence for Samuel, son of Samuel, being in Plymouth in 1627 is the inscription on his gravestone, which shows him dying in his seventy-first year on 17 August 1695, thus having him born ca. 1624. However, gravestone inscriptions frequently contain some error, and if this one overstated his age by a few years, he might not even have been born by the 1627 division. Samuel Fuller, the son of Edward, died at Barnstable 31 October 1683. He dated his will 29 October 1683, inventory 14 November 1683, and in it he named his sons Samuel and John, and his daughters Elizabeth Taylor, Hannah Bonham, Mary Williams, and Sarah Crowe. (*MD* 2:237). He had other children who died young. His daughter Hannah, who married Nicholas Bonham, moved with her husband to Piscataway, New Jersey, thus bringing the Edward Fuller line there at an early date.

GARDINER, RICHARD—Bradford wrote that Richard Gardiner, a 1620 *Mayflower* passenger, became a seaman and died in England or at sea. He had no known descendants. *Three Visitors*, p. 47, gives a letter from Altham mentioning that Richard Gardiner asked for the vacant master's position on Altham's ship, claiming it was his due by place, but some felt he was not qualified for the job. Altham said that Gardiner, who had been willing to help with the ship, felt bad that the company would not pay him wages with the seamen. Gardiner received one share in the 1623 land division.

GIBBS, THOMAS – First recorded on the 1643 ATBA list for Sandwich, Thomas Gibbs died shortly before 27 March 1692/93. The name of his wife is unknown, and he had seven children: John, Thomas, Samuel, Sarah, Job, Bethia, and Mary. Their descendants are given by Lydia B. (Phinney) Brownson and Maclean W. McLean, "Thomas 1 Gibbs of Sandwich, Mass. (ca. 1615-1693)," *NEHGR* 123:54, 129, 205, 266, 124:70, 128:305.

GIFFORD, WILLIAM – Almon E. Daniels and Maclean W. McLean, "William Gifford of Sandwich, Mass. (D. 1687)," starting in *NEHGR* 128:241, and continuing for many years, gives a comprehensive family history of this family which spread over much of southeastern Massachusetts and nearby Rhode Island.

GILSON, WILLIAM – William Gilson was on the original 1633 freeman list, and in that year he was an Assistant. He was an early resident of Scituate, owning one of the nine houses that John Lothrop found there on his arrival in late September 1634, and Gilson was among the original members of the church Lothrop organized there 8 January 1634/35 (*NEHGR* 10:42, 9:279). His servant Thomas Boiden joined the church on 17 May 1635. He was one of a committee who obtained on 22 January 1638/39 a land grant at Sippican (later canceled). He remained at Scituate when the Lothrop group left. His will dated 26 January 1639/40, inventory 1 February 1639/40, named his wife Frances, his cousin John Damon, who worked for him as a servant, his cousin Hannah Damon, and his cousin Daniel Romeball; he also left £5 to Mr. John Lothrop (*MD* 3:160). On 7 June 1649 Humphrey Turner, Henry Cobb, Henry Rowley, and Bernard Lumbert testified, in connection with a request by John Damon for his rights to Gilson's lands, that they had asked Gilson why he wanted so much land, being old and having no issue of his body to inherit from him, and he said that he had brought two of his sister's children to New England with him, and he was bound in conscience to provide for them as if they were his own (*PCR* 2:142-43).

GLASS, JAMES – James Glass was a servant to Henry Cogan of Barnstable, and on 13 February 1639/40 the rest of his term was transferred to Manasseh Kempton of Plymouth (*PCR* 1:139). He married Mary Pontus, daughter of William and Wybra (Hanson) Pontus 31 October 1645 (*PCR* 2:88; *MD* 11:92). G. E. McCracken (*NEHGR* 111:178) gives their children as Hannah, who died young; Wybra, who married Joseph Bumpus; Hannah, who married Isaac Billington; and Mary, who married Samuel Hunt; and he shows that James Glass was probably a son of James and Mary (Cogan) Glass of Taunton, Somerset; that he came to New England as a servant to his uncle Henry Cogan, q.v., and that he was a nephew to Judith Cogan, the first wife of Gyles Rickard, q.v.. The same source gives added information on two of James's brothers who came to New England, Roger Glass, who was a servant to his aunt Frances (Cogan) Whetcomb's husband John Whetcomb in Scituate (Roger left no known issue), and Henry Glass, who was a servant in Essex County in the Bay Colony (not known if he left issue); also, James's sister, Amy Glass, came to New England and married at Plymouth (1) Richard Willis and (2) Edward Holman (*NEHGR* 111:177). James Glass probably was one of the seven unnamed men servants accompanying Henry Cogan to New England in 1637.

GODBERTSON, GODBERT—see Cuthbert Cuthbertson.

GOODMAN, JOHN—A 1620 *Mayflower* passenger, John Goodman was not the same person as the later Plymouth settler, Deacon John Dunham, in spite of some claims to the contrary. He left no known descendants, but his death is somewhat a mystery. *Bradford (Ford)* 2:410 puts him in a group of men whom he says died shortly after arrival in the general sickness. Certainly he was alive on 19 January 1620/21 when he is recorded as successfully fighting off two wolves (*Mourt's Relation*, p. 29). He would also seem to have been alive at the time of the 1623 land division, when he was recorded as one of the sharers. He was gone by the 1627 division, and had probably died in the meantime. Dexter (p. 16) wrote that Goodman was the widower of Mary Backus who had married (2) Sarah Hooper at Leiden 10 October 1619, accompanied by Samuel Fuller, but the actual Leiden records list the name as Jan Codmoer.

GRAY, EDWARD—He arrived in Plymouth ca. 1643 and became a merchant, among the wealthiest in Plymouth Colony. He married (1) Mary Winslow a granddaughter of John and Mary (Chilton) Winslow, and Gray's children by her are given in the Chilton part of *MF* 2:15-6 as Desire, Mary, Elizabeth, Sarah, John, and Anna. He married (2) Dorothy Lettice and had six more children: Edward, Thomas, Samuel, Susanna, Rebecca, and Lydia. He died at Plymouth the last of June 1681, age ca. fifty-two.

HANFORD, THOMAS—see Eglin Hatherly.

HARDING, MARTHA—Widow Harding was on the 25 March 1633 tax list for the minimum amount, nine shillings. Martha Harding died before 28 October 1633 and John Doane presented her inventory and was administrator on behalf of her son (*PCR* 1:18). Her inventory was valued at a little over £20, and among her debts were £20 to three of her husband's brothers in England. It was noted that she died without a will, leaving one son to the custody of Mr. John Doane (*MD* 1:82-83), and *Dawes-Gates* 2:302 gives good reason to think that she may have been Doane's sister. Her son, Joseph Harding, later married Bethiah Cooke (*PCR* 8:27), daughter of Josiah Cooke, q.v. There were other Hardings in the area, such as the John Harding on the 1643 ATBA for Duxbury; the Phebe Harding who married John Browne on 26 March 1634 (*PCR* 1:26); and the Winifred Harding who married Thomas Whitton on 22 November 1639 (*PCR* 1:134); but no relationship is known with Martha Harding.

HARLOW, WILLIAM—Savage and Pope were wrong in their treatment of William Harlow and were corrected by George Ernest Bowman,
"Sergeant William Harlow of Plymouth and William Harlow of Sandwich
Were Not the Same Person," *MD* 12:193. The William Harlow of Plymouth
town died 25 August 1691 in his sixty-seventh year (*Ply. Town Recs.* 1:202;
Ply. Ch. Recs. 1:271), and thus was born ca. 1624. He was on the 1643 ATBA
for Plymouth; he was a grandjuror on 7 June 1653 (*PCR* 3:32); and he
became a freeman on 6 June 1654 (*PCR* 3:48). In 1656 he was a highway
surveyor for Plymouth, and in 1661 he was a constable for Plymouth (*PCR*
3:100, 215). He was among those granted land on 3 June 1662 at Taunton
(*PCR* 4:20). By the late 1660s he was known as Sergeant Harlow. On 1 June
1669 Sgt. William Harlow was a selectman for Plymouth (*PCR* 5:19), and
on 15 September 1673 he became a deputy (*PCR* 5:135).

He married (1) on 20 December 1649 Rebecca Bartlett, daughter of
Robert Bartlett and his wife Mary Warren (daughter of Richard Warren);
(2) 15 July 1658 Mary Faunce, daughter of John Faunce; and (3) 25 January 1665/66 Mary Shelley (*PCR* 8:8, 21, 26). In the settlement of his estate,
dated 9 September 1691, his widow is Mary Harlow, and his surviving children are sons Samuel, William, Nathaniel, and Benjamin, and seven
unnamed daughters (*MD* 12:195). On 12 April 1667 Sgt. William Harlow
made an agreement with Secretary Nathaniel Morton and his wife Lydia
to put out his son Nathaniel Harlow, near two and one-half years old, with
the Mortons until he was twenty-one (*PCR* 5:10). The agreement between
Harlow and Morton showed that the Mortons "desired" the child, and it
provided that in case Nathaniel Morton died before the child was seven
years old, William Harlow would pay £10 to Lydia Morton to help in the
maintenance of the child. Nathaniel Morton in his 1685 will gave a young
cow and calf to his kinsman Nathaniel Harlow, son of William, and
requested his loving kinsman Sgt. William Harlow to be a supervisor of
his will (*Ply. Colony LR* 5:350). The kinship between Harlow and Morton
would have been through Harlow's second wife, Mary Faunce, whose
mother, Patience Morton, was a sister of Nathaniel Morton, and thus
Nathaniel Harlow would have been Nathaniel Morton's nephew.

William Harlow's children by his first wife were William, Samuel,
Rebecca, and William; by his second wife, Mary, Repentance, John, and
Nathaniel; and by his third wife Hannah, Bathsheba, Joanna, Mehitabel,
Judith, and Benjamin (*MD* 12:195). An early article, Theodore P. Adams,
"The Harlow Family," *NEHGR* 14:227, is undocumented and has known
errors. The house of William Harlow is still standing in Plymouth and may
be visited during the summer; it is said to contain original beams from
Plymouth's first meetinghouse-fort, and is known as the "Harlow Old Fort
House."

HARMON, JOHN—The son of Edmond Harmon of London, tailor,
John Harmon became an apprentice to Francis Cooke for seven years
beginning 1 October 1636 (*PCR* 1:46-47). His name was on a 28 October
1645 list of Plymouth soldiers who went on the campaign against the

Narragansetts (*PCR* 2:90). On 24 April 1644 John Harmon bought six acres of land from William Browne for fifty shillings and on 24 September 1645 he sold the same land to Webb Adey for thirty shillings (*PCR* 12:113-14). According to Pope, he died 16 March 1661.

HARRIS, WALTER—Walter Harris had bound himself by indenture to Mr. John Atwood under the command of Mr. John Doane for five years, and on 8 April 1633 Doane sold his service, with Harris's consent, to Henry Howland for £14 (*PCR* 1:12-13). This is the only time he appears in the records, although Pope shows a Walter Harris in Dorchester in 1641. As sheer speculation, one might wonder if the name Walter is a recording mistake, and if he might not be identical with Arthur Harris (also called Harrison). On 31 August 1640 Arthur Harrison was granted twenty-five acres of land in Duxbury due him for his service (*PCR* 1:160), but no record of his working earlier as a servant is available—see Pope for additional information on him.

HATCH, WILLIAM—Elizabeth French, "Genealogical Research in England—Hatch," *NEHGR* 70:256, has taken the Hatch family back to John at Hecche of Kent, England, born ca. 1415. Elder William Hatch was born ca. 1598, probably in County Kent, the son of William and Anne Hatch. He sailed for Plymouth in March 1634/35 in the *Hercules,* with his second wife, Jane (Young), five children and six servants, and he settled at Scituate. He became a freeman on 5 January 1635/36, and in 1643 he was chosen the first ruling elder of the Second (Vassall's) Church at Scituate. In 1643 he also became a lieutenant in the Scituate military company. He died at Scituate 6 November 1651. His first wife is unknown. His widow Jane married (2) Elder Thomas King of Scituate. Hatch had seven children, six by his second wife, two of whom died young in England. Other members of his family came to Plymouth Colony, including his brother Thomas Hatch and Thomas's wife Lydia, and to Scituate; his sister Elizabeth (Hatch) Soan who became the second wife of John Stockbridge of Scituate; and his cousin Lydia Huckstep, who came to Scituate with her husband Nathaniel Tilden. In a footnote, p. 256, Miss French removes some of the confusion concerning two Thomas Hatches who settled in Plymouth Colony. This second Thomas Hatch, apparently unrelated to the above Hatch family, settled first in Dorchester, then in Yarmouth, and finally in Barnstable, leaving a widow Grace and children.

HATHERLY, EGLIN—Born in Devonshire ca. 1589, Eglin Hatherly probably died at Scituate after 1653. Her first two husbands, (_____) Downe and Jeffrey Hanford, died in England, and she sailed on 10 April 1635 from London to Boston on the *Planter,* then age forty-six, with her daughters Margaret, sixteen, and Elizabeth, fourteen. She resided in Scituate, and she and her children joined Lothrop's Church there. She married (3) 15 December 1637 Richard Sillis (Sealis), but they had no children. Her Hanford children were named in the will of her brother, Timothy Hatherly, q.v. Additional information on her can be found in Mary Lovering Holman, *Ancestry of Col. John H. Stevens. . .* (Concord, N.H., 1948),

1:485-87, which gives Eglin's children by Jeffrey Hanford as Susanna, who married (1) John Whiston and (2) William Brooks; Lettice, who married (1) Edward Foster and (2) Edward Jenkins; Margaret, who married Isaac Robinson, q.v.; Elizabeth, who married Nicholas Wade, q.v.; and Thomas, who married (1) Hannah Newberry and (2) Mary (Miles) Ince.

HATHERLY, TIMOTHY—One of the London Adventurers, he was a felt maker of St. Olaves, Southwark, Surrey (see John Irish). He visited Plymouth in 1623, but came as a settler in 1632 on the *William and Mary*, residing at Scituate, where the General Court had given him large land allotments. He was frequently an Assistant, apparently one of the liberal ones, as is shown in the text. He was notable for his opposition to the persecution of the Quakers. He died childless, but the line was carried on via his sister Eglin Hatherly, q.v., who also lived in Scituate. See also Pope. He died 24 October 1666. His will, dated 12 December 1664, proved 30 October 1666, named his wife Lydia (widow of Nathaniel Tilden); Edward Jenkins, his wife and children (his niece's family); Nicholas Wade, his wife and children (another niece's family); Susanna, wife of William Brooks, and children (niece); Timothy and Elizabeth Foster (niece's children); Thomas Hanford (nephew); Fear, the wife of Samuel Baker, and the other three children of Isaac Robinson, John, Isaac, and Mercy (children of a deceased niece); Lydia Garrett, his wife's daughter, and her four children; George Sutton, his wife and children; the wife of William Bassett, his wife's daughter; widow Preble, his wife's daughter; Lydia Lapham; Thomas Lapham; Stephen Tilden; Nicholas Baker; "my man Thomas Savory"; and Lydia Hatch, daughter of William Hatch; with his friend Joseph Tilden as executor (*MD* 16:158).

HEARD, WILLIAM—William Heard arrived at Plymouth in 1623 and received one share in the 1623 land division. He does not appear in the 1627 cattle division.

HEDGE, WILLIAM—William Hedge is stated to have been the son of Elisha and Ann (Ward) Hedge of Northamptonshire (*NEHGR* 111:319). He settled first in Lynn, where he became a freeman in 1634 (Savage). He moved to Sandwich, and on 5 November 1638 he sold the remaining term of his servant Robert Wickson to Gov. Thomas Prence for £12 (*PCR* 1:102). In 1638 he was fined for keeping a hog unringed (*PCR* 1:107). In 1640 he received fourteen acres of meadow land in Sandwich which was granted to some sixty people according to quality and estate of the grantee and condition of the land. Only six other grantees received as much or more land as he. (*PCR* 1:149-50). By 1643 he had moved to Yarmouth (*PCR* 2:62). In 1648/49 he was presented by the grand jury for letting an Indian have a gun, powder, and shot, and for receiving stolen goods, but he was cleared on both counts (*PCR* 2:137), and in 1650 was chosen constable of Yarmouth (*PCR* 2:153). In 1652 he was presented for selling wine and strong waters without a license (*PCR* 3:17), and in 1658 he was fined ten shillings for threatening to have the blood of Edward Sturges (*PCR* 3:150). It appears that he may have been associated with Sturges in keeping an ordinary, for after this date Hedge is in the records for approval to bring large amounts of liquor into Yarmouth, sometimes with Edward Sturges (*PCR* 4:28, 52). He also served at times as a grandjuror (*PCR*, passim). In 1653 he became ensign of Yarmouth's military company, and in 1659 he became its captain (*PCR* 3:38, 169). Because of vagaries in the spelling of names, he is easy to confuse with William Hedges (or Hedge, Hodges) of Taunton, though when the name is preceded by "Mr." it is usually William of Yarmouth. Savage and Torrey give him an unidentified first wife, and Savage calls his second wife Blanch (_____), widow of Tristram Hull, who had died 20 December 1666. Hedge dated his will 30 June 1670, inventory taken 15 July 1670, and he bequeathed to sons Abraham, Elisha, William, John, and Lemuel, and daughters Sarah Matthews, Elizabeth Barnes, Mary Sturges, and Mercy. He also named his beloved sister Brooks in Virginia and his deceased brother Brooks. He gave his wife Blanch twelve pence plus what he had received of hers because she "hath dealt falcly with with mee in the Covenant of Marriage in Departing from mee" (*MD* 18:252).

HEWES, JOHN—John Hewes (the surname could probably also be Hughes) was taxed at Plymouth in 1633 and 1634. On 1 April 1633 he and his wife Joan were sentenced to sit in the stocks for having a child conceived before matrimony (*PCR* 1:12). He was probably the Goodman Hewes who had one of the nine houses existing at Scituate before Lothrop's arrival in late 1634, and he built another house there in 1636 (*NEHGR* 10:42). In 1650 he was accused of stealing and in 1652 he became a highway surveyor for Scituate (*PCR* 2:160, 3:32). He was on a jury in 1653 and became a constable for Scituate in 1659 (*PCR* 3:28, 163). He was joined by wife Joan in a 1654 deed where he was identified as "Sr." (*MD* 15:179). The will of John Hewes of Scituate was dated 6 February 1671, sworn 22 February 1674; he named his wife "Joanna," son John Hewes, and son-in-law Jeremiah Hatch (*MD* 34:112; Pope is wrong in calling the son James Hewes.) His daughter was Mary Hewes, who married Jeremiah Hatch on 29 December 1657 (*MD* 2:34).

HICKS, EPHRAIM—A son of Robert and Margaret, Ephraim was apparently born after their arrival at Plymouth; see article under Robert Hicks. Ephraim married Elizabeth Howland, q.v., but died three months later.

HICKS, LYDIA—A daughter of Robert and Margaret; Lydia arrived in 1623 with her mother on the *Anne*. Lydia later married Edward Bangs, q.v. See the article under Robert Hicks.

HICKS, MARGARET—Margaret Hicks arrived at Plymouth in 1623 on the *Anne* with her children Samuel and Lydia to join her husband Robert, q.v. In her will dated 8 July 1665, exhibited 6 March 1665/66, the widow Margaret Hicks of Plymouth named her son Samuel Hicks, daughter-in-law Lydia Hicks, son Samuel's seven children, grandchild John Bangs, and the children of her loving deceased daughter Phebe, who had married George Watson (*MD* 16:157-58).

HICKS, ROBERT—He arrived in 1621 on the *Fortune*. Banks called him a fellmonger of Bermondsey and Southwark, County Surrey. Robert S. Wakefield, "The Children of Robert Hicks," *TAG* 51:57, shows that Hicks had at least nine children. See also R. G. Rider, "More on the Robert Hicks Ancestry: Clues to the Identity of his Spouse," *TAG* 54:31, which should be read with a bit of caution. His wife was Margaret Hicks, q.v. Some interesting background is given on Hicks in the deposition of Clement Briggs of Weymouth, fellmonger, taken at New Plymouth 29 August 1638. Briggs said that about twenty-two years earlier he was dwelling (and working for) Mr. Samuel Latham in Bermondsey Street, Southwark, London, and a Thomas Harlow was dwelling with (and working for) Mr. Robert Hicks. Harlow and Briggs often discussed how many pelts their masters pulled a week. Hicks pulled 300 a week and sometimes 600 or 700, and he sold his sheep's pelts for forty shillings a hundred to Mr. Arnold Allard, whereas Mr. Samuel Latham sold his to the same man for fifty shillings a hundred, even though Mr. Hicks's pelts were better ware (*PCR* 12:35). In Plymouth, Hicks recorded with the court on 13 July 1639 a release whereby Thomas Heath of London, cooper, on 13 July 1619 had acquitted Robert Hicks, formerly a citizen and leatherseller of London, of all debts, including £180 pounds which Hicks had owed Heath (*PCR* 12:43). Hicks died at Plymouth 24 May 1647, and in his will, dated 28 May 1645, inventory 5 July 1647, he named his wife Margaret, oldest son Samuel, son Ephraim, grandson John Bangs, John Watson, and a number of nonrelative Plymouth residents (*MD* 8:143).

HICKS, SAMUEL—A son of Robert and Margaret, Samuel arrived at Plymouth in 1623 on the *Anne* with his mother. He later married Lydia Doane, daughter of John Doane, q.v. See the article under Robert Hicks. On 7 June 1661 the General Court noted that there were differences between Samuel Hicks and his mother Margaret Hicks, widow, arising from the will of his father Robert Hicks, and also about some goods of his younger brother Ephraim. Samuel agreed to pay his mother £10 in full satisfaction of all differences, and he also promised that in case he left Plymouth he would not put anyone in the house who would be injurious or offensive to his mother (*PCR* 3:206, 217).

HILAND, THOMAS—Elizabeth French, "Genealogical Research in England—Hyland," *NEHGR* 66:61, takes Thomas Hiland's family back several generations in England, where he was baptized at Waldron, Sussex, 23 April 1604. He later moved to Tenderden, Kent, where his first five children were born. The baptism of his daughter Annah on 17 January 1635/36 is the last record of him in England. His wife Deborah _____ accompanied him to New England. He was on Reverend Lothrop's list of homeowners in Scituate in 1637 as Goodman Hyland (*NEHGR* 10:43), and he was one of twenty-one men who took the Oath of Fidelity at Scituate 1 February 1638/39. In 1646 he was a grandjuror (*PCR* 2:102), and in the same year he was one of three grandjurors fined twenty shillings each for not attending court (*PCR* 2:110). In 1648 he was chosen, but not sworn in, as a constable for Scituate (*PCR* 2:124). In 1648 he bought a one-thirtieth share in Mr. Hatherly's tract of land at Scituate (*PCR* 12:158). A document of June 1650 has Mary Lapham, widow (see under Nathaniel Tilden), acknowledging that her husband Thomas Lapham had sold during his lifetime to Thomas Hiland a house and one-half acre of land in Tenterden, County Kent (*PCR* 12:194). On 7 June 1653 Thomas Hiland, Sr. and Thomas Hiland, Jr. started legal action against Mr. Charles Chauncy, Mr. Anthony Eames, Samuel Jackson, and John Saffin, but later acknowledged that they had defamed these men by doing so, and at Mr. Chauncy's request the acknowledgment was recorded (*PCR* 3:46).

In a will dated 14 February 1682/83, inventory 3 May 1683, Hiland mentioned his son Thomas; grandson Thomas, son of son Thomas; John, brother of his grandson Thomas; his four daughters Elizabeth James, Sarah Turner, Mary Bryant, and Deborah Tichnor; his grandson Philip James, son of Francis James of Hingham; Isabel Witherell, sometime wife to his son Samuel, but now wife to Samuel Witherell; his grandson Benjamin Bryant, son of his daughter Mary Bryant; his granddaughter Elizabeth Bryant; his grandson Joseph Studson; and his daughter Studson (who was not necessarily living at the time). He left to his heirs his house at Waldron in old England and his house at Tenterden in Kent. He also mentioned "All my right in the undivided land in Scituate as I am an ancient Planter coming in by order and all that is wanting, to make up my accommodations, that by order of Court of right belongs to me" (*Ply. Colony PR* 4:2:33). His son Thomas married Elizabeth Stockbridge, daughter of John Stockbridge, q.v. Grandson Thomas, who died in the 1690 Canadian expedition, predeceased his father (*MD* 30:71). The testator Thomas Hiland also had daughters Annah and Ruth who were not mentioned in his will, and Miss French in the *NEHGR* article suggests that Ruth might have been the mother of his grandson "Joseph Studson" (more usually spelled Stetson), and Torrey has Ruth Hiland married to a Joseph Stetson (see under Robert Stetson).

HILL, JOHN—In a letter from Governor Bradford to Governor Winthrop dated 6 February 1631, John Hill is mentioned as one who moved from Plymouth Colony to the Bay Colony (*MD* 9:1-3).

HILTON, WILLIAM—William Hilton arrived at Plymouth in 1621 on the *Fortune*, and received one acre for himself in the 1623 land division, while his wife and two children, who arrived in 1623, were given an additional three acres. The children were probably William, Jr. and Mary Hilton (*MQ* 40:58). The family did not appear in the 1627 cattle division, and most likely they had left Plymouth in the aftermath of the Lyford confrontation. Hubbard, *General History*, p. 93-94, wrote about the Lyford troubles that "some of their [Lyford and Oldham] friends yet surviving do affirm, upon their own knowledge, that both. . .were looked upon as seemingly, at least, religious: and that the first occasion of the quarrel with them was, the baptizing of Mr. Hilton's child, who was not joined to the church at Plymouth." The baptizing would have been done by Lyford.

Hilton and his family moved north of Plymouth, and not long after he joined his brother Edward Hilton, who headed the small group of traders at Piscataqua (*Bradford [Ford]* 2:175). William Hilton is known for writing several letters, one of which was written to England from New Plymouth in November or December 1621, and in this letter he highly praised the new colony, "We found all our friends and planters in good health. . .the Indians around us peaceable and friendly, the country very pleasant and temperate . . .I know not any thing a contented mind can here want" (*Bradford [Ford]* 1:240).

HINCKLEY, SAMUEL—His English origins are shown by Elizabeth French, "Genealogical Research in England—Hinckley," *NEHGR* 65:287, 314, 68:186). He was of Tenterden, Kent, and came to New England in the *Hercules* in March 1634/35, accompanied by his wife Sarah and four unnamed children. He lived in Scituate, but apparently did not become a member of Lothrop's church, for only his wife is shown as having joined, being recorded as "Goody Hinckley" on 30 August 1635. They had a daughter Elizabeth baptized at Scituate 6 September 1635 (*NEHGR* 9:281-82). Samuel became a freeman 2 January 1637/38, and on the same date he was a trial juror (*PCR* 1:74). On 4 December 1638 he was among several men of Scituate who were presented for receiving strangers into their houses without license from the government (*PCR* 1:106). On 4 June 1639 he was a grandjuror (*PCR* 1:126). Since his son Samuel was baptized at Barnstable on 24 July 1642 (*NEHGR* 9:282), it would appear that he accompanied Lothrop in the move there. On 5 June 1644 he was a high-way surveyor for Barnstable (*PCR* 2:72), a position he held many times. He dated his will 8 October 1662, proved 4 March 1662/63, and he named his wife Bridget (second wife, Bridget Bodfish); sons Thomas, Samuel, and John; daughters Susanna, Sarah, Mary, and Elizabeth; his son Thomas's children Samuel, Mary, Thomas, Bathsheba, and others unnamed; and Samuel and Jonathan Cobb, sons of his daughter Cobb; and he named son Thomas executor and son-in-law Henry Cobb overseer (*MD* 12:203).

HINCKLEY, THOMAS—The last governor of Plymouth Colony, he was the son of Samuel Hinckley, q.v. Thomas married (1) Mary Richards 7 December 1641 (*MD* 6:98) or 4 December 1641 (*PCR* 8:44) and (2) Mary Glover 16 March 1659/60. *PCR* 8:44 also gives his children as Mary, Sarah, Meletiah, Hannah, Samuel, Thomas, Bathsheba, and Mehitabel, and, by his second wife, Admire and Ebenezer.

HOLMAN, EDWARD—Edward Holman arrived at Plymouth on the *Anne* in 1623. Banks thought he came from Clapham, County Surrey. He was in both the 1623 and 1627 divisions, and he was a Purchaser, but, strangely, he was not made a freeman. Pope thought he had returned to England in the early years and that he was identical with the Edward Holman who embarked from England for New England on 22 June 1632. On 26 August 1636 he charged John Jenney with refusing to pay him for a gun Holman lost while in Jenney's service, but the court acquitted Jenney (*PCR* 1:43). On 4 October 1636 Holman was fined twenty shillings for breaking the Sabbath (*PCR* 1:44). In 1637 he was a volunteer for the Pequot War (*PCR* 1:61). On 30 November 1640 John Barnes was ordered to to repay six shillings he wrongfully took from Holman in a land transaction, and on the same day Holman and Barnes made an agreement in court, Holman paying Barnes twenty shillings and promising to deliver a boat to Plymouth of of which he had sold a one-third part to Barnes (*PCR* 1:167-68). Holman and three others were ordered to answer charges that they had taken goods from a shipwreck, and on 4 January 1641/42 he confessed that he had taken canvas to make a main sail, a pair of drawers, a waistcoat, and a shirt (*PCR* 2:29, 31). On 9 June 1653 he was fined for being drunk. On 2 February 1657/58 John Barnes complained that Holman entertained Barnes's servant, John Wade, and took him to Duxbury in Holman's boat without Barnes's consent. The court found Holman faulty on this and similar past charges, and fined him ten shillings (*PCR* 3:126). He was fined ten shillings on 2 March 1657/58 for telling a lie in court (*PCR* 3:129). On 10 June 1661 he was fined ten shillings for being convicted of drunkenness a second time (*PCR* 3:222).

Holman was an original purchaser of land at Dartmouth on 7 March 1652/53 (*MD* 4:187-88). On 4 January 1661/62 he sold one-half of his land at Dartmouth to Hugh Cole (*MD* 16:208), and on 31 January 1664/65 he sold one-half of his remaining half share to Richard Kerby of Sandwich (*Ply. Colony LR* 3:48). On 17 June 1667 Edward Holman of Plymouth, a seaman, sold his one-fourth lot of land at Dartmouth to Mr. John Almy of Portsmouth, Rhode Island (*Ply. Colony LR* 4:287). Edward Holman of Plymouth, a seaman, confirmed on 23 April 1675 a sale of land at Manomet Pond that he had sold to Thomas Clarke, then of Plymouth, twenty-eight years earlier (*Ply. Colony LR* 4:21).

Holman married Amy (Glass) Willis before 17 April 1644 (*PCR* 12:113). She was baptized at Taunton, Somerset, 10 December 1618, daughter of James and Mary (Cogan) Glass, and widow of Richard Willis (*NEHGR* 111:177) – the article gives Edward and Amy a son Edward, born in 1647, but this could be based on a misreading of *Plymouth Col. LR* 4:21, and there is no evidence that they had children. On 24 January 1648/49 Holman put out his stepson Richard Willis, age seven, as an apprentice weaver with Gyles Rickard, and it would seem that Amy Holman was dead by this time (*PCR* 12:157). On 4 May 1652 the court ordered Holman not to visit the house of Thomas Shrive, and ordered Shrive and his wife not to visit Holman's house, and on 9 June 1653 Holman and Martha Shrive were ordered not to keep company with each other or they would be whipped (*PCR* 3:6, 37).

It would not seem that Edward Holman would be related to the more prosperous John Holman, gentleman, of Dorchester in the Bay Colony; however, there is at least a link via married John Holman married Anne Bishop, whose sister Abigail Bishop married Henry Cogan, q.v. (*NEHGR* 111:175). Henry Cogan's sister Mary (Cogan) Glass was the mother of Amy (Glass) Willis, who married (2) Edward Holman. John Holman was apparently from the general area of Bridport, Dorset, for he gave his father-in-law Thomas Bishop a power of attorney to collect rents for him in the parish of Swyre, Dorset (Pope).

HOLMES, JOHN – John Holmes arrived at Plymouth before 16 October 1632, when he bought a house and six acres of land from William Palmer (*PCR* 12:18). In 1638 he was appointed Messenger of the Court, and his duties included being summons server, jailer, and executioner. His wife was probably Sarah Holmes, and he had two sons, John Holmes, who married (1) Patience Faunce, daughter of John and Patience (Morton) Faunce and (2) Patience Bonham, daughter of George and Sarah (Morton) Bonham; and Nathaniel Holmes, who married Mercy Faunce, sister of Patience Faunce. Both sons had large families, and thus there are many descendants. The first four generations of this family are given by Eugene A. Stratton, "The Descendants of Mr. John Holmes, Messenger of the Plymouth Court," in the June and September 1986 issues of *NGSQ*.

HOLMES, JOHN – For mention of Rev. John Holmes of Duxbury, see under William Holmes, below. He married Mary Atwood daughter of John Atwood (also called Wood) of Plymouth 11 December 1661 (*PCR* 8:23). Vinton, *Giles Memorial*, pp. 184-85, observes that this John Atwood should not be confused with the Plymouth Colony Assistant. Holmes succeeded Ralph Partridge as minister of the Duxbury Church. He had studied at, but not graduated from, Harvard College. He died 24 December 1675, and in his will he named his wife Mary, and children Joseph, Mary, and Isaac (*Ply. Colony PR* 3:1:169); he named his trusty and beloved friends, John Alden, Constant Southworth, and Josiah Standish, as overseers.

HOLMES, OBADIAH – Obadiah Holmes is shown in the text as a persecuted baptist minister sometimes associated with Rehoboth and also Salem, but he lived most of his New England years in Rhode Island. His English origins as the son of Robert and Katherine (Johnson) Hulme, baptized at Didsbury, Lancashire, 18 March 1609/10, are given by J. T. Holmes, "The English Ancestry of Rev. Obadiah Holmes," *NEHGR* 64:237. He married Katherine Hyde. Edith May Tilley, "The Will of Rev. Obadiah Holmes, With a Few Extracts From His Manuscripts," *NEHGR* 67:21, shows that he dated his will at Newport, Rhode Island, 9 April 1681 sworn 4 December 1682. A family history is given by J. T. Holmes, *The American Family of Reverend Obadiah Holmes* (1915).

HOLMES, WILLIAM – There were two contemporary William Holmeses in Plymouth Colony, one of whom was Maj. William Holmes, the leader of the Plymouth forces in the Pequot War. He died at Boston 12 November 1649, and in his will he named Margaret, Mary, Rachel, and Bathsheba Holmes, daughters of his deceased brother Thomas Holmes, and Thomas's widow Margaret Webb, alias Holmes – thus it appears he left no direct descendants (see Pope; Vinton, *Giles Memorial;* and *MD* 14:153). Vinton, devotes a major section of the *Giles Memorial* to the descendants of the other William Holmes, who lived in Scituate, and Vinton speculated that he might have been a nephew of Maj. William Holmes, but it would seem strange for a childless man not to mention a nephew who lived that close in his will. William of Scituate married an Elizabeth _____, and in his will dated 4 March 1677/78, proved 25 February 1678/79, he named his sons Israel, Isaac, Josiah, and Abraham, and daughters Elizabeth, Mary, Sarah, and Rebecca, and he also mentioned all his (unnamed) grandchildren. He does not mention a son John, but Vinton in a footnote, p. 184, believed that there was a good case for Rev. John Holmes being a son of William and Elizabeth Holmes, showing that a grant of land was made to Rev. John Holmes at Pinquine-hole in Sandwich "in the right of his father," a strong indication that his father lived in Plymouth Colony. Vinton also noticed that Rev. John Holmes named a son Isaac (and William Holmes had a son Isaac). For these reasons, Vinton includes the descendants of Rev. John Holmes with the descendants of the other children of William Holmes. The Vinton material is good, but some errors have been corrected in the Stratton article mentioned above under Messenger John Holmes.

HONEYWELL, WILLIAM – On 25 July 1633 William Honeywell contracted to serve Thomas Prence as an apprentice for seven years, at the end of which time Prence would give him twenty-five acres of unmanured land and twelve bushels of corn (*PCR* 1:16). Though this time was extended because Honeywell at various times absented himself from service, Prence agreed on the last day of February 1639/40 to release him from the contract on consideration of his working some acres Prence owned in return for half the crop. Honeywell would stay with Thomas Atkinson, whom Prence would pay for room and board (*PCR* 1:139-40). On 1 June 1641 Honeywell was granted the land due him for his service (*PCR* 2:16). On 6 March 1665/66 William Honeywell was tried on suspicion of buggery with a beast, but denied it, and there being insufficient evidence, he was freed (*PCR* 4:116). No record has been found of his having a wife or children in Plymouth Colony.

HOPKINS, CONSTANCE – A daughter of Stephen Hopkins, q.v., Constance accompanied him on the 1620 *Mayflower* to Plymouth, and later married Nicholas Snow, q.v.

HOPKINS, DAMARIS – A daughter of Stephen Hopkins, q.v., Damaris was with him on the 1620 *Mayflower*, and she died at Plymouth during the early years. The Damaris Hopkins who married Jacob[2] Cooke, son of Francis, was a second daughter of that name born in Plymouth almost certainly after the death of the first Damaris. Bowman, in the article cited under Stephen Hopkins, gives the indirect evidence for this conclusion.

HOPKINS, ELIZABETH – The wife of Stephen Hopkins, q.v., Elizabeth's maiden name was probably Fisher. She accompanied Hopkins on the 1620 *Mayflower*.

HOPKINS, GILES – A son of Stephen Hopkins, q.v., Giles came to Plymouth with his father on the 1620 *Mayflower*, and on 9 October 1639 he married Catherine Wheldon (*PCR* 1:134; *MD* 13:85). The will of Giles

Hopkins of Eastham, dated 19 January 1682/83, codicil 5 March 1688/89, proved 16 April 1690, mentioned his wife "Catorne," and sons Stephen, William, Caleb, and Joshua (*MD* 1:110). *MD* 7:236-37 gives the births of his children, as later recorded at Eastham, as Mary, November 1640; Stephen, September 1642; John, 1643 (died at age of three months); Abigail, October 1644; Deborah, June 1648; Caleb, January 1650/51; Ruth, June 1653; Joshua, June 1657; William, 9 January 1660/61; and Elizabeth, November 1664 (died one month old).

HOPKINS, OCEANUS—A son of Stephen Hopkins and his wife Elizabeth, q.v., Oceanus was born on the 1620 *Mayflower* while at sea—hence the first name. He died without issue before the 1627 division.

HOPKINS, STEPHEN—He most likely was the Stephen Hopkins who sailed on the *Seaventure* to Virginia in 1609, but was shipwrecked in Bermuda, where he was almost hanged for mutiny. He spent two years in Jamestown, where he learned much of later use to the Plymouth colonists (*Adventurers of Purse and Person—Virginia 1607-1625*, ed. by Annie Lash Jester with Martha Woodroof Hiden, 2nd ed. (1964), p. 213-17). See also the excellent account of his family in *Dawes-Gates* 2:443-51, which includes the reasoning for believing that the Stephen Hopkins of Virginia was identical with the one of Plymouth.

Hopkins arrived at Plymouth on the 1620 *Mayflower* accompanied by his wife, Elizabeth, and his sons Giles and Oceanus, and daughters Constance and Damaris, Oceanus having been born at sea on the *Mayflower*, plus two servants, Edward Doty and Edward Leister. Damaris died during the early years, and Hopkins and his wife later had a second daughter Damaris. He was probably also one of the dissenters at Plymouth whose actions led to the necessity for drafting the Mayflower Compact. *Bradford (Ford)* 1:219, and *Mourt's Relation*, p. 40, tell how in 1621 the colonists sent Mr. Edward Winslow and Mr. Stephen Hopkins on a mission to visit Massasoit. *Mourt's Relation*, pp. 7-8, also shows how Hopkins warned colonists on an early expedition about an Indian trap to catch deer, and how Bradford, not hearing the warning, stepped on the trap and was immediately caught by his leg. When Samoset first came to the settlement on 16 February 1620/21, the Englishmen were suspicious of him, and they "lodged him that night at Steven Hopkins house, and watched him" (*Mourt's Relation*, p. 33). Hopkins was an Assistant at least as early as 1633, and he continued in 1634, 1635, and 1636. He was on the original freeman list, and he was a volunteer in the Pequot War (*PCR* 1:61).

Keeping in mind the delicate balance in Plymouth between "covenant" and "noncovenant" colonists, it is reasonable to assume that Hopkins must have been a leader of the non-Separatist settlers, and in his career at Plymouth can be seen some of the ambiguity that attached to the non-Separatists living in a Separatist colony. On 7 June 1636, at a time when Hopkins was an Assistant, the General Court found him guilty of battery against John Tisdale, and he was fined £5, and ordered to pay Tisdale forty shillings, the court observing that he had broken the King's peace, "wch he ought after a speciall manner to have kept" (*PCR* 1:42). On 2 October 1637 he was presented twice, first for suffering men to drink in his house on the Lord's day before meeting ended, and for allowing servants and others to drink more than proper for ordinary refreshing, and second for suffering servants and others to sit drinking in his house contrary to orders of the court, and to play at shovel board and like misdemeanors (*PCR* 1:68). On 2 January 1637/38 Hopkins was presented for suffering excessive drinking in his house "as old Palmer, James Coale, & William Renolds" (*PCR* 1:75). On 5 June 1638 he was presented for selling beer for two pence a quart which was not worth a penny a quart, and for selling wine at excessive rates "to the oppressing & impovishing of the colony"; he was fined £5 for some of these offenses, including selling strong waters and nutmegs at excessive rates (*PCR* 1:87, 97). In the Dorothy Temple case (see text) he was "committed to ward for his contempt to the Court, and shall so remayne comitted untill hee shall either receive his servant Dorothy Temple, or els pvide for her elsewhere at his owne charge during the terme shee hath yet to serve him" (*PCR* 1:112). On 3 December 1639 he was presented for selling a looking glass for sixteen pence which could be bought in the Bay Colony for nine pence, and he was also fined £3 for selling strong water without license" (*PCR* 1:137). Jonathan Hatch, who from the records seems to have been a recurring disciplinary problem in the colony, on 5 April 1642 was ordered by the court to dwell with Mr. Stephen Hopkins, "& the said Mr Hopkins to have a speciall care of him" (*PCR* 2:38).

He dated his will 6 June 1644, inventory 17 July 1644, and mentioned his deceased wife; sons Giles and Caleb; daughter Constance, wife of Nicholas Snow; daughters Deborah, Damaris, Ruth and Elizabeth; and grandson Stephen, son of his son Giles (*MD* 2:12). Ralph D. Phillips, "Hopkins Family of Wortley, Gloucestershire—Possible Ancestry of Stephen Hopkins," *TAG* 39:95, suggests that he might have come from the parish of Wotten-under-Edge, Gloucestershire, but the evidence is not sufficient to say positively. Some writers, such as Banks in *English Ancestry*, pp. 61-64, and Jacobus in *Waterman Family*, 1:86, have felt that his wife, Elizabeth, may have been Elizabeth Fisher, whom a Stephen Hopkins married at London 19 February 1617/18—*Mourt's Relation*, p. 15, states that he was of London. If so, she would have been a second wife, for the births of some of his children would predate this marriage. *Dawes-Gates* 2:443, citing the London marriage record, states that his wife was "undoubtedly" Elizabeth Fisher. Timothy Hopkins, "Stephen Hopkins of the Mayflower and Some of His Descendants," *NEHGR* 102:46, 98, 197, 257, 103:24, 85, 166, 304, 104:52, 123, 213, 296, 105:32, 100, covers some of his early generations, but it is not documented. George E. Bowman wrote an article in *MD* 5:47 to consolidate much of the early information known about his family. A popularized biography of Stephen Hopkins was written by Margaret Hodges, *Hopkins of the Mayflower—Portrait of a Dissenter* (New York, 1972). Claims that a John Hopkins of Hartford, Connecticut, was his son are baseless. By his first wife he had Constance, who married Nicholas Snow, and

Giles, who married Catherine Wheldon. By Elizabeth Fisher he had the Damaris, who died young; Oceanus, who died young; Caleb, who died at Barbados as an adult without issue; Deborah, who married Andrew Ring; the second Damaris, who married Jacob Cooke, son of Francis; Ruth, who died without issue; and Elizabeth, who died without issue (*Dawes-Gates*, 2:449).

HOUSE, SAMUEL—One of the original members of the Scituate Church on 8 January 1634/35 (*NEHGR* 9:279), Samuel House was probably in the Lothrop group that had just arrived at Scituate. J. Gardner Bartlett shows in *NEHGR* 66:357 that Samuel House of Scituate, a shipwright, in 1649 made Thomas Tarte of Scituate his attorney to represent him regarding the will of Thomas House of London, watchmaker. According to Bartlett, a competent genealogist, House, or Howse, was the son of Rev. John Howse. Samuel was a brother to Hannah House, the first wife of Rev. John Lothrop. Samuel married at Scituate ca. 1635 an Elizabeth, daughter of William and Elizabeth (Paine) Hammond of Watertown, Massachusetts. He was with the Lothrop group at Barnstable, but later returned to Scituate. His inventory was taken there in 1661 (*MD* 15:59). Bartlett also observes that Thomas House of Yarmouth may have been a brother of Samuel House.

HOWLAND, ARTHUR—A brother of 1620 *Mayflower* passenger John Howland, q.v., Arthur Howland arrived in Plymouth much later. The first mention of him in New England records is in *Lechford's Notebook*, p. 297-99, where he is described in 1640 as a Duxbury planter. Robert S. Wakefield and Robert M. Sherman, "Arthur Howland of Plymouth, Mass. 1640, and his Wife Margaret (_____) Walker, and Their Children," *NGSQ* 71:84, give a comprehensive presentation of his family, including his children Deborah, Mary, Martha, Elizabeth, and Arthur, together with what is known about the grandchildren. It was son Arthur who married Elizabeth Prence and acquired a somewhat reluctant father-in-law, Gov. Thomas Prence (see text). Arthur, Sr. is mentioned in Plymouth records as a Quaker. He was buried at Marshfield 30 October 1675. See also George E. McCracken, "The Will of Arthur Howland, Senior, of Marshfield," *NEHGR* 104:221.

HOWLAND, HENRY—A brother of 1620 *Mayflower* passenger, John Howland, Henry Howland was in Plymouth at least as early as 25 March 1633, when his name appears on the tax list, and he was also on the original freeman list. On 8 April 1633, Walter Harris had his indenture transferred to Henry Howland (*PCR* 1:13). On 5 January 1635/36 Henry became the constable of Duxbury (*PCR* 1:36). He was frequently a member of trial and grand juries (*PCR*, passim). On 3 June 1657 he, John Tompson, Morris Truant, Ralph Allen, and Thomas Greenfield refused to serve on the grand jury (*PCR* 3:115). On 2 March 1657/58, the same day his brother Arthur was fined £4 for permitting a Quaker meeting in his house and £5 for resisting the constable of Marshfield in the execution of his office, Henry Howland was fined ten shillings for entertaining a meeting in his house contrary to court orders (*PCR* 3:129). On 7 June 1659 the court, referring to an order disenfranching Quakers and other offenders, gave notice to four men to appear in court the following August, and on 6 October 1659 Howland had his freeman status taken away from him (*PCR* 3:167, 176). On 1 May 1660 Henry Howland was charged with entertaining another man's wife in his house after her husband had complained to him, and for permitting a Quaker meeting in his house and entertaining a foreign Quaker. He stiffly denied the first charge, and the court noted that the evidence "did not appeer to make it out," but he was convicted on the Quaker charges. On the same day Lt. Samuel Nash complained against Howland for stopping up a highway (*PCR* 3:186). On 2 October 1660 he was fined £4 for twice having Quaker meetings at his house (*PCR* 3:201). On 3 June 1668 he was a highway surveyor for Duxbury (*PCR* 4:181). He made his will 28 November 1670, inventory 14 January 1670/71, and he named his wife Mary (her surname is not known; they were possibly married in England), his sons Zoeth, Joseph, John, and Samuel, and his daughters Sarah, Elizabeth, Mary, and Abigail (*MD* 19:32). An article by Robert S. Wakefield and the late Robert M. Sherman, "Henry Howland of Duxbury, Mass., 1633, His Children and His Grandchildren," will appear in a forthcoming issue of *NGSQ*.

HOWLAND, JOHN – The son of Henry Howland of Fenstanton, Huntingdonshire, John came to Plymouth on the 1620 *Mayflower* as a servant to John Carver. After the death of Carver, he rose rapidly as a leader in the colony. In 1627 he was the head of one of the twelve companies which divided the livestock, and he was one of the eight Plymouth Undertakers who assumed responsibility for the colony's debt to the Adventurers in return for certain monopoly trade privileges. He was on the 1633 freeman list, and by 1633, if not earlier, was an Assistant, being reelected to this position in 1634 and 1635 (*PCR*, passim). In 1634 he was in charge of the colony trading outpost on the Kennebec River when Talbot and Hocking were killed (see text). He received a good number of land grants, was elected a deputy for Plymouth, served on numerous special committees, and was an important lay leader of the Plymouth Church. The Reverend John Cotton related how at his own ordination as pastor of the church in 1669 "the aged mr John Howland was appointed by the chh to Joyne in imposition of hands" (*Ply. Ch. Recs.* 1:144). Howland died on 24 February 1672/73 in his eightieth year, and John Cotton noted his passing, "He was a good old disciple, & had bin sometime a magistrate here, a plaine-hearted christian" (*Ply. Ch. Recs.* 1:147; see also Nathaniel Morton's eulogy in the text).

John Howland married, probably ca. 1626, Elizabeth Tilley, q.v. In his will, dated 29 May 1672, inventory 3 March 1672/73, he mentioned his wife Elizabeth; oldest son John Howland; sons Jabez and Joseph; youngest son Isaac; daughters Desire Gorham, Hope Chipman, Elizabeth Dickenson, Lydia Browne, Hannah Bosworth, and Ruth Cushman; and granddaughter Elizabeth Howland, daughter of his son John (*MD* 2:70). His widow

Elizabeth died at the home of her daughter Lydia Browne, wife of James, at Swansea on 21 December 1687, and in her will, dated 17 December 1686, proved 10 January 1687/88, she said she was seventy-nine years old, and mentioned her sons John, Joseph, Jabez, and Isaac; daughters Lydia Browne, Elizabeth Dickenson, and Hannah Bosworth; son-in-law Mr. James Browne; and grandchildren James Browne, Jabez Browne, Dorothy Browne, Desire Cushman, Elizabeth Bursley, and Nathaniel the son of Joseph Howland (*MD* 3:54). Franklyn Howland, *A Brief Genealogical and Biographical History of Arthur, Henry, and John Howland and their Descendants. . .* (New Bedford, Mass., 1885), contains many errors. It is debatable whether John Howland or John Alden has the greatest number of descendants living today, but certainly the number of both is high. Elizabeth Pearson White, former editor of the *Mayflower Quarterly*, is compiling a comprehensive family history of the first five generations of John Howland's family.

HURST, JAMES—Davis (2:64) states that Henry Cobb married James Hurst's daughter Patience in 1631, which would have Hurst arriving in Plymouth between 1627 and 1631. Cobb's first child by his wife Patience was born 7 June 1632, which would tend to confirm a 1631 marriage (*PCR* 8:42). Dexter, p. 617, shows that a Jacob Hurst was living in Leiden, Holland, in 1609 and 1622, and Jacob is the Dutch form of James. This Jacob was a linen-weaver, and he had a wife Margaret, children Isaac, Mary, and Silvester, and a maid, but he was "too poor to be taxed." The name Hurst can be associated indirectly with Leiden another way, for the wife of 1620 *Mayflower* passenger John Tilley was Joan Hurst of Henlow, Bedfordshire, and *Bang's Pilgrims*, p. 16, shows that John Masterson, a Leiden Separatist who stayed behind, also came from Henlow, Bedfordshire. It is clear that in Plymouth James Hurst had a wife named Garteud or similar, for his will of 10 December 1657, inventory 24 December 1657, named his wife "Garteud" and his grandchildren John Cobb, Gershom Cobb, James Cobb, Eliezer Cobb, Mary Dunham, Hannah Cobb, and Patience Cobb (*MD* 14:228). On 30 May 1670 an inventory taken of the property of "Gartherew" Hurst, widow, deceased, was exhibited by John Cobb, who referred to "Grandmother Hurst," and she owned half a share in a cow in the hands of Gershom Cobb (*MD* 18:251). Hurst was a deacon of the Plymouth Church, as is shown by a deed dated 21 March 1647/48 (*PCR* 12:153; see also text). He was on the 1633 freeman list, and he frequently served on juries and committees (*PCR*). There is no known relationship between James Hurst and a contemporary William Hurst who was living in Sandwich.

HURST, JOAN—The wife of John Tilley, Joan accompanied him on the 1620 *Mayflower*, and they died soon after arrival at Plymouth. She is shown by the Ward articles, cited under John Tilley, to have been the daughter of William, and probably Rose, Hurst of Henlow, Bedfordshire. She had earlier been widowed from a Thomas Rogers, but this was not the *Mayflower* Thomas Rogers.

IRISH, JOHN – An indenture dated 20 April 1629 between John Irish of the parish of Clisden, County Somerset, England, laborer, and Timothy Hatherly of the parish of St. Olave, County Surrey, feltmaker, bound Irish as a servant to Hatherly for five years at Plymouth, New England; besides board and lodging, Irish was to receive £5 per annum and at the expiration of his term of service was to receive twenty-five acres of land and twelve bushels of wheat (*Bristol County, Mass. LR* 2:120). Willis and Stella Irish, *Descendants of John Irish, The Immigrant, 1629-1963, and Allied Families* (Freeport, Maine, 1964), a good, though not sufficiently documented family history, on p. 11 assumes that John Irish arrived on the *Talbot*, which is reasonable, since that ship was known to be carrying servants for Plymouth. In 1634 at Kennebec, he was one of the four men sent by John Howland to cut the moorings of Hocking's boat at the time when Moses Talbot was killed (*MD* 2:11). In 1637 he was one of the volunteers in the war against the Pequots (*PCR* 1:61). Moving to Duxbury, Irish and Henry Wallis made a covenant that the survivor of them would get the other's five acres of land by Stony Brook in Duxbury; in 1641 the court gave him, as survivor, such land (*PCR* 2:12-13). Duxbury town records of 1639 show that the people of Duxbury promised William Hiller and George Pollard certain concessions for setting up a grist mill on Stony Brook, and one concession was to "do our best endeavours to procure the lands of John Irish and Henry Wallis," offering them an exchange elsewhere, or to give Hiller and Pollard £6 toward the purchase of same (*PCR* 12:73). On 11 June 1641 John Irish gave his ten acres at Stony Brook to Hiller and Pollard for Hiller's house and garden lot (*PCR* 12:74). On 5 March 1643/44 the court ordered that John Irish was to have his twenty-five acres of land, due for his service, made up by Duxbury men, for it had been agreed that such servants promised land by covenant would have it provided for by the towns where they lived (*PCR* 2:69).

Apparently Irish did not get the land in Duxbury, and on 29 September 1658 the court ordered that John Irish of Duxbury could search out land according to his indenture, with Constant Southworth to help him find it (*PCR* 3:149). His name was on the 1662 list of former servants and ancient freemen to be granted land at Saconett Neck (*PCR* 4:18). There is no record that he ever became a freeman of Plymouth Colony. Although no will was found, the court on 5 March 1677/78 ordered a division of the land owned by John Irish, deceased, at Saconett, which he had "bequeathed" to his two sons, John, Jr. and Elias (*PCR* 5:252); however, from the same court records it appears that son Elias had died earlier, for on 30 October 1677 William Witherell of Taunton (Elias's wife Dorothy's father) was given the administration of his estate (*PCR* 5:247), and it is the same William Witherell who was given the divided share of Elias, who is called William Witherell's "child." John Irish, Jr. became constable in Middleborough in 1672, and in Saconett in 1678 (*PCR* 5:91, 265). The Irish family history states that John, Sr. married Elizabeth Risley ca. 1640, but the authority for her surname is not known. That his wife's name was Elizabeth is shown by a deed of 7 December 1659 whereby John Irish of Duxbury, roper, sold Guydo Bayley land in Bridgewater (*MD* 14:91). The Irish family history has John Irish, Jr. marrying (1) Elizabeth Savory and (2) Priscilla (Southworth), widow of Samuel Talbot and daughter of Edward and Mary (Pabodie) Southworth of Duxbury; a clue toward finding contemporary support for the marriage to Priscilla Southworth may come from Mrs. Charles L. Alden, "Alden Genealogy," *NEHGR* 54:181, where she states that on or about 17 February 1719/20 Col. Benjamin Church "'went on a visit to the only surviving sister' of his wife, Priscilla (Southworth) [Talbot] Irish, wife of John Irish, who lived in Little Compton"—See also Robert S. Wakefield, "The Children and Purported Children of Richard and Elizabeth (Warren) Church," *TAG* 60:138-39. The Irish family history gives John [1] Irish two daughters, Elizabeth Irish and Lydia Irish, stating that Lydia married a _____ Gray, and they made their home in France (but no evidence or reason for this is given). Daughter Elizabeth married Philip Washburn (evidence is given under his name).

JACKSON, ABRAHAM—Abraham Jackson was born probably in England ca. 1623-28, based on his being admitted to the Plymouth Church on 14 March 1708, when he was said to be "upwards of eighty years of age" (*Ply. Ch. Recs.* 1:207). Savage stated that he was an apprentice to Nathaniel Morton. The earliest mention of him in the records was when he married Remember (or Remembrance) Morton on 18 November 1657 (*MD* 17:72). That she was the daughter of court secretary Nathaniel Morton is shown by *Ply. Co. LR* 5:231, where on 16 February 1703/04 Abraham and Remember Jackson sold land to Benjamin Warren that they had received of their honored father Nathaniel Morton. There is another 1657 record showing that Jackson had taken the Oath of Fidelity that year and was a resident of Marshfield (*PCR* 8:178). In 1661 the guns and swords of Plymouth were disposed of, including a short gun and a sword given to Nathaniel Morton for the use of Abraham Jackson (*PTR* 1:44). There were other Jacksons in early Plymouth, such as Samuel of Scituate and Thomas, but there is no indication of any relationship with Abraham. Abraham was admitted a freeman on 1 June 1658 (*PCR* 3:136). On 7 May 1662 the court heard his complaint that Rose, wife of Thomas Morton, had called him a lying rascal and rogue, and she confessed her fault and promised to be more careful of her words (*PCR* 4:11). On 3 June 1662 he became a constable of Plymouth (*PCR* 4:14). He frequently served on juries, and sometimes was a surveyor of the highways for Plymouth (*PCR, PTR*, passim).

In 1665 he was ordered to pay eight shillings to William Nelson to end a controversy about the keeping of two sheep (*PCR* 4:105). One of his occupations was producing and selling tar, and in 1665 he was fined £5 for ruining several barrels of tar by putting dirt in them (*PCR* 4:111). On 6 March 1665/66 the court allowed Giles Rickard, Jr. ten shillings from Abraham Jackson concerning a controversy between them over a parcel of tar, and on 1 May 1666 the court heard a complaint by Jackson that Nathaniel Warren detained a barrel of tar delivered by Jackson for town use

(*PCR* 4:117, 120). On 1 June 1669 he petitioned the court to remit his forfeiture of three barrels of tar to the government for breaching a law prohibiting the making of tar, and the court, referring to his poor condition and many losses, ordered that he should have seven bushels of corn paid for by the treasurer (*PCR* 5:21). He obtained various grants of land in the Plymouth area (*PTR* 1:45, 48, 53, 61, 94, 127), and he bought and sold land on a number of occasions (*PTR*, *PCR*, passim). He lived near the north side of Town Brook, as is shown by a deed of 1689 whereby John Cole sold land there to William Shurtleff excepting a parcel forty by fifty feet which was the house and land of Abraham Jackson (*MD* 32:36). His wife Remember died on 24 July 1707 in her seventieth year (*Ply. Ch. Recs.* 1:205), and Abraham died on 4 October 1714 (*MD* 16:84). He left descendants living in Plymouth, and Lydia Jackson, a nineteenth century descendant, became the second wife of Ralph Waldo Emerson, the marriage taking place in the house which now serves as the headquarters of the General Society of Mayflower Descendants in Plymouth.

JENNEY, JOHN – John Jenney arrived at Plymouth in 1623 on the *Little James* with his wife Sarah and children Samuel, Abigail, and Sarah. Captain Altham of the *Little James* (*Three Visitors*, p. 24) noted that "Good wife Jennings was brought abed of a son aboard our ship." Banks called Jenney a cooper of Norwich, County Norfolk, but Leiden records of his 1614 marriage to Sarah Carey, of Monk's Soham, County Suffolk, call him a brewer's man from Norwich (Dexter, p. 619), and Winslow also called him a brewer and noted that he was among those Englishmen in Holland who could speak Dutch and would sometimes take communion in the Dutch Church (*Hypocrisie Unmasked*, p. 63). He owned a grain mill in Plymouth, and he was a Purchaser, but not an Undertaker, as has been written. He was one of the colony's leaders, however, serving as an Assistant. After he and his wife died, his family moved to Dartmouth, with which the name Jenney became associated. See the article in *TAG* 35:70 by Bertha Clark, whose excellent manuscript on the Jenney family is at NEHGS in Boston. Also of interest is the account given of the Jenney family in *Small Descendants* 2:646; see also Frederick G. Jenny, "John Jenny," *NEHGR* 115:233. John's son Samuel, apparently the son born on the *Little James*, married Susanna Wood; daughter Sarah married Thomas Pope as his second wife; and daughter Abigail married Henry Wood and lived in Yarmouth and Middleborough (see Bowman, "Mistress Sarah Jenny's Will and Inventory," *MD* 8:171). In John Jenney's will, dated 28 December 1643, he cautioned, "Whereas Abigaile my eldest Daughter had somewhat given her by her grandmother and Henry Wood of Plymouth aforesaid is a suter to her in way of marriage my will is that if shee the said Abigaile will Dwell one full yeare wth mr. Charles Chauncey of Scittuate before her marriage (pvided he be willing to entertaine her) that then my said Daughter Abigall have two of my cowes and my full consent to marry wth the said Henry Wood" (*MD* 6:170); however, the marriage took place four months later on 28 April 1644 (*MD* 13:86).

KEMPTON, EPHRAIM—On 7 March 1642/43 Ephraim Kempton, Sr. of Scituate was fined twenty shillings for unclean speeches and carriages toward Mr. Hatherly (*PCR* 2:54). Kempton apparently arrived at Plymouth with his son, Ephraim, Jr., for on 4 June 1645, following the death of Ephraim, Sr., the court noted that Ephraim, Jr. and his father had labored together in partnership "since their comeing over into this countrey," and therefore Ephraim, Jr. owned one-half of their joint property, with the other one-half to be considered the estate of Ephraim, Sr. (*PCR* 2:85). Direct evidence is lacking of a relationship between Ephraim Kempton and Manasseh Kempton, but on 28 October 1645 Manasseh Kempton and the younger Ephraim were appointed administrators of the property of Ephraim, Sr., the court noting that Manasseh was owed £21 from the estate (*PCR* 2:89), and on 30 October Manasseh joined Ephraim, Jr. at the latter's request as a surety for Ephraim, Sr.'s estate (*PCR* 12:125). There is thus a suggestion of a relationship, and possibly Manasseh and Ephraim, Sr. were brothers. Ephraim, Jr. married on 28 January 1645/46 Joanna Rawlings, daughter of Thomas Rawlings (*PCR* 8:17), and they had Joanna, Patience, Ephraim, and Manasseh (*PCR* 8:18). Ephraim, Jr. died in 1655 (*PCR* 8:49). Pope is wrong in attributing four children to Ephraim, Sr., for it was in the settlement of the estate of Ephraim, Jr. on 8 June 1658 that four minor children (only one, Ephraim, by name) were mentioned (*MD* 12:213).

KEMPTON, MANASSEH—Arriving at Plymouth in 1623 on the *Anne,* Manasseh Kempton was originally from Colchester, County Essex, England. He was listed erroneously as "Manasseh & John Fance" in the 1623 land division, but there was no Manasseh Faunce. By the 1627 division he was married to Juliana (Carpenter), q.v., widow of George Morton (evidence of her identity is found in *PCR* 12:204, where in a deed of 22 February 1650/51 Kempton refers to his "sons" Ephraim, Nathaniel, and John Morton). He did not leave any known descendants, and these three were his stepsons. He died 14 January 1662/63, having done "much good in his place the time God lent him" (*PCR* 8:23), and his widow Juliana, age eighty-one, died 19 February 1664/65, "a faithfull servant of God" (*PCR* 8:25). See also Ephraim Kempton.

KING, SAMUEL—The son of William and Judith (Cogan) King, Samuel King was born in England ca. 1619, and he came to Plymouth with his mother and her second husband, Giles Rickard (Mrs. John E. Barclay, "Samuel King Family of Plymouth, Plympton and Halifax, Mass.," *TAG* 30:11), probably in 1637, as one of the three children traveling with Giles and Judith (*NGSQ* 71:176). Mrs. Barclay showed that he married Anne Finney, and in her article she gave additional details on their four children. Samuel King died in August 1705 (*Ply. Ch. Recs.* 1:201).

LANGFORD, RICHARD—Richard Langford died at Plymouth 14 September 1633, and his inventory included a one-half interest in a boat, another one-half interest in a canoe, corn in the field, and many smaller items (*MD* 1:83-86). There is nothing in the records to show that he left a wife or children.

LANGMORE, JOHN – A 1620 *Mayflower* passenger, John Langmore traveled as a servant to Christopher Martin and died in the early months after reaching Plymouth (*Bradford [Ford]* 2:399, 405). He left no known issue.

LATHAM, WILLIAM – A 1620 *Mayflower* passenger, he was described by *Bradford (Ford)* 2:399, 401-02, as a servant boy, who after more than twenty years in Plymouth went to England and from there to the Bahamas, where he died with others for lack of food. He is shown in *Lechford's Notebook* (p. 421) in 1641 as "William Latham of Duxbury, planter aged about 32 yeares." He shared in the 1627 Division of Cattle, and he was on both the 1633 and the 1634 tax lists. On 5 June 1638 he was fined forty shillings for entertaining John Phillips in his house contrary to law (*PCR* 1:87). On 6 July 1638 John Phillips gave his share of a corn crop he had with William Latham to William Reynolds in exchange for half of a black heifer (*PCR* 12:31). On 5 November 1638 Latham was charged with drunkenness (*PCR* 1:101). On 26 December 1639 William Latham of Duxbury, planter, sold his house, twenty acres of land, and one acre of meadow to Mr. Ralph Partridge (*PCR* 12:54). On 4 June 1645 Roger Cooke and William Latham charged that John and Ann Barker burned their house by accident to the damage of £20, but the jury could not give a verdict, and Barker paid them twenty shillings toward their losses (*PCR* 7:41). There is no indication in the records that Latham married or had children, and no relationship is known to the other Lathams in New England (such as Cary Latham in Cambridge and the Robert Latham who arrived later to reside at Marshfield).

LEE, TRYPHOSA – She was the wife of Stephen Tracy, q.v.

LEISTER, EDWARD – A 1620 *Mayflower* passenger, Edward Leister was called by Bradford (*Ford* 2:400, 411), a servant of Stephen Hopkins who "after he was at liberty, went to Virginia, and ther dyed." See also Edward Doty, a fellow servant with whom he had a duel.

LETTICE, THOMAS – He is first mentioned in the records on 7 March 1636/37 when Francis Cooke brought charges against Thomas Lettice, James Walker, John Browne the younger, and Thomas Teley, who being in the service of John Browne the elder and Thomas Willet, who were also charged, abused Cooke's cattle; he was awarded £3 damages and thirteen shillings six pence for costs (*PCR* 7:5). In several actions of 1641 against James Luxford, Thomas Lettice (twice) and other complainants were awarded property belonging to Luxford which was in the hands of others. (*PCR* 7:25, 27). On 2 December 1639 William Fallowell, Robert Finney, John Finney, and Thomas Lettice were assigned garden places near Webb's Field (*PCR* 1:136). Thomas Lettice became a freeman in 1654 (*PCR* 3:48). In 1659 he brought charges against Thomas Pope for abusive carriages at the mill at Plymouth, and Pope was fined ten shillings to the use of the colony (*PCR* 3:173). Lettice served at times on juries and as surveyor of highways (*PCR*, passim). In 1651 a John Lettice was constable for Plymouth (*PCR* 2:167), but this may have been a clerical error for Thomas Lettice, since John Lettice is otherwise unknown (except for an error in the index of *PCR* 3, where in the text Thomas Lettice served on a 1660 coroner's jury (*PCR* 3:196), but was indexed as John Lettice). Thomas bought a house and seven acres of land in Plymouth from Thomas Cushman on 24 March 1641 (*PCR* 12:77), and on 27 August 1679 he was living on New Street (now called North Street) in Plymouth (*PCR* 6:161).

Savage thought he might have been the Thomas Lettyne, age twenty-three, who appears in Hotten, p. 60, as sailing for New England in the *Elizabeth* on 15 April 1635, but there is no way to confirm or refute this. In his will dated 1678, confirmed by him 25 October 1681, and sworn October 1682, Lettice named his wife Anne, and his daughters Anne, wife of Samuel Jenney; Elizabeth Cooke, widow; and Dorothy, wife of Edward Gray (*MD* 14:64). His son Thomas died 3 November 1650 (*PCR* 8:11). His daughter Elizabeth married (1) 18 October 1655 William Shurtleff (*PCR* 8:17) (2) Jacob Cooke, son of *Mayflower* passenger Francis Cooke, as his second wife and (3) Hugh Cole, as his second wife (*PCR* 8:32; *MD* 13:204.

LITTLE, THOMAS — Thomas Little first appears in Plymouth records on the 1633 tax list. On 19 April 1633 he married Ann Warren, daughter of *Mayflower* passenger Richard Warren and his wife Elizabeth (*PCR* 1:13). On 7 October 1633 Little sold his dwelling house to Richard Higgins for twenty-one bushels of corn (*PCR* 1:16). On 28 May 1635 he made a gift of land to his brother-in-law Robert Bartlett (*PCR* 1:34). On 12 March 1638/39 William Taylor (son of William Taylor of Boddington, County Cornwall, carpenter) transferred his indenture with the consent of all from Mr. John Atwood to Thomas Little (*PCR* 1:119). Little moved to Marshfield, where he became constable on 3 June 1662 (*PCR* 4:15). He bought farm land in Marshfield which had belonged to Maj. William Holmes, deceased, and on 3 June 1662 the court ordered that in view of his many improvements of the land, if anyone should show better title in the future, such person would have to pay him fully for his improvements (*PCR* 4:16). On 9 June 1665 he was fined £1/10 for not keeping secret the proceedings of the grand jury, of which he was a member (*PCR* 4:101). When he refused to pay rents claimed by Mrs. Rachel Davenport for the land of the late William Holmes, the court on 1 May 1666 awarded her £15, which, because of his improvements, was less than she had claimed (*PCR* 4:119). On 14 August 1672 administration of the estate of Thomas Little of Marshfield was given to his widow, Anna Little (*PCR* 5:101). His will dated 12 May 1671, inventory 4 April 1672, mentioned his wife; his sons Isaac, Ephraim, Thomas, and Samuel; his grandson John Jones; and his servant Sarah Bonney (*MD* 4:161). His son Thomas died in King Philip's War at Rehoboth, and in his will (*MD* 4:164) we learn that his father Thomas also had daughters Ruth, Hannah, Patience, and Mercy. The younger Thomas died without having married. The senior Thomas Little also had a daughter Abigail, who married Josiah Keene and predeceased her father (*MD* 8:191-92, 19:128, 28:5-6).

LOMBARD, BERNARD – The name is also seen as Lumbart, Lumbert and similar variations. Bernard Lombard was born probably at Thorncombe, Dorset, ca. 1608. On 20 February 1668/69 he deposed that he was about age sixty (*MD* 17:109). Bernard was the son of Thomas Lombard, q.v., and much of the information below is from Robert S. Wakefield, "The Lombard Family of Barnstable, Mass.," *TAG* 52:136-39. Bernard was first at Dorchester with his father. Moving to Plymouth County, he lived at Scituate, where he and his wife joined Lothrop's church 19 April 1635; he had a house at Scituate by 1636, and his daughter Mary was baptized there 8 October 1637 (*NEHGR* 10:42, 9:279, 281). He became a Plymouth freeman 3 January 1636/37 (*PCR* 1:48). In 1639 he moved to Barnstable with the Lothrop group. On 10 October 1643 the court ordered that if the townsmen of Barnstable did not appoint a place for their defense, it would have Mr. Thomas Dimmack, Anthony Annable, Henry Cobb, Henry Cogan, and Bernard Lombard do it (*PCR* 2:65). On 2 June 1646 Bernard Lombard was on the grand jury (*PCR* 2:102), a position he held a number of times. On 5 October 1652 he was approved by the court as ensign for the Barnstable military company (*PCR* 3:17). On 9 June 1653 Gyles Rickard was presented for lascivious carriage toward Mary Lombard, the daughter of Bernard Lombard (*PCR* 3:36). His children were Thomas, who married Elizabeth Derby; Abigail (also called Abia), who married James Claghorn; Mary, who married George Lewis; Martha, who married John Martin; and Jabez, who married Sarah Derby. In his 1668/69 deposition, Bernard called William Clark of Yarmouth "Father Clarke" and testified to Clarke's nuncupative will leaving everything he had to Joseph Benjamin, Bernard's brother-in-law (*MD* 17:109).

LOMBARD, THOMAS – The Wakefield article (see Bernard Lombard above) shows that Thomas Lombard was baptized at Thorncombe, Dorset, 2 February 1581/82, the son of Thomas Lombard. He had a brother, Bernard, baptized there 2 July 1580, but the Bernard found in New England records is Thomas's son. Thomas married more than once, perhaps three times, and had children by at least two wives. He probably came to New England on the *Mary and John*, settling at Dorchester, where he appears on Dorchester records, including the baptism of his son Jobaniah on 23 June 1639, and thus he arrived in Plymouth Colony several years after his son Bernard. On 3 December 1639 Thomas was licensed to keep an ordinary and sell wine at Barnstable for entertaining strangers, provided that he would keep order in the house (*PCR* 1:137). He was a surveyor of the highways for Barnstable on 6 June 1649 (*PCR* 2:139). The court ordered on 2 October 1660 that since Jedidiah, the son of Thomas Lombard, Sr., had acted stubbornly against his father, Jedidiah, with the consent of his father, could place himself with some other honest and godly family, if he could do so, but if he did not, then Mr. Hinckley would so dispose of him (*PCR* 3:201).

On 7 March 1664/65 administration of the estate of Thomas Lombard was given to his widow, Joyce, and his sons Jedidiah and Caleb (*PCR* 4:81).

His will, dated 23 March 1662/63, inventory 8 February 1664/65, mentioned his wife; his sons Caleb, Jedidah, Benjamin, Bernard, and Joshua; his sons-in-law Joseph Benjamin and Edward Coleman; his daughters Margaret Coleman and Jemima; and his granddaughter Abigail Benjamin (*MD* 16:124). Three sons predeceased him: two sons named Thomas baptized at Thorncombe, one of whom must have died young. The other, who came to New England with him, appeared on the 1643 ATBA list, and died without known issue, before his father made his will; and Jobaniah, who died young. Son Joshua married Abigail Linnel; Jedidiah married Hannah Wing; Benjamin married (1) Jane Warren (2) Sarah Walker, and (3) widow Hannah Whetstone; and Caleb, whose wife's name is unknown. Daughter Margaret married Edward Coleman, and Jemima married Joseph Benjamin. Additional information on the Lombard family can be found in the Amos Otis Papers, which are not well documented.

LONG, ROBERT—Robert Long arrived at Plymouth in 1623 and was in the 1623 land division sharing three acres of land with Patience Brewster and Fear Brewster. He was not in the 1627 division.

LOTHROP, JOHN—E. B. Huntington, *A Genealogical Memoir of the Lo-Lathrop Family in This Country Embracing. . ."* (Ridgefield, Conn., 1884), is a well presented family history, especially for John Lothrop's life in England and America. Lothrop's family can be traced back a number of generations in England, and his own baptism is recorded at Etton, Yorkshire, 20 December 1584. He graduated from Cambridge University with a B.A. in 1605, and M.A. in 1609. He became curate of the church at Egerton, County Kent from ca. 1611 to 1623. In 1623 he was called to succeed Rev. Henry Jacob (who had left for Virginia) at the First Independent Church in Southwark, Surrey. Independent worship being illegal, Lothrop's services were conducted in secret. In 1632 he was imprisoned, but released on bail in 1634. Nathaniel Morton (*New Englands Memoriall*, p. 140-41) relates some of his background, including the death of his first wife in England. Huntington, p. 25, quotes from Governor Winthrop's *Journal* under date of 18 September 1634 "The Griffin and another ship now arriving with about 200 passengers. Mr. Lathrop and Mr. Sims, two godly ministers coming in the same ship." That same year Lothrop went to Scituate, where he formed the first church there, and then in 1639 the church divided and Lothrop went with the group that settled at Barnstable, becoming minister there, too. His records of some activities and events at Scituate and Barnstable are in *NEHGR* 9:279-87, 10:37-43; also see text. Two of his letters of 1638 to Governor Prence mention in rather vague terms the forthcoming move from Scituate (Huntington, p. 28-32). One of the letters is also signed by Anthony Aniball, _____ (no doubt Henry) Cobb, and _____ (no doubt Isaac) Robinson "In behalf of the church." He became a freeman on 7 June 1637 (*PCR* 1:60).

He married (1) Hannah House (sister of Samuel House, q.v.) and (2) Ann _____, who has variously been thought to be a Hammond or a Dimmock; since his son Barnabas was born 6 June 1636, he married his second wife probably in 1635 (see Torrey, and Wakefield, *Marriages*). His will (*MD* 11:42) dated 10 August 1653, inventory 8 December 1653, names his sons Thomas, John (in England), and Benjamin and daughters Jane and Deborah; "to the rest of my Children both mine and my wives my will is that every of them shall have a Cow." His children were to have a choice of one of his books each, and the rest were to be sold, with the money divided among them. Some of his lands were to be sold, with the money to be divided among the children "that have the least portions." The wording of the will is unfortunate, for it leaves open the question as to how many children survived him. There is a possibility he may have been the father of Elizabeth, the unwanted wife of John Williams, q.v. *PCR* 4:107 shows that on 3 October 1665 "Mr. Barnabas Laythorpe hath seen cause, in the behalfe of his sister [Elizabeth Williams] and those related to her, to revive the former complaint [against John Williams]." For reasons too lengthy to give in detail, Barnabas Laythorpe could only be the son of Rev. John Lothrop, and sister in this context could only mean blood sister or sister-in-law. Since Barnabas's wife was Susanna Clark, daughter of Thomas Clark, q.v., and there was no Elizabeth in the Thomas Clark family, the term probably meant blood sister. Otis/Swift, *Barnstable Families*, devotes some fifty pages to Lothrop and his descendants, but is not well documented. See also *NEHGR* 84:437.

LUCE, HENRY — A "Harke" Luce is on the 1643 ATBA for Scituate, but no relationship is known. Henry Luce served on a jury 31 October 1666 to divide land in Scituate (*PCR* 4:139). Banks in his *History of Martha's Vineyard* 3:246-47, states that Henry was born ca. 1645 and brought up in Wales; he married Rebecca Munson, and settled in Martha's Vineyard, being the immigrant ancestor of the numerous Luce family found in Martha's Vineyard and elsewhere. Banks also wrote that Henry and Harke Luce were from Horton, Gloucestershire, and settled first at Scituate. Whether Banks is entirely or partly wrong on Henry Luce cannot be determined; however, it is certain that Henry Luce's wife was Remember, daughter of Lawrence and Judith (Dennis) Litchfield of Scituate. A court order of 27 October 1674 required Josias Litchfield "without any further delay" to make payment to his sisters Remember Lewes and Dependance Litchfield from the estate of his brother Experience Litchfield (*PCR* 5:154). The will of William Dennis (*MD* 14:113), dated 16 February 1649/50, proved 5 March 1656/57, names his daughter Judith (then remarried to William Peaks) and Remember Litchfield, Dependance Litchfield, and Experience Litchfield, all under age and unmarried; the will of William Peaks (*Ply. Colony PR* 4:2:41), dated 31 October 1682, declaring that he was first "penitant, and Sorry from the botome of my hart for my Sines past," names his sons Israel, Eleazer, and William; wife (Judith); "daughter-in-law [stepdaughter] Dependance Litchfield;" and "Grandchildren experience Luce and Remember Luce," two of the children of Henry and Remember Luce — see also Gerald James Parson, "The Will of William Dennis of Scituate, Mass.," *TAG* 33:153. Further information on the Litchfield family can be found in Wilford J.

Litchfield, *The Litchfield Family in America* (2 vols., 1901, 1906), and on the Henry Luce family in Martha McCourt, *The American Descendants of Henry Luce*, (rev. 1984), both of which are insufficiently documented. The Luce family reentered the Plymouth area via Ebenezer [3] Luce, son of William Luce and his wife Ann Crosby (daughter of Rev. Thomas Crosby, q.v.), who married Sarah [4] Doty (great-granddaughter of *Mayflower* passenger Edward Doty) and had children at Rochester—see Stratton, "The Elusive Luces—A Doty Line," *MQ* 47:23.

LYFORD, JOHN—In a letter to Bradford dated 24 January 1623/24, Robert Cushman informed him that the Adventurers were sending over a preacher, "an honest plaine man, though none of the most eminente and rare," whom the colonists could chose as their pastor at their discretion. Cushman said that he and Winslow "gave way" to sending Lyford "to give contente to some hear, and we see no hurt in it, but only his great charge [expense] of children" (*Bradford [Ford]* 1:357-58). That there was in fact some hurt in it can be seen from the text. After being expelled from Plymouth, Lyford went to Nantasket, then Cape Ann, and finally moved to Virginia, where he died. An English minister who had also lived in Ireland, Lyford apparently wanted to practice Anglican rites at Plymouth, and one of the marks the Plymouth authorities had against him was his baptism of the child of William Hilton, who was not a member of the Plymouth Church (Hubbard, *General History*, p. 92-94, 102, 107; *Bradford [Ford]* 1:416-23). After Lyford's death, his widow Sarah married Edmond Hubbard of Hingham. Savage gave Lyford four children, but only three are known, Ruth, who married James Bate (*Suffolk Deeds*, 1:27); Obadiah, a clergyman who died a young man in Ireland; and Mordecai, who at the age of about fourteen in 1639 chose his stepfather Edmond Hubbard as his guardian. Edmond Hubbard, his wife Sarah and Mordecai Lyford were involved in legal matters regarding lands that John Lyford left in Ireland, and Sarah Hubbard, sometime wife of John Lyford, was described as age about fifty-three in 1639 (*Lechford's Notebook*, p. 140-42). Morton in *New Englands Memoriall*, p. 53-61, gives additional details on Lyford's objectionable activities at Plymouth, including an assertion that Lyford's wife, fearing God's judgment, related to the Plymouth colonists that Lyford had had a bastard child by another woman, and following another similar incident he had been forced to leave Ireland, and so came to New England.

MANLOVE—see MENDLOVE.

MANN, RICHARD—The name of Richard Mann is first recorded on a list of 15 January 1644/45 of thirty-two Scituate men who had taken the Oath of Fidelity (*PCR* 8:183). However, the 1643 ATBA for Scituate contains a first name Richard without a surname, and considering all those known to be there both immediately before and after the ATBA, it is most likely that this was Richard Mann. He was one of the twenty-six men buying the Hatherly tract in 1648, and he was described in the deed as a planter (*PCR* 12:158). On 16 February 1655/56 a coroner's jury found that Richard Mann drowned by falling through the ice as he walked over a pond beside his house (*PCR* 3:92-93). On 6 May 1656 administration of his estate was given to his wife (*PCR* 3:98). His wife was Rebecca _____, who married (2) 31 March 1656 John Corwin, or Cowen (*MD* 2:33). The fact that Mann's first known child, Nathaniel, was born 25 September 1646 might indicate that he married Rebecca in New England. Their other children were Thomas, born 15 August 1650; Richard, born 5 February 1652/53; and Josiah, born 10 December 1654 (*Scituate VR* 1:242-43). On 5 July 1670 the court settled a case between John Cowin and Nathaniel Mann about the house and land in Cowin's possession which by right belonged to Nathaniel Mann since his becoming of age, and Cowin was allowed to retain the house five more years on payment of rent to Mann (*PCR* 5:44-45). On 30 October 1671 Thomas Mann and Richard Mann, for Josiah Mann and themselves, acknowledged receipt of their portions of the estate of their father Richard Mann from their "father-in-law" (stepfather) John Cowin (*PCR* 5:174). (As an interesting aside, John Cowin, a Scot, was tried in 1671 for speaking contemptible words against the royal dignity of England, in that he said he scorned to be in subjection to any Englishman; however, the jury found him not guilty [*PCR* 5:54, 61]). Of Richard Mann's children, only Thomas and Richard are known to have had issue. Eugene A. Stratton, "Mann-Ensign Notes," *TAG* 61:46, shows some evidence that Richard Mann may have come from Cornwall, and also some evidence that Thomas [2] Mann's wife, Sarah _____, was the daughter of Thomas and Elizabeth (Wilder) Ensign. A good family history for its time was George S. Mann, *Mann Memorial, A Record of the Mann Family in America* (Boston, 1884). Robert S. Wakefield, "Additions and Corrections to Austin's Genealogical Dictionary of R.I.," *TAG* 52:168, corrects an earlier article by G. Andrews Moriarty (*TAG* 27:220, 39:2) in which Moriarty erroneously identified a Thomas Mann of Rehoboth as the son of Richard Mann of Scituate. Deane, *Scituate*, identified Richard Mann with *Mayflower* passenger Richard More, but they were in fact two individuals.

MARTIN, CHRISTOPHER – Christopher Martin, a leader of the "Strangers," represented the Adventurers and was governor of the *Mayflower* in 1620 when it first sailed, possibly continuing in this position after the *Speedwell* had to stay back in England, or possibly relinquishing the position of governor of the *Mayflower* to Carver (see text). He acted as purchasing agent at Southampton, but could not account for the money entrusted to him. Bradford wrote, "He so insul[t]eth over our poore people, with shuch scorne and contempte, as if they were not good enough to wipe his shoes. It would break your hart to see his dealing." Bradford said he came from Billerica, County Essex, and he brought with him his wife and two servants, Solomon Prower and John Langmore. He died on 8 January 1621, and Bradford wrote that "he and all his, dyed in the first infection" (*Ford* 1:117, 118 [fn], 128, 136 [fn], 142, 144, 2:399, 405). His death probably eliminated a source of much potential trouble in the delicate life of the new colony. R. J. Carpenter, *Christopher Martin, Great Burstead and The Mayflower* (Chelmsford, Essex, 1982), a fourteen-page pamphlet, gives some of his background in County Essex, and notes that he left a son Nathaniel in England. He is shown in Essex as engaging in Puritan activities—see the book review in *MQ* 49:144.

MARTIN, possibly MARIE—The wife of Christopher, she sailed on the 1620 *Mayflower* and died in the early months of the colony. She has been called Marie Prower, a widow who married Martin, and one of Martin's servants was Solomon Prower, who was also called her son and Martin's stepson (Banks, *English Ancestry*, p. 70).

MASTERSON, RICHARD—A Separatist, Richard Masterson was recorded at Leiden as a woolcarder from Sandwich, England. He had been a surety for Robert Cushman in buying a house in Leiden. He married 23 November 1619 Mary Goodale. There was also a John Masterson living in Leiden, who married in 1633 Catherine Lisle, but it is not known if they were related (Dexter, p. 624-25). He came to Plymouth in 1629 or 1630, and he died in the 1633 sickness, being noted by Bradford as one of their ancient friends from Holland (*Bradford [Ford]*, 2:171). His widow Mary married Rev. Ralph Smith, and in 1649 as Mary Smith, sometime wife of Richard Masterson, she made over to her son Nathaniel Masterson and her daughter Sarah, wife of John Wood, her interest in a house in Leiden that had belonged to her deceased husband (*PCR* 12:176-77). Along with Francis Jessopp, Thomas Nash, Thomas Blossom, and Roger White, Masterson had been one of the signers of a letter dated 30 November 1625 from Leiden to Bradford and Brewster in which they said sadly that if they were to rejoin their brethren in Plymouth, it would have to be accomplished by the means of the Plymouth group (*Bradford Letter Book*, p. 21). Nathaniel Morton called Masterson one of the deacons of the Leiden Church who had given part of his estate for the good of the Separatists (*Ply. Ch. Recs.* 1:83).

MAY, DOROTHY—The first wife of Gov. William Bradford, q.v., Dorothy May crossed the sea with him on the 1620 *Mayflower*, but drowned at Cape Cod on 7 December 1620 (George E. Bowman, "Governor William Bradford's First Wife Dorothy May Bradford Did Not Commit Suicide," *MD* 29:97, and "Dorothy May's Death," *MD* 31:105). In her marriage intention at Amsterdam in November 1613, she gave her age as sixteen, and thus would have been born ca. 1597. Charles Hervey Townshend, "Dorothy May and Her Relations," *NEHGR* 50:462, calls her the daughter of John and Cordelia (Bowes) May of Wisbech, Cambridgeshire—however, see below. David H. Kelley, "A Royal Line from Edward I to Dorothy May Bradford of Plymouth, Mass.," *TAG* 46:117, 47:87 (erroneously attributed to another in *TAG* 46, and corrected in *TAG* 47), constructs a royal line for her, which he acknowledges needs more evidence, but aside from that is dependent on Dorothy being the daughter of Cordelia Bowes, the wife of John May, and this is not yet a proven fact.

Though we know little of her, she is a classic example of why secondary sources must be used very cautiously. The story of her supposed suicide was first made by Jane Goodwin Austin, "William Bradford's Love Life," *Harper's New Monthly Magazine*, June 1869, long, long after the facts or after the story could have been accurately transmitted by oral history. Even such a careful historian as Samuel Eliot Morison seems to have been taken in by this hoax, for in *Bradford (Morison)*, p. xxiv, he writes, "It may be that [Bradford] suspected (as we do) that Dorothy Bradford took her own life, after gazing for six weeks at the barren dunes of Cape Cod." It should be noted that the *Mayflower* first landed at Cape Cod on 11 November 1620, and Dorothy May drowned on 7 December 1620 (Bowman, *MD* 29:99 from Rev. Thomas Prince from Bradford's "register" and Mather's *Magnalia*). She hardly had the chance to gaze on those barren dunes for six weeks. Bowman meticulously analyzed every contemporary scrap of information available, concluding that there was no evidence to support Mrs. Austin's story. That should have been sufficient, but two years later Bowman was able to add to his debunking of this strange tale. In *MD* 31:105, Bowman writes of his discovery that in the 1892 revision of her article, Mrs. Austin confessed that her youth "perhaps in the first flush of delight and surprise" at contemplating the "romance" of Plymouth history, may have been under a "certain fermentation of fancy, suggesting rather what 'might have been,' than what is known to have been. Certainly , the author recalls with rather rueful mirth the reproof received from an aged relative who, after vainly inquiring for 'the documents in the case' of William Bradford, remarked: 'You have no right to defraud people by pretending to have what you have not.' "

In the Townshend article we find, "In a letter to Governor Bradford from Roger White, a brother-in-law of the Rev. John Robinson, written from Holland in December 1625, mention is made of John May, your (Governor Bradford's) 'father-in-law.' " In *Bradford (Ford)* 1:396-97 (fn) we find, "Bradford gave an account of these troubles to his father-in-law, Henry May, which produced some hesitation among those at Leyden about going. Roger White speaks of. . .your letter to your father-in-law, Mr. May." Well, now, which was her father, John May or Henry? Both writers seem to be basing their information on contemporary facts. How do we find what the facts were? Again, we refer to Mr. Bowman, who, in *MD* 9:115-17, gives both the original Dutch language and the English translation of the Bradford-May marriage intentions: "geassisteet met herrij Maijr" and "assisted [a better translation would be attended] by Henry May." So there is nothing here to say that Henry May was her father; he could have been a brother, or cousin, or, conceivably, an unrelated May. Bowman was also responsible for the reprinting of *Bradford's Letter Book*, where, on p. 20, we find the Roger White letter, and the pertinent part "your letter to your father-in-law, Mr. May." No first name appears in the letter. Nowhere in the contemporary evidence is there anything to tell us whether Dorothy May's father was John or Henry. We may conclude that a Henry May was in Leiden at the time, and that Dorothy May's father was probably in Leiden at the time, but they may have been either one person or two. Does Ford gives us any additional information? On p. 2:404 he states again

that Dorothy was the daughter of Henry May, but he cites as his source —
the Townshend article! (Experience Mitchell, q.v., received a letter dated
24 July 1662 from his cousin Thomas Mitchell, living in Amsterdam, Holland, in which the latter said that he had delivered Experience's letter to
Preserved May, and added that Mr. John May had died.)

MAYHIEU, HESTER — The wife of *Mayflower* passenger Francis Cooke,
Hester came to Plymouth in 1623 on the *Anne*. She was a Huguenot who
had lived in Canterbury and Leiden. See G. Andrews Moriarty, "Hester
Le Mayhieu, Wife of Francis Cooke," *NEHGR* 107:61, for information on
her background. Winslow said she was of the French Walloon (Huguenot)
Church and took communion with the Separatist Church (*Hypocrisie
Unmasked,* p. 64). Her admission to the French Reformed Church in Leiden
in 1603 is shown in *MD* 27:147.

MENDLOVE, MARK — The name is also found as Manlove and other
variations. George Ely Russell, "The Migrations of Mark Manlove
(ca. 1617-1666) in New England, Virginia, and Maryland," *TAG* 61:71-76,
consolidates much of the information available on him. A William Mendlove, servant to William Palmer, was whipped at Plymouth on 23 July 1633
for attempting uncleanness with Palmer's maidservant, and at the same
time Palmer sold Mendlove's remaining time of service to Richard Church
for £3. As part of the contract, Church was to teach Mendlove carpentry.
William Mendlove then disappears from Plymouth records, but a Mark
Mendlove appears in a context which leads Mr. Russell to believe that they
were one and the same man. In 1637 Mark Mendall (another variation of
Mendlove), a laborer, gave a bond to appear at court, and Richard Church
was his surety. Later in the year Mark Menlove, a carpenter, was bonded
again. In 1639 Mark Mendlove bought land from William Hiller, and in
1640 he sold his land to John Barnes. Sometime in the 1640s he moved to
Stamford, Connecticut, and by 1653 he had settled in Virginia. He married again in Virginia, and in 1665 moved to Maryland, where he died in
1666. His first wife was a Hannah, and he probably had by her his children John, Mary, Ann, Hannah, Christopher, Abiah, Thomas, William,
and Mark. His second wife was Elizabeth Roberts, and by her he had
George, Persis, and Luke. Some of his children later moved into Delaware.
The references given by Mr. Russell will be very helpful to anyone seeking further information on Manlove-Mendlove families. Note that there
was also a Robert Mendlove living in Plymouth Colony.

MERRICK, WILLIAM — Born ca. 1600 (see will below), William Merrick
first appears in Plymouth records 5 October 1636, when he was one of four
men fined £5 after William Bradford charged them with trespass (*PCR* 1:44).
Dawes-Gates 2:581-86 has an excellent account of what is known of him,
though the speculation that he did not marry until ca. 1642, because he
might have been in servitude until this time, does not hold. That he was
probably a servant on arrival is backed up by his 1673 deed, when he sold
land at Saconett and mentioned that the land had been granted to the Old
Servants of which he was one; also in 1686 he made his "kinsman John

Partridge of Duxbury" his attorney for land in the Saconett purchase, Merrick being one of the first purchasers and one of the "Old Servants in the infancy of this jurisdiction" (*Ply. Colony LR* 4:260, 5:517). However, on 6 October 1636 he was one of several men granted land at Powder Point in Duxbury (*PCR* 1:45), and on 2 October 1637 he was granted twenty acres at Green's Harbor (*PCR* 1:66). Thus he would have been released from servitude prior to 6 October 1636, and he was quite possibly one of the servants who came over on the *Talbot* in 1629. By 1649 he was known as Sgt. William Merrick (*PCR* 12:178). On 5 June 1651, and again on 4 May 1652, he was proposed for freeman status, but did not become a freeman until 1 June 1658 (*PCR* 2:167, 3:7, 137). On 4 October 1652 William Merrick of Eastham sold his land in Duxbury to George Partridge (*MD* 1:135). On 1 June 1663 Ens. William Merrick was approved as lieutenant of the Eastham military company (*PCR* 4:41).

He married Rebecca Tracy, daughter of Stephen Tracy, ca. 1642 (*Dawes-Gates* 2:801, 584). In his will dated 3 December 1686, inventory 17 February 1688/89, he called himself about eighty-six years of age, and he named his wife Rebecca, oldest son William, son Stephen, "all my children," and grandchild Ruth Freeman (*MD* 10:7). His children, recorded at Eastham, though the first three or four must have been born at Duxbury, were William, Stephen, Rebecca, Mary, Ruth, Sarah, John, Isaac, Joseph, and Benjamin (*PCR* 8:28, 30; *MD* 5:23, 7:19). *Dawes-Gates* 2:585 states that son William married (1) Abigail Hopkins, daughter of Giles [2] Hopkins and (2) Elizabeth, the widow of Jabez Snow; Stephen married (1) Mercy Bangs and (2) Anna Wilbore; daughter Mary married Stephen Hopkins, son of Giles [2]; Ruth married Edmond [3] Freeman; Sarah married John [3] Freeman; Joseph married (1) Elizabeth Hawes and (2) Elizabeth (Freeman) Remick, daughter of Samuel [2] Freeman (Samuel [1]).

MINTER, DESIRE – A servant to John Carver, Desire Minter arrived at Plymouth on the 1620 *Mayflower*. She was said to have "returned to her friends, and proved not very well, and dyed in England" (*Bradford [Ford]* 2:401). Dexter, p. 625, 633, shows that there was a William Minter from Norwich, England, and his wife Sarah Willet, daughter of Thomas Willet, living in Leiden between 1613 and 1616 (William died and his widow Sarah married Roger Simmons and died at Leiden in 1629). If Desire were a daughter of William and Sarah, she would also have been a niece of Thomas Willet, who arrived later in Plymouth Colony.

MITCHELL, EXPERIENCE – Experience Mitchell arrived in Plymouth in 1623 on the *Anne*, and Banks writes that he was from Duke's Place, London. Underhill (*Small Descendants*, 1:510), based in part on Dexter (p. 625), thought Experience was the son of Thomas Mitchell of Cambridge, England, who was a member of Francis Johnson's church at Amsterdam, and that Experience was born in Leiden in 1611. Experience received a letter dated 24 July 1662 from his nephew Thomas Mitchell in Amsterdam in which Thomas mentions having received Experience's letter dated 23 April 1661, and says, "I do also wish my cousin Elizabeth much joy with her daughter that God has given her to her six sons. I do also wish my cousin Sarah much joy in her married estate" (*PN&Q* 3:102-03). Experience was a Purchaser and was on the 1633 freeman list. He later moved to Duxbury, where he became a highway surveyor on 3 March 1639/40 (*PCR* 1:141); he also served on various juries (*PCR*, passim). On 7 June 1659 he was fined ten shillings for refusing to serve on the grand jury (*PCR* 3:168). He married, probably not long after the 1627 cattle division, Jane Cooke, daughter of 1620 *Mayflower* passenger Francis Cooke; though there is no record of their marriage, their son Thomas Mitchell in a deed of 1 August 1672 refers to some land given him by his grandfather Francis Cooke (*MD* 3:104). By his first wife Jane, Mitchell had Thomas and Elizabeth, but indirect evidence indicates that the rest of his children were probably by his second wife Mary _____. See John B. Threlfall, "Comments on the Two Wives of Experience Mitchell of Plymouth, Mass.," *NEHGR* 127:94; Robert S. Wakefield, "Not All the Children of Experience Mitchell Are Mayflower Descendants," *TAG* 59:28; and Barbara L. Merrick, "Some Descendants of Francis Cooke, Mayflower Passenger," *MQ* 49:130. Also see Merton Taylor Goodrich, "Gaining Experience—A Problem in the Mitchell Family," *TAG* 12:193 (see also *TAG* 19:226 and *NEHGR* 83:457). In his will, dated 5 December 1684, inventory 14 May 1689, Mitchell named his wife Mary; sons Edward and John; grandsons Experience and Thomas; granddaughter Mary Mitchell; and daughters Mary Shaw, Sarah Hayward, and Hannah Hayward (*MD* 32:97). His daughter Elizabeth, who married John Washburn, and his son Jacob, who married Susanna Pope, predeceased him.

MORE, ELLEN—see Richard More.

MORE, JASPER—see Richard More.

MORE, MARY—see Richard More.

MORE, RICHARD—Baptized at Shipton, Shropshire, 13 November 1614, Richard More was a son of Catherine (More) More, wife of Samuel More. He sailed on the *Mayflower* as a young ward to Elder Brewster. Sir Anthony Wagner, "The Origin of the Mayflower Children: Jasper, Richard and Ellen More," *NEHGR* 114:163 and "The Royal Descent of a Mayflower Passenger," *NEHGR* 124:85, shows that the More children (including a fourth sibling, whom Bradford called a boy, but who probably was Mary, known sister to the other three) were born of an adulterous relationship of their mother. The husband, to spare them future disgrace, put the children out with John Carver and Robert Cushman to go to the New World. Wagner traced the mother back to royalty, making the More children the only ones on the *Mayflower* of proven royal descent. Richard was the only More child to survive that first winter, and he later disappeared from Plymouth records, leaving some writers to identify him with Richard Mann of Scituate. However, it was later discovered that he moved to Salem and became a sea captain (*MD* 22:49, 74; *MQ* 43:45). Richard's son, Caleb More, testified in 1678 that his father "bought out of a London ship in Virginia," Mary, who later became the wife of Giles Corey (who was later executed as a "wizard" at Salem) (Essex County Quarterly Courts 7:148). The discovery that

Richard More of Plymouth and Richard More of Salem were identical was made by Dr. Edwin A. Hill in 1905 and published in *NYGBR* 36:213, 291.

Richard More married (1) Christian Hunter and had a number of children, but descent today can be traced only through his granddaughter Susanna Dutch, who married Benjamin Knowlton. Mrs. John F. Barclay, "Notes on the Hollingsworth, Hunter, More and Woodbury Families of Salem, Mass.," *TAG* 40:77, shows that his first wife's name was Hunter, not Hunt, as has been written at times. More married (2) Jane (_____) Crumpton, but had no issue by her. Richard D. Pierce, ed., *The Records of the First Church in Salem, Massachusetts 1629-1736* (Salem, 1974), p. 166, shows that in 1688 "Old Captain More having been for many years under suspicion and a common fame of lasciviousness, and some degree at least of incontency and therefore was at severall times spoke to, by sundry brethren and also by the Elders in a private way, because for want of proof we could go no further. He was at last left to himselfe so farr as that he was convicted before justices of peace by three witnesses of gross unchastity with another mans wife and was censured by them." His written and verbal repentences were accepted in 1691 and he was "by the vote of the Church forgiven and restored to his former state." His first five generations are given in *MF* 2.

More's reputation in the Salem Church tends to confirm an English parish record noted by the late Robert M. Sherman, FASG, from St. Dunstan's, Stepney, Middlesex, showing that Richard Moore of Salem in New England, a mariner, married on 23 October 1645 Elizabeth Woolno of Limehouse, at a time when he was already married to Christian Hunter. There are other indications that he made at least several trips to England, and the fact that he had living wives on both sides of the Atlantic might strengthen a conjecture that he was a trans-Atlantic sea captain.

MORGAN, BENEDICT—Benedict Morgan received one share in the 1623 land division as one who arrived on the *Fortune* in 1621, but he was no longer in Plymouth at the time of the 1627 division of livestock. See also Peter Wilson Coldham, FASG, "Edward Winslow and Bennet Morgan of Plymouth, 1624," *NGSQ* 63:295.

MORTON, GEORGE—In the Leiden record of his betrothal to Juliana Carpenter on 6 July 1612 (married 23 July 1612), George Morton is said to have come from York, England, and his brother Thomas Morton was one of the witnesses (Dexter, p. 626). There have been attempts to connect him with Morton families of Austerfield or Bawtry, but the evidence is insufficient. His brother Thomas may have been the Thomas Morton who arrived at Plymouth on the *Fortune* in 1621, and the Thomas Morton, Jr. who arrived at Plymouth on the *Anne* in 1623 may have been Thomas's son and George's nephew. There is no known or suspected relationship with Thomas Morton of Merrymount. George has been called the Mourt of *Mourt's Relation* (it having been common to cut off the end syllable of some names (e.g., Coop-Cooper, Hunt-Hunter), the name G. Mourt appearing at the end of the preface, and this is likely, but not proven.

However, Edward Winslow was the author of most of this work, with probably some part done by Bradford, and Mourt would have been the one who arranged publication in England. George Morton arrived in Plymouth in 1623, probably on the *Anne,* though Banks says on the *Little James.* He had been one of the most important of the Separatist leaders in Leiden, and he would have played a leading role in the development of Plymouth Colony, but he died in June 1624. His widow Juliana married Manasseh Kempton, and in the 1627 cattle division she and her second husband are in Bradford's company, along with her children by George Morton: Nathaniel, John, Ephraim, and Patience. Another daughter, Sarah Morton, was born in Leiden, and in 1627 she was in Francis Eaton's company. *Moore Families,* p. 391-98, gives a well documented account of his life. Some of his early descendants are given in John K. Allen, *George Morton of Plymouth Colony and Some of his Descendants* (privately printed, 1908), which contains errors, some of which are resolved by *Plymouth Co. LR* 12:72. *MD* 17:45 transcribes additional original documents concerning George Morton and his family.

MORTON, NATHANIEL—Born at Leiden ca. 1613 (he died at Plymouth 28 June 1685 in his seventy-third year—*Ply. Ch. Recs.* 1:160), the son of George and Juliana Morton, Nathaniel Morton arrived with his parents at Plymouth in 1623. Following his father's death in 1624 he was taken into the home of his uncle, William Bradford. He became a freeman on 3 January 1636/37 (*PCR* 1:48). He married (1) on 25 December 1635 Lydia Cooper (*PCR* 1:35), the sister of John Cooper, q.v., of Scituate and Barnstable, who had married Nathaniel's aunt, Priscilla (Carpenter) Wright. He married Hannah (Pritchard) Templar (*PCR* 8:35), daughter of Richard and Anne Pritchard, and widow of Richard Templar (Pope) on 29 April 1674. He was a grandjuryman in 1639 and 1646 (*PCR* 1:126, 2:102). In 1647 he became Secretary (title later changed to Clerk) of the Plymouth General Court (*PCR* 2:120), a position he kept until his death. Since he was custodian of the records, and also probably had access to the papers of his uncle, William Bradford, he was able to write some of the history of Plymouth Colony, especially in his 1669 *New Englands Memoriall* and his *A Breife Eclesiasticall History of the Church of Christ Att Plymouth Anno Domi 1680* (see text, and also appendix D, which shows indications that he probably rearranged the sequence of signers of the Mayflower Compact to suit his own purposes). In his writings he showed himself to be a very orthodox member of his community, and he was most intolerant of anyone holding views different from his own.

He dated his will 22 April 1685, inventory July 1685, and specified that he wanted to be buried near his first wife, Lydia Morton. He named his second wife Ann Morton; his daughters Remember Jackson, Lydia Elliston, Hannah Bosworth, and Joanna Prince; his sisters Patience and Sarah; his grandson Nathaniel Bosworth, son of Nathaniel Bosworth; his grandsons Eleazer Dunham and Nathaniel Dunham; his kinsman Nathaniel Harlow; his brother Lt. Ephraim Morton; and his kinsman Sgt. William Harlow

(*Ply. Colony LR* 5:350). Children who had predeceased him were Mercy, who had married Joseph Dunham (*PCR* 8:17); Eleazer (*PCR* 8:8); a still-born daughter (*PCR* 8:11); Nathaniel (*PCR* 8:31); and Elizabeth, who had married Nathaniel Bosworth (*PCR* 8:33).

MORTON, THOMAS – Thomas Morton arrived on the *Fortune* in 1621 and received one share in the 1623 land division. His name was in the 1627 cattle division, but then crossed out, indicating that he died around this time. He was probably the father of the Thomas Morton, Jr., q.v., who arrived in 1623. Neither should be confused with Thomas Morton of Merrymount, who was not a resident of Plymouth Colony, but whose career was at times interwoven with the life of Plymouth, to the dislike of the latter (see text).

MORTON, THOMAS, Jr. – Arriving on the *Anne* in 1623, Thomas Morton, Jr. was probably a son of the Thomas Morton who had arrived on the *Fortune* in 1621 and died before the 1627 division. The senior Thomas was most likely the brother who witnessed the betrothal of George Morton, q.v., in Leiden in 1612. The junior Thomas Morton married at Plymouth, Rose _____, possibly ca. 1645 when he purchased a farm, and she died 31 November 1685 (*MD* 15:213). He apparently left no issue, and he deeded his whole estate to his faithful servant, Samuel Gardiner, whom he brought up from childhood (*PN&Q* 5:122).

MULLINS, ALICE – A 1620 *Mayflower* passenger, Alice accompanied her husband William to Plymouth, and she died during the first year, sometime after 5 April 1621.

MULLINS, JOSEPH – A 1620 *Mayflower* passenger, Joseph accompanied his parents, William and Alice Mullins, to Plymouth, and he died during the first year, sometime after 5 April 1621.

MULLINS, PRISCILLA – A 1620 *Mayflower* passenger, Priscilla accompanied her parents, William and Alice Mullins, to Plymouth. She married John Alden, q.v., and left many descendants.

MULLINS, WILLIAM – A 1620 *Mayflower* passenger, William Mullins came from Dorking, County Surrey, and he brought his wife Alice, his children Joseph and and Priscilla, and his servant Robert Carter, with him. Mullins died 21 February 1620/21 (*MD* 30:3). His will (*MD* 1:230) shows that he also left a son William and a married daughter Sarah (Mullins) Blunden, in England, and George E. Bowman, "The Estates of William [2] Mullins and His Daughter Sarah [3] (Mullins) (Gannett) (Savill) Faxon and of Her Three Husbands" (*MD* 7:37, 179) shows that William [2] came to Plymouth Colony sometime after his father's death. From the probate documents it appears that granddaughter Sarah left no descendants, and the only proven Mullins descendants living today are via daughter Priscilla, who married John Alden. Though Bradford wrote that Mullins, his wife, his son, and his servant all died during the first winter, Bowman shows in *MD* 1:230 that the wife and son must have been alive when the *Mayflower* set sail again for England in April 1621, but died before the arrival of the *Fortune* in November 1621. Bradford called him "Mr. William Mullins," and he was one of the more prosperous of the original settlers. See also Robert S. Wakefield, "William Mullins's Grandchildren in England," *MQ* 39:83.

NASH, SAMUEL – A freeman on the 1633 list, Samuel Nash in 1637 was one of the volunteers against the Pequot Indians (*PCR* 1:61). He was a surveyor of the highways in 1640/41 (*PCR* 2:9), and a grandjuror several times (*PCR, passim*). He was a sergeant from Duxbury in the 1645 expedition against the Narragansetts, and in the same year he was made a lieutenant (*PCR* 2:90, 88). Several times he posted bond as surety for others to appear in court, and on one occasion in 1647 when George Wright did not appear after Nash and Richard Church had given bond of £20 each for him, the court gave them license to apprehend Wright (*PCR* 2:113). It appears that they lost their money, for on 7 June 1648 the court gave Lieutenant Nash and Sergeant Church authority to collect a £5/8 debt owed Wright toward recovering their loss as a result of Wright breaking his bond (*PCR* 2:127). In 1652 he was made chief marshal for the colony, and in 1653 he became a deputy for Duxbury (*PCR* 3:12, 23). In 1658 he was one of those selected by the Council of War to be an adviser to the colony's major (*PCR* 3:153). In 1664 he and John Sprague were fined £3 each for signing as witnesses a document made by William Pabodie for separating William and Mercy Tubbs from their wedding bond (*PCR* 4:66). In 1666 he complained that the constable of Duxbury did not pay him part of his salary as marshal, and the court told him to buy ten shillings worth of corn at the expense of John Bourne, who was the original cause of the neglect of payment (*PCR* 4:121).

On 6 July 1682 Nash testified that he was age eighty or thereabouts and that he had been sent years earlier by Governor Bradford to accompany Edward Winslow to go to the trading post at Sowamset where Thomas Prence was in charge (*PCR* 7:257). Thus he was born ca. 1602. His wife is not known. Because he was aged and not able to care for himself alone, he put his estate in the hands of his daughter Martha's husband, William Clarke, and the estate was appraised by John Soule and Philip Leonard, chosen by Clarke and approved by Nash. He died before 5 March 1683/84, when the court gave Martha Clarke some personal estate of Nash valued at about £19 as her due for her pains in looking after her father (*PCR* 6:126). By his will dated 2 June 1681 he gave his dwelling house and some lands to Martha Clarke, other lands to his deceased grandson Samuel Sampson's two sons, Samuel and Ichabod Sampson, and the rest of his estate to his daughter Martha, and his granddaughters Elizabeth Delano and Mary Howland (*Ply. Colony PR* 4:2:112). Clarence Almon Torrey, "A Nash-Sampson-Delano-Howland Problem," *TAG* 15:165, uses this will and other information to show that Samuel Sampson, the deceased grandson of Lt. Samuel Nash was a son of Abraham Sampson of Duxbury, and thus that Abraham Sampson had married a daughter of Samuel Nash. Since Nash did not mention other sons of Abraham Sampson, it appeared that Abraham had two wives, with the other wife unidentified. Nash's daughter Martha Clarke was childless. With no indication that Nash had any other married children, Torrey felt it safe to assume that the granddaughters were daughters of Abraham Sampson by his first wife, and he identified them as Elizabeth Sampson, wife of Philip 2 Delano, and Mary Sampson, wife of Samuel 2 Howland (Henry 1).

NEWCOMEN, JOHN – *Bradford (Ford)* 2:112 named John Newcomen as the young man waylaid and shot to death by John Billington in 1630 "about a former quarrel." Morton, *New England Canaan,* reversed it and stated in a typical punning way that Billington killed him after being pursued by some "carelesse fellow that was new come into the land." John G. Hunt, *NEHGR* 113:68, speculated that Newcomen might have been a relative of Elder Brewster's wife.

NEWMAN, SAMUEL – Born at Banbury, County Oxford, 10 May 1602, the son of Richard Newman, Samuel graduated from Trinity College, Oxford, 17 October 1620. In 1625 he became rector of the church at Ecclesfield, West Riding, Yorkshire. He came to Dorchester in the Bay colony about 1636, and he was the first minister of the church at Weymouth from 30 January 1638/39 until 1643. He moved with many Weymouth families to Rehoboth and was ordained minister there in 1644. He compiled a concordance to the Bible. Newman married at Banbury, 25 December 1623, Sybil _____, who was born there 21 November 1604 and died at Rehoboth 2 November 1672. He died at Rehoboth 5 July 1663. His children, all born in England except for the last, who was born at Weymouth, were Samuel, born 6 July 1625; Antipas, born 15 October 1627; Noah, born 10 January 1631; and Hopestill, born 29 May 1641 (married Rev. George Shove of Dorchester and Taunton). The above is from Chamberlain, *History of Weymouth,* 4:444, which is not documented, and could contain errors, but is probably generally correct, and is given here for background purposes. It is a letter of Samuel's son the Reverend Noah Newman, that furnishes the names of those killed at the Pawtucket massacre on 26 March 1676 (see *TAG* 60:236).

NEWTON, ELLEN – Arriving on the *Anne* in 1623 as Ellen Newton, by the time of the 1627 division she had married John Adams, q.v. After the death of Adams, she married Kenelm Winslow, q.v., brother of Edward Winslow, and she had children by both husbands.

NICOLAS, AUSTEN – Austen Nicolas arrived at Plymouth in 1621 on the *Fortune,* and received one share in the 1623 land division. He was not in the 1627 cattle division.

NORRIS, MARY – A 1620 *Mayflower* passenger, Mary (Norris) accompanied her husband Isaac Allerton to Plymouth, where she died 25 February 1620/21. Dexter, p. 601, shows from Leiden records that she was from Newbury, Berkshire, and she was married to Allerton at Leiden 4 November 1611. On 22 December 1620, when the *Mayflower* was at anchor in Plymouth Harbor, she was delivered of a stillborn son (*Mourt's Relations,* p. 24).

OLDHAM, JOHN—He arrived at Plymouth in 1623 on the *Anne* with his family, including his sister Lucretia Oldham, q.v. Though the relationship between John Oldham and Lucretia (Oldham) Brewster has been questioned, there is a letter from Jonathan Brewster dated 30 April 1636 to John Winthrop, Jr. in Connecticut in which Brewster writes "and if my brother Oldam be at the rivers mouth" (*Winthrop Papers*, p. 67). It is interesting that there was a Margaret Oldham at Leiden, who was betrothed on 29 July 1611 to William Bassett (Dexter, p. 603). While this in itself proves nothing, it is surprising to note how many of the surnames of people in early Plymouth show up in Leiden. In the 1623 land division, John Oldham and "those joyned with him" received ten shares, an unusually large grouping. Those joined with him presumably included his wife and children, his sister, and other individuals "on their particular" (see text). John Oldham was a coconspirator with Rev. John Lyford in 1624 and as a consequence was exiled from Plymouth Colony. He first went to Nantasket (Hull), but in 1625 returned to Plymouth in spite of his banishment. There, Bradford writes (*Ford*, 1:411-14) they "apointed a gard of musketers which he was to pass throw, and ever one was ordered to give him a thump on the brich, with the but end of his musket." The Dorset group employed him to help colonize Cape Ann in 1625, but he became dissatisfied and later went to Virginia. He returned to Hull and showed himself repentant to the Plymouth leaders, so much so that they put him in charge of Thomas Morton of Merrymount when they sent the latter back to England in 1630. Oldham returned from England with the Bay Colony settlers and became a deputy at Watertown. He was killed by Indians while on a trading voyage to Block Island in 1636. As related in the text, Oldham's murder was one of the immediate causes of the Pequot War.

Bradford (*Ford* 1:412) noted that among those with him then, "2 litle boys that were his kinsmen were saved." Pope states that John and Thomas Oldham, ages twelve and ten in 1635, came to New England on the *Elizabeth and Ann,* and settled in Plymouth Colony, and they may have been related to John Oldham. John Oldham's baptism has not been found in All Saints parish, Derby, Derbyshire (though a baptism probably pertaining to his sister Lucretia was—see below), but the records of All Saints do show that among the children of Thomas and Elizabeth Oldham were John, baptized 9 April 1622, and Thomas, baptized 23 August 1624. These would be possibilities for John Oldham's young "kinsmen."

OLDHAM, LUCRETIA—She was the sister of John Oldham, q.v., and wife of Jonathan Brewster, q.v. *The Brewster Book* (*MD* 1:8) records that Jonathan Brewster married "Lucretia Oldam of Darby the 10th Aprill 1624." A note by John G. Hunt (*NEHGR* 111:242) shows a baptized Lucretia, daughter of William Ouldham, in the Parish of All Saints, Derby, Derbyshire, on 14 January 1600/01. William Ouldham had married Philippa Sowter there on 17 November 1588.

PALMER, WILLIAM—Much error has been written about the William Palmer family, but Mrs. John E. Barclay, "Notes on the Palmer Family of

Plymouth," *TAG* 32:39, helps sort out the facts. Palmer arrived at Plymouth in 1621 on the *Fortune* with his son William, and two years later his wife Frances arrived on the *Anne* to join him. He moved to Duxbury in the 1630s, having sold his house and six acres at Reed Pond to John Holmes for £35 on 16 October 1632 (*PCR* 12:18). He was a "nailer" by occupation. He was on the 1633 list of freemen, and his son William, Jr. became a freeman on 1 January 1634/35 (*PCR* 1:32). William, Sr. was prosperous enough to have servants. On 23 July 1633 William Mendlove (see under Mark Mendlove) was whipped for attempting uncleanness with Palmer's maid and for running away from his master (*PCR* 1:15). On 15 August 1633 Robert Barker transferred his apprenticeship status from John Thorpe, deceased, to William Palmer (*PCR* 1:16). On 2 January 1637/38 Stephen Hopkins was presented by the grand jury for suffering excessive drinking in his house by several men, including "old Palmer," who must have died shortly after the event and before the grand jury's presentment. Widow Palmer and "Widdow Palmers man" were among the testifying witnesses (*PCR* 1:75).

He dated his will 7 November 1637, proved 13 November 1637 (*MD* 2:147). His wife Frances had died earlier, and Mrs. Barclay shows hints that he may have had an earlier wife. His last wife was Mary _____, described in his will thusly: "whereas I have married a young woman who is dear unto me." He had left at least two children behind in England, and he had a daughter who had married Henry Rowley, but died before 17 October 1633. His son William Palmer, Jr. married Elizabeth Hodgkins, and by her he had one child, Rebecca Palmer, before he died in 1636, predeceasing his father. By his (third?) wife, William, Sr. had posthumously another William Palmer, born 26 June 1638. Mrs. Barclay gives good reasons for thinking that William Palmer's widow Mary later married Robert Paddock. The son of the young wife Mary, the posthumous William Palmer, married a Susanna, who has been variously confused in published material as Susanna Hathaway or Susanna Cooke. Her correct identity is shown by Carlton A. Palmer, Jr., "Susannah (Briggs) Palmer of Plymouth Colony and Little Compton, Rhode Island," *MQ* 50:188, as a daughter of John and Sarah (Cornell) Briggs and this Susanna married (2) John Northway. The family history by Horace Wilbur Palmer, *Palmer Families in America*, vol. 3 (Somersworth, N.H., 1973), has some significant errors.

PENN, CHRISTIAN—Christian Penn arrived on the *Anne* in 1623. At the time of the 1627 division she was married to *Mayflower* passenger Francis Eaton, and after his death she married *Mayflower* passenger Francis Billington. Information on her three children by Eaton, and their descendants, is given in *MF-1*, and on her nine children by Billington in Wakefield, *TG* 3:228. She died probably at Middleborough ca. 1684.

PERRY, EZRA—Ezra Perry was not in the 1643 ATBA, but is first in the records in 1644 as among those contributing to the repair of the Sandwich meetinghouse. He married 12 February 1651/52, Elizabeth Burges, daughter of Thomas and Dorothy Burges of Sandwich, and they had seven children. Lydia B. Phinney Brownson and Maclean W. McLean, "Ezra

Perry of Sandwich, Mass. (ca. 1625-1689)," *NEHGR* 115:86, 181, 268, 116:27, 100, 191, 117:313, gives a comprehensive account of Perry's early descendants.

PHILIPS, JOHN—In Bradford's letter to Governor Winthrop of 6 February 1631/32 he wrote that the government warned all Plymouth people not to receive any people from the Bay as servants or otherwise unless such people had letters of dismissal from a Bay Church. He mentioned that John Philips was sick when he came to Plymouth, saying that his Bay Colony master had sent him to seek new employment, and had he not been given help he might have died. His master came later and sold his remaining term to a Plymouth resident (*MD* 9:1-3). He was a volunteer in the Pequot War (*PCR* 1:61). On 5 June 1638 William Latham was presented for entertaining John Philips into his house contrary to an act of the court (*PCR* 1:87). He received several land grants (*PCR* 1:145, 153, 165). On 2 August 1653 he sued Joseph Roes for a £6 debt (*PCR* 3:39). In 1655 he was a highway surveyor for Marshfield, and in 1657 he was a constable for Marshfield (*PCR* 3:79, 116). He was sent as constable in 1657 to break up a Quaker meeting at Arthur Howland's house, and Howland threatened that he would have either a gun or a sword in his belly (*PCR* 3:124-25). In 1659 he was proposed as a freeman (*PCR* 3:163), but there is no record that he became one.

He married (1) Grace (_____), widow of William Holloway (Torrey), and on 31 October 1666 he was willing to pay £10 to Grace Holloway (his stepdaughter), who was then of age, as the portion due her from her deceased father (*PCR* 4:136). He married (2) on 14 March 1666/67 Faith (Clarke) Doty, widow of *Mayflower* passenger Edward Doty (*PCR* 8:31). On 23 February 1666/67 he and Faith Doty had made a marriage agreement that the children of each would remain under the control of the natural parent only, that Faith could dispose of her own property as she saw fit, and that if Philips should predecease her, she would have a life interest in one-third of his real and personal property (*PCR* 4:163-64). On 3 June 1668 Mary Philips and Jane Holloway were each fined three shillings, four pence, for striking each other (*PCR* 1:187). In his will dated 20 October 1691, sworn 16 May 1692, John Philips of Marshfield, age about eighty-nine, named his sons Samuel (the older son) and Benjamin; his daughter Mary Philips (unable to maintain herself because of weakness of reason and understanding); grandson John Philips, son of his son Benjamin; and the rest of his grandchildren, who were the sons of his sons Samuel and Benjamin (*Ply. County PR* 1:140). For the will of his second wife, who died before he did, see under Faith Clarke.

PHIPS, WILLIAM—William Phips, the late servant of the partners, sold on 31 August 1636 to Josiah Winslow the land due him on completion of his apprenticeship (*PCR* 1:43), and thus most likely he had come to Plymouth a number of years before 1636. There is no other mention of him in Plymouth records.

PICKWORTH, JOHN—In Bradford's letter to Governor Winthrop of 6 February 1631/32 he wrote that John Pickworth came from the Bay to Plymouth as a sojourner to work for a few weeks, and he got a wife in Plymouth "& so is longe since returned duble, & hath no cause to complaine, except he hath goot a bad wife" (*MD* 9:1-3). Pope identifies him with the John Pickworth of Salem, who, in his will of 1663, had a wife Ann.

PIERCE, ABRAHAM—Abraham Pierce (or Peirce, with variations) is believed to have come to Plymouth in 1623 on the *Anne*, and to be one of the two men listed in the 1623 land division as "Mr Perces 2 ser:" (see Robert C. Anderson, "A Clue to the English Ancestry of Abraham Pierce of Plymouth and Duxbury," *TAG* 54:164, which gives reasons for thinking that he might have been a relative of the London merchant and Adventurer John Peirce). He was named in the 1627 cattle division, and on 28 September 1629 he sold to Thomas Clarke one acre of land abutting Hob's Hole (*PCR* 12:7), precisely where the two servants of Mr. Peirce had been given land in 1623. by 1638 he owned land on the Jones River (*PCR* 1:111-12), and in 1640 he was granted forty acres at the North River (*PCR* 1:165). He was on the 1643 ATBA twice, once as a resident of Plymouth and once as a resident of Duxbury, indicating that he probably moved about this time (Shurtleff put his name on the Plymouth list preceded and followed by "double plus" marks, indicating that this entry had been canceled in the original record).

It is this 1643 Plymouth record which has led to controversy, for Shurtleff put on one line "Abraham Pearse, the blackamore," though the original record takes two lines, one for the name and one for "the blackamore" (*PCR* 8:187). In recent years Shurtleff's error was taken by some groups to mean that Pierce was a black, and thus that there was a black at Plymouth at least as early as 1627, perhaps 1623, and, though he appears frequently in other records, becoming a prosperous landowner with a large family, but never again referred to as a black, that he lived a colorblind existence with his white cosettlers. Although the ATBA list clearly indicates that there was a black in Plymouth as early as 1643, Richard L. Ehrlich and James W. Baker, "Abraham Pearse of Plymouth Colony," *MQ* 49:57, give the results of much research by Plimoth Plantation to show there is insufficient evidence for believing that Abraham Pearce was a black.

Pierce was one of the Purchasers, and he was on the 1633 freeman list. He was active in acquiring and selling land (*PCR, Duxbury Records,* passim). On 2 March 1651/52 the grand jury presented him for spending the Sabbath slothfully and negligently and for not frequenting public worship, a charge from which he was later excused, but with a warning to mend his ways (*PCR* 3:5). He married Rebecca _____, whose sister Hannah _____ was the wife of John Scudder (*NEHGR* 9:284). In 1660 Pierce's son James was killed by lightning while fishing in Plymouth Harbor (*PCR* 3:195-96). In 1663 his son Abraham Pierce, Jr. was summoned before magistrates to answer for abusive speeches to his father (*PCR* 4:47). He died before 3 June 1673, when administration of his estate was given to his son Abraham, Jr., who granted twenty-two acres of land to his brother Isaac, and twenty shillings each to his sisters Rebecca Wills, Mary Baker, and Alice Baker (*PCR* 5:116-17). There is a published, but inadequately documented family history, Ebenezer W. Peirce, *The Peirce Family of the Old Colony: or the Lineal Descendants of Abraham Peirce, Who Came to America as Early as 1623* (1870).

PITT, WILLIAM—The names Pitt and Pitts were sometimes used interchangeably. William Pitt arrived at Plymouth in 1621 on the *Fortune*, and in the 1623 land division he and William Wright shared two acres of land. He was not in the 1627 cattle division. A William Pitt was later in Marblehead as a merchant (Pope), but no relationship between the two is known. The Marblehead William Pitt married Susanna Alley (Aealy, Ely), widow of Philip Alley, and administration of the estate of Susanna Pitts, the former Susanna Ely, was granted to John Bundy, q.v., of Taunton, who appeared to be her nearest kin (Pope).

PITTS, EDITH—She first appears in the records on 3 January 1636/37 as a servant to Samuel Jackson of Scituate, and she was to appear in court as a witness against John Emerson, who had been accused of abusing her (*PCR* 1:48-49).

PITTS, PETER—Born in England ca. 1622-27, Peter Pitts married ca. 1655 Mary (Andrews) Hodges, daughter of Henry and Mary Andrews of Taunton, and widow of William Hodges, who died 2 April 1654 (*MD* 12:246). Pitts signed an agreement with his wife-to-be before marriage binding him to "maintain [her] two children until they come to the age of fifteen or sixteen years." He was one of the shareholders in the Taunton Iron Works. He died 1692 and his inventory, taken 9 January 1692/93, included household goods, wearing clothes, flax comb and wheel, farm tools, sheep, oxen, steers, swine, leather, hemp, wool, and a cowbell. His children were Samuel Pitts, who married Sarah Bobbit; Mary Pitts, who married Isaac Hathaway; Sarah Pitts (unmarried 1697); Peter Pitts, who married Bethiah Robinson; Alice Pitts, who married John Wilbore; and Ebenezer Pitts, who married Elizabeth Haskins. An excellent, well-documented family history is by Frances Davis McTeer and Julia Bumpas Berndt, *Some Descendants of Peter Pitts of Taunton, Mass.* (1979).

Peter Pitts was on the 1643 ATBA for Taunton. He was a member of the grand jury in 1655 and other years, was constable for Taunton in 1658, and was made a freeman in 1658 (*PCR* 3:78, 136-37). On 3 June 1656 Timothy Halway of Taunton was presented and admonished for threatening to strike Peter Pitts with a pitchfork, saying that he did not care if he were hanged for it (*PCR* 3:102). On 3 June 1668 an Indian named Powas complained that Peter Pitts had taken away his gun in a dispute about Powas digging some ground for Pitts, and the court ordered Powas to dig up about twenty rods of ground, following which Pitts should give him back his gun (*PCR* 4:183). The will of Alice Paine of Rehoboth, wife of Stephen Paine and former wife of William Parker, dated 5 June 1672, mentioned her cousin Richard Harte of Rhode Island, and her cousin Peter Pitts, Sr. of Taunton, and five children of Peter Pitts: Samuel Pitts, Peter Pitts, Jr., Mary Pitts, Sarah Pitts, and Alice Pitts (*Ply. Colony PR* 4:2:38).

PLUMMER, Anne–The wife of Henry Sampson, q.v., Anne Plummer was probably the sister of Mary Plummer.

PLUMMER, MARY–The first wife of John Barnes, q.v., Mary Plummer was probably the sister of Anne Plummer.

PONTUS, WILLIAM–William Pontus was one of the Leiden Separatists, being found in the records there as a fustian weaver (Dexter, p. 629). He was betrothed to Wybra Hanson 13 November 1610, with William Brewster among the witnesses. The Dutch records describe him in 1622 as living with his wife and daughter Mary, and being too poor to be taxed. He was on the 1633 list of Plymouth freemen, but was not on the 1633 and 1634 tax lists, nor on the 1643 ATBA, which might indicate that he was then over sixty years of age. He died 9 February 1652/53, having made his will on 9 September 1650, proved 4 March 1652/53, in which he named his daughters Mary and Hannah. Mary married (1) James Glass and (2) Philip Delano. Hannah married (1) John Churchill and (2) Giles Rickard. Much of what is known about William Pontus was written up and documented in *Moore Families*, p. 423-28.

PRATT, JOSHUA–Joshua Pratt arrived at Plymouth on the *Anne* in 1623, and was in the 1623 land division and the 1627 cattle division. He was a Purchaser and was on the 1633 list of freemen. He was on the committee of 3 January 1627/28 to lay out the twenty-acre allotments (*PCR* 12:14). He was chosen as messenger of the court and constable for Plymouth on 1 January 1633/34, and he continued as constable after the messenger position was given to Mr. John Holmes on 4 December 1638 (*PCR* 1:21, 105). He obtained a good number of land grants and engaged in frequent land transactions (*PCR*, passim). On 7 March 1652/53 he was one of the purchasers of land in Dartmouth (*MD* 4:186-87). Administration of his estate was granted to his wife Bathsheba on 5 October 1656 (*PCR* 3:108)–her surname is unknown, and she may have been a second wife. He has been called a brother of Phineas Pratt, q.v., and in the 1623 land division he was paired with Phineas, but proof of a relationship is lacking. His widow married (2) John Dogged 29 August 1667 (*PCR* 8:31). His children are thought to be Benajah, who married Persis Dunham; Hannah, who married William Spooner; Jonathan, who married Abigail Wood; and Bathsheba, who married Joshua Rice.

PRATT, PHINEAS–Arriving on the *Sparrow* in 1622, Phineas Pratt was one of an advance group sent out by Thomas Weston, and after the arrival of the full company in the *Charity* and the *Swan*, they began the ill-fated settlement of Wessagusset. Bowman in *MD* 4:87, 129 relates much of what is known about Pratt, including details on his part in alerting Plymouth about the plight of the Wessagusset settlers, and he makes frequent use in his article of Pratt's own "Petition," which can be found in Mass.

Historical Society Collections, 4th Ser. 4:479. Pratt decided to remain in Plymouth, where he married Mary Priest, daughter of *Mayflower* passenger Degory Priest and his wife, Sarah, the sister of Isaac Allerton. Pratt did not have a wife at the time of the 1627 livestock division, but he was married before 11 November 1633 when he was appointed to take possession of the personal property of Cuthbert Cuthbertson and his wife Sarah (*PCR* 1:19). Since Sarah (Allerton) (Vincent) Priest married (3) Cuthbert Cuthbertson, Mary Priest was a stepdaughter to Cuthbertson, a relationship shown in *PCR* 1:159, where the court acknowledged that John Coombe, gentleman, and Phineas Pratt, joiner, had been given land by Cuthbertson because of their respective marriages with his "daughters." Pratt was a Purchaser, and he was on the 1633 freeman list. On 5 November 1644 Thomas Bunting, who had been dwelling with Pratt, put himself, with Pratt's consent, as a servant to John Cooke, Jr., who had paid Pratt a milk cow valued at £5, plus forty shillings in money, for Bunting's indenture (*PCR* 2:78). Pratt later moved to Charlestown in the Bay Colony, where he died 19 April 1680, age about ninety years. He dated his will 8 January 1677/78, proved 15 June 1680, and from the probate papers it can be seen that his children were John, Mary, Samuel, Daniel, Mercy, Joseph, Peter, and Aaron (*MD* 4:137-38). Also see *MD* 3:1.

PRENCE, THOMAS – Thomas Prence was born ca. 1600, for he was in his seventy-third year at his death on 29 March 1673 (*PCR* 8:34). His father was Thomas Prence (or Prince – the Plymouth man always spelled it Prence) who had lived at Lechlade, Gloucestershire, but was a carriage maker of All Hallows Barking, London, when he made his will 31 July 1639 and named his "son Thomas Prence now remayninge in New England" (*Dawes-Gates* 2:683, gives an excellent documented account of Prence's life). Prence arrived at Plymouth Colony in 1621 on the *Fortune*, and from the beginning seemed to have taken a leading role in Plymouth affairs. Of the eight Plymouth Undertakers, who seemed to be the most important men in the colony in 1627, Prence was the only one who had not arrived on the *Mayflower*. He became governor in 1634, and was elected an Assistant in 1635, and from then on he was either an Assistant or governor every year for the rest of his life. He also served as treasurer, as president of the Council of War, and in various other capacities. With the death of Bradford in 1657, Prence became without doubt the most important and influential man in the colony. He was of a conservative nature, as is shown by his siding with Bradford and Winslow in the 1645 Vassall controversy, and by his actions against the Quakers. He was involved in several law suits which were decided in his favor, such as 1650, when Strong Furnell of Boston submitted a written humble apology to the court for having evilly slandered Mr. Prence after the latter sued him for £200 damage (*PCR* 2:152). In 1665 as compensation for having required Prence, as governor, to reside in Plymouth, the court ordered that he would be paid £50 per year as long as he remained governor, and he was given a house in the Plain Dealing area of Plymouth as a residence (in 1668, at his request, the court sold him that house for £150) (*PCR* 4:108, 184). He engaged in many land transactions, and he died a wealthy man, leaving a personal estate in excess of £400 and some eleven tracts of land, at least two of them containing 100 acres each (*MD* 3:206).

He married (1) Patience Brewster, daughter of Elder Brewster on 5 August 1624 (2) on 1 April 1635 Mary Collier, daughter of William Collier; (3) between 1662 and 1668 Apphia (Quicke) Freeman; and (4) before 1 August 1668 Mary (_____) Howes, widow of Thomas Howes (Ella Florence Elliot, "Gov. Thomas Prence's Widow Mary, Formerly the Widow of Thomas Howes, and the Inventory of Her Estate," *MD* 6:230; *Dawes-Gates* 2:692 gives other dates for (3) and (4) and supplies the name Quicke). His children by Patience Brewster were Rebecca, who married Edmond Freeman; Mercy, who married John Freeman; Hannah, who married (1) Nathaniel Mayo and (2) Jonathan Sparrow; and Thomas, who died before 13 March 1672/73 in England. His children by Mary Collier were Jane, who married Mark Snow as his second wife; Mary, who married John Tracy; Sarah, who married Jeremiah Howes; Elizabeth, who married Arthur Howland; and Judith, who married (1) Isaac Barker and (2) William Tubbs (*Dawes-Gates* 2:693). In his will dated 13 March 1672/73, proved 5 June 1673, he named his wife Mary; his seven surviving daughters, Jane, the wife of Mark Snow; Mary Tracy; Sarah Howes; Elizabeth Howland; Judith Barker; Hannah; and Mercy; his grandson Theophilus Mayo; his granddaughter Susanna Prence, the daughter of his deceased son Thomas; his son John Freeman; Lydia Sturtevant; and his brother Thomas Clarke (*MD* 3:203). His chagrin over Arthur Howland's eventually successful suit for the hand of his daughter Elizabeth is related in the text, and he probably was not happy over the marriage of two of his daughters to sons of Edmond Freeman. The mention in his will of his deceased son Thomas's daughter Susanna Prence would indicate that he died without surviving male issue in the Prence line.

Mary Walton Ferris makes the point in *Dawes-Gates* 2:686-87 that his reputation for intolerance, particularly toward the Quakers, has clouded over his extensive service to the colony. She especially notes that he presided over the court in the very sane and reasonable handling of Plymouth's first witchcraft trial in 1661; that he dealt in a humane way with the Indians, and missionary Thomas Mayhew wrote of his "gentle and kind dealing" with them (Prence also presided over the court as governor in 1638 when the momentous decision was made to execute the white men who had murdered an Indian); that he showed wisdom in 1637 when he negotiated with the Massachusetts men who unjustly demanded much of the land on the Connecticut River that Plymouth had purchased from the Indians; and that he advocated and brought about a free school system in the colony.

PRIEST, DEGORY—A 1620 *Mayflower* passenger, Degory Priest was in Leiden records as from London, a hatmaker, who married Sarah (Allerton) Vincent, sister of Isaac Allerton, at Leiden 4 November 1611, and he was age forty in 1619 (Dexter, p. 630). He died at Plymouth 1 January 1620/21, leaving his widow and two daughters, who had come over from Leiden to Plymouth in 1623. See John G. Hunt, "Origin of Digory Priest, Early Settler in Plymouth, New England," *NEHGR* 111:320, for a clue as to his origin, but it should be kept in mind that the name is not as unique as it may seem, at least in the Devonshire area. His daughters Mary and Sarah are given below. His widow married Cuthbert Cuthburtson.

PRIEST, MARY – A daughter of Degory Priest, q.v., Mary Priest arrived with her mother on the *Anne* in 1623, and she later married Phineas Pratt, q.v. (*MD* 4:94).

PRIEST, SARAH – A daughter of Degory Priest, q.v., Sarah Priest arrived with her mother on the *Anne* in 1623, and she later married John Coombs, q.v., (*MD* 4:96).

PROWER, SOLOMON – A servant to Christopher Martin, possibly his stepson, Solomon Prower sailed on the 1620 *Mayflower* and died at Plymouth on 24 December 1620. He was erroneously recorded as Solomon Martin in Prince's Annals (*MD* 30:3). He left no known issue.

RANDE, JAMES – James Rande arrived at Plymouth in 1623 and received one share in the 1623 land division, but he was not in the 1627 cattle division.

RATTLIFE, ROBERT – Robert Rattlife arrived at Plymouth in 1623 and received two shares in the 1623 land division, which would indicate that his wife was with him. He was not in the 1627 cattle division.

RICKARD, GILES – Giles Rickard sailed on the *Speedwell* leaving Weymouth, Dorset, on 22 April 1637, for New England, with his wife and three children, plus one boy and one maid, the same ship taken by his wife's brother, Henry Cogan, q.v., and some other West England people who settled in Plymouth Colony, such as Elizabeth Poole, Walter Harris, John Crocker, and Thomas Farwell (*NGSQ* 71:176). Mrs. Barclay shows in *TAG* 30:11 that Rickard married at West Hatch, County Somerset, 7 January 1623/24 Judith (Cogan) King, the widow of William King. G. E. McCracken shows in *NEHGR* 111:172 that Judith Cogan was the daughter of Henry and Joane (Boridge) Cogan, who was baptized at Taunton, Somerset, 13 June 1594. The three children accompanying him were his sons Giles Rickard and John Rickard, and his wife's son Samuel King, q.v., by her earlier marriage. Judith died at Plymouth 6 February 1661/62 (*PCR* 8:23). Giles married (2) Joan (_____) Tilson, widow of Edmond Tilson (*MD* 17:183; Torrey, p. 624), and (3) Hannah (Pontus) Churchill, widow of John Churchill and daughter of William and Wybra (Hanson) Pontus (*MD* 18:57; *PCR* 2:79; *Ply. Ch. Recs.* 1:269); there was no issue by his second and third wives.

On 4 December 1637 Giles Rickard was granted seven acres of land in Plymouth, which he could not alienate, and if uninhabited would be returned to the town; on 2 January 1637/38 Giles Rickard and John Barnes (who had also been granted seven acres on the same day in the same area) were sureties for £20 each for William Corvanel to appear at court; on 6 March 1637/38 Giles Rickard petitioned to be admitted a freeman; on

4 September 1638 he was on the jury that convicted four Englishmen of murdering an Indian; on 16 April 1639 he and John Barnes were sureties for £20 each for the appearance at court of Richard Derby, gentleman (*PCR* 1:70-71, 75, 79, 96, 121). On 27 May 1639 he was a surety for £5 for Richard Willis, the husband of Amy (Glass) Willis, who was a niece of Giles's first wife (*PCR* 1:122). On 1 June 1641 he was on a grand jury, and on 7 September 1641 he was admitted a freeman (*PCR* 2:16, 23). On 1 March 1641/42 he was made a constable and surveyor of highways for Plymouth town (*PCR* 2:34). On 4 October 1648 he was on a trial jury that convicted Alice Bishop of murdering her daughter (*PCR* 2:134). Notwithstanding his frequent membership on grand juries, on 9 June 1653 he was presented by a grand jury for "lascivious carriages towards Mary, the daughter of Barnard Lumberd, of Barnstable" (*PCR* 3:36); yet, on 1 June 1658 he was selected again as constable for Plymouth (*PCR* 3:135). On 1 March 1658/59 he was granted a license to keep an ordinary at Plymouth for entertaining visitors, but not for the use of the townspeople; this was renewed on 7 March 1659/60, with a provision that he could also sell wine and strong liquors to townspeople, but only to be consumed in their own houses, and another renewal was granted 10 June 1661 (*PCR* 3:159, 181, 219). On 5 March 1660/61 he was fined ten shillings for selling wine to Indians (*PCR* 3:207). He was fined or given short jail sentences for other offences, such as for allowing John Barnes to be drunk in his house, and for swearing. On 31 October 1666 his liquor license was revoked, though after he complained that the liquor on hand would be lost, he was allowed to sell his remaining stock to out-of-towners, or to townspeople "for the reliefe of the weake or sicke" (*PCR* 4:136).

Giles Rickard was a weaver by trade (*MD* 11:18, 12:132). His residence in Plymouth was a little south of the bridge over Town Brook, with the highway to Sandwich cutting between his lands and those of John Barnes (*Ply. Town Recs.* 1:84 fn). Barnes is frequently mentioned with him in the records, and Rickard's son John married an Esther Barnes, whom John Barnes named in his will as a "kinswoman." Giles Rickard dated his will 8 January 1684/85 and the witnesses, Ephraim Morton and William Harlow, swore to it on 5 March 1684/85 (*Ply. Colony PR* 4:2:101-02). In his will he called himself a weaver, and named his wife Hannah, who was to get the lower and upper rooms, garret, and little bedroom of his house in Plymouth, plus one-half of his shop and barn, and the benefit of one-half of his land and orchard, plus his second best bed, suitable furniture, bedclothes, a pewter platter, other household items, and two cows. He also left bequests to his grandson John Rickard, son of his son John, and to Giles and John Rickard, sons of his son Giles. The residue of his estate was left to his son Giles. His inventory of 6 February 1684/85 consisted of several pieces of real estate valued at £95, and about £66 in livestock and personal property, including some small books and two Bibles. Additional information on his family can be found in Eugene A. Stratton, "Which John Rickard Married Mary Cooke?" *MQ* 49:122. Mrs. Barclay shows convincingly in "Rebecca, Wife of Reverend Isaac Cushman," *TAG* 26:144 that Cushman's wife was not, as some others have stated, of Giles Rickard's family. There is no evidence that the Sarah Rickard who married George Pidcock on 16 May 1640 was his daughter (*PCR* 1:153), and it is most unlikely. A three-generation genealogy of Giles Rickard's family is being compiled for journal publication by Ginger K. W. Stratton.

RIGDALE, ALICE—The wife of John Rigdale, Alice accompanied him on the 1620 *Mayflower* and died in the early months of Plymouth Colony.

RIGDALE, JOHN—Arriving with his wife Alice on the 1620 *Mayflower*, John Rigdale died in the early months of Plymouth Colony, leaving no known descendants.

RING, MARY—The William Ring who turned back to England in 1620 on the *Speedwell* with Robert Cushman (*Bradford [Ford]* 1:145) probably died later in Leiden. It was most likely his wife, Mary Ring, who witnessed the betrothal of Samuel Terry in Leiden in 1614 (Dexter, p. 630), and she is probably the Mary Ring who arrived at Plymouth ca. 1629 with children Elizabeth, Susanna, and Andrew (John Insley Coddington, "The Widow Mary Ring, of Plymouth, Mass., and Her Children," *TAG* 42:193). Mr. Coddington builds a tentative pedigree to show that William Ring quite likely was the man of that name of Pettistree, County Suffolk, who married at Ufford, County Suffolk, 21 May 1601 Mary Durrant of Ufford; a daughter Elizabeth was baptized at Ufford 23 February 1602/03. Mary Ring died at Plymouth 15 or 19 July 1631, and in her will she named her daughters Elizabeth Deane and Susan Clark, her son-in-law Stephen Deane, a child of Stephen and Elizabeth Deane, and her son Andrew Ring, who was a minor. She named her friends Samuel Fuller and Thomas Blossom as overseers of the will (*MD* 1:29); both Fuller and Blossom had been members of the Leiden congregation. Son Andrew married (1) Deborah Hopkins daughter of *Mayflower* passenger Stephen Hopkins and (2) Lettice (_____) Morton, widow of John Morton. The children of Mary Ring's children are given in Mr. Coddington's article.

ROBINSON, ISAAC—Although Pastor John Robinson and his wife, Bridget (White) Robinson, did not get to Plymouth, their son Isaac, born ca. 1610, did, arriving in 1631 according to a note of Judge Sewall's conversation with him (Pope). Somehow one might expect that the son of the Separatists' beloved pastor would have been given special privileges, but though he became a freeman by 7 March 1636/37 (*PCR* 1:52), he was not on the original freeman list, nor was he made a Purchaser. He became a resident of Scituate, joining the church there on 7 November 1636, having a dismissal from the Plymouth Church, and he had a new house in Scituate in 1637. On 27 June 1636 he entered married intentions at Mr. Hatherly's house with Margaret Hanford, daughter of Hatherly's sister Eglin Hanford (*NEHGR* 9:280, 10:43, 9:286). Mary Lovering Holman, "The Robinson Family," *TAG* 18:45, shows that Isaac's second wife was not, as some claim, Mary Faunce, or an Elizabeth, and Mrs. Holman pointed out that although the second wife was believed to have been a

Mary, there was no proof. However, Robert S. Wakefield, "Isaac Robinson's Second Wife Mary," *TAG* 56:147, cites *Plymouth Colony LR* 3:154 to show that in a deed of 1669 Isaac Robinson of Saconesett (Falmouth) was joined by his wife Mary. His children by Margaret Hanford were Susanna, who died young; John, who married Elizabeth Weeks; Isaac, who married a Mary, but drowned apparently without issue; Fear, who married Rev. Samuel Baker as his first wife; Mercy, who married William Weeks; and Margaret, who died young. His children by Mary were Isaac, who was born Israel but had his name changed to Isaac after his half-brother Isaac drowned, and who married Anne Cottle; Jacob, who married (1) a Mary and (2) Experience Rogers; Peter, who married (1) Mary Manter and (2) an Experience; and Thomas, who disappears from the records (Mrs. Holman shows that he was probably not the Thomas Robinson of Guilford, Connecticut) (*TAG* 18:45). See also Mary Lovering Holman, *Ancestry of Col. John H. Stevens,. . .*, vol. 1 (Concord, N.H., 1948), p. 487. Robinson moved with the Lothrop group to Barnstable in 1639, and he died there age ninety-four in 1704 (*TAG* 18:45).

He served on the grand jury in 1639 (*PCR* 1:126); he was tax collector for Barnstable in 1646 (*PCR* 2:105); and he had several like positions. He was a deputy for Barnstable in 1645 and 1651 (*PCR* 2:94. 168). On 3 May 1659 John Cogan, minor son of the deceased Henry Cogan, selected Capt. James Cudworth and Isaac Robinson as his guardians (*PCR* 3:161). On 1 March 1658/59 Isaac Robinson and Giles Rickard, Sr. complained to the court that Henry Cogan's two children who were living with John Finney of Barnstable were being wrongly treated (*PCR* 3:156). On 7 March 1659/60 the court took notice of "sundry scandals and falchoods in a letter of Isacke Robinsons, tending greatly to the prejudice of this govment, and incurragement of those commonly called Quakers," and also noted that such an offence could result in disfranchisement, but the court would forbear until further inquiry (*PCR* 3:183). However, on 6 June 1660 the court disfranchised Robinson and Captain Cudworth for being manifest opposers of the law. An addition to the records states that "There being some mistake in this, att his request, hee, the said Isacke Robinson, is reestablished, and by generall voat of the Court accepted againe into the association of the body of the freemen" (*PCR* 3:189). The date of the addition is unknown, but on 4 July 1673 the court voted to restore him to freeman status (*PCR* 5:126), and thus he might have been without the vote for some 13 years. On 8 April 1664 John Cogan, having come of age, discharged his "loveing frinds" James Cudworth and Isaac Robinson from accountability as his guardian (*PCR* 4:77). On 7 February 1664/65 Mr. Isaac Robinson was approved by the court to keep an ordinary at Saconesett (*PCR* 4:80). He continued to receive various land grants along with others, but otherwise is mostly unmentioned in the records during the last decades of his life.

ROGERS, THOMAS – A 1620 *Mayflower* passenger, Thomas Rogers was a camlet merchant in Leiden, where he became a citizen in 1618. He sold his house there in 1620 (Dexter, p. 632). His son Joseph accompanied him to Plymouth, and survived him when Thomas died during the early illnesses. The wife of Thomas, Elizabeth or Elsgen, stayed at Leiden, and she was mentioned there in a tax list of 1622 with her children, John, Lysbeth, and Grietgen; she probably died at Leiden. Son John came to Plymouth after the 1627 division. John married Anna Churchman, and his brother Joseph married Hannah _____ (see *MF* 2). *Bradford (Ford)* 2:400, 409, stated that Thomas's "other children came afterwards," and "The rest of Thomas Rogers [children] came over, and are maried, and have many children." One of the "rest" of his children, of course, was son John, but there must have been at least one other, possibly more, who have not yet been identified. See Samuel Eddy for some speculation on this matter.

ROWLEY, HENRY—On 17 October 1633 Henry Rowley married Anna Blossom, widow of Thomas Blossom (*PCR* 1:16). He became a freeman 1 January 1634/35 (*PCR* 1:32). He and his wife joined Lothrop's Scituate Church at its origin on 8 January 1634/35, and he was probably one of those who had been dismissed at the same time from the Plymouth Church for this purpose; he had one of the nine houses at Scituate existing before Lothrop's arrival in September 1634, and he acquired Henry Cobb's house at Scituate between September 1634 and October 1637 (*NEHGR* 9:279, 10:42). He was among those given land at Sippican (*PCR* 1:108), and he accompanied the Lothrop group to Barnstable, where he was constable on 2 March 1640/41 (*PCR* 2:9). He was a deputy for Barnstable on 29 August 1643. He died intestate, and an inventory of his property was exhibited to the court in July 1673 by his son Moses (*MD* 24:137). Moses Rowley married Elizabeth Fuller, granddaughter of *Mayflower* passenger Edward Fuller (*PCR* 8:47; *MD* 13:8). Torrey suggests a prior wife as mother of Moses, and this seems reasonable if Anna Blossom had prevously been married by 1610 or earlier.

SABIN, WILLIAM—Though the name has been taken to indicate a Huguenot origin, William Henry Waldo Sabine, "The Surname Sabin(e) Its Origin and Development from Circa 1200," *NEHGR* 101:264, cites evidence to show that the name is found in England centuries before there were Huguenots. Mr. Sabine also shows the concentration of the name around Tichfield, Hampshire, and he cites an entry in the Tichfield parish register of 6 October 1609 of the baptism of William Sabin, probably the son of William and Mary (Bushe) Sabine, as most likely pertaining to the Plymouth Colony immigrant of that name. William is first found in Plymouth records in a 1643 list of Rehoboth inhabitants giving their net worth for the purpose of obtaining future land grants and paying taxes— his "estate" of £53 was among the lowest on the list. His first wife died ca. 1660-63, and he married (2) on 22 December 1663 Martha Allen, daughter of James and Anne Allen of Medfield. He was a deputy to the General Court in 1657, 1659, 1660, 1661, 1670, and 1671, a constable in Rehoboth in 1672, a selectman in 1685 and 1686, and he was often on juries. He died 9 February 1686/87, mentioning an unnamed wife and his surviving children in his will (*Suffolk County PR*, 1582). By his first wife he had Samuel,

Elizabeth, Joseph, Benjamin, Nehemiah, Experience, Mary (or Mercy), Abigail, Hannah, Patience, Jeremiah, and Sarah. By his second wife he had James, John, Hezekiah, Noah, Mehitabel, Mary, Sarah, and Margaret. Much of this material is from an unpublished compilation by John B. Threlfall. Torrey suggests that Sabin's first wife might have been _____ Wright. An early article on Sabin and his family is in *NEHGR* 36:52.

SAMSON, ABRAHAM—It had long been thought that Abraham Samson was a brother to 1620 *Mayflower* passenger Henry Samson, but in Robert Leigh Ward's first article shown under Henry Samson below, there is no mention of Abraham in Henlow parish records. However, in "Henry Sampson's Paternal Grandfather" (*TAG* 56:141), Ward shows Henry's father James had a brother Laurence, who married Mary Shabery, and among their children was an Abraham Samson born at Campton, Bedfordshire, 14 August 1614, who would thus be a good candidate for the Plymouth Colony Abraham Samson. Abraham first appears in Plymouth records as a resident of Duxbury who was presented on 4 December 1638 for striking John Washburn, Jr. at the meeting house on the Lord's day (*PCR* 1:107). In 1646/47 he was fined for being drunk, and in 1648 he was made a surveyor of the highways for Duxbury (*PCR* 2:111, 124). He became a freeman in 1654 (*PCR* 3:48). He was one of the former servants and ancient freemen given land at Saconnet Neck in 1662 (*PCR* 4:18). In 1662/63 he was fined ten shillings for being drunk (*PCR* 4:33). Mrs. Barclay, "The Early Sampsons," *TAG* 28:1, shows that there is no record of his death, nor of the births of his children. Since Henry Samson named his children in his will, there is a strong assumption that the other Samsons of the right age in Duxbury must be Abraham's sons, and these include Samuel, George, Abraham, and Isaac, all of whom left descendants. Clarence Almon Torrey, "A Nash-Sampson-Delano-Howland Problem," *TAG* 15:165, gives indirect evidence to show that Abraham Samson had by his first wife (who was a daughter of Samuel Nash, q.v.) daughters Elizabeth, who married Philip 2 Delano, and Mary, who married Samuel 2 Howland, and he may have had other daughters. Torrey showed that Abraham's son Samuel was also by his first wife, but the other sons were probably by an unidentified second wife.

SAMSON, HENRY—Robert Leigh Ward, "English Ancestry of Seven Mayflower Passengers: Tilley, Sampson, and Cooper," *TAG* 52:198, traces Henry Samson back to Henlow, Bedfordshire, England, where he was baptized 15 January 1603/04, the son of James and Martha (Cooper) Samson. Bradford called him a child, and a cousin to Edward and Ann Tilley and to Humility Cooper, all of whom sailed with him on the 1620 *Mayflower*. In "Henry Sampson's Paternal Grandfather," *TAG* 56:141, Ward analyzes additional evidence on his grandparents. See also Ward, "The Baronial Ancestry of Henry Sampson, Humility Cooper, and Ann (Cooper) Tilley," *TG* 6:166. In Plymouth Henry Samson married on 6 February 1635 Anne Plummer (*PCR* 1:36). He was one of the Purchasers and over the years received generous land grants (*PCR*, passim). He became a freeman before

7 March 1636/37, and he was a volunteer in the Pequot War (*PCR* 1:53, 61). On 5 January 1640/41 he bought from John Cooke the remaining term of indenture of Philip Davis (*PCR* 2:6). He served on grand and trial juries, as constable of Duxbury, and as a tax collector, and he assisted in laying out grants of land on behalf of the court (*PCR*, passim). He made his will 24 December 1684, sworn 5 March 1684/85, and he named his sons Stephen, John, James, and Caleb, and daughter Elizabeth, wife of Robert Sprout; Hannah, wife of Josias Holmes; the wife of John Hanmore; Mary, wife of John Summers; and Dorcas, wife of Thomas Bonney. Mrs. Barclay, "The Early Sampsons," *TAG* 28:1, sorts out some of the confusion over the descendants of Henry and Abraham Samson. An article "Robert [1] Sprout of Scituate, MA, and His Wife Elizabeth Samson," by Robert M. Sherman and Robert S. Wakefield, will appear in *TAG* 61:200.

SARGENT, WILLIAM—Baptized at Northampton, Northamptonshire, on 20 June 1602, William Sargent died at Barnstable, 16 December 1682. His first wife Hannah _____ died in England, as did probably his second wife Mary _____. He was last recorded in England on 22 January 1636/37 (baptism of a daughter) and first recorded in New England at Charlestown, where he and his third wife Sarah were admitted as church members 10 March 1638/39. An entry in *Lechford's Notebook*, p. 224, gives a certificate by Governor Winthrop regarding William Sargent of Charlestown, a haberdasher of hats, from Northampton, England, and his wife Sarah, widow of William Minshall of Whitchurch, County Salop. Sargent moved first to Malden, and then, ca. 1656 or 1657, to Barnstable. He was made a Bay freeman in 1639 and was a lay preacher in Malden and Barnstable. G. Andrews Moriarty gives documentary evidence in a series of articles in *NEHGR* 74:231, 267, 75:57, 129, 79:358, tracing William Sargent's line back to English royalty.

Sargent almost always appears in the records with the title "Mr." On 1 June 1658 he was made a freeman by the Plymouth General Court (*PCR* 3:137). A fairly good, but mostly undocumented, family history is Aaron Sargent, *Sargent Genealogy* (Somerville, Mass., 1895)—some errors in the early generations have been corrected by the Moriarty articles. This book also transcribes William Sargent's will. His children by his first wife were Elizabeth (died young), Hannah (married Henry Felch of Reading, Mass.), Elizabeth (married [1] David Nichols of Boston and [2] Thomas Bill of Boston), and Mary (died young). By his second wife, Sargent had Sarah and Mary, both of whom probably died young. By his third wife he had John (married [1] Deborah Hillier of Barnstable and [2] Lydia Chipman, daughter of John and Hope [Howland] Chipman, and granddaughter of *Mayflower* passenger John Howland); Ruth (married [1] Jonathan Winslow, son of Josiah and nephew of Gov. Edward Winslow, [2] Richard Bourne of Sandwich, q.v., and [3] John Chipman [after the death of his wife Hope]; and Samuel (died unmarried). Sargent has many descendants living today.

SAVORY, THOMAS—He may have been related to the Anthony Savory who was on the 1633 freeman list, and who apparently died in the

1630s. Thomas was one of the four men sent by John Howland in 1634 on the Kennebec River to cut the moorings of Hocking's ship, Hocking having aimed his gun first at Savory, but then shooting and killing Moses Talbot instead (*MD* 2:11). In October 1636 Savory was found guilty of drunkenness, and was sentenced to be whipped (*PCR* 1:44). In 1641 Joshua Pratt was granted some land near the house he had bought of Thomas Savory at "Squerrell" (*PCR* 2:27). In 1652 Samuel Nash was appointed chief marshal and Thomas Savory under marshal, or executioner, of Plymouth Colony (*PCR* 3:12). In 1659/60 Savory was fined five shillings for being drunk (*PCR* 3:181). On 7 May 1661 Ann, the wife of Thomas Savory, was found guilty for being at home on the Lord's day with Thomas Lucas during the time of public worship and for being found drunk at the time under a hedge in an uncivil and beastly manner, and she was sentenced to sit in the stocks and fined five shillings for drunkenness and ten shillings for profaning the Lord's day (*PCR* 3:212). In the will of Timothy Hatherly, dated 20 December 1664, fifty shillings was to be given to "my man Thomas Savory. . .when his service is expired" (*MD* 16:158); this was likely Savory's son Thomas, then about sixteen years old. In 1665 Thomas, Sr. was a surety for George Barlow, who was accused of attempting the chastity of Abigail, wife of Jonathan Pratt (*PCR* 4:88). On 7 June 1665 Savory was granted one share in the Major's Purchase in Middleborough "for his children" (*PCR* 4:95). On 7 June 1670 he was dismissed from his office of under marshal, having been found several times unfaithful to the office and especially for letting Joseph Turner escape, but on his petition he was restored to office on 5 July 1670 (*PCR* 5:40, 44).

Thomas Savory made his will 6 April 1674, sworn 7 March 1675/76, and he left all his estate to his wife, Ann, also called Annis. He also desired "my deare wife to Consider; my son Aron att her decease; if shee have any thinge left; and the Reason why I Give all to my wife is because I have little my debts being payed" (*Ply. Colony PR* 3:1:172). The wording might indicate that son Aaron was by an earlier wife, but not necessarily. On 7 March 1675/76 Ann Savory, widow, was given administration of her late husband Thomas Savory's estate. His children, probably by Ann, included Moses, Samuel, Jonathan, and Mara, born between 1649 and 1654 (*PCR* 8:8, 12, 14, 16). The births of older children were not recorded. Savory's son Thomas, five years old in March 1653, was put out as an apprentice carpenter to Thomas Lettice on 2 August 1653 (*MD* 3:139-41), and a son Benjamin, eight years old in March 1653, was put out on 3 November 1653 to John and Alice Shaw, Shaw paying Thomas Savory thirty shillings (*MD* 5:90-91). Another son, Anthony, is mentioned in a deed of 22 March 1677/78 in which Ann Savory, widow, gave land to her sons Anthony Savory and Aron Savory which belonged to her deceased husband Thomas Savory by exchange with "our brother in law Samuell Eedey" (*Ply. Colony LR* 4:311). Note under Samuel Eddy the speculation that his wife Elizabeth might have been a daughter of Thomas Rogers. A Margaret Savory in

Leiden in 1613 and in 1619 (Dexter, p. 633) would have been too old to have been an earlier wife of Thomas Savory, but it does show that the surname was found there.

SHAW, JOHN—Arriving at Plymouth between 1623, when he was not named in the division of land, and 1626, when he was a Purchaser, John Shaw became the leader of one of the companies in the 1627 cattle division, and he was on the 1633 freeman list. It is likely that he had one or more children born in England, though any family would have arrived after the 1627 list, for he was alone at that time. He was later known to have a wife Alice, surname unknown, and it is not known if she came from England, or if he might have had an earlier wife in England. Shaw engaged in a number of land transactions, was a leader of the group that cut the passage between Green's Harbor and the bay in 1633 (*PCR* 1:13-14), and was a highway surveyor for Plymouth in 1643 and 1644 (*PCR* 2:53, 72). In 1653 John and Alice Shaw agreed to raise Benjamin Savory, son of Thomas and Annis Savory, and if they died before Benjamin reached twenty-one, Jonathan Shaw, John's son, was to do it, and was also to teach Benjamin reading and writing (*MD* 5:90). On 26 March 1658 John Shaw of Plymouth, planter, gave his son, Sgt. James Shaw, one-half of his land at Cushena, but another son, John Shaw, would get half of the land given James if he came before 1 March 1661/62 (*MD* 10:34). On 30 January 1663/64 John Shaw, Sr. gave his son-in-law Stephen Bryant land at Namassakett and Rehoboth, and he gave one-half of his land at Cushena to his son James, and one-fourth of the same land each to his son Jonathan Shaw and his son-in-law Stephen Bryant; he gave his daughter Abigail Bryant his furniture after his death (*MD* 10:35). On 22 March 1663/64 George Watson and John Shaw, Sr. were granted a lot on Puncateesett Necke (*Ply. Town Recs.* 1:67). Benjamin Shurtleff wrote an undocumented history of his family, *John Shaw of Plymouth, Massachusetts* (Kenilworth, Ill.).

SHERMAN, WILLIAM—Mary Lovering Holman, *Descendants of William Sherman of Marshfield, Massachusetts* (Concord, N.H., 1936), is a model for the presentation of a family history. Little is known about William Sherman before he appeared on the 1633 tax list. He married in 1638 Prudence Hill, possibly a sister of Ralph Hill. In 1640 Sherman was granted land in Marshfield and he resided there the rest of his life. In 1653 he served on a committee to arrange for the building of a bridge over the South River, and in 1657 he was a grandjuror. He died intestate, and there is no probate record of his estate. From land records given by Holman, there is evidence to show that he had sons William, Samuel, and John, and Holman shows by another land record and the probate record of Edward Stephens that William Sherman had a daughter, possibly named Sarah or Hannah, who was the wife of Edward Stephens.

SHURTLEFF, WILLIAM—The name Shurtleff has been spelled many ways, and on 2 September 1634 "William Shetle hath put himselfe an aprentise to Thomas Clarke for the terme of eleven yeares from the 16 of May last" (*PCR* 1:31). On 5 June 1644 William Shertcliffe was fined five shillings for breaking the peace on John Smyth (*PCR* 2:73), and on 2 October 1650 James Cole was presented for making a battery on Shirtleff, but was cleared (*PCR* 2:162). Shurtleff was a surveyor of the highway for Plymouth and a member of a coroner's jury in 1656 (*PCR* 3:100, 109). In 1659 he had a dispute with Thomas Pope about the bounds of their respective lands at Strawberry Hill, or the Reed Pond, in Plymouth township (*PCR* 3:169). On 7 June 1659 he was proposed as a freeman, and on the same day he was chosen as constable of Plymouth (*PCR* 3:163). On 27 March 1660 he sold an acre of land in Doten's Meadow, Plymouth, to Gabriel Fallowell, and at that time Shurtleff was described as a resident of Marshfield (*MD* 14:145). On 6 June 1660 he became a freeman (*PCR* 3:188). In 1662 he was one of the servants and ancient freemen given land at Saconett (*PCR* 4:18). In 1664/65 he complained against Thomas Little for taking away timber trees from his land (*PCR* 4:79). In 1666 the court ordered that he "be accommodated with land amongst the servants neare unto the Bay line" (*PCR* 4:131).

On 18 October 1655 William Shurtleff married Elizabeth Lettice (*PCR* 8:17), daughter of Thomas Lettice. He died in 1666 and was buried on 24 June 1666, having been killed by lightning (*MSR*, p. 248; see documentation in Shurtleff book below, 2:1064). His widow married (2) Jacob Cooke 18 November 1669 (*PCR* 8:32), and she was in her father's will dated 1678 as Elizabeth Cooke, widow (*MD* 14:64). She married (3) Hugh Cole on 1 January 1688/89 (*MD* 13:204). A full-size family history is Benjamin Shurtleff, *Descendants of William Shurtleff of Plymouth and Marshfield, Massachusetts*, 2 vols. (Revere, 1912; 2nd ed. San Francisco, 1976), which is not sufficiently documented and contains a number of errors (for correction of one major error, see Eugene A. Stratton, "Mary, Wife of Nathaniel Atwood," *MQ* 48:127). In the first edition, Benjamin Shurtleff has the immigrant William Shurtleff most likely identical with a William Shurtleff said to have been baptized at Hallamshire, Ecclesfield, West Riding, Yorkshire, on 16 May 1624. However, in the second edition, Roy Lothrop Shurtleff states that after extensive checking he was not able to confirm the identification, and must conclude that it is not yet possible to go further back than the immigrant William. William was known to have had three sons, William, Thomas, and Abiel, and has many descendants today through William and Abiel.

SIBSEY, JOHN—Bradford (*Morrison*, p. 189-92) called Mr. John Sibsey and Mr. Fells the chief among many passengers aboard the *Sparrowhawk* bound for Virginia in 1627 when it was wrecked off Cape Cod. All the passengers were allowed to stay at the colony until they could get another ship for Virginia, and in the meantime were permitted to plant a crop for their subsistence. Most of these passengers were servants, many of whom came from Ireland. Apparently all this group left the colony when they were able. They would have been present during the 1627 cattle division, but did not share in it.

SILVESTER, RICHARD – According to Banks (*Planters* 2:91), Richard Silvester came to New England in 1630 on the *Mary and John,* the ship carrying West Country passengers who founded Dorchester in the Bay Colony, but this has not been confirmed. He settled briefly at Dorchester, and then went to Weymouth. It was around this time that he married Naomi _____, for they had their first child at Weymouth on 8 December 1633. He became a Bay Colony freeman on 1 April 1634. According to Albert Henry Silvester, "Richard Silvester of Weymouth, Mass., and Some of His Descendants," *NEHGR* 85:247, 357, 86:84, 120, 286, 87:84, 128:202, a good but insufficiently documented family history, he was fined in 1638 for selling strong water, and he was fined again in 1639 for speaking against a law about hogs and against a particular magistrate. On 13 March 1638/39 he was disenfranchised and fined £2 for association with John Smyth in attempting to organize a new church. Deane (*History of Scituate,* p. 347-48) states that Shurtleff gained notoriety for espousing liberal religious sentiments. While at Weymouth, Shurtleff's young son, about six years old, accidentally shot and killed himself with a pistol.

In 1650 Silvester sold his property in Weymouth and moved to Marshfield in Plymouth Colony. He was proposed as a Plymouth freeman in 1651 (*PCR* 2:167), but he was not on the 1658 list of freemen. In 1654 he became a surveyor of the highways for Marshfield (*PCR* 3:50), and in 1655 he became a constable of Marshfield (*PCR* 3:78). On 5 March 1661/62 his daughter Dinah was charged with falsely accusing the wife of William Holmes of being a witch, and on 9 May 1661 Dinah was sentenced to be publicly whipped or pay £5 to William Holmes. Her recorded apology said in part, "I doe freely acknowlidg I have wronged my naighbour, and have sined against God in soe doeing; though I had entertained hard thoughts against the woman, for it had bine my dewty to declare my grounds, if I had any, unto some majestrate in a way of God, and not to have devoulged my thoughts to others, to the womans defamation" (*PCR* 3:205-07, 211). In 1667 Dinah was fined £10 for fornication (*PCR* 4:162). Richard Silvester's will was dated 16 June 1663, proved 2 October 1663, and he named his sons John, Joseph, Israel, Richard, and Benjamin, and his daughters Lydia, Dinah, Elizabeth, Naomi, Hester, and Charity (*MD* 15:60). He left his wife Naomi the residue of his estate, after debts and other bequests were paid, but only £15 if she remarried. However, on 5 October 1663 the court noted that the wording of the will in fact left her an inconsiderable part of his estate, and, as appeared by the testimony of some of her neighbors, she was a frugal and laborious woman who had contributed significantly to the acquisition of Richard's estate. Therefore the court determined to take some (unspecified) prudent course to improve the situation (*PCR* 4:46). Naomi died before 26 November 1668, when her inventory was taken (*MD* 17:110). Though Naomi has been called a Torrey, there is no evidence for this or any other surname for her. What appears to be a mistake in the records (*Weymouth Town Records* 1:196) gives Richard Silvester's wife's first name as "Emline" on 15 September 1651 (see Silvester article, above, p. 266-68); however, he had named a child Naomi before this date, and he certainly had a wife Naomi after this date.

SIMONSON, MOSES—Moses Simonson arrived on the *Fortune* in 1621. Though not on the 1633 freeman list, he became a freeman no later than 7 March 1636/37 (*PCR* 1:53). He was in Leiden with the Separatists, and Winslow called him a member of the Dutch Church who could speak English and who took communion with the Separatist Church (*Hypocrisie Unmasked*, p. 63). He also went by the name Moses Simons, and on 13 December 1660 Moses Simons of Duxbury and his wife Sarah sold his right of lands in Bridgewater to Nicholas Byram (*MD* 34:85). He dated his will 17 June 1689, calling himself "aged and full of decay," and his inventory was taken 10 September 1691 (*MD* 31:60). He mentioned his sons Aaron and John; and his daughters Mary, wife of Joseph Alden; Elizabeth, wife of Richard Dwelly; and Sarah, wife of James Nash. He also had a son Moses, Jr. of Scituate, who predeceased him (*Ply. Colony PR* 3:2:62-63).

SMITH, RALPH—A 1613 graduate of Christ College, Cambridge, Ralph Smith sailed to Salem in the Talbot with the Higginson Fleet (*Bradford [Ford]* 2:87). A letter from Craddock to Endicott showed that Smith had differences of view with other Bay Colony ministers, inclining toward Separatism. Bradford wrote about 1629 that "Ther was one Mr. Ralfe Smith, and his wife and familie, that came over into the Bay of the Massachusets, and sojourned at presente with some stragling people that lived at Natascoe . . . . He ernestly desired that they would give him and his, passage for Plimoth. . . . He was here accordingly kindly entertained and housed, and had the rest of his goods and servants sente for, and exercised his gifts amongst them, and afterwards was chosen into the ministrie, and so remained for sundrie years" (*Ford* 2:87-88). In a footnote, Ford cites Hubbard to show that the Plymouth Church was dissatisfied with its first pastor, and that perhaps he was invited more because of his Separatist tendencies than for any fitness of office, "being much over-matched by him [Brewster] that he was joined with in the presbytery, both in point of discretion to rule, and aptness to teach, so as through many infirmities, being found unable to discharge the trust committed to him with any competent satisfaction, he was forced soon after to lay it down. Many times it is found that a total vacancy of an office is easier to be borne, than an underperformance thereof." See also the text on this matter.

His wife died and after the death of Richard Masterson he married Masterson's widow Mary (Goodall) Masterson, as is shown by a deed (*PCR* 12:176) of 1649 in which Mary Smith, sometime the wife of Richard Masterson, deceased, gave to her son Nathaniel Masterson and her daughter Sarah, wife of John Wood, all her interest in a house in Leiden. Smith left his ministry in 1637, and remained in Plymouth Colony until about 1645, when he became minister at Manchester; Smith later moved to Salem, and died at Boston 1 March 1660/61. Administration of his estate was granted to Nathaniel Masterson, his late wife's son (*Suffolk County Wills* (Baltimore, 1984), p. 189, 365.

SNOW, ANTHONY – Of the three Snows who married into *Mayflower* families, Anthony came over the latest, being first recorded on 7 May 1638 when he requested three acres of land from the court (*PCR* 1:83). On 9 November 1639 he married Abigail Warren, daughter of *Mayflower* passenger Richard Warren (*PCR* 1:134). He served on the grand jury and in other public capacities. He moved to Marshfield, and later, on 5 June 1651, he became a freeman (*PCR* 2:167). He served as a constable for Marshfield and as a Marshfield deputy. He died in August 1692, having made his will 28 December 1685, codicil 8 August 1692, and in it he named his wife Abigail; his son Josias Snow; his daughters Lydia, Sarah, and Alice; his grandson James Ford; his daughter Abigail's children; his granddaughters Hannah and Abigail Ford; his son Josias's wife; and his brother Joseph Warren was to be one of the overseers (*MD* 5:1). His daughter Abigail had married Michael Ford. Anthony also had a son who died young. As is shown by a deed (*PCR* 12:176) from Thomas Church to Anthony Snow and Richard Church, Snow was a feltmaker by trade.

SNOW, NICHOLAS – Nicholas arrived on the *Anne* in 1623, and by the time of the 1627 division he was married to *Mayflower* passenger Constance Hopkins, daughter of Stephen. Banks wrote that he was of Hoxton, County Middlesex. He was a Purchaser and was on the 1633 freeman list. On 5 January 1634/35, the servant of Nicholas Snow, unnamed, was willing to serve out his time with John Cooper, according to the terms of the indenture (*PCR* 1:33). Twyford West, whose indenture had been assigned by Edward Winslow to Nicholas Snow, complained to Winslow that he disliked being with Snow, and on 11 February 1635/36 voluntarily increased his indenture from six to seven years in consideration of Winslow reacquiring his indenture from Snow (*PCR* 1:37). Snow served as highway surveyor, on the grand jury, and in other similar positions, and as a Purchaser he enjoyed various land grants. On 1 December 1640 he was one of several highway surveyors presented for not mending the highways (*PCR* 2:5). He was one of the Plymouth residents moving to Nauset in the 1640s, and he was a surveyor, deputy, tax collector, constable, and selectman there (*PCR*, passim). In 1664 he was among those allowed to bring liquors into Eastham (*PCR* 4:100). He died 15 November 1676, having made his will 14 November 1676, and he named his wife Constant and his sons Mark, Joseph, Stephen, John, and Jabez, and after his wife's death his livestock and moveable estate would be divided among all his children (*MD* 3:167). He also had married daughters Mary, Sarah, Elizabeth, and Ruth, and Bowman thought he had three other probably married daughters. For additional information see Mrs. M. L. T. Alden, "The Snow Genealogy," *NEHGR* 47:81, 186, 341, 48:71, 188, 49:71, 202, 451, 51:204, 64:284, which should be used cautiously.

SNOW, WILLIAM – On 31 August 1638 William Snow, "lately brought out of old England by Mr. Richard Derby," had his indenture transferred to Edward Doty and was to serve Doty seven years (*PCR* 1:94). Inasmuch as Derby had contracted specifically with Doty at Plymouth on 12 July 1637 to procure "one able man servant to serve the said Edward Doty" (*PCR* 12:21), and inasmuch as Derby returned to his home in Sturtle, near Burfort, Dorsetshire, at this time (see John Chipman), we have a clue that Snow may have come from this area, too. William Snow was tried in court on 8 June 1651 for vain, light, and lascivious carriage, and he was admonished on 7 October 1651 for the same (*PCR* 2:170, 172). Ca. 1654 he married Rebecca Browne, daughter of *Mayflower* passenger Peter Browne, q.v., and on 25 March 1667/68 William Snow of Bridgewater, husbandman, sold to Ephraim Tinkham one-third share of land at Dartmouth which had been granted by the court to Peter Browne, a Purchaser (*Ply. Colony LR* 3:111). On 7 November 1679 Snow sold to John Brown another one-third of his land formerly belonging to Peter Browne, and his wife Rebecca consented to the sale (*Ply. Colony LR* 5:197). Snow dated his will 9 March 1698/99, proved 4 March 1708/09, and he mentioned an unnamed wife, his sons William, Joseph, and Benjamin, and his daughters Mary, Lydia, Hannah, and Rebecca (*MD* 8:101). He also had a son James who died in 1690 on the Canadian expedition (*Genealogical Advertiser* 2:62). Although Mitchell, *Bridgewater*, p. 27, stated that William Snow was on a 1657 freeman list for Bridgewater, he actually took the Oath of Fidelity as a resident of Bridgewater in 1657, which was not the same thing, and there is no record that he ever became a freeman (*PCR* 8:185), nor was his name on the 1658 list which is believed to be of all the colony's freemen (*PCR* 8:197-202).

SOULE, GEORGE – A 1620 *Mayflower* passenger, George Soule arrived as a servant to Edward Winslow. He became a Purchaser and was on the 1633 list of freemen. He moved to Duxbury and acquired considerable amounts of land in other places. Soule was a volunteer in the Pequot War and in 1642 was a duputy for Duxbury. He married a Mary, whose surname possibly was Becket. He died in 1679. His will, dated 11 August 1677, with codicil 20 September 1677, proved 1679, named his sons Nathaniel, George, and John, and his daughters Elizabeth, Patience, Susannah, and Mary. He also had sons Zachariah and Benjamin who predeceased him. *MF* 3, with its necessary Addendum, gives his first five generations. The Soule family history compiled by Gideon T. Ridlon is not reliable.

SOUTHWORTH, CONSTANT – Constant Southworth, the son of Edward and Alice (Carpenter) Southworth, was probably born at Leiden ca. 1614-16, for his parents married there 28 May 1613 (Leiden Records, as in *MD* 10:2). The same records show that Edward Southworth had a brother Thomas then living in Leiden. Edward Southworth died, and his widow Alice came to Plymouth and married Gov. William Bradford on 14 August 1623. Constant came to Plymouth in 1628, probably on the *White Angel,* and a contemporary account shows that the Plymouth Company paid twenty shillings for his passage and four shillings, eight pence per week for eleven weeks for his food (*MHS Collections,* 3rd Series, 1:199). It is assumed that he, and his brother Thomas, who must have come over later, lived with their mother and step-father, Governor Bradford. The

Southworth family was apparently of gentle birth, but claims that Edward Southworth was identical with the Edward Southworth, son of Thomas and Rosamond (Lister) Southworth, or Samlesbury Hall, Lancashire, are not adequately supported.

Constant Southworth married Elizabeth Collier, daughter of William Collier (*PCR* 1:68). In his will, dated 27 February 1678/79, inventory 15 March 1678/79, he named his wife Elizabeth; son Edward; son Nathaniel; son William; daughter Mercy Freeman; daughter Alice Church; daughter Mary Alden; daughter Elizabeth Southworth, provided she did not marry William Fobes; daughter Priscilla Southworth; grandson Constant Freeman; cousin Elizabeth Howland; and his brother Thomas. Constant held many important posts, including treasurer, Assistant, and ensign in the Duxbury military company. Samuel G. Webber, *A Genealogy of the South-wards (Southards) Descendants of Constant Southworth* (Boston, 1905), is a good family history, though insufficiently documented.

SOUTHWORTH, THOMAS—A brother of Constant Southworth, q.v., Thomas was probably born at Leiden ca. 1616-20, and he came to Plymouth sometime after 1627, most likely living with his mother, Alice, and her husband, Gov. William Bradford. He married 1 September 1641 Elizabeth Reyner, perhaps kin to Rev. John Reyner, and they had one child, Elizabeth, who married Joseph Howland (*PCR* 2:23). On 28 October 1641 William Bradford gave a house and land "unto my sone-in-law [stepson] Thomas Southworth" (PCR 12:76-77). Thomas occupied important positions, including Assistant, deputy, commissioner of the United Colonies, and military captain (*PCR*, passim). He died 8 December 1669 (*PCR* 8:32). His will, dated 18 November 1669, proved 1 March 1669/70, named his wife and his daughter Elizabeth Howland, and her husband Joseph, and left gifts to Thomas Faunce, Deborah Morton, William Churchill, and "my brother Constant Southworth" (*MD* 18:185-86). The Thomas Southworth who came to Plymouth should not be confused with his uncle, Thomas Southworth, who stayed behind in Leiden.

SPARROW, RICHARD—Richard Sparrow was on the 1633 freeman list. He served in various public capacities, such as juryman, highway surveyor, and constable for Plymouth (*PCR*, passim). On 24 June 1639 Mary Moorecock, with the consent of her father-in-law (probably step-father), apprenticed herself to Richard Sparrow and his wife Pandora for nine years (*PCR* 1:128-9). On 2 October 1650, Thomas Shrive was presented for pilfering corn from Richard Sparrow's barn, and Sparrow was presented for concealing Shrive's crime (*PCR* 2:162). Sparrow moved to Eastham, where he was elected a deputy 6 April 1653 (*PCR* 3:24). In his will dated 19 November 1660, inventory 22 January 1660/61, he named his wife Pandora, son Jonathan, and grandchildren John Sparrow, Priscilla Sparrow, and Rebecca Sparrow (*MD* 12:57). A more complete account is given in *Dawes-Gates* 2:763-68, which shows that he had only one known child, Jonathan, who married (1) Rebecca Bangs (2) Hannah (Prence) Mayo and (3) Sarah (Lewis) Cobb, having six children by his first wife and three children by his second wife. The Richard Sparrow house is one of the oldest houses remaining in Plymouth today.

SPRAGUE, FRANCIS – Arriving in 1623 on the *Anne*, Francis Sprague had three shares in the 1623 land division, and he was in the 1627 cattle division with Anna Sprague and Mercy Sprague, the latter known to be his daughter, but his relationship to Anna, possibly a wife or another daughter, is not known. His son John Sprague was born in Plymouth and married Ruth Basset, daughter of William Basset (Maclean W. McLean, "John 2 Sprague (c. 1635-1676) of Duxbury, Mass.," *TAG* 41:178, gives the next two generations). Mary Lovering Holman, *The Scott Genealogy* (1919), p. 241, gives him four children. In addition to a son John, Francis had Mercy Sprague, who married 9 November 1637 William Tubbs (*PCR* 1:68); Anna Sprague, who married before 1 April 1644 William Lawrence (*PCR* 12:138 shows that on that date Francis Sprague sold fifty acres of land to his son-in-law William Lawrence); and Dorcas Sprague, who married before 26 October 1659 Ralph Earle (*MD* 14:90-91 shows that on that date Sprague sold land to his son-in-law Ralph Earle). Though William Lawrence's wife was a daughter of Francis Sprague, it is assumed that her first name was Ann, and if it should later be learned that the Anna in the 1627 division was Sprague's wife, then the first name of Lawrence's wife is unknown. A family history is W. V. Sprague, *Sprague Families of America* (1913, with supplements 1940, 1941). One of the Purchasers, Sprague was on the 1633 and 1634 tax lists and became a freeman 7 June 1637. On 2 January 1637/38 he was presented for beating William Halloway, erstwhile servant to William Bassett (*PCR* 1:75). In 1638 he was licensed to keep an ordinary at Duxbury; his license was suspended in 1640, but he was licensed again in 1646 (*PCR* 1:99, 153, 2:104). In 1650 he became a constable for Duxbury (*PCR* 2:153). On 27 April 1661 Francis Sprague of Duxbury deeded his dwelling house and land to his son John Sprague with the provision that John would not take possession until his father died (*MD* 19:107). Francis was listed in the 29 May 1670 list of freemen in Duxbury, but his name was crossed out (*PCR* 5:275), which would seem to indicate that he died shortly after that date. The Anthony Sprague who married Elizabeth, daughter of Robert Bartlett, and the Joanna Sprague who married Caleb Church, were not of this family, but were children of William Sprague of Hingham.

STANDISH, MYLES – Young, *Planters*, p. 33-34, gives an excerpt from Hubbard that "Captain Standish had been bred a soldier in the Low Countries, and never entered the school of our Saviour Christ, or of John Baptist, his harbinger," and this is the evidence that Myles Standish never joined the Separatist Church. He was acquainted with the Leiden Church, though, and Nathaniel Morton writes (*Memoriall* p. 143) that "In his younger time he went over into the Low-Countreys, and was a Souldier there, and came acquainted with the Church of Leyden, and came over into New-England with such of them as at the first set out for the Planting of the Plantation of New-Plimoth, and bare a deep share of their first

Difficulties, and was alwayes very faithful to their Interest." After he rescued the Englishmen at Wessagusset, and killed a number of Indians in
the process, some of the Plymouth company criticized Standish. Bradford,
in a letter of 8 September 1623, defended him, "As for capten Standish we
leave him to answare for him selfe; but this we must say, he is as helpfull
an instrument as any we have, and as carefull of the generall good" (*Bradford [Ford]* 1:368-69 footnote). Pastor Robinson in a letter from Leiden of
19 December 1623 was also critical of the killings at Wessagusset, writing
"ther is cause to fear. . .ther may be wanting that tendernes of the life of
man (made after Gods image) which is meete. It is also a thing more glori-
ous in mens eyes, then pleasing in Gods, or conveniente for Christians,
to be a terrour to poore barbarous people." Robinson felt that under the
circumstance one or two Indians killed would have been enough, and he
was distressed at the total number. Still he emphasized his personal feelings for Standish, "whom I love, and am perswaded the Lord in great mer-
cie and for much good hath sent you him, if you use him aright. He is a
man humble and meek amongst you, and towards all in ordinarie course"
(*Ford* 1:368).

Standish arrived at Plymouth on the 1620 *Mayflower* with his wife Rose,
who died in the early months, and he married again before the 1627 division Barbara _____ by whom he had all his known children. In his
position as the colony's chief military officer, he had to be rechosen each
year, and though a few might have voted against him, such as Billington,
Oldham, and Lyford, Standish held an uninterrupted term of office as captain. He was also an Assistant for many years, as well as treasurer for some.
He was Acting Governor on at least one occasion, when the Court of Assistants met on 3 May 1653 under Capt. Myles Standish, who had been
"deputed, in the absence of the Governor, to bee in his place" (*PCR* 3:27).
Although he was entirely faithful to the colony, on at least one occasion
he differed from the other leading officials—Bradford, Winslow, and
Prence—when in 1645 he sided with Vassall in the controversy over freedom of religion (see text). He died on 3 October 1656. His will was dated
7 March 1655, proved May 1657, and he named his wife Barbara; his sons
Alexander, Myles, Charles, and Josias; his deceased daughter Lora and
daughter-in-law Mary (who was a daughter of John Dingley, q.v.); Mercy
Robinson "whom I tenderly love for her grandfathers [Pastor John Robin-
son] sake"; and his servant John Irish, Jr. (*MD* 3:153). He appointed his
loving friends Mr. Timothy Hatherly and Capt. James Cudworth
supervisors of his will. His inventory shows by the books he left a most
impressive range of interests. The last part of his will itemizing lands
"Surruptuously Detained from mee my great grandfather being a second
or younger brother from the House of Standish of Standish" has provoked
many a study to determine his precise origins—see Thomas Porteus, "Some
Recent Investigations Concerning the Ancestry of Capt. Myles Standish,"
NEHGR 68:339, and G. V. C. Young, *Pilgrim Myles Standish: First Manx
American* (Isle of Man, 1984), and "Pilgrim Myles Standish: His European

Background," Bangs's *Pilgrims*, pp. 35-43. It does appear that Standish probably had his origin in the Isle of Man, and though his parentage does not yet seem fully proven, the studies of Mr. Young and others are continuing. It is likely that Standish was somehow of the Standish of Standish family, for he was too honest to lie about it, and too intelligent to be mistaken on an essential aspect of his own recent generations. Myles Standish, *The Standishes of America*, 2nd ed. (1895), is neither particularly accurate or complete. Merton Taylor Goodrich, "The Children and Grandchildren of Capt. Myles Standish," *NEHGR* 87:149 gives information on his early descendants, but more research is needed. See also Norman Weston Standish, "Standish Lands in England," *MQ* 52:109.

STATIE, HUGH—Hugh Statie arrived at Plymouth in 1621 on the *Fortune*, and he received one share in the 1623 land division. He was not in the 1627 cattle division. A Hugh Stacy later appeared in Salem and Dedham, and since the pronunciation of Statie and Stacy could be quite similar, there is a possibility that the two were identical.

STETSON, ROBERT—Deane (*Scituate*, p. 340) stated that Robert Stetson received a grant of a considerable amount of land on the North River in 1634 from the Plymouth Court, but court records do not show the event. Stetson first appears in Plymouth records on the occasion of the birth of his first child in June 1639 (*PCR* 8:18). He was a constable for Scituate in 1642/43 (*PCR* 2:53), and a grand jury member in 1652 (*PCR* 3:10). He became a freeman on 7 June 1653 (*PCR* 3:30), and he became a deputy (probably for Scituate) for the first of many times on 7 March 1653/54 (*PCR* 3:44). He was confirmed on 6 October 1659 as the cornet for the colony's troop of horse (*PCR* 3:174).

His first wife is given by Torrey as Honor _____, and his second wife was Mary (Hiland), widow of John Bryant. Stetson made his will 4 September 1702, proved 5 March 1702/03 (Pope). His children, as given by Underwood (*Small Descendants*, 2:873) were Joseph, who married Prudence _____; Benjamin, who married Bethia Hawke; Thomas, who married Sarah Dodson; Samuel, who married (1) Lydia _____ and (2) Mercy or Mary _____; John, who married Abigail _____; Eunice, who married Timothy Rogers; Lois, who probably died without issue; Robert, who married Joanna Brooks; and Timothy, who probably died without issue. The births of the first eight at Scituate between 1639 and 1653 are given in *PCR* 8:18, and the baptism of Timothy in 1658 is found in the records of the Second Scituate Church (*Mayflower Source Records*, p. 316). All nine children were by Stetson's first wife. His son Joseph Stetson married Prudence (see above) probably as his second wife, and had married a first wife Ruth Hiland, and thus would have been the father of the "Joseph Studson" named as a grandson in the will of Thomas Hiland, q.v. A family history is *The Descendants of Cornet Robert Stetson of Scituate, Massachusetts* (1933).

STEVENS, WILLIAM—Although he arrived at Plymouth in 1623 on the *Little James*, he was not named among those sharing the 1623 land division. Perhaps he was included with others who received shares without being named; however, it is quite possible that he was left out because he had been specifically hired to work for the company for a five-year period, along with Thomas Fell, q.v. Fell and Stevens were sent home in 1624, apparently because they behaved badly when the *Little James* sank. For additional details see chapter 1, note 18.

STEWARD, JAMES – James Steward arrived at Plymouth in 1621 on the *Fortune* and received one share in the 1623 land division. He was not in the 1627 cattle division.

STOCKBRIDGE, JOHN – A well documented study of his family is given by Roger D. Joslyn, "The Descendants of John [1] Stockbridge," *NEHGR* 133:93, 187, 286, 134:70, 135, 228, 291, 135:36, 121. John Stockbridge was born in England ca. 1608, and at age twenty-seven he sailed for New England on 17 June 1635 on the *Blessing* with his wife Ann, twenty-one, and son Charles, one. He settled at Scituate where he was recorded as a wheelwright. His wife joined the Scituate Church in 1637, and she was part of the Vassall group in 1640. In June 1638 John Stockbridge was fined for disgraceful speeches against the government and those who attempted to reprove him, and in September 1638 he was fined again for contemptuous words against the government. He was presented in December 1638 for receiving strangers and foreigners, but the charges were dismissed. He continued speaking against the government, and, though he was proposed as a freeman, there is no record that he was ever granted the franchise. He served at various times as constable and grandjuryman, and he bought and sold land, and purchased a one-half interest in a grist mill, which was later expanded into a sawmill. His house was the main garrison in Scituate during King Philip's War. His first wife Ann died, and on 9 October 1643 he married (2) Elizabeth (Hatch) Soan (or Soane), a sister of William Hatch, q.v., and widow of Robert Soan. Probably ca. 1654 he married his third wife Mary _____, whose surname was possibly Broughton. Shortly after 1656 Stockbridge moved to Boston, where he died 13 October 1657. In his will dated 4 July 1657, inventory 3 February 1658, Stockbridge mentioned his wife Mary, son Charles; a younger son John; daughters Elizabeth, Mary Stockbridge, Esther Stockbridge, Sarah Stockbridge, and Hannah Ticknor; and Hannah's husband William Ticknor (*Suffolk County Wills* (Baltimore, 1984), p. 136). Roger D. Joslyn, "The English Origin of John Stockbridge and His First Wife Ann," *NGSQ* 74:111 gives John's parentage and shows that his first wife was Ann Kendall.

SYMONS, THOMAS – Thomas Symons (or Simons) was mentioned in the will of Samuel Fuller dated 30 July 1633 as Fuller's servant (*MD* 1:26). On 1 February 1641/42 Edward Doty, who was taking care of a steer and two cows for Thomas Symons, was ordered to be responsible for any damage they might cause to other men's corn (*PCR* 2:33).

TALBOT, MOSES – Moses Talbot was the man serving under John Howland at the Kennebec trading post who was killed in April 1634 by John Hocking (*MD* 2:11).

TALBOT, PETER – Peter Talbot must have been at Plymouth for some years earlier than 22 August 1636, when he made over his right to James Skiff for five acres of land which he had earned by his indenture to Edward Doty (*PCR* 1:43).

TENCH, WILLIAM – William Tench arrived at Plymouth in 1621 on the *Fortune*, and in the 1623 land division he and John Cannon, q.v., received a two-acre share between them. Tench was not in the 1627 cattle division.

THORPE, JOHN – Robert Barker complained on 20 January 1632/33 that his master, John Thorp, did not give him enough clothes (*PCR* 1:7). On 1 April 1633 John Thorp and his wife Alice were fined and ordered to sit in the stocks for conceiving a child before marriage, but they were given twelve months to pay the fine because of their poverty (*PCR* 1:12). By 15 August 1633 Thorpe had died, and his widow Alice turned over the remaining time of his apprentice Robert Barker, who was to have learned carpentry from him, to William Palmer (*PCR* 1:16). Thorpe's widow Alice, who must have been young, disappears from the records after 1633.

TILDEN, NATHANIEL – Nathaniel Tilden was baptized at Tenterden, County Kent, 28 July 1583, the son of Thomas and Alice (Biggs) Tilden. Background on his family is given in *NEHGR* 65:322, 75:226, and 114:153. Tilden came to New England in the *Hercules* 1634/35, accompanied by his wife Lydia (Huckstep), seven children, and seven servants. He settled in Scituate and he probably died there between May and July 1641. All the children of Nathaniel and Lydia Tilden were born in England, five dying there prior to the family's departure. The children were Thomas, who died young; Mary, who married Thomas Lapham; Joseph, who died young; Sarah, who married George Sutton; Joseph, who married Alice or Elizabeth Twisden; Stephen, who died young; Thomas, who married Elizabeth (Bourne) Waterman; Judith, who married Abraham Preble; Winifred, who died young; Lydia, who died young; Lydia, who married Richard Garrett; and Stephen, who married Hannah Little. Mary and Sarah were married on the same day, 13 March 1636/37 (*NEHGR* 9:286), and their husbands were Tilden's servants. After his death, his widow Lydia married Timothy Hatherly. Elizabeth French shows in *NEHGR* 70:256 that Lydia (Huckstep) (Tilden) Hatherly was a cousin of Thomas Hatch, q.v., who also came to New England in the *Hercules* and settled at Scituate. Tilden was of the gentry and addressed as "Mr.," and he was one of the wealthier Scituate residents. He dated his will 25 May 1641, inventory 31 July 1641, and he named his wife Lydia and his children Stephen; Lydia; Joseph; Thomas; Judith; Mary, the wife of Thomas Lapham; and Sarah, the wife of George Sutton; and he also mentioned his two indentured servants, Edward Jenkins and Edward Tarte (*MD* 3:220).

TILDEN, THOMAS – Thomas Tilden arrived at Plymouth in 1623 and received three shares in the 1623 land division, indicating that he was quite likely accompanied by a wife and child (Torrey gives him a wife Ann, and wondered if he had returned to England). Tilden was not in the 1627 cattle division. The name Thomas occurs in the family of Nathaniel Tilden, q.v., (who had a father, brother, and son named Thomas), but no connection has been found between the two families.

TILLEY, ANN – The wife of Edward Tilley, her maiden name was Ann (or Agnes) Cooper, q.v.

TILLEY, EDWARD – A 1620 *Mayflower* passenger, Edward Tilley arrived at Plymouth with his wife Ann (Cooper), his brother John, and two cousins, the children Henry Sampson and Humility Cooper. Edward and his wife died shortly after arrival, leaving no known descendants. More and more we are learning that *Mayflower* passengers not previously known to have been in Leiden in fact had been there. Mr. Ward (*TG* 6:166) shows that Humility Cooper, q.v., was born in Holland, and Dr. Bangs (*MQ* 52:7) seems to prove that Edward Tilley was in Leiden at least by 1616. It also seems likely, though evidence has not yet been found, that John Tilley, the wives of Edward and John, and the young Henry Sampson might have been in Leiden, too. See also under Edward's brother John Tilley.

TILLEY, JOAN – The wife of John Tilley, her maiden name was Joan Hurst, q.v.

TILLEY, JOHN – A 1620 *Mayflower* passenger, John Tilley arrived at Plymouth with his wife Joan (Hurst), his daughter Elizabeth Tilley, and his brother Edward Tilley, q.v. A most valuable discovery by Robert Leigh Ward, "English Ancestry of Seven Mayflower Passengers," *TAG* 52:198, gives the Tilley origin in Henlow, Bedfordshire, and shows that John and Edward were the sons of Robert and Elizabeth (_____) Tilley. John and his wife left children in Bedfordshire who could conceivably have left descendants, though none living today is yet known. This article, plus Ward's subsequent articles, "Henry Sampson's Paternal Grandfather," *TAG* 56:141; "Further Traces of John Tilley of the Mayflower," *TAG* 60;171; and "The Baronial Ancestry of Henry Sampson, Humility Cooper, and Ann (Cooper) Tilley," *TG* 6:166, show much interrelationship among the Tilleys, Coopers, Sampsons, and Hursts. There were Hursts, also, living in Leiden (see under James Hurst), and Bangs's *Pilgrims*, p. 16, shows that a John Masterson, a Separatist who remained at Leiden, also came from Henlow, Bedfordshire. George E. Bowman, "'Jan Tellij' of Leyden Was Not John Tilley of the Mayflower," *MD* 10:65, comments on a record of a person with a similar name in Holland. Robert L. French, "John Tilley, Jr., 1599-1636," *MQ* 49:16, suggests that a John Tilley who appeared at Cape Ann was a son of the *Mayflower* John Tilley, but proof is lacking.

TILLEY, ELIZABETH – A daughter of John and Joan (Hurst) Tilley, Elizabeth accompanied her parents on the 1620 *Mayflower*. She had been baptized at Henlow, Bedfordshire, on 30 August 1607. At Plymouth she married John Howland, and they have many descendants living today.

TINKER, THOMAS – Passengers on the 1620 *Mayflower*, Thomas Tinker, his wife, and son died shortly after their arrival at Plymouth, leaving no known descendants. Dexter (p. 636) thought he might have been identical with Thomas Tinker who was in Leiden in 1617. Banks believed he was either from Tickhill, Yorkshire, or was the Thomas Tinker, carpenter, of Neatishead, County Norfolk, who was born at Thurne, Yorkshire, in 1581 (Banks, *English Ancestry,* p. 89).

TINKER, _____ – A 1620 *Mayflower* passenger, she was the wife of Thomas Tinker, q.v.

TINKER, _____ – A 1620 *Mayflower* passenger, he was the son of Thomas Tinker, q.v.

TINKHAM, EPHRAIM – On 23 July 1634 Mr. Timothy Hatherly turned over the remaining term of his servant, Ephraim Tinkham, to John Winslow, and Winslow was obligated to perform the conditions expressed in the indenture (*PCR* 1:31). On 2 August 1642 Tinkham was granted twenty-five acres of land due him for his service by indenture, and, the indenture being lost, its terms were affirmed by Timothy Hatherly and John Winslow (*PCR* 2:43). Probably ca. 1645 or 1646 Tinkham married Mary, daughter of *Mayflower* passenger Peter Browne, and on 27 October 1647 Ephraim Tinkham and his wife Mary sold to Henry Sampson their one-third part of land in Duxbury formerly belonging to Peter Browne, deceased (*PCR* 12:146). On 1 May 1655 Ephraim Tinkham and Arthur Hathaway asked permission to live with their families on the lands of John Barnes at Lakenham (a section of Plymouth) (*PCR* 3:76-77). Tinkham was a highway surveyor for Plymouth on 3 June 1656, and he took the Oath of Fidelity in 1657 (*PCR* 3:100, 8:181). He and Stephen Bryant asked on 5 May 1663 to have some differences about the bounds of their lands settled (*PCR* 4:35), and on 1 August 1665 Tinkham and Major Winslow had a dispute about a horse (*PCR* 4:103). On 5 June 1666 the court granted twelve acres of upland at Whetstones Vinyard Brook to Sgt. Ephraim Tinkham (*PCR* 4:130), and he received various other land grants (*PCR,* passim), probably because his wife was one of the first-born children. On 13 August 1679 Tinkham sold to John Browne of Duxbury two acres of land he had in the right of his wife Mary, the daughter of Peter Browne, deceased, and his wife consented to the sale (*Ply. Colony LR* 5:197). On 1 June 1675 Tinkham was a selectman for Plymouth, but was fined on the same day for coming to court drunk (*PCR* 5:164, 173). He was on the 29 May 1670 freeman list for Plymouth (*PCR* 5:274). The will of Ephraim Tinkham, Sr. of Plymouth, dated 17 January 1683/84, inventory 20 May 1685, named his wife Mary; oldest son Ephraim; sons Ebenezer, Peter, Helkiah, John, and Isaac; and daughter Ruth Tomson (*MD* 4:122-25). Son Helkiah has been said to have married Ruth Cooke, daughter of Jacob[2] (Francis[1]) Cooke, but though Helkiah's wife was a Ruth there is no evidence for her surname. The early generations of Ephraim and Mary (Browne) Tinkham are given by Robert S. Wakefield, "Peter Browne of the Mayflower and His Descendants for Four Generations," *Mayflower Families in Progress* (Plymouth, Mass., 1986).

TRACY, STEPHEN – Arriving in 1623 on the *Anne,* Stephen Tracy had been a say-weaver among the Separatists at Leiden, where he married Tryphosa Lee on 6 January 1621 (Dexter, p. 636). He was baptized at Great Yarmouth, County Norfolk, on 25 December 1596, the son of

Stephen and Agnes (Erdley) Tracy (Robert S. Wakefield, "The Adventurous Tryphosa (Lee) Tracy," and "Further on Tryphosa Tracy," *TAG* 51:71, 242). His wife probably arrived on the *Jacob* with their daughter Sarah in 1625. Stephen Tracy was on the 1633 freeman list, and he served on various public committees and juries (*PCR*, passim). On 7 July 1638 he hired John Price to work for him four months (*PCR* 1:92). On 5 March 1638/39 he became a constable for Duxbury (*PCR* 1:116). He later returned to England and was residing at Great Yarmouth on 20 March 1654/55 when he gave a power of attorney to Mr. John Winslow of Plymouth to dispose of his estate in New England for the benefit of his son John Tracy, daughters Ruth Tracy and Mary Tracy, and the rest of his five children (*MD* 10:143). Daughters Sarah and Rebecca had been in the 1627 livestock division. Sarah Tracy married George Partridge (*MD* 13:84). Rebecca Tracy married William Merrick (*Dawes-Gates* 2:801). John Tracy married Mary Prence, daughter of Governor Thomas and Mary (Collier) Prence, and later moved to Windham, Connecticut. Also see *Dawes-Gates* 2:799-802, some of which has been updated by Mr. Wakefield's articles.

TREVOR, WILLIAM—A seaman on the 1620 *Mayflower* who was hired to remain one year with the settlers at Plymouth, William Trevor returned to England, probably on the *Fortune*, and no descendants are known.

TURNER, HUMPHREY—Humphrey Turner was on the 1633 freeman list, and on 18 May 1633 he sold his right to a piece of land near the Plymouth fort to Josias Winslow for £8 (*PCR* 1:13). He probably moved to Scituate about this time, for he was one of nine men with a house there when Lothrop arrived in September 1634. Turner was an original member of the church Lothrop formed on 8 January 1634/35. Turner's daughter Mary was baptized at Lothrop's house on 25 January 1634/35, and his wife joined the church on 10 January 1635/36 (*NEHGR* 10:42, 9:279-81). In 1638 he was among those fined for nonappearance at court, in his case paying three shillings for each of the three times he failed to appear (*PCR* 1:104). On 5 January 1635/36 he was elected constable of Scituate for the first of several times (*PCR* 1:36, passim). He did not go to Barnstable with the Lothrop group, and on 30 November 1640 Turner, Mr. Timothy Hatherly, and Edward Foster were appointed to apportion new land to such people of Scituate as they thought fit (*PCR* 1:168). On 2 June 1640 Turner was elected a deputy for Scituate (*PCR* 1:155), and he often served on juries. By trade he was a tanner, and on 18 January 1643/44 James Till of Scituate was found guilty by the court of having received from Mr. Hanbury two hides to be delivered to Humphrey Turner for tanning, but selling them to Joseph Tilden instead (*PCR* 2:68). He made his will 28 February 1669, sworn 5 June 1673, and named his oldest son John Turner; his son John Turner the younger; his sons Joseph, Daniel, Nathaniel, and Thomas Turner; his daughters Mary Parker and Lydia Doughty; his grandchildren Humphrey Turner and Mary Doughty; the sons of his oldest son, Jonathan, Joseph, and Ezekiel Turner; and the daughter of his son Nathaniel, Abigail Turner (*MD* 24:42). He was one of very few men having two living sons with the same name, and it is likely that they were by different wives, although no second wife is known. Torrey called his only known wife Lydia (?Gamer). Turner's son John the older married Mary Brewster, daughter of Jonathan [2] Brewster, and his son John the younger married Ann James.

TURNER, JOHN—Passengers on the 1620 *Mayflower,* John Turner and his two sons died shortly after arrival at Plymouth. Bradford wrote around 1650 that he also had a daughter who came later and was married and living in Salem; however, no descendants are known. Some additional information can be found in Robert S. Wakefield, "Mayflower Passengers Turner and Rogers: Probable Identification of Additional Children," *TAG* 52:110, which shows that Turner had lived among the Separatists at Leiden, and that his daughter who married and lived in Salem was named Elizabeth.

TURNER, _____—A 1620 *Mayflower* passenger, he was the son of John Turner, q.v.

TURNER, _____—A 1620 *Mayflower* passenger, he was the son of John Turner, q.v.

VASSALL, WILLIAM—William Vassall was born ca. 1593, the son of John Vassall, an alderman of London. William and his brother Samuel Vassall were among the original patentees of the Massachusetts Bay Company. William came to New England in 1630 as a Bay Colony Assistant, but returned to England after a short while, and from his subsequent behavior it appeared that he differed with the Winthrop government. In 1635 he sailed aboard the *Blessing,* at age forty-two, with his wife Ann, age forty-two; and children Judith, sixteen; Frances, twelve; John ten; Ann, six; Margaret, two; and Mary, one; and settled at Roxbury in the Bay Colony. Shortly after, however, he moved to Scituate, the Plymouth Colony town closest to the Bay Colony (*NEHGR* 17:56; Deane, *Scituate,* p. 366; Pope). His involvement in the religious and political life of both colonies can be seen in the text. He left in 1646 for England in connection with the Child petition, and never returned to New England. He later moved to Barbadoes, where he was quite prosperous, and he died there in 1655. In his will, dated 13 July 1655, he named his son John, and his daughters Judith, Frances, Ann, Margaret, and Mary (*NEHGR* 17:57). Vassall's wife was Ann King, and she was possibly related to the Thomas King who also sailed on the *Blessing* and settled at Scituate; see *NEHGR* 109:95. Of their children, Judith married *Mayflower* passenger Resolved White and their descendants can be found in *MF* 1, and Frances married James Adams, son of John Adams, q.v. Son John Vassall was on the 1643 ATBA for Scituate, and in 1652 he was a lieutenant under Capt. James Cudworth, but later left the colony. Daughter Ann married Nicholas Ware, and daughter Margaret married Joshua Hubbard (also seen as Hobart) (Torrey, p. 377). There is a good account of some of William Vassall's family in Annie Lash Jester and Martha Woodroof Hiden, ed., *Adventurers of Purse and Person, Virginia, 1607-1625* (2nd ed.; n.p., Order of First Families of Virginia, 1964), pp. 334-35. Though William himself seems to have had no Virginia connection, his son John and his daughter Anne, wife of Nicholas Ware, were residents of Rappahannock County, Virginia, and his brother Samuel died on a voyage to Virginia. Additional information on William Vassall is given in Roger D. Joslyn, "The English Origin of John Stockbridge and His First Wife Ann," *NGSQ* 74:111; the references given here are especially helpful for researching the Vassall family.

VINAL, ANNA—A Stephen Vinal was proposed as a freeman on 5 March 1638/39 (*PCR* 1:116), and Lothrop recorded a "Goodman Vinall" acquiring a house in Scituate between 1634 and 1637 (*NEHGR* 10:42). On 1 December 1646 Ann Vinal, "Spinster" (which could be used by a widow), bought one of the thirty shares of land at Scituate owned by Timothy Hatherly (*PCR* 12:158). On 1 June 1658 Stephen Vinal and John Vinal became freemen (*PCR* 3:137). On 7 March 1664 Stephen Vinal and John Vinal were given the administration of the estate of Ann Vinal, deceased (*PCR* 4:81). Thus it appears that Stephen Vinal, Sr. was an early resident of Scituate with his wife and two sons, and that he died not long after their arrival there. For the early generations of this family, see Mrs. Barclay, "Corrections Concerning the Vinal Family, Scituate, Massachusetts," *TAG* 39:41.

VINAL, STEPHEN—See Anna Vinal.

WADE, NICHOLAS—He was among those taking the Oath of Allegiance at Scituate 1 February 1638/39 (*PCR* 1:110). There is no record of him becoming a member of Lothrop's Church. On 6 October 1657 he was licensed to keep an ordinary at Scituate (*PCR* 3:123). In 1662 he was among those former servants and ancient freemen being given land at Saconett Neck (*PCR* 4:18). Since there is no record of him becoming a freeman, he might have come to Scituate as a servant; however, inclusion on a preferred list for land grants was sometimes based on a person's connection to a family which had made early contributions to the colony, and Wade's marriage in the 1640s to the niece of Timothy Hatherly, Elizabeth Hanford, could indicate that he fitted into this category. In his will dated 7 February 1683/84, inventory 11 March 1683/84, Wade mentioned an unnamed wife (his wife Elizabeth presented the inventory); eldest son John Wade; son Thomas Wade; daughter Susanna White (who had received her portion during her former husband Wilcom's days); son Nicholas Wade; son Nathaniel Wade; his "sonns" children Nicholas, Nathaniel, Elizabeth, and Hannah; and daughter Elizabeth (*Ply. Colony PR* 4:2:136). Savage gives him two other children, Joseph, killed in King Philip's War, and Jacob. A Joseph Wade was among those killed in the war on 26 March 1676 (Bowen, *Early Rehoboth* 3:14-15), as was John Ensign, whose family was closely connected with the Wades. A forthcoming article by Eugene A. Stratton will present the evidence for believing that the Joseph Wade killed in the war was the son of Nicholas and Elizabeth (Hanford) Wade; that he married Sarah Ensign, daughter of Thomas and Elizabeth (Wilder) Ensign and sister of the John Ensign who was killed in the war; and that his widow Sarah later married Thomas [2] Mann. See also Eglin Hatherly.

WADSWORTH, CHRISTOPHER – Christopher Wadsworth was on the 1633 freeman list, and he served on various juries and received a number of land grants (*PCR*, passim). On 16 September 1633 he witnessed William Wright's will (*MD* 1:200). On 1 January 1633/34 he was chosen constable for the "ward" bounded between the Jones River and Greens Harbor, and he was chosen constable for Duxbury again in 1637 and 1638 (*PCR* 1:21, 80, 86). He became a deputy in 1640 for Duxbury (*PCR* 1:154), and in 1666 he became a selectman for Duxbury (*PCR* 4:124). He dated his will 31 July 1677, sworn 27 October 1680, and he named his wife Grace, and his sons Joseph and John (*Ply. Colony PR* 4:1:69). His widow Grace Wadsworth dated her will 13 January 1687, proved 13 June 1688, and she named her sons Joseph and John; the children of her son Samuel Wadsworth, deceased; her daughter Mary Andrews; and her grandchildren John, Mary, and Abigail Wadsworth (*PN&Q* 4:123). Torrey thought Wadsworth's wife's maiden name might be Cole.

WALLEN, JOYCE – Joyce Wallen was the wife of Ralph Wallen, q.v.

WALLEN, RALPH – Arriving in 1623 on the *Anne* Ralph Wallen was accompanied by his wife Joyce. He was on the 1633 freeman list, and he was a Purchaser, but he does not seem to have held any public office. He died before 27 February 1643, when the inventory of the estate of John Atwood showed a debt owing to the widow Wallen (*MD* 5:158). A deed of 9 June 1660 showed John Jenkins of Barnstable selling land which belonged to him as the heir apparent of Ralph Wallen of Plymouth, deceased (*MD* 14:234). Samuel Fuller in his will dated 30 July 1633 directed that "my daughter Mercy be and remaine with goodwife Wallen so long as she will keep her at a reasonable charge" (*MD* 1:24). A Thomas Wallen was recorded on 4 April 1650 along with others as being arrested for helping two women run away from their husbands (*PCR* 2:149), but whether he was related to Ralph and Joyce Wallen cannot be determined.

WARREN, RICHARD – A 1620 *Mayflower* passenger, Richard Warren is unusual because, although Bradford in his "decreasing and increasings" gives him the honorific title "Mr.," he does not mention him at all in the text of his history, and very little is known about him except for a few brief mentions elsewhere. In *Mourt's Relation*, p. 15, Winslow lists ten men on an early expedition at Cape Cod, three of whom, including Richard Warren, were from London. Judging from land transactions (see, for example, *MD* 3:45-51 and *PCR* 12:28) of his widow, Elizabeth, who came over in 1623 on the *Anne* with daughters Abigail, Anna, Elizabeth, Mary, and Sarah, the family appears to have been one of the wealthier ones at Plymouth. However, he was not one of the eight select Undertakers in 1627. Nathaniel Morton wrote for the year 1628 "This Year died Mr. Richard Warren, who. . .was an useful Instrument and during his life bare a deep share in the Difficulties and Troubles of the first Settlement of the Plantation of New-Plimouth" (*Memoriall*, p. 68). His widow, Elizabeth Warren, was given the unique distinction of having a law passed unanimously by the whole court to give her the Purchaser status her deceased husband had had, "hee dying before he had performed the bargaine, the said Elizabeth performed the same after his decease, and also for the establishing of the lotts of lands given formerly by her unto her sonnes in law, Richard Church, Robert Bartlett, and Thomas Little" (*PCR* 1:54). The three sons-in-law had married respectively daughters Elizabeth, Mary, and Anna, and the other two daughters were married later, Sarah to *Mayflower* passenger John Cooke, and Abigail to Anthony Snow. Richard and Elizabeth Warren had two sons born at Plymouth, Nathaniel, who married Sarah Walker, and Joseph, who married Priscilla Faunce — see the second revision (1986) of the *Families of the Pilgrims* booklet on Warren. Widow Elizabeth Warren's servant, Thomas Williams, was charged with speaking profane and blasphemous speeches to her, but the court released him with a warning after he made a humble acknowledgment of his offence (*PCR* 1:35). She died at Plymouth 2 October 1673, aged above ninety years, "having lived a godly life, came to her grave as a shoke of corn fully ripe" (*PCR* 8:35). The English origin of the Warrens, though much searched for, has not yet been found, but she was definitely not Elizabeth Jowett, as some have claimed. Although Warren's granddaughter Elizabeth Warren had a child by Joseph [2] Doty, she did not, as has been written, marry him. Some early generations are given by Claude W. Barlow, "Richard and Elizabeth Warren," *MQ* 42:125, 43:12. See also Mrs. Washington A. Roebling, "Richard Warren of the Mayflower and Some of His Descendants," *NEHGR* 55:70, which contains some errors. See also Ruth Berg Walsh, "The Search for Pilgrim Richard Warren's Parentage," *MQ* 51:109).

WASHBURN, JOHN—John Washburn was in Plymouth Colony at least as early as 2 January 1632/33, when he sued Edward Doty (*PCR* 1:6). He came from Bengeworth, near Evesham, County Worcester, where he was baptized 2 July 1596, the son of John and Martha (Timbrell) (Stephens) Washburn; he married 23 November 1618 Margery Moore (parish records, p. 47-48 of James Davenport, *The Washburne Family of Little Washburne & Wichenford in the County of Worcester* [London, 1907]). John's family later joined him in Plymouth, and they are shown by Hotten, p. 57, to have sailed on the *Elizabeth*, which left England for New England on 13 April 1635 with certificates from the mayor of Evesham: Margerie Washborn, age forty-nine, and her two sons John Washborne, age fourteen, and Philip Washborne, age eleven. Margery (Moore) Washburn was baptized at Bengeworth 3 November 1588, the daughter of Robert and Ellen (Taylor) Moore (Davenport, p. 51).

Davenport supports the claim of some American Washburn descendants that John Washburn is a descendant of the Washburns of Wichenford, who have a proven royal line; however, he offers no valid evidence, and the claim must be considered unproven and probably false. E. A. B. Barnard, *Some Notes on the Evesham Branch of the Washbourne Family*

(Evesham, 1914), points out that there were Washburns in the neighborhood of Evesham centuries before a descendant of the Wichenford family is claimed to have moved there. Numerous errors have appeared on the Washburn family, such as the claim that the immigrant John Washburn was identical with the John Washburn who was the secretary in England of the Plymouth (England) Company until 1628, which Davenport denies, pointing to handwriting specimens of each, and noting that the Plymouth immigrant was a churchwarden in Bengeworth as recently as 1625. It is, however, possible that William Washburn, who died on Long Island in 1659, might have been either a brother or cousin to the immigrant John Washburn; see Davenport, p. 54, and John G. Hunt, "Clues to Origin of Washburne. . .of Hempstead, L.I., etc.," *TAG* 36:62-64.

In Plymouth Colony John Washburn moved from Plymouth to Duxbury and became a freeman on 2 June 1646. He and his two sons were in the 1643 ATBA list from Duxbury. He served in various minor capacities, as shown in *PCR* volumes. On 3 June 1662 he was granted what appears to be a double portion of land at Saconnet (Little Compton) by virtue of his being both an ancient freeman and a former servant, though the records do not indicate to whom he was a servant (*PCR* 4:18; this would certainly seem to refute any claim that he had been secretary of the Plymouth Company). There is no record that he lived in Saconnet, but he moved from Duxbury to Bridgewater sometime after 26 May 1666. George E. Bowman, "Washburn Notes," *MD* 15:247-53, 16:248-53, helps sort out some of the misconceptions about the early Washburns, and he shows (16:248) that John, Sr. must have died shortly before 17 March 1670/71. Inasmuch as John's son John had all his children by his first wife, a *Mayflower* descendant, and John's son Philip's only son, John [3], married as his only wife a *Mayflower* descendant, there is a strong presumption that thereafter all Washburns in colonial Plymouth are probably *Mayflower* descendants.

WASHBURN, JOHN — The son of John and Margery (Moore) Washburn (see father for additional pertinent information), the younger John Washburn was baptized at Bengeworth, County Worcester, on 26 November 1620, and he arrived at Plymouth with his mother and brother, Philip, in 1635. He married (1) on 6 December 1645 Elizabeth Mitchell, daughter of Experience and Jane (Cooke) Mitchell (*PCR* 2:94). Bowman shows (*MD* 15:247) that he married (2) between 1684 and 1686 Elizabeth (_____) Packard, widow of Samuel Packard, but he had no children by her. His children by his first wife have sometimes been confused to include those of his brother Philip, q.v. John was probably the John Washburn (rather than his father) who was sent from Duxbury in the campaign against the Narragansetts in August 1645 (*PCR* 2:90). He was made a freeman on 6 June 1654 (*PCR* 3:48), and became a constable of Duxbury 7 June 1659 (*PCR* 3:163). He dated his will 30 October 1686, sworn 14 September 1687, and he named his wife Elizabeth; sons John, Thomas, Joseph, Samuel, Jonathan, Benjamin, and James; and his daughters Mary, Elizabeth and "her husband," Jane, and Sarah (*MD* 15:248). See also Mrs. John E. Barclay, "Rebecca Lapham, Wife of Samuel 3 White or John 3 Washburn," *NEHGR* 115:83, and "The Ancestry of Experience, Wife of Cornelius 4 Washburn of Bridgewater, Mass.," *NEHGR* 119:22.

WASHBURN, PHILIP—The son of John and Margery (Moore) Washburn (see his father for additional information), Philip's baptism is not recorded at Bengeworth, but he was eleven years old when he arrived in Plymouth with his mother and brother in 1635. Bowman gives (*MD* 16:248) two deeds proving who Philip's father was. Unlike his brother John, Philip did not become a freeman, and a Bridgewater town meeting record of 8 May 1685 (*MD* 16:249) shows that he was incapable at that time of taking care of himself, and his nephew Joseph Washburn agreed to take care of him. Philip's brother John had directed in his will that "my Son John take Care of my Brother Phillip," and this is probably part of the reason why many people (e.g., Davis, Savage, Mitchell) have stated that Philip had no children of his own. The fact is, though, that Philip married late in life Elizabeth Irish, daughter of John and Elizabeth Irish, and they had a son John, who married Lydia Billington, and daughters Margery, who married Josiah Leonard; Mary, who married Daniel Pratt, and Elizabeth, who married Joseph Amory (*MD* 15:247). Bowman (*MD* 16:249) refers to a 1702 lawsuit regarding Philip's children's suit against their uncle John Irish. Proof that Philip had a son John is found in *Ply. Co. LR* 10:1:466, in which John Washburn on 8 December 1708 sold land to Samuel Bradford, "which my honored grandfather John Irish deceased" formerly possessed. Philip was still living on 19 August 1700, when he was mentioned in a Bridgewater town record (*MD* 16:253).

WEBB, ADEY—see Webb Adey.

WESTON, EDMOND—See Stratton, "The Descendants of Edmund Weston, Revisited," *NGSQ* 71:41, for a three-generation family history. Nothing is known about Weston's English antecedents, though Banks felt he came from Cornwell, Oxfordshire, or Shustoke, Warwickshire. He arrived in Boston in 1635 on the *Elizabeth and Ann*, and his age was given as thirty. On 2 November 1636 Mr. John Winslow transferred the services of Weston for the next two years to Nathaniel Thomas on behalf of his father William Thomas. He lived in Duxbury and had various land grants, including an original proprietorship in the Bridgewater grant. He became a freeman on 7 June 1648 and he served in such offices as grandjuryman and highway surveyor. He seems to have married late in life; his wife's name is unknown, though there is speculation he might have married a daughter of Philip Delano. His will was dated 16 April 1686, sworn 3 June 1686, and he named his sons Elnathan, Edmond, and John, and his daughter Mary, the wife of John Delano.

WHITE, PEREGRINE—Born to William and Susanna White aboard the *Mayflower* at Provincetown Harbor, Peregrine White died at Marshfield 20 or 22 July 1704, age eighty-three years, eight months. He married Sarah Bassett, daughter of William and Elizabeth Bassett. In 1655 he was granted land as the "first of the English that was borne in these ptes." His children were Daniel, Jonathan, Peregrine, Sarah, Sylvanus, Mercy, and a child that died young. Their spouses and descendants are given in *MF* 1.

WHITE, RESOLVED – A 1620 *Mayflower* passenger traveling with his parents, William and Susanna White, he was born ca. 1615 in either England or Holland, and he was living at Marshfield in 1684, and probably still living 19 September 1687. He married (1) Judith Vassall daughter of William and Ann (King) Vassall, and (2) Abigail (_____) Lord at Salem on 5 October 1674. All his children were by his first wife, and they were William, John, Samuel, Resolved, Anna, Elizabeth, Josiah, and Susanna. *MF* 1 gives their spouses and descendants.

WHITE, WILLIAM – A 1620 *Mayflower* passenger, William White arrived at Plymouth with his wife and two sons, Resolved and Peregrine, the latter born on ship at Provincetown Harbor, and he was also accompanied by two servants, William Holbeck and Edward Thompson. Bradford gives him the honorific prefix "Mr.," and he apparently was one of the wealthier Separatists at Leiden. He died at Plymouth 21 February 1620/21. His wife was Susanna, who later married Edward Winslow, but her parentage has been controversial. Certainly she would not seem to be a sister to Edward and Samuel Fuller, who had a sister Anna, but no Susanna, and Anna's birth ca. 1578 would have made her most likely too old to have been Edward Winslow's second wife. A William White was betrothed to Ann Fuller, spinster from England, on 27 January 1612 at Leiden, and Samuel Fuller was one of the witnesses, which hints at some relationship between Ann and Samuel, but there were at least two, if not three, William Whites in the English community at Leiden. A William White continued to appear in Leiden records, such as being a witness at the betrothal of Godbert Godbertson to Sarah (Allerton) (Vincent) Priest on 25 October 1621, which was after the death at Plymouth of the *Mayflower* William White. Edward Winslow wrote a letter 30 October 1623 to his "uncle Mr. Robert Jackson," who lived in Spalding, Lincolnshire, and desired to be remembered to his father-in-law, adding "Almost two yeares since I wrote to my father-in-law declaring the death of his soon White & the continued health of his daughter and her two children" (*NEHGR* 109:242). This letter, of course, is a clue to the ancestry of William White's wife; it also shows that not only was her father living at the time of the letter, but also a "brother and sisters." The descendants of William and Susanna White are given in *MF* 1.

WILLET, THOMAS – The son of Thomas and Alice Willet of Leiden (Dexter, p. 639), Thomas Willet stated on 26 April 1671 that he was going on sixty-four years of age (*MD* 26:80), and thus was born ca. 1607. He arrived at Plymouth prior to 1 January 1633/34, when he became a freeman (*PCR* 1:21). On 6 July 1636 he married Mary Browne (*PCR* 1:43), daughter of Mr. John Browne. On 6 February 1636/37 he, John Jenney, and George Watson were fined for trading with the Indians for corn (*PCR* 1:50). On 7 June 1637 he was one of eight men appointed to advise the governor and Assistants on the matter of the beaver trade, which was likely to go to decay (*PCR* 1:62). On 5 June 1638 he was chosen for the grand jury (*PCR* 1:87). In 1641/42 he purchased a one-sixteenth part of a ship to be built with an estimated cost of £200 (*PCR* 2:31). In 1646 he was on a commission to determine how to raise money by taxing wine, etc. (*PCR* 2:101). In 1646 he was a deputy for Plymouth, and in 1649 a highway surveyor for Plymouth (*PCR* 2:104, 139). He became captain of the Plymouth military company in 1647/48 (*PCR* 2:121). On 8 June 1649 the court let out the Kennebec trade to Mr. William Bradford, Mr. Edward Winslow, Mr. Thomas Prence, Mr. Thomas Willet, and Mr. William Paddy (*PCR* 2:144). On 5 June 1651 he was elected an Assistant for the first of many times (*PCR* 2:166). He was a member of the colony's Council of War and a Plymouth commissioner of the United Colonies (*PCR*, passim). On 20 June 1654 he was chosen by the Plymouth government to be an adviser to the English colonial forces which were preparing to assist England in the war against the Dutch at Manhattan (*PCR* 3:55-56). He had had dealings with the Dutch earlier, was well respected for honesty and fairness, and after the English defeated the Dutch and took over New Amsterdam, renaming it New York, Willet in 1664 became the first English mayor of the city (*Bradford [Ford]* 2:84 footnote), following which he returned to Plymouth.

On 7 March 1659/60 the court noted that the town of Seekonk had earlier objected to a grant of 500 acres of land for commonage to Thomas Willet, feeling that it would be prejudicial to them, but now Seekonk was willing that he get the grant (*PCR* 3:183). He acquired considerable land over the years, lived at Swansea, was the Plymouth magistrate for his area, and exercised considerable influence there (*PCR*, passim, and text). Willet attended the Swansea Baptist Church, probably without being a member. He was sent by the court on several diplomatic missions to the Indians, but died at Swansea and was buried 3 August 1674 (*PCR* 8:51) before King Philip's War began. He dated his will 26 April 1671, sworn 12 August 1674, and he named his sons James, Hezekiah, Andrew, and Samuel; his daughters Esther Willet, Mary Hooker, and Martha Saffin; his sons-in-law John Saffin and Samuel Hooker; his brother-in-law James Brown; Samuel Hooker's six sons; John Saffin's four sons, not already mentioned, by Willett's daughter Martha; granddaughter Sarah Eliot; grandsons Samuel Hooker and Thomas Saffin; Rev. John Myles; and his old servant John Padduck (*MD* 26:80).

WILLIAMS, ROGER—The founder of Rhode Island, Roger Williams came to Massachusetts Bay Colony in 1630, and moved to Plymouth probably in 1632 (see text). He was probably the Mr. Williams who was allotted meadow land for hay in Plymouth on 1 July 1633 (*PCR* 1:15). Samuel Fuller in his will dated 30 July 1633 gave two acres of land in Plymouth to his son Samuel "if mr Roger Williams refuse to accept of them as formerly he hath done" (*MD* 1:25). As Bradford noted (see text), he left Plymouth abruptly in 1633, with his wife and family. Much has been written on him, but he is more associated with Rhode Island than Plymouth.

WINSLOW, EDWARD – The son of Edward and Magdalene (Oliver) Winslow of Droitwich, Worcestershire, Edward Winslow was baptized there on 19 October 1595. He received a good education in the cathedral school at Worcester, and he later went to Leiden, where he became associated with William Brewster in the printing business. Winslow was betrothed at Leiden on 28 April 1618 to Elizabeth Barker from Chatsum (Chattisham, Suffolk), and he was described as a printer and accompanied by Isaac Allerton, Jonathan Brewster, Mary Allerton, and Jane Hazel, the bride's niece. With Bradford, Allerton, and Samuel Fuller, he wrote a letter from Leiden to Carver and Cushman in England on 10 June 1620 (*MD* 8:100; Dexter, p. 640). He arrived at Plymouth on the 1620 *Mayflower* with his wife, and she died on 24 March 1620/21 (*MD* 30:3). Bradford recorded in his register (*MD* 30:4) that the first marriage at Plymouth was of Mr. Edward Winslow on 12 May 1621 to Susanna White, widow of William White, q.v. Winslow had no known children by his first wife, and by his second wife he had Edward, John, Josias (who became a governor of Plymouth Colony), and Elizabeth – the first two died young, and the other two had but few surviving descendants, so that Edward Winslow probably has fewer descendants living today than any other of the *Mayflower* passengers from whom descent can be traced.

Winslow's life in Plymouth as a principal diplomat and trade negotiator, Assistant, and governor, is given in the text. A good article on his activities on behalf of Cromwell's Commonwealth after he left Plymouth is G. D. Scull, "Edward Winslow," *NEHGR* 38:21. Other articles of interest are Lemuel Shattuck, "Genealogical Memoir of the Descendants of Edward Winslow, Governor of Plymouth Colony," *NEHGR* 4:297; John H. Sheppard, "Genealogy of the Winslow Family," *NEHGR* 17:159; William S. Appleton, "English Ancestry of the Winslow Family," *NEHGR* 21:209, 24:329, 43:433; and John G. Hunt, "The Mayflower Winslows – Yeomen or Gentlemen?," *NEHGR* 121:25, 122:175, 124:182. Some of these contain information about his brothers also, but should be used cautiously, for there are known errors. The chart given by Appleton, for example, going back to John Winslow and Agnes Throckmorton is sheer fantasy; Agnes Throckmorton married a Thomas Winslow, but there is no known connection between this Thomas and the father or grandfather of Edward Winslow. Because Edward Winslow seemed to be the most aristocratic of the *Mayflower* passengers, genealogists and historians have tried to find an aristocratic background for him, but to no avail. His father, Edward Winslow, was a prosperous salt merchant, but his grandfather Kenelm Winslow described himself in his will as a "yeoman," and no one has been able to discover Kenelm's ancestry with any certainty. There have been attempts to find an aristocratic origin for Edward's mother, Magdalene Oliver – see, for example, John G. Hunt, "Clues to the Ancestry of Winslow of Droitwich," *TAG* 41:168, "Governor Edward Winslow's Mother's Family, the Olivers," *TAG* 42:52, "A Note on the Winslow Births in England," *TAG* 42:186 (which was a response to Meredith B. Colket's commentary "The

Winslow 'Royal Line' " *TAG* 42:56), and "A Winslow Pilgrim Note — Addendum," *TAG* 43:239. Davis P. and Frances K. Holton, *The Winslow Memorial*, 2 vols. (1887, 1888), is the only book-size family history so far, and includes the descendants of his brothers, but is not reliable.

Another article of interest is Peter Wilson Coldham, "Edward Winslow and Bennet Morgan of Plymouth 1624," *NGSQ* 63:295, which provides an interesting note on the original financial arrangements for the founding of Plymouth by showing that Winslow, in addition to his shares in the original enterprise for bringing himself and his wife over, invested £60 for six additional shares. It has been thought that some of the wealthier first colonists, such as Richard Warren, must have invested some of their money as well as their persons, but this is the first direct evidence of a specific sum.

WINSLOW, GILBERT — A brother of Edward Winslow, Gilbert Winslow arrived with him at Plymouth on the 1620 *Mayflower*. He received one acre of land in the 1623 land division, but was not in the 1627 cattle division, and Bradford stated that he returned to England and died there. No descendants are known. The inventory of another brother, Kenelm Winslow, mentioned that he had one-half of the share of land granted by the court to him and his brother Josias on account of their brother Gilbert being a "first comer" (*MD* 24:42). On 1 June 1663 the court acknowledged that Gilbert Winslow, deceased, who was one of the "first comers," had a right to land, and allowed his heirs to look for some (*PCR* 4:40).

WINSLOW, JOHN — A brother of Edward Winslow, q.v., John Winslow was born at Droitwich, Worcestershire, on 16 April 1597 (*MD* 3:129), and he arrived at Plymouth in 1621 on the *Fortune*. He was a Purchaser and he was on the 1633 freeman list. On 25 July 1633 the court noted that John Beavan had covenanted to serve John Winslow as an apprentice for six years (*PCR* 1:15-16). On 23 July 1634 Mr. Timothy Hatherly turned over his servant Ephraim Tinkham to John Winslow for the rest of his term (*PCR* 1:31). On 3 March 1634/35 Winslow was on a committee to assess colonists for the costs of the watch and other charges (*PCR* 1:33). On 5 January 1635/36 he was on a committee to set the prices of goods and labor (*PCR* 1:36). In 1636 he turned over the services of Edmond Weston for two years to Nathaniel Thomas (*PCR* 1:45). In 1637 he was on a committee to assess taxes for the cost of sending men to the Pequot War (*PCR* 1:61). In 1638 he and his brother Kenelm were witnesses against Stephen Hopkins for selling wine at excessive rates (*PCR* 1:87). He served on various other committees and juries and as a deputy for Plymouth. On 28 July 1640 he sold for £12 the services of Joseph Grosse for five years to John Howland (*PCR* 1:158). On 17 October 1642 he was one of several men appointed to grant lands for the town of Plymouth (*PCR* 2:48). In 1653 he was appointed to the Council of War (*PCR* 3:26). Around 1655 he moved to Boston, where he became a wealthy merchant and shipowner, though he still retained lands at Plymouth, and in 1662 he was on a list of "first born" men of Plymouth to share in a land distribution (*PCR* 4:19).

John married *Mayflower* passenger Mary Chilton, q.v., and their descendants are given in *MF-2*. He dated his will 12 March 1673/74, proved 21 May 1674, and he mentioned his wife Mary; his sons John, Isaac, Benjamin, Edward, and Joseph; William Payne, the son of his daughter Sarah Middlecott; Parnell Winslow, daughter of his son Isaac; the daughters of his daughter Latham; granddaughter Susanna Latham; son Edward's children; the children of Edward Gray by his daughter Mary; son Joseph's two children; granddaughter Mercy Harris's two children; kinsman Josiah Winslow, the Governor of Plymouth; brother Josiah; kinswoman Eleanor Baker, the daughter of his brother Kenelm; Mr. Paddy's widow; and his negro girl Jane (*MD* 3:129). He left personal property valued at about £3,000, a good part of it in money, and this was a substantial sum for the time. His widow Mary survived him, but died before May 1679, and she dated her will 31 July 1676. In it she named her sons John, Edward, Joseph, and Samuel (Samuel had not been mentioned in his father's will); daughters Susanna Latham and Sarah Middlecott; grandson William Paine; granddaughter Susanna Latham; granddaughter Ann Gray; son Edward's daughter Mary Winslow; son Edward's children; grandchildren Parnell Winslow and Chilton Latham; granddaughter Mercy Harris; son Joseph's daughter Mary Winslow; and granddaughter Mary Pollard (*MD* 1:65).

WINSLOW, JOSIAS – A brother of Edward Winslow, q.v., Josias Winslow was the accountant whom Bradford, in writing about 1631, said that "Mr. Sherley would needs send them. . . . He had made mention of shuch a thing the year before, but they write him word, that their charge was great allready. . . . Yet he now sente one, which they did not refuse, being a yonger brother of Mr. Winslows, whom they had been at charge to instructe at London before he came. He came over in the White Angell with Mr. Allerton, and ther begane his first imploymente." Bradford continued that the arrangements by Mr. Sherley and Mr. Allerton to send goods were much more costly than need be, "And if Josias Winslow had not been ther, it had been worse, for he had the invoyce, and order to send them to the trading houses" (*Ford* 2:135-36). Later Bradford wrote that "the new accountante, which they in England would needs presse upon them, did wholy faile them, and could never give them any accounte; but trusting to his memorie, and lose papers, let things rune into shuch confusion, that neither he, nor any with him, could bring things to rights" (*Ford* 2:230), and still later, in a document of 1641 between Mr. Atwood, in Mr. Sherley's behalf, and the colony, it was stated that "the accounts of the said partnership are found to be confused, and cannot orderley appeare (through the defaulte of Josias Winslow, the booke keeper)" (*Ford* 2:297).

Josias became a freeman on 1 January 1632/33 (*PCR* 1:5). He later moved to Marshfield, where he was constable on 2 March 1640/41 (*PCR* 2:9). He served in other public positions, such as juror, deputy, and highway surveyor, and on committees to regulate land, to decide the Kennebec trade, and to determine tax revenues. On 4 June 1645 he was chosen as a member of a committee to revise the colony's laws (*PCR* 2:85). On

5 June 1671 Mr. Josias Winslow, Sr. was a member of the Council of War (*PCR* 5:64). He was buried 1 December 1674 in his sixty-ninth year (he had been baptized at Droitwich, Worcestershire, on 16 February 1605/06). He dated his will 12 April 1673, inventory 17 December 1674, and he named his wife Margaret, his son Jonathan, his four daughters, his granddaughter Hannah Miller, his grandchildren, and his loving friend Mr. Samuel Arnold, and he appointed Capt. William Bradford and his loving nephew Maj. Josias Winslow as overseers (*MD* 34:33). On 1 March 1674/75 the court ruled that because he had during his life already given his lands in Marshfield without restriction to his son Jonathan on the latter's marriage to Ruth, the daughter of Mr. William Sergeant, but in his will left the same lands to Jonathan in fee tail (which basically meant that he could not sell them), that part of the will was void, but the rest would stand (*PCR* 5:159-60). His wife Margaret was the daughter of Thomas Bourne, and was mentioned in Bourne's will of 1664 as "my daughter Winslow" (*MD* 16:24). Pope confused the name of his son, calling him Josiah when it should have been Jonathan. The Maj. Josias Winslow in his will, who became a governor of Plymouth Colony, was the son of his brother Edward.

WINSLOW, KENELM – A brother of Edward Winslow, q.v., Kenelm was not in the 1627 division, but arrived at Plymouth before 1 January 1632/33 when he became a freeman (*PCR* 1:5). On 8 January 1632/33 Francis Eaton confirmed that he had sold his dwelling house to Kenelm and Josias Winslow (*PCR* 1:8). On 6 January 1633/34 Samuel Jenny, son of John Jenny, was apprenticed to Kenelm Winslow, joyner, for four years (*PCR* 1:24). On 22 January 1633/34 Josias Winslow sold his part of the dwelling he had purchased from Francis Eaton (*PCR* 1:24). Kenelm Winslow married in June 1634 Ellen (or Eleanor) (Newton) Adams, widow of John Adams, q.v. (*PCR* 1:30); she died at Marshfield 5 December 1681, eighty-three years old (*Marshfield VR*). At the time of this marriage, Kenelm Winslow of Marshfield put up security to pay James Adams, son of John, £5 when he became of age, and this was done and recorded on 26 December 1651 (*PCR* 2:176). On 22 February 1635/36 John Gardiner, a servant of Kenelm Winslow, had the rest of his time turned over to George Kenrick (*PCR* 1:37). Kenelm received various land grants and served on committees and juries (*PCR*). On 1 December 1640 he was fined for neglecting his duty as an elected highway surveyor (*PCR* 2:4).

On 4 June 1645 a committee (consisting of Myles Standish, William Paddy, Edmond Eddenden, Edward Case, Anthony Annable, Anthony Thacher, and Thomas Tupper) to examine a complaint of injustice by Kenelm Winslow, reported that Kenelm's charge was untrue. He had charged that he could not be heard in a case between himself and John Maynard, but the committee found the Bench and jury without fault, and the court ordered him to be imprisoned and fined £10. On his petition the same day in which he acknowledged his offence and sorrow for same, he was released from imprisonment, and his fine was suspended for one year and then, if he showed good behavior, it would be remitted (*PCR* 2:85).

On 5 May 1646 Kenelm was sued by Roger Chandler for detaining his daughter's clothes on pretence that she owed further service, and the court ordered him to return the clothes; on the same day the court ordered Kenelm to find sureties for his good behavior for uttering opprobrious words against the Marshfield Church, "saying they were all lyers, etc.," and when he refused to do so, he was sentenced to prison, where he remained until the next court (*PCR* 2:98). On 1 June 1647 he was chosen constable for Marshfield (*PCR* 2:115). From 1649 onward he was frequently a deputy from Marshfield (*PCR*). On 7 March 1653/54 Kenelm complained against John Soule for speaking falsely of his daughter and scandalizing her in carrying false reports between her and Josias Standish (*PCR* 3:46). He dated his will 8 August 1672, proved 5 June 1673, and named his oldest son Kenelm, son Nathaniel, wife Ellinor, son Job, grandchild Kenelm Baker, and daughter Ellinor, and he asked his wife to give Mary Adams an equal share of his personal property with the rest of his grandchildren (*MD* 24:41). He died 12 September 1672 (*MD* 24:42), and was buried at Salem 13 September 1672 (*Marshfield VR*, p. 427).

WRIGHT, WILLIAM—William Wright arrived at Plymouth on the *Fortune* in 1621, and participated in the 1623 and 1627 divisions. He married at Plymouth Priscilla Carpenter, q.v., who arrived after the 1627 division. Wright was on the 1633 freeman list, but he died shortly after. In his will dated 16 September 1633, inventory 6 November 1633, he named his wife Priscilla, Elder William Brewster, his "brother Will Bradford," and his "brother Fuller" (*MD* 1:200).

Bibliography

I t cannot be overemphasized that information has to originate some-
where. Ultimately, information comes from the senses, usually eyes
or ears. As Donald Line Jacobus said, the best evidence is to be able
to say, "I was there, I saw it, and thus I know it to be true." Since we cannot transport ourselves back to Plymouth Colony, our best sources are the
writings of people who were there and who saw or heard things with their
own eyes or ears. These are our primary sources. Especially in history and
genealogy, where so much erroneous information has been committed to
print, secondary sources—people writing about events that occurred years
or centuries earlier when they could have had no personal knowledge of
the facts—must be used with considerable caution. Historians and genealogists today refuse to rely on secondary sources any further than the references these sources cite.

In the case of Plymouth Colony, our primary sources are few, our reliable secondary sources are not much greater in number, and our unrelia-
ble secondary sources are legion. Those who would undertake the study
of Plymouth Colony are well advised to learn to use primary sources whenever possible. The listing below is divided into primary and secondary
sources that will be of general interest to the readers of this book. More
specialized books and articles cited in the text, or family histories used as
references in the biographical sketches, are not repeated below. Additional
information on primary sources, including unpublished ones, can be found
in chapter 14. The reader should keep in mind also that even primary writings can be subject to either original or transcription error; ordinarily,
though, a primary source is accepted at face value unless there is reason
to suspect it, or it is inconsistent with other sources of known reliability.

PRIMARY SOURCES

Bradford, William. *Governor William Bradford's Letter Book*. Although
published as a booklet by the Massachusetts Society of Mayflower Descendants (Boston, 1906), the booklet is not easily found. Much easier to obtain
(in such places as the genealogical sections of large libraries) will be the
transcription in volumes 5, 6, and 7 of the *Mayflower Descendent* (see below).

This collection of letters written by and to Bradford, some not available elsewhere, is most valuable for supplementary information to that found in Bradford's *Of Plymouth Plantation.*

Bradford, William. *Of Plimouth Plantation 1620-1647.* There are many editions, but the best are the two-volume edition edited by Worthington C. Ford and published by the Massachusetts Historical Society in 1912, and the one-volume edition edited by Samuel Eliot Morison (New York, 1952). Ford keeps to the original spelling and punctuation used by Bradford, and gives extremely informative, wide-ranging footnotes. Morison, while keeping to the original sense, has edited Bradford's writing into something more easily understood by modern readers, and Morison's footnotes have the benefit of more recent resarch than Ford's, but are not as comprehensive. The beginning reader will find Morison's version to be a better introduction, but scholars will find Ford's to be more valuable.

Copy of the Old Records of the Town of Duxbury, Massachusetts 1642-1770 (Plymouth, 1893). Much of these records have to do with land transactions and town meetings, and some are helpful for determining genealogical relationships.

Genealogical Advertiser, edited by Lucy Hall Greenlaw (reprinted as a single volume, Baltimore, 1974). A genealogical journal transcribing many original documents from Plymouth Colony, it contains some material not available in any other publication, and thus it should be included in any thorough historical or genealogical research.

Hinckley, Thomas. "The Hinckley Papers," *Collections of the Massachusetts Historical Society,* 4th Series, volume 5 (Boston, 1861). These letters to and from Plymouth Colony's last governor show quite impressively the circumstances leading to the absorption of Plymouth by Massachusetts Bay.

Hubbard, William. *A General History of New England* (Cambridge, 1815). The publication date notwithstanding, this book was actually written in the second half of the seventeenth century by a Bay Colony minister who was a younger contemporary of many of the early Plymouth colonists. His work is based in part on other writings of his times, such as Bradford's *Of Plimouth Plantation,* but also contains valuable information on the history of Plymouth not available elsewhere. Some of Hubbard's information must have come directly from participants or eye-witness observers of the events he narrates. He is generally sympathetic to the actions of the Plymouth leaders, except in his criticism of their relations with the Indians.

Mayflower Descendant. Originally published under the editorship of George Ernest Bowman of the Massachusetts Society of Mayflower Descendants in thirty-four volumes between 1899 and 1937, it has recently been revived by the same publisher with Alicia C. Williams as editor. Long out of print, the original thirty-four volumes can now be obtained on microfiche from the publisher, and the current journal is available by subscription from 101 Newbury Street, Boston, MA 02116. These journals contain an unparalleled collection of original source material (vital records, wills, deeds, inventories, letters, and more) together with some documented articles of genealogical interest, and is indispensable for any serious study of the history or genealogy of colonial Plymouth (that is, it covers much more than the Plymouth Colony period, but goes up to about the time of the American Revolution, and in some cases a little beyond). See also *Pilgrim Notes and Queries*, below.

Mayflower Source Records, selected by Gary Boyd Roberts (Baltimore, 1986). This book contains reprints of many articles from the *New England Historical and Genealogical Register* giving primary source information. For the serious scholar it is a valuable adjunct to the information in the *Mayflower Descendant*. Some of the information in the book can be obtained elsewhere, but not all, and genealogists wanting to be thorough in checking original material for southeastern Massachusetts, Cape Cod, Nantucket, and Martha's Vineyard will want to refer to this book.

Morton, Nathaniel. *New Englands Memoriall* (Cambridge, 1669; reprint Boston, 1903). Nathaniel Morton was secretary to the colony court for many years and had access to official colony records as well as to Governor Bradford's private records. His book repeats much from Bradford's *Of Plimouth Plantation*, but is of some interest for supplementary information.

Morton, Thomas. *New English Canaan* (1637; reprint, Boston, 1883). A fancifully written account of early New England settlements by a man who had good reason to dislike the Plymouth colonists, who had destroyed his free-living trading post at Merrymount and sent him back a prisoner to England. The book is useful to show us that there was "another side" to the Plymouth story, and for little side remarks which help fill in gaps in other knowledge.

Mourt's Relation: A Relation or Journal of the Beginning and Proceedings of the English Plantation Settled at Plymouth in New England. . . . Another indispensable source for knowledge on early Plymouth, this book is discussed in chapter 14. There are a number of versions, including the Readex Microprint of the original text available from Pilgrim Hall in Plymouth, Massachusetts (recommended for those with more than casual interest), and one put in modern language by Dwight B. Heath (New York, 1969). A new, annotated version recently became availble, edited by Jordan D. Fiore (Marlborough, N.H., 1986).

Pilgrim Notes and Queries. These five volumes published between 1913 and 1917 by the publisher and editor of the *Mayflower Descendant* (see above) are a companion publication to the latter, containing much the same type of original source material. It is included as part of the microfiche version of the *Mayflower Descendant*.

Plymouth Church Records, 2 volumes (New York 1620-1623; reprint, Baltimore, 1975). This book includes William Bradford's "Dialogue or the sume of a Conference between som younge men borne in New England and sundery Ancient men that cam out of Holland and old England anno dom 1648," which gives information on the origin of the Separatist Church. A history of the Plymouth Church by Nathaniel Morton repeats much from

Bradford's *Of Plimouth Plantation 1620-1647,* but also gives a few additional details not available elsewhere. There are also in volume 1 some of the church and vital records maintained by the Reverend John Cotton during the Colony period. Volume 2 is entirely outside the Colony period.

Plymouth Scrap Book, compiled by Charles Henry Pope (Boston, 1918). A collection of some of the oldest wills, inventories, deeds, and miscellaneous documents from Plymouth Colony, this book starts with an index of names, so that a researcher can quickly determine if there is any material of particular interest in it.

Prince, Thomas. *Chronological History of New England in the Form of Annals,* volume 1 (Boston, 1736). This work draws much on contemporary and older writings, including some that are no longer available to us in the original. It is, for example, the only trace we have of a "register" of vital statistics maintained by Bradford, and this valuable information on Plymouth from Prince is reprinted in volume 30 of the *Mayflower Descendant.*

Purchas, Samuel. *Purchas, His Pilgrims* (London, 1626). Among other items of historic interest, this book contains some informative accounts of early voyages to New England.

Records of the Colony of New Plymouth in New England (1620-1691), edited by Nathaniel B. Shurtleff and David Pulsifer, 12 volumes (Boston, 1855-61; reprinted as 12 volumes in 6 books, New York, 1968). Along with Bradford's *Of Plimouth Plantation,* this set of original court records (see description in chapter 14) is our most valuable source of knowledge for the history of Plymouth Colony, and is also valuable to genealogists as a supplement to the vital records, wills, and deeds of the colony.

Records of the Town of Plymouth, 3 volumes (Plymouth, 1889). Only volume 1 is of interest for Plymouth Colony. These original town records start in 1636 and are especially helpful in presenting land transactions. Genealogical relations are sometimes shown, or can be deduced, from these records.

Smith, John. *The Complete Works of Captain John Smith, 1580-1631,* edited by Philip L. Barbour, 3 volumes (University of North Carolina, 1986). Though Plymouth Colony plays only a small part in Smith's most interesting writings, the additional information he gives which is not available elsewhere concerning the early years of Plymouth is helpful for an understanding of the colony. Mr. Barbour's edition of Smith's works is the definitive one.

Three Visitors to Early Plymouth, edited by Sydney V. James, Jr. (Plimoth Plantation, 1963). This book puts together seven letters written in the 1620s by three visitors to Plymouth, Emmanuel Altham, John Pory, and Isaac de Rasieres (see chapter 14). These views by outsiders add much to our knowledge of the colony.

Winthrop, John. *The History of New England from 1630 to 1649,* 2 volumes (Boston, 1853). Though much more concerned with Massachusetts Bay Colony than Plymouth, Governor Winthrop's contemporary writings add some information to the history of Plymouth which would otherwise not be known. Some of Edward Winslow's letters to Winthrop published in *Collections of the Massachusetts Historical Society* (as shown in the text) are especially revealing of behind-the-scenes attitudes and actions of Plymouth leaders.

Winslow, Edward. *Good Newes from New England* (London, 1623). In effect, this is a continuation of *Mourt's Relation*, and of much value to anyone with an interest in the history of Plymouth (see chapter 14). It is included in volumes 4 and 5 of *Pilgrim Notes and Queries* and volumes 25 and 26 of the *Mayflower Descendant*.

Winslow, Edward. *Hypocrisie Unmasked* (London, 1646). Written mainly as propaganda in favor of orthodoxy in the Bay Colony and Plymouth, this book is especially of interest to historians. It was reissued in 1649 as The Danger of Tolerating Levellers in a Civil State (see chapter 14).The book is included in volume 27 of the *Mayflower Descendant*.

Winslow, Edward. *New Englands Salamander, Discovered by. . .* (London, 1647). A polemic written to defend the Bay Colony and Plymouth against attacks by William Vassall and his adherents, the book contains much of historical value (see chapter 14). It is reprinted in the *Collections of the Massachusetts Historical Society*, volume 2 of the 3rd Series, Cambridge, 1830, pp. 110-45.

Young, Alexander. *Chronicles of the Pilgrim Fathers* (Boston, 1844; reprint, Baltimore, 1974). This book contains excerpts from contemporary writings, such as from Bradford and *Mourt's Relation*, and accordingly is by nature a sampler; most of the complete works from which the excerpts come are readily available.

SECONDARY SOURCES

Bangs, Jeremy D., editor. *The Pilgrims in the Netherlands—Recent Research* (Leiden, 1984). This fifty-six page booklet contains some interesting material on current research in the Netherlands concerning the English Separatists who lived there before moving to Plymouth.

Banks, Charles E. *English Ancestry and Homes of the Pilgrim Fathers. . . .* (1929; reprint, Baltimore with corrections, 1984); *Planters of the Commonwealth* (1930; reprint, Baltimore, 1984); *Topical Dictionary of 2885 English Immigrants to New England 1620-1650* (1930; reprint, Baltimore, 1980). Colonel Banks did a considerable amount of research on the English origins of Plymouth and other early New England settlers, and these books are valuable as clues for further research. However, as with other sources, nothing should be assumed to be necessarily correct without adequate contemporary documentation. The *Topical Dictionary* in particular should be used with caution, having been published from Banks's notes after his death by one who was not as careful as Banks himself.

Bliss, Leonard, Jr. *The History of Rehoboth* (Boston, 1836). Bliss used many original records for his history, such as Proprietors' Records, some of which he quotes verbatim. The book is quite helpful from the historical point of view, and also as genealogical background.

Bowen, Richard L. *Early Rehoboth*, 4 volumes (Rehoboth 1945-50). Bowen updates Bliss and gives much valuable additional information.

Davis, William T. *Ancient Landmarks of Plymouth*, 2nd ed. (Boston, 1899), the second part of which (of most interest to genealogists) is available as *Genealogical Register of Plymouth Families* (Baltimore, 1985). Loved by beginning genealogists because it gives so much genealogical information on Plymouth families, and frequently looked down on by experienced genealogists because it contains such a high percentage of error, it can be a very valuable research aid provided that readers use it only for clues and never claim a line just because it was found in Davis.

Deane, Samuel. *History of Scituate, Massachusetts* (Boston, 1831). Deane gives helpful historical and geographical information on Scituate. Where he cites original records, such as on the Vassall controversy, he is very good, but his genealogical sketches contain much error and should not be relied on.

DeForest, L. Effingham, and Anne DeForest. *Moore and Allied Families* (New York, 1938). Many Plymouth people are in the family histories covered by this book. It has a generally good bibliography, though it lacks item-by-item documentation, and some errors have been noted.

Demos, John. *A Little Commonwealth—Family Life in Plymouth Colony* (New York, 1970). This book shows very interestingly a historian's use of the methodology of genealogy to present the physical settings, everyday household life, family relationships, and other intimate background of the Plymouth colonists. It should be required reading for any serious Plymouth Colony scholar, and is also an excellent book for the general reader.

Dexter, Harry Martyn, and Morton Dexter. *The England and Holland of the Pilgrims* (London, 1906; reprint, Baltimore, 1978). This is a pioneering effort which gives us much information on those Plymouth colonists who had earlier lived in Leiden. Some of the work represents the conclusions of the Dexters, and has been updated by more recent investigations.

Ferris, Mary Walton. *Dawes-Gates Ancestral Lines*, 2 volumes (1943, 1931). A well researched collection of family histories of many families, including some from Plymouth Colony.

Genealogies of Mayflower Families, selected by Gary Boyd Roberts, 3 volumes (Baltimore, 1985). These volumes contain articles published originally in the first 138 volumes of the *New England Historical and Genealogical Register*, and were selected for their bearing on the genealogies of Plymouth Colony and County families. Some of them were written in the years when even good genealogists did not pay special attention to documentation, and some of them contain known errors. The articles in general are of much use to Plymouth scholars, but the usual rule of paying attention to the adequacy of the documentation holds true as always.

Langdon, George D., Jr. *Pilgrim Colony: A History of New Plymouth 1620-1691* (New Haven, 1966). An outstanding history of Plymouth Colony, this book should be read by anyone with interest in American colonial history.

Langdon, George D., Jr. "Bibliographic Essay," *Occasional Papers in Old Colony Studies* (Plimoth Plantation, 1969). In this monograph Dr. Langdon describes a selection of the published and manuscript sources he used for his book *Pilgrim Colony* (see above). The essay was not printed in the first edition of the book, but was included in the second. This is required reading for anyone wishing to do research on Plymouth Colony, and it has been very helpful in the preparation of this book. It is different from this Bibliography, particularly in covering some general background historial sources in more detail, and genealogical sources in much less detail.

Leach, Douglas Edward. *Flintlock and Tomahawk — New England in King Philip's War* (1958; reprint, paperback 1966). This is the definitive coverage of King Philip's War, both the overall war and the part that Plymouth played in it.

Mayflower Ancestral Index, compiled by Milton E. Terry and Anne B. Harding, volume 1 (Plymouth, 1981). This index covers the descendants of the families of eight *Mayflower* passengers: Eaton, S. Fuller, White, Chilton, More, Rogers, Soule, and Brewster. Each entry gives the name of a descendant, together with spouse, plus reference to a number leading to the line-carrying parent (or parents, if both were *Mayflower* descendants), and thus one can "chain" backwards or forwards to trace a line. Such an index is obviously good for clues, but the index is not documented and is known to contain many errors. Inclusion of a line in the index is not sufficient in itself as evidence of a *Mayflower* line.

Mayflower Families Through Five Generations. This is a continuing series published by the General Society of Mayflower Descendants to show the first five generations of *Mayflower* passengers known to have descendants today. Documentation is given collectively, rather than item-by-item, for each family group, and of course the authenticity of any claimed descendant in these books must depend on the adequacy of the particular documentation. Some errors have been found in the books, especially in volume 3, and addenda have been compiled for them. The volumes published thus far are:

Volume One, edited by Lucy Mary Kellogg (Plymouth, 1975), consisting of the following families: Francis Eaton (complied by Lee D. van Antwerp); Samuel Fuller (compiled by Arthur H. and Katharine W. Radasch); and William White (complied by Robert M. and Ruth W. Sherman).

Volume Two, edited by Robert M. Sherman (Plymouth, 1978), consisting of the following families: James Chilton (compiled by Robert M. Sherman and Verle D. Vincent); Richard More (compiled by Robert S. Wakefield and Lydia R. Finlay); and Thomas Rogers (compiled by Alice W. A. Westgate).

Volume Three, edited by Anne Borden Harding (Plymouth, 1980), consisting of the family of George Soule (compiled by John E. Soule and Milton E. Terry).

Mayflower Quarterly (MQ). The official journal of the General Society of Mayflower Descendants, this publication serves to disseminate news of Society events. Over the years, it has also published a good number of articles of genealogical interest, and it often gives information on current *Mayflower* passenger and Plymouth Colony research activities.

McIntyre, Ruth A. *Debts Hopeful and Desperate* (Plimoth Plantation, 1963). This is an excellent, well-researched exposition and untangling of the economic origins and continuing problems of early Plymouth.

Mitchell, Nahum. *History of the Early Settlement of Bridgewater* (Boston, 1840; reprint, Baltimore, 1983). As with Davis, this book is good for clues, but bad to cite as evidence.

Morison, Samuel Eliot. *Builders of the Bay Colony* (1930; revised Boston, 1958). An understanding of the founding and the continued life of the Bay Colony, Morison's work is most helpful to an understanding of Plymouth Colony, and this book is an excellent way to begin on the Bay Colony.

National Genealogical Society Quarterly (NGSQ). Although this journal does not feature as many New England articles as do some of the other named genealogical magazines, over the years it has published some valuable articles on Plymouth Colony genealogy. It may be obtained by subscription from 4527 17th Street, North; Arlington, VA 22207.

New England Historical and Genealogical Register (NEHGR). The dean of American genealogical journals, NEHGR over its 140 years has printed many articles of interest to Plymouth Colony historians and genealogists. The Register is known for its high level of scholarship, though some of the articles contain known errors, and all must depend ultimately on the adequacy of their documentation. Many of the most pertinent articles having to do with Plymouth are reprinted in *Genealogies of Mayflower Families*, and some Plymouth Colony source records are reprinted in *Mayflower Source Records* (see respectively under Secondary Sources and Primary Sources). Other articles with some bearing on Plymouth families have been reprinted in *English Origins of New England Families*, Series 1 and 2, 3 volumes each series (Baltimore, 1984, 1985). NEHGR may be obtained by subscription from 101 Newbury Street, Boston, MA 02116.

Plimoth Plantation. Not usually given as a secondary source, since it is not a publication, nonetheless this life-size re-creation of Plymouth Colony as it existed in 1627, complete with costumed human "interpreters" of the people known to have lived in Plymouth at the time, is something everyone with any interest in the history and people of Plymouth Colony should visit. If it were just another "theme" outdoor museum, it would not be included in this Bibliography. What makes it different is its continuing scholarly research and painstaking attention to detail aimed at immersing people of today into the lives and surroundings of people of a by-gone age. A nonprofit enterprise to which admission requires a fee to help pay for upkeep, Plimoth Plantation offers the visitor an excellent opportunity to relive the past in an authentic setting, and the visitor cannot help but be richer and better educated for the experience. With a remarkable specialized library and staff, the Plantation strives for accuracy in building early Plymouth houses, designing clothes, planting crops, displaying artifacts, portraying customs and celebrations, and much else based on 1627 Plymouth. It is located about three miles south of the town of Plymouth on a slope similar to that of the original settlement.

Plooij, Daniel. *The Pilgrim Fathers from a Dutch Point of View* (New York, 1932). Plooij gives additional information on the Engish Separatists in Holland to continue the research started by Dexter. Although listed under Secondary Sources, many primary source documents are found in this book. Samuel Eliot Morison called Plooij the principal authority on the Plymouth people in Leiden.

Pope, Charles H. *The Pioneers of Massachusetts* (Boston, 1900; reprint, Baltimore, 1986). Pope gives a short biographical-genealogical entry on seventeenth-century Massachusetts immigrants, including those residing in Plymouth Colony. His work was based in part on the works of his predecessors (such as Savage) and in part on original research. That it contains a significant number of errors should not detract from its overall value as clues for further genealogical research (and indeed Pope sometimes shows where to look for further information). The usual caveat stands, though, that "proof" depends on adequate primary source documentation, and inclusion of a genealogical relationship in Pope is not in itself proof.

Richards, Lysander Salmon. *History of Marshfield* (Plymouth, 1901). The book is good background information on the town, and cites and quotes original documents.

Rutman, Darrett B. *Husbandmen of Plymouth — Farms and Villages in the Old Colony 1620-1692* (Boston, 1967). Another excellent monograph published by Plimoth Plantation, it presents an in-depth treatment of various phases of the agrarian life of Plymouth Colony.

Savage, James. *A Genealogical Dictionary of the First Settlers of New England,* 4 volumes (Boston, 1860-62; reprint, Baltimore, 1986). One of the first places to check for genealogical information on seventeenth-century New England families, this was an enormous undertaking for its time. Though it has many errors, and it cannot be acceptable as adequate evidence, it remains of considerable value for clues.

Sherman, Ruth Wilder, and Robert S. Wakefield. *Plymouth Colony Probate Guide* (Warwick, R.I., 1983). Probate and land records are the heart of effective genealogical research, and this book shows where to find some 800 probate records of the residents who died during the colony period. Accordingly it is an invaluable research aid, and it should be consulted by anyone doing research on Plymouth Colony genealogy or history.

The American Genealogist (TAG). Founded by one of America's greatest genealogists, Donald Lines Jacobus, and dedicated to the use of scientific method in genealogy, this journal has been in existence since 1922. During the ensuing years it has presented a good number of articles on families of Plymouth Colony, many of them written by some of the best scholars in the field. Especially notable for Plymouth Colony, among others, are the many articles of Florence Barclay and Robert S. Wakefield. Some most interesting articles showing or giving clues regarding the English origin and ancestry of early Plymouth immigrants have been presented by John G. Hunt. This journal has traditionally shown much willingness to publish articles to correct errors discovered in articles of itself or other genealogical journals. Currently under the editorship of Ruth Wilder Sherman and David L. Greene, *TAG* may be obtained by subscription from 128 Massasoit Drive, Warwick, RI, 02888. It is especially recommended to genealogists on all levels, and beginners would do well to study the standards and techniques of its writers.

The Genealogist (TG). Although relatively new in the field, this journal has acquired an excellent reputation among scholars for its high standards and its willingness to print occasional genealogical articles which might not appear elsewhere because of size or esoteric subject matter. It has published a number of most useful articles concerning Plymouth Colony. It may be obtained from P.O. Box 1058, Rockefeller Center Station, New York, NY 10185.

Torrey, Clarence Almon. *New England Marriages Prior to 1700* (Baltimore, 1985). Compiled from Torrey's handwritten records by Elizabeth Petty Bentley for the Genealogical Publishing Company, this book is in effect an index to the original Torrey collection at the New England Historic Genealogical Society (which is also available on microfilm and can be seen at various libraries or purchased from NEHGS). The original collection gives the many sources Torrey used in compiling his comprehensive marriage data, which is of tremendous value to genealogists. The book is a short cut useful to determine whether or not Torrey had source information on a given marriage. Readers are cautioned that reference to Torrey in the Biographical Sketches of the instant book is not an assurance that the information is correct, but rather is intended to point to where additional information may be obtained; that is, the Torrey collection itself. Torrey collected data from all kinds of sources: primary, secondary with documentation, and secondary without documentation. "Proof" of a given marriage, together with vital record information on years of birth, marriage, death, and first known child, must depend on the validity of the particular sources given by Torrey, not on the mere fact of inclusion in Torrey's work.

Wakefield, Robert S. *Plymouth Colony Marriages to 1650* (Warwick, R.I., 1978; reprint, 1980). This book lists the most determinable marriages of the people in early Plymouth, and gives sources. It is bound together in a volume which also contains Charles T. Libby, *Mary Chilton's Claim to Celebrity*, an aspect of several interesting aspects of Plymouth.

Weston, Thomas. *History of the Town of Middleboro, Massachusetts* (Boston, 1906). The book is good background for a history of the town. Weston is not particularly good as a genealogist.

Willison, George F. *Saints and Strangers* (New York, 1945). This book has been as popular among general readers as it has been unpopular among historians and experienced genealogists. Mr. Willison, a good researcher, accumulated a tremendous amount of information on Plymouth Colony, but he presented it so intermixed with conjecture and fiction that it must be used with extreme caution.

Winsor, Justin. *History of the Town of Duxbury, Massachusetts* (Boston, 1849; reprint, Baltimore, 1985). As with Davis, this book is good for clues, but bad to cite as evidence.

Wright, Otis Olney. *History of Swansea, Massachusetts 1667-1917* (Swansea, 1917). The book has good background information and cites and quotes original documents.

List of Appendices

A. The 1621 Peirce Patent
B. The 1629 Bradford Patent
C. Bradford's *Mayflower* Passenger List
D. The Mayflower Compact
E. The 1623 Division of Land
F. The 1626 Purchasers
G. The 1627 Division of the Cattle
H. The 1633 and 1634 Tax Lists
I. A Compiled List of Arrivals between 1627 and 27 March 1634
J. The 1643 List of Men between the Ages of 16 and 60 Able to Bear Arms
K. The Will and Inventory of John Barnes

The 1621 Peirce Patent

T he first Peirce Patent of 1620 has disappeared, both document and text, and we know little more than that it was granted in February 1619/20 by the Virginia Company to John Peirce, one of the Adventurers who was representing the whole company, to start a new settlement in Virginia territory. On the return of the *Mayflower* in May 1621, the company of Adventurers learned that the colonists settled at Plymouth and that they had drawn up the Mayflower Compact. Accordingly, the Adventurers quickly obtained a new patent, this time from the Council for New England, dated 1 June 1621. This "second Peirce Patent" was granted to John Peirce and "his Associates," and it specifically allowed the settlers to take some of the actions they had already taken.

The text, given below, is taken from *Bradford (Ford)* 1:246-51:

This Indenture made the First Day of June 1621 And in the yeeres of the raigne of our soueraigne Lord James by the grace of god King of England Scotland Fraunce and Ireland defendor of the faith etc. That is to say of England Fraunce and Ireland the Nynetenth and of Scotland the fowre and fiftith. Betwene the President and Counsell of New England of the one partie And John Peirce Citizen and Clothworker of London and his Associates of the other partie Witnesseth that whereas the said John Peirce and his Associates have already transported and vndertaken to transporte at their cost and chardges themselves and dyvers persons into New England and there to erect and build a Towne and settle dyvers Inhabitantes for the advancem[en]t of the generall plantacon of that Country of New England Now the sayde President and Counsell in consideracon thereof and for the furtherance of the said plantacon and incoragem[en]t of the said Vndertakers haue agreed to graunt assigne allott and appoynt to the said John Peirce and his associates and euery of them his and their heires and assignes one hundred acres of grownd for euery person so to be transported besides dyvers other pryviledges Liberties and commodyties hereafter menconed. And to that intent they haue graunted allotted assigned and confirmed, And by theis pre[sen]ntes doe graunt allott assigne and confirme vnto the said John Peirce and his Associates his and their heires and assignes and the heires and assignes of euery of them seuerally and respectyvelie one hundred seuerall acres of grownd in New England for euery person so transported or to be transported, Yf the said John Peirce or his Associates contynue there three whole yeeres either at one or seuerall tymes or dye in the meane season after he or they are shipped with intent there to inhabit. The same Land to be taken and chosen by them their deputies or assignes in any place or places wher-soeuer not already inhabited by any English and where no English person or persons are already placed or settled or haue by order of the said President and Councell made choyce of, nor within Tenne myles of the same, vnles it be the opposite syde of some great or Navigable Ryver to the former particuler plantacon, together with the one half of the Ryver or Ryvers, that is to say to the middest thereof as shall adioyne to such landes as they shall make choyce of together with all such Liberties pryviledges proffittes and commodyties as the said Land and Ryvers which they shall make choyce of shall yeild together with free libertie to fishe in and vpon the Coast of New England and in all havens portes and creekes Therevnto belonging and that no person or persons whatsoeuer shall take any benefitt or libertie of or to any of the grownds or the one half of the Ryvers aforesaid, excepting the free vse of highwayes by land and Naviga-ble Ryvers, but that the said vndertakers and planters their heires and assignes shall haue the sole right and vse of the said grownds and the one half of the said Ryvers with all their proffittes and appurtennces. And foras-much as the said John Peirce and his associates intend and haue vnder-taken to build Churches, Schooles, Hospitalls Towne howses, Bridges and such like workes of Charytie As also for the maynteyning of Magistrates and other inferior Officers, In regard whereof and to the end that the said John Peirce and his Associates his and their heires and assignes may haue wherewithall to beare and support such like charges. Therefore the said President and Councell aforesaid to graunt vnto the said Vndertakers their heires and assignes Fifteene hundred acres of Land more over and aboue the aforesaid proporcon of one hundred the person for euery vndertaker and Planter to be ymployed vpon such publique vses as the said Vnder-takers and Planters shall thinck fitt. And they do further graunt vnto the said John Peirce and his Associates their heires and assignes, that for euery person that they or any of them shall transport at their owne proper costes and charges into New England either vnto the Lands hereby graunted or adioyninge to them within Seaven Yeeres after the feast of St. John Bap-tist next comming Yf the said person transported contynue there three whole yeeres either at one or seuerall tymes or dye in the mean season after he is shipped with intent there to inhabit that the said person or per-sons that shall so at his or their owne charges transport any other shall haue graunted and allowed to him and them and his and their heires respectyvelie for euery person so transported or dyeing after he is shipped one hundred acres of Land, and also that euery person or persons who by contract and agream[en]t to be had and made with the said Vndertakers shall at his and their owne charge transport him and themselves or any

other and setle and plant themselves in New England within the said
Seaven Yeeres for three yeeres space as aforesaid or dye in the meane tyme
shall haue graunted and allowed vnto euery person so transporting or
transported and their heires and assignes respectyvely the like nomber of
one hundred acres of Land as aforesaid the same to be by him and them
or their heires and assignes chosen in any entyre place together and
adioyning to the aforesaid Landes and not straglingly not before the tyme
of such choyce made possessed or inhabited by any English Company or
within tenne myles of the same, except it be on the opposite side of some
great Navigable Ryver as aforesaid Yeilding and paying vnto the said President and Counsell for euery hundred acres so obteyned and possessed by
the said John Peirce and his said Associates and by those said other persons and their heires and assignes who by Contract as aforesaid shall at
their owne charges transport themselves or others the Yerely rent of Two
shillinges at the feast of St. Michaell Tharchaungell to the hand of the Rent-
gatherer of the said President and Counsell and their successors foreuer,
the first paym[en]t to begyn after the expiracon of the first seaven Yeeres
next after the date hereof And further it shal be lawfull to and for the said
John Peirce and his Associates and such as contract with them as aforesaid their Tennantes and servantes vpon dislike of or in the Country to
returne for England or elsewhere with all their goodes and chattells at their
will and pleasure without lett or disturbaunce of any paying all debtes that
justly shalbe demaunded And likewise it shalbe lawfull and is graunted
to and for the said John Peirce and his Associates and Planters their heires
and assignes their Tennantes and servantes and such as they or any of
them shall contract with as aforesaid and send and ymploy for the said
plantacon to goe and returne trade traffique inport or transport their goodes
and merchaundize at their will and pleasure into England or elswhere paying onely such dueties to the Kinges ma[jes]tie his heires and succesors
as the President and Counsell of New England doe pay without any other
taxes Imposicons burthens or restraintes whatsoeuer vpon them to be
ymposed (the rent hereby reserved being onely excepted) And it shalbe
lawfull for the said Vndertakers and Planters, their heires and successors
freely to truck trade and traffique with the Salvages in New England or
neighboring thereabouts at their wills and pleasures without lett or disturbaunce. As also to haue libertie to hunt hauke fish or fowle in any place
or places not now or hereafter by the English inhabited. And the said President and Counsell do covenant and promyse to and with the said John
Peirce and his Associates and others contracted with as aforesaid his and
their heires and assignes, That vpon lawfull survey to be had and made
at the charge of the said Vndertakers and Planters and lawfull informa-
con geven of the bowndes, meetes, and quantytie of Land so as aforesaid
to be by them chosen and possessed they the said President and Counsell vpon surrender of this p[rese]nte graunt and Indenture and vpon
reasonable request to be made by the said Vndertakers and Planters their
heires and assignes within seaven Yeeres now next coming, shall and will

by their Deede Indented and vnder their Common seale graunt infeoffe and confirme all and euery the said landes so sett out and bownded as aforesaid to the firme all and euery the said landes so sett out and bownded as aforesaid to the said John Peirce and his Associates and such as contract with them their heires and assignes in as large and beneficiall manner as the same are in theis p[rese]ntes graunted or intended to be graunted to all intentes and purposes with all and euery particuler pryviledge and freedome reservacon and condicon with all dependances herein specyfied and graunted. And shall also at any tyme within the said terme of Seaven Yeeres vpon request vnto the said President and Counsell made, graunt vnto them the said John Peirce and his Associates Vndertakers and Planters their heires and assignes, Letters and Grauntes of Incorporacon by some vsuall and fitt name and tytle with Liberty to them and their successors from tyme to tyme to make orders Lawes Ordynaunces and Constitucons for the rule governement ordering and dyrecting of all persons to be transported and settled vpon the landes hereby graunted, intended to be graunted or hereafter to be granted and of the said Landes and proffittes thereby arrysing. And in the meane tyme vntill such graunt made, Yt shalbe lawfull for the said John Peirce his Associates Vndertakers and Planters their heires and assignes by consent of the greater part of them to establish such lawes and ordynaunces as are for their better governem[en]t, and the same by such Officer or Officers as they shall by most voyces elect and choose to put in execucon And lastly the said President and Counsell do graunt and agree to and with the said John Peirce and his Associates and others contracted with and ymployed as aforesaid their heires and assignes, That when they haue planted the Landes hereby to them assigned and appoynted, That then it shalbe lawfull for them with the pryvitie and allowaunce of the President and Counsell as aforesaid to make choyce of and to enter into and to haue an addition of fiftie acres more for euery person transported into New England with like reservacons condicons and pryviledges as are aboue granted to be had and chosen in such place or places where no English shalbe then setled or inhabiting or haue made choyce of and the same entered into a booke of Actes at the tyme of such choyce so to be made or within tenne Myles of the same, excepting on the opposite side of some great Navigable Ryver as aforesaid. And that it shall and may be lawfull for the said John Peirce and his Associates their heires and assignes from tyme to tyme and at all tymes hereafter for their seuerall defence and savetie to encounter expulse repell and resist by force of Armes aswell by Sea as by Land and by all wayes and meanes whatsoeuer all such person and persons as without the especiall lycense of the said President or Counsell and their successors or the greater part of them shall attempt to inhabit within the seuerall presinctes and lymmyttes of their said Plantacon, Or shall enterpryse or attempt at any tyme hereafter distruccon, Invation, detryment or annoyaunce to the said Plantacon. And the said John Peirce and his associates and their heires and assignes do covennant and promyse to and with the said President and Counsell and their successors, That they the said John Peirce and his Associates from tyme to tyme during the said Seaven Yeeres shall make a true Certificat to the said President and Counsell and their successors from the chief Officers of the places respectyvely of euery person transported and landed in New England or shipped as aforesaid to be entered by the Secretary of the said President and Counsell into a Register book for that purpose to be kept And the said John Peirce and his Associates Jointly and seuerally for them their heires and assignes do covennant promyse and graunt to and with the said President and Counsell and their successors That the persons transported to this their particuler Plantacon shall apply themselves and their Labors in a large and competent manner to the planting setting making and procuring of good and staple commodyties in and vpon the said Land hereby graunted vnto them as Corne and silkgrasse hemp flaxe pitch and tarre sopeashes and potashes Yron Clapbord and other the like materialls. In witnes whereof the said President and Counsell haue to the one part of this p[rese]nte Indenture sett their seales And to th'other part hereof the said John Peirce in the name of himself and his said Associates haue sett to his seale geven the day and yeeres first aboue written.

LENOX HAMILTON WARWICK SHEFFIELD FERD: GORGES

The 1629/30 Bradford Patent

I saac Allerton obtained in England Plymouth's third patent, dated 13 January 1629/30, granted to William Bradford and his associates by the Council for New England. This was the patent which Bradford formally surrendered to the General Court of Freemen on 2 March 1640/41. It remained the justification for Plymouth's existence until the usurpation of Andros in 1686. The text below was taken from William Brigham, *The Compact with the Charter and Laws of the Colony of New Plymouth. . .*, (Boston, 1836), p. 21-26:

To all to whom these presents shall come greetinge: — Whereas our late sovereigne lord King James for the advancemente of a colonie and plantacon in the cuntry called or knowne by the name of New-Englande in America, by his highnes letters pattents under the greate seale of Englande bearinge date att Westminster the third day of November in the eighteenth yeare of his highnes raigne of England &c. did give graunte and confirme unto the right honoble Lodowicke late lord duek of Lenox, George late lord marques of Buckingham, James Marques Hamilton, Thomas earle of Arundell, Robert earle of Warwicke and Ferdinando Gorges, knight, and divers others whose names are expressed in the said letters pattents and their successors that they should bee one bodie pollitique and corporate perpetually consistinge of forty persons, and that they should have perpetuall succession and one common seale to serve for the said body and that they and their successors should be incorporated called and knowne by the name of the Councell established at Plymouth in the county of Devon for the plantinge ruelinge orderinge and governinge of New Englande in America, and alsoe of his spetiall grace certaine knowledge and meere motion did give graunte and confirme unto the said presidente and councell and their successors forever under the reservations limitations and declaracons in the said letters pattents expressed, all that part and portion of the said cuntry now called New-England in America scituate, lyinge and beinge in breadth from ffourty degrees of northerly latitude from the aquinoctiall line to ffourty eight degrees of the said northerly latitude inclusively, and in length of and in all the breadth aforesaide throughout the maine lande from sea to sea, together alsoe with all the firme landes soyles

399

grounds creeks inletts havens portes seas rivers islands waters fishinges mynes and mineralls as well royall mines of gold and silver as other mines and mineralls pretious stones quarries and all and singuler the commodities jurisdiccons royalties privileges ffranchises and preheminencies both within the said tracte of lands upon the maine, as alsoe within the said islands and seas adioyninge: To have hold possesse and enjoy all and singuler the foresaid continente landes territories islands hereditaments and prcints sea waters fishinges with all and all manner their commodities royalties privileges preheminences and proffitts that shall arise from thence, with all and singuler their appurtenaces and every parte and parcell thereof unto the said councell and their successors and assignes forever: To be holden of his Matie, his heirs and sucessors as of his mannorr of East Greenwiche in the county of Kent in free and common soccage and not *in capite* nor by knights service yeeldinge and prayinge therefore to the said late King's Matie, his heires and successors the fifte parte of the oare of gold and silver which from tyme to tyme and att all tymes from the date of the said letters pattents shalbe there gotten had and obtained for and in respect of all and all manner of duties demands and services whatsoever to be done made and paid unto his said late Matie, his heirs and successors as in and by the said letters pattents amongst sundry other privileges and matters therein contained more fully and at large it doth and may appeare. Now knowe yee that the said councell by virtue and authority of his said late Mats letters pattents and for and in consideracon that William Bradford and his associatts have for these nine yeares lived in New Englande aforesaid and have there inhabited and planted a towne called by the name of New Plimouth att their own proper costs and charges: And now seeinge that by the speciall providence of god, and their extraordinary care and industry they have increased their plantacon to neere three hundred people, and are uppon all occasions able to relieve any new planters or others his Mats subjects whoe may fall uppon that coaste; have given graunted bargained sould enfeoffed allotted assigned and sett over and by these presents doe cleerely and absolutely give graunt bargaine sell alien enfeoffe allott assigne and confirme unto the said William Bradford, his heires, associatts and assignes all that part of New-Englande in America aforesaid and tracte and tractes of lande that lye within or betweene a certaine rivolet or rundlett there commonly called Coahassett alias Conahassett towards the north, and the river commonly called Naragansets river towards the south; and the great westerne ocean towards the east, and betweene and within a straight line directly extendinge upp into the maine land towards the west from the mouth of the said river called Naragansetts river to the utmost limitts and bounds of a cuntry or place in New Englande called Pokenacutt alias Sowansett westward, and another like straight line extendinge itself directly from the mouth of the said river called Coahassett alias Conahassett towards the west so farr up into the maine lande westwardes as the utmost limitts of the said place or cuntry commonly called Pokencott alias Sowamsett doe extend, togeather with one half of the said river called Naragansetts and the said rivolett or rundlett called Coahassett alias Conahassett and all lands rivers waters havens creeks ports fishings fowlings and all hereditiments proffitts comodities and emoluments whatsoever situate lyinge and beinge or ariseinge within or betweene the said limitts and bounds or any of them. And for as much as they have noe conveniente place either of tradinge or ffishinge within their own precints whereby (after soe longe travell and great paines,) so hopefull a plantacon may subsiste, as alsoe that they may bee incouraged the better to proceed in soe pious a worke which may especially tend to the propagation of religion and the great increase of trade to his Mats realmes, and advancemente of the publique plantacon, the said councell have further given graunted bargained sold enfeoffed allotted assigned and sett over and by these presentes doe cleerely and absolutely give graunte bargaine sell alien enfeoffe allott assigne and confirme unto the said William Bradford his heires associats and assignes all that tracte of lande or parte of New England in America aforesaid wch lyeth within or betweene and extendeth itself from the utmost limits of Cobbiseconte alias Comasee-Conte which adjoineth to the river of Kenebeke alias Kenebekike towards the westerne ocean and a place called the falls att Mequamkike in America aforesaid, and the space of fifteene Englishe miles on each side of the said river commonly called Kenebek river, and all the said river called Kenebek that lies within the said limitts and bounds eastward westward northward or southward laste above mentioned, and all lands grounds soyles rivers waters fishings hereditaints and proffitts whatsoever situate lyinge and beinge arisinge happening or accrueinge, or which shall arise happen or accrue in or within the said limitts and boundes or either of them together with free ingresse egresse and regresse with shipps boates shallopps and other vessells from the sea commonly called the westerne ocean to the said river called Kennebek and from the said river to the said westerne ocean, togeather with all prerogatives rights royalties jurisdiccons, priviledges ffranchises liberties and ymunities, and alsoe marine liberty with the escheats and casualties thereof the Admiralty Jurisdiccon excepted with all the interest right title claime and demande whatsoever which the said councell and their successors now have or ought to have an claime or may have and acquire hereafter in or to any the said porcons or tractes of land hereby menconed to be graunted, or any the premisses in as free large ample and beneficiall manner to all intents, construccons and purposes whatsoever as the said councell by vertue of his Mats said letters pattents may or can graunte; to have an to holde the said tracte and tractes of lande and all and singular the premisses above menconed to be graunted with their and every of their appurtenances to the said William Bradford his heires associatts and assignes forever, to the only proper and absolute use and behoofe of the said William Bradford his heires associats and assignes forever; Yeeldinge and payinge unto our said soveraigne Lord the Kinge, his heires and successors forever one-fifte parte of the oare of the mines of gold and silver and one other fifte parte thereof to the presidente and councell, which shall be had possessed and obtained within the precints aforesaid for all services and demands whatsoever. And the said councell doe further graunt and agree to and with the said William Bradford his heires associatts and assignes and every of them, his and their ffactors agents tenants and servants and all such as hee or they shall send and employ aboute his said particular plantacon, shall and may from tyme to tyme ffreely and lawfully goe and returne trade and traffique as well with the Englishe as any of the natives within the precincts aforesaid, with liberty of fishinge uppon any parte of the sea coaste and sea shoares of any the seas or islands adjacente and not beinge inhabited or otherwise disposed of by order of the said presidente and councell: alsoe to importe exporte and transporte their goods and merchandize att their wills and pleasures paying only such duty to the kings Matie, his heires and successors as the said Presidente and councell doe or ought to pay without any other taxes impositions burdens and restraints uppon them to be imposed. And further the said councell doe graunt and agree to and with the said William Bradford his heires associatts and assignes, that the persons transported by him or any of them shall not be taken away, ymployed or commanded either by the Governor for the tyme beinge of New Englande or by any other authority there, from the buisnes and employmente of the said William Bradford and his associats his heires and assignes; necessary defence of the cuntry preservacon of the peace suppressinge of tumults within the lands, trialls in matters of justice by appeale uppon spetiall occasion only excepted. Alsoe it shall be lawful and free for the said William Bradford his associats his heires and assignes att all tymes hereafter to incorporate by some usuall or fitt name and title, him or themselves or the people there inhabitinge under him or them with liberty to them and their successors from tyme to tyme to frame, and make orders ordinances and constitucons as well for the better governmente of their affairs here and the receavinge or admittinge any to his or their society, as alsoe for the better governmt of his or their people and affaires in New England or of his and their people att sea in goeinge thither, or returninge from thence, and the same to putt in execucon or cause to be putt in execucon by such officers and ministers as he and they shall authorise and depute: Provided that the said laws and orders be not repugnante to the lawes of Englande, or the frame of governmente by the said presidente and councell hereafter to be established. And further it shall be lawful and free for the said William Bradford, his heires, associats and assignes to transporte cattle of all kinds, alsoe powder shot ordnance and municon from tyme to tyme as shal be necessary for their strength and safety hereafter for their severall defence; to encounter expulse repell and resiste by force of armes as well by sea as by lande, by all waies and meanes whatsoever. And by vertue of the authority to us derived by his said late Mats letters pattents to take apprehand seize and make prize of all such persons their shipps and goods as shall attempt to inhabite or trade with the savage people of that cuntry within the severall precincts and limitts of his and their severall plantacon, or shall enterprise or attempt att any tyme destruccon invasion detriment or annoyance to his and their said plantacon; the one moiety of which goods soe seized and taken it shalbe lawfull for the said William Bradford his heires associats and assignes to take to their own use and behoofe; the other moyety thereof to be delivered by the said William Bradford his heires associats and assignes to such officer and officers as shalbe appointed to receave the same for his Mats use. And the said councell doe hereby covenante and declare that it is their intente and meaninge for the good of this plantacon that the said William Bradford his associats his or their heires or assignes shall have and enjoy whatsoever privilege or privileges of what kinde soever, as are expressed or intended to be graunted in and by his said late Mats letters pattents, and that in as large and ample manner as the said councell thereby now may or hereafter can graunt, coynnige of money excepted. And the said councell for them and their successors doe covenante and graunte to and with the said William Bradford, his heires associates and assignes by these presents, that they the said councell shall at any time hereafter uppon request att the only proper costs and charges of the said William Bradford, his heires associats and asignes doe make suffer execute and willingly consent unto any further acte or actes, conveyance or conveyances, assurance or assurances whatsoever, for the good and perfect investinge assureinge and conveyinge and sure makinge of all the aforesaid tracte and tractes of landes royalties mines mineralls woods fishinges and all and singuler their appurtenances, unto the said William Bradford his heires associats and asignes as by him or them or his or their heires and assignes, or his or their councell learned in the lawe shalbe devised, advised and required. And lastly know yee that wee the said counsell have made constituted deputed authorized and appointed Captaine Miles Standish, or in his absence Edward Winslowe, John Howlande and John Alden, or any of them to be our true and lawful attorney and attornies jointly and severally in our name and steed to enter into the said tracte and tractes of lande and other the premisses with their appurtennances, or into some parte thereof in the name of the whole for us and in our names to take possession and seisin thereof, and after such posession and seisin thereof or of some parte thereof in the name of the whole had and taken; then for us and in our names to deliver the full and peacable possession and seisin of all and singuler the said menconed tobe graunted premisses unto the said William Bradford his heires associatts and assignes or to his or their certaine atturney or atturnies in that behalf ratifyinge alloweinge and confirminge all whatsoever our said atturney doe in or about the premisses. In witness whereof, the said councell established att Plimouth in the county of Devon for the plantinge ruleinge orderinge and governinge of New England in America have hereunto putt their seale the thirteenth day of January in fifte yeare of the raigne of our Soveraigne Lord Charles by the grace of God, Kinge of Englande Scotland Fraunce and Ireland defender of the ffaithe &c. Anno Domi 1629.

R. WARWICKE.

Bradford's Mayflower Passenger List

We could deduce from some other original records, such as *Mourt's Relation*, the names of a few of the passengers on the 1620 *Mayflower*, but our only complete list, if it is complete, is dependent upon the notes made by Gov. William Bradford some thirty years after the fact, presumably based on his memoranda as well as his memory. For the most part his list is consistent with all other known facts. In one case he wrote "Richard More; and another of his brothers," when research by Sir Anthony Wagner indicates that that "brother" might have been a sister. In another case he gave a group of people as dying in sickness of the first winter, but the inclusion of one name, John Goodman, on the 1623 land division list would indicate that Goodman lived longer that Bradford stated. All in all, Bradford's list has held up quite well to the test of time, and anyone contradicting the inclusion or exclusion of a given name on or from the list must assume the burden of proof from other original records.

Since we have Bradford's list in his own handwriting, we know that the sequencing of names is as he intended them, and this sequencing is probably a good indication of how important Bradford thought the passengers were in 1620, a better indication of importance than Nathaniel Morton's transcription of the signers of the Mayflower Compact. Bradford's list is actually two lists, the first a grouping of the people who were on the *Mayflower*, usually under a head of family, followed by a repetition of the same names and sequencing with additional comments on who was still living at the time Bradford wrote, who had died, what had happened to some, and their "increasings"; that is, the number of their descendants at the time Bradford wrote. The following list is from *Bradford (Ford)* 2:399-411:

Mr. John Carver; Kathrine, his wife; Desire Minter; and • 2• man-servants, John Howland, Roger Wilder; William Latham, a boy; and a maid servant, and a child that was put to him, called Jasper More.

Mr. William Brewster; Mary, his wife; with • 2• sons, whose names were Love and Wrasling; and a boy was put to him called Richard More; and another of his brothers. The rest of his children were left behind, and came over afterwards.

Mr. Edward Winslow; Elizabeth, his wife; and •2• men servants, caled Georg Sowle and Elias Story; also a litle girle was put to him, caled Ellen, the sister of Richard More.

William Bradford, and Dorothy, his wife; having but one child, a sone, left behind, who came afterward.

Mr. Isaack Allerton, and Mary, his wife; with •3• children, Bartholomew, Remember, and Mary; and a servant boy, John Hooke.

Mr. Samuell Fuller, and a servant, caled William Butten. His wife was [left] behind, and a child, which came afterwards.

John Crakston, and his sone, John Crakston.

Captin Myles Standish, and Rose, his wife.

Mr. Christopher Martin, and his wife, and •2• servants, Salamon Prower and John Langemore.

Mr. William Mullines, and his wife, and •2• children, Joseph and Priscila; and a servant, Robart Carter.

Mr. William White, and Susana, his wife, and one sone, caled Resolved, and one borne a ship-bord, caled Peregriene; and •2• servants, named William Holbeck and Edward Thomson.

Mr. Steven Hopkins, and Elizabeth, his wife, and •2• children, caled Giles, and Constanta, a doughter, both by a former wife; and •2• more by his wife, caled Damaris and Oceanus; the last was borne at sea; and two servants, called Edward Doty and Edward Litster.

Mr. Richard Warren, but his wife and children were lefte behind, and came afterwards.

John Billington, and Elen, his wife; and •2• sones, John and Francis.

Edward Tillie, and Ann, his wife; and •2• children that were their cossens, Henery Samson and Humillity Coper.

John Tillie, and his wife; and Eelizabeth, their doughter.

Francis Cooke, and his sone John. But his wife and other children came afterwards.

Thomas Rogers, and Joseph, his sone. His other children came afterwards.

Thomas Tinker, and his wife, and a sone.

John Rigdale, and Alice, his wife.

James Chilton, and his wife, and Mary, their dougter. They had an other doughter, that was maried, came afterward.

Edward Fuller, and his wife, and Samuell, their sonne.

John Turner, and •2• sones. He had a doughter came some years after to Salem, wher she is now living.

Francis Eaton, and Sarah, his wife, and Samuell, their sone, a yong child.

Moyses Fletcher, John Goodman, Thomas Williams, Digerie Preist, Edmond Margeson, Peter Browne, Richard Britterige, Richard Clarke, Richard Gardenar, Gilbart Winslow.

John Alden was hired for a cooper, at South-Hampton, wher the ship victuled; and being a hopefull yong man, was much desired, but left to his owne liking to go or stay when he came here; but he stayed, and maryed here.

John Allerton and Thomas Enlish were both hired, the later to goe m[aste]r of a shalop here, and the other was reputed as one of the company, but was to go back (being a seaman) for the help of others behind. But they both dyed here, before the shipe returned.

There were allso other •2• seamen hired to stay a year here in the country, William Trevore, and one Ely. But when their time was out, they both returned.

These, bening aboute a hundred sowls, came over in this first ship; and began this worke, which God of his goodnes hath hithertoo blesed; let his holy name have the praise.

And seeing it hath pleased him to give me to see •30• years compleated since these beginings; and that the great works of his providence are to be observed, I have thought it not unworthy my paines to take a view of the decreasings and increasings of these persons, and such changes as hath pased over them and theirs, in this thirty years. It may be of some use to such as come after; but, however, I shall rest in my owne benefite.

I will therfore take them in order as they lye.

Mr. Caruer and his wife dyed the first year; he in the spring, she in the sommer; also, his man Roger [Wilder], and the litle boy Jasper [More] dyed before either of them, of the commone infection. Desire Minter returned to her freinds, and proved not very well, and dyed in England. His servant boy Latham, after more then •20• years stay in the country, went into England, and from thence to the Bahamy Ilands in the West Indies, and ther, with some others, was starved for want of food. His maid servant maried, and dyed a year or tow after, here in this place. His servant, John Howland, maried the doughter of John Tillie, Elizabeth, and they are both now living, and have •10• children, now all living; and their eldest daughter hath •4• children. And ther •2• daughter, one, all living; and other of their children mariagable. So •15• are come of them.

Mr. Brewster lived to very old age; about •80• years he was when he dyed, having lived some •23• or •24• years here in the countrie; and though his wife dyed long before, yet she dyed aged. His sone Wrastle dyed a yonge man unmaried; his sone Love lived till this year •1650• and dyed, and left •4• children, now living. His doughters which came over after him are dead, but have left sundry children alive; his eldest sone is still liveing, and hath •9• or •10• children; one maried, who hath a child or •2•

Richard More his brother dyed the first winter; but he is maried, and hath •4• or •5• children, all living.

Mr. Ed: Winslow his wife dyed the first winter; and he maried with the widow of Mr. White, and hath •2• children living by her marigable, besides sundry that are dead.

One of his servants dyed, as also the litle girle, soone after the ships arivall. But his man, Georg Sowle, is still living, and hath •8• children. and he maried againe; and hath four children, •3• whereof are

William Bradford his wife dyed soone after their arivall; maried.

Mr. Allerton his wife dyed with the first, and his servant, John Hooke. His sone Bartle is maried in England, but I know not how many children he hath. His doughter Remember is maried at Salem, and hath •3• or •4• children living. And his doughter Mary is maried here, and hath •4• children. Him selfe maried againe with the doughter of Mr. Brewster, and hath one sone living by her, but she is long since dead. And he maried againe, and hath left this place long agoe. So I account his increase to be •8• besides his sons in England.

Mr. Fuller his servant dyed at sea; and after his wife came over, he had tow children by her, which are living and growne up to years; but he dyed some •15• years agoe.

John Crakston dyed in the first mortality; and about some •5• or •6• years after, his sone dyed; having lost him selfe in the wodes, his feet became frosen, which put him into a feavor, of which he dyed.

Captain Standish his wife dyed in the first sicknes, and he maried againe, and hath •4• sones liveing, and some are dead.

Mr. Martin, he and all his, dyed in the first infection; not long after the arivall.

Mr. Molines, and his wife, his sone, and his servant, dyed the first winter. Only his dougter Priscila survied, and maried with John Alden, who are both living, and have •11• children. And their eldest daughter is maried, and hath five children.

Mr. White and his •2• servants dyed soone after ther landing. His wife maried with Mr. Winslow (as is before noted). His •2• sons are maried, and Resolved hath •5• children, Peregrine tow, all living. So their increase are •7•

Mr. Hopkins and his wife are now both dead, but they lived above •20• years in this place, and had one sone and •4• doughters borne here. Ther sone became a seaman, and dyed at Barbadoes; one daughter dyed here, and •2• are maried; one of them hath •2• children; and one is yet to mary. So their increase which still survive are •5• But his sone Giles is maried, and hath •4• children.

His doughter Constanta is also maried, and hath •12• children, all of them living, and one of them maried.

Mr. Richard Warren lived some •4• or •5• years, and had his wife come over to him, by whom he had •2• sons before [he] dyed; and one of them is maryed, and hath •2• children. So his increase is •4• But he had •5• doughters more came over with his wife, who are all maried, and living, and have many children.

John Billinton, after he had bene here •10• yers, was executed for killing a man; and his eldest sone dyed before him; but his •2• sone is alive, and maried, and hath •8• children.

Edward Tillie and his wife both dyed soon after their arivall; and the girle Humility, their cousen, was sent for into England, and dyed ther. But the youth Henery Samson is still liveing, and is maried, and hath •7• children.

John Tillie and his wife both dyed a litle after they came ashore; and their daughter Elizabeth maried with John Howland, and hath isue as is before noted.

Francis Cooke is still livng, a very olde man, and hath seene his childrens children have childen; after his wife came over, (with other of his children,) he hath •3• still living by her, all maried, and have •5• children; so their encrease is •8• And his sone John, which came over with him, is maried, and hath •4• children living.

Thomas Rogers dyed in the first sicknes, but his sone Joseph is still living, and is maried, and hath •6• children. The rest of Thomas Rogers [children] came over, and are maried, and have many children.

Thomas Tinker, and his wife and sone, all dyed in the first sicknes. And so did John Rigdale, and his wife.

James Chilton and his wife also dyed in the first infection. But their daughter Mary is still living, and hath •9• children; and one daughter is maried, and hath a child; so their increase is •10•

Edward Fuller and his wife dyed soon after they came ashore; but their sone Samuell is living, and maried, and hath •4• children or more.

John Turner and his •2• sones all dyed in the first siknes. But he hath a daugter still living at Salem, well maried, and approved of.

Francis Eeaton his first wife dyed in the generall sicknes; and he maried againe, and his •2• wife dyed, and he maried the •3• and had by her •3• children. One of them is maried, and hath a child; the other are living, but one of them is an ideote. He dyed about •16• years agoe. His sone Samuell, who came over a sucking child, is allso maried and hath a child.

Moyses Fletcher, Thomas Williams, Digerie Preist, John Goodman, Edmond Margeson, Richard Britterige, Richard Clarke. All these dyed sone after their arivall, in the generall sicknes that befell. But Digerie Preist had his wife and children sent hither afterwards, she being Mr. Allertons sister. But the rest left no posteritie here.

Richard Gardinar became a seaman, and died in England, or at sea.

Gilbert Winslow, after diverse years aboad here, returned into England, and dyed ther.

Peter Browne maried twise. By his first wife he had •2• children, who are living, and both of them maried, and the one of them hath •2• children; by his second wife he had •2• more. He dyed about •16• years since.

Thomas English and John Allerton dyed in the generall siknes.

John Alden maried with Priscila, Mr. Mollines his doughter, and had issue by her as is before related.

Edward Doty and Edward Litster, the servants of Mr. Hopkins. Litster. Litster after he was at liberty, went to Virginia, and ther dyed. But Edward Doty by a second wife hath •7• children, and both he and they are living.

Of these •100• persons which came first over in this first ship together, the greater halfe dyed in the genreall mortality; and most of them in •2• or •3• monthes time. And for those which survi[v]ed, though some were ancient and past procreation, and others left the place and cuntrie, yet of those few remaining are sprunge up above •160• persons, in this •30• years, and are now living in this presente year, •1650• besides many of their children which are dead, and come not within this account.

And of the old stock (of one and other) ther are yet living this present year, •1650• nere •30• persons. Let the Lord have the praise, who is the High Preserver of men.

The Mayflower Compact

The Mayflower Compact was signed while the *Mayflower* was anchored at Cape Cod (Provincetown Harbor) on 11 November 1620 (21 November 1620 New Style). It was signed by all free adult males and some, not all, servants. *Bradford (Ford)* 1:191 gives the wording of the compact as taken directly from Bradford's manuscript. However, Bradford does not give any list, or even hint, as to the names of the signers. Nathaniel Morton in *New Englands Memoriall*, pp. 15-16, gives both the compact and a list of signers, and many people have taken this list as if it were a faithful reproduction of the names of all the signers and in the sequence of their signing, and they have further deduced the relative importance of each given signer from his position in Morton's list.

Ford's footnote to the compact quotes Deane and adds his own comment, and because of its pertinence will be given in its entirety: "'Bradford gives no list here of the signers of this compact. Morton [*Memoriall*, 15] must have had some other authority than this History for the names he has appended to it in the Memorial, or else he supplied them by conjecture from Bradford's list of passengers in the Appendix. If we suppose this compact to have been signed by all the adult male passengers, it would seem that other names besides those Morton has given should have been included.' DEANE

"Morton follows quite closely the order of names given in Bradford's list, which in itself offers a fair argument for his having copied from Bradford and not from the original sheet on which the compact had been written and signed. A few variations may be laid to errors in copying or in printing. As to names in the Bradford list which are not to be found in that of Morton, they represent servants who may have been under age or closely bound by articles of indenture, and member of families whose head had already signed."

Morton from his writings seems a rather dull fellow, very orthodox in his beliefs, and not one to care about precise transcriptions. The version of the compact below is from Bradford, but Morton's differences are given in brackets. The list of "signers" of course must come from Morton. After each name will be given the position of the signer in Bradford's list, for various people are listed together in a group with the head of family or other person. If the signer is not the head of family or group, his name will be followed by "(w/number)," to indicate his group. Any analysis of the sequencing of names of signers as given by Morton must conclude that if he used accurate information to determine who the signers were, he still did not list them in the sequence of actual signing, for it is inconceivable, for example, that John Alden in 1620 would have ranked with Allerton and Standish, and would have been ahead of such important (in 1620) people as Samuel Fuller, Christopher Martin, William Mullins, William White, Richard Warren, and so on. It is also doubtful that John Howland, in 1620 a servant to John Carver, would have signed in the position given him by Morton. It seems likely, as hinted by Deane and Ford, that Morton sequenced his names roughly in the order given by Bradford's passenger list (which, for all we know, could have been similar to the actual signing as well), but he gave a higher position to a few signers, such as Alden and Howland, who were living in 1669 when Morton wrote his book. The line between two groups of signers represents the division between two pages of Morton's book. The text of the compact is:

In the name [Name] of God, Amen. We whose names [Names] are underwriten [under-written], the loyall subjects [Loyal Subjects] of our dread soveraigne [Soveraign] Lord, King [Lord King] James, by the grace of God, of [God of] Great Britaine [Britain], Franc, and [France and] Ireland king [Ireland, King], defender [Defendor] of the faith [Faith], etc.

Haveing [Having] undertaken, for [undertaken for] the glorie [glory] of God, and advancemente [advancement] of the Christian faith, and honour [Faith, and the Honour] of our king [King] and countrie [Countrey], a voyage [Voyage] to plant the first colonie [Colony] in the Northerne [Northern] parts of Virginia, [;] doe [Do] by these presents [Presents] solemnly and mutually [mutually,] in the presence of God, and one of [God and one] another, covenant and combine [Covenant and Combine] our selves togeather [together] into a civill body politick [Civil Body Politick], for our better ordering and preservation [,] and furtherance of the ends aforesaid; [:] and by vertue hearof [virtue hereof] to enacte [do enact], constitute, and [constiture and] frame shuch [such] just and equall [equal] lawes [Laws], ordinances [Ordinances], acts [Acts], constitutions, [Constitutions] and offices [Officers], from time to time, as shall be thought most meete [meet] and convenient for the generall [general] good of the Colonie, [Colony;] unto which we promise all due submission and obedience. In witnes wherof [witness whereof] we have hereunder [hereunto] subscribed our name [Names] at Cap-Codd [Cape Cod,] the .11. [eleventh] of November, in the year of the raigne [in the Reign] of our soveraigne lord, King [Soveraign Lord King] James, of England, France, and Ireland, the [France and Ireland the] eighteenth, and of Scotland the fiftie [fifty] fourth. Anno [fourth, Anno] Dom. 1620.

John Carver (1)   Samuel Fuller (6)   Edward Tilly (15)
William Bradford (4)   Christopher Martin (9)   John Tilly (16)
Edward Winslow (3)   William Mullins (10)   Francis Cook (17)
William Brewster (2)   William White (11)   Thomas Rogers (18)
Isaac Allerton (5)   Richard Warren (13)   Thomas Tinker (19)
Miles Standish (8)   John Howland (w/1)   John Ridgdale (20)
John Alden (26)   Steven Hopkins (12)   Edward Fuller (22)

John Turner (23)   Digery Priest (w/25)   Richard Clark (w/25)
Francis Eaton (24)   Thomas Williams (w/25)   Richard Gardiner (w/25)
James Chilton (21)   Gilbert Winslow (w/25)   John Allerton (27)
John Craxton (7)   Edmond Margeson   Thomas English (w/27)
                                        (w/25)
John Billington (14)   Peter Brown (w/25)   Edward Doten (w/12)
Moses Fletcher (25)   Richard Bitteridge (w/25) Edward Liester (w/12)
John Goodman (w/25) George Soule (w/3)

The 1623 Division of Land

T he 1623 Division of Land is valuable because it tells us, more or less, who was in Plymouth in 1623, and which of these residents were respectively passengers of the 1621 *Fortune* and the 1623 *Ann* and *Little James*. Robert S. Wakefield, "The Plymouth 1623 Land Division," *MQ* 40:7-13, 55-62, analyzes what he calls a "reconstructed 1623 census of Plymouth" to devise rules for how he believes the allotments were made. This analysis can be revised in the light of subsequently obtained information. For example, we now know that Edward Winslow, in addition to his person, invested £60 in the Plymouth venture, and thus his four acres would not be explained by his number of shares in the company.

The number given after each name represented the number of acres a "head of family" was entitled to, and certainly was at least partially based on the number of members, including servants, in that person's family. John Oldham received the largest number of acres, ten, and they must have represented one each for himself, his wife, his children, his sister Lucretia, and others associated with him. The list given below is from *PCR* 12:4-6, the original pages of which are in the handwriting of Gov. William Bradford:

The Falles of their grounds which came first over in the May Floure, according as thier lotes were case .1623.

	Robart Cochman	1 the number [of]
	Mr William Brewster	6 akers to [each]
	William Bradford	3 one.
	Richard Gardener	1
these lye on the	Frances Cooke	2
South side of	George Soule	1
the brooke to	Mr Isaak Alerton	7
the baywards.	John Billington	3
	Peter Browen	1

Samuell Fuller	2
Joseph Rogers	2

these containe .29. akers.

These lye one the South side of the brook to the woodward opposite to the former.	John Howland	4
	Steuen Hobkins	6
	Edward ∧	1
	Edward ∧	1
	Gilbard Winslow	1
	Samuell ffuller Juneor	3

these containe .16. akers besides

Hobamaks ground which lyeth betwene Jo: Howlands & Hobkinses.

this .5. akers lyeth behind the forte to the litle ponde.	William White	5

	Edward Winslow	4
	Richard Warren	[2]
these lye one the north side of the towne nexte adjoyning to their gardens which came in the Fortune.	John Goodman	X
	John Crackston	X
	John Alden	X
	Marie Chilton	X
	Captin Myles Standish	2
	Francis Eaton	4
	Henerie Samson	1
	Humillitie Cooper	1

The fales of their grounds which came in the Fortune according as their Lots were cast 1623.

these lye to the sea, eastward.		These lye beyond the f[irst] to the wood we[st]ward.	
William Hilton	1	William Wright &	2
John Winslow	1	William Pitt	
William Coner	1	Robart Hickes	1
John Adams	1	Thomas Prence	1
William Tench &	2	Steuen Dean	1
John Cannon		Moyses Simonson &	2
		Philipe de la Noye	
		Edward Bompass	1
these folowing lye		Clemente Brigges	1
beyonde the .2. brooke.		James Steward	1

		William Palmer	2
		Jonathan Brewster	1
Hugh Statie	1	Benet Morgan	1
William Beale & Thomas Cushman	2	Thomas Flauell & his son,	2
Austen Nicolas	1	Thomas Morton	1
Widow Foord	4	William Bassite	2
	15. akers		19. akers

The fales of their grounds which came ouer in the shipe called the Anne according as their/ were cast. 1623.

	Akers	These to the sea eastward.	akx.
James Rande	1	Francis Spragge	3

these following lye beyond the brooke to Strawberie-hill.

Edmond Flood	1	Edward Burcher	2
Christopher Connant	1	John Jenings	5
Francis Cooke	4	goodwife Flauell	1
		Manasseh & John Fance	2
these but against the swampe & reed-ponde.		this goeth in wth a corner by ye ponde.	
George Morton & Experience Mitchell	8	Allice Bradford	1
Christian Penn	1	Robart Hickes his wife & children	4
Thomas Morton Junior	1	Brigett Fuller	1
William Hiltons wife & .2. children	3	Ellen Newton	1
		Pacience & Fear Brewster, wth Robart Long	3
		William Heard	1
		Mrs Standish	1

These following lye on the other side of the towne towards the eele-riuer.

Marie Buckett adioyning to Joseph Rogers	1	Robart Rattlife beyonde the swampie & stonie ground	[2]
Mr Ouldom & those joyned with him	10	These butt against Hobes Hole.	
Cudbart Cudbartsone	6		
Anthony Anable	4	Nicolas Snow	X
Thomas Tilden	3	Anthony Dixe	X
Richard Waren	5	Mr Perces .2. Ser:	X
Bangs	4	Ralfe Walen,	X
South side.		North side.	
Steph: Tracy three acres	3	Edw: Holman 1. acre	1
Tho. Clarke one acre	1	ffrance wife to Wit Palmer	1
Robt Bartlet one acre	1	Josuah Prat & Phineas Prat	2

The 1626 Purchasers

I saac Allerton negotiated in England an agreement dated 26 October 1626 between the Adventurers and himself as "one of the planters resident at Plymoth afforesaid, assigned, and sent over as agent for the rest of the planters ther," whereby the Adventurers for £1,800 sold to the planters, later known as the Purchasers, all the "said stocks, shares, lands, marchandise, and chatles" which had belonged to the Adventurers (*Bradford [Ford]* 2:4). The list we have of the Purchasers is from *PCR* 2:177, and was obviously compiled sometime after the 1626 agreement, for Richard Warren died in 1628, and his wife replaced him on the list, and John Billington was hanged in 1630, and his share is represented on the list by his surname only. Though the following year the fifty-eight Purchasers in turn assigned both the shares in the company and the debt to the eight Plymouth and four London Undertakers, the list of Purchasers continued to be an important one for, in general, these people were privileged above all others in future land grants in the colony. The list, consisting of fifty-three Plymouth names plus the names of five London men, is as follows:

The Names of the Purchasers

Mr Wm Bradford	Abraham Pearse
Mr Thom Prence	Steeven Tracy
Mr Wm Brewster	Joseph Rogers
Mr Edw Winslow	John Faunce
Mr John Alden	Steeven Deane
Mr John Jenney	Thom Cushman
Mr Isaack Allerton	Robte Hicks
Capt Miles Standish	Thom Morton
Mr Wm Collyer	Anthony Annable
Mr John Howland	Samuell Fuller
Manasseth Kempton	Franc Eaton
Francis Cooke	Willm Basset
Jonathan Brewster	Francis Sprague
Edward Banges	The Heires of John Crackstone
Nicholas Snow	Edward Bumpas
Steven Hopkins	Willm Palmer

Thomas Clarke
Raph Wallen
Willm Wright
Elizabeth Warren, widow
Edward Dotey
Cutbert Cutbertson
John Winslow
John Shaw
Josuah Pratt
John Adams
 ∧   Billington
Phineas Pratt
Samuell Fuller
Clement Briggs

Peter Browne
Henry Sampson
Experience Michell
Phillip Delanoy
Moyses Symonson
Georg Soule
Edward Holman
                    .53
Mr James Sherley
Mr Beauchampe
Mr Andrewes
Mr Hatherley
Mr Wm Thomas
              In all 58.

The 1627 Division of the Cattle

" **A** t a publique Court held the 22th of May [1627] it was concluded by the whole Companie, that the cattell wch were the Companies, to wit, the Cowe, & the Goates should be equally divided to all the psonts of the same company & soe kept untill the expiration of ten yeares after the date above written (*PCR* 12:9)." It is believed that the list includes the name of every resident then at Plymouth (not some transients who were known to be there at the time). Residents included servants and children, and note the inclusion of Mary Brewster, daughter of Jonathan and Lucretia Brewster, who had been born just five weeks prior to the division on 16 April 1627 (*MD* 1:7). For convenience, the division was made into twelve lots consisting of thirteen people, often related, in each. The following is from *PCR* 12:9-13:

    i. The first lot fell to ffrancis Cooke & his Companie Joyned to him his wife Hester Cooke

        3 John Cooke
        4 Jacob Cooke
        5 Jane Cooke
        6 Hester Cooke
        7 Mary Cooke
        8 Moses Simonson
        9 Phillip Delanoy
      10 Experience Michaell
      11 John ffance
      12 Joshua Pratt
      13 Phinihas Pratt

    To this lot fell the least of the 4 black heyfers Came in the Jacob, and two shee goats.

    2 The second lot fel to Mr Isaac Allerton & his Companie joyned to him his wife ffeare Allerton.

        3 Bartholomew Allerton
        4 Remember Allerton

    5 Mary Allerton
    6 Sarah Allerton
    7 Godber Godberson
    8 Sarah Godberson
    9 Samuell Godberson
    10 Marra Priest
    11 Sarah Priest
    12 Edward Bumpasse
    13 John Crakstone

To his lot fell the Greate Black cow came in the Ann to which they must keepe the lesser of the two steers, and two shee goats.

3 The third lot fell to Capt Standish & his companie Joyned to him

    2 his wife Barbara Standish
    3 Charles Standish
    4 Allexander Standish
    5 John Standish
    6 Edward Winslow
    7 Susanna Winslow
    8 Edward Winslow
    9 John Winslow
    10 Resolued White
    11 Perigrine White
    12 Abraham Peirce
    13 Thomas Clarke

To this lot fell the Red Cow wch belongeth to the poore of the Colonye to wch they must keepe her Calfe of this yeare being a Bull for the Companie. Also to this lott Came too she goats.

4 The fourth lot fell to John Howland & his company Joyned to him

    2 his wife Elizabeth Howland
    3 John Howland Junor
    4 Desire Howland
    5 William Wright
    6 Thomas Morton Junor
    7 John Alden
    8 Prissilla Alden
    9 Elizabeth Alden
    10 Clemont Briggs
    11 Edward Dolton
    12 Edward Holdman
    13 Joh. Alden

To this lot fell one of the 4 heyfers Came in the Jacob Called Raghorne.

5 The fift lot fell to Mr Willm Brewster & his companie Joyned to him

    2 Loue Brewster
    3 Wrestling Brewster
    4 Richard More
    5 Henri Samson
    6 Johnathan Brewster
    7 Lucrecia Brewster
    8 Willm Brewster
    9 Mary Brewster
   10 Thomas Prince
   11 Pacience Prince
   12 Rebecka Prince
   13 Humillyty Cooper

To this lot ffell one of the fower Heyfers Came in the Jacob Caled the Blind Heyfer & 2 shee goats.

6 The sixt lott fell to John Shaw & his companie Joyned

    1 to him
    2 John Adams
    3 Eliner Adams
    4 James Adams
    5 John Winslow
    6 Mary Winslow
    7 Willm Basset
    8 Elizabeth Bassett
    9 Willyam Basset Junor
   10 Elyzabeth Basset Junor
   11 ffrancis Sprage
   12 Anna Sprage
   13 Mercye Sprage

To this lot fell the lesser of the black Cowes Came at first in the Ann wth which they must keepe the bigest of the 2 steers. Also to this lott was two shee goats.

7 The seauenth lott fell to Stephen Hopkins & his companie Joyned to

    2 him his wife Elizabeth Hopkins
    3 Gyles Hopkins
    4 Caleb Hopkins
    5 Debora Hopkins
    6 Nickolas Snow
    7 Constance Snow
    8 Willam Pallmer
    9 ffrances Pallmer
   10 Willm Pallmer Jnor
   11 John Billington Senor
   12 Hellen Billington
   13 ffrancis Billington

To this lott fell A black weining Calfe to wch was aded the Calfe of this yeare to come of the black Cow, wch pueing a bull they were to keepe it vngelt 5 yeares for common vse & after to make there best of it. Nothing belongeth of thes too, for ye copanye of ye first stock: but only half ye Increase.

To this lott ther fell two shee goats: which goats they posses on the like terms which others doe their cattell.

8 The eaight lot fell to Sameull ffuller & his company Joyned to him hiw wife

    2 Bridgett ffuller
    3 Samuell ffuller Junior
    4 Peeter Browne
    5 Martha Browne
    6 Mary Browne
    7 John fford
    8 Martha fford
    9 Anthony Anable
   10 Jane Anable
   11 Sara Anable
   12 hanah Anable
   ~~13 Thom Morton Senor~~
   13 Damaris Hopkins

To this lott fell A Red eyfer Came of the Cow wch belongeth to the poore of the Colony & so is of that Consideration. (viz) thes psonts nominated, to haue halfe the Increace, the other halfe, with the ould stock, to remain for the vse of the poore.

To this lott also two shee goats.

9 The ninth lot fell to Richard Warren & his companie Joyned wth

    2 him his wife Elizabeth Warren
    3 Nathaniell Warren
    4 Joseph Warren
    5 Mary Warren
    6 Anna Warren
    7 Sara Warren
    8 Elizabeth Warren
    9 Abigall Warren
   10 John Billington
   11 George Sowle
   12 Mary Sowle
   13 Zakariah Sowle

To this lott fell one of the 4 black Heyfers that came in the Jacob caled the smooth horned Heyfer and two shee goats.

10 The tenth lot fell to ffrancis Eaton & those Joyned wth him his

   2 wife Christian Eaton
   3 Samuell Eaton
   4 Rahell Eaton
   5 Stephen Tracie
   6 Triphosa Tracie
   7 Sarah Tracie
   8 Rebecka Tracie
   9 Ralph Wallen
  10 Joyce Wallen
  11 Sarah Morton
  ~~12 Edward Fludd~~
  12 Robert ~~Hilton~~ Bartlet
  13 Tho: Prence

To this lott fell an heyfer of the last yeare called the white belyd heyfer & two shee goats.

11 The eleuenth lott ffell to the Gouernor Mr William Bradford and

   2 those with him, to wit, his wife Alles Bradford and
   3 William Bradford, Junior
   4 Mercy Bradford
   5 Joseph Rogers
   6 Thomas Cushman
   7 William Latham
   8 Manases Kempton
   9 Julian Kempton
  10 Nathaniell Morton
  11 John Morton
  12 Ephraim Morton
  13 Patience Morton

To this lott fell An heyfer of the last yeare wch was of the Greate white back cow that was brought ouer in the Ann, & two shee goats.

12 The twelueth lott fell to John Jene & his companie joyned to him,

   2 his wife Sarah Jene
   3 Samuell Jene
   4 Abigall Jene
   5 Sara Jene
     Robert
   6 Robert Hickes
   7 Margret Hickes
   8 Samuell Hickes
   9 Ephraim Hickes
  10 Lidya Hickes
  11 Phebe Hickes

12 Stephen Deane
13 Edward Banges

To this lott fell the greate white backt cow wch was brought ouer with the first in the Ann, to wch cow the keepeing of the bull was joyned for thes psonts to puide for. heere also two shee goats.

The 1633 and 1634 Tax Lists

On 25 March 1633 the following people were rated (that is, taxed) the following amounts, as determined by William Bradford, Capt. Myles Stanidsh, John Alden, John Howland, John Doane, Stephen Hopkins, William Gilson, Samuel Fuller, Sr., John Jenney, Cuthbert Cuthbertson, and Jonathan Brewster (*PCR* 1:9-11):

	£ sh d
Edward Wynslow, Govr	02:05:00
Mr. Will Bradford	01:16:00
Capt Myles Standish	00:18:00
Will Brewster	01:07:00
Isaack Allerton	03:11:00
Thomas Prence	01:07:00
John Howland	00:18:00
John Alden	01:04:00
John Done	01:07:00
Sam: Fuller, Senior	00:18:00
John Jenny	01:16:00
Stephen Hopkins	01:07:00
Jonathan Brewster	01:07:00
William Gilson	00:12:00
France Weston	00:15:00
Robt Heekes	00:18:00
John Wynslow	00:18:00
Manasseh Kempton	00:18:00
Godbert Godbertson	00:18:00
John Coombs	00:12:00
Phineas Pratt	00:09:00
George Sowle	00:09:00
Thomas Clarke	01:04:00
John Washburne	00:09:00
Nicholas Snow	00:18:00
Mr Hatherlies two men	00:18:00

Edward Bangs	00:12:00
John Browne	00:09:00
Stephen Tracy	00:18:00
Widow Warren	00:12:00
Robert Bartlet	00:09:00
Anthony Annable	00:18:00
France Eaton	00:09:00
Raph Wallen	00:09:00
France Sprage	00:18:00
John Dunham	00:09:00
Roger Chandler	00:09:00
Samuell Nash	00:09:00
Stephen Deane	00:09:00
William Basset	01:07:00
Expience Michaell	00:18:00
Edward Dowty	01:07:00
Peter Browne	00:18:00
Humfrey Turner	00:09:00
Sam: Eedy	00:09:00
Will Palmer	01:07:00
John Holmes	00:18:00
John Barnes	00:09:00
John Fance	00:09:00
Thomas Pope	00:09:00
John Shawe	00:18:00
Richard Lanckford	00:09:00
John Adams	00:09:00
Abraam Peirce	00:09:00
Christopher Wadsworth	00:12:00
France Billington	00:09:00
France Cooke	00:18:00
Moses Symons	00:09:00
Widdow Blossome	00:09:00
James Hurst	00:09:00
Henry Cobb	00:09:00
Henry Howland	00:09:00
Phillip Delanoy	00:18:00
Edward Bumpasse	00:09:00
Joseph Rogers	00:09:00
John Rogers	00:09:00
William Sherman	00:09:00
John Thorp	00:18:00
Samuell Chandler	00:09:00
Richard Church	01:16:00
William Richards	00:09:00
Thomas Little	00:18:00

William Bennet	∧ ∧ ∧
Addy Web	00:09:00
Mr Colliers men	00:18:00
Richard Sparrow	00:09:00
William Latham	00:09:00
Richard Higgins	00:09:00
Edward Foster	00:09:00
Richard Seer	00:09:00
Thomas Boreman	00:09:00
Edward Holman	00:18:00
Kenelme Wynslow	00:12:00
Widow Harding	00:09:00
∧ Rowland	00:09:00
John Bowman	00:09:00
John Hewes	00:09:00
∧ Rowly	00:09:00
Nathaniell Morton	00:09:00

On 27 March 1634 the following people were rated the following amounts, as determined by Gov. Thomas Prence, William Bradford, Capt. Myles Standish, John Howland, Stephen Hopkins, John Doane, William Gilson, William Collier, John Jenney, Robert Hicks, Jonathan Brewster, Kenelm Winslow, and Stephen Deane (*PCR* 1:26-29):

	£ sh d
Edw: Wynslow	02:05:00
Mr Will Bradford	01:07:00
Capt Myles Standish	00:18:00
Mr Will Brewster	01:07:00
Isaack Allerton	01:16:00
Joh Howland	01:04:00
Joh Alden	01:04:00
Steph Hopkins	01:10:00
Mr Will Collier	02:05:00
Joh Done	01:07:00
Joh Jenny	01:07:00
Jonath Brewster	01:04:00
Will Gilson	01:07:00
Robt Heeke	00:12:00
John Wynslow	00:18:00
Menasseh Kempton	00:18:00
John Coombs	00:09:00
Phineas Pratt	00:09:00
George Sowle	00:09:00
Tho: Clarke	01:07:00
Nicholas Snow	00:12:00
Mr Hatherlies men	∧ ∧ ∧

Edw: Bangs	00:12:00
John Browne	00:09:00
Stephen Tracy	00:18:00
Widow Warren	00:09:00
Robert Barlet	00:09:00
Anthony Annable	00:09:00
France Sprague	00:18:00
John Dunham	00:09:00
Roger Chandler	00:09:00
Samuell Nash	00:09:00
Stephen Deane	00:12:00
William Bassett	01:07:00
Expience Michaell	00:09:00
Edw: Dowty	00:18:00
Widow Browne	00:09:00
Widow Fuller	00:09:00
Samuell Fuller	00:09:00
Humphrey Turner	00:09:00
Samuell Edy	00:09:00
Will Palmer	00:18:00
Will Palmer, Junior	00:09:00
James Cole	00:09:00
John Holmes	00:18:00
John Barnes	00:18:00
John Fance	00:09:00
Tho Pope	00:09:00
John Shaw	00:09:00
Widow Adams	00:09:00
Abr Peirce	00:09:00
France Billington	00:09:00
France Cooke	00:09:00
John Cooke	00:09:00
John Cooke, Senior	00:09:00
Moses Symonson	00:09:00
∧ Rowly	00:18:00
Henry Howland	00:18:00
Phillip Delanoy	00:09:00
Edw: Bumpasse	00:09:00
Joseph Rogers	00:09:00
Sam Chandler	00:09:00
Rich Church	01:07:00
Will Richard	00:09:00
Tho Little	00:18:00
Ady Web	00:09:00
Rich Sparrow	00:09:00
Will Latham	00:09:00

Richard Higgens	00:12:00
Edw: Foster	00:09:00
Kenelm Wynslow	00:18:00
John Hewes	00:09:00
Nathaniell Morton	00:09:00
John Bowman	00:09:00
Raph Fogge	00:12:00
Isaack Robbinson	00:09:00
Josias Cooke	00:09:00
Walter Woodart	00:09:00
James Hurst	00:09:00
Henry Cob	00:09:00
Richard Clovfe	00:12:00

The 1627-1634 Arrivals

T his is not a contemporary list, but is one compiled by Robert S. Wakefield and Eugene A. Stratton from a number of original source documents to show the people who are known or presumed to have arrived at Plymouth sometime between 22 May 1627, date of the Division of the Cattle, and 27 March 1634, date of the 1634 Tax List. These people are also given (or included under someone else) in the biographical sketches. This list is undoubtedly incomplete, but it is hoped that future research will allow additions to it. In general, childen born abroad who came over during this period to join their parents are included, but children born in Plymouth Colony are not.

ADEY, WEBB
BAKER, WILLIAM
BARKER, ROBERT
BARNES, JOHN
BEAVAN, JOHN
BENNET, WILLIAM
BLOSSOM, ANNA—wife of Thomas
BLOSSOM, ELIZABETH—daughter of Thomas
BLOSSOM, THOMAS
BLOSSOM, THOMAS—son of Thomas
BOREMAN, THOMAS
BOWMAN, JOHN
BRADFORD, JOHN, son of William
BRIAN, THOMAS
BROWNE, DOROTHY, wife of John
BROWNE, JAMES, son of John
BROWNE, JOHN
BROWNE, JOHN—another John Browne; married Phebe Harding
BROWNE, JOHN—son of the first John Browne
BROWNE, MARY—the second wife of Peter Browne
BROWNE, MARY, daughter of John
BROWNE, WILLIAM, son of John
BUMPUS, HANNAH, wife of Edward

CHANDLER, EDMOND
CHANDLER, ISABELLA, wife of Roger
CHANDLER, MARTHA, daughter of Roger
CHANDLER, MARY, daughter of Roger
CHANDLER, ROGER
CHANDLER, SAMUEL
CHANDLER, SARAH, daughter of Roger
CHURCH, RICHARD
CLOUGH, RICHARD
COBB, HENRY
COLE, HUGH
COLE, JAMES
COLE, JAMES, son of James
COLE, JOB
COLE, JOHN
COLE, MARY, wife of James
COLLIER, ELIZABETH, daughter of William
COLLIER, JANE, wife of William
COLLIER, MARY, daughter of William
COLLIER, REBECCA, daughter of William
COLLIER, SARAH, daughter of William
COLLIER, WILLIAM
COLLIER (Mr. Collier's Men) — They were taxed before the
    arrival of William Collier on his behalf. One was probably John Cole.
CONVERSE, SARAH
COOKE, JOHN, SR.
COOKE, JOSIAS
COMBES, JOHN
COWLES, ELIZABETH
COWLES, ROBERT
DOANE, JOHN
DUNHAM, ABIGAIL, wife of John
DUNHAM, ABIGAIL, daughter of John
DUNHAM, JOHN
DUNHAM, JOHN, son of John
DUNHAM, PERSIS, daughter of John
DUNHAM, SAMUEL, son of John
DUNHAM, THOMAS, son of John
EDDY, JOHN, brother of Samuel
EDDY, SAMUEL
FOGGE, RALPH
FOSTER, EDWARD
GILSON, FRANCIS, wife of William
GILSON, WILLIAM
GRINDER, ALICE, servant to Isaac Allerton in 1633 (*PCR* 1:20)

GYLES, "Goodman," mentioned in the will of Mary Ring (*MD* 1:29-31), possibly the Edm. Giles mentioned in her inventory (*MD* 1:31-34), who was also mentioned in the inventory of John Thorp (*MD* 1:158-61).

HARDING, MARTHA

HARDING, PHEBE, married John Brown 26 March 1634.

HARDING, _____, son of widow Martha Harding; mentioned in court 28 October 1633 (*PCR* 1:18).

HARRIS, WALTER

HATHERLY (Mr. Hatherly's Men)—They were taxed on Mr. Hatherly's behalf in both 1633 and 1634.

HATHERLY, TIMOTHY

HEWS, JOAN, wife of John

HEWS, JOHN

HIGGENS, THOMAS

HIGGINS, RICHARD

HILL, JOHN

HODGKINS, ELIZABETH, married William Palmer, Jr. 27 March 1634

HOLMES, JOHN

HOLMES, WILLIAM

HONEYWELL, WILLIAM

HOWLAND, ARTHUR, possibly came over in this period

HOWLAND, HENRY

HURST, GARTEND, wife of James

HURST, JAMES

HURST, PATIENCE, daughter of James

IRISH, JOHN

LANCKFORD, RICHARD

LITTLE, THOMAS

MASTERSON, MARY, wife of Richard

MASTERSON, NATHANIEL, son of Richard

MASTERSON, RICHARD

MASTERSON, SARAH, daughter of Richard

MENDLOVE, WILLIAM

NASH, SAMUEL

NEWCOMEN, JOHN

PALMER'S MAID SERVANT, mentioned in *PCR* 1:15.

PHILIPS, JOHN

PHIPS, WILLIAM

PICKWORTH, (ANN?), wife of John

PICKWORTH, JOHN

PLUMMER, ANN, married Henry Sampson

PLUMMER, MARY, married John Barnes

PONTUS, HANNAH, daughter of William

PONTUS, MARY, daughter of William

PONTUS, WILLIAM

PONTUS, WYBRA, wife of William

POPE, THOMAS
PRATT, BATHSHEBA, wife of Joshua
RAY, DANIEL
REYNOLDS, WILLIAM
RICHARDS, WILLIAM
RING, ANDREW, son of Mary
RING, ELIZABETH, daughter of Mary
RING, MARY
RING, SUSANNA, daughter of Mary
ROBINSON, ISAAC
ROGERS, ELIZABETH, daughter of Thomas, possibly in Plymouth,
  and possibly married Samuel Eddy.
ROGERS, HANNAH, married Joseph Rogers
ROGERS, JOHN, son of Thomas
ROGERS, MARGARET, daughter of Thomas, possibly in Plymouth
ROGERS, Mr.
ROWLAND, (William?)
ROWLEY, HENRY
ROWLEY, MOSES, son of Henry
ROWLEY, SARAH, probably daughter of Henry
SAMPSON, ABRAHAM—possibly came over in this period
SAVERY, ANTHONY
SAVERY, THOMAS
SEARS, RICHARD
SHAW, ABIGAIL, daughter of John
SHAW, (ALICE?), wife of John
SHAW, JAMES, son of John
SHERMAN, WILLIAM
SHURT, ABRAHAM
SMITH, JOHN
SMITH, Mrs., wife of Ralph
SMITH, RALPH
SOUTHWORTH, CONSTANT
SOUTHWORTH, RICHARD
SYMONS, THOMAS (also called Simmons)
TALBOT, MOSES
TALBOT, PETER
THORP, ALICE, wife of John
THORP, JOHN
TURNER, HUMPHREY
TURNER, JOHN, the elder, son of Humphrey
TURNER, JOHN, younger, son of Humphrey
TURNER, LYDIA, wife of Humphrey
TURNER, LYDIA, daughter of Humphrey
TURNER, THOMAS, son of Humphrey
WADSWORTH, CHRISTOPHER

WADSWORTH, GRACE, wife of Christopher
WASHBURN, JOHN
WESTON, FRANCIS
WILKES, WILLIAM
WILLET, THOMAS
WILLIAMS, ROGER
WINSLOW, JOSIAS
WINSLOW, KENELM
WOODWARD, WALTER
WRIGHT, PRISCILLA, wife of William

The 1643 Able to Bear Arms (ATBA) List

T he United Colonies in their Constitution of 19 May 1643, among other matters, provided that each colony's commissioners would submit from time to time "a true accounte and number of all their males. . .of what qualitie or condition soever they be, from 16 years old to 60" resident in their respective colonies (*Bradford [Ford]*) 2:356). Note on the following list the names of "Mr. Bradford," the governor, and ministers such as Mr. John Reyner and Mr. Charles Chauncy. The records show that the court excused specifically only a few men from this list because they were not able bodied, such as George Pidcock (*PCR* 2:67). Thus the list would seem to be fairly complete in giving us the names of almost all adult males in Plymouth in 1643, and that of course is its value. A bit of caution is necessary, though, for not all names were necessarily entered in 1643, and some may have been put on the list in 1644 or later. Some men are on the list for two towns, indicating that in 1643 they lived in one town, but later moved to another and had their names added to the other's. The list is found in *PCR* 8:187-96.

In transcribing the list, Shurtleff used certain symbols to indicate the way the names actually appeared on the original records, but these have been omitted from the list given below. The main meaning of these symbls was to indicate that a name had been cancelled, or sometimes interlined. In at least one case, concerning "the blackamore," Shurtleff made a significant error in his transcription. In some cases, names had numbers after them, but again the numbers are not given here. The list as given here is intended to show who was living where in or sometime after 1643. Anyone needing to make an analysis for other purposes is referred to the original record in Plymouth.

August, 1643. The Names of all the Males that are able to beare Armes from xvj. Yeares, wthin the sevrall Towneshipps.

Plymouth

Mr. Willm Hanbury	Robte Eldred
Raph Jones John Jenkine	Robte Wickson
Charles Thurstone	George Crips

439

John Howland, Sen
John Howland, Jun
Francis Cooke
Jacob Cooke
John Cooke, Jnr, his boy
Samuell Eaton
William Spooner
Phineas Pratt
George Clarke
Francis Billington
Benjamin Eaton
Abraham Pearse
the blackamore
Mathew Fuller
John Bundy
Thurston Clark, Jun.
Gregory Armestrong
Robte Lee
Nicholas Hodges
Thomas Gray
John Shawe, Sen
James Shawe
John Shawe Jun.
Stephen Bryan
John Harman
John Winslow
Samuell Kinge
Edward Dotey
Willm Snowe
John Holmes
Willm Hoskine
James Hurst
George Lewes
Mr John Atwood
Willm Crowe
Thomas Southwood
Mr John Done
James Cole, Sen.
James Cole, Jun.
Heugh Cole
Thomas Lettis
John Grome
& Brick
Thomas Willet
John Cooke, Sen.
Samuell Hicks

Ephraim Hicks
Richard Knowles
James Renell
James Adams
John Yeonge
Edward Holman
Caleb Hopkins
John Heyward
Willm Baker
Richard Bashop
John Gorame
Mr Wm Paddy
Henry Atkins
Mr Bradford
John Bradford
Samuell Stertevant
Samuell Cutbert
Mr Thomas Prence
Thom Roberts
Willm Nelson
John Smyth
Nathl Sowther
Mr John Reynor
Samuell Fuller
Samuel Eddy
Richard Sparrow
John Kerby
John Jenney, Sen.
Samuell Jenney
John Jenney, Jur
Richard Smyth
Josias Cooke
John Wood
Henry Wood
Steephen Wood
Robte Paddock
Josuah Pratt
Richard Wright
Andrew Ringe
Gabriell Fallowell
Thomas Cushman
Thom Sauory
John Finney
Webb Addey
Thomas Pope
Giles Rickett, Sen.

John Rickett
Giles Rickett, Junr
Georg Watson
John Barnes
Edward Edwards
John Jordaine
John Dunhame
Thom Dunhame
Samuell Dunhame
Edmond Tilson
John Smaley
Francis Goulder
Thomas Whitney
Ezra Couell
Anthony Snow
Richard Higgens
John Jenkine
Nathaniell Morton
Manasseth Kempton
John Morton
Ephraim Morton
James Glasse
Edward Banges
Joseph Ramsden
Jeremiah Whitney

Nicholas Snow
Marke Snow
Willm Fallowell
Robte Finney
John Smith, Senr
Thom Clarke
Georg Bonum
Willm Shercliffe
John Churchell
Joseph Greene
Thomas Morton
Thomas Williams
John Faunce
Richard Church
Gabriell Royle
Nathaniell Warren
Joseph Warren
Robte Bartlett
Thom Shreeue
Thom Little
John Tompson
Ephraim Tinkham
Willm Browne
Thomas Tiley
Wm Hartopp

Duxborrow, 1643

Moyses Symons
Samuell Tompkins
James Lyndall
Thom Ouldame
Edmond Weston
Willm Hillier
Wm Foard
Francis West
Francis Godfrey
Solomon Lenner
John Irish
Phillip Delanoy
Mr John Alden, Sen
John Alden, Jun
Jos: Alden
Morris Truant
John Vobes
Willm Sherman
Samuell Nash

Abraham Sampson
Georg Soule
Zachary Soule
Wm Maycumber
Wm Tubbs
Wm Paybody
Experience Michell
Henry Howland
Henry Sampson
John Browne
Edmond Hunt
Willm Brett
John Phillips
Thomas Gannett
Wm Mullens
John Tisdale
Nathanell Chaundor
John Harding
John Aymes

Francis Goole
John Wsborne, Sen
John Washbore, Jun
Phillip Washborne
Wm Bassett, Sen
Wm Bassett, Jun
Francis Sprague
Willm Laurance
John Willis
Jonathan Brewster
Willm Brewster
Loue Brewster
Constant Southworth
Capt Standish
Alexander Standish
John Heyward
John Farneseed
Yong Jo: Brewster
Haden   ∧
Thom Bonney
Robte Hussey
Richard Wilson

Thom Heyward, Sen
Thom Heyward, Jun
Th: Robins
Arthur Harris
Edward Hall
Christopher Waddesworth
Willm Clarke
Mr Comfort Starr
John Starr
Daniell Turner
Georg Patrich
John Maynard
Steephen Bryan
John Roger
Joseph Rogers
Joseph Pryor
Benjamin Reade
Abraham Pearse
Wm Merick
Will: Hartub
Sam: Chanler

1643 Scittuate

Mr Charles Chauncey
Thomas Hanford
Robert Haward
Raph Clenes
Nathaniell Mote
Henry Advard
Willm Parker
John Hollett
Gowen White
Willm Perrie
Willm Holmes
Thomas Ensigne
Georg Willerd
Richard   ∧
Walter Briggs
John Hore
John Wadfield
Thomas Allen
John Hewes
James Cudworth
John Whistons
Nicholas Wade

John Tilton
Thomas Symons
Edward Foster
Thomas Rawlins, Sen
Thomas Rawlins, Jun
Robte Brelles
John Witherden
John Beamont
Richard Toute
Georg   ∧
Thomas Tarte
John Dammon
John Hammon
Christopher Winter
Henry Merrite
John Merrite
Isaack Chittenden
Joseph Collman
John Whitcombe
Thomas Lapham
Edmond Eddenden
Thomas Hyland

John Rogers
Thomas Chambers
Richard Curtis
Willm Curtis
Joseph Tilden
Thom Tilden
Edward Tarte
Georg Sutton
Symon Sutton
Thomas Pynson
Richard Gannett
Willm Randle
Willm Hatch
John Lewes
Thomas Wyborne
John Winter
Humfrey Turner
John Turner
John Turner
John Hewes
John Williams, Sen
John Williams, Jun
Edward Williams
James Cushman
James Till
Jeremie ∧
Peter Collemore
Willm Wills
Samuell Fuller
Isaack Buck
Willm Hatch

Walter Hatch
Harke Luse
Thomas Clay
Goodman Read
Thomas Robinson
Edward ∧
Ephraim Kempton, Sen
Ephraim Kempton, Jur
Walter Woodworth
Isaack Stedman
Georg Russell
Georg Moore
Mr Willm Vassell
John Vassell
Resolued White
Willm Pakes
Jacob ∧
Thomas King
Mr Weatherell
Thomas Byrd
Edward Jenkins
George Kennerick
Mr Garrat
Henry Mason
Elisha Besbeach
John Bryant
John Hatch
John Stockbridg
Robte Stutson
∧   Glasse

1643. Sandwitch

Henry Feake
Daniell Wing
Peter Gaunt
Thomas Johnson
Miles Black
Nicholas Wright
Edward Dillinghame
John Fish
Richard Kerby
Thomas Launder
Henry Saunderson
John Winge
Willm Wood

John Ellis
Thomas Nichols
Anthony Bessy
Joseph Winsor
Nathaniell Willis
Anthony Wright
Richard Chadwell
Jonathan Fish
Samuell Arnold
Georg Allen
Richard Burges
Henry Cole
Joseph Holly

[Sherjashubb Bourne, – John Nye –
tooke this oath, anno 1673.]
John Bell
Peter Hanbury
Thom Burges, Senr
Thomas Burges, Junr
Thomas Tuper
Hery Dillingham
Henry Sephen
Thomas Butler
James Skiffe
Laurance Willis
John Presbury
John Freeman
Edmond Clarke
Willm Swyft
Michaell Turner
Peter Wright
Stephen Winge
Thoms Bordman
Raph Allen
Francis Allen

Thomas Gibbs
Edmond Freeman, Jur
Nathaniell Fish
Robte Botefish
Thomas Greenfeild
Mathew Allen
John Johnson
John Greene
Richard Burne
Thomas Shillingsworth
John Dingley
John Vincent
John Joyce
Willm Newland
Edmond Berry
George Buitt
John Newland
Benjamin Noy
Georg Knott
John Blakemore
Mr Willm Leuerich
Mr Edmond Freeman, Sen.

Barnistable. 1643.

Mr John Lathrope
Mr John Mayo
Thomas Dimmock
Richard Foxwell
Nathaniell Bacon
Samuell Mayo
John Scudder
Roger Goodspeed
Henry Cobb
Barnard Lumbard
Thomas Huckings
Edward Fitzrandle
Georg Lewes
Isaack Wells
Henry Rowley
Thomas Lothrope
John Hall
Thomas Lumbard
Robte Linnett
Willm Casley
John Bursley
Thomas Allen

Samuell Jackson
Willm Tilly
Samuell Hinckley
Thomas Hinckley
John Smyth
James Cudworth
Mr Nicholas Symkins
James Hamblin
Henry Coggen
Henry Borne
Willm Crocker
Austine Bearse
Thomas Shawe
John Cooper
Thomas Hatch
Robert Shelly
Willm Pearse
Willm Beetes
John Crocker
Abraham Blush
Henry Ewell
Dolor Davis, & his sonns

Laurance Lichfeild
Thomas Boreman
Anthony Annable
John Casley
John Russell
John Foxwell
Thomas Blossome
Samuell Lothrope
Joseph Lothrope

David Linnett
Nathaniell Mayo
Richard Berry
John Blower
Francis Crocker
Benjamin Lothrope
John Davis
Nicholas Davis

Yarmouth. 1643.

Robert Dennis
Thomas Flaune
Nicholas Sympkins
Willm Chase, Senr
Willm Chase, Junr
Anthony Thacher
Andrew Hellot, Jun
Samuell Williams
John Derbey
Thomas Payne
Willm Twyneing
James Mathews
Yelverton Crowe
John Crowe
Tristrame Hull
Edward Sturges
Anthony Berry
Thomas Howe
Thomas Falland
Nicholas Wadiloue
Samuell Hellott
Willm Palmer
Richard Taylor
Willm Lumpkine
Willm Grause
Henry Wheildon

Samuell Rider
Richard Prichett
Richard Temple
Thomas Starre
Benjamin Hamond
James Bursell
Willm Edge
Robert Davis
Richard Seeres
Heugh Norman
Peter Worden
Willm Nicholsone
John Burstall
Emanuell White
Willm Norcutt
Mr Marmaduke Mathews
Richard Hore
Roger Else
John Gray
Andrew Hellott, Sen
Job Cole
Daniell Cole
Heugh Tilly, al Hillier
John Joyce
Wm Pearse
∧ Boreman

Taunton. 1643.

Mr John Browne
Mr Willm Poole
John Browne
James Browne
James Walker
Oliu Purchase
Thomas Gilbert
Richard Stacye

Willm Hollway
Tymothy Hollway
Willm Parker
Peter Pitts
John Parker
Willm Hailstone
Wm Hodges
Willm Phillips

John Maycumber
Thoms Coggin
James Wyatt
Edward Rew
Thom Harvey
James Chichester
Willm Seward
Aron Knapp
John Barratt, Richard Williams
Nicholas Hart
Willm Powell
Edward Bobbett
Richard Paule
Anthony Slocome
Edward Case
Thomas Farewell
Tobias Saunders
Henry Andrewes
John Gallop

John Gilbert, Junr
John Stronge
Thom Cassell
John Deane
Edward Abbott
Walter Deane
Wm Wetherrell
Hezekiah Hore
George Macie
Georg Hall
John Perry
Benjamin Wilson
Mr Street
Richard Williams
Willm Evans
Christopher Thrasher
Thomas Cooke
Thom Cooke, Jr
John Gingell

1643. Marshfeild.

Mr Edward Winslow
John Thomas
Robte Chambers
Arthur Hadaway
Twyford West
Edward Bumpas
John Rowse
Robte Carver
Leiftennant Nathaniell Thomas
Anthony Watters
Thomas Roberts
Henry Draton
Raph Trumle
Allexander Williams
James Pittney
John Dingley
Thomas Chillingsworth
Mr Edward Buckley
Willm Hayle
Tymothy Williams
John Bourne
Willm Launder
Roger Cooke
Robte Waterman
Josias Winslow
  x Lillye

  x Russell
Kenelme Winslowe
James Adams
Arthur Howland
Willm Halloway
Edward Brough
John Barker
Thomas Howell
Raph Chapman
Robte Barker
Willm Barden
Willm Brookes
Gilbert Brookes
Nathaniell Biell
Richard Beare
Jos: Winslow
Anthony Snow
John Goarum
Josphe Bidle
  ∧ Putle
  ∧ Sherman
John Walker
Mr Win: man
Wm Lathame
  ∧ Laurence

The Will and Inventory of John Barnes

T hese are given as examples of what can be found in Plymouth Colony wills and inventories. John Barnes's will is more typical than his inventory in that the inventory, he being a general merchant, is much larger and more varied than the average inventory. His will names his wife Joan (from other sources we know she was his second wife); his son Jonathan; a grandson John Marshall; a cousin, the wife of Henry Sampson; a deceased daughter Lydia; his grandchildren "now in being"; and his kinswoman Esther Rickard. Since *PCR* 1:16 shows that John Barnes married Mary Plummer on 12 September 1633, we can assume that his "cousin," the wife of Henry Sampson, was probably a cousin, or more likely a sister, to Barnes's wife, for we know that Henry Sampson married Anne Plummer on 6 February 1635. *PCR* 8:22 shows that Mr. Robert Marshall married Mary Barnes, probably in 1660, and this fits nicely with the mention in the will of a grandson John Marshall. Barnes's kinswoman Esther Rickard is undoubtedly the "Hester" Barnes (Esther and Hester were interchangeable) who married John Rickard on 31 October 1651 (*PCR* 8:13); though "kinswoman" was used at times for a granddaughter, in this case the chronology and other known facts indicate that Esther was not a granddaughter, and the best guess is that she might have been a somewhat close relative, such as the daughter of a brother or cousin.

The will also shows Barnes's concern that there might be strife between his second wife and his son, Jonathan, by his first wife, and there might also be problems between son Jonathan and the heirs of his deceased daughter Lydia. The information in the will also fits nicely with information from a land record (*PCR* 12:214) in which Barnes recorded his gift of cattle on 24 August 1651 to his children Jonathan, Mary, Hannah, and Lydia. Since neither Hannah nor any heirs of Hannah are mentioned in Barnes's will, we can assume that Hannah probably died without surviving issue; however, that fact that the land record shows he disposed of some of his property during his lifetime leaves the possibility that Hannah might have already had a sufficient portion so as not to be mentioned in the will.

The inventory shows a considerable assortment of clothes, household items, tools, weapons, food (including a bag of pepper), and various miscellaneous items. It is interesting to note that of his five books, one was an English Bible, one an Indian Bible, and one a psalmbook. A detailed analysis of the significance of all the items in his inventory could probably take up an entire book. The will and inventory, as found in Charles Henry Pope, *The Plymouth Scrap Book* (Boston, 1918), p. 56, 102-08, are given below:

The Will of John Barnes
6th of March 1667/68
New England

The Last will & Testament of John Barn's
which is as ffollows.

To All whome these may concern. (Know you That I John Barn's (being of my Sound Understandinge: doe declaire This to be my Last will and Testament. Knowing not how soon ye lord may call me out of this world. doe theirfore Labor to give noe occasion of strife unto those that shall survive me. But that peace may be Among them. 1. In the first place I doe desire that my body; be decently buryed (and) that Funerall charges to be Expended out of my psonall Estate. — 2. That all Legacys be payd. before any division of my estate by mayd. — 3. I doe apoynt yt my dear wife Joan Barn's & my son Jonathan Barn's be ye Execotrs of this my Last will and Testament. — 4. I doe Bequeath unto my wife Joan Barn's half of Every pt. and pcell of my housing and Lands yt I doe now psess in ye Township of new Plimoth dureing The Tearme of her life. — 5. I doe bequeath unto my sonn unto my sonn Jonathan the other half part of my above said housing Lands &c. unless my sayd Sonn shall forfitt it on condittions as follow's in any oyr pt of this my will. — 6. I doe bequeath all my Land lying near to Road Island unto my grand-Sonn John Marshall, as also ye silver dish yt I doe usually use to Eat in. — 7. I doe bequeath to my Cozen ye wife of henery Samson forty shilling's out of my Estate to be payd Beffore division of my Estate. — 8. I doe Bequeath my moveable Estate as follow's one third to my wife for ever in Case she shall not molest any pson to whome I have fformerly sould any Lands unto in Case she shall so doe, yn it shall fall to my Sonn or grandson John Marshall. ye Next third I doe bequeath to my Sonn Jonathan In Case he doe not demand any pt of That Estate yt fformerly I gave to my daughter Lyddyah: Now deceased. in case he shall Soe doe yt third shall fall unto my grandson John Marshall ffor ever. The Next third I doe bequeath to my grandchildren now in being togeither wth my Kinswoman Ester Ricket to pay to each of ym an Equall pt of yt my Estate. hoping That my Last will may be an instrument of peace; shall cease waiting for ye Time of my chang. — 9. I doe Further Request and desire Elder Thomas Couchma Lt. Ephraim Morton and Joseph Warren to be the overseers of this my Last will and Testament

Signed and Sealed In	his mark
ye prsence of	John X Barnes
george Soule Senr:	(Seal)
Saml: Seaburij	
Samuell hunt	

The Inventory of Estate of John Barnes

A true Inventory of the estate of Mr John Barnes lately deceased taken and aprised by us whose names are underwritten this 30th day of August Anno Dom 1671 as followeth

	£.s.d.
Imprs. his apparell one [Parropus] Coate	00-15-00
Item a sadcullered Carsey suite	01-15-00
Item a broadcloth Coate	01-00-00
It. a serge heire Cullered suite	01-05-00
It. a gray serge Coate	01-00-00
It. a broadcloth suite and a troopers Coate all of them worn	01-10-00
It. a great Russed Cloth Coate	01-05-00
It. 2 old troopers Coates and an old paire of briches	01-05-00
It. 3 Red wascoates	00-18-00
It. 4 paire of drawers	00-18-00
Ite. a night uper garment and a tufted fustian wascoate	00-07-00
Item 3 old dubletts	00-12-00
Item 3 paire of wosted stockens	00-10-00
Item 6 paire of stockens 1 of them holland	00-10-00
Item a black demicaster of the new fashion; & 1 old satten capp	00-12-00
Item 2 Cullerd hatts	00-06-00
Item 4 old hatts	00-04-00
Item 2 new Cullered hatts	00-10-00
Item 1 hatt more	00-02-06
Item 5 blacke silke hatt bands	00-03-00
Item 2 paire of Cotton gloves and 2 paire of lether gloves fringed	00-07-00
Item 1 Remnant of sad cullered cloth in bitts and one pair of gater lashes	00-05-00
Item a paire of mittens and a paire of blacke Garters	00-01-00
Item 2 dowlis shirts almost new	00-16-00
Item 2 shirts more	00-16-00
Ite. 2 shirts more	00-10-00
Ite: half a dozen of bands and band stringes and an old wrought capp	00-12-00
Item a silk neckcloth.	
His cash.	

Item 10s. sent into the bay by George Watson and by him Returned:	00-10-00
Item in cash more which we find exstant	05-08-07
Item a set of silver buttons and a silver thimble	00-06-00
Item 7 whole silver spoones and 2 broken ones	03-04-00
Item a silver bason	03-00-00
Item a silver beer bowle	03-00-00
Item a silver dram cupp:& 2 other small peeces of broken silver	00-16-00
Item a smale psell of Gould and silver case	00-03-00
Item a knot of silver buttons	00-03-00
Item 2 bibles one English and another Indian	01-00-00
Ite old Psalme booke and 2 other old bookes	00-01-06
Item 3 Cowes	07-10-00
his cattle Item 2 two year old steeres	03-10-00
Item a Calfe	00-10-00
Item 27 sheep	09-00-00
Item 4 mares and a Colt att prsent appeering	13-10-00
his Armour	
Item 2 guns 1 of them brasse muskett and an other great gun	03-00-00
Item 1 matchlocke and one another little old gun Carbine	01-08-00
Item a pistoll	00-06-00
Item 1 sword and belt	00-08-00
Item 2 old daggers and a paire of bandeleeres	00-05-00
Item a small prsell of powder 3 powder hornes a Cartrich a small powder barrell: bullets & shott about a dozen pound	00-06-00
Item 3 paire of shooes	00-08-00
Item a paire of bootes	00-10-00
Brasse in the kitchen	
Item 2 brasse panns	01-10-10
Item 2 great brasse Kettles	04-00-00
Item 2 brasse kettles	00-12-00
Item 4 brasse skillets 1 and old one	01-10-00
Item 1 warming pann	00-06-00
Item 1 Chaffing	00-05-00
Item a brasse ladle & Candle sticks & a bottom of a warming pan	00-05-00
Item a copper pestell 1 morter and an other belmettle pestell and morter	01-00-00
Item a brasse skimer and a little peece of a brasse lampe and a peece of a brasse ladle	00-03-00
Pewter in the Kitchen	
Item 12 Pewter platters 2 of them bigger than the others	03-00-00
Item 2 great Pewter platters	00-12-00
Item 7 Pewteer platters and smale dishes	00-17-06

Item 5 basons and a pewter dish	00-14-00
Item 2 flaggons and 2 pint potts	01-00-00
Item 9 porringers	00-09-00
Item 3 pint potts a half pint pott a quarter of one and a half quarter	00-12-00
Item 1 Candle cupp 2 Candle sticks 2 small sawcers and a salt Cellar	00-09-06
Item a Cokernutt sett with pewter and an old peece of pewter	00-02-06
Item 2 old quart potts a wrought salt Cellar 2 great old basons 2 lesser old basons	00-14-00
Item 4 other pewter platters a little sawcer another old bason	01-00-00
Item 2 new Chamber potts & 2 old ones	00-07-00
Item 2 old peeces of old pewter & a bason	00-02-00
Tinine ware	
Item 2 tinnine kittles and a dripping pann and 2 other old things with an apple Toster	00-05-00
Iron Item 2 Iron potts 1 other little Iron pot hookes	01-10-00
Item 5 pot hangers	00-15-00
Item 2 Iron spitts 2 paire of tongges 2 fier shovells	00-13-00
Item a paire of Andirons	00-10-00
Item a paire of Andirons faced with brasse	00-18-00
Item a paire of smale Andjrons	00-04-00
Item 3 Iron wedges 4 augers a wrybitt a hand saw an adds a bilhooke 2 sickles a drawing knife 3 augers a hatchett 2 marking Irons 3 other axes without helves a brest wimble 2 Chissells	01-10-00
Item a thwart saw 2 agers a Cooper adds 1 Iron – an old box of thinges to mend shooes as aules &c. 2 agers more 2 Gouges 2 hoes a hammer a drawing knife 3 Cowbells 3 Spades one shovell	01-15-00
Item a smoothing Iron and heaters	00-02-00
Item 2 looking glasses and an houre glasse	00-08-00
In the Parlour	
Item a pound of thrid a knife and kniting needles Item a bagg of pepper a pound and halfe of thrid more small things in it	00-06-00
Item 2 yards of blew linine	00-03-00
Item 3 little Remnants of Red Cotton	00-03-00
Item 2 peeces of homespone cloth	00-05-00
Item pins with a hank of thred a lock and (lasses) and a box	00-04-00
Item woolen yarne and basket in which it is	00-05-00
Item another bag with cloak buttons in it with thrid and lasse with 2 papers of hooks and eyes and a prsell of thrid	

Item a smale prsell of buttons and a prsell of green silke lasse with black Ribbons 1 old hatband and a prsell of Manchester and a prsell of tape	00-03-00
Item 2 hankers of silke and 40 skeines of silk	00-03-10
Item a bag with some smale householdments	00-02-00
Item another little bag with Implements	00-03-00
Item another little bag with smale thinges in it	00-01-06
Item another bag with a smale box in it with a gallypot and a little cloth	00-07-00
Item another little box with a locke and key to it and a bagg of wampum	00-10-00
Item a Compas diall	00-02-00
Item another box of things a case with tooth pickes a paire of spectacles with a prsell of Ribband in a bag in which it is	00-11-00

THE SAME CONCLUDED

Item 2 hankes	00-08-00
Item 5 sheets 3 homade and one holland, dowlis	02-10-00
Item 2 Table clothes	00-15-00
Item 2 pillowbeers	00-10-00
In the Parlour Item halfe a dozen of Napkins	00-06-00
Item another damask Napkin	00-01-00
Item a settle in the Parlour	00-08-00
Item a paire of stillyardes with scales & a bag of waightes	01-00-00
Item 15 little glasses 9 little Gally potts	00-01-06
Item Tobacco pipes stainds and other lumber	00-03-00
In the Leanto over the sellar Item a Chist	00-08-00
Item in it halfe a dozen of Napkins	00-06-00
Item two pillowbeers	00-09-00
Item a table cloth	00-05-00
Item 2 towells and Chimney Cloth	00-05-00
Item a table Cloth and halfe a dozen of Napkins	00-10-00
Item a paire of sheets Canvas and 1 Course holland	01-12-06
Item another Table cloth and a halfe a dozen of Napkins	01-06-00
Item a smale Neckcloth	00-01-06
Item a feather bed and bolster a Rugg and a paire of sheets, 2 pillows and pillow beers on them	13-00-00
Item the Curtaine and Vallence	00-03-00
7 Ephagyes or picktures	00-07-00
Item 2 Iron backes for Chimneys	01-10-00
Item a Chist with severall Earthen potts with divers smale thinges in them	00-05-00
Item 2 lether Chaires	00-16-00
Item 2 other Chaires	00-12-00
Item 2 Joyne stooles	00-05-00

Item 7 Cushen	00-14-00
Item a Table and Karpett	01-05-00
In the Chamber over the Parlour	
Item a paire of Shooes of No 12 s	00-05-00
Item 12 yards of Cloth	01-10-00
Item 4 yards of blew trading cloth	01-02-00
Item a green blankett	00-15-00
Item a blankett of Cape cloth	01-00-00
Item 4 yards of sacking	00-04-00
Item a Beare skin 1 buckskin	00-12-00
Item a box and Cards and other thinges	00-05-00
Item 1 old chist with hobnailes and other Nailes	01-04-06
Item more in Nailes	01-00-00
Item 2 paire of bellowes	00-03-00
Item a prsell of sheeps wool	04-03-06
Item Cotton wool	00-04-06
Item a sadle and pannell and another old saddle	01-10-00
Item a box of drawers with ffish hookes & sparrow bills	00-05-00
Item lines and ledds	00-05-00
Item a pillion saddle	00-10-00
Item a peece of lether	00-05-00
Item a fflaskett and a bitt of sayle Cloth	00-05-00
Item a little case box with a little box in it with an. . .Commoditie in it	00-02-00
Item 4 new pothangers 1 old style and an iron Crow	00-07-00
Item hopps in a bag and 2 blanketts	00-15-00
Item a little hanger for a sword a pair of sheep sheeres and 7 Indian basketts	00-07-00
Item a chist with Candles in it and a gally pott	01-00-00
Item a firkin of Tallow and another old cask with Tallow in it	02-00-00
Item a little thinge with Ginger in it	00-02-00
Item four little old. . .with six bottles	00-06-00
Item a old cask	00-04-00
Item another glasse Case with 9 bottles in it	00-04-00
Item a firkin with hogsfatt and 1 earthen pot	00-10-00
Item 2 earthen potts with butter	00-15-00
Item 2 halfe hogsheads	00-05-00
Item 3 tubbs and three snale old Casks	00-05-00
Item 6 earthen vessells with an earthen bason	00-05-00
Item a Cherne & 4 smale Rundeletts	00-05-00
Item 5 (kimuells) and 6 trayes	00-10-00
Item 1 bowle and 1 tunnell dish 2 Cheeseffatts 1 tray	00-05-00
Item 2 dozen of trenchers	00-02-00
Ite: andiron driping pan and a gridiron	00-05-00

Item 2 pitchers 2 earthen potts 1 Cheeseladder a Roling pin	00-01-06
Item 5 pailes a wooden ladle and a spinning wheel	00-10-00
Item a frying pan and 2 old Casks	00-05-00
In the middle room Item a great scifting trough 4 scives an old one	00-12-00
Item 4 Chaires 1 old smale table and 3 Cushens	00-12-00
Napkins a table clothe a towell	00-06-00
Item Corne on the Ground	02-00-00
Item a quire of paper	00-06-00
Seven Cheese	00-10-00
Item in the Chamber over the (. . .)	
Item a feather bed 2 bolsters a pillow 2 blanketts 1 Rugg 1 paire of sheets & a Cortaine Rod & Cortaine	10-00-00
Item another feather bed and a bolster and Rugg	03-00-00
Item an old pillow	00-02-06
Item a bagg	00-02-00
Item in a half pipe about 5 bushells of Indian Corn	00-16-00
Item a hogshead of feathers and barrell of feathers	02-10-00
Item another half pipe and 3 old barrells	00-08-00
Item a hogshead a barrell a halfebushell and a Cart Saddle	00-05-00
Item a meal trough a seine a bagg and a bushell of Indian Corne in it 3 Caskes & Rye in them about five bushells and a halfe	01-06-00
Item a baskett and woole and three lines 1 old Coller 1 old Lanthorne & other old lumber	00-10-00
Item a share and coulter a spade and a plaine a pickaxe a wrybitt a smoothing plaine and old iron	00-12-00
a forme and a Chaire table	00-10-00
in the little Roome att the south end of the house	
Item 2 venice glasses 3 other glasses 1 stone Jugg 3 earthen potts another white Gally pott a drinking pott another drinking pott a pewter tunnell a little white bottle and a white drinking cupp and other old earthen ware	00-07-00
Item a feather bed two bolsters 2 pillowes 2 blanketts a Coverlid and a paire of sheets a Curtaine Red Curtaines and vallence	10-00-00
Item a Course pillow beare with a sheet & some other linnen	01-10-00
Item an old Chist with some old things in it	00-05-00
Item a Chist	00-10-00
Item in this chist a Canvas sheet	00-05-00
Item 7 Napkins a little table Cloth 2 towells	00-11-00
Item another Canvas sheet a paire of drawers and 2 Capps	00-08-00
Item a paire of Cotton sheets	00-10-00
Item another paire of Cotton sheets	00-15-00

Item a Table Cloth and a towell a table Cloth and a Canvas pillow beer	00-10-00
Item a paire of Canvas sheets	01-00-00
Item a trundle bedsted with a feather bed a bolster 3 blanketts a little Rugg	05-10-00
Item a window Curtaine and about 2 pound of woolen yearne	00-03-00
Item a pillion	00-10-00
Item a blankett	00-10-00
Item 2 milk panns 9 earthen potts a grindstone	00-14-00
a sun dial 3 hoes a ( ) a sheet and a table cloth	01-14-00
In the bake house An Iron pott 2 tubbs a paile 1 old hogshead 2 old barrells and an halfe bushell	01-00-00
Item without dors a paire of wheels and a Cart	01-00-00
In the slaughter house	
1 old shovell 2 pichforkes 1 dungforke and old winnow sheet a latter a. . .of barly	00-12-00
Item without doors	
Item a pitchforke & some spikes	01-00-00
Item 14 boards	01-00-00
Item a tubb 2 boards & a wooden shovell	00-05-00
In the ware house	
Item a barrell and a halfe of salt	01-00-00
Item 9 empty barrells 3 of them tarr barrells and 2 hogsheads	01-10-00
Item a. . .cask with Ginger in it	01-00-00
Item a cask with lime in it	00-05-00
Item a bagg with Cotton wool in it	01-00-00
Item a peece of an old Grapnell hemp and oates 1 old (. . .) 3 old casks a bushell of oates and a halfe a bushell of Indian Corne	00-06-00
besides 4 yards of Cotton and woolen Cloth	06-06-00
Item 2 dosen of hoes Chayers	01-06-00
	50-19-01
	24-07-04
	38-14-06
	38-00-00
	72-00-00
	02-16-00
	226-18-08

Aprised by us
    Nathaniel : Morton
    John Morton
    Gyles Rickard Senor
    Samuell donham
    Mistris Barnes before shee took oath did mension about seaven pound of English money not in the Inventory above mentioned; and a broken. . .that was broken with a Chaine in which shee hangs her. . .of which shee made a smale Cup. . .that is extant and a brake to brake flax;
.This Inventory is Reccorded according to order p me Nathaniel : Morton Secretary see book of Wills and Inventoryes Recorded folio 31; 32: 33:E

Index